XML

Primer Plus

Nicholas Chase

SAMS

201 West 103rd St., Indianapolis, Indiana, 46290 USA

XML Primer Plus

Copyright ©2003 by Sams Publishing

All rights reserved. No part of this book shall be reproduced, stored in a retrieval system, or transmitted by any means, electronic, mechanical, photocopying, recording, or otherwise, without written permission from the publisher. No patent liability is assumed with respect to the use of the information contained herein. Although every precaution has been taken in the preparation of this book, the publisher and author assume no responsibility for errors or omissions. Nor is any liability assumed for damages resulting from the use of the information contained herein.

International Standard Book Number: 0-672-32422-9

Library of Congress Catalog Card Number: 2002102791

Printed in the United States of America

First Printing: November 2002

05   04   03   02   4   3   2   1

Trademarks

All terms mentioned in this book that are known to be trademarks or service marks have been appropriately capitalized. Sams Publishing cannot attest to the accuracy of this information. Use of a term in this book should not be regarded as affecting the validity of any trademark or service mark.

Warning and Disclaimer

Every effort has been made to make this book as complete and as accurate as possible, but no warranty or fitness is implied. The information provided is on an "as is" basis. The authors and the publisher shall have neither liability or responsibility to any person or entity with respect to any loss or damages arising from the information contained in this book or from the use of the CD or programs accompanying it.

ASSOCIATE PUBLISHER
Michael Stephens

MANAGING EDITOR
Charlotte Clapp

ACQUISITIONS EDITORS
Michelle Newcomb
Todd Green

DEVELOPMENT EDITOR
Robin Drake

PROJECT EDITOR
George E. Nedeff

COPY EDITOR
Matt Wynalda

INDEXER
Bill Meyers

PROOFREADER
Jody Larsen

TECHNICAL EDITORS
Danny Kalev
Andy Lester
Jason Pellerin
Jeff Spotts

TEAM COORDINATOR
Lynne Williams

MULTIMEDIA DEVELOPER
Dan Scherf

INTERIOR DESIGNER
Gary Adair

COVER DESIGNER
Aren Howell

PAGE LAYOUT
Susan Geiselman
Julie Parks

CONTENTS AT A GLANCE

INTRODUCTION   1

PART I: XML Fundamentals   15

CHAPTER 1   Basic XML Document Structure 17

CHAPTER 2   Designing XML Documents and Applications 47

CHAPTER 3   Manipulating Documents: The Document Object
Model (DOM) 87

CHAPTER 4   Advanced DOM Techniques 133

CHAPTER 5   XML Streams: The Simple API for XML (SAX) 161

CHAPTER 6   Validation 255

CHAPTER 7   Document Type Definitions (DTDs) 291

CHAPTER 8   XML Schemas 323

CHAPTER 9   Extensible Stylesheet Language Transformations (XSLT) 375

CHAPTER 10   Transformation and Applications 419

CHAPTER 11   Selecting Data: XML Path Language (XPath) 473

PART II: Using XML   521

CHAPTER 12   Browser-Based XML: Cascading Style Sheets (CSS) 523

CHAPTER 13   Browser-Based XML: XHTML 553

CHAPTER 14   XML Linking Language (XLink) 601

CHAPTER 15   XForms 637

CHAPTER 16   XML and Publishing: Formatting Objects with XSL 681

CHAPTER 17   XML and Web Services 719

CHAPTER 18   XML Data Binding 763

CHAPTER 19   XML and Databases: Relational Databases 793

CHAPTER 20   XML and Databases: Native XML Databases 813

CHAPTER 21   Where We Go from Here 857

PART III: Appendixes   867

    APPENDIX A   Resources 869

    APPENDIX B   XML Information Set 879

    APPENDIX C   Answers to Review Questions and Sample Exercise Solutions . . .885

INDEX   967

TABLE OF CONTENTS

INTRODUCTION 1

PART I: XML Fundamentals   **15**

CHAPTER 1: Basic XML Document Structure 17
The Structure of an XML File 18
The XML Declaration 19
The DOCTYPE Declaration 20
The Root Element 20
Elements 20
Nesting Elements 21
Handling Whitespace 21
Attributes 25
Restrictions on Attribute Values 26
Whitespace in Attributes 26
Common Attribute Types .26
Beyond Elements and Attributes 27
Entities 28
CDATA Sections 30
Processing Instructions 31
Comments 32
Well-Formed Versus Valid Documents 33
Valid Documents 33
Requirements for a Well-Formed Document 36
Namespaces 38
Specifying a Namespace .39
URN Versus URI Versus URL 40
The Default Namespace .41
Namespace Scope 42
Namespaces and Attributes 44
Summary 45
Review Questions 46
Programming Exercises 46

CHAPTER 2: Designing XML Documents and Applications 47
The Planning Process 48
Defining the Goals and Objectives 48
Gathering the Team 50
Determining Methodology 51

Gathering Information 51
    Scope 52
    Data Sources and Destinations 52
    Industry Standards 53
    Potential Structures 54
Function/Process Modeling 54
    The Basic Functions 55
    Decomposing the Function 56
    Events 58
    Reviewing the Model 58
Data Modeling 61
    Defining Data Entities 62
    Determining Data Attributes 63
    Determining Relationships 65
    Entity-Relationship Diagrams (ERDs) 66
Checking the Model 68
    Cross-checking the Models 68
    Completeness Checks 69
    Redundant Data Entities 69
    User Approval 69
Creating the Structure 70
    Tree Diagrams 70
    Elements or Attributes? 72
    Attributes and Data Normalization 73
    Grouping Elements 75
    Allowing for Presentational and Data Issues 76
    How Tight Is Tight Enough? 77
The Final Structure 78
    Testing the Final Structure 79
Summary 83
Review Questions 84
Programming Exercises 85
CHAPTER 3: Manipulating Documents: The Document Object Model (DOM) . .87
What Is the Document Object Model? 88
    A Set of Interfaces 88
    The Importance of Nodes 89
    The Different Recommendations 91
The DOM Structure 92
    Getting Ready 93
    The Source Document 93
    Parsing the Document 94

Checking for Supported Features 98
Examining the Structure of the Document 101
Child Nodes, NodeLists, and Node Types 107
Navigating a DOM Document 109
Retrieving Elements by Name 109
NamedNodeMaps 111
Attributes 112
Working with Text Nodes 113
Testing for Children 114
Retrieving an Element by ID 115
Changing Content 117
Changing Text 117
Changing Attributes 119
Creating New Content 120
Creating an Element 120
Adding the Element 121
Creating a New Document 122
Saving the Document 124
The Result 129
Summary 130
Review Questions 130
Programming Exercises 131
CHAPTER 4: Advanced DOM Techniques 133
Additional Features of the DOM Level 2.0 Core .133
Using Siblings 134
Outputting the Tree 141
Normalization and Canonicalization 147
DOM Level 2.0 Traversal 148
NodeIterators 148
Configuring a NodeIterator 151
TreeWalkers 151
NodeFilters 153
DOM Level 3.0 Load and Save 156
Loading the Document 156
Saving the Document 157
Summary 158
Review Questions 159
Programming Exercises 159
CHAPTER 5: XML Streams: The Simple API for XML (SAX) 161
What Is SAX? 161
Event-Based Versus Object-Based APIs 161

A Simple Stream 162
Pros and Cons 163
Creating the Parser 163
The Lay of the Land 163
Creating the XMLReader .164
The ContentHandler 169
Parsing the Document 179
The ErrorHandler 182
Other Handlers 186
Handling Events 187
The Source Document 187
Document Events 188
Element Events 191
Text Events 199
Other Events 207
Creating the Application 208
Detecting Votes 208
Determining the Winner .209
Stopping When You've Had Enough 210
Filters and Chains 224
What Does a Filter Do? 224
Creating the Filter 225
Inserting the Filter into the Stream 238
Affecting the Data 239
The Final Step 251
Summary 252
Review Questions 253
Programming Exercises 253
CHAPTER 6: Validation 255
What Is Validation? 255
A Basic DOCTYPE 256
Defining the Elements 256
Defining the Attributes 257
External DTDs 258
Validating Documents 258
SAX Features 258
Turning on Validation in SAX 259
Running the SAX Application 261
Creating an Error Handler 262
Types of Problems 264
DOM and Validation 265

Schema Validation 267
   Schema Overview 267
   Specifying a Schema 268
   Turning on Schema Validation .268
Working with Errors 281
   Errors and SAX 281
   Handling the Errors 287
   Changes After the Fact 289
Summary 290
Review Questions 290
Programming Exercises 290

CHAPTER 7: Document Type Definitions (DTDs) 291
Types of DTDs 291
   External DTDs 292
   Internal DTDs 295
Creating Elements and Content Models 296
   Content Modifiers 297
   Element Choices 298
   Mixed Content 299
   Whitespace, Mixed Content, and DOM 300
   ANY Elements 301
   Empty Elements 301
   Empty Elements and Browsers .302
Creating Attributes 303
   Default Values 303
   Enumerated Attributes 305
   ID and **IDREF** Attributes 307
   NMTOKEN Attributes 309
   ENTITY Attributes 310
General Entities 310
   Custom Entities 311
   Named Entities Versus Numerical Entities 313
   External Entities 314
Parameter Entities 317
   Making Decisions 318
   Customization 319
Summary 321
Review Questions 321
Programming Exercises 322

CHAPTER 8: XML Schemas 323
Schema Structure 323

Basic Structure 323
Documenting the System 324
Using the Schema Document 325
Simple Elements 325
Built-in Data Types 326
Fixed and Default Values 328
Complex Elements 329
Defining Child Elements 329
Number of Occurrences 331
Mixed Content 333
Catchall Elements 334
Referencing Predefined Elements 335
Scope 337
Element Groups 339
Adding Attributes 340
Optional and Default Attribute Values 342
Named Attributes and Attribute Groups 343
Creating New Types 345
Named Types 346
Restriction 347
Adding Attributes to Simple Types by Extension 351
Deriving Custom Types 352
Deriving via Restriction 354
Data Integrity 358
Unique Keys 358
Keys and Keyrefs 360
Namespaces 361
noNamespaceSchemaLocation 361
The targetnamespace 362
Multiple Namespaces 367
Other Schema Proposals 368
Abstract Schema and Load and Save 369
RELAX NG 371
Schematron 371
Summary 372
Review Questions 372
Programming Exercises 373
CHAPTER 9: Extensible Stylesheet Language Transformations (XSLT) 375
XSL, XSLT, and XSL-FO 376
Basic Style Sheet Transformations 383
The Style Sheet Document 383

Outputting a Value 384
Testing the Style Sheet 385
An Overview of XPath 386
Children and Descendants 386
The Document Root 388
Attributes 389
Testing Criteria 389
Templates 391
Creating a Template 391
Applying Templates 393
Built-in Templates 397
Creating Content 398
Dynamic Elements 399
Dynamic Attributes 400
XML-to-XML Conversion 401
Adding Comments 402
Processing Instructions 404
Sorting Data 404
Creating a Loop 405
copy-of Versus value-of 405
Variables and Parameters 408
Named Templates 408
Parameters 409
Parameters and Named Templates 410
Variables 411
Flow Control 412
If-Then 412
Choose 413
Modes 414
Summary 416
Review Questions 417
Programming Exercises 417
CHAPTER 10: Transformation and Applications 419
Transformation Methodologies 420
Transformation API for XML (TrAX) .420
Language-Specific Issues 420
Transforming Streams 421
Transforming Data 422
Sources 422
Results 424
The `TransformerFactory` 425

Determining the Style Sheet 426

Creating the Transformer and Transforming the Data 431

Templates and Parameters 433

Creating a Template 433

Using a Parameter 435

Transforming Multiple Files 437

Transformations and SAX 439

Source and Style Sheet 439

SAX as Input 440

The Transformer as ContentHandler 443

SAX as a Result 445

Chaining Transformations 455

SAX and XMLFilters 457

Programming Within a Style Sheet 459

Extension Functions 460

Extension Elements 464

Element Context 466

External Classes 468

Summary 470

Review Questions 470

Programming Exercises 471

CHAPTER 11: Selecting Data: XML Path Language (XPath) 473

What Is XPath? 473

How XPath Works 474

Testing the Results 474

Location Steps 476

Context 477

Types of Returned Data 478

Functions 478

Axes 478

Child 478

Self 480

Parents 481

Siblings 483

Descendants 485

Preceding and Following 488

Attribute 490

Namespace 491

Node Tests 493

Names 493

Text Nodes 495

Comment and Processing Instruction Nodes 496

All Nodes 498

Location Paths 499

Combining Steps and the Context Node 499

Some Examples 501

The Abbreviated Form 504

Relative Versus Absolute Paths 505

Predicates 506

Existence 506

Equality 509

Context Size and Position 511

Functions 511

Boolean Functions 512

Node Functions 513

String Functions 514

Number Functions 517

Summary 518

Review Questions 518

Programming Exercises 518

PART II: Using XML   **521**

CHAPTER 12: Browser-Based XML: Cascading Style Sheets (CSS) 523

Gathering the Pieces 524

The Source File 524

Creating a Style Sheet 526

Selectors 527

Element Selectors 528

Descendant Selectors 528

Sibling Selectors 530

Classes and IDs 530

Properties 532

Types of Properties 532

Shorthand Properties 532

Combining Properties 532

Controlling Appearance 533

Color 533

Text Size 535

Font Appearance 536

Layout and Flow 537

Borders 537

Margins and Padding 539

Size 540

Position 542

Flow 545

Removing Objects from the Flow 547

Other Media 550

Summary 550

Review Questions 551

Programming Exercises 551

CHAPTER 13: Browser-Based XML: XHTML 553

XHTML Overview 553

What Is XHTML? 554

Basic Page Structure 554

XHTML Versions 555

Validating Documents 555

Basic XHTML 556

Whitespace 556

Simple Formatting 561

Links 563

Images 566

Tables 570

CSS in XHTML 573

XHTML Forms 576

Text Elements 576

Choice Elements 578

Button Types 581

Presetting Form Information 583

Submitting Form Information 585

Converting XML to XHTML with XSLT .587

The Style Sheet 587

XSLT in the Browser 589

XSLT Style Sheets on the Server 590

Outputting HTML 590

HTML DOM in the Browser 593

Accessing Form Values 593

Changing Page Content and Presentation 596

Summary 598

Review Questions 599

Programming Exercises 599

CHAPTER 14: XML Linking Language (XLink) 601

XLink Overview 602

Link Types 603

The **actuate** Attribute 603
The **show** Attribute 604
Seeing XLinks in Action 604
Link-Building Basics 605
XHTML Hyperlinks 605
Simple XLinks 606
The **show** Attribute: Replace, New, or Embed? 608
Extended XLinks 610
Extended Links 611
Anatomy of an Extended XLink 612
One Resource, Multiple Arcs 615
One Arc, Multiple Destinations 617
Multidirectional Links 618
Linkbases 625
Creating a Linkbase 626
Using Linkbase Information on a Page 628
Linkbase Behaviors 630
XPointer 630
Forms 631
Points 632
Ranges 633
Schemes, and Using XPointer in URIs 634
Functions 635
Summary 635
Review Questions 636
Programming Exercises 636
CHAPTER 15: XForms 637
XForms Basics 637
A Simple Form 638
Anatomy of an XForms Form 641
Getting Ready 642
Form Controls 642
Text 644
Choices 649
Uploads 652
Ranges 654
Boolean 655
Submitting the Form 656
submitInfo 656
Form Values 658
Setting Initial Values 658

Schemas 660
Binding 663
Relevance 665
Form Structures 666
Repeating Structures 666
Itemsets and Attributes 668
Grouping 671
Multiple Forms and Form Submissions 672
Creating a Second Form Model 673
Associating Controls with the Appropriate Form Model 674
Importing Additional Data 675
Form Events 675
Events Overview 675
Creating the Action 676
Create the Listener 677
Triggering the Event 678
Summary 679
Review Questions 679
Programming Exercises 680
CHAPTER 16: XML and Publishing: Formatting Objects with XSL 681
Overview 681
Uses for XSL 681
Layouts, Flows, and Blocks 682
Properties 683
Setting Up 684
Creating a Basic Document 685
Creating the Page Master 685
Building the Page Sequence Master 686
Generating the Page 687
Controlling Page Flow and Page Breaks 689
Adding Static Content 691
Inserting Page Numbers 693
Styling the Content 694
Types of Properties 694
Text Properties 694
Spacing 696
Borders 697
Colors 698
Tables and Lists 699
Tables 699
Lists 702

Images and Links 704
    External Images 704
    External Links 706
    Internal Links 707
Advanced Page Management 708
    Multiple Page Sequence Masters 709
    Multiple Pages 711
    Page Alternatives and Page Position 711
    Odd/Even Pages 714
Summary 716
Review Questions 717
Programming Exercises 717

CHAPTER 17: XML and Web Services 719
Overview 719
    What Are Web Services? 720
    How Do You Use Web Services? 720
    How Do You Find Web Services? 721
    How Do You Secure Web Services? 721
The Web Server 721
    Installing the Web Server 722
    Starting and Testing the Server 722
    Testing the Server 722
    Installing the SOAP Toolkit 723
    Testing the SOAP Installation 725
A Simple Web Service 726
    The Application 726
    Preparing for Deployment 734
    Deploying the Application 736
Using SOAP to Call a Web Service 737
    What Is SOAP? 737
    The SOAP Message 739
    SOAP Messaging 739
    Creating the SOAP Message 740
    Populating the Message 743
    Sending the Message 746
    Reading the Reply 748
Web Services Description Language (WSDL) 751
    The Overall Architecture 751
    Services 752
    Bindings 752
    Port Types 754

Operations 754

Messages 755

Types 756

Putting It Together 756

Document Versus RPC 759

Universal Description, Discovery, and Integration (UDDI) 760

Redundancy 760

Business Information 760

Service Information 761

The UDDI API 761

Summary 762

Review Questions 762

Programming Exercises 762

CHAPTER 18: XML Data Binding 763

Overview 763

How Bound Classes Can Be Used 764

Data Binding Products 765

Creating a Class 765

A Simplified Set of Data 766

The Simplified DTD 766

The Binding Schema 766

Generating the Classes 767

The Generated Classes 767

Using the Classes 768

Unmarshalling the Data 768

Retrieving the Objects 769

Reading the Data 770

Changing Data 771

Marshalling the Data 774

The New Data 775

Creating and Removing Elements 775

Creating and Adding a New Element .776

When Good Data Goes Bad 777

Removing an Existing Element 778

A Closer Look at Binding Structures 779

The Actual File 780

The New Data Structure 780

The New Binding Schema 781

Multiple Levels and Datatypes 782

The Full Structure 782

Binding to Different Types 784

The Generated Classes 785
Objects as Properties 785
Referential Integrity 787
Summary 789
Review Questions 789
Programming Exercises 789

CHAPTER 19: XML and Databases: Relational Databases 793
Types of Systems 793
Middleware 794
Relational Databases 794
Native XML Databases 795
Other Options 795
Types of Data 796
Data-Centric XML 796
Document-Centric XML 798
What the Type of Data Means to You 799
XML Relational Mapping Models 799
CLOBs 799
Object-Relational Storage 801
Collections of Tables 802
XML-Enabled Databases 803
Oracle 803
DB2 805
SQL Server 807
Summary 812
Review Questions 812
Programming Exercises 812

CHAPTER 20: XML and Databases: Native XML Databases 813
Overview of Native XML Databases 813
Why Use a Database at All? 814
Text-Based NXDs Versus Model-Based NXDs 815
Round-Tripping 815
Queries 817
Updates 817
Accessing the Database via an API 818
NXD Basics 818
Installing an XML Database 818
Creating a Collection 819
Adding Documents 820
Retrieving Documents 820
Running Queries 820

Using the XML:DB API 821
   Connecting to the Database and the Collection 822
   Adding a Resource 823
   Returning a Resource 827
   Querying Resources 831
XQuery 1.0 and XPath 2.0 834
   FLWR Statements 834
   Sources 841
   Multiple Sources and Joins 841
   Conditional Processing 842
   Type Management 843
   Functions 844
   Custom Functions 845
XUpdate 846
   Using the XML:DB API with XUpdate 846
   Removing Information 848
   Changing Information 849
   Creating New Information 851
   Variables 853
Summary 855
Review Questions 856

CHAPTER 21: Where We Go from Here 857
The 10,000-Foot View 857
   Core Standards 857
   Associated Standards 858
   Applications 859
Existing Vocabularies 859
   MathML 859
   Scalable Vector Graphics (SVG) and Synchronized Multimedia Integration
     Language (SMIL) 860
   Resource Definition Framework (RDF) 861
   Wireless Markup Language (WML) 862
   XML-based User Interface Language (XUL) 863
   Open eBook (OEB) 863
   Business Process Modeling Language (BPML) .863
Where We're Going 863
   Old Recommendations, New Versions 864
   Document Management 864
   Security 864
Last Words 865

PART III: Appendixes **867**

  APPENDIX A: Resources 869

    Introduction 869

    Chapter 1 869

    Chapter 2 870

    Chapter 3 870

    Chapter 4 871

    Chapter 5 871

    Chapter 7 871

    Chapter 8 872

    Chapters 9–10 872

    Chapter 11 873

    Chapter 12 873

    Chapter 13 873

    Chapter 14 874

    Chapter 15 874

    Chapter 16 874

    Chapter 17 875

    Chapter 18 875

    Chapter 19 876

    Chapter 20 876

    Chapter 21 877

  APPENDIX B: XML Information Set 879

    The `document` Information Item 879

    The `element` Information Item 880

    The `attribute` Information Item 880

    The `processing instruction` Information Item 881

    The `unexpanded entity reference` Information Item 881

    The `character` Information Item 882

    The `comment` Information Item 882

    The `Document Type Definition` Information Item 882

    The `unparsed entity` Information Item 882

    The `notation` Information Item 883

    The `namespace` Information Item 883

  APPENDIX C: Questions and Answers 885

    Chapter 1 885

      Review Questions 885

      Programming Exercises 886

    Chapter 2 887

      Review Questions 887

      Programming Exercises 888

Chapter 3 890
    Review Questions 890
    Programming Exercises 891
Chapter 4 895
    Review Questions 895
    Programming Exercises 895
Chapter 5 898
    Review Questions 898
    Programming Exercises 899
Chapter 6 906
    Review Questions 906
    Programming Exercises 907
Chapter 7 908
    Review Questions 908
    Programming Exercises 909
Chapter 8 911
    Review Questions 911
    Programming Exercises 911
Chapter 9 917
    Review Questions 917
    Programming Exercises 918
Chapter 10 923
    Review Questions 923
    Programming Exercises 924
Chapter 11 927
    Review Questions 927
    Programming Exercises 928
Chapter 12 930
    Review Questions 930
    Programming Exercises 931
Chapter 13 932
    Review Questions 932
    Programming Exercises 933
Chapter 14 935
    Review Questions 935
    Programming Exercises 936
Chapter 15 938
    Review Questions 938
    Programming Exercises 938
Chapter 16 949
    Review Questions 949

Programming Exercises 949
Chapter 17 953
Review Questions 953
Programming Exercises 953
Chapter 18 956
Review Questions 956
Programming Exercises 957
Chapter 19 965
Review Questions 965
Programming Exercises 966
Chapter 20 966
Review Questions 966
INDEX 967

ABOUT THE AUTHOR

Nicholas Chase has been involved in Web site development for companies such as Lucent Technologies, Sun Microsystems, Oracle, and the Tampa Bay Buccaneers. Nick has been a high school physics teacher, a low-level radioactive waste facility manager, an online science fiction magazine editor, a multimedia engineer, and an Oracle instructor. More recently, he was the chief technology officer of an interactive development company, and is the author of several books on XML and on Web development.

DEDICATION

To my mother, Judy, for pushing me along the road.

ACKNOWLEDGMENTS

There are so many people I'd like to thank that I could probably fill up an entire book with just the acknowledgments. First and foremost, I want to thank my wife, Sarah, not only for helping me to retain my sanity, but also for making it possible for me to keep working with a broken collarbone and shoulder blade. (I do *not* want to thank the horse that *broke* my collarbone and shoulder blade.) Even more, I want to thank Sarah for helping me by coming up with the Vanguard Station examples throughout the book. If they're funny, they're hers. If they're not, they're mine.

I also want to thank my son, Sean, for putting up with long hours and understanding that this book will be finished Real Soon Now. Honest.

This book could not possibly have been written without the help and support of several individuals inside and outside Sams Publishing. Specifically, I want to thank the acquisitions editor Michelle Newcomb, for making me call her when my emails sounded panicky, and for forcing me to fill out schedules that actually made sense. I also want to thank Development Editor Robin Drake for understanding my sense of humor and for her voluminous knowledge on just about everything. I also want to thank eagle-eyed Technical Editors Danny Kalev, Andy Lester, and Jeff Spotts for looking over my shoulder, and Copy Editor Matt Wynalda for making sure it all makes sense. Thanks to George Nedeff for keeping all the many pieces in order, and to Todd Green for pitching in when Michelle had, um, more important things to do. (Mother and baby are doing just fine.)

Many thanks to Jason Pellerin and company for contributing the PHP, Perl, VB, and C++ code examples. It's impossible to keep up with everything, and they did a great job of making what we were doing here accessible to programmers outside the Java fold.

And last, but not least, thank you for reading this acknowledgment. I hope you find in this book a resource to take with you to the next level in your work.

WE WANT TO HEAR FROM YOU!

As the reader of this book, *you* are our most important critic and commentator. We value your opinion and want to know what we're doing right, what we could do better, what areas you'd like to see us publish in, and any other words of wisdom you're willing to pass our way.

As an executive editor for Sams Publishing, I welcome your comments. You can email or write me directly to let me know what you did or didn't like about this book—as well as what we can do to make our books better.

Please note that I cannot help you with technical problems related to the *topic* of this book. We do have a User Services group, however, to which I will forward specific technical questions related to the book.

When you write, please be sure to include this book's title and author as well as your name, email address, and phone number. I will carefully review your comments and share them with the author and editors who worked on the book.

Email: feedback@samspublishing.com

Mail: Michael Stephens
           Associate Publisher
           Sams Publishing
           201 West 103rd Street
           Indianapolis, IN 46290 USA

For more information about this book or another Sams Publishing title, visit our Web site at www.samspublishing.com. Type the ISBN (excluding hyphens) or the title of a book in the Search field to find the page you're looking for.

INTRODUCTION

Undoubtedly, you've heard of Extensible Markup Language, commonly known as XML. You may have even seen some of it, though you might not have been aware of it at the time. One thing's fairly certain, however: You'll be seeing a lot more of it in the future.

My certainty is based on the fact that XML is beginning to spread at a pace that almost justifies the hype that accompanied its introduction, now that commercial vendors have discovered its potential. XML is showing up everywhere from configuration files to content management, from electronic data interchange to Web services to...well, you get the idea.

This book talks about all of these things, and does it in such a way that you'll be off and running pretty quickly, ready to start tackling your own projects. Before we get too far, though, let's talk about what XML actually is, so you'll have a feel for what you're doing here.

The Historical Perspective

Okay, there's a scientist in Denmark. He's got a brilliant paper that he wants to share with his colleague in Finland. The trouble is, he and his colleague don't use the same word processing software. He could just send the information in plain text, but then he would lose all of his formatting, and the information would become garbled as style information was lost.

The answer? Well, he could just give up the whole thing, move to Finland, and do the research over again, but that's a little bit drastic. He could print the paper out and mail it, but he really wants his colleague's feedback right now. He could fax it, but then she wouldn't be able to make changes without retyping the whole thing.

Instead, he could send the text along with instructions on how to format each piece, indications of where the equations are, and so on. As long as his colleague could read and understand his notes, everything would be okay. He could even share his data with her, with similar indications within the file as to the meaning of each piece of information.

In advertising agencies, the process of making these handwritten indications on a document or ad layout is known as "marking up" the page. Similarly, the instructions included in a file are known as *markup*.

For example, our scientist wants to quickly pass on some information to his colleague. It might look something like listing I.1.

LISTING I.1   A Simple Message

```
<message>
    <heading>Preliminary Results</heading>
    <paragraph>
        Upon initial investigation, it seems that the subject could,
        under proper stimuli, be induced to emit sounds similar to those
        of the <species>canis familiaris</species>. Results to follow.
    </paragraph>
</message>
```

It's not pretty, but it's intelligible. What's more, if the scientist's colleague has a program that understands the meaning of each markup item, it can interpret and display it properly. For example, the software might understand that headings should be large and bold, that paragraphs belong in a block of their own, and that a species should be rendered in italic.

If you've ever built a Web page, this probably sounds familiar to you. After all, it's very much like Hypertext Markup Language (HTML). In HTML, we could have written the message shown in listing I.2.

LISTING I.2   The Message in HTML

```
<html>
<head><title>Preliminary Results</title></head>
<body>
    <h1>Preliminary Results</h1>
    <p>Upon initial investigation, it seems that the subject could,
    under proper stimuli, be induced to emit sounds similar to those of the
    <i>canis familiaris</i>. Results to follow.</p>
</body>
</html>
```

Any browser can display this properly, because it understands the meanings of the markup, as shown in Figure I.1.

FIGURE I.1

As long as a software application understands the markup, it can render it intelligently.

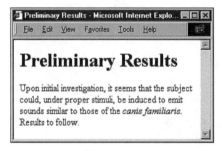

HTML defines a set of tags that have specific meanings. A *tag* is a series of characters between two angle brackets (< and >), and comes in two varieties: *start tags* and *end tags*. The italics tag, for example, is represented by <i> and </i>.

Take the term *canis familiaris* in Listing I.2. When the browser encounters the `<i>`, it renders the following content in italics, stopping when it gets to the end tag, `</i>`.

Although both pages might be rendered the same way, there's a fundamental difference between them. The markup in the first example provides information about structure, whereas the markup in the second example provides information about presentation. An application searching through our scientist's correspondence could easily list the species referenced in each message, because it could look for the `<species>` tag. In the HTML example, however, that information is lost. Most other portable formats, such as Rich Text Format (RTF) and Portable Document Format (PDF), suffer from the same limitation.

Why is this important? For several reasons:

- Even with the amount of complexity that has been added to HTML in the last few years, it is still a barely adequate publishing solution. Every day designers come up with new ideas for presenting information and wind up twisting themselves in knots to accomplish them. In many cases, they practically abandon HTML altogether, relying on related technologies such as cascading style sheets to provide the desired effect.

- The environment for content display is becoming increasingly diverse. The complex pages that can be built for a browser on a typical desktop PC are, in most cases, useless when viewed with the browser in a mobile phone or PDA. If content only exists in HTML, there is little that can be done about this. On the other hand, if the content exists in the more generalized way that XML provides, technologies such as XSL Transformations (XSLT) can create custom presentations for each situation.

- Using XML enables us to create much more than simply content to display. For example, we could use XML for our scientist's results, as shown in Listing I.3.

LISTING I.3 Data as XML

```
<results>
    <trial attempt="1">
        <date>12/31/2001 3:15:00pm</date>
        <stimulus>Request</stimulus>
        <duration>5 minutes</duration>
        <response>none</response>
    </trial>
    <trial attempt="2">
        <date>12/31/2001 3:25:00pm</date>
        <stimulus>Polite request</stimulus>
        <duration>5 minutes</duration>
        <response>none</response>
    </trial>
    <trial attempt="3">
        <date>1/3/2001 1:35:00pm</date>
        <stimulus>Hypnosis</stimulus>
        <duration>15 minutes</duration>
        <response>Bark</response>
    </trial>
</results>
```

Encoding the information in this way provides several advantages. In addition to the fact that the scientist's colleague can now read the data even without the application that produced it, and the fact that we can display it any way we want, the data can be processed easily by an application designed to analyze the data.

For all these reasons, the World Wide Web Consortium (W3C), the de facto Internet standards body, undertook to create XML starting in 1996. Designed to overcome HTML's limitations, XML is based on an ISO standard, Standard Generalized Markup Language (SGML). The XML 1.0 Recommendation was approved in 1998 and, like many XML-related recommendations, is currently maintained by the W3C.

This book focuses on getting you ready to write applications that work with XML data, either producing or analyzing it.

The Basic Nature of XML

In their simplest form, XML documents consist of two basic units: elements and attributes. Think of an *element* as a tag and its contents. Let's look at our sample data in Listing I.4, for example.

LISTING I.4   A Simple XML Fragment

```
<trial attempt="1">
    <date>12/31/2001 3:15:00pm</date>
    <stimulus>Request</stimulus>
    <duration>5 minutes</duration>
    <response>none</response>
</trial>
```

In this example, we have five elements: `trial`, `date`, `stimulus`, `duration`, and `response`, denoted by an opening tag, a closing tag, and the content in between. Four of those elements, `date`, `stimulus`, `duration`, and `response` are simple elements, containing only text. The fifth, `trial`, contains the other elements. This makes `trial` the *parent* element of the other four, and they are its *children*. This parent-child structure is essential to the XML hierarchy, and we'll discuss it at length in many of this book's chapters.

Attributes are name-value pairs, such as `attempt="1"` in Listing I.4, which appear within the start tag of an element and provides information about that element. An element may carry any number of attributes, and in fact, some applications use only attributes to convey information. One good example is HTML's `img` (image) tag:

```
<img src="images/logo.gif" height="30" width="75">
```

There is no closing tag for an image. In HTML, this is not a problem—in fact, it's the proper way to add an image to the page—but XML requires a closing tag. It would be silly to write this:

```
<img src="images/logo.gif" height="30" width="75"></img>
```

So instead, XML specifies an abbreviation:

```
<img src="images/logo.gif" height="30" width="75" />
```

When we add the slash within the opening tag, this becomes an *empty* element, which doesn't need a closing tag.

An Extra Space

XML doesn't require a space before the closing slash of an empty element, but many browsers will not perform properly if it's left out.

There is much more to the structure of an XML document, which we'll discuss in Chapter 1, "Basic XML Document Structure."

Some Sample Applications of XML

By its very nature, XML is flexible enough to be useful in a whole slew of environments, from the browser to the server to communication between machines around the world running different applications on different operating systems in different languages. A number of related technologies have sprung up to aid in these uses.

XML in the Browser

Probably the most familiar implementation of XML for most people is XHTML. XHTML is a reformulation of HTML using the new rules of XML, such as case-sensitivity of element names (in tags) and the requirement that attribute values be enclosed in quotes. An XHTML document may be virtually indistinguishable from a well-written HTML document. In fact, we can convert Listing I.2 into an XHTML document by simply adding an XML declaration to the top of the file, as shown in Listing I.5.

Being Bold

Throughout the book, code changes that need your attention appear in **bold**.

LISTING I.5   The Message in XHTML

```
<?xml version="1.0"?>
<html>
<head><title>Preliminary Results</title></head>
<body>
   <h1>Preliminary Results</h1>
   <p>Upon initial investigation, it seems that the subject could,
   under proper stimuli, be induced to emit sounds similar to those of the
   <i>canis familiaris</i>. Results to follow.</p>
```

LISTING I.5   Continued

```
</body>
</html>
```

We'll discuss XHTML in detail in Chapter 13, "Browser-Based XML: XHTML."

Some browsers enable an author to go one step further, using XML directly in the browser and simply styling it using cascading style sheets (CSS). The CSS Recommendation, originally developed for HTML, enables an author to control the presentation of content. For example, we can get virtually the same result as Listing I.5 by adding CSS information to the original XML message. In Listing I.6, we add a reference to a separate file containing CSS information.

LISTING I.6   `message.xml`

```
<?xml version="1.0"?>
<?xml-stylesheet href="messages.css" type="text/css"?>
<message>
    <heading>Preliminary Results</heading>
    <paragraph>
        Upon initial investigation, it seems that the subject could,
        under proper stimuli, be induced to emit sounds similar to those
        of the <species>canis familiaris</species>. Results to follow.
    </paragraph>
</message>
```

The `messages.css` file shown in Listing I.7 contains instructions on how to present the information.

LISTING I.7   `messages.css`

```
heading { display: block;
          font-weight: bold;
          font-size: 24pt;
          padding-bottom: 19px }
paragraph { display: block;}
species { font-style: italic }
```

The result, shown in Figure I.2, is virtually identical to the original HTML version shown in Figure I.1.

FIGURE I.2

We can use cascading style sheets to control the appearance of XML data.

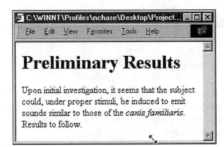

Cascading style sheets are just one way we can control the appearance of XML information. In some cases, the browser isn't capable of handling such information, and an entirely different version of the content is needed.

That's where *Extensible Stylesheet Language Transformations (XSLT)* comes in. An XSL Transformation enables us to take an XML document and remove, rearrange, and alter data before presenting it to the client. For example, we could take the same XML message and transform it for text-only browsers, such as the ones contained in mobile phones. Listing I.8 shows the XSL style sheet.

LISTING I.8   `messages.xsl`

```
<?xml version="1.0"?>
<xsl:stylesheet xmlns:xsl="http://www.w3.org/1999/XSL/Transform" version="1.0">

<xsl:template match="/">
<html>
    <head>
        <title>
            <xsl:value-of select="message/heading"/>
        </title>
    </head>
    <body>
        <xsl:value-of select="message/paragraph"/>
    </body>
</html>
</xsl:template></xsl:stylesheet>
```

This style sheet creates a simple page showing only text, as shown in Figure I.3.

FIGURE I.3
XSLT style sheets enable the use of one XML document in many contexts.

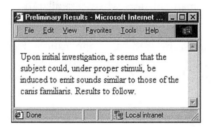

We'll cover XSLT in detail in Chapter 9, "Extensible Stylesheet Language Transformations (XSLT)."

We can also use XML to create documents for display in other media (such as paper) using XSL Formatting Objects, which are discussed in Chapter 16, "XML and Publishing: Formatting Objects with XSL."

XML on the Server

As useful as XML is in the browser, where it really comes into its own is on the server, where it can be manipulated in any number of ways. Several programming models exist, and we'll look at a few of them.

One common use for XML is in application configuration files. These files are simple to manipulate, and human-readable. Because they can contain specific, human-friendly element names, they're easier to work with than a simple file with information on random lines all by itself. Take for example the snippet from an ASP.NET configuration file shown in Listing I.9.

LISTING I.9   `Web.config`

```
<configuration>
  <configSections>
    <sectionGroup name="system.web">
      <section name="trace"
               type="System.Web.Configuration.TraceConfigHandler">
    </sectionGroup>
  </configSections>
  <system.web>
    <trace enabled="true" requestLimit="20" pageOutput="true"
           traceMode="SortByTime" localOnly="true" />
  </system.web>
</configuration>
```

Because the file is in XML, it is easy for a human to decipher and alter it, and for an application to predictably interpret it.

In addition to using XML for configuration files, applications can process XML directly, both for read-only analysis and for manipulation, whether similar to XSLT or along entirely different lines.

These lines might involve analysis by Web-based applications such as servlets or Java Server Pages, or might include something as basic as a database, like those featured in Chapter 19, "XML and Relational Databases," and Chapter 20, "XML Databases and Datastores."

XML also lends itself to data binding, as we'll discuss in Chapter 18, "Data Binding." In this case, the data can be manipulated in order to act like an object, such as a Java object. This binding of the data to an object enables non-XML programmers to execute their business logic without worrying about the underlying structure of the data.

For example, the Java snippet in Listing I.10 shows the creation of an object that represents an XML document, the setting of an element value, and the retrieval of an element value.

LISTING I.10   Data Binding Snippet

```
...
    Car birthdayPresent = new Car();
    float theirPrice = birthdayPresent.getPrice();
```

LISTING I.10   Continued

```
        birthdayPresent.setOffer(new java.math.BigDecimal(theirPrice/2));
...
```

The application reads an XML document to create an instance of the `Car` class, which matches the structure of the document. After manipulation, the data can be written back out as XML.

Perhaps the most exciting use of XML is to simplify the exchange of data between applications, even on different platforms. Because it's text and is thus portable between applications and platforms, XML is a good choice for sending data between applications. Several means, such as the Simple Object Access Protocol (SOAP) and .NET, use XML in this way to send data from location to location. We'll cover these in detail in Chapter 17, "XML and Web Services."

How Does It All Fit Together?

Programming with XML involves using many different but related technologies and standards. We will cover the most important of those currently on the market in this book, getting you up and running with your own programs as quickly as possible.

The following sections describe the contents of each of this book's chapters.

Part I, "XML Fundamentals"

In Part I, we're going to build a foundation. You'll learn what XML is and to get a good handle on its structure. You'll also get a grounding in the basic means for programming XML, such as DOM and SAX, on which most other applications are built. By the end of this part, you'll be ready to build your own applications from scratch.

Chapter 1, "Basic XML Document Structure"

This chapter begins to explain the concepts behind XML as a structure for data. It provides a glimpse into much of what is to follow, covering elements, attributes, and other types of XML information, as well as concepts such as well-formedness, validation, and namespaces.

Chapter 2, "Designing XML Documents and Applications"

Before actually building any applications, we'll discuss the process for deciding exactly what we're building and how we might structure it. We'll give examples to demonstrate the planning process and show how it leads to a finished plan. We'll also look at some typical situations and the types of XML structures they generate.

Chapter 3, "Manipulating Documents: The Document Object Model (DOM)"

Here we'll begin to build simple applications, with examples in Java, VB, C++, PHP, and Perl. By the end of the chapter, you'll have a good idea of how the structure of an XML document works, and how it can be manipulated programmatically using the Document Object Model (DOM), a way of looking at the data based on the hierarchy of information.

Chapter 4, "Advanced DOM Techniques"

This chapter examines the direction of new and future DOM work in order to facilitate more extensive work with XML. We'll look at programming techniques such as the use of `TreeWalkers`, `NodeIterators`, and `NodeFilters`. We'll also look ahead to DOM events and DOM Level 3.

Chapter 5, "XML Streams: The Simple API for XML (SAX)"

This chapter provides a different look at XML structures, demonstrating the use of XML streams in which you analyze the data sequentially, as it appears in the document. This method is faster and less resource-intensive than DOM, but is read-only. We'll also look at chaining streams together.

Chapter 6, "Validation"

Now that you've got an understanding of how XML data can be used within an application, we'll discuss the importance of data integrity, along with techniques for enforcing data integrity.

Chapter 7, "Document Type Definitions (DTDs)"

Here we'll look at the most basic way of creating and reading the Document Type Definitions (DTDs) that specify the structural requirements enforced in the previous chapter.

Chapter 8, "XML Schemas"

This chapter moves one step further than DTDs, examining the further capabilities provided by W3C XML Schemas. It also discusses some of the more advanced features and how and why you should use them, and takes a brief look at other XML Schema proposals, such as RELAX.

Chapter 9, "Extensible Stylesheet Language Transformations (XSLT)"

Once data has been expressed in an XML document, it can be manipulated in a variety of ways, including transformations. This chapter covers the building of XSL style sheets.

Chapter 10, "Transformation and Applications"

Transformations can be handled by some browsers, but are even more useful when they are incorporated into an application. This chapter demonstrates the use of XSLT from within an application.

Chapter 11, "Selecting Data: XML Path Language (XPath)"

XSL Transformations (and other, later technologies) depends on the ability to specify particular data within a document. This chapter covers XPath, which allows programmers to perform such selections. It also covers XPath's more complex, useful abilities, and how and when to use them.

Part II, "Using XML"

By this point in the book, you'll have a good understanding of how XML works, and how you can use it in your own applications. Up until now, most of what we'll have looked at will have been fairly well settled—or at least complete enough for us to work with. In Part II, we'll be stepping into a world where standards are still being defined and implementations are not always complete. For at least the foreseeable future, XML "standards" will be perpetually under development, and if you wait for them to be set in stone, you'll be left far behind. Instead, the chapters in this part look at various areas of XML as they exist at the moment, giving you a solid understanding of how they work. This way, when the standard or specification or recommendation is ready, you will be too, even if names have been changed here and there.

Chapter 12, "Browser-Based XML: Cascading Style Sheets (CSS)"

In this chapter, you'll see firsthand the separation of content and presentation that XML represents as we look at the direct manipulation of XML content in the browser using Cascading Style Sheets (CSS) and their power to control presentation.

Chapter 13, "Browser-Based XML: XHTML"

It's natural to compare XML and HTML, particularly with XHTML in the picture. Now that you have an understanding of XML away from the Web, and of the various presentation properties that can affect it, this chapter discusses some of the ways that XML is used within the browser, including XHTML and client-side scripting using JavaScript.

Chapter 14, "XML Linking Language (XLink)"

XML Linking Language provides a much more robust means for linking information than is currently available in Web pages. This chapter discusses some of these capabilities, and looks at how and when to implement them. It also includes a discussion of XPointer, a means for specifying a particular piece or range of information within an XML document.

Chapter 15, "XForms"

An extension of currently available Web technologies, XForms greatly increases data collection capabilities and flexibility, separating presentation from content in a way that provides functionality inaccessible today without complex and unreliable scripting. This chapter demonstrates how to build such forms and how to use them to your advantage.

Chapter 16, "XML and Publishing: Formatting Objects with XSL"

The separation of presentation and content that is inherent in XML enables us to create complex presentations using XSL Formatting Objects. These documents can then be converted to PDF documents, making them more widely available.

Chapter 17, "XML and Web Services"

The Holy Grail of XML is universally understandable data. This chapter demonstrates the use of Web services, which enable machines differing in both geography and operating system to communicate.

Chapter 18, "XML Data Binding"

This chapter discusses the concepts behind data binding, such as marshaling and unmarshaling data and manipulating the resulting objects.

Chapter 19, "XML and Databases: Relational Databases"

Any significant application is likely to have a database behind it, and in the majority of cases that database is relational. This chapter looks at the XML capabilities of some existing relational databases.

Chapter 20, "XML and Databases: Native XML Databases"

As XML becomes more prevalent in the marketplace, databases built around XML become more common. This chapter describes the different types of XML databases and discusses how to use them.

Chapter 21, "Where We Go From Here"

Part III, "Appendixes"

Appendixes A and B provide information that you might find useful independent from the rest of the book. Appendix C supplies answers to the review questions provided at the end of each chapter, along with sample solutions to the chapter exercises.

Appendix A, "Resources"

XML covers much more ground than could ever be discussed in a single book. This appendix provides you with pointers to both online and offline sources for more information on the topics covered in each chapter.

Appendix B, "XML Information Set"

With so many initiatives attempting to define XML-related standards and recommendations, it was necessary to define a common vocabulary for discussing XML structures. This appendix provides a look at that vocabulary, known as the XML Information Set.

Appendix C, "Answers to Review Questions and Sample Exercise Solutions"

After each chapter, you'll have a chance to apply what you've learned and make sure that you understand each of the concepts presented. Rather than leaving you on your own, this appendix provides the answers to the review questions and sample solutions for the exercises at the end of each chapter, in case you get stuck.

What You Do and Don't Need to Know

This book makes certain assumptions about the skill set that you bring to the table. First, we'll assume that you're familiar with at least one programming language; you won't be able to program using XML without one! XML is a structure for storing information that is easily manipulated via an application, but is not a programming language in itself.

We'll start out in the first several chapters by giving examples in Java, C++, VB, PHP, Perl, and possibly other languages here and there. Once the pattern is established, we'll show each new example in only one or two languages. You can then adapt the concept to your own applications.

A Note About the Sample Code

Throughout the book, I'll be providing sample code in various languages. While I've tried to make sure there are no errors, it's important to understand that the sample code is for demonstration only, to show you how various concepts work in different environments. When you build your own applications, you may run into issues involving network setup, security settings, and so on. Because this is a book about XML rather than VB, C++, PHP, Perl, and so on, we must leave these issues to you.

We won't assume that you know anything at all about XML, or even that you've used HTML before, though experience with either would certainly make your life easier.

Conventions

This book uses a few typographical conventions:

- *Italics* are used for emphasis and to introduce new terms.

- Program text, functions, URLs, and other "computer language" are set in a fixed-pitch font—for example, `<!ELEMENT woodwind (#PCDATA)>` or `www.ibm.com`.

- Placeholders within syntax lines appear in *`monospace italic`*. For example, in the following syntax, the words *`{name}`* and *`{content model}`* will be replaced with the name of the element and the applicable content model, respectively.

  ```
  <!ELEMENT {name} ({content model})>
  ```

- Sometimes a line of code contains more characters than can possibly fit within the margins of a printed book. In those cases, the [ic:ccc] symbol appears at the beginning of a line that is a continuation of the previous line, as in the following example:

  ```
  <!ENTITY concertpieces SYSTEM
  ➥"http://www.nicholaschase.com/musicapp/getmusic.asp?date=4.23.04">
  ```

This symbol merely indicates that we ran out of room on the page. We've tried to place these code continuation arrows as helpfully and unobtrusively as possible.

- As we progress through each example, new sections of code will be indicated in bold, so you'll know what you have to add. For example:

```
<xforms:itemset model="employees" nodeset="people/person">
    <xforms:caption ref="personname" />
    <xforms:value ref="@pid" />
</xforms:itemset>
```

PART I

XML FUNDAMENTALS

1 Basic XML Document Structure

2 Designing XML Documents and Applications

3 Manipulating Documents: The Document Object Model (DOM)

4 Advanced DOM Techniques

5 XML Streams: The Simple API for XML (SAX)

6 Validation

7 Document Type Definitions (DTDs)

8 XML Schemas

9 Extensible Stylesheet Language Transformations (XSLT)

10 Transformation and Applications

11 Selecting Data: XPath

CHAPTER 1

BASIC XML DOCUMENT STRUCTURE

You will learn about the following in this chapter:

- The structure of an XML file
- Elements
- Attributes
- Entities, CDATA sections, processing instructions, and comments

- Well-formed versus valid documents
- Namespaces

*I*n some ways, the structure of an XML file may seem obvious; it's a series of elements and attributes arranged in a parent-child hierarchy. The specifics of that structure aren't so simple, however.

There are several ways to look at a document. The Document Object Model (DOM) organizes the document into different types of nodes, while the Simple API for XML (SAX) looks at an XML document as a series of events, such as start tags, characters, and end tags. In fact, there are so many ways to refer to the different parts of an XML file that the World Wide Web Consortium (W3C) has produced the XML Information Set Recommendation (*XML Infoset*, for short), which provides a set of definitions for use by other specifications.

XML Infoset URI

You can find the Recommendation at `http://www.w3.org/TR/xml-infoset/`. For more details on the XML Infoset, see Appendix B.

In this chapter, we'll build a foundation by looking at the structure of an XML document as it's defined in the XML 1.0 Recommendation. Before we do, however, let's take a moment to get a handle on how a document such as the XML 1.0 Recommendation comes into existence.

Like most Internet-related technologies, XML is shepherded by the World Wide Web Consortium (W3C), an organization formed for the purpose of providing a single point of focus. The W3C has different Working Groups, each of which concentrates on a particular area. A document is produced as a Working Draft, which is then made available for implementers. These are the people and companies that will actually be building software based on the eventual document. Discussion takes place among members and in forums such as the xml-dev mailing list, and the feedback goes into producing subsequent drafts.

Finally, the group produces a Candidate Recommendation, which is voted on and either accepted or rejected. If rejected, it may move back to Working Draft status. If accepted, it becomes a Proposed Recommendation, and finally a W3C Recommendation.

The Structure of an XML File

The XML 1.0 Recommendation defines a series of conditions that must be followed for XML data to be considered *well-formed*. Well-formedness is the basis for an XML document; if it's not well-formed, it's not XML.

Well-formedness in XML is based on two types of information contained within a document: *character data* and *markup*. In general, the markup is any information that is part of a tag, and the content is any information that isn't.

For example, in the following text, only the word **open** is actually character data:

```
<airlock id="level1"><status>open</status></airlock>
```

Everything else on the line is markup that provides information about the content of the document. *Parsing* is the process of extracting the information represented by the combination of markup and character data.

Tags are not the only type of markup, however. Let's look at the overall structure of the simple file in Listing 1.1 before we move on to discuss the different types of information a document can contain.

LISTING 1.1   A Simple XML Document

```
<?xml version="1.0" encoding="ISO-8859-1" standalone="no"?>
<!DOCTYPE airlocksystem SYSTEM "airlocks.dtd">
<airlocksystem>
    <airlock lockid="A23b">
        <size height="320" width="500" />
        <type>Bronson</type>
        <location>Level 2 aft</location>
        <status>open</status>
    </airlock>
    <airlock lockid="Q36d">
        <size height="200" width="300" />
        <type>Perch</type>
        <location>Level 15 starboard</location>
        <status>closed</status>
    </airlock>
</airlocksystem>
```

The XML Declaration

In most cases, the very first line of an XML file is the *XML declaration*. The declaration can specify a number of different pieces of information. Take the declaration from our sample file:

```
<?xml version="1.0" encoding="ISO-8859-1" standalone="no"?>
```

The use of the question mark tells any application that this is not simply a tag. This declaration has four separate and distinct pieces of information:

Information	Description
<?xml	The first five characters notify the application that this is, in fact, the XML declaration, and not the start of other content. (This comes in handy when using other encodings, as you'll see shortly.)
version="1.0"	Next comes the version information. This information is included in anticipation of a time when more than one version may exist. Although there are no plans at this time to revamp XML and produce a new version, there may be a time when this happens; if it does, including the version information will enable an application to reject a document written in a version it doesn't understand.
encoding="ISO-8859-1"	After the version declaration comes the encoding information. XML has been designed specifically to allow the use of various international character sets. It requires that all applications support the Unicode standard, which provides encoding information for most of the world's major languages. The application needs to know how to interpret the characters it sees. In this case, we've specified the Latin-1 character set, ISO 8859-1. Perhaps the most common encoding used with XML files is UTF-8, which includes encodings for most of the world's common alphabets.
	Of course, this raises the question: How does the application read the encoding information if it doesn't know what encoding to use? The answer lies in the first five characters of the XML declaration. If it doesn't understand the encoding, it goes back to the beginning and tries to determine what encoding would make the first five characters <?xml. From there, it can make an educated guess about the encoding.
standalone="no"	Finally, we have the standalone declaration. This declaration determines whether the document contains any external entities. These entities are part of the Document Type Definition (DTD), which we'll discuss briefly later in this chapter, and fully in Chapter 7.

Information Order

Although you'll see that the order in which attributes appear *in an element* is not important, their order is important in the XML declaration.

In general, the XML declaration is optional, but if you do decide to use one, remember that an XML document can carry only one. So if you will be combining documents, it's a good idea to leave out the declaration to prevent conflicts. Remember, however, that any document using an encoding other than UTF-8 or UTF-16 *must* have an XML declaration so the application can figure out how to read the rest of the document.

The DOCTYPE Declaration

Immediately following the XML declaration is the optional **DOCTYPE** declaration:

```
<!DOCTYPE airlocksytem SYSTEM "airlocks.dtd">
```

This declaration is not required for an XML document unless you want to verify the content through validation. Validation is covered in detail in Chapter 6, "Validation," Chapter 7, "Document Type Definitions (DTDs)," and Chapter 8, "XML Schemas." In its simplest form, validation entails specifying a file that contains a series of definitions to which the document must conform. These definitions may be contained within the document itself, in which case they're internal, or in a separate file, in which case they're external.

The Root Element

Finally, we come to the XML data itself. The first requirement is that the document must consist of a single *root element*. In other words, no matter how much information you have, it must all be contained between a single start tag and end tag, such as `<airlocksystem>` and `</airlocksystem>` in Listing 1.1. Of course, this doesn't mean that you have a giant mess, with individual pieces of information scattered about. It means that all of your nicely organized sections, such as each `airlock` record, are contained within a single root element.

Elements

Elements are the backbone of an XML document. In fact, a document that doesn't have at least one element is not considered well-formed.

An element typically consists of a start tag, character data, and an end tag:

```
<type>Perch</type>
```

The name of the element is the prominent feature of the markup that defines an element. In this example, the name of the element is `type`. XML element names have simple rules:

- The name must start with a letter or the underscore character (_).

- The end tag must contain exactly the same name as the start tag. This includes case; XML is case sensitive.

- Names *should not* contain colons. Officially, they're allowed, but as you'll see when we get to namespaces later in the chapter, the colon has a special meaning and should not be used under other circumstances.

- Names *must not* contain spaces.

Understandable Names

Although it's not a technical requirement that XML elements have names that fit their functions, part of the advantage of XML is the fact that humans can understand the data. Make sure that unless you're deliberately trying to obscure the data, you name your elements in such a way that an outsider can understand your intent.

Nesting Elements

Of course, a single element would be of limited use. In an XML document, elements are *nested*, meaning that each element is contained within other elements—except for the root element, of course!

If you're going to nest XML elements, you must do it properly. If the start tag of an element is contained within another element, the end tag must be within that element as well. Let's compare two examples.

Correct:

`<sentence>These elements are nested <adverb>properly</adverb></sentence>.`

Incorrect:

`<sentence>These elements are nested <adverb>improperly</sentence></adverb>.`

Elements must be nested properly for the document to be well-formed.

When one element is nested within another, it's said to be the *child* of that element, and the element that contains it is said to be its *parent*. In the preceding example, the `sentence` element is the parent, and the properly nested `adverb` element is its child.

Handling Whitespace

In XML, whitespace is often added to make a document more readable. For example, a document may be formatted as shown in Listing 1.2, or in the more readable format shown in Listing 1.3. This is known as *pretty printing*.

LISTING 1.2   The XML Data Without Convenient Spacing

```
<?xml version="1.0"?><airlocksystem><airlock lockid="A23b">
<size height="320" width="500" /><type>Bronson</type>
<location>Level 2 aft</location><status>open
</status></airlock></airlocksystem>
```

LISTING 1.3   The Pretty Printed Document

```
<?xml version="1.0"?>
<airlocksystem>
  <airlock lockid="A23b">
    <size height="320" width="500" />
    <type>Bronson</type>
    <location>Level 2 aft</location>
    <status>open</status>
  </airlock>
</airlocksystem>
```

Although they contain the same data, Listings 1.2 and 1.3 are not equivalent. The spaces and tabs are considered character data within the elements. In actual processing, however, the spaces and tabs in the `airlocksystem` and `airlock` elements in Listing 1.3 are not really relevant, and although an application is required to pass on these spaces, tabs, and line feeds, they're typically ignored. For example, consider the HTML page in Listing 1.4.

LISTING 1.4   A Sample HTML Page

```
<html>
<head>
    <title>
        Preserving space
    </title>
</head>
<body>
    <p>
        Impressionist paintings are just that:
        <b>impressions</b>
        of a single moment in time.
    </p>
</body>
</html>
```

When this page is displayed in a browser, all the whitespace within its elements is collapsed, including the whitespace within the paragraph element (`<p></p>`), as shown in Figure 1.1. Collapsing whitespace consists of converting tabs, line feeds, carriage returns, line feed/carriage return combinations, and multiple spaces into a single space.

FIGURE 1.1

Whitespace within elements is collapsed.

It makes sense to collapse the space *between* elements, but why *within* them? Well, it turns out that there's really little distinction between *within* and *between*. All elements are "within" the root element, so all whitespace is "within" an element.

In the <p> element, for example, we have character data, then markup (the <b> and </b> tags) indicating another element and its character data, then more character data within the <p> element. In the <body> element, we have character data (the whitespace), then markup (the <p> and </p> tags) indicating another element and its character data, then more character data (the whitespace).

So what happens if we really *want* the whitespace? In HTML, we can use a special set of tags, <pre> and </pre>, to indicate to the browser that the text is *preformatted*, and the browser should preserve the spaces. For example, if we made the additions shown in bold in Listing 1.5, we would get the result shown in Figure 1.2.

LISTING 1.5   Preserving Whitespace in an HTML Document

```
<html>
<head>
   <title>
        Preserving space
   </title>
</head>
<body>
   <pre>
        Impressionist paintings are just that:
        <b>impressions</b>
        of a single moment in time.
   </pre>
</body>
</html>
```

In XML, we don't have the advantage (or disadvantage) of a single predefined element to inform the application that the whitespace within a particular element is significant. Instead, we can tell the application that the spaces within a particular element are significant by adding an attribute called xml:space. We'll deal more with attributes in the next section, but for now you just need to understand that an *attribute* is a name-value pair added to the start tag of an element.

FIGURE 1.2
Certain elements, such as
`<pre>`, preserve white-
space.

The `xml:space` attribute is predefined in XML, and can take one of two values: `preserve`, in
which all whitespace characters are considered "significant," and `default`, in which the application can handle the spaces as though the `xml:space` attribute weren't specified.

Another Predefined Attribute

XML also defines the `xml:lang` attribute, which is discussed in Chapter 2, "Designing XML
Documents and Applications."

Browsers don't currently support the `xml:space` attribute, but when they do, it will look like
Listing 1.6 and Figure 1.3.

LISTING 1.6   Using the `xml:space` Attribute

```
<html>
<head>
    <title>
        Preserving space
    </title>
</head>
<body>
    <p xml:space="preserve">
        Impressionist paintings are just that:
        <b>impressions</b>
        of a single moment in time.
    </p>
</body>
</html>
```

FIGURE 1.3
Using the `xml:space`
attribute to signal significant whitespace.

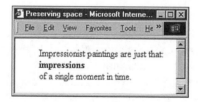

Attributes

As you have already seen, it's possible to add name-value pairs to a start tag in order to provide additional information to an element. These name-value pairs are called *attributes*, and they can be an integral part of your XML documents.

Attributes enable you to add information to an element independent of the element's character data. In fact, you can replace the character data altogether using attributes, resulting in empty elements. Take these examples:

```
<size>
    <height>320</height>
    <width>500</width>
</size>

<size height="320" width="500" />
```

Both provide the same information, but in different ways.

Elements or Attributes?

The decision regarding whether to use elements or attributes is a thorny one. We'll discuss the issue thoroughly in Chapter 2.

Like element names, attribute names have certain requirements:

- Attribute names must conform to the same rules as element names.

- The names must be unique.

This doesn't mean that an attribute name can be used only once in a document, but it does mean that an attribute name can be used only once within a specific *element*. So the following example is incorrect:

```
<job employee="Bob Jones" employee="John Smith">Accountant</job>
```

But this example is correct:

```
<job employee="Bob Jones">Accountant</job>
<job employee="John Smith">Accountant</job>
```

And so is this one:

```
<job employee="Bob Jones">Accountant</job>
<office employee="Bob Jones">102B</office>
```

Namespaces and Duplicate Attribute Names

To be strictly accurate, an element cannot contain two attributes with the same name in the same namespace. We'll discuss this further in the "Namespaces" section, later in this chapter.

Restrictions on Attribute Values

Although both elements and attributes can contain information, restrictions exist on the types of information that an attribute can contain.

Also, attribute values are not parsed, so it might be tempting to try and slip an element or two into an attribute, but the fact that an attribute value can't contain the < character prevents you from adding any markup.

Whitespace in Attributes

The way in which an application handles whitespace in attributes differs from the way in which it handles whitespace for elements:

- In an element, line feeds, carriage returns, and so on are converted into a single space.

- In an attribute, each whitespace character, including spaces, tabs, line feeds, carriage returns, and line feed/carriage return combinations, is converted to a single space, which may result in an attribute value that contains a sequence of spaces. Whether the application collapses this sequence of spaces to a single space depends on the type declared for the attribute.

Common Attribute Types

In Chapter 7, we'll be declaring actual types for our attribute values. These types won't much matter until we begin to validate our documents, but knowing what's available can affect our initial document structure designs. Let's look briefly at the different attribute types defined in the XML 1.0 Recommendation.

The most common type of attribute is **CDATA**, or character data. Character data isn't parsed. It's presented exactly as it exists (after whitespace conversion). **CDATA** allows us to include text, spaces, and most other forms of content to provide information meaningful to a human reader. For example:

```
<maintenance lastdone="2/17/2325" responsible="Frank Madison">
    Once per month
</maintenance>
```

ID and **IDREF** are another pair of common attribute types. The **ID** attribute acts like the primary key on a database table, providing a value that can be referenced by the **IDREF** attribute. For example, we might break out maintenance personnel into their own elements, as in Listing 1.7.

LISTING 1.7   Using **ID** and **IDREF** Attribute Types to Cross-Reference Attributes

```
<?xml version="1.0" encoding="ISO-8859-1" standalone="no"?>
<!DOCTYPE airlocksystem SYSTEM "airlocks.dtd">
<airlocksystem>
    <airlock lockid="A23b">
```

LISTING 1.7   *Continued*

```
        <size height="320" width="500" />
        <type>Bronson</type>
        <location>Level 2 aft</location>
        <status>open</status>
        <maintenance responsible="M83">
            <lastdone>2/23/2325</lastdone>
            <frequency>Once per month</frequency>
        </maintenance>
    </airlock>
    <airlock lockid="Q36d">
        <size height="200" width="300" />
        <type>Perch</type>
        <location>Level 15 starboard</location>
        <status>closed</status>
        <maintenance responsible="D59">
            <lastdone>2/17/2325</lastdone>
            <frequency>Once per month</frequency>
        </maintenance>
    </airlock>
    <personnel badge="M83">
        <name>Frank Madison</name>
        <department>Maintenance</department>
    </personnel>
    <personnel badge="D59">
        <name>Angus Doyle</name>
        <department>Maintenance</department>
    </personnel>
</airlocksystem>
```

If we were defining the attribute types in a Document Type Definition (as we'll do later, in Chapter 7), the `badge` attribute would be defined as an `ID`, and the `responsible` attribute would be defined as an `IDREF`. This means that any value for `responsible` must match an existing value for `badge`. In this way, we can link elements together. In this example, by simply referring to the maintenance person responsible for a particular airlock, we can add or remove information associated with that person without touching the actual `airlock` element, simply by changing the referenced `personnel` element.

`CDATA`, `ID`, and `IDREF` are just a few of the attribute types available. We'll discuss others in Chapter 7.

Beyond Elements and Attributes

Let's stop for a moment and look at our sample document as it currently exists:

```
<?xml version="1.0" encoding="ISO-8859-1" standalone="no"?>
<!DOCTYPE airlocksystem SYSTEM "airlocks.dtd">
<airlocksystem>
    <airlock lockid="A23b">
```

```
        <size height="320" width="500" />
        <type>Bronson</type>
        <location>Level 2 aft</location>
        <status>open</status>
        <maintenance responsible="M83">
            <lastdone>2/23/2325</lastdone>
            <frequency>Once per month</frequency>
        </maintenance>
    </airlock>
    <airlock lockid="Q36d">
        <size height="200" width="300" />
        <type>Perch</type>
        <location>Level 15 starboard</location>
        <status>closed</status>
        <maintenance responsible="D59">
            <lastdone>2/17/2325</lastdone>
            <frequency>Once per month</frequency>
        </maintenance>
    </airlock>
    <personnel badge="M83">
        <name>Frank Madison</name>
        <department>Maintenance</department>
    </personnel>
    <personnel badge="D59">
        <name>Angus Doyle</name>
        <department>Maintenance</department>
    </personnel>
</airlocksystem>
```

While this is certainly helpful, it's just a start to what we can do with XML data. This file serves as the basis for our airlock control system. We can use this file to do so much more than simply hold information, by using information items other than elements and attributes in our XML file.

Entities

What would happen if you needed to add information in your XML file that *looked* like markup? Say we wanted to add a reference to signage for our airlocks:

```
<signage><DANGER!> Open Airlock</signage>
```

The trouble here is that the document is no longer well-formed. The application assumes that DANGER! is markup, so it looks for an end tag.

Fortunately, there's a way around this. XML allows us to use the ampersand (&) and semicolon (;) to "escape" characters, or provide equivalents that are converted to the actual values when the data is used. We sometimes see this in HTML pages. For example, Listing 1.8 shows an HTML page that displays the airlock signage.

LISTING 1.8   Escaping Characters

```
<html>
<head>
    <title>Signage</title>
</head>
<body>
    <p>Signage for airlock A23b:</p>
    <p>&lt;DANGER!&gt; Open Airlock</p>
</body>
</html>
```

As Figure 1.4 shows, the browser converts the < and > back into less-than (<) and greater-than (>) signs.

FIGURE 1.4

The browser converts < and > back to < and >.

These escaped values are called *entities*. In its simplest form, an entity enables us to add information to XML by means of a reference to a predefined value.

XML defines five entities that can be used automatically, as shown in the following table.

Entity	Resulting Symbol	Description
&lt;	<	Less than sign
&gt;	>	Greater than sign
&amp;	&	Ampersand
&quot;	"	Quotation mark
&apos;	'	Apostrophe (single quote)

All these entities are necessary to allow a full range of expression:

- The < and > entities allow us to add information that only looks like markup (< and >) within an element or attribute.

- ' and " allow us to add single quotes (') and double quotes (") within an attribute value without prematurely terminating the attribute.

- & allows us to use an ampersand (&) without the application assuming that we're trying to create an escaped character.

These are not the only entities we can use, however. For example, you may be familiar with HTML's non-breaking space ( ), which is not collapsed like a normal space. In fact, in Chapter 7, we'll see that XML allows us to define our own entities. This can be useful for characters that are not easily typed, or for entire sections of text we want to use in several places.

CDATA Sections

Sometimes even escaping the characters doesn't really solve the problem. Perhaps there is simply too much data to escape, or escaping it is inconvenient. Maybe escaping it is fine, but unescaping it to use it is difficult. This is often the case when scripts are added to Web pages as part of a file.

To solve this problem, we can use a CDATA section. As we said in the discussion of attributes, CDATA is short for *character data*. Like an attribute value, a CDATA section is not parsed by the application, so we can add anything we like to it.

We add a CDATA section using special formatting. For example, we could have solved the signage issue in the previous example as follows:

```
<signage><![CDATA[<DANGER!> Open Airlock]]></signage>
```

Or perhaps we want to add scripting that is associated with the data, as in Listing 1.9.

LISTING 1.9   CDATA Sections Allow the Use of Characters That Are Normally Considered Markup

```
<?xml version="1.0" encoding="ISO-8859-1" standalone="no"?>
<!DOCTYPE airlocksystem SYSTEM "airlocks.dtd">
<airlocksystem>
    <airlock lockid="A23b">
        <size height="320" width="500" />
        <type>Bronson</type>
        <location>Level 2 aft</location>
        <status>open</status>
        <maintenance responsible="M83">
            <lastdone>2/23/2325</lastdone>
            <frequency>Once per month</frequency>
        </maintenance>
        <signage>
            <signtext><![CDATA[<DANGER> Open Airlock]]></signtext>
            <checkscript type="text/javascript">
                <![CDATA[
                function checkSign() {
                  var now = new Date();
                  var targetDate = new Date("3/23/2325")
                  if (targetDate.valueOf() < now.valueOf(){
                      alertString = "DANGER! Airlock maintenance"
                      alertString = alertString + "is overdue!";
                      alert(alertString);
                  }
                }
                ]]>
```

LISTING 1.9   Continued

```
            </checkscript>
        </signage>
    </airlock>
...
</airlocksystem>
```

The **CDATA** section allows us to add necessary items without worrying about affecting the well-formed nature of the content.

Processing Instructions

Another common type of information added to XML is the *processing instruction*. A processing instruction includes information that's passed to the application that's processing the data. It typically contains a target, along with an instruction passed to the target. For example:

```
<?environment checkAtmosphere?>
```

The **<?** at the beginning tells the application that this is the start of a processing instruction. Next comes the target, then the instruction.

The XML Declaration Is a Special Case

Note that even though the XML declaration also starts with **<?** and ends with **?>**, it is *not* considered a processing instruction.

In most cases, the "instruction" takes the form of a name-value pair, or several name-value pairs. Perhaps the most common form of processing instruction at the time of this writing is the style sheet directive. For example, we can add a style sheet to the XML file, as shown in Listing 1.10.

LISTING 1.10   Adding a Processing Instruction

```
<?xml version="1.0" encoding="ISO-8859-1" standalone="no"?>
<!DOCTYPE airlocksystem SYSTEM "airlocks.dtd">
<?xml-stylesheet href="airlocks.xsl" type="text/xsl"?>
<airlocksystem>
    <airlock lockid="A23b">
        <size height="320" width="500" />
        <type>Bronson</type>
...
```

When a browser processes this file, it sees the processing instruction, and knows to apply the style sheet to the data. In this case, I've created a style sheet called **airlocks.xsl** that arranges the data into a report. (You'll learn more about this type of style sheet in Chapter 9, "Extensible Stylesheet Language Transformations [XSLT].") The results of performing the transformation are shown in Figure 1.5.

FIGURE 1.5

Processing instructions tell the browser to apply a style sheet to the page.

We can use processing instructions for other purposes as well. For example, we can create references to Java classes that we can then call within a style sheet, as you'll see in Chapter 9.

Comments

This being a programming book, I would be remiss if I left out the most underused type of XML information: the comment. A comment is a section of a document that starts with <!-- and ends with --> and is effectively ignored by the processor, so it allows us to do two things:

- Add information that's intended to be read by a human looking at the file.

- Use comments to effectively "remove" certain sections of a document.

Both uses are illustrated in Listing 1.11.

LISTING 1.11   Comments Add Information or Remove It

```
...
<airlock lockid="A23b">
    <size height="320" width="500" />
    <type>Bronson</type>
    <location>Level 2 aft</location>
    <status>open</status>
    <maintenance responsible="M83">
        <lastdone>2/23/2325</lastdone>
        <frequency>Once per month</frequency>
    </maintenance>
    <signage>
        <signtext><![CDATA[<DANGER> Open Airlock]]></signtext>
        <!-- CheckScript currently under review. Removed until
            review completion.  NC 3/1/2325 -->
        <checkscript type="text/javascript">
        <!--
```

LISTING 1.11   Continued

```
            <![CDATA[
            function checkSign() {
              var now = new Date();
              var targetDate = new Date("3/23/2325");
              if (targetDate.valueOf() < now.valueOf()) {
                  alertString = "DANGER! Airlock maintenance"
                  alertString = alertString + "is overdue!";
                  alert(alertString);
              }
            }
            ]]>
        -->
        </checkscript>
      </signage>
    </airlock>
...
```

In this case, we've added a comment about the status of the CheckScript. We've also effectively removed the contents of the **checkscript** element by enclosing it within a comment. Because it's within a comment, the processor will ignore it.

Well-Formed Versus Valid Documents

Throughout the discussion so far, we've talked about well-formed documents, with the occasional mention of valid documents. The connotations of the words themselves are similar, and might give you the impression that they mean the same thing; in fact, there is a significant difference between well-formed and valid documents:

- A *well-formed* document satisfies the requirements for a basic XML document, but can contain any elements, in any order, with any type of content.

- A *valid* document conforms to certain definitions of which elements and attributes may appear, and where.

A well-formed document doesn't have to be valid, but all valid documents must also be well-formed.

Think of it this way: A box can be rectangular (it has four sides) without being square (all four sides are the same length). But if a box is square, it's automatically rectangular, because the definition of a square is simply that it's a rectangle with all four sides the same length. In the same way, a document can be well-formed without necessarily being valid. But a valid document *must* be well-formed.

Valid Documents

Some requirements for a well-formed document only make sense in the context of a document with a Document Type Definition (DTD), so let's first discuss DTDs briefly.

A DTD is one way to provide the standard against which a document being validated is judged. The DTD provides information on elements and attributes that a document can contain. We'll discuss DTDs in detail in Chapter 7, but we can look at a brief example in our airlock document.

Listing 1.12 shows an internal DTD along with the document as we've built it.

LISTING 1.12 An Internal DTD

```
<?xml version="1.0" encoding="ISO-8859-1" standalone="no"?>
<!DOCTYPE airlocksystem [

<!ELEMENT airlocksystem (airlock+,personnel+)>

<!ELEMENT airlock (size, type, location, status, maintenance, signage)>
<!ATTLIST airlock lockid CDATA #IMPLIED>

<!ELEMENT size (#PCDATA)>
<!ATTLIST size height CDATA  #IMPLIED
               width CDATA   #IMPLIED>

<!ELEMENT type (#PCDATA)>
<!ELEMENT location (#PCDATA)>
<!ELEMENT status (#PCDATA)>

<!ELEMENT maintenance (lastdone, frequency)>
<!ATTLIST maintenance responsible IDREF #REQUIRED>
<!ELEMENT lastdone (#PCDATA)>
<!ELEMENT frequency (#PCDATA)>

<!ELEMENT personnel (name, department)>
<!ATTLIST personnel badge ID #REQUIRED>
<!ELEMENT name (#PCDATA)>
<!ELEMENT department (#PCDATA)>

<!ELEMENT signage (signtext, checkscript)>
<!ELEMENT signtext (#PCDATA)>
<!ELEMENT checkscript (#PCDATA)>
<!ATTLIST checkscript type CDATA #REQUIRED>
]>
<airlocksystem>
   ...
   <airlock lockid="Q36d">
      <size height="200" width="300" />
      <type>Perch</type>
      <location>Level 15 starboard</location>
      <status>closed</status>
      <maintenance responsible="D59">
         <lastdone>2/17/2325</lastdone>
         <frequency>Once per month</frequency>
      </maintenance>
      <signage>
```

LISTING 1.12   Continued

```
            <signtext>Airlock Closed</signtext>
            <!-- CheckScript currently under review. Removed until
                review completion.  NC 3/1/2325 -->
            <checkscript type="text/javascript">
            <!--
                <![CDATA[
                function checkSign() {
                    ...
                }
                ]]>
            -->
            </checkscript>
        </signage>
    </airlock>
    <personnel badge="M83">
        <name>Frank Madison</name>
        <department>Maintenance</department>
    </personnel>
    ...
</airlocksystem>
```

Each element specification defines the children of that element. Can it contain other elements, or should it just hold text? If it can contain other elements, what are they, how many can it hold, and in what order?

A DTD can also define entities, as mentioned previously. These entities can be internal or external, as shown in Listing 1.13.

LISTING 1.13   Definition of Internal and External Entities

```
<?xml version="1.0" encoding="ISO-8859-1" standalone="no"?>
<!DOCTYPE airlocksystem [
<!ELEMENT airlocksystem (airlock+,personnel+)>
<!ELEMENT airlock (size, type, location, status, maintenance, signage)>
<!ATTLIST airlock lockid CDATA #IMPLIED>
...
<!ELEMENT checkscript (#PCDATA)>
<!ATTLIST checkscript type CDATA #REQUIRED>
<!ENTITY signagetext "<![CDATA[<DANGER> Open Airlock]]>">
<!ENTITY checkscriptfunction SYSTEM "checkscripttext.txt">
]>
<airlocksystem>
    <airlock lockid="A23b">
...
        <maintenance responsible="M83">
            <lastdone>2/23/2325</lastdone>
            <frequency>Once per month</frequency>
        </maintenance>
        <signage>
            <signtext>&signagetext;</signtext>
```

LISTING 1.13   Continued

```
            <checkscript type="text/javascript">
                &checkscriptfunction;
            </checkscript>
        </signage>
    </airlock>
    <airlock lockid="Q36d">
    ...

        <maintenance responsible="D59">
            <lastdone>2/17/2325</lastdone>
            <frequency>Once per month</frequency>
        </maintenance>
        <signage>
            <signtext>Airlock Closed</signtext>
            <checkscript type="text/javascript">
                &checkscriptfunction;
            </checkscript>
        </signage>
    </airlock>
    ...
</airlocksystem>
```

Notice that the **&signagetext;** entity is defined within the document, so no other files are necessary to replace it within the **signtext** element. The **&checkscriptfunction;** entity, on the other hand, refers to an external file, so it's known as an *external entity*. In both cases, the replacement text will be substituted for the entity reference before any other processing is done on the data.

DTDs are far from the only way to validate a document. Several proposals exist for XML Schemas. These Schemas are methods for specifying the contents of an XML file that are themselves in the familiar XML syntax, which a DTD is not, as you can see in Listing 1.12. We'll discuss XML Schemas such as the W3C XML Schema Recommendation and RELAX NG in Chapter 8.

Requirements for a Well-Formed Document

Most of the requirements for a well-formed document are fairly straightforward, such as proper nesting and a single root element. Some are more esoteric. All are listed here:

- The document must have a single root element that contains all other elements.

- All elements must be nested properly. If an element's start tag is contained within an element, the end tag must be contained within that same element.

- All attribute values must be enclosed in quotation marks. These may take the form of single primes (or "straight apostrophes" [']) or double primes (or "straight quotes" ["]). If you're creating files in a word processing program, make sure that it doesn't attempt to be "helpful" and change your straight quotes (" ") to curly quotes ("").

- Attribute values cannot contain the < character.

- An element cannot have more than one attribute with a particular name.

- All characters in the document must be legal characters. Legal characters for an XML document include most of the 65,000 or so characters defined by the Unicode standard, but remember that the characters must match any encoding specification in the document. If you specify ISO 8859-1 (Latin-1), for example, you must stay with characters in that set.

Included Unicode Characters

The actual definition of "legal characters" includes the whitespace characters `#x9`, `#xA`, `#xD`, and `#x20`, `#x21–#xD7FF`, `#xE000–#xFFFD`, and `#x10000–#x10FFFF`.

Common "Illegal" Characters

Several characters inserted into documents by Microsoft Word, such as the em dash (—) in place of two hyphens (- -) and the ellipsis (…) in place of three periods (. . .), are not legal XML characters.

- If you declare the document as `standalone="yes"`, all entities used within the data must be declared within the body of the document, and not externally.

External Entities and Non-Validating Parsers

Not all parsers are validating parsers, which makes a difference when dealing with external entities. A *validating parser* will always attempt to retrieve an external entity, but a *non-validating parser* won't necessarily retrieve the definition of an external entity. This only applies to files that are not specified as `standalone="yes"`, because files specified as `standalone="yes"` must not contain references to external entities anyway.

- An attribute value cannot refer to an external entity.

- A special type of entity, called a *parameter entity*, can be referenced within the DTD, but not within the document. (We'll deal with parameter entities in Chapter 7.)

- A parameter entity cannot refer to itself.

- A parsed entity (including all entities we've covered so far) cannot contain a reference to an unparsed entity, such as a reference to a graphics file, as you'll see in Chapter 7.

Some well-formedness constraints, such as the requirement of unique attribute names, are affected by the use of XML namespaces. See the next section for details.

Namespaces

The concept of *namespaces* is not something that was concocted for XML. It has been a part of programming for decades, in fact. The idea behind namespaces is that at any given time, a single name should refer to a single item, whether that item is a variable, a function, or a file. There should never be any confusion about what a name refers to.

For example, in many professional sports, a player is identified by a number on his or her uniform. Within each team, only one player can wear each number, but it's not uncommon for a single number to be in use by two teams playing against each other. Because the number is also associated with a team, however, there is no problem identifying the player.

Namespaces are in many ways like these teams; they provide a realm in which names must be unique, but they also provide a way to mix names without causing confusion.

In programming, we tend to see namespaces used in several ways. For example, you can have several files with the same name, as long as they're in different directories. You can have several Java classes with the same name, as long as they're in different packages.

In XML, we can use namespaces to allow the combination of elements from different sources without causing confusion.

One excellent example of namespace usage is an XSL style sheet, where some elements provide instructions to the processor and others are merely content that will be output. Listing 1.14 shows a simple example.

LISTING 1.14   A Simple Namespace Example

```
<?xml version="1.0"?>
<xsl:stylesheet xmlns:xsl="http://www.w3.org/1999/XSL/Transform" version="1.0">

<xsl:template match="/">
<html>
    <head>
        <title>
            <xsl:value-of select="message/heading"/>
        </title>
    </head>
    <body>
        <xsl:value-of select="message/paragraph"/>
    </body>
</html>
</xsl:template>

</xsl:stylesheet>
```

The elements in bold are part of the **xsl** namespace, so they're handled differently from those not in bold.

Let's take a look at Listing 1.14 step by step.

The first thing we need to do is declare the namespace itself. We do this in the main `xsl:stylesheet` element using the `xmlns:xsl` attribute:

```
<xsl:stylesheet xmlns:xsl="http://www.w3.org/1999/XSL/Transform"
                                            version="1.0">
```

Here we have declared not only the namespace (`http://www.w3.org/1999/XSL/Transform`) but also an alias (`xsl`) that refers to the namespace. It's important to note that although the alias is referenced in each element, the namespace itself is the full location, or URI. (The URI is only for uniqueness, and doesn't necessarily refer to an actual Web address, as you'll see shortly.)

Namespaces do more than prevent name clashes; in some ways, they can act like version numbers. XSL style sheets provide a perfect example of this function.

The first XSL processors, which were produced before the XSL Transformations Recommendation was complete, used a working draft of the Recommendation, and handled style sheets accordingly. Once the Recommendation was complete, however, several significant changes had been made, and a style sheet written for the working draft would not work properly under a processor expecting one written for the Recommendation.

Fortunately, namespaces had been built into the Recommendation from the beginning. The older style sheets (and processors) used this namespace:

```
http://www.w3.org/TR/WD-xsl
```

The newer style sheets (and processors) used this one:

```
http://www.w3.org/1999/XSL/Transform
```

By looking at the namespace, the processor knew whether it could handle the style sheet, and how to go about doing so.

Specifying a Namespace

It's often a good idea to add namespace information to your documents, particularly if there's a chance that your data will be mixed with data from another source at some point. For example, at some point the airlock data from our earlier example may be mixed with life-support system data. The combined document might look something like Listing 1.15.

LISTING 1.15   Combining Namespaces

```
<?xml version="1.0" encoding="ISO-8859-1" standalone="no"?>
<airlocksystem xmlns:ls="http://www.example.com/lifesupport/" >
   <airlock lockid="A23b">
      <size height="320" width="500" />
      <type>Bronson</type>
      <location>Level 2 aft</location>
      <status>open</status>
      <maintenance responsible="M83" ls:supervisor="D59">
         <lastdone>2/23/2325</lastdone>
```

LISTING 1.15   Continued

```
        <frequency>Once per month</frequency>
        <ls:checkmethod>Negative pressure</ls:checkmethod>
    </maintenance>
    <signage>
...
```

It's important to note that we're not limited to a single namespace. We could actually set up a namespace for each set of data, as shown in Listing 1.16.

LISTING 1.16   Showing Multiple Namespaces

```
<?xml version="1.0" encoding="ISO-8859-1" standalone="no"?>
<air:airlocksystem xmlns:air="http://www.example.com/airlocksystem/"
                   xmlns:ls="http://www.example.com/lifesupport/" >
    <air:airlock air:lockid="A23b">
        <air:size air:height="320" air:width="500" />
        <air:type>Bronson</air:type>
        <air:location>Level 2 aft</air:location>
        <air:status>open</air:status>
        <air:maintenance air:responsible="M83" ls:supervisor="D59">
            <air:lastdone>2/23/2325</air:lastdone>
            <air:frequency>Once per month</air:frequency>
            <ls:checkmethod>Negative pressure</ls:checkmethod>
        </air:maintenance>
        <air:signage>
...
```

URN Versus URI Versus URL

When choosing a namespace for their data, many people worry about what form it should take. The most common form of namespace is a *uniform resource identifier* (URI), formerly known in many circles as a *uniform resource locator* (URL). Because of the word *locator*, many people assume that the application somehow retrieves information from this address as to how to process the data. This is simply not true.

The sole purpose of a namespace is to provide a unique identifier. URIs are often used because they offer infinite variety and enable companies to choose one of their own URIs (assuming that they have a domain name under their control). This prevents different companies from inadvertently using the same namespace.

In some cases, such as the XSL example in Listing 1.14, there actually is information at the end of the line, but this is more for convenience than for any technical reason. All that's required is a unique address.

Current discussions center around whether to choose a URI or a *uniform resource name* (URN). A URN doesn't actually provide information on where to find a resource; it just provides a way to refer to it. Whereas URIs typically start with a protocol such as `http://` or `ftp://`, URNs start with `urn:` and take this form:

`urn:{namespace}:{specificstring}`

Here are some examples:

`urn:AIRLOCKSYSTEM:lifesupport`

`urn:AIRLOCKSYSTEM:airlocks`

`urn:MANAGEMENT:humanresources`

The Default Namespace

Many XML documents don't contain any namespace information, and are said to contain "no namespace." Even in a document where a namespace has been declared, unaliased elements and attributes can still be considered to have no namespace. Take Listing 1.17, for example.

LISTING 1.17   Elements with No Namespace

```
<?xml version="1.0" encoding="ISO-8859-1" standalone="no"?>
<airlocksystem xmlns:ls="http://www.example.com/lifesupport/" >
   <airlock lockid="A23b">
      <size height="320" width="500" />
      <type>Bronson</type>
      <location>Level 2 aft</location>
      <status>open</status>
      <maintenance responsible="M83" ls:supervisor="D59">
         <lastdone>2/23/2325</lastdone>
         <frequency>Once per month</frequency>
         <ls:checkmethod>Negative pressure</ls:checkmethod>
      </maintenance>
      <signage>
...
```

In this example, the `airlock`, `size`, `type`, and other elements and their attributes that aren't in boldface print have no namespace, while the `checkmethod` element and `supervisor` attribute are considered part of the `lifesupport` namespace.

On occasion, we want elements to be part of a namespace, but we don't want to specify an alias in every element, making a mess like Listing 1.16. In this case, we can create a default namespace to which any unaliased elements will belong. To declare a default namespace, simply omit the alias declaration. For example, we can add a default namespace to Listing 1.17, as shown in Listing 1.18.

LISTING 1.18   Using a Default Namespace

```
<?xml version="1.0" encoding="ISO-8859-1" standalone="no"?>
<airlocksystem xmlns="http://www.example.com/airlock/"
               xmlns:ls="http://www.example.com/lifesupport/" >
```

LISTING 1.18   Continued

```
<airlock lockid="A23b">
  <size height="320" width="500" />
  <type>Bronson</type>
  <location>Level 2 aft</location>
  <status>open</status>
  <maintenance responsible="M83" ls:supervisor="D59">
      <lastdone>2/23/2325</lastdone>
      <frequency>Once per month</frequency>
      <ls:checkmethod>Negative pressure</ls:checkmethod>
  </maintenance>
  <signage>
...
```

In this case, the bold elements are considered part of the `airlock` namespace.

There is one important distinction, however. Notice that the attributes are not bold. Attributes are *never* considered part of the default namespace. So although the `airlock` element is part of the `airlock` namespace, the `lockid` attribute is still considered to have no namespace.

Namespace Scope

A namespace declaration affects an element and all of its children, unless it's overridden by another declaration. Take Listing 1.19, for example.

LISTING 1.19   Inheriting Namespaces—Or Not

```
<?xml version="1.0" encoding="ISO-8859-1" standalone="no"?>
<air:airlocksystem xmlns:air="http://www.example.com/airlock/"
                 xmlns:ls="http://www.example.com/lifesupport/" >
   <air:airlock xmlns:air="http://www.example.com/airlockReports/"
                 lockid="A23b">
     <size height="320" width="500" />
     <type>Bronson</type>
     <location>Level 2 aft</location>
     <status>open</status>
     <maintenance responsible="M83" ls:supervisor="D59">
         <lastdone>2/23/2325</lastdone>
         <frequency>Once per month</frequency>
         <ls:checkmethod>Negative pressure</ls:checkmethod>
     </maintenance>
     <signage>
...
```

The `airlocksystem` element is part of the `airlock` namespace, which is http://www.example.com/airlock/. But its child element, `airlock`, resets the definition of the `air:` alias, so the `airlock` element is part of the `airlockReports` namespace, http://www.example.com/airlockReports/.

Notice that we can't simply declare a namespace for a parent and assume that the children fall into the same namespace. The `airlock` element is in the `airlockReports` namespace, but its child, the `size` element, isn't. In fact, the `size` element has no namespace at all.

This is one situation in which the default namespace comes into play. In Listing 1.20, the `size` element is part of the default namespace, even though its parent, the `airlock` element, is part of the `airlockReports` namespace.

LISTING 1.20   Inheriting the Default Namespace

```
<?xml version="1.0" encoding="ISO-8859-1" standalone="no"?>
<airlocksystem xmlns="http://www.example.com/airlock/"
               xmlns:ls="http://www.example.com/lifesupport/" >
   <air:airlock xmlns:air="http://www.example.com/airlockReports/"
                lockid="A23b">
      <size height="320" width="500" />
      <type>Bronson</type>
      <location>Level 2 aft</location>
      <status>open</status>
      <maintenance responsible="M83" ls:supervisor="D59">
          <lastdone>2/23/2325</lastdone>
          <frequency>Once per month</frequency>
          <ls:checkmethod>Negative pressure</ls:checkmethod>
      </maintenance>
      <signage>
...
```

Like any other namespace, the default namespace can be changed in a child element, as in Listing 1.21.

LISTING 1.21   Changing the Default Namespace

```
<?xml version="1.0" encoding="ISO-8859-1" standalone="no"?>
<airlocksystem xmlns="http://www.example.com/airlock/"
               xmlns:ls="http://www.example.com/lifesupport/" >
   <airlock xmlns="http://www.example.com/airlockReports/"
                lockid="A23b">
      <size height="320" width="500" />
      <type>Bronson</type>
      <location>Level 2 aft</location>
      <status>open</status>
      <maintenance responsible="M83" ls:supervisor="D59">
          <lastdone>2/23/2325</lastdone>
          <frequency>Once per month</frequency>
          <ls:checkmethod>Negative pressure</ls:checkmethod>
      </maintenance>
      <signage>
...
```

In this example, the `airlocksystem` element is part of the `airlock` namespace, whereas the `airlock` element and all of its unaliased children are part of the `airlockReports` namespace.

We can also "undeclare" the default namespace by setting the value to empty quotes (""), as shown in Listing 1.22.

LISTING 1.22   Undeclaring the Default Namespace

```
<?xml version="1.0" encoding="ISO-8859-1" standalone="no"?>
<airlocksystem xmlns="http://www.example.com/airlock/"
               xmlns:ls="http://www.example.com/lifesupport/" >
    <airlock xmlns="" lockid="A23b">
       <size height="320" width="500" />
       <type>Bronson</type>
       <location>Level 2 aft</location>
       <status>open</status>
       <maintenance responsible="M83" ls:supervisor="D59">
           <lastdone>2/23/2325</lastdone>
           <frequency>Once per month</frequency>
           <ls:checkmethod>Negative pressure</ls:checkmethod>
       </maintenance>
       <signage>
...
```

In this case, the `airlocksystem` element is part of the `airlock` namespace, but the `airlock` element and all of its children have no namespace.

Namespaces and Attributes

Namespace declarations affect attributes in two ways. First, as mentioned earlier, it's important to understand that the default namespace is not inherited by an attribute, so an element in the default namespace and its unaliased attribute are not in the same namespace.

A related effect is that even though two attributes in a single element can't share the same name, attributes can have the same names if they appear in different namespaces. For example, Listing 1.23 shows a perfectly legal and well-formed document.

LISTING 1.23   Namespaces and Duplicate Attribute Names

```
<?xml version="1.0" encoding="ISO-8859-1" standalone="no"?>
<airlocksystem xmlns="http://www.example.com/airlock/"
               xmlns:ls="http://www.example.com/lifesupport/" >
    <airlock lockid="A23b">
       <size height="320" width="500" />
       <type>Bronson</type>
       <location>Level 2 aft</location>
       <status>open</status>
       <maintenance responsible="M83" ls:responsible="D59">
           <lastdone>2/23/2325</lastdone>
           <frequency>Once per month</frequency>
           <ls:checkmethod>Negative pressure</ls:checkmethod>
```

LISTING 1.23   Continued

```
        </maintenance>
        <signage>
...
```

Remember, though, that a namespace is determined not by the alias, but by the actual URI or URN. Listing 1.24 shows a document that is *not* well-formed.

LISTING 1.24   Incorrect Use of Namespaces and Duplicate Attribute Names

```
<?xml version="1.0" encoding="ISO-8859-1" standalone="no"?>
<airlocksystem xmlns="http://www.example.com/airlock/"
               xmlns:ls="http://www.example.com/lifesupport/"
               xmlns:maint="http://www.example.com/lifesupport/" >
    <airlock lockid="A23b">
        <size height="320" width="500" />
        <type>Bronson</type>
        <location>Level 2 aft</location>
        <status>open</status>
        <maintenance maint:responsible="M83" ls:responsible="D59">
            <lastdone>2/23/2325</lastdone>
            <frequency>Once per month</frequency>
            <ls:checkmethod>Negative pressure</ls:checkmethod>
        </maintenance>
        <signage>
...
```

Even though the `maint` alias and `ls` alias are different, they both refer to the `http://www.example.com/lifesupport/` namespace, so both attributes are part of the same namespace and can't share the same name.

Summary

The most basic XML data consists of elements (set off from the character data by tags similar to those seen in HTML) and attributes (name-value pairs specified in the start tag of an element), but there are many other types of information. These other types include processing instructions, which allow you to send information to other applications; entities, which allow you to refer to other content; and comments, which allow you to leave information for those who come after you.

The actual data in an XML document can be segregated into different namespaces, enabling you to distinguish between different types of data and to avoid naming conflicts.

An XML document must be well-formed, which means that, among other things, its elements are properly nested and its attribute values are enclosed in quotes. Some XML documents are also valid, which means that they have been compared to some sort of standard, such as a Document Type Definition, to ensure that they have the proper structure and content.

Review Questions

1. What is an XML element?

2. What is an attribute?

3. How do you nest elements?

4. How many root elements can there be in a document?

5. What is the difference between a well-formed document and a valid document?

6. What is an entity?

7. Give an example of a processing instruction.

8. What is a DTD used for?

9. What is a namespace?

10. What is a child element?

Programming Exercises

1. Create a simple XML document to describe yourself. Make sure that it is well-formed.

2. Create an XML file to describe a hobby of yours. Make sure that the data is at least three levels deep.

3. Create an XML file that uses ID and IDREF attributes to link elements together conceptually. (Do not include a DTD at this time.)

4. Add a second namespace to one of your documents and add information that is part of that namespace.

CHAPTER 2

DESIGNING XML DOCUMENTS AND APPLICATIONS

You will learn about the following in this chapter:

- The planning process
- Defining goals and objectives
- Gathering the team
- Gathering information
- Function/process modeling

- Data modeling
- Checking the model
- Creating the structure
- The final structure

Before we actually build anything, let's look at planning the structure of the data. Yes, yes, I know, you're anxious to get your hands dirty, and so am I, but planning is an essential part of any application, and XML-related applications are no exception. The structure of your documents is the underpinning for your entire system. If you don't take the time to understand exactly what you're building, and more importantly, why you're building it, you're setting yourself up for failure.

In this chapter, we're going to discuss the various aspects of planning for the data and structure to be included in a collection of XML documents. If you've already got a structure in mind, or if one has been imposed on you and you feel that you must skip ahead to Chapter 3, well, I suppose I can forgive you, but you may find it helpful to at least glance at the "Checking the Model" section of this chapter to make sure you haven't missed anything. This chapter will still be here the next time you have to design from scratch.

This isn't a book on project management, but we'll cover the essentials of managing a project as we design an XML data structure for an outer space tourist resort. Feel free to choose one of your own projects and follow along.

Functions and Methods

In this chapter we'll talk a lot about functions and methods. Rather than object methods and functions, however, we're referring to functions carried out by a business and the methods by which a business does something.

The Planning Process

Because XML is inherently simple, the temptation is to simply create the structure as you go along, a process known as "designing at the keyboard." As tempting as this may be, a multitude of reasons exists for avoiding it.

Unless your process is extremely small, self-contained, and completely independent of any other documents or systems, you're going to need other people's feedback to make sure that your designs truly capture the system that you're trying to replicate or produce. In most cases, these people are not technical, and will need documentation geared more toward the layman than toward other engineers.

This documentation is the main deliverable, or required output, of the planning process. It gives you a chance to confirm the appropriateness of the model that you have produced before you write thousands of lines of code to manipulate a model that doesn't reflect the actual data.

The planning process involves the following basic steps:

1. Define goals and objectives.

2. Gather the team.

3. Gather information.

4. Create preliminary models.

5. Validate the models.

6. Make changes as appropriate.

7. Create the XML document structure.

8. Deploy.

9. Maintain.

In this chapter, we will deal with the first seven steps, taking the design through the analysis and into the actual structure. It's important to note at this point that the usual process is to create a Document Type Definition or other document against which XML data can be validated, but because we won't cover DTDs until Chapter 7, we will stop with the prototype document in this chapter.

Defining the Goals and Objectives

It may seem silly to start defining goals and objectives before we gather the team, and indeed, there will be situations where building the team is the very first task. In many cases, however, the goals and objectives of the project directly affect the composition of the team, as you'll see in the next section.

First, let's talk about the difference between goals and objectives. Simply put, a *goal* is an overall result that you want to accomplish, while an *objective* is a measurable step on the way to that goal. Note the word *measurable*. If something can't be measured, it's not an objective. (It might still be a goal, however.)

For example, you might have a goal of increasing business. While it would seem that that is easy to measure, it really isn't. Increase what kind of business? As measured by what? And increased by how much? It should be easy to tell whether you've successfully defined an objective with no "wiggle room." For example, either you've increased sales to existing customers by 25% or you haven't.

In our fictional example, the Vanguard Space Resort has been experiencing low turnout for events, even among visitors who are already on the station. Market research reveals that visitors are skittish about safety. The management team decrees that this project should fulfill the following two goals:

- Enhance visitors' perception of safety on and around the station

- Increase visitor participation in excursions and events

The project team eventually breaks these goals down into specific objectives:

Goal	Objectives
Enhance visitors' perception of safety on and around the station	Formalize and publish maintenance schedules and results
	Improve maintenance signage
	Automatically disable equipment that is beyond its maintenance period
	Prevent scheduling of events during maintenance
Increase visitor participation in excursions and events	Make scheduling available to visitors from the terminals in their rooms
	Allow users to make their own appointments using room and public terminals rather than having to contact resort personnel
	Personalize ads in visitors' rooms based on preferences and past activities

Write down the goals and objectives for your project. Review the objectives to make sure they really are specific and measurable. For example, the "Improve maintenance signage" objective is still too general and unmeasurable. We can rephrase it as follows:

Post signage on all applicable equipment stating date of last maintenance, results, and next maintenance due date.

Note that in many cases, we determine goals and objectives not prior to choosing the team, but concurrent with it, as the existing team refines the objectives and spots expertise holes that must be filled.

Gathering the Team

Any project team has several "roles" that must be filled, though there's nothing that says that a single person can't have more than one job. These roles include

- **Project manager**—This person is responsible for making sure that staff are assigned, deadlines are met, and problems are resolved.

- **Team leader**—This person is responsible for the overall direction of the group.

- **Interviewer**—This person is responsible for gathering information from users and other subject matter experts.

- **Recordist**—This person is responsible for recording information from both interviews and meetings. The recordist is often the most skilled person in the group, because he or she needs to be able to determine what information must be recorded.

- **Committee members**—These people are responsible for analyzing the information presented, using it to determine the components that must be accounted for, and creating the overall structure.

- **Subject matter experts**—These are the people who actually use the data, either in its original form (such as the legacy databases in which it's stored) or in its intended form (such as the target system). They won't necessarily be involved in the day-to-day workings of the committee, but can be called in when their expertise is needed.

- **Stakeholders**—These are the people who have something to gain from the project, whether it's better data, improved quality of work life, or an improved image within the company.

In general, you'll want to keep the number of participants manageable—in most cases, more than 6 to 8 committee members is a recipe for disaster—but it's important to make sure that all the stakeholders are represented in some way.

Remember, in smaller projects, there's no reason that one or two people can't fill all or most of these roles. In larger projects, there's no reason to include on the committee a person from every department that will be affected if doing so will swell the team to an unmanageable size. You'll also need the unbiased opinions of reviewers who aren't involved in the actual design process as the project moves along.

Our resort project team consists of

- A project manager, from the project management office.

- A consultant contracted and brought to the station to perform the actual analysis and design the system to be built. The consultant will act, in this case, as both the interviewer and the recorder, but will not implement the actual system.

- A representative from the maintenance department.

- The activities director.

- The assistant safety director.

- A longtime visitor to the resort.

Determining Methodology

Once you've gathered the team together, it's time to make some decisions about how you're going to work, and how often you're going to meet. It's important to set expectations early so individuals can adjust their own workflows and schedules, and make sure that their time is allocated to the project. Otherwise, participation will be spotty, and your project will stall. Remember to allow for time between meetings so members can analyze and prepare information.

How will decisions be made, particularly in the face of conflict? Don't fall into the trap of requiring consensus on all decisions; there will always be cases where mutually exclusive opinions are strongly held.

You may opt to give the team leader the final decision. In many cases this works, but in some situations it can lead to sabotage later on. If the people who are going to use the system don't buy into it from the beginning, they'll do everything they can to avoid it. Many perfectly good systems fail because they simply aren't used by the people they were intended to help.

One methodology that works well is the majority (more than 50%) or supermajority (2/3 majority) vote, because it forces people to explain their position in the hopes of swaying others to their way of thinking. That dissenting voice may be right!

Our resort team will meet twice a week (because we're in a hurry) and will resolve conflicts via supermajority vote.

In most cases, the ultimate deliverable is an analysis report that includes not only the rationale for all decisions, but also a Document Type Definition or XML Schema document. For this example, however, our final product will be a sample document illustrating our chosen structure.

Gathering Information

Now that we've got the team assembled and we know how we're going to work and what it is that we're trying to accomplish, it's time to begin the analysis phase of the project.

Any project involves a number of factors, some of which have to do with the project itself and some of which are imposed by outside limitations. In this phase, we'll gather information on constraints to which we must conform and systems (electronic and otherwise) into which we must integrate.

Scope

The scope of a project is at once the most obvious aspect that must be resolved and the one that is most often overlooked because it's considered to be so obvious. Unfortunately, when two people talk, they frequently aren't speaking the same language.

For example, when the stated goal is to "integrate all of our systems into a single interface," does that mean all of the existing systems? All systems built from now on, including some that may replace legacy systems? Is it only to include work from this point on, or will you need to include all legacy documents? How far back? For what departments?

Determine the scope of your project and document it. Our resort team decides that the scope of the project includes the creation of a new system that integrates with the existing maintenance and activities scheduling systems. Because the overall goals of the system involve public perception of the present condition, our team decides not to include any legacy activities data, but to include legacy maintenance data up to one year old. The system encompasses all future data for both maintenance and activities.

Data Sources and Destinations

In an integration project, many of the original data sources are obvious; they're the systems to be integrated. But this step is rarely that simple. Are there any other potential sources for data? What about paper documents? Will users be creating new data in the new system that doesn't conform to any of the old systems? What happens to the data when you're finished with it?

In many cases, we're using XML to facilitate communication between different companies, in which case this aspect of the project is crucial. Where is the data coming from, and in what form? Is there a structure for it when it arrives, and is that structure XML based? Will you have to process it before you can use it? Will you be performing any processing on it before you send it on to its final destination? What is the final form and destination? Is it XML? How will it get there? Over a network, or (heaven forbid) on paper?

This part of the discussion shouldn't encompass only systems. Your users are a "destination" for the data. How will they be using it, and what is their level of sophistication? Do they understand XML, or will you need to build an application that hides the details from them?

The resort team determines that they're dealing with the following data sources:

- Existing maintenance records in the legacy system

- Incoming maintenance reports entered into the new system via handheld terminals by maintenance personnel

- Activity schedules from the legacy system

- New activities scheduled through the new system by activities personnel on their terminals

- Appointments made by users through their terminals

- Visitor preferences from the existing marketing database

The team determines that the data will proceed to the following destinations:

- Visitors will see the data (appropriately transformed for presentation) on the terminals in their rooms.

- Maintenance personnel will see the data (appropriately transformed for presentation) on their handheld terminals.

- Activities personnel will see the data (appropriately transformed for presentation) on their terminals.

- Maintenance reports will be transferred to the legacy maintenance system.

- New activities will be transferred to the legacy activities system.

The team also determines that users will not interact directly with the data, but will interact with it through a software interface.

Legal Requirements

When looking at the constraints that may affect your application, it's important to remember that not all of them will be technical. Your legal department may have a say in either including or excluding information from the system. For example, many European countries have strict personal privacy requirements, and this may have an effect on the types of information that can be transferred between systems. A hazardous waste reporting system may have specific regulatory information that must be included. Be aware of constraints that may exist, and don't be afraid to contact the legal department. Any hassle on the front end is worthwhile, so long as you don't have to redesign the entire system after it's already been built! (This is one case where it is *not* easier to ask for forgiveness than for permission.)

Industry Standards

Information transferred between companies is often in a form that complies with an industry standard. Hundreds of "standard" DTDs and XML Schema documents exist, and your system may be required to comply with one or more of them, if data is coming from or going to a partner that uses these standards.

Even if data will remain internal, it's never a bad idea to check for the existence of an industry standard structure. This document can serve as a sanity and completeness check for you later in the process.

One word of warning, however. Now is the time to document any such requirements, but it's not the time to actually study the document. You may come up with a better approach than the standard's authors, and your business may have idiosyncrasies that make the standard unworkable, or at least inadequate. There will be plenty of time for checking the model after the analysis and modeling are done.

The resort team determines that while the data will all remain internal and will not conform to any particular industry standard, they will check the Space Station Maintenance Language standard for guidance.

Potential Structures

Through the analysis, you may come to the conclusion that no one structure is going to satisfy everybody. The users need something simple, the database needs to conform to a particular format, and two of your trading partners—companies with which you do business and exchange information—use different industry standard DTDs, while the third insists on using their own in-house proprietary model.

Don't panic.

It's perfectly normal, particularly in large-scale XML projects, for a system to need to conform to multiple structures. The idea is to make sure that all of them are compatible with each other.

For example, you might have a situation in which the application can be built most effectively using one structure, but a completely different structure is necessary to efficiently import data into the database. At the same time, the complexity of both of these models might completely overwhelm the users who are going to actually create the initial data.

To satisfy all these seemingly contradictory needs, you can create several structures:

- **Reference structure**—The reference structure is the overall model with which every structure must be compatible.

- **Authoring structure**—This is typically a scaled-down version of the reference structure.

- **Conversion structure**—This may be an intermediate form for data that's in the process of being transformed into something else.

- **Interchange structure**—This can include any number of structures into which the data must be converted for transfer to your trading partners.

Function/Process Modeling

The two major types of modeling that we'll cover in this book are *function/process modeling* and *data modeling*. While it may seem that data modeling is more appropriate for an XML project, because the focus of this book is XML programming, there's some impetus to begin with function/process modeling. We'll cover data modeling in the next section.

The Basic Functions

The first step in function/process modeling is to determine the basic functions that must be accomplished in the course of doing business. Note that we're not talking about the functions that the application or project must accomplish. In fact, there's no mention in process modeling of how something is accomplished—just the fact that it is accomplished.

The reason for this is that we're performing a problem-solving task, and often things are done in a certain way "because we've always done it that way." Removing the mechanism from the function allows us to think about the problem in a different way.

For example, say the maintenance team has been filling out paper maintenance reports because they need a signed copy for the regulatory files. Another person then enters these reports into the computer system. If the mechanism for these functions were included in the function statements, they would read as follows:

```
Complete maintenance report form and sign.
Enter the maintenance report data into the system.
```

This doesn't leave a lot of room for alternatives. On the other hand, if the same statements were written without any mechanism, we could create a system in which maintenance personnel enter their report data directly into the system, then print out a copy and sign it:

```
Obtain signed maintenance record.
Record maintenance data.
```

Notice that the order in which functions are recorded is not necessarily relevant.

Start by determining the basic functions that need to be accomplished and document them by creating a function hierarchy model, where each function is represented by a box with rounded corners, as in Figure 2.1.

FIGURE 2.1

A basic function
hierarchy diagram.

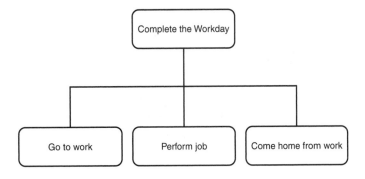

After some discussion, the resort team determines the basic functions that they feel fall within the scope of the project, as shown in Figure 2.2.

FIGURE 2.2
The resort team's basic functions.

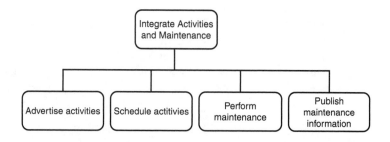

Of course, this is a very high-level look at what's going on, and doesn't provide a lot of useful information. It does provide a starting point, however.

Decomposing the Function

Once you have your basic functions, you can begin to *decompose* them. This process involves breaking them down into the individual subfunctions needed to accomplish the overall function.

> **Function Order**
>
> Note that although it makes sense to document functions in order, there's nothing about the function hierarchy diagram that mandates any particular order. In other words, don't assume from the order in the diagram that this is the order in which actions must occur.

For example, we might break the basic function "Make dinner" into subfunctions "Obtain ingredients," "Mix ingredients," and "Cook ingredients," as shown in Figure 2.3.

FIGURE 2.3
Decomposing a function.

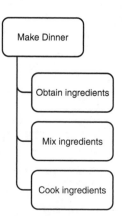

Decomposition continues until we reach the most atomic level practical for the project. In general, if you're writing functions with more than one or two verbs in them, you probably need to break them down further.

For example, the resort team can break down the "Schedule activities" function as shown in Figure 2.4.

FIGURE 2.4
Decomposing the "Schedule activities" function.

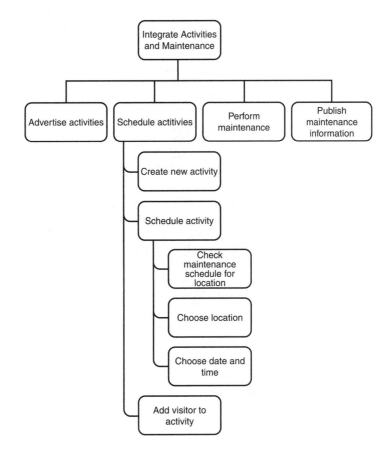

Sometimes there's simply too much information to convey conveniently in one place. In such cases, use an ellipsis (…) to indicate that there's more information on another page, as shown in Figure 2.5. The additional information is shown in Figures 2.6 and 2.7.

FIGURE 2.5
Use an ellipsis to indicate that more information is available elsewhere.

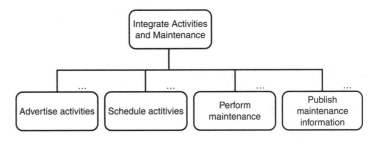

FIGURE 2.6
The resort team's activity-related functions.

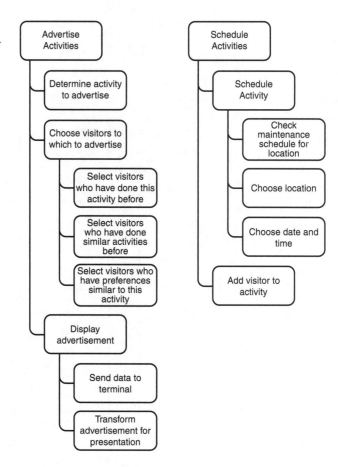

Events

In some cases, a function is triggered by an outside event. For example, an airlock must be inspected when its maintenance period expires. Such events are shown as the outline of an arrow pointing to the function that they trigger, as shown in Figure 2.8.

Check your hierarchy for events masquerading as functions. For example, the so-called function "Maintenance period expires" in Figure 2.7 really should be an event rather than a function, as shown in Figure 2.9.

Reviewing the Model

Once your preliminary process model is complete, have it checked by an objective third party for completeness and reasonableness. You should be able to answer the following questions:

- Would the CEO of the company recognize the company, or is it so generic it could refer to any company?

FIGURE 2.7
The resort team's maintenance-related functions.

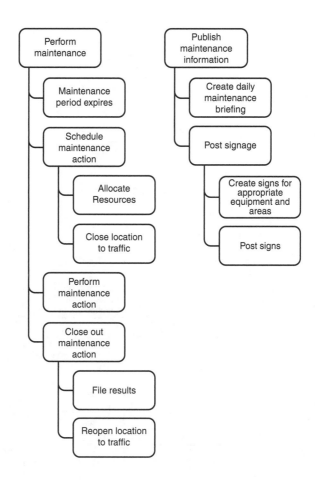

Remove any events from your hierarchy and add them back as event arrows.

- Did you remember the most obvious functions?

- Can all project objectives be accomplished through functions in your hierarchy?

- Are all functions phrased in such a way that they are independent of the method used to accomplish them, except perhaps as an example for clarification?

When you can answer all of these questions satisfactorily, you're ready to move on to the next step.

Upon review, the resort team discovers that they didn't include a function to actually create an activity to schedule. To fix the problem, they make the changes shown in Figure 2.10.

The team also needs to consider how to remove activities or other objects. What process is involved with canceling an activity? What is involved with removing equipment from service?

FIGURE 2.8
An event is shown as an arrow pointing to the function it triggers.

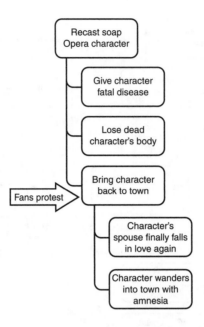

FIGURE 2.9
Sometimes functions are really events.

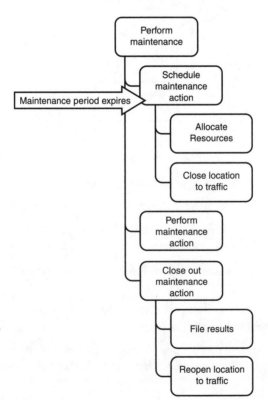

FIGURE 2.10

The preliminary function hierarchy.

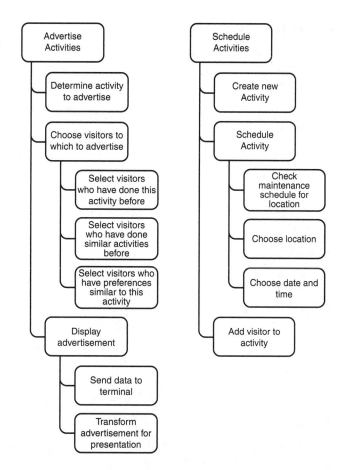

Data Modeling

Now that we've looked at what the business does, let's look at the data it uses.

In *data modeling*, there are three kinds of information: entities, attributes, and relationships. An *entity* is something of importance, either physical or conceptual, about which we need information, such as an employee or a customer's order. An *attribute* is information about that entity, such as the employee name or order number. A *relationship* describes how two entities are connected to each other. For example, an order must have one or more order items, and an order item must belong to exactly one order.

In the database world, entities can be likened to tables and attributes can be likened to columns in those tables. Relationships roughly correspond to foreign keys.

Because the words *entity* and *attribute* have specific meanings in XML, in this context we'll call them *data entities* and *data attributes* to avoid confusion as much as possible.

Defining Data Entities

You can also think about data entities as anything that needs to be created, edited, interacted with, or destroyed. Think about the types of "things" your project will deal with and list them. Don't worry about relationships or duplicates right now—just brainstorm.

The resort team comes up with an initial list of 13 potential entities:

- Activity
- Location
- Maintenance action
- Maintenance personnel
- Activities personnel
- Visitor
- Equipment
- Reservation
- Advertisement
- Terminal
- Maintenance report
- Maintenance briefing
- Signage

Now look at your list. Are there any entries in your list that are really just different types of a more general data entity? For example, the resort team realizes that maintenance personnel, activities personnel, and visitors are really just different types of people, so they alter the list:

- Activity
- Location
- Maintenance action
- Person
- Equipment
- Reservation
- Advertisement
- Terminal
- Maintenance report

- Maintenance briefing
- Signage

Personal Preference

Most structures can be built in various ways. Some designers would choose to represent personnel as employees and keep visitors separate. The "right" choice depends on the system you're building.

Determining Data Attributes

One of the enduring issues surrounding XML data modeling is the question of whether data should be represented in attributes or elements. Don't get hung up on this issue at this stage. We'll discuss it fully in the section "Creating the Structure," but for right now we're just determining the properties of the potential data entities we defined in the previous step.

For each data entity on your list, determine any properties you may need, either to interact with the data entity or as storage for future use. The resort team's list shapes up as follows:

- Activity
  - Name
  - Description
  - Date
  - Location
  - Activity type
  - Participant limit
- Location
  - Name
  - Deck
  - Designation
- Maintenance action
  - Location
  - Equipment
  - Personnel
  - Date
  - Action performed

- Results
- Comments
- Person
    - First name
    - Last name
    - Type
    - Department
    - Visit start date
    - Visit end date
- Equipment
    - Name
    - Location
    - Maintenance interval
    - Last maintenance
    - Signage
- Reservation
    - Visitor
    - Activity
    - Attended
- Advertisement
    - Activity
    - Content
- Terminal
    - Person
    - Type
- Maintenance report
    - Maintenance action
    - Report format
    - Report status

- Maintenance briefing
  - Start date
  - End date
  - Maintenance action
- Signage
  - Content

For each data entity, create a data entity information form that lists general information about the entity, all of its data attributes (or potential data attributes), and the rationale behind every decision affecting the data entity. If you decide to remove a data attribute, document the reason why. Even if you decide not to use the data entity, keep the form and document your reasons.

Determining Relationships

As you determine your data entities, you'll notice that many of them make sense only in the context of others. For example, a maintenance briefing couldn't exist without maintenance reports. In this section, we'll document these requirements, also known as *relationships*, as part of an entity-relationship diagram (ERD), so let's start to get a handle on what relationships exist in our project.

A relationship can be stated as a sentence that indicates whether the relationship is required or optional and includes the data entity names, a verb describing the relationship, and a quantity. For example:

```
A piece of equipment must exist in one and only one location.
```

Relationships work in both directions, but it's important to note that the terms are frequently very different. For example:

```
A location may have one or more pieces of equipment.
```

Note that the first relationship is a mandatory one-to-one relationship, while the second is an optional one-to-many relationship.

Begin by writing down the sentences that express the relationships between your data entities. The resort team lists the following relationships:

```
A piece of equipment must exist in one and only one location.
A location may have one or more pieces of equipment.
An activity must be held in one and only one location.
A location may host one or more activities.
An activity may be attended by one or more persons.
A person may attend one or more activities.
A maintenance action must be performed by one and only one person.
A person may perform one or more maintenance actions.
A maintenance action must apply to one and only one piece of equipment.
A piece of equipment may be the subject of one or more maintenance actions.
```

```
A maintenance action must be documented by one and only one maintenance report.
A maintenance report must document one and only one maintenance action.
A maintenance action may appear in one or more maintenance briefings.
A maintenance briefing may describe one or more maintenance actions.
A person may make one or more reservations.
A reservation must be for one and only one person.
A reservation must apply to one and only one activity.
An activity may have one or more reservations.
A person may receive one or more advertisements.
An advertisement must be targeted to one or more persons.
A person may use one and only one terminal.
A terminal may be used by one or more persons.
A maintenance report must be signed by one and only one person.
A person may sign one or more maintenance reports.
A piece of equipment must have one or more pieces of signage.
A piece of signage may hang on one or more pieces of equipment.
An advertisement must advertise one or more activities.
An activity may be the subject or one or more advertisements.
An advertisement must be sent to one or more terminals.
A terminal may receive one or more advertisements.
```

These prose-based relationship statements are helpful for non-technical subject matter experts because they don't require the experts to interpret diagrams. For example, the resort team originally stated that

```
A piece of equipment must be the subject of one or more maintenance actions.
```

Upon review with the maintenance department, however, they discover that some pieces of equipment have long maintenance periods, and are frequently replaced before they actually have to be maintained. They therefore change the relationship to read as follows:

```
A piece of equipment may be the subject of one or more maintenance actions.
```

Include your relationships on the data entity information form for each relevant data entity.

Entity-Relationship Diagrams (ERDs)

The purpose of entity-relationship diagrams, or ERDs, is to give you an easy way to review the structure of the model you're proposing by formalizing the means for expressing data entity relationships.

In an ERD, a data entity is represented by a box with rounded corners, and a relationship is represented by one of a variety of lines, depending on the type of relationship. If the line is solid, it represents a "must" relationship. If it's dashed, it represents a "may" relationship. For example, Figure 2.11 represents a mandatory one-to-one relationship between horses and the stalls in which they sleep.

FIGURE 2.11
A simple pair of relation-ships.

We can "read" this diagram to re-create the relationships it represents. In the case of Figure 2.11, the relationships are

`Each horse must sleep in one and only one stall.`

and

`Each stall must hold one and only one horse.`

Of course, relationships aren't always reciprocal. For instance, if there are more stalls than horses, there will be stalls without horses, but each horse can still be in only one stall. You can see this mix of "must" and "may" relationships in Figure 2.12.

FIGURE 2.12
Mixing optional and mandatory relationships.

We would read these relationships as

`Each horse must sleep in one and only one stall.`

and

`Each stall may hold one and only one horse.`

Both of these examples show a one-to-one relationship. In an ERD, one-to-many (or many-to-many) relationships are represented by forked connections. For instance, to express that one pasture may support more than one cow, we create the diagram shown in Figure 2.13.

FIGURE 2.13
A one-to-many relationship.

These relationships read

`Each cow must graze in one and only one pasture.`

and

`Each pasture may support one or more cows.`

To get a good overall picture of your model, translate your relationship statements into an ERD. The resort team's ERD is shown in Figure 2.14.

FIGURE 2.14
The resort team's entity-
relationship diagram.

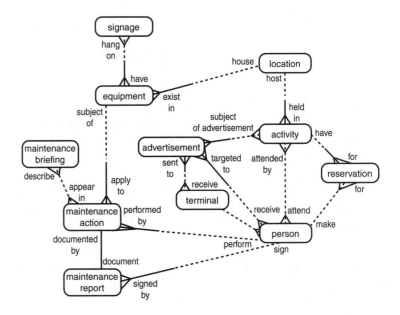

Checking the Model

Presumably, you've been checking the pieces of the model as you have gone along by consulting the people who are actually going to use the data (or who already do) to make sure that the pieces are correct. Now it's time to check the model as a whole.

Cross-checking the Models

Part of the reason for doing both function/process modeling and data modeling is that it gives us the opportunity to cross-check the models against each other. This will help us recognize areas that were left out of one or the other.

Look at your models and ask yourself these questions:

- Are there functions that relate to concepts or data entities not mentioned in the ERD? For example, the function hierarchy refers to user preferences, but user preferences have not been identified as a type of data entity.

- Are there functions to create, update, and delete every data entity, data attribute, and relationship in the ERD? For example, the function hierarchy gives no indication as to how various types of signage are created.

Cross-check your models and make sure that everything is accounted for.

Completeness Checks

The second round of completeness checks deals with documentation outside the model itself.

First, go back through the data entity information forms and make sure that every decision you made is represented in the model. Is every data entity you decided to keep reflected in the ERD? Is every data entity you decided not to keep left out of the ERD?

Are the relationships shown in the ERD documented on the information forms, and vice versa? Remember, non-technical people may find it easier to read the information forms than the ERD. Also, decisions regarding changes must be documented, and it's inconvenient to do so on the ERD itself.

Once you've reconciled your own documentation, it's time to pull out the interchange structure, if you'll be required to conform to one. Check to see whether there are any data entities that you haven't considered, but before you add them to your model, consider this: Do they really represent something your business (and specifically your project) needs to deal with? If not, leave them out of the model. You can worry about the conformation when you build the actual structure.

Localization

Don't forget to consider other languages and geographical and cultural concerns. Will you need to provide alternate content? XML provides a standard attribute, `xml:lang`, that you can use to designate a particular language for content. Language-aware tools can check this attribute against a list of standard values (such as `en` for English and `fr` for French) and display the proper content. You can also distinguish between different variations of a language, such as American, British, and Australian English.

Redundant Data Entities

Do you have objects or concepts that are described more than once within the model, but in different ways?

One common issue is relationships masquerading as entities. For example, the `reservation` data entity may really be just an expression of the fact that the user has signed up for a particular activity.

Be careful before pruning your model, however. There may be a distinction, for example, between a user who has made a reservation for an activity and one who has actually attended. In that case, you will need to keep the `reservation` data entity.

User Approval

Once you've completed your checks, it's time to put all the information together and put it in front of users. You must let users review the model before you actually build anything, or you are doomed to hours, days, or even weeks of rebuilding from comments afterwards. Why build something you'll have to change later when it's just as easy to have users review it while it's still in plain language?

Gather all the function hierarchy diagrams, entity-relationship diagrams, and data entity information forms, and package them together with an overall report describing the proposed system. Depending on the sophistication of those who will be reviewing the material, you may find it helpful to give a presentation explaining the material, rather than simply dropping it on their desks.

If users dislike the model, ask them to detail, in writing, the reasons why, and explain that these reasons will be included in the documentation, whether or not the changes are made. This way, when the system has been in place for a year and questions are asked, the reasons will be clear.

The resort team presents their model and entertains suggestions for several changes. The team eventually decides not to make the changes, but they document the requests, the reasons for them, and the reasons the changes are not made. This way, if the same requests are made a year from now, they won't have to be rehashed.

Creating the Structure

Now that the model is complete and has been approved by the users, it's time to translate it from a structure into a grammar. We can then use this grammar to validate our XML documents. Again, we haven't covered DTDs or XML Schemas yet, so in this section, we'll create a tree diagram and a sample document that conforms to it. In Chapter 7, "Document Type Definitions (DTDs)," and Chapter 8, "XML Schemas," we'll see how to translate this diagram into an actual grammar that a parser can use to validate documents.

Tree Diagrams

At this point, you may be wondering why we're going to look at yet another type of diagram, when we already have an ERD. Well, besides the advantage we get from looking at a problem in several different ways, tree diagrams give us some capabilities that ERDs don't.

While we could clutter up an ERD with data attributes, this still wouldn't solve the problem of element order. XML allows us to specify the order in which elements can appear, and there's no way to represent that in an ERD. Similarly, an ERD doesn't always accurately represent the hierarchical nature of an XML document.

In a tree diagram, elements are represented by rectangles, with the attributes listed alongside. Lines indicate the relationships. Figure 2.15 shows an initial translation of the resort ERD into a tree diagram. Keep in mind that this is just the first pass, and will likely change significantly.

Notice that while the relationship between `activity`, `advertisement`, and `person` shows two individual lines, the relationship between `equipment`, `signage`, and `maintenance action` shows a single line with rectangular branches. The rectangular branches indicate that order is important, so the `signage` and `maintenance action` elements must appear in the order specified (from left to right), whereas the `advertisement` and `person` elements can appear within the `activity` in any order.

FIGURE 2.15
The first pass at a tree diagram.

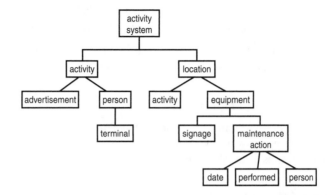

To indicate whether an element is optional and whether it can be repeated, we'll use the ?, *, and + symbols in the diagram. They have the following meanings:

Symbol	Meaning
?	Indicates that an element may appear zero times or one time.
+	Indicates that an element must appear at least once.
*	Indicates that an element may appear any number of times, including zero.

An element that has no modifier must appear exactly once.

Check your model and add modifiers as necessary. The changes to the resort diagram are shown in Figure 2.16.

FIGURE 2.16
Modifiers indicate whether elements are optional or repeatable.

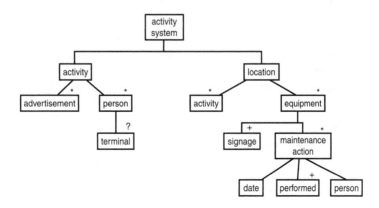

The `maintenance action` element must contain one or more `performed` elements, as indicated by the **+** modifier. The `person` element can have zero or one `terminal` elements, as indicated by the **?** modifier. Much of this model allows zero, one, or many elements to appear, as indicated by the ***** modifier. A notable exception is the `person` element within a `maintenance report`—there must be exactly one, as indicated by the absence of a modifier.

Note that this is just the initial model. In addition to other structural issues, we still have to solve the perpetual question of elements versus attributes.

Elements or Attributes?

Unless you're completely new to the idea of creating an XML structure, at some point you've wondered whether it would be better to add a particular piece of information to your structure as an element or as an attribute. For example, the XML elements

```
<dog>
    <species>Yorkshire Terrier</species>
    <name>Razzle Dazzle</name>
</dog>
```

and

```
<dog species="Yorkshire Terrier" name="Razzle Dazzle"/>
```

both contain the same information, but the first shows all the information as child elements, whereas the second one shows all the information as attributes. So which is the right way to do it?

Both. Or neither. It depends.

In terms of "correctness," there really is no right or wrong answer. It simply depends on personal preference. But there are factors that might influence your decision one way or the other.

First, consider the information that will be contained in each value. If an information item has children, you must make it an element because attributes can't contain children. Similarly, if you're dealing with a large amount of content, particularly if it spans more than one line, you'll probably want to make it an element. Remember also that attributes can't contain the **<** character, so a `CDATA` section should be part of an element.

Space issues may also come into play if you're storing or moving a large amount of data over a network. Because elements need start and end tags, they lead to larger file sizes. Even in the simple example earlier in this section, the element version has 36% more characters, and thus takes up 36% more space than the attribute version.

Sometimes the deciding factor is out of your hands, such as when an application requires data in a particular form. For example, some applications don't recognize attributes (though these are not actually XML compliant), or a database might expect each row to have an element with its columns specified as attributes.

One important factor has less to do with the data itself than with how the data is used. The following examples both convey the same information. In the first one, the `seasonname` is an attribute of the **event**'s parent element, and in the second, it's a sibling element, at the same level as the **event**:

```
<season seasonname="Summer">
    <event>
        <eventname>Seafood Fest</eventname>
        <eventdates>8/25/03-8/30/03</eventdates>
    </event>
</season>

<season>
    <seasonname>Summer</seasonname>
    <event>
        <eventname>Seafood Fest</eventname>
        <eventdates>8/25/03-8/30/03</eventdates>
    </event>
</season>
```

When we begin to explore programming that accesses these documents in Chapter 3, "Manipulating Documents: the Document Object Model (DOM)," we'll see that encoding the information as a sibling rather than an attribute of the parent can make processing more complicated.

It's often helpful to encode information about the element as an attribute, and to encode the information contained by the element as child elements. But wait a minute—isn't all information "about" the element? After all, isn't that why it's there? Yes, but what we're talking about here is information about the actual element itself, and not the object that the element describes. Some designers choose to interpret this rule by using attributes to identify a particular element, while including the rest of the information as elements. For example, the resort team could restructure the **location** element as shown in Figure 2.17.

FIGURE 2.17
Using attributes for
identification only.

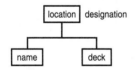

One special case of this rule is an attribute that refers back to another element, as seen in data normalization.

Attributes and Data Normalization

One thing that you may have noticed about the resort team's model is that several elements, such as an advertisement, appear in multiple places in the model. If all the information for each advertisement is included in each location, it will lead not only to huge file sizes, but also to a data maintenance nightmare.

In database structures, *normalizing* the data often solves this problem. Normalizing data basically refers to the process of structuring the data so that it's referenced in a single location, rather than repeated. In XML, these references are often accomplished through the use of attributes. Listing 2.1 shows a document that is not normalized.

LISTING 2.1   Non-Normalized Data

```xml
<?xml version="1.0"?>
<maintenance>
    <equipment>
        <name>Airlock 37r</name>
        <location>
            <name>Back Door</name>
            <deck>37</deck>
            <designation>37Aft</designation>
        <location>
        <signage>
            <content>Warning! Airlock may open suddenly!</content>
        </signage>
    </equipment>
    <equipment>
        <name>Nutrition Wall 37A</name>
        <location>
            <name>Back Door</name>
            <deck>37</deck>
            <designation>37Aft</designation>
        </location>
        <signage>
            <content>Warning: The chili has been reported to bite back.</content>
        </signage>
    </equipment>
</maintenance>
```

Notice that all information for the location exists in both places. Listing 2.2 shows normalization of both location and signage information.

LISTING 2.2   Normalized Data

```xml
<?xml version="1.0"?>
<maintenance>
    <location designation="37Aft">
        <name>Back Door</name>
        <deck>37</deck>
    </location>
    <signage signid="1">
        <content>Warning! Airlock may open suddenly!</content>
    </signage>
    <signage signid="2">
        <content>Warning: The chili has been reported to bite back.</content>
    </signage>
    <equipment location="37Aft" signage="1">
        <name>Airlock 37r</name>
    </equipment>
    <equipment location="37aft" signage="2">
```

LISTING 2.2   Comtinued

```
                <name>Nutrition Wall 37A</name>
        </equipment>
</maintenance>
```

All the information still exists, but it's accessible in a different way. In data-intensive applications, this means of encoding data often makes more sense.

Grouping Elements

Another issue that comes up periodically is the depth to which elements should be nested. Is it better to have a shallow or deep document? Again, the answer is "it depends."

In Listing 2.2, we see a good reason for nesting, or container elements. We can rewrite Listing 2.2 as shown in Listing 2.3.

LISTING 2.3   Grouping Elements

```
<?xml version="1.0"?>
<maintenance>
    <locations>
        <location designation="37Aft">
            <name>Back Door</name>
            <deck>37</deck>
        </location>
    </locations>
    <signs>
        <signage signid="1">
            <content>Warning! Airlock may open suddenly!</content>
        </signage>
        <signage signid="2">
            <content>Warning: The chili has been reported to bite back.</content>
        </signage>
    </signs>
    <equipment location="37Aft" signage="1">
        <name>Airlock 37r</name>
    </equipment>
    <equipment location="37aft" signage="2">
        <name>Nutrition Wall 37A</name>
    </equipment>
</maintenance>
```

Overall, it's typically easier to get to elements that are higher up in the document hierarchy, but the "best" structure depends on how the data will be used, and who is going to use it. For example, programmers typically prefer nested elements, so they can reference a single element, such as signs, and have a collection of information available. Non-programmers, however, typically prefer a relatively flat document, because it seems more flexible to them. Keep in mind that this flexibility can cause problems for authors—the people actually creating the documents—who are overwhelmed by too many choices. In these cases, it's often helpful to provide container elements that limit their choices.

Keep in mind that you don't need to change the reference structure just because you add these containers for the convenience of authors. You can also create an authoring structure and then transform the data to remove the containers before adding the data back into your system, if you'd like.

Beware the Unintended Consequences!

If you use containers, remember that if you remove a container element from the document, you're also removing all of its children.

Allowing for Presentational and Data Issues

On the other end of the spectrum, a lack of complexity can lead to a situation where you can't use the data in the way in which you would like without breaking it up further. This process is known as a *second-level parse*.

Second-level parsing often occurs in situations where data is either presented in a certain manner or used for calculations. For example, you may have an element like the one shown in Listing 2.4.

LISTING 2.4   A Simple Element

```
<address>
    John Smith
    123 Main Street
    Anytown, IN 34523
</address>
```

If you want to present this data on a Web page as shown in Figure 2.18, you need to add the code in Listing 2.5.

LISTING 2.5   Adding Presentation Information

```
<html>
<head><title>John Smith</title></head>
<body>
<p>
    <b>Smith, John</b><br/>
    123 Main Street<br/>
    Anytown, IN 34523
</p>
</body>
</html>
```

FIGURE 2.18
Displaying data.

You could certainly create a program to do this, but if you know (or suspect) that your data will be used in this way, it's much better to create a structure like Listing 2.6, which allows you to directly transform it into the new format.

LISTING 2.6   Structuring Content to Prevent a Second-Level Parse

```
<address>
    <firstname>John</firstname>
    <lastname>Smith</lastname>
    <street>123 Main Street</street>
    <city>Anytown</city>
    <state>IN</state>
    <postalcode>34523</postalcode>
</address>
```

The same process applies for data. Suppose you store the maintenance interval like this:

```
<interval>30 days</interval>
```

Now if you need to determine whether the maintenance data has passed, you have to do a second-level parse on the data to get the number (**30**) and the unit (**days**). Instead, consider representing the data as follows:

```
<interval>
    <length>30</length>
    <unit>days</unit>
</interval>
```

How Tight Is Tight Enough?

In some cases, you might find that the restrictions you've placed on your data are too strict for the users creating it. For example, the advertising department might not know which visitors are going to receive an advertisement when they create it because the advertisement will be added to the system before the data regarding those users. In this case, you might consider creating an authoring structure that loosens this requirement. Similarly, one department might need the restriction, while another might not. In this case, the authoring structure will be stricter than the reference structure.

The general rule is this: Your structure should be tight enough to prevent sloppiness and tag abuse, but not so tight that it becomes annoying to users.

The Final Structure

Keeping all these considerations in mind, the resort team decides to make changes to the model as shown in Figure 2.19.

FIGURE 2.19
The final model.

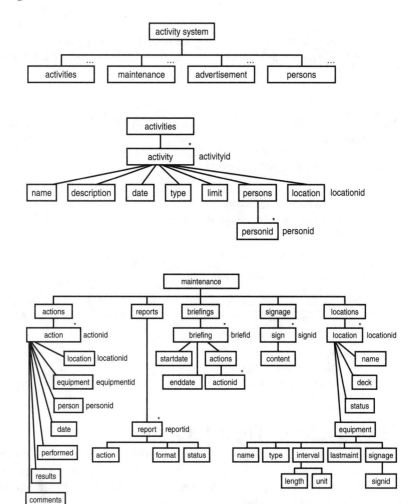

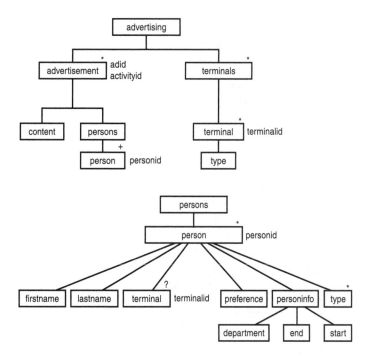

Testing the Final Structure

The final test of a structure is to mark up several of the target documents or pieces of target data. You'll need to do this again after the DTD or schema has been created, but even now it's helpful. I found several errors in the model as I'd originally drawn it by creating this sample file, including the complete omission of maintenance reports! Because we're marking up data rather than documents, we'll create a sample document holding sample data, as shown in Listing 2.7.

LISTING 2.7   The Final Document

```xml
<?xml version="1.0"?>
<activitysystem>
    <activities>
        <activity activityid="A1">
            <name>Zero-G Volleyball</name>
            <description>
                Even better than beach volleyball!
```

LISTING 2.7   Continued

```
            </description>
            <date>4.30.45</date>
            <type>Sports</type>
            <limit>18</limit>
            <location locationid="L1"/>
            <persons>
                <person personid="P2"/>
                <person personid="P1"/>
            </persons>
        </activity>
        <activity activityid="A2">
            <name>Stargazing</name>
            <description>
                Learn the visible constellations.
            </description>
            <date>4.29.45</date>
            <type>Educational</type>
            <limit>5</limit>
            <location locationid="L2"/>
            <persons>
            </persons>
        </activity>
    </activities>
    <maintenance>
        <actions>
            <action actionid="A1">
                <location locationid="L1"/>
                <equipment equipid="E1"/>
                <person personid="P3"/>
                <date>4.26.45</date>
                <performed>Routine check</performed>
                <results>OK</results>
            </action>
            <action actionid="A2">
                <location locationid="L2"/>
                <equipment equipid="E2"/>
                <person personid="P3"/>
                <date>4.27.45</date>
                <performed>Changed light bulb.</performed>
                <results>OK.</results>
                <comments>
                    Security needs to check for vandals.
                </comments>
            </action>
        </actions>
        <reports>
            <report>
                <action actionid="A1"/>
                <format>Short</format>
                <status>Complete</status>
            </report>
            <report>
```

LISTING 2.7   Continued

```
                <action actionid="A2"/>
                <format>Long</format>
                <status>Awaiting signature</status>
            </report>
    </reports>
    <briefings>
        <briefing briefid="B1">
            <startdate>4.1.45</startdate>
            <enddate>4.30.45</enddate>
            <actions>
                <action actionid="A1"/>
                <action actionid="A2"/>
            </actions>
        </briefing>
        <briefing>
            <startdate>3.1.45</startdate>
            <enddate>3.31.45</enddate>
            <actions>
            </actions>
        </briefing>
    </briefings>
    <signage>
        <sign signid="S1">
            <content>
                This equipment includes no dangerous parts.
            </content>
        </sign>
        <sign signid="S2">
            <content>
                Warning! Airlock may open unexpectedly!
            </content>
        </sign>
        <sign signid="S3">
            <content>Danger! Low Ceiling!</content>
        </sign>
    </signage>
    <locations>
        <location locationid="L1">
            <name>Zero-G Sports Arena</name>
            <deck>25</deck>
            <status>Closed</status>
            <equipment>
                <name>Volleyball net</name>
                <type>S</type>
                <interval>
                    <length>1</length>
                    <unit>year</unit>
                </interval>
                <lastmaint>2.13.45</lastmaint>
                <signage>
                    <sign signid="S1"/>
                </signage>
```

LISTING 2.7   Continued

```
                </equipment>
                <equipment>
                    <name>Airlock F25</name>
                    <type>A</type>
                    <interval>
                        <length>1</length>
                        <unit>month</unit>
                    </interval>
                    <lastmaint>4.3.45</lastmaint>
                    <signage>
                        <sign signid="S2"/>
                        <sign signid="S3"/>
                    </signage>
                </equipment>
            </location>
        </locations>
    </maintenance>
    <advertising>
        <advertisement adid="AD1" activityid="A1">
            <content>
                Enjoy the sensations of Zero-G volleyball ...
            </content>
            <persons>
                <person personid="P1"/>
                <person personid="P2"/>
            </persons>
        </advertisement>
        <advertisement adid="AD2" activityid="A2">
            <content>
                Relax and learn about the stars around you ...
            </content>
            <persons>
                <person personid="P2"/>
            </persons>
        </advertisement>
        <terminals>
            <terminal terminalid="T1">
                <type>Full</type>
            </terminal>
            <terminal terminalid="T2">
                <type>Full</type>
            </terminal>
            <terminal terminalid="T3">
                <type>Text Only</type>
            </terminal>
        </terminals>
    </advertising>
    <persons>
        <person personid="P1">
            <firstname>Luke</firstname>
            <lastname>Hamill</lastname>
```

LISTING 2.7   Continued

```
                    <terminal terminalid="T1"/>
                    <preference>Sports</preference>
                    <type>V</type>
                    <personinfo>
                        <visitstart>4.15.45</visitstart>
                        <visitend>5.15.45</visitend>
                    </personinfo>
                </person>
            </persons>
            <persons>
                <person personid="P2">
                    <firstname>Lee</firstname>
                    <lastname>Fisher</lastname>
                    <preference>Sports</preference>
                    <preference>Educational</preference>
                    <type>V</type>
                    <personinfo>
                        <visitstart>4.3.45</visitstart>
                        <visitend>4.20.45</visitend>
                    </personinfo>
                </person>
            </persons>
            <persons>
                <person personid="P3">
                    <firstname>Harry</firstname>
                    <lastname>Solo</lastname>
                    <terminal terminalid="T3"/>
                    <type>S</type>
                    <personinfo>
                        <department>Maintenance</department>
                    </personinfo>
                </person>
            </persons>
        </activitysystem>
```

Summary

The process of creating a structure for XML data involves several steps, no matter where the data is coming from or where it's going:

1. Define goals and objectives.

2. Gather the team.

3. Gather information.

4. Create preliminary models.

5. Validate the models.

6. Make changes as appropriate.

7. Create the XML document structure.

8. Deploy.

9. Maintain.

Be sure to gather feedback from the people who are ultimately going to use the structure, or your project has little hope of success. This feedback comes during the analysis phase, when you're documenting the functions that are to be performed by the system that you're building, and during the data modeling phase, when you're defining the data entities that the system will handle and their data attributes.

When you have enough information, create a model of the basic structure. When this is approved by users, create sample documents, or in the case of existing data or documents, mark up several randomly chosen but representative documents with the new model to confirm that it's appropriate and usable.

Review Questions

1. What's the difference between a goal and an objective?

2. What are the six roles involved in planning a design?

3. Can one person perform more than one of these functions?

4. What is the scope of a project?

5. What are three possible sources of data for an XML system?

6. What are three possible destinations for data in an XML system?

7. What is an interchange structure?

8. What is a reference structure?

9. What does function modeling document?

10. What is an event?

11. When should you review the model with users?

12. What is a data entity?

13. What is a data attribute?

14. What is a relationship?

15. What are you looking for when you cross-check the function hierarchy and entity-relationship diagrams?

16. What is the meaning of the ?, +, and * modifiers?

17. What is data normalization?

18. What is one reason for grouping similar elements using a container element?

Programming Exercises

1. Create a function hierarchy diagram for making a major purchase, such as a car or a house.

2. Create an entity-relationship diagram for a school.

3. Translate the ERD in the previous exercise into an appropriate tree model.

4. Create a sample document based on the model.

MANIPULATING DOCUMENTS: THE DOCUMENT OBJECT MODEL (DOM)

You will learn about the following in this chapter:

- The various DOM Recommendations

- The difference between elements and nodes

- The DOM API and what it represents

- Navigating the DOM tree

- Creating a DOM document from a file

- Creating and manipulating DOM data

- Saving a DOM document to a file

When new XML users go to the W3C site (`http://www.w3.org`) and look up the Document Object Model (DOM), very often they're overwhelmed from the start. This is not surprising; there are three different levels, each of which has separate recommendations (or modules). So what is it that you're actually supposed to *do* with this stuff?

Simply put, the Document Object Model is a way of looking at a tree of XML data, and a group of APIs for reading and manipulating it. These APIs are common among DOM-compliant applications, so what works in one environment should work in another.

Your software determines the version of DOM available to you. At the time of this writing, most implementations (but not all) are at Level 2.0, with some support for Level 3.0. In most cases, you'll use the Core module, but there are situations in which each of the other modules will be useful.

This chapter provides an overview of all the recommendations, and focuses on the DOM Level 2.0 Core. In Chapter 4, "Advanced DOM Techniques," and Chapter 13, "XML in the Browser: XHTML," we'll look at some of the other modules.

What Is the Document Object Model?

The Document Object Model actually sprang out of browsers scripting HTML pages. Back when this sort of scripting (now known as DHTML, or Dynamic HTML) was new, each browser implemented it in its own way. For example, thinking of a form as an object was a fairly obvious choice, but how would you represent the value of a form input called `username`? Would it be one of the following?

```
document.forms.myForm.username
```

```
document.forms.myForm.username.value
```

```
document.forms["myform"].username
```

```
document.forms[0].elements[3].value
```

The list wasn't exactly endless, and some of these choices were functionally equivalent, but there were enough differences in what was supported between different browsers (and even versions of the same browser) to cause a nightmare for Web developers who needed to make sure their pages worked everywhere that scripting was available.

The result was the development of the Document Object Model, a (sort-of) standard way of looking at HTML. This unofficial version, based on version 3.x browsers, is known as DOM Level 0.

The first official version, DOM Level 1.0, created a basic structure of nodes, elements, and attributes that allowed navigation around a document. Even from the beginning, however, everyone knew that this was just a starting point, and since then DOM Level 2.0, which incorporates more functionality, has been (mostly) approved, and DOM Level 3.0, which takes things a step further, is in the works.

As I said before, it's easy to get confused with all these recommendations. Let's start simple, with the Core Recommendation.

A Set of Interfaces

In some ways, it's misleading to say that the Document Object Model defines a set of objects. Actually, it defines a set of interfaces *to* objects. An interface is a set of the following:

- Properties or data that an object holds

- Methods or actions that an object can take

- Parameters that you can pass to an object or method

- The type of object that a method returns, if any

A programmer can implement these interfaces by creating objects that conform to them. This way, when another programmer wants to use these objects, he or she will know how, because they're based on these well-defined interfaces.

For example, the DOM Core Recommendation defines an interface called `Element`, with a method called `getAttribute()`. The interface specifies that when the `getAttribute()`

method is called with the name of an attribute, it should return the value of the attribute. This means that if I create an object based on this `Element` interface, you can use it secure in the knowledge that if you want the value of an attribute, you can use the `getAttribute()` method.

Because the interfaces are standard, the implementation itself takes on less importance. All you care about is that if you call `getAttribute("month")` on the `birthday` element, you're going to get the value of the `month` attribute. This portability is the purpose of the Document Object Model.

The Importance of Nodes

When you come right down to it, all of DOM is based on the node. Documents, elements, attributes, text, and even processing instructions and comments are all special cases of the `Node` interface.

For example, the XML document

```
<?xml version="1.0"?>
<friend>
    <handle degree="close">Harold</handle>
</friend>
```

actually represents at least 8 nodes of different types:

- one document node
- two element nodes (`friend` and `handle`)
- four text nodes (`close`, `Harold`, and the line feeds before and after the `name` element)
- one attribute node (`degree`)

These nodes are arranged in parent-child relationships, as shown in Figure 3.1.

FIGURE 3.1

The parent-child relationships of a simple document.

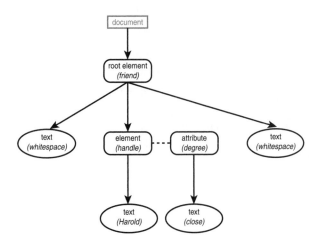

Notice that the elements and the text they contain are separate nodes; the element node acts as the parent and the text node as the child, as indicated by the arrows. Notice also that the attribute node is *not* a child of the element node.

The Document Object Model defines 12 different node types, each of which implements the `Node` interface, and each of which adds methods that are peculiar to itself.

For example, the `Node` interface specifies the `getNodeValue()` method, because it's applicable to most node types. The `getTarget()` method, on the other hand, applies only to processing instructions, and as such is part of the `ProcessingInstruction` interface.

The Document Object Model specifies the following interfaces:

- `Node`—The overall type that applies to everything. The `Node` interface includes methods for getting information about the `Node`, such as `getParentNode()` and `getNodeName()`, and for manipulating the structure of a document or individual node, such as `insertBefore()` and `removeChild()`. It also defines numeric values for each node type, enabling you to determine what type of node you're dealing with even if the object type itself is `Node`.

- `Document`—The `Node` that begets almost all other types of nodes. While the `Node` interface carries the methods that are used to move nodes around, the `Document` interface carries the methods that are used to actually create them, such as `createElement()` and `createTextNode()`.

- `Element`—The type of node that can be associated with `Attr` nodes. This interface contains convenience methods such as `getElementsByTagName()`.

- `Attr`—This node, whose name is short for *attribute*, can have either `Text` nodes or `EntityReferences` as children.

- `Text`—This is a string with no markup. This means that a mixed-content text node is broken up into separate `Text` and `Element` nodes.

- `CDATASection`—This node type "hides" markup. Unlike a `Text` node, markup within the value will not cause a separate `Element` node to be created.

- `DocumentType`—This node type contains all the information that would normally be contained in the internal subset of a DTD as a string value. It also contains the name of the specified root element and any system or public identifiers that point to external subsets of the DTD.

- `Comment`, `Notation`, `Entity`, `EntityReference`, and `ProcessingInstruction`—These nodes simply model their namesakes, providing the appropriate information about themselves.

Entities

We'll deal with entities, entity references, and notations in detail in Chapter 7, "Document Type Definitions (DTDs)."

Some DOM interfaces don't correspond to actual node types within the document, but are provided to make your life easier when you're working with documents:

- `DocumentFragment`—This implementation of the `Node` interface doesn't actually have any of its own methods at all, and instead acts as a sort of mini-document or container for other groups of nodes you may want to move around. For example, if you insert a `DocumentFragment` into a document, only the child nodes are actually inserted.

- `DOMImplementation`—This interface provides a means to determine whether certain actions are supported using the `hasFeature()` method. It also allows you to create `Document`s and `DocumentType`s.

- `DOMException` and `ExceptionCode`—These interfaces provide a way for the application to tell you that something has gone wrong, and what it is.

- `NodeList` and `NamedNodeMap`—These two utility interfaces are essential in actually working with a DOM document, as you'll see when we start building the application. `NodeList` provides an ordered list of results, such as the children of a node, and `NamedNodeMap` provides a list that is unordered but accessible by name, such as the attributes of an element.

The Different Recommendations

All these interfaces are part of the DOM Level 1.0 Recommendation. Minor changes were made to Level 1.0 to create the DOM Level 2.0 Core Recommendation.

DOM Level 2.0 includes five other module recommendations, each of which has a specific purpose:

- **DOM Level 2.0 Traversal and Range**—This module includes two new interfaces, `NodeIterator` and `TreeWalker`, that provide alternative means for navigating the document. It also defines a means for referring to a particular portion of a document. (We'll talk about ranges in Chapter 14, "`XML Linking Language (XLink)`."

- **DOM Level 2.0 HTML**—This module includes specialized versions of the definitions in the Core Recommendation, such as `HTMLDocument` and `HTMLFormElement`. These interfaces are most commonly implemented in a browser, where JavaScript or other client-side scripting controls an HTML page.

- **DOM Level 2.0 Style Sheets**—This module specifies interfaces that deal with cascading style sheets and the data they contain.

- **DOM Level 2.0 Views**—This module provides a way to distinguish between different versions of a document. For example, a cascading style sheet may change the data within a document, creating a different view. (As of the time of this writing, this module has been removed from DOM Level 3.0.)

- **DOM Level 2.0 Events**—This module stems from work on browser scripting, and provides a way to determine the behavior of objects when some action, such as a mouse click, affects them, their ancestors, or their descendants.

DOM Level 3.0, which is still in the Working Draft stage at the time of this writing, includes revisions of the Core and Events modules, as well as two new modules:

- **DOM Level 3.0 Load and Save**—This module attempts to actually detail the loading and saving of documents (which is, as of Level 2.0, still up to the individual implementers).

- **DOM Level 3.0 Validation**—This module provides a way to validate an existing `Document` object against a specific associated grammar, and to require that it remain valid throughout its existence.

- **DOM Level 3.0 XPath**—This module allows greater flexibility in the use of XPath expressions to locate and specify nodes within a document. It's not an update of XPath, but rather a way to use XPath 1.0 with a DOM document.

Determining Support

So with all these different versions and implementations and modules, how do you know whether a particular method or interface is available for your application?

The answer lies in the `DOMImplementation` interface and its `hasFeature()` method. Each of these modules has a standard name and version, so to determine whether the `TreeWalker` interface is available, you can check the following value:

`myDOMImplementation.hasFeature("Traversal", "2.0")`

We'll see an example of this in the next section, once we've actually created a DOM document to work with.

The DOM Structure

Now that we've gotten the lay of the land, it's time to actually do some programming.

Here we hit a crossroads. Nowhere in the preceding discussion do you see any mention of a programming language. In fact, eliminating language dependence is one of the major benefits of XML.

So how do we decide what language to use? Simple. We don't. I'm going to show you all the examples in Java, but I'm also going to provide some examples in languages such as C++ and Visual Basic .NET just to get you started. Once we're on the road, you can adapt the changes we make to the Java application to your own language. (This shows the advantage of a common API.)

In the last chapter, we looked at planning an application for increasing guest participation in activities at our outer space tourist resort. In this chapter, we're going to write a small portion of that application, and look at displaying the activities and taking reservations.

Getting Ready

Before you can build any DOM application, you'll need to have an implementation of the Document Object Model installed and ready to go. For the main examples, I'll be using the Java API for XML, or JAXP 1.2. Here are some other implementations:

Platform	DOM Implementation(s)
Java	JAXP, Apache Xerces-Java
C++	Microsoft Visual C++ .NET—COM and MSXML 4.0
Visual Basic	Microsoft Visual Basic .NET—MSXML 4.0
Perl	Apache Xerces, with XML::Xerces for DOM 2.0 support (XML::DOM supports only DOM 1.0, and won't work with the complete sample application, but is fine for general use.)
PHP	PHP 4.2.1 or later, compiled with DOM XML support (requires Gnome libxml2)

Make sure your software is installed and tested.

MSXML SDK

The MSXML SDK is undergoing many changes that will enable it to provide support for the various XML standards. SDK version 4.0 (the current release at the time of this writing) is required for the samples in this book. You can download the latest release of the SDK from the `http://www.microsoft.com` Web site in the Downloads area.

The Source Document

The application in this chapter is based on the document that we developed in the last chapter, which describes activities, people, and locations. The relevant portions of this document are shown in Listing 3.1.

LISTING 3.1   The Source Document

```xml
<?xml version="1.0"?>
<activitysystem>
    <activities>
        <activity activityid="A1">
            <name>Zero-G Volleyball</name>
            <description>
                Even better than beach volleyball!
            </description>
            <date>4.30.45</date>
            <type>Sports</type>
```

LISTING 3.1   Continued

```
            <limit>18</limit>
            <locationRef locationid="L1"/>
            <persons>
                <person personid="P2"/>
                <person personid="P1"/>
            </persons>
        </activity>
        <activity activityid="A2">
            <name>Stargazing</name>
            <description>
                Learn the visible constellations.
            </description>
            <date>4.29.45</date>
            <type>Educational</type>
            <limit>5</limit>
            <locationRef locationid="L1"/>
            <persons></persons>
        </activity>
    </activities>
    <maintenance>
...
        <locations>
            <location locationid="L1">
                <name>Zero-G Sports Arena</name>
                <deck>25</deck>
                <status>Closed</status>
                <equipment>
...
                </equipment>
                <equipment>
...
                </equipment>
            </location>
        </locations>
    </maintenance>
    <advertising>
...
    </advertising>
    <persons>
...
    </persons>
</activitysystem>
```

Parsing the Document

Before we can actually do anything with this data, we will need to parse it, or analyze it to determine the actual structure and content of the data. How we actually go about this will vary by implementation, because actually loading the document is one area where the specifics are not included in the DOM Level 2.0 Recommendation. Even within a single implementation, you may have several options for parsing a file to create a DOM document.

In this section, we'll look at how a number of different implementations go about creating a DOM document from an XML file.

Java

The JAXP implementation makes use of a `DocumentBuilder` to create the document, and a `DocumentBuilderFactory` to create the `DocumentBuilder`. The entire process is shown in Listing 3.2a.

Listing Numbers

Whenever the same process is performed in several languages, the listings will share a common number, but will be given a letter designation (for example, Listing 3.2a for Java, Listing 3.2b for C++, and so on).

LISTING 3.2a   Parsing the Document Using Java

```java
import javax.xml.parsers.DocumentBuilder;
import javax.xml.parsers.DocumentBuilderFactory;
import java.io.File;
import org.w3c.dom.Document;

public class ActivityListing {

    public static void main (String args[]) {

        File docFile = new File("activities.xml");
        Document doc = null;

        try {

            DocumentBuilderFactory dbf = DocumentBuilderFactory.newInstance();
            DocumentBuilder db = dbf.newDocumentBuilder();
            doc = db.parse(docFile);

        } catch (Exception e) {
            System.out.print("Problem parsing the file.");
        }

    }
}
```

Here we start with the basic application. First, instantiate the `DocumentBuilderFactory` using the static `newInstance()` method. Once it's created, the `DocumentBuilderFactory` creates the `DocumentBuilder` object using the `newDocumentBuilder()` method. The `DocumentBuilder` itself then parses the file, which you specified earlier. Compile and execute the application to check for errors.

Remember, the only part of this process that is part of the DOM Recommendation is the actual `Document` object. Let's look at the other implementations in the following sections.

C++

Listing 3.2b shows the same functionality as Listing 3.2a, but uses Microsoft Visual C++ and COM instead of Java.

LISTING 3.2b Parsing the Document Using C++

```cpp
#include "stdafx.h"
#import "C:\windows\system32\msxml2.dll"
using namespace MSXML2;

int _tmain(int argc, _TCHAR* argv[])
{
    ::CoInitialize(NULL);
    try
    {
        HRESULT hr;

        CComPtr<MSXML2::IXMLDOMDocument>  pDomDocument;
        hr = pDomDocument.CoCreateInstance(__uuidof(MSXML2::DOMDocument));
        hr = pDomDocument->load("activities.xml");

    }
    catch(...)
    {
        wprintf(L"Caught the exception");
    }
    ::CoUninitialize();
    return 0;
}
```

In this example, `msxml.dll` is in the `system32` directory of the Windows installation. Change the path to match your configuration. I modified the `stdafx.h` file so that I can use COM, so it now looks like this:

```cpp
#define WIN32_LEAN_AND_MEAN
#define _WIN32_DCOM
#include <stdio.h>
#include <tchar.h>
#define _ATL_CSTRING_EXPLICIT_CONSTRUCTORS

#include <windows.h>
#include <comdef.h>
#include <atlbase.h>
```

To get started, create a Win32 project and modify the Application Settings tab so the application type is Console Application. Select the ATL Support check box.

Visual Basic .NET

In Visual Basic, Microsoft's MSXML uses `DOMDocument` to load the file and parse it. To get started, create a new `Windows Application` project in VB and draw a pushbutton in the default form. From the `Project` menu, select `Add Reference`, and select `Microsoft XML`,

v4.0 as the available reference. Then, in the click event of the pushbutton, we can add the code shown in Listing 3.2c.

LISTING 3.2c   Pushbutton Code Using VB

```
Private Sub Button1_Click(ByVal sender As System.Object,
                          ByVal e As System.EventArgs) _
                          Handles Button1.Click
    Dim xmldoc As New MSXML2.DOMDocument40()
    xmldoc.async = False
    xmldoc.load("activities.xml")
End Sub
```

We have created a new **DOMDocument** using the namespace MSXML2.

PHP

PHP's DOM support is very much in flux. The examples in this chapter use the new functions introduced in version 4.2.1, which for the most part are closer to DOM compliance than previous versions. However, as of version 4.2.1, PHP's DOM support is still incomplete, and function names (and functionality) may change in later versions. If you have a later or earlier version and the examples in this chapter don't work, check the DOM XML section of the PHP manual (listed in Appendix A, "Resources") for more information.

Listing 3.2d uses PHP to parse the **activities.xml** file.

LISTING 3.2d   Parsing the Document Using PHP

```
<?php

$file = "activities.xml";
if (!$doc = domxml_open_file($file)) {
  trigger_error("Failed to open or parse XML file '$file'", E_USER_ERROR);
}

?>
```

Perl

Perl file loading and parsing are done through the XML::Xerces::DOMParser interface. First create an input source from the target file, and then instantiate a parser. Use that parser to parse the file, and then retrieve the **Document**, as in Listing 3.2e.

LISTING 3.2e   Executing the Document Using Perl

```
use XML::Xerces;
use XML::Xerces::DOMParse;

my $file   = XML::Xerces::LocalFileInputSource->new("activities.xml");
my $parser = XML::Xerces::DOMParser->new();
```

LISTING 3.2e   Continued

```
eval { $parser->parse($file); };
XML::Xerces::error($@) if $@;

my $doc = $parser->getDocument();
```

XML::DOM

In case you don't have access to or can't install the Apache Xerces library and XML::Xerces, there is an alternative DOM implementation for Perl, called XML::DOM. XML::DOM is based on the expat parser, which is included with many Linux distributions, so Linux users may find it much easier to install than XML::Xerces. However, XML::DOM supports only DOM level 1.0; the full application described in this chapter *will not work* with XML::DOM.

That caveat aside, XML::DOM presents a DOM interface almost indistinguishable from XML::Xerces (as long as you only use DOM 1.0 features).

To parse the file with XML::DOM, use the following:

```
use XML::DOM;

my $parser = new XML::DOM::Parser;
my $doc    = $parser->parsefile("activities.xml");
```

Checking for Supported Features

With all of these differences, how do you know whether your implementation can do what you want it to? The answer is the `DOMImplementation` object. Implementations typically provide a nonstandard way to create a `DOMImplementation` without a `Document` object, but DOM also specifies that we can obtain a `DOMImplementation` from the `Document` itself, either as an object property or through a method.

Once you have the `DOMImplementation`, you can use it to test for specific modules. For example, our implementations should all support the DOM Level 2.0 Core module, but unless this book has been around for a while, they won't support Level 5.0. Listings 3.3a–e demonstrate the use of the `DOMImplementation` object.

Java

LISTING 3.3a   Checking for Support

```
import javax.xml.parsers.DocumentBuilder;
import javax.xml.parsers.DocumentBuilderFactory;
import java.io.File;
import org.w3c.dom.Document;
import org.w3c.dom.DOMImplementation;

public class ActivityListing {

    public static void main (String args[]) {
        File docFile = new File("activities.xml");

        Document doc = null;
```

LISTING 3.3a   Continued

```
    try {

        DocumentBuilderFactory dbf = DocumentBuilderFactory.newInstance();
        DocumentBuilder db = dbf.newDocumentBuilder();
        doc = db.parse(docFile);

        DOMImplementation domImpl = doc.getImplementation();
        if (domImpl.hasFeature("Core", "2.0")) {
            System.out.println("2.0 is supported.");
        } else {
            System.out.println("2.0 is not supported.");
        }

        if (domImpl.hasFeature("Core", "5.0")) {
            System.out.println("5.0 is supported.");
        } else {
            System.out.println("5.0 is not supported.");
        }

    } catch (Exception e) {
        System.out.print("Problem parsing the file.");
    }

  }

}
```

Executing and running the program should provide the following output:

```
2.0 is supported.
5.0 is not supported.
```

C++

Listing 3.3b shows the earlier C++ example extended to show the supported features.

LISTING 3.3b   Checking for Support with C++

```
#include "stdafx.h"
#import "C:\windows\system32\msxml2.dll"
using namespace MSXML2;

int _tmain(int argc, _TCHAR* argv[])
{
    ::CoInitialize(NULL);
    try
    {
        HRESULT hr;
        CComPtr<MSXML2::IXMLDOMDocument>  pDomDocument;
        CComPtr<MSXML2::IXMLDOMImplementation>  pDomImpl;

        hr = pDomDocument.CoCreateInstance(__uuidof(MSXML2::DOMDocument));
```

LISTING 3.3b   Continued

```
        hr = pDomDocument->load("activities.xml");
        hr = pDomDocument->get_implementation(&pDomImpl);

        if (SUCCEEDED(hr) && pDomImpl)
        {
            VARIANT_BOOL vtHasFeature = VARIANT_FALSE;
            vtHasFeature = pDomImpl->hasFeature(_bstr_t("MS-DOM"),
                                                _bstr_t("2.0") );
            if (vtHasFeature == VARIANT_TRUE)
                wprintf(L"2.0 is supported\n");
            else
                wprintf(L"2.0 is not supported\n");
            vtHasFeature = VARIANT_FALSE;
            vtHasFeature = pDomImpl->hasFeature(_bstr_t("MS-DOM"),
                                                _bstr_t("5.0") );
            if ( vtHasFeature == VARIANT_TRUE )
                wprintf(L"5.0 is supported\n");
            else
                wprintf(L"5.0 is not supported\n");
        }
    }

    catch(...)
    {
        wprintf(L"Caught the exception");
    }
    ::CoUninitialize();
    return 0;
}
```

For MSXML, which is the Microsoft implementation of DOM standards, the supported feature
is MS-DOM instead of Core.

Visual Basic

We can perform the same exercise in Visual Basic, as shown in Listing 3.3c. We'll extend the
previous VB application to examine the supported features.

LISTING 3.3c   Checking for Support with VB

```
    Private Sub Button1_Click(ByVal sender As System.Object,
                              ByVal e As System.EventArgs) _
                    Handles Button1.Click
        Dim xmldoc As New MSXML2.DOMDocument40()
        xmldoc.async = False
        xmldoc.load("activities.xml")
        Dim objXMLDOMImpl As MSXML2.IXMLDOMImplementation
        objXMLDOMImpl = xmldoc.implementation
        If objXMLDOMImpl.hasFeature("MS-DOM", "2.0") Then
            MsgBox("2.0 is supported")
        Else
            MsgBox("2.0 is not supported")
        End If
        If objXMLDOMImpl.hasFeature("MS-DOM", "5.0") Then
```

LISTING 3.3c   Continued

```
            MsgBox("5.0 is supported")
        Else
            MsgBox("5.0 is not supported")
        End If
    End Sub
```

PHP

PHP supports most core DOM 2.0 functions, though with a nonstandard naming convention (PHP DOM functions `look_like_this`, `notLikeThis`). One thing *not* supported is the `hasFeature()` function; as of the current stable version of PHP (4.2.1 at the time of this writing), there is no way to query the implementation to find supported features.

Perl

Here, the Perl interface using XML::Xerces is almost identical to Java's JAXP. Syntax differences aside, you'll find that to be the case most of the time when you're working *within* a document.

LISTING 3.3d   Checking for Support with Perl

```
use XML::Xerces;
use XML::Xerces::DOMParse;

my $file   = XML::Xerces::LocalFileInputSource->new("activities.xml");
my $parser = XML::Xerces::DOMParser->new();
eval { $parser->parse($file); };
XML::Xerces::error($@) if $@;

my $doc = $parser->getDocument();

my $impl = $doc->getImplementation();

print "2.0 is supported.\n"    if $impl->hasFeature( 'Core', '2.0' );
print "5.0 is supported.\n"    if $impl->hasFeature( 'Core', '5.0' );
```

You should see output like the following:

```
2.0 is supported.
```

Examining the Structure of the Document

Now let's start looking at the actual document. Earlier we talked about the fact that elements and text are different types of nodes, with text nodes being the children of their element parents. Before we start building the application, let's take a look at how that shakes out in the actual document. In Listings 3.4a–e, we'll look at the names and values of several nodes.

We're going to see two important concepts in action:

- Elements exist independently of their content.

- Nodes exist in a parent-child relationship.

Java

LISTING 3.4a   Element and Text Nodes

```
...
import org.w3c.dom.Element;
import org.w3c.dom.Node;

public class ActivityListing {

   public static void println(String arg) {
      System.out.println(arg);
   }

   public static void main (String args[]) {
      File docFile = new File("activities.xml");
      Document doc = null;
      try {
         DocumentBuilderFactory dbf = DocumentBuilderFactory.newInstance();
         DocumentBuilder db = dbf.newDocumentBuilder();
         doc = db.parse(docFile);
      } catch (Exception e) {
         System.out.println("Problem parsing the file.");
      }

      println("Get the document element.");
      Element root = doc.getDocumentElement();
      println("--The name of the document root is "
                                          +root.getNodeName());
      println("--The value of the document root is "+
                              "["+root.getNodeValue()+"]");

      println(" ");
      println("Get the first child of the root element.");
      Node firstChild = root.getFirstChild();
      println("--The name of the first child is "
                                    +firstChild.getNodeName());
      println("--The value of the first child is "+
                          "["+firstChild.getNodeValue()+"]");

      println(" ");
      println("Get the second child of the root element.");
      Node secondChild = firstChild.getNextSibling();
      println("--The name of the second child is "
                                  +secondChild.getNodeName());
      println("--The value of the second child is "+
                          "["+secondChild.getNodeValue()+"]");
   }
}
```

Conventions

Throughout this and future chapters, we'll be using the same applications over and over, with changes and additions. Sections marked in bold are new, and sections that haven't changed and aren't relevant to the current discussion have been replaced with an ellipsis (. . .).

Figure 3.2 shows the relevant portions of the XML document.

FIGURE 3.2

The relevant portions of the document.

```
<?xml version="1.0" ?>
- <activitysystem>
  - <activities>
    + <activity activityid="A1">
    + <activity activityid="A2">
    </activities>
  + <maintenance>
  + <advertising>
  + <persons>
  </activitysystem>
```

Here's the output of this application:

```
Get the document element.
--The name of the document root is activitysystem
--The value of the document root is [null]

Get the first child of the root element.
--The name of the first child is #text
--The value of the first child is [
    ]

Get the second child of the root element.
--The name of the second child is activities
--The value of the second child is [null]
```

The first step is to retrieve the document element, also known as the root element. As expected, this is the **activitysystem** element, as we can see when we retrieve the name of the node. The value of the node, however, might be a little surprising. Notice that because **root** is an **Element** node, it has a name, but not a value. The value of an **Element** node is always **null**, whether or not it has any content. If it does have content, the content is represented by its child nodes.

Root Element Versus Document Root

Note that the root element and the document root are *not* the same thing. The document root is the root of the document itself, and is actually the parent of the root element. The choice of `getDocumentElement()` as the name of the method that retrieves the root element is unfortunate, but don't let it confuse you!

Next, retrieve the first of those child elements. It may not be what you expect. The first child is not the **activities** element, but rather the whitespace node that precedes the **activities** element. This node doesn't have a name, but it has a value (between the brackets).

The **activities** element is actually the second child, as you'll see if you retrieve the next sibling. Again, because **activities** is an **Element** node, we have a name, but a value of **null**.

Now let's look at how we'd do the same thing in other languages.

C++

Listing 3.4b shows the retrieval of nodes using C++.

LISTING 3.4b Accessing Elements and Text Nodes in C++

```
...
    hr = pDomDocument->load("activities.xml");
    // now let us get the elements and the text nodes
    CComBSTR bstrNodeName;
    CComPtr<MSXML2::IXMLDOMElement> pDomElement;
    hr = pDomDocument->get_documentElement(&pDomElement);
    hr = pDomElement->get_nodeName(&bstrNodeName);
    wprintf(L"Get the document element.\n");
    wprintf(L"--The name of the document root is %s \n", bstrNodeName);
    _variant_t  vtValue;
    pDomElement->get_nodeValue(&vtValue);
    if ( vtValue.vt == VT_NULL )
        wprintf(L"--The value of the document root is [null]\n\n");
    else
    {
        CComBSTR bstrValue(vtValue.bstrVal);
        wprintf(L"--The value of the document root is [%s]\n\n",
            bstrValue);
    }

    CComPtr<MSXML2::IXMLDOMNode>  pFirstChild;
    pDomElement->get_firstChild(&pFirstChild);
    if (pFirstChild)
    {
        CComBSTR  bstrFirstChildNodeName;
        pFirstChild->get_nodeName(&bstrFirstChildNodeName);
        wprintf(L"Get the first child of the root element.\n");
        wprintf(L"--The name of the first child is %s \n",
            bstrFirstChildNodeName);
        _variant_t vtFirstChildValue;
```

LISTING 3.4b   Continued

```
    pFirstChild->get_nodeValue(&vtFirstChildValue);
    if (vtFirstChildValue.vt == VT_NULL)
        wprintf(L"--The value of the first child is [null]\n\n");
    else
    {
        CComBSTR bstrFirstChildValue(vtFirstChildValue.bstrVal);
        wprintf(L"--The value of the first child is [%s]\n\n",
                bstrFirstChildValue);
    }
    CComPtr<MSXML2::IXMLDOMNode>  pSecondChild;
    pFirstChild->get_nextSibling(&pSecondChild);
    if (pSecondChild )
    {
        CComBSTR  bstrSecChildNodeName;
        pSecondChild->get_nodeName(&bstrSecChildNodeName);
        wprintf(L"Get the second child of the root element.\n");
        wprintf(L"--The name of the second child is %s\n",
                bstrSecChildNodeName);
        _variant_t vtSecChildValue;
        pSecondChild->get_nodeValue(&vtSecChildValue);
        if (vtSecChildValue.vt == VT_NULL)
            wprintf(L"--The value of the second child is [null]\n\n");
        else
        {
            CComBSTR bstrSecChildValue(vtSecChildValue.bstrVal);
            wprintf(L"--The value of the second child is [%s]\n\n",
                    bstrSecChildValue);
        }
    }
    }
  }
  ...
```

Visual Basic

Listing 3.4c shows node access in Visual Basic.

LISTING 3.4c   Accessing Elements and Text Nodes in VB

```
    ...
        hr = xmldoc.load("activities.xml")
        Dim root As MSXML2.IXMLDOMElement
        root = xmldoc.documentElement
        Dim text As String
        text = "The name of the document root is "
        text = text & root.baseName
        MsgBox(text)

        Dim text2 As String
        text2 = "The value of the document root is "
        text2 = text2 & "[" & root.nodeValue & "]"
        MsgBox(text2)
```

LISTING 3.4c Continued

```
               Dim firstchild As MSXML2.IXMLDOMNode
               firstchild = root.firstchild
               Dim firstchildname As String
               firstchildname = "The name of the first child is "
               firstchildname = firstchildname & firstchild.nodeName
               MsgBox(firstchildname)

               Dim firstchildvalue As String
               firstchildvalue = "The value of the first child is "
               firstchildvalue = firstchildvalue & "[" & firstchild.nodeValue & "]"
               MsgBox(firstchildvalue)

               Dim secondchild As MSXML2.IXMLDOMNode
               secondchild = firstchild.nextSibling
               Dim secondchildname As String
               secondchildname = "The name of the second child is "
               secondchildname = secondchildname & secondchild.nodeName
               MsgBox(secondchildname)

               Dim secondchildvalue As String
               secondchildvalue = "The value of the second child is "
               secondchildvalue = secondchildvalue &"["& secondchild.nodeValue & "]"
               MsgBox(secondchildvalue)
          End Sub
```

PHP

One thing to watch out for in the PHP implementation (see Listing 3.4d) is the non-standard naming of methods. Instead of the mixed-case style used in Java and Perl—where function names take the form `getDocumentElement()`—PHP generally uses underscores to separate individual "words" in method names, leading to methods with names like `document_element()`. You'll also notice that the PHP implementation of DOM drops the `get` from some functions, such as `getDocumentElement()` and `getFirstChild()`, but leaves it for others, such as `getElementsByTagName()`. In general, you'll probably have to check the PHP manual the first time you use a method to see how the name has been changed.

LISTING 3.4d Accessing Elements and Text Nodes in PHP

```
<?php

$file = "activities.xml";
if (!$doc = domxml_open_file($file)) {
  trigger_error("Failed to open or parse XML file '$file'", E_USER_ERROR);
}

echo ("Get the document element.<br />");
$root = $doc->document_element();
echo ("--The name of the document root is " .
      $root->node_name() . "<br />");
echo ("--The value of the document root is [" .
      $root->node_value() . "]<br /><br />");
```

LISTING 3.4d   Continued

```
echo ("Get the first child of the root element.<br />");
$first_child = $root->first_child();
echo ("--The name of the first child is " .
    $first_child->node_name() . "<br />");
echo ("--The value of the first child is [" .
    $first_child->node_value() . "]<br /><br />");

echo ("Get the second child of the root element.<br />");
$second_child = $first_child->next_sibling();
echo ("--The name of the second child is " .
    $second_child->node_name() . "<br />");
echo ("--The value of the second child is [" .
    $second_child->node_value() . "]<br />");
?>
```

Perl

Listing 3.4e shows the Perl version.

LISTING 3.4e   Accessing Elements and Text Nodes in Perl

```
...
my $doc = $parser->getDocument();

print "Get the document element.\n";
my $root = $doc->getDocumentElement();
print "--The name of the document root is "
  . $root->getNodeName() . "\n";
print "--The value of the document root is ["
  . $root->getNodeValue() . "]\n\n";

print "Get the first child of the root element.\n";
my $first_child = $root->getFirstChild();
print "--The name of the first child is "
  . $first_child->getNodeName() . "\n";
print "--The value of the first child is ["
  . $first_child->getNodeValue() . "]\n\n";

print "Get the second child of the root element.\n";
my $second_child = $first_child->getNextSibling();
print "--The name of the second child is "
  . $second_child->getNodeName() . "\n";
print "--The value of the second child is ["
  . $second_child->getNodeValue() . "]\n";
```

Child Nodes, NodeLists, and Node Types

Before we get into the actual application, let's take one more look at the difference between element nodes and text nodes.

Every node has a type, which corresponds to one of the numeric constants defined within the Node interface. These constants are listed here:

```
ELEMENT_NODE                     = 1
ATTRIBUTE_NODE                   = 2
TEXT_NODE                        = 3
CDATA_SECTION_NODE               = 4
ENTITY_REFERENCE_NODE            = 5
ENTITY_NODE                      = 6
PROCESSING_INSTRUCTION_NODE      = 7
COMMENT_NODE                     = 8
DOCUMENT_NODE                    = 9
DOCUMENT_TYPE_NODE               = 10
DOCUMENT_FRAGMENT_NODE           = 11
NOTATION_NODE                    = 12
```

This means that the value of getNodeType() for an element will be 1, the value for a text node will be 3, and so on. This allows us to compare the actual node type against the defined types in order to determine what sort of node we're dealing with.

In Listing 3.5, we'll retrieve a NodeList of all the children of the activitysystem element. DOM defines the NodeList interface, which contains an ordered list of objects. We'll then loop through the NodeList and examine the type for each node we find.

LISTING 3.5   Examining Node Types

```
...
import org.w3c.dom.NodeList;

public class ActivityListing {
...
   public static void main (String args[]) {
...
      Element root = doc.getDocumentElement();
      NodeList children = root.getChildNodes();
      for (int i=0; i < children.getLength(); i++) {

          Node thisNode = children.item(i);
          if (thisNode.getNodeType() == thisNode.ELEMENT_NODE) {

             println("Element: "+thisNode.getNodeName());

          } else if (thisNode.getNodeType() == thisNode.TEXT_NODE) {

             println("Text: "+thisNode.getNodeValue());

          }
      }

      Node firstChild = root.getFirstChild();
      Node secondChild = firstChild.getNextSibling();
   }
}
```

If you're working in a language other than Java, you should be able to use what you've learned so far to adapt this code to your application.

The `children NodeList` holds all the child nodes of `root`, and for each one, compares the type against the standard types, outputting the appropriate content:

```
Text:

Element: activities
Text:

Element: maintenance
Text:

Element: advertising
Text:

Element: persons
Text:
```

Note that because there's no general `else` clause, nodes other than `Text` or `Element` won't show up at all.

Navigating a DOM Document

At this point we have an application, we've parsed the document, we've looked at node types, and we've obtained an object that represents the `activities` element. It's time to move on to the next step: displaying information on available activities.

In the real world, of course, you would have any number of options for displaying this information. The ultimate destination might be a browser, or it might be some other client-side application. Because you might be using any of several languages in your environment, we'll keep the functionality simple and just retrieve the information and output it to the default location. What you do with it from there is up to you.

Retrieving Elements by Name

We retrieved the `activities` element by working our way down the list of children of `activitysystem`, but there's a better way. DOM enables you to retrieve a list of child elements based on their names, eliminating not only any extraneous elements, but also the whitespace between them.

Listing 3.6 shows the retrieval of all `activity` children of the `activities` element and their subsequent passing to the `displayActivity()` method. The method is just a placeholder for now, but to keep things clean, this is where we'll put the logic to retrieve and display information about an individual activity.

LISTING 3.6   Retrieving the Activities

```
...
        Element root = doc.getDocumentElement();

        Node firstChild = root.getFirstChild();
        Node secondChild = firstChild.getNextSibling();

        Element activitiesElement = (Element)secondChild;
        NodeList activitiesList =
                    activitiesElement.getElementsByTagName("activity");
        for (int i=0; i < activitiesList.getLength(); i++) {
            Node thisNode = activitiesList.item(i);
            displayActivity(thisNode);
        }
    }

    public static void displayActivity(Node thisAct) {

        println("Activity node");

    }
}
```

Notice that because the `getElementsByTagName()` method is defined as part of the `Element` interface, we first have to convert the `secondChild` `Node` to an `Element` object. Next, we create a `NodeList` containing all the `activity` children of `activities`, and loop through it, displaying static text for each. As you'll see in a little while, the `NodeList` keeps the nodes in their original document order.

PHP

PHP doesn't support the `NodeList` interface. Instead of returning a `Nodelist` interface, PHP returns an array:

```php
<?php

...

$first_child   = $root->first_child();
$activities_el = $first_child->next_sibling();

$activities_list  = $activities_el->get_elements_by_tagname("activity");
$count_activities = count($activities_list);

for ($i = 0; $i < $count_activities; $i++) {
  display_activity($activites_list[$i]);
}
function display_activity (&$act)
{
  echo("Activity mode<br>\n");
}
?>
```

Perl

Perl supports the `NodeList` interface, but can also return a native Perl array, if called in list context. The following code shows the native array:

```
...
my $activities_el = $first_child->getNextSibling();
for my $act ( $activities_el->getElementsByTagName("activity") ) {
    display_activity($act);
}

sub display_activity {
    print "Activity Element\n";
}
...
```

Here's the standard `NodeList`:

```
...
my $activities_el = $first_child->getNextSibling();
my $activities_list = $activities_el->getElementsByTagName("activity");

for ( my $i = 0 ; $i < $activities_list->getLength() ; $i++ ) {
    display_activity( $activities_list->item($i) );
}
...
```

NamedNodeMaps

DOM also defines an interface called `NamedNodeMap`, which provides an unordered representation of a group of nodes that are accessible by name. For example, Listing 3.7 shows the `activity` element's attributes retrieved and stored as a `NamedNodeMap`.

LISTING 3.7   A NamedNodeMap

```
...
    public static void displayActivity(Node thisAct) {

        NamedNodeMap actAttrs = thisAct.getAttributes();
        println("Activity node: " + actAttrs.getNamedItem("activityid"));

    }
...
```

The `getAttributes()` method returns a `NamedNodeMap` of all the attributes on the element. In this case, of course, there is only one attribute, but that doesn't matter to the map. When we execute this application, notice the result:

```
Activity node: activityid="A1"
Activity node: activityid="A2"
```

Why did we get both the name and the value? Because the `getNamedItem()` method of `NamedNodeMap` returns a node, not a string value. That node is an `Attr` node.

Attributes

Attributes seem simple. After all, they're just a name and a value, right? Well, yes, they are just a name and a value, but they're far from simple.

First of all, as mentioned previously, attributes are not considered the children of the elements that carry them, but rather they're viewed as properties of sorts. Because of this, they're not considered part of the DOM tree.

Second, while attribute nodes have text children that contain their values, they also return their values directly through both the `getValue()` method, which is specific to `Attr` nodes, as well as the `Node` interface's `getNodeValue()` method. More commonly, however, attribute values are retrieved directly from the element, as shown in Listing 3.8.

LISTING 3.8   Retrieving Attribute Values

```
...
    public static void displayActivity(Node thisAct) {

        NamedNodeMap actAttrs = thisAct.getAttributes();
        Node thisActNode = actAttrs.getNamedItem("activityid");
        Attr thisActAttr = (Attr)thisActNode;

        println(thisActAttr.getValue());
        println(thisActAttr.getNodeValue());
        println(thisActAttr.getFirstChild().getNodeValue());

        Element thisActElement = (Element)thisAct;
        thisActAttr = thisActElement.getAttributeNode("activityid");
        println(thisActAttr.getValue());

        println(thisActElement.getAttribute("activityid"));

    }
...
```

Let's look at what we have here. We're extracting the attribute `Node` from the `NamedNodeMap`, then casting it to an `Attr` so we can access `Attr`-specific methods such as `getValue()`. The `getNodeValue()` method also returns the value, as does retrieving the `Text` node child and getting that value.

The other option is to work directly from the element. First we convert the `activity` node to an `Element` node, then we use `getAttributeNode()` to retrieve the actual attribute node. Note that at this point, `thisActAttr` represents the same `Attr` object it represented in the first section, and can be treated accordingly.

We can also retrieve the value directly from the `Element` using the `getAttribute()` method.

Working with Text Nodes

All right, enough preliminaries. We want to display the information on activities, so we're going to need to access the text child nodes of our elements. The code in Listing 3.9 retrieves the main text nodes, as shown in Figure 3.3.

LISTING 3.9   Retrieving the Text Nodes

```
...
    public static void displayActivity(Node thisAct) {

        Element thisActElement = (Element)thisAct;
        String activityCode =
                        thisActElement.getAttribute("activityid");

        NodeList nameElements =
                        thisActElement.getElementsByTagName("name");
        Node nameElement = nameElements.item(0);
        Node nameText = nameElement.getFirstChild();
        String name = nameText.getNodeValue();

        String description =
                thisActElement.getElementsByTagName("description")
                            .item(0).getFirstChild()
                            .getNodeValue();

        String date = thisActElement.getElementsByTagName("date")
                                    .item(0).getFirstChild()
                                    .getNodeValue();

        String type = thisActElement.getElementsByTagName("type")
                                    .item(0).getFirstChild()
                                    .getNodeValue();

        String limit = thisActElement.getElementsByTagName("limit")
                                    .item(0).getFirstChild()
                                    .getNodeValue();
        int limitNum = Integer.parseInt(limit);
    }
}
```

Here we're creating **String** variables and assigning the values of their corresponding text nodes. Later, we'll output these variables to display the activity information.

Let's look at it step by step as we retrieve the name of the activity. First we're getting all name children of the **activity** element, and retrieving the first (and only) item in the list from the zero-based array. This is the **name** element itself. Next, we get the first child of that element, which is the text node. Finally, we retrieve the value of the text node.

We'll do the same for the subsequent values, but we'll use Java's shorthand capabilities.

FIGURE 3.3
The main activity
elements.

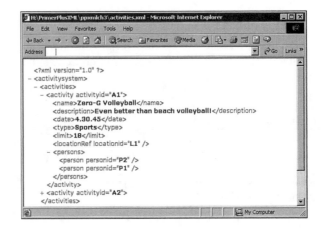

Testing for Children

The last item, `limit`, defines how many participants the activity can have. All current participants are noted as children of the `persons` element, so we can use `getElementsByTagName()`
to tell us how many people are already signed up. Before we bother getting a count, however,
we can use the `hasChildNodes()` method to determine whether there are any children, as
shown in Listing 3.10.

LISTING 3.10   *Counting Children*

```
...
        String limit = thisActElement.getElementsByTagName("limit")
                                     .item(0).getFirstChild()
                                     .getNodeValue();
        int limitNum = Integer.parseInt(limit);

        int currentNum = 0;

        Node personsNode = thisActElement
                            .getElementsByTagName("persons").item(0);
        Element personsElement = (Element)personsNode;

        if (personsElement.hasChildNodes()) {

            currentNum = personsElement.getElementsByTagName("person")
                                                        .getLength();

        };

        int spacesLeft = limitNum - currentNum;

    }
}
```

First we initialize the `currentNum` variable, then we get a reference to the `persons` element, just as we did with the previous elements. The difference here is that rather than retrieving the child node value, we're checking for children, then retrieving the number of child nodes (if any).

Watch That Structure!

This is one case in which it's important that those designing the application and those designing the structure communicate. If you're counting on there being a `persons` element present and the DTD designer decides to indicate a lack of participants by leaving it out, you're going to have a problem. Of course, a truly fault-tolerant application should take these potential issues into account.

It's important to note that while there will be situations where performance dictates a structure like this, the check was unnecessary in this case; if there are no children, the length of the `NodeList` will simply be zero.

Retrieving an Element by ID

Now that we have the information on the activity itself, we want the information about the location. The location information, however, is stored in a separate `location` element that is only referenced by the `locationRef` element. To get that information, we want to be able to retrieve the `location` element directly, preferably by some kind of unique identifier.

The `getElementById()` method on the `Document` object will select an element by its unique ID value, but first we have to create that ID. We'll talk more about ID values in Chapter 7, "Document Type Definitions (DTDs)," but for now understand that Listing 3.11 shows the specification of the `location` element's `locationid` as a unique identifier.

LISTING 3.11 Creating the ID within `activities.xml`

```
<?xml version="1.0"?>
<!DOCTYPE activitysystem [
    <!ATTLIST location locationid ID #REQUIRED>
]>
<activitysystem>
    <activities>
...
```

Now we can reference the ID directly, as in Listing 3.12.

LISTING 3.12 Retrieving an Element by ID

```
...
        int spacesLeft = limitNum - currentNum;

        Node locationRefNode =
            thisActElement.getElementsByTagName("locationRef").item(0);
```

LISTING 3.12   Continued

```
          Element locationRefElement = (Element)locationRefNode;
          String locationRef = locationRefElement.getAttribute("locationid");

          Document doc = locationRefElement.getOwnerDocument();
          Element locationElement = doc.getElementById(locationRef);

          String locationName = locationElement.getElementsByTagName("name")
                                       .item(0).getFirstChild()
                                       .getNodeValue();
          String locationDeck = locationElement.getElementsByTagName("deck")
                                       .item(0).getFirstChild()
                                       .getNodeValue();
      }
  }
```

First, we retrieve the value of the `locationid` attribute from the `locationRef` element, just as we retrieved the `activityCode` attribute earlier.

Next, we have to work around a little problem. Because we declared the `doc` variable in the `main()` method, it's not defined within the `displayActivity()` method. Fortunately, we can get a reference to the `Document` object itself by calling the `getOwnerDocument()` method for any of our elements.

Once we get the document, we can call the `getElementById()` method to get a reference to the `location` element that matches our `locationRef`. From there, we can retrieve the information just as we did for all of our other elements.

Finally, now that we have all the information, we can display it, as shown in Listings 3.13 and 3.14.

LISTING 3.13   Displaying the Results

```
    ...
          String locationDeck = locationElement.getElementsByTagName("deck")
                                       .item(0).getFirstChild()
                                       .getNodeValue();

      println("Activity:");
      println("("+activityCode+") "+name+" -- "+date);
      println("Type: "+type);
      println(description);
      println("Spaces left: "+spacesLeft);
      println("Location: "+locationName+", Deck "+locationDeck);
      println("\n");
    }
  }
```

LISTING 3.14   The Results

```
Activity:
(A1) Zero-G Volleyball -- 4.30.45
Type: Sports

                Even better than beach volleyball!

Spaces left: 16
Location: Zero-G Sports Arena, Deck 25


Activity:
(A2) Stargazing -- 4.29.45
Type: Educational

                Learn the visible constellations.

Spaces left: 5
Location: Zero-G Sports Arena, Deck 25
```

Changing Content

Now that we've successfully read information from various places in a DOM document, we'll look at changing some of that information.

Using the application we've already built, we'll first modify it so that if a location is listed as Closed, the date of the event will be changed to TBD. Then we'll change the value of the locationid to TBD.

In the next section, we'll build a document from scratch to hold participant information.

Changing Text

We'll begin by checking the value of the **status** element and if it's Closed, we'll reset the **date** element's content. Because the result affects the rest of the application (specifically the value of the **date** variable), we'll move the location check to the top of the method, as shown in Listing 3.15.

LISTING 3.15   Checking the Location and Setting the Date

```
...
    public static void displayActivity(Node thisAct) {

        Element thisActElement = (Element)thisAct;

        Node locationRefNode = thisActElement
                        .getElementsByTagName("locationRef").item(0);
        Element locationRefElement = (Element)locationRefNode;
        String locationRef = locationRefElement.getAttribute("locationid");
```

LISTING 3.15   *Continued*

```
Document doc = locationRefElement.getOwnerDocument();
Element locationElement = doc.getElementById(locationRef);
String locationName = "TBD";
String locationDeck = "TBD";
String status = locationElement.getElementsByTagName("status")
                                    .item(0).getFirstChild()
                                    .getNodeValue();

if (status.equals("Closed")) {

    Node thisDate = thisActElement.getElementsByTagName("date")
                                    .item(0);
    Node thisDateText = thisDate.getFirstChild();
    thisDateText.setNodeValue("TBD");

} else {

    locationName = locationElement.getElementsByTagName("name")
                                    .item(0).getFirstChild()
                                    .getNodeValue();
    locationDeck = locationElement.getElementsByTagName("deck")
                                    .item(0).getFirstChild()
                                    .getNodeValue();
}

String activityCode =
                thisActElement.getAttribute("activityid");
```

```
...
```

First, we get the value of the **status** text, just as we've retrieved all the other text values. If the value is **Closed**, we make the change to the **date** element's content. To do this, we retrieve the element itself by choosing the first item in **getElementsByTagName()**, just as we did before. Because it's actually the value of the text node child we want to change, we get that next. Finally, we set the value of the text node using **setNodeValue()**.

In Java, we could have accomplished all of this in a single step, using

```
thisActElement.getElementsByTagName("date").item(0)
                .getFirstChild().setNodeValue("TBD");
```

The rest of the application continues on as before, so the new value of TBD is retrieved for the date. The results are as follows:

```
Activity:
(A1) Zero-G Volleyball -- TBD
Type: Sports

            Even better than beach volleyball!

Spaces left: 16
```

```
Location: TBD, Deck TBD


Activity:
(A2) Stargazing -- TBD
Type: Educational

            Learn the visible constellations.

Spaces left: 5
Location: TBD, Deck TBD
```

Persistence

It's crucial to understand that we have just made a change to the in-memory copy of the XML document, as opposed to the original file. You can verify this by checking the file after you've run the application.

Nothing we have done here affects the original file unless and until we save the information, which we'll take care of at the end of the chapter.

Changing Attributes

Changing the value of an attribute is much more straightforward, as shown in Listing 3.16.

LISTING 3.16   *Setting an Attribute Value*

```
...
    if (status.equals("Closed")) {

        Node thisDate = thisActElement.getElementsByTagName("date")
                                    .item(0);
        Node thisDateText = thisDate.getFirstChild();
        thisDateText.setNodeValue("TBD");

        locationRefElement.setAttribute("locationid", "TBD");

    } else {

        locationName = locationElement.getElementsByTagName("name")
                                    .item(0).getFirstChild()
                                    .getNodeValue();
        locationDeck = locationElement.getElementsByTagName("deck")
                                    .item(0).getFirstChild()
                                    .getNodeValue();
    }
...
```

The `setAttribute()` method takes the name of the attribute and the desired value. If the named attribute doesn't exist, `setAttribute()` creates it, then sets the value.

Creating New Content

At this point we've read and modified simple information such as attributes and text nodes. Modifying the content of an element is a bit more complex, and requires adding or removing nodes.

In this section, we'll start by creating a new **person** element, giving it an attribute, and adding it to the **persons** element for each **activity**. We'll then create a new document and populate it with the participant information for each activity.

Finally, we'll look at some of the ways that current implementations persist (save) a **Document** object.

Creating an Element

Before you can add an element to a document, you must first create it. Creating elements and other nodes is the responsibility of the **Document** object.

In Listing 3.17, we'll create a method for adding the new **person**, and execute it before displaying the activity information so the number of available spaces is correct.

LISTING 3.17   Creating an Element

```
...
      NodeList activitiesList =
                activitiesElement.getElementsByTagName("activity");
      for (int i=0; i < activitiesList.getLength(); i++) {

         Node thisNode = activitiesList.item(i);
         addNewParticipant(thisNode, "P4");
         displayActivity(thisNode);
      }
   }
...
   public static void addNewParticipant(Node thisAct, String thisPerson) {

      Element thisActElement = (Element)thisAct;

      Node thisPersons = thisActElement.getElementsByTagName("persons").item(0);
      Element thisPersonsElement = (Element)thisPersons;

      Document doc = thisPersonsElement.getOwnerDocument();

      Element thisPersonElement = doc.createElement("person");
      thisPersonElement.setAttribute("personid", thisPerson);
   }
}
```

First, we establish the parent node for the new child node. In this case, that's the **persons** element within each **activity** element. Next, we need to create the actual element node, which means that we need the `Document` object. As before, we need to get a reference from the element itself because we're out of the original `Document` object's scope.

The `Document` creates the element (and we assign it a `personid` attribute) but at this moment, the element is in limbo. It's not yet a part of the tree.

Adding the Element

To make a newly created element part of the tree, we have to add it to the structure. There are several ways to do this. The first, and most common, is to simply append it to the content of the parent element, as shown in Listing 3.18.

LISTING 3.18 Appending a Child

```
...
    public static void addNewParticipant(Node thisAct, String thisPerson) {

        Element thisActElement = (Element)thisAct;

        Node thisPersons = thisActElement.getElementsByTagName("persons").item(0);
        Element thisPersonsElement = (Element)thisPersons;

        Document doc = thisPersonsElement.getOwnerDocument();
        Element thisPersonElement = doc.createElement("person");
        thisPersonElement.setAttribute("personid", thisPerson);

        thisPersonsElement.appendChild(thisPersonElement);
    }
}
```

In this case, we simply add the new element to the content that already exists. Before, the `persons` element may have looked like the following:

```
<persons>
    <person personid="P2"/>
    <person personid="P1"/>
</persons>
```

Now it looks like this:

```
<persons>
    <person personid="P2"/>
    <person personid="P1"/>
    <person personid="P4"/>
</persons>
```

The `Node` interface also provides two other construction-type methods.

The first, `insertBefore()`, takes two arguments: the node being added, and the node that it's to precede. So if `P1Element` represents the `person` with a `personid` of `P1`, the statement

```
thisPersonsElement.insertBefore(thisPersonElement, P1Element);
```

results in a structure of

```
<persons>
    <person personid="P2"/>
    <person personid="P4"/>
    <person personid="P1"/>
</persons>
```

Note that a node may only appear in a `Document` once, so if `thisPersonElement` already exists somewhere else, it's automatically removed, and then placed in its new position.

The second additional method is `replaceChild()`, where a call to

```
Element replacedChild =
            thisPersonsElement.replaceChild(thisPersonElement, P1Element);
```

results in a structure of

```
<persons>
    <person personid="P2"/>
    <person personid="P4"/>
</persons>
```

In this case, `replacedChild` is also equal to `P1Element`, as `replaceChild()` returns the node that was replaced.

Creating a New Document

Now we're ready to create a new document. Overall, there's just one new technique: actually creating the document. Again, this is not the standard way of doing things; in the case of the Java implementation, the `DocumentBuilder` creates a new `Document` object.

The rest of Listing 3.19 simply shows another use for the techniques we covered earlier in this chapter.

LISTING 3.19   Creating the New Document

```
...
public class ActivityListing {

    public static void println(String arg) {
        System.out.println(arg);
    }

    public static void main (String args[]) {
        File docFile = new File("activities.xml");
        Document doc = null;
        Document newDoc = null;

        try {

            DocumentBuilderFactory dbf = DocumentBuilderFactory.newInstance();
            DocumentBuilder db = dbf.newDocumentBuilder();
            doc = db.parse(docFile);

            newDoc = db.newDocument();
```

LISTING 3.19   *Continued*

```
   } catch (Exception e) {
     System.out.println("Problem parsing the file.");
   }

   Element newRoot = newDoc.createElement("roster");
   newDoc.appendChild(newRoot);

   Element root = doc.getDocumentElement();

   Node firstChild = root.getFirstChild();
   Node secondChild = firstChild.getNextSibling();

   Element activitiesElement = (Element)secondChild;
   NodeList activitiesList =
             activitiesElement.getElementsByTagName("activity");
   for (int i=0; i < activitiesList.getLength(); i++) {

     Node thisNode = activitiesList.item(i);
     addNewParticipant(thisNode, "P4");
     displayActivity(thisNode);

     Element thisActivity = (Element)thisNode;
     String thisActivityId = thisActivity.getAttribute("activityid");

     Element newActivity = newDoc.createElement("activity");
     newActivity.setAttribute("activityid", thisActivityId);

     Element personsElement =
           (Element)thisActivity.getElementsByTagName("persons").item(0);
     NodeList participants = personsElement.getElementsByTagName("person");

     for (int j=0; j < participants.getLength(); j++) {
         Element thisPerson = (Element)participants.item(j);
         String thisPersonId = thisPerson.getAttribute("personid");

         Element thisNewPerson = newDoc.createElement("person");
         Node thisPersonText = newDoc.createTextNode(thisPersonId);
         thisNewPerson.appendChild(thisPersonText);

         newActivity.appendChild(thisNewPerson);
     }

     newRoot.appendChild(newActivity);

   }
  }
...
```

(If you're working in one of the other languages, stay with me for a moment. We'll cover the creation of a document in the next section.)

A document isn't well-formed XML until it has a root element, so next we create a new `Element` node with the name `roster` and append it to the document itself.

Now we're ready to start adding new nodes to the document. We simply pull information from the old document just as we did before, then add it to the new document. For example, we retrieve the `activityid` using the `getAttribute()` method, then create a new element and add the attribute to it.

The `person` elements are a bit different, because we're changing the `personid` from an attribute to the text of the element. Because of this, creating the new `person` element involves creating a new text node, then appending it as a child to the element. As each `person` element is completed, append it to the `activity`.

Finally, append each `activity` to the new root element.

Which Document?

When creating new elements, be sure that you use the right document to do it. Nodes are not easily transferable between documents, so create the node using the document that will ultimately contain it.

Saving the Document

The DOM Level 2.0 doesn't specify a means for saving an XML document (though that's planned for Level 3.0), so it's up to the implementation to decide how to do so. The following subsections provide some examples.

Java

The JAXP specification doesn't include a standard way to save documents, but it's recommended that you use the package's XSL transformation abilities. We'll cover transformation in detail in Chapter 10, "Transformations Within an Application." For now, understand that we're transforming a document, but we're not providing a style sheet, so the document comes through unchanged. Listing 3.20a demonstrates the process.

LISTING 3.20a   Saving the Document

```
...
import javax.xml.transform.TransformerFactory;
import javax.xml.transform.Transformer;
import javax.xml.transform.dom.DOMSource;
import javax.xml.transform.stream.StreamResult;

public class ActivityListing {
...
   public static void main (String args[]) {
...
        newRoot.appendChild(newActivity);
```

LISTING 3.20a Continued

```
    }

    try {

        TransformerFactory transformerFactory =
                        TransformerFactory.newInstance();
        Transformer transformer =
                    transformerFactory.newTransformer();

        DOMSource origDocSource = new DOMSource(doc);
        StreamResult origResult = new StreamResult("updated.xml");
        transformer.transform(origDocSource, origResult);

        DOMSource newDocSource = new DOMSource(newDoc);
        StreamResult newResult = new StreamResult("roster.xml");
        transformer.transform(newDocSource, newResult);

    } catch (Exception e) {
        println("Could not save document.");
    }
}

public static void displayActivity(Node thisAct) {
...
```

When transforming documents, a `Transformer` takes the source and sends it to the result after applying the instructions specified by the style sheet with which the `Transformer` was created. Because there is no style sheet in this case, the `Transformer` makes no changes and simply sends the original document to the result, which in this case is a file.

C++

In C++, creating an XML document is as simple as calling the **save** function with the destination filename.

LISTING 3.20b Saving the Document in C++

```
#include "stdafx.h"
#import "C:\windows\system32\msxml2.dll"
using namespace MSXML2;

int _tmain(int argc, _TCHAR* argv[])
{
    ::CoInitialize(NULL);
    try
    {
        HRESULT hr;
        CComPtr<MSXML2::IXMLDOMDocument>  pDomDocument;

        // We create the initial empty DOMDocument
        hr = pDomDocument.CoCreateInstance(__uuidof(MSXML2::DOMDocument));
```

LISTING 3.20b Continued

```
        // We load the XML file into the DOMDocument
        hr = pDomDocument->load("activities.xml");

        // Here we can place code that makes modifications to the DOMDocument

        // Now, we save the DOMDocument as some other XML file
        hr = pDomDocument->save("new_activities.xml");
    }

    catch(...)
    {
        wprintf(L"Caught the exception");
    }
    ::CoUninitialize();
    return 0;
}
```

Visual Basic

The VB process is as simple as in VC++, as Listing 3.20c shows.

LISTING 3.20c Saving the Document in VB

```
    Private Sub Button1_Click(ByVal sender As System.Object,
                              ByVal e As System.EventArgs) _
                              Handles Button1.Click

        'We create the initial empty DOMDocument
        Dim xmldoc As New MSXML2.DOMDocument40()
        Dim hr As Boolean

        'We load the XML file into the DOMDocument
        xmldoc.async = False
        hr = xmldoc.load("activities.xml")

        'Here we can place code that makes modifications to the DOMDocument

        'Now, we save the DOMDocument as some other XML file
        xmldoc.save("new_activities.xml")
    End Sub
```

PHP

Creating a new document and writing DOM structures to disk are both easy using PHP, but at the time of this writing the current version of PHP, 4.2.1, has two bugs to watch out for. First, formatting the output removes whitespace nodes, and second, the PHP version of getElementById(), get_element_by_id(), doesn't actually search for an element with an attribute of *type* ID. Instead, it searches for an element *named* ID. This behavior will likely be fixed in future versions, but I've included a workaround as part of Listing 3.20d.

Output Formatting and Apache

If you're running PHP version 4.2.2 or earlier as an Apache module, beware of letting `dump_file()` or `dump_mem()` format your XML output; the formatting changes (such as removing whitespace nodes) persist across requests, even if you load the source XML document again.

LISTING 3.20d   Saving the Document in PHP

```php
<?php

...

$new_doc  = domxml_new_doc('1.0');
$new_root = $new_doc->create_element('roster');

$first_child       =& $root->first_child();
$activities_el     =& $first_child->next_sibling();
$activities_list   = $activities_el->get_elements_by_tagname("activity");
$count_activities = count($activities_list);

for ($i = 0; $i < $count_activities; $i++) {
  $act =& $activities_list[$i];
  add_new_participant($act,"P4");
  display_activity($act);

  $act_id = $act->get_attribute("activityid");
  $new_act = $new_doc->create_element("activity");
  $new_act->set_attribute("activityid",$act_id);

  $persons_el_list = $act->get_elements_by_tagname("persons");
  $persons_el       =& $persons_el_list[0];
  $person_list      = $persons_el->get_elements_by_tagname("person") ;
  $count_persons    = count($person_list);
  for ($j = 0; $j < $count_persons; $j++) {
    $person          = $person_list[$j];
    $person_id       = $person->get_attribute("personid");
    $new_person      = $new_doc->create_element("person");
    $new_person_text = $new_doc->create_text_node($person_id);
    $new_person->append_child($new_person_text);
    $new_act->append_child($new_person);
  }

  $new_root->append_child($new_act);
}

$new_doc->append_child($new_root);

$doc->dump_file("updated.xml",false,false);
$new_doc->dump_file("roster.xml",false,false);

...
```

LISTING 3.20d   Continues

```
function add_new_participant (&$act, $person)
{
  $act_persons_list = $act->get_elements_by_tagname("persons");
  $act_persons_el   =& $act_persons_list[0];

  $doc            =& $act_persons_el->owner_document();
  $new_person_el = $doc->create_element("person");
  $new_person_el->set_attribute("personid",$person);
  $act_persons_el->append_child($new_person_el);
}

function & get_element_by_id(&$doc, $tagname, $attr_name, $value)
{
  $tags       = $doc->get_elements_by_tagname($tagname);
  $count_tags = count($tags);

  for ($i = 0; $i < $count_tags; $i++) {
    $el =& $tags[$i];
    if ($el->get_attribute($attr_name) == $value) {
      return $el;
    }
  }

  return false;
}
?>
```

Perl

Creating a `Document` object in Perl is a bit more complex than it is in Java. Instead of using a document builder or factory object, with XML::Xerces you use the `DOMImplementation` object to create a new, empty document type based on a DTD. (The DTD document doesn't have to exist, but you do have to put a DTD name in the command.) Then you can create an instance of that `DocumentType`, get the root `Document` object, and add elements.

On the other hand, saving the file is much easier. Instead of using an XSLT transform, just open a `FileHandle` for writing, format the document, and print it to the open `FileHandle` (see Listing 3.20e).

LISTING 3.20e   Saving the Document in Perl

```
use FileHandle;
use XML::Xerces;
use XML::Xerces::DOMParse;

my $file   = XML::Xerces::LocalFileInputSource->new("activities.xml");
my $parser = XML::Xerces::DOMParser->new();
eval { $parser->parse($file); };
XML::Xerces::error($@) if $@;
```

LISTING 3.20e   *Continued*

```perl
my $doc  = $parser->getDocument();
my $root = $doc->getDocumentElement();

my $first_child  = $root->getFirstChild();
my $activities_el = $first_child->getNextSibling();

my $impl     = XML::Xerces::DOM_DOMImplementation::getImplementation();
my $new_dt   = $impl->createDocumentType( 'roster', '', 'roster.dtd' );
my $new_doc  = $impl->createDocument( 'roster', 'roster', $new_dt );
my $new_root = $new_doc->getDocumentElement();
for my $act ( $activities_el->getElementsByTagName("activity") ) {
    add_new_participant( $act, "P4" );
    display_activity($act);

    ...

}

my $updated = new FileHandle( "updated.xml", "w" );
$XML::Xerces::DOMParse::INDENT = "  ";
XML::Xerces::DOMParse::format($doc);
XML::Xerces::DOMParse::print( $updated, $doc );
$updated->close;

my $roster = new FileHandle( "roster.xml", "w" );
$XML::Xerces::DOMParse::INDENT = "  ";
XML::Xerces::DOMParse::format($new_doc);
XML::Xerces::DOMParse::print( $roster, $new_doc );
$roster->close;
...

sub add_new_participant {
    my $act    = shift;
    my $person = shift;

    my $act_persons_el = $act->getElementsByTagName("persons")->item(0);

    my $doc            = $act_persons_el->getOwnerDocument();
    my $new_person_el = $doc->createElement("person");
    $new_person_el->setAttribute( "personid", $person );
    $act_persons_el->appendChild($new_person_el);
}
```

The Result

The result of all the work we've done in this chapter is an XML document with **activity** and **person** elements, as shown in Listing 3.21. (I've added whitespace to make the document a bit more readable.)

LISTING 3.21   The Resulting Document

```xml
<?xml version="1.0" encoding="UTF-8"?>
<roster>
   <activity activityid="A1">
      <person>P2</person>
      <person>P1</person>
      <person>P4</person>
   </activity>
   <activity activityid="A2">
      <person>P4</person>
   </activity>
</roster>
```

Summary

The Document Object Model was developed to give people writing XML applications common ground on which to build. By creating a series of interfaces representing different node types such as elements and attributes, DOM makes it likely that an application written for one implementation will be able to run in another implementation with only minor changes.

DOM centers around the premise that everything in a document is a `Node`. A `Document` is a `Node`, as is an `Element` and the `Text` node that is its child. To add content to an element, you must create a new node and add it using methods such as `appendChild()` and `insertBefore()`.

Using methods such as `getChildNodes()` and `getElementsByTagName()`, you can create a `NodeList` of nodes and evaluate them one by one.

Attributes are not part of the DOM tree, because they're not considered children of the elements that carry them. Instead, they're properties of the elements. They can be selected as `NamedNodeMap`s and retrieved by attribute name.

The current version of DOM, Level 2.0, doesn't specify a standard means for loading or saving a `Document` object, so these functions are left to implementers.

Review Questions

1. What is the purpose of the Document Object Model?

2. What is the relationship between DOM and browsers?

3. What are the DOM Level 2.0 modules?

4. What is the main interface in the DOM Level 2.0 Core module?

5. Which interface is generally used to create nodes?

6. Which interface is generally used to move nodes around?

7. What two essential operations are not defined by DOM Level 2.0?

8. How many nodes are involved with an element that has text content and two attributes?

Programming Exercises

These exercises assume that you have a file called **aliens.xml** with the following content:

```xml
<?xml version="1.0"?>
<aliens>
  <alien>
      <classification>GS3</classification>
      <species>Isaboreans</species>
      <planet>Isabore 3</planet>
      <range confirmed="yes">3000000</range>
  </alien>

  <alien>
      <classification>PPW</classification>
      <species>Rowaria</species>
      <planet>Roware 9</planet>
      <range confirmed="no">400000</range>
  </alien>

  <alien>
      <classification>IOPO</classification>
      <species>Discoria</species>
      <planet>Bearost 4</planet>
      <range confirmed="yes">9000</range>
  </alien>

</aliens>
```

1. Using your chosen language, create a **Document** object.

2. Alter your application to retrieve the root element and output its name.

3. Display the species names.

4. For each **alien** element, display the name and text of each element node.

5. Make sure all confirmed attributes have a value of **yes**.

CHAPTER 4

ADVANCED DOM TECHNIQUES

You will learn about the following in this chapter:

- Sibling relationships
- Normalization and canonical form
- NodeIterators

- TreeWalkers
- NodeFilters
- DOM Level 3.0 Load and Save

*I*n Chapter 3, "Manipulating Documents: The Document Object Model (DOM)," you learned how to think of your XML data in terms of a tree of nodes. You learned how to navigate around those nodes, and how to add, subtract, and change them.

In this chapter, we're going to look at some of the more sophisticated techniques for manipulating DOM documents.

These techniques come from the DOM Level 2.0 Core module and the DOM Level 2.0 Traversal and Range module. We'll also take a peek at the upcoming DOM Level 3.0 Load and Save module.

Additional Features of the DOM Level 2.0 Core

In Chapter 3, we covered the very basic issues behind the Document Object Model. Now let's look at it a little more carefully. In this section, we'll go beyond `NodeList`s in navigating through the document and we'll work with node types other than text, elements, and attributes. In the process, we'll output the entire document to the screen.

We'll also look at different ways to represent a DOM document, and the effects of normalization and canonical representation (or *canonicalization*).

Most of the examples in this chapter use a portion of the airlock system document that we discussed in Chapter 2, "Designing XML Documents and Applications." It is shown in Listing 4.1.

LISTING 4.1   The Source Document

```
<?xml version="1.0" encoding="ISO-8859-1" standalone="no"?>
<!DOCTYPE airlocksystem SYSTEM "airlocks.dtd">
<?xml-stylesheet href="airlocks.xsl" type="text/xsl"?>
<airlocksystem>
    <airlock lockid="A23b">
        <size width="500" height="320" />
        <type>Bronson</type>
        <location>Level 2 aft</location>
        <status>open</status>
        <maintenance responsible="M83">
            <lastdone>2/23/2325</lastdone>
            <frequency>Once per month</frequency>
        </maintenance>
        <signage>
            <checkscript type="text/javascript">
                &checkscript;
            </checkscript>
            <signtext><![CDATA[<DANGER> Open Airlock]]></signtext>
        </signage>
    </airlock>
    <personnel badge="D59">
        <name>Angus Doyle</name>
        <department>Maintenance</department>
    </personnel>
</airlocksystem>
```

Using Siblings

In Chapter 3, we navigated the document by creating **NodeList**s and iterating through them based on the length of the list. This is a perfectly serviceable way of doing things, but doesn't really mesh with the structure of the document. Another method, shown in Listing 4.2, involves looking directly at the siblings. (We'll look at other languages as soon as we've mastered the concept.)

LISTING 4.2   Navigating a Document Using Siblings

```
import javax.xml.parsers.DocumentBuilder;
import javax.xml.parsers.DocumentBuilderFactory;
import java.io.File;
import org.w3c.dom.Document;
import org.w3c.dom.Node;

public class DocumentListing {

    public static void println (String arg) {
        System.out.println(arg);
    }

    public static void main (String args[]) {
        File docFile = new File("airlocks.xml");
```

LISTING 4.2   Continued

```
        Document doc = null;
        try {
           DocumentBuilderFactory dbf = DocumentBuilderFactory.newInstance();
           DocumentBuilder db = dbf.newDocumentBuilder();

           doc = db.parse(docFile);

        } catch (Exception e) {
           System.out.print("Problem parsing the file.");
        }

        Node root = doc.getDocumentElement();
        for (Node child = root.getFirstChild();
             child != null;
             child = child.getNextSibling()) {

            int type = child.getNodeType();
            String name = child.getNodeName();
            String value = child.getNodeValue();

            println("(" + type + ") " + name + ": " + value);

        }
    }
}
```

In this example, we parse the document and get the root element as usual. Normally, we would then get a `NodeList` of the children of the `root` element, then use that list to create a `for` loop that iterates through them one by one, based on the index of each item in the list. In other words, we would use the following code:

```
for (int i = 0;
     i < childNodeList.getLength();
     i++) {

   Node thisNode = childNodeList.item(i);
   ...

}
```

Here we start with the first item, and as long as the index is less than the length of the list, we increase the index by 1. The "current" node is determined by choosing the item out of the list based on the index.

Using children and siblings requires virtually the same algorithm, but different objects:

```
for (Node child = root.getFirstChild();
     child != null;
     child = child.getNextSibling()) {

   Node thisNode = child;
   ...

}
```

In this case, we start with the first child, and as long as there are still children, we keep moving to the next sibling. Because we're moving through the list directly, the current node is the child node itself.

The output shows the text and element nodes that are direct children of the root element:

```
(3) #text:

(1) airlock: null
(3) #text:

(1) personnel: null
(3) #text:
```

Using this method, we can crawl through the entire tree, examining each node as we come to it, as shown in Listings 4.3a–e.

Java

Stepping through the entire tree involves creating a method and calling it recursively, as in Listing 4.3a.

LISTING 4.3a   Stepping Through the Tree in Java

```java
...
    public static void main (String args[]) {
        File docFile = new File("airlocks.xml");

        Document doc = null;
        try {
            DocumentBuilderFactory dbf = DocumentBuilderFactory.newInstance();
            DocumentBuilder db = dbf.newDocumentBuilder();

            doc = db.parse(docFile);

        } catch (Exception e) {
            System.out.print("Problem parsing the file.");
        }

        stepThrough(doc);

    }

    public static void stepThrough(Node thisNode) {

        int type = thisNode.getNodeType();
        String name = thisNode.getNodeName();
        String value = thisNode.getNodeValue();

        println("(" + type + ") " + name + ": " + value);

        for (Node child = thisNode.getFirstChild();
                child != null;
```

LISTING 4.3a   Continued

```
                child = child.getNextSibling()) {

            stepThrough(child);

        }
    }
}
```

The idea is to recursively step through the children of each node, so we'll break the logic out into a separate method, **stepThrough()**. We'll start with the **Document** node itself, outputting the type, name, and value and then moving through each of its children. We'll also step through all the children of each child. Let's see what this looks like in other languages, and then look at the results.

C++

In C++, the same example can be written as shown in Listing 4.3b.

LISTING 4.3b   Stepping Through the Tree in C++

```cpp
#include "stdafx.h"
// Change the path to msxml.dll per your machine configuration
#import "C:\windows\system32\msxml2.dll"
using namespace MSXML2;

HRESULT stepThrough(MSXML2::IXMLDOMNode *pNode)
{
        MSXML2::DOMNodeType eType;
        pNode->get_nodeType(&eType);
        CComBSTR nodeName;
        pNode->get_nodeName(&nodeName);
        CComVariant nodeValue;
        pNode->get_nodeValue(&nodeValue);
        if (V_VT(&nodeValue) == VT_NULL)
            nodeValue = L"null";
        wprintf(L"(%d) %s: %s\n", (int)eType, nodeName, V_BSTR(&nodeValue));

        // Access the child nodes and so on
        for (pNode->get_firstChild(&pNode);
            pNode != NULL;
            pNode->get_nextSibling(&pNode))
        {
            stepThrough(pNode);
        }
        return S_OK;
}

int _tmain(int argc, _TCHAR* argv[])
{
    ::CoInitialize(NULL);
```

LISTING 4.3b   Continued

```
    try
    {
        CComPtr<MSXML2::IXMLDOMDocument>  pDomDocument;
        pDomDocument.CoCreateInstance(__uuidof(MSXML2::DOMDocument));
        pDomDocument->load("airlocks.xml");

        CComQIPtr<MSXML2::IXMLDOMNode> pDocNode(pDomDocument);
        stepThrough(pDocNode);
    }
    catch(...)
    {
        wprintf(L"Caught the exception");
    }
    ::CoUninitialize();
    return 0;
}
```

Visual Basic

Listing 4.3c shows the Visual Basic version.

LISTING 4.3c   Stepping Through the Tree in VB

```
Private Sub Button1_Click(ByVal sender As System.Object, ByVal e As
                  System.EventArgs) Handles Button1.Click
    Dim xmldoc As New MSXML2.DOMDocument40()
    xmldoc.async = False
    xmldoc.load("c:\\activities.xml")
    Dim thisNode As MSXML2.IXMLDOMNode
    thisNode = xmldoc
    stepThrough(thisNode)
End Sub

Public Function stepThrough(ByVal thisNode As MSXML2.IXMLDOMNode)
    Dim nodeType As Integer
    nodeType = thisNode.nodeType
    Dim nodeName As String
    nodeName = thisNode.nodeName
    Dim nodeValue As String
    nodeValue = nodeValue & thisNode.nodeValue
    If (nodeValue.Length() = 0) Then
        nodeValue = "null"
    End If
    Dim MsgString As String
    MsgString = "(" & nodeType & ") " & nodeName & ": " & nodeValue
    MsgBox(MsgString)

    Dim childCounter As Integer
    childCounter = thisNode.childNodes.length
    Dim childNode As MSXML2.IXMLDOMNode
    Dim currentNode As Integer
```

LISTING 4.3c   Continued

```
          currentNode = 0
          childNode = thisNode.firstChild
          If Not (childNode Is Nothing) Then
               stepThrough(childNode)
          End If
          Do While currentNode < childCounter
               childNode = childNode.nextSibling
               If Not (childNode Is Nothing) Then
                    stepThrough(childNode)
               End If
               currentNode = currentNode + 1
          Loop
     End Function
```

PHP

The PHP version is straightforward, as shown in Listing 4.3d.

LISTING 4.3d   Stepping Through the Tree in PHP

```php
<?php

$file = "airlocks.xml";
if (!$doc = domxml_open_file($file)) {
  trigger_error("Failed to open or parse XML file '$file'", E_USER_ERROR);
}

$root = $doc->document_element();

step_through($root);

function step_through (&$node)
{
  $type  = $node->node_type();
  $name  = $node->node_name();
  $value = $node->node_value();

  echo "($type) $name: $value<br>\n";

  for ($child =& $node->first_child();
       $child != null;
       $child =& $child->next_sibling())
    {
      step_through($child);
    }

}

?>
```

Perl

Perl requires just a bit more code (see Listing 4.3e).

LISTING 4.3e   *Stepping Through the Tree in Perl*

```perl
use XML::Xerces;
use XML::Xerces::DOMParse;

my $file   = XML::Xerces::LocalFileInputSource->new("airlocks.xml");
my $parser = XML::Xerces::DOMParser->new();
my $error_handler = XML::Xerces::PerlErrorHandler->new();
$parser->setErrorHandler($error_handler);
eval { $parser->parse($file); };
XML::Xerces::error($@) if $@;

my $doc  = $parser->getDocument();
my $root = $doc->getDocumentElement();

step_through($root);

sub step_through {
    my $node = shift;

    my $type  = $node->getNodeType();
    my $name  = $node->getNodeName();
    my $value = $node->getNodeValue();

    print "($type) $name: $value\n";

    for (
        my $child = $node->getFirstChild() ;
        defined($child) ;
        $child = $child->getNextSibling()
      )
    {
        step_through($child);
    }
}
```

Even though we're not validating, XML::Xerces insists on having the DTD file present when it parses the file. Feel free to simply create an empty file called **airlocks.dtd**, although this works better with a DTD that defines the entity used in the XML document.

The Results

The partial results in Listing 4.4 show the sequence of events.

LISTING 4.4   *Partial Results*

```
(9) #document: null
(10) airlocksystem: null
(7) xml-stylesheet: href="airlocks.xsl" type="text/xsl"
(1) airlocksystem: null
(3) #text:

(1) airlock: null
(3) #text:

(1) size: null
(3) #text:

(1) type: null
(3) #text: Bronson
(3) #text:

(1) location: null
(3) #text: Level 2 aft
(3) #text:

(1) status: null
(3) #text: open
(3) #text:

(1) maintenance: null
...
```

The first pass outputs the document itself, which has no name or value. The second outputs the three children of the document: the `DOCTYPE` definition, the style sheet directive or processing instruction, and the root element.

The first two children, the `DOCTYPE` and processing instruction, have no children, but the `airlocksystem` element does. These children are processed one by one—first the text node, then the `airlock` element. The `airlock` element has children of its own, so they're processed before any siblings of `airlock`.

This process continues. For example, the `type` element's text child is processed before the `type` element's sibling, `location`. In this way, we can traverse the entire tree structure.

Later, we'll see how the Traversal module automates a lot of this process using a `TreeWalker`.

Outputting the Tree

Now that we have a convenient way to access all the tree's nodes, let's look at using it to output the contents of a tree. Along the way, we'll take a look at the special methods for less common node types, such as `DOCTYPE`s and processing instructions.

Let's start by simply creating the element and text nodes, and outputting the basic information on almost everything else, as in Listing 4.5.

LISTING 4.5   The Basic Document

```
...
public class DocumentListing {

   public static void print (String arg) {
      System.out.print(arg);
   }

...
   public static void stepThrough (Node thisNode) {

      if (thisNode.getNodeType() == thisNode.ELEMENT_NODE) {

         print("<" + thisNode.getNodeName() + ">");

         for (Node child = thisNode.getFirstChild();
              child != null;
              child = child.getNextSibling()) {

            stepThrough(child);

         }

         print("</" + thisNode.getNodeName() + ">");

      } else if (thisNode.getNodeType() == thisNode.TEXT_NODE) {

         print(thisNode.getNodeValue());

      } else {

         int type = thisNode.getNodeType();
         String name = thisNode.getNodeName();
         String value = thisNode.getNodeValue();

         println("(" + type + ") " + name + ": " + value);

         for (Node child = thisNode.getFirstChild();
              child != null;
              child = child.getNextSibling()) {

            stepThrough(child);

         }

      }

   }

}
```

Here we're simply looking at the node type for each node, and handling it appropriately. Text nodes are simply output; they don't require special formatting, and they have no children. Element nodes, on the other hand, need start and end tags.

The results are shown in Listing 4.6.

LISTING 4.6   The Results

```
(9) #document: null
(10) airlocksystem: null
(7) xml-stylesheet: href="airlocks.xsl" type="text/xsl"
<airlocksystem>
   <airlock>
      <size></size>
      <type>Bronson</type>
      <location>Level 2 aft</location>
      <status>open</status>
      <maintenance>
          <lastdone>2/23/2325</lastdone>
          <frequency>Once per month</frequency>
      </maintenance>
      <signage>
          <checkscript><DANGER> Open Airlock
                         (4) #cdata-section:
              function checkSign() {
                var now = new Date();
                var targetDate = new Date("3/23/2325");
                if (targetDate.valueOf() < now.valueOf()) {
                    alertString = "DANGER! Airlock maintenance"
                    alertString = alertString + "is overdue!";
                    alert(alertString);
                }
              }


          </checkscript>
          <signtext>(4) #cdata-section: <DANGER> Open Airlock
</signtext>
      </signage>
   </airlock>
   <personnel>
      <name>Angus Doyle</name>
      <department>Maintenance</department>
   </personnel>
</airlocksystem>
```

Strictly speaking, the result isn't a well-formed XML document for two reasons. First, the first three lines are text nodes outside the root node, and second, the CDATA section includes the less-than character (<), but here it's not enclosed in the <![CDATA[ ]]> section. Instead, it appears as text, and that's a violation of XML's well-formedness constraints. It does, however, give us an idea of what the finished product will look like.

There are two important items to note:

- The element's children must be sent off to `stepThrough()` in order to be processed.

- Because attributes are not children of the element, they won't be output by this method—yet.

Before we get to the attributes, let's take care of the unspecified child nodes, shown in bold in Listing 4.7.

LISTING 4.7   The Remaining Child Nodes

```
...
import org.w3c.dom.DocumentType;
import org.w3c.dom.ProcessingInstruction;

public class DocumentListing {

...
    public static void stepThrough (Node thisNode) {

        if (thisNode.getNodeType() == thisNode.ELEMENT_NODE) {
...
        } else if (thisNode.getNodeType() == thisNode.TEXT_NODE) {

            print(thisNode.getNodeValue());

        } else if (thisNode.getNodeType() == thisNode.DOCUMENT_NODE) {

            println("<?xml version=\"1.0\"?>");
            for (Node child = thisNode.getFirstChild();
                 child != null;
                 child = child.getNextSibling()) {
               stepThrough(child);
            }

        } else if (thisNode.getNodeType() == thisNode.CDATA_SECTION_NODE) {

            CDATASection thisCdataNode = (CDATASection)thisNode;
            print("<![CDATA[" + thisCdataNode.getNodeValue() + "]]>");

        } else if (thisNode.getNodeType() == thisNode.DOCUMENT_TYPE_NODE) {

            DocumentType thisDocNode = (DocumentType)thisNode;
            print("<!DOCTYPE " + thisDocNode.getName() );

            if (thisDocNode.getSystemId() != null) {
                print(" SYSTEM " + thisDocNode.getSystemId());
            } else if (thisDocNode.getPublicId() != null) {
                print(" PUBLIC " + thisDocNode.getPublicId());
            }

            if (thisDocNode.getInternalSubset() != null) {
```

LISTING 4.7   *Continued*

```
        print(thisDocNode.getInternalSubset());
    }

    println(">");

} else if (thisNode.getNodeType() ==
                              thisNode.PROCESSING_INSTRUCTION_NODE) {

    ProcessingInstruction thisProcNode = (ProcessingInstruction)thisNode;
    println("<?" + thisProcNode.getTarget() + " "
                              + thisProcNode.getData() + "?>");

} else {
...
    }

  }

}
```

The `Document` node is easy; we're simply outputting the XML declaration, then processing the child nodes. The `CDATASection` is even easier; we simply output the value within the `CDATA` delimiters.

When we come down to the `DocumentType` node, however, things get a little more complicated. This is the node in the document that reads

```
<!DOCTYPE airlocksystem SYSTEM "airlocks.dtd">
```

In order to get to methods such as `getSystemId()`, we need to cast the node to a `DocumentType` object. From there, we can get the name, which represents the root node name, and the system ID (or formal public identifier, as the case may be). If the document carries an internal DTD subset (as we'll discuss in Chapter 7, "Document Type Definitions (DTDs)"), the `getInternalSubset()` method returns it as a string we can output directly.

`ProcessingInstruction`s are fairly straightforward, though they, too, must be cast to their specific object in order to access the proper methods. The target of the processing instruction represents the application for which the instruction is meant, and the data carries a string representing all name-value pairs present in the processing instruction.

That leaves us with just the attributes. Because the `Node` interface specifies a `getAttributes()` method, we don't actually have to cast the `Node` to an `Element` to get a `NamedNodeMap` of attributes, as shown in Listing 4.8.

LISTING 4.8   *Retrieving the Attributes*

```
...
    public static void stepThrough (Node thisNode) {

    if (thisNode.getNodeType() == thisNode.ELEMENT_NODE) {
```

LISTING 4.8   Continued

```
                print("<" + thisNode.getNodeName());

                NamedNodeMap attributes = thisNode.getAttributes();
                for (int i=0; i < attributes.getLength(); i++) {
                   print(" " + attributes.item(i).getNodeName() + "=\""
                              + attributes.item(i).getNodeValue() + "\"");
                }

                print(">");
...
```

The complete results are shown in Listing 4.9.

LISTING 4.9   The Results

```
<?xml version="1.0"?>
<!DOCTYPE airlocksystem SYSTEM airlocks.dtd>
<?xml-stylesheet href="airlocks.xsl" type="text/xsl"?>
<airlocksystem>
    <airlock lockid="A23b">
        <size height="320" width="500"></size>
        <type>Bronson</type>
        <location>Level 2 aft</location>
        <status>open</status>
        <maintenance responsible="M83">
            <lastdone>2/23/2325</lastdone>
            <frequency>Once per month</frequency>
        </maintenance>
        <signage>
            <checkscript type="text/javascript">
                <![CDATA[
                function checkSign() {
                  var now = new Date();
                  var targetDate = new Date("3/23/2325");
                  if (targetDate.valueOf() < now.valueOf()) {
                      alertString = "DANGER! Airlock maintenance"
                      alertString = alertString + "is overdue!";
                      alert(alertString);
                  }
                }
                ]]>
            </checkscript>
            <signtext><![CDATA[<DANGER> Open Airlock]]></signtext>
        </signage>
    </airlock>
    <personnel badge="D59">
        <name>Angus Doyle</name>
        <department>Maintenance</department>
    </personnel>
</airlocksystem>
```

Normalization and Canonicalization

You may have noticed that while the information contained in the outputted document is the same, the form is slightly different. The text nodes were carried through, but what about empty elements? For example, the element

```
<size width="500" height="320" />
```

becomes

```
<size height="320" width="500"></size>
```

These elements are functionally equivalent, but the different representations make it difficult to compare the two. Similarly, it's difficult to tell by looking at it how many text node children of the `frequency` element are represented by the following:

```
<frequency>Once per month</frequency>
```

This could easily be two, three, or even more nodes, but because they're rendered together, it's impossible to tell.

Why does it matter?

It matters because in certain situations, such as a DOM application or an XPath or XPointer expression, the application may be looking for a specific numbered node. In this case, we might look for

```
FrequencyElement.getFirstChild()
```

If the first child doesn't contain all the text, we're going to have a problem. Normalization involves cleaning up extra and empty text nodes. Any empty text nodes are removed, and any adjacent text nodes are merged into one.

It's important to keep in mind that **CDATA** sections are treated differently from text nodes in this respect. Adjacent **CDATA** sections are *not* merged.

This doesn't entirely solve the problem of documents that are functionally equivalent, but textually different. Here we run into the issue of canonical XML.

Canonical XML is a series of rules for making decisions about handling XML when multiple options are available. For example, order matters for elements, but attributes may appear on the start tag for an element in any order. For a document to be represented as canonical XML, it must conform to a set of rules that includes the following:

1. XML declarations and DTDs must be removed.

2. Attributes must be listed in alphabetical order.

3. Namespace declarations must appear only on the outermost element of the set for which they are applicable.

4. In text nodes, <, &, >, and #xD characters must be replaced with <, &, >, and , respectively.

5. In attribute nodes, <, &, ", **#x9**, **#xA**, and **#xD** characters must be replaced with <, &, ", 	,
, and , respectively.

6. Extra spaces within the start tag of an element must be removed.

DOM Level 2.0 Traversal

The Document Object Model Level 2.0 Traversal module provides two new ways to navigate through a document. The first, `NodeIterator`, is similar to `NodeList`. It provides a "flattened" view of a node, allowing you to simply visit each node in document order without regard to hierarchical concepts such as parents and children. The second, `TreeWalker`, is similar to the method of navigating we saw in the first half of the chapter. The `TreeWalker` visits each node in descendant order, allowing navigation based on hierarchy.

Both provide advantages over the manual methods we've been using, because they work with `NodeFilter`s that provide a simple way to affect which nodes are presented.

NodeIterators

A `NodeIterator` takes a flattened view of the document or node being viewed—it simply visits each node in turn without any regard for relationships to other nodes. In fact, the `NodeIterator` is not even aware of the parent-child relationships between nodes.

Java

Let's look at the sample `NodeIterator` shown in Listing 4.10a.

LISTING 4.10a   Using a `NodeIterator` in Java

```java
import javax.xml.parsers.DocumentBuilder;
import javax.xml.parsers.DocumentBuilderFactory;
import java.io.File;
import org.w3c.dom.Document;
import org.w3c.dom.Node;
import org.w3c.dom.traversal.DocumentTraversal;
import org.w3c.dom.traversal.NodeIterator;
import org.w3c.dom.traversal.NodeFilter;

public class ShowDocument {

    public static void main (String args[]) {
        File docFile = new File("airlocks.xml");

        Document doc = null;
        try {
            DocumentBuilderFactory dbf = DocumentBuilderFactory.newInstance();
            DocumentBuilder db = dbf.newDocumentBuilder();

            doc = db.parse(docFile);
```

LISTING 4.10a *Continued*

```
        } catch (Exception e) {
            System.out.print("Problem parsing the file.");
        }
        Node root = doc.getDocumentElement();

        DocumentTraversal traversal = (DocumentTraversal)doc;
        int whattoshow = NodeFilter.SHOW_ALL;
        NodeFilter nodefilter = null;
        boolean expandreferences = false;

        NodeIterator iterator = traversal.createNodeIterator(root,
                                                whattoshow,
                                                nodefilter,
                                                expandreferences);

        Node thisNode = null;
        thisNode = iterator.nextNode();
        while (thisNode != null) {
            System.out.println(thisNode.getNodeName()+": "+thisNode.getNodeValue());
            thisNode = iterator.nextNode();
        }
    }
}
```

Before we look at the specifics of creating the `NodeIterator`, let's look at what it actually does. We create it with a root node, which can be any node within the document (or the document itself). It's this node that the `NodeIterator` traverses.

For example, if the root node is

```
<appliances>
    <clock status="working">cuckoo</clock>
    <television status="broken">black and white</television>
</appliances>
```

the current settings (which we'll discuss in a moment) yield a `NodeIterator` that starts out with no context node at all. Instead, the reference position is immediately before the first node. The first call to `nextNode()` moves it forward to the first node, the `appliance` element.

The loop then assigns each node as the context node in document order, so the result is

```
appliances: null
#text:

clock: null
#text: cuckoo
#text:

television: null
#text: black and white
#text:
```

The `nextNode()` method returns `null` when it runs out of nodes to return. Similarly, the `previousNode()` method moves the `NodeIterator` backwards in the list. These two methods, however, are the only ways to move the pointer. A `TreeWalker` provides much more flexibility, but before we move on, let's look at the status of `NodeIterators` in other languages, and the values that control their creation.

C++/VB

At the time of this writing, MSXML has some support for DOM Level 2.0, but doesn't include support for the Traversal module, so `NodeIterators` and `TreeWalkers` are not available in C++ or Visual Basic. To find out the current state of Microsoft XML Core Services, search the MSDN site (`http://msdn.Microsoft.com`) for the term *MSXML*.

PHP

PHP currently doesn't support any DOM 2.0 traversal features.

Perl

The XML::Xerces traversal interface is similar to the Java JAXP interface, except that you can use the document object itself to create the `NodeIterator` (or `TreeWalker`) objects, and you *must* subclass `XML::Xerces::PerlNodeFilter` and pass a valid filter object to `createNodeIterator()`. (We'll talk about `NodeFilters` in the next section.)

LISTING 4.10b   Using a `NodeIterator` in Perl

```perl
use FilterAccept;
use XML::Xerces;
use XML::Xerces::DOMParse;

my $file   = XML::Xerces::LocalFileInputSource->new("airlocks.xml");
my $parser = XML::Xerces::DOMParser->new();
my $error_handler = XML::Xerces::PerlErrorHandler->new();
$parser->setErrorHandler($error_handler);
eval { $parser->parse($file); };
XML::Xerces::error($@) if $@;

my $doc  = $parser->getDocument();
my $root = $doc->getDocumentElement();

my $to_show  = $XML::Xerces::DOM_NodeFilter::SHOW_ALL;
my $filter   = FilterAccept->new();
my $iterator = $doc->createNodeIterator( $root, $to_show, $filter, 0 );
my $node     = $iterator->nextNode();
while ( defined($node) ) {
    print $node->getNodeName() . ": " . $node->getNodeValue . "\n";
    $node = $iterator->nextNode();
}
```

For this example, we've created a `NodeFilter` subclass that accepts all nodes:

```
package FilterAccept;

@ISA = qw(XML::Xerces::PerlNodeFilter);

sub acceptNode {
    return $XML::Xerces::DOM_NodeFilter::FILTER_ACCEPT;
}

1;
```

(See Listing 4.14 for an example of a `NodeFilter` that actually filters.)

Remember, this goes in a file called `FilterAccept.pm`, located either in the same directory as the main file or in a Perl library directory so the application can find it.

Configuring a `NodeIterator`

The `whattoshow` value can be set to a number of static values within the `NodeFilter` interface. These values, such as **SHOW_ALL** or **SHOW_TEXT**, provide a way to quickly limit the nodes visible to the `NodeIterator` by type.

To be more specific, you can create a `NodeFilter`. This is a special class that evaluates each node before determining whether it belongs in the resultset. We'll look at `NodeFilter`s after looking at `TreeWalker`s, but for now we'll set the `NodeFilter` to `null` in the Java example, and a generic filter in the Perl example.

Finally, the `expandreferences` argument affects how entities are treated. If this value is set to `true`, all the children of an entity reference will be included. For example, if our test file includes an entity that references a whole tree of elements, the `NodeIterator` will see each element. On the other hand, if it's set to `false`, only the entity reference node itself will be seen. The child nodes will be invisible to the `NodeIterator`.

TreeWalkers

While `NodeIterator`s can be useful, the "flat" nature of their view can be considered a problem, as it limits what can be done with the `NodeIterator`. The `TreeWalker` has a much more flexible set of methods, such as `getParent()`, `getLastChild()`, and `getNextSibling()`.

Sound familiar? The `TreeWalker` walks the tree in much the same way as we did in the first half of the chapter; it processes the child nodes of each node in the tree before moving on to any sibling nodes, but it does so much more simply.

Listing 4.11 shows a `TreeWalker` performing the same work as the `NodeIterator`.

LISTING 4.11   Using a TreeWalker

```
...
import org.w3c.dom.traversal.TreeWalker;
import org.w3c.dom.traversal.NodeFilter;
```

LISTING 4.11   Continued

```
public class ShowDocument {

...

        DocumentTraversal traversal = (DocumentTraversal)doc;
        int whattoshow = NodeFilter.SHOW_ALL;
        NodeFilter nodefilter = null;
        boolean expandreferences = false;

        TreeWalker walker = traversal.createTreeWalker(root,
                                            whattoshow,
                                            nodefilter,
                                            expandreferences);

        Node thisNode = null;
        thisNode = walker.nextNode();
        while (thisNode != null) {
            System.out.println(thisNode.getNodeName()+": "+thisNode.getNodeValue());
            thisNode = walker.nextNode();
        }
    }
}
```

Functionally, all we've really changed here is the fact that we're creating a `TreeWalker` instead of a `NodeIterator`. Everything else is the same. The advantage is that we get to navigate through the document "deeply," by processing a node's children before its siblings, but we don't have to create a new method and call it recursively, as we did when we were using `getNextSibling()` manually.

The results are slightly different from those for the `NodeIterator`, however. Unlike a `NodeIterator`, the `TreeWalker` doesn't actually return the root element to start with, so the output of this application is

```
#text:

clock: null
#text: cuckoo
#text:

television: null
#text: black and white
#text:
```

The interface defines the following methods for a `TreeWalker`:

```
parentNode();
firstChild();
lastChild();
previousSibling();
nextSibling();
previousNode();
nextNode();
```

The way in which they're implemented depends on the language; in Java, the `firstChild()` method is represented as `getFirstChild()`.

NodeFilters

In addition to the "what to show" value, which can limit the nodes visible to a `NodeIterator` or `TreeWalker` based on nodes' types, you can create a custom `NodeFilter`. The `NodeFilter` allows you to pick and choose from the available nodes, returning only those you really want.

For example, Listing 4.12 shows a `NodeFilter` that prevents the `TreeWalker` from outputting any appliance that's broken.

LISTING 4.12   The `NodeFilter`

```
import org.w3c.dom.traversal.NodeFilter;
import org.w3c.dom.Node;
import org.w3c.dom.Element;

public class ShowFilter implements NodeFilter {

    public short acceptNode(Node thisNode) {
        if (thisNode.getNodeType()==Node.ELEMENT_NODE) {
            Element thisElementNode = (Element)thisNode;
            if (thisElementNode.getAttribute("status").equals("broken")) {
                return NodeFilter.FILTER_SKIP;
            }
        }
        return NodeFilter.FILTER_ACCEPT;
    }
}
```

The `NodeFilter` interface specifies a single method: `acceptNode()`. This method decides what should be done with each node. The options are `FILTER_ACCEPT`, `FILTER_SKIP`, and `FILTER_REJECT`.

Let's look at these choices by adding the `NodeFilter` to the application, as shown in Listing 4.13.

LISTING 4.13   Adding the `NodeFilter`

```
    ...
        DocumentTraversal traversal = (DocumentTraversal)doc;
        int whattoshow = NodeFilter.SHOW_ALL;
        NodeFilter nodefilter = new ShowFilter();
        boolean expandreferences = false;

        TreeWalker walker = traversal.createTreeWalker(root,
                                                whattoshow,
                                                nodefilter,
                                                expandreferences);

    ...
```

LISTING 4.13   Continued

Now if we run the application, the results look like this:

```
#text:

clock: null
#text: cuckoo
#text:

#text: black and white
#text:
```

Notice that the television element node is gone, as expected, but that its child, the `black and white` text node, is still present. This is because we chose `FILTER_SKIP` instead of `FILTER_REJECT`. The former skips the node itself, while the latter skips the node and all of its children.

Java

We can change the `NodeFilter` to use `FILTER_REJECT`, as in Listing 4.14a.

LISTING 4.14a   Using `FILTER_REJECT` in Java

```
    ...
            if (thisNode.getNodeType()==Node.ELEMENT_NODE) {
                Element thisElementNode = (Element)thisNode;
                if (thisElementNode.getAttribute("status").equals("broken")) {
                    return NodeFilter.FILTER_REJECT;
                }
            }
    ...
```

Now when we run the original application, we get this result:

```
#text:

clock: null
#text: cuckoo
#text:

#text:
```

Notice two things here:

- We can change the nodes returned by the `TreeWalker` without touching the application that actually uses the `TreeWalker`—a major benefit of using `NodeFilter`s.

- The entire `television` element, with its children, is now gone.

Or is it?

Here we can see a major difference between the way `TreeWalker`s and `NodeIterator`s work. If we change the application back to a `NodeIterator`, the result is

```
#text:

clock: null
#text: cuckoo
#text:

#text: black and white
#text:
```

Notice that the `black and white` text node is back, even though the `NodeFilter` uses `FIL-TER_REJECT`. Why? Remember when we said that the `NodeIterator` isn't aware of the parent-child relationship between nodes? This is one time when this matters. Because it has no concept of the relationship between `television` and `black and white`, it doesn't know to leave out `black and white` when it leaves out `television`. A `NodeIterator` treats `FILTER_REJECT` the same way it treats `FILTER_SKIP`, and simply leaves out the current node.

Perl

We can also change the `NodeFilter` to use `FILTER_REJECT` in Perl, as shown in Listing 4.14b.

LISTING 4.14b   Using `FILTER_REJECT` in Perl

```perl
use FilterShowWorking;

...

my $to_show = $XML::Xerces::DOM_NodeFilter::SHOW_ALL;

my $filter = FilterShowWorking->new();
my $walker = $doc->createTreeWalker( $root, $to_show, $filter, 0 );
my $node = $walker->nextNode();
while ( defined($node) ) {
    print $node->getNodeName() . ": " . $node->getNodeValue . "\n";
    $node = $walker->nextNode();
}

package FilterShowWorking;

@ISA = qw(XML::Xerces::PerlNodeFilter);

sub acceptNode {
    my $self = shift;
    my $node = shift;

    if (   $node->getNodeType() == $XML::Xerces::DOM_Node::ELEMENT_NODE
        && $node->getAttribute("status") eq "broken" )
    {
        return $XML::Xerces::DOM_NodeFilter::FILTER_REJECT;
    }
    return $XML::Xerces::DOM_NodeFilter::FILTER_ACCEPT;
}
```

DOM Level 3.0 Load and Save

Now let's take a quick look at some of the functionality being developed for the Document Object Model Level 3.0. Specifically, we're going to look at the loading and saving features of the DOM Level 3.0 Load and Save module.

You may remember that in Chapter 3 we talked a lot about how the Document Object Model doesn't specify a way to parse a file to create a document or save it, so it is up to the individual implementers. The DOM Level 3.0 Load and Save module attempts to fill in these holes by providing a standard set of interfaces for loading and saving a document.

Complete implementations of DOM Level 3.0 are not available at the time of this writing, but partial support is available in Xerces-Java 2.0.1. Because the recommendations aren't final yet, it's possible that the information in this section will change slightly (or not so slightly). If you run into problems, check the documentation for your parser.

Loading the Document

Loading the document involves a series of steps:

1. Create the `DOMImplementationLS`, which contains the factory methods to create everything else.

2. Create the `DOMBuilder`.

3. Create the `DOMInput` and specify its source.

4. Use the `DOMBuilder` to parse the `DOMInput` and return the DOM `Document`.

Let's look at how this works in Listing 4.15.

LISTING 4.15   Loading a Document

```
import org.w3c.dom.Document;
import org.apache.xerces.dom.DOMImplementationImpl;
import org.apache.xerces.dom3.ls.DOMImplementationLS;
import org.apache.xerces.dom3.ls.DOMBuilder;
import org.apache.xerces.dom3.ls.DOMInputSource;
import org.w3c.dom.Node;

public class LoadSave {

    public static void main (String args[]) {

        Document doc = null;
        try {
            DOMImplementationLS DOMLS = new DOMImplementationImpl();

            short synch = 1;
            DOMBuilder db = DOMLS.createDOMBuilder(synch);
```

LISTING 4.15   Continued

```
                DOMInputSource dinput = DOMLS.createDOMInputSource();
                dinput.setSystemId("airlocks.xml");

                doc = db.parse(dinput);

        } catch (Exception e) {
            System.out.print("Problem parsing the file.");
        }

        Node root = doc.getDocumentElement();
        System.out.println(root.getNodeName());
    }
}
```

First, create the `DOMImplementationLS`. How you do this will depend on the implementation, but the Recommendation suggests casting it from a `DOMImplementation` object. Notice that here it's simply instantiated from an implementation class.

Next, determine whether the `DOMBuilder` will be synchronous (with a value of **1**) or asynchronous (with a value of **2**) and pass this value to the `createDOMBuilder()` method of the `DOMImplementationLS`.

Synchronous or Asynchronous?

Whether a `DOMBuilder` is synchronous or asynchronous determines whether other actions can go on while the document is loading. For example, if the `DOMBuilder` is asynchronous, another part of the application can be working on the document before it's fully loaded. On the other hand, if the `DOMBuilder` is synchronous, the application must wait until the document has been fully loaded before working with it.

Next, create the `DOMInputSource`. A `DOMInputSource` can represent a stream, a file or URI (using a system identifier), a Formal Public Identifier, or even a string of text. Set the source of the data to be parsed.

Finally, parse the `DOMInputSource` to create the `Document`. At this point, you have a normal DOM `Document` node that can be manipulated as though it were created with the implementation-specific methods of DOM Level 2.0.

Saving the Document

Persisting or saving a `Document` or other `Node` involves a process similar to that for loading the `Document`, as shown in Listing 4.16.

LISTING 4.16   Saving the Document

```
import org.w3c.dom.Document;
import org.apache.xerces.dom.DOMImplementationImpl;
import org.apache.xerces.dom3.ls.DOMImplementationLS;
```

LISTING 4.16 *Continued*

```
import org.apache.xerces.dom3.ls.DOMBuilder;
import org.apache.xerces.dom3.ls.DOMInputSource;
import org.apache.xerces.dom3.ls.DOMWriter;
import org.apache.xerces.dom3.ls.DOMOutputStream;
import org.w3c.dom.Node;

public class LoadSave {

   public static void main (String args[]) {
      File docFile = new File("activities.xml");

      Document doc = null;
      try {
...
         doc = db.parse(dinput);

         Node root = doc.getDocumentElement();
         System.out.println(root.getNodeName());

         DOMWriter dw = DOMLS.createDOMWriter();

         DOMOutputStream doutput = DOMLS.createDOMOutputStream();
         doutput.setSystemId("output.xml");

         dw.writeNode(doutput, doc.getDocumentElement());

      } catch (Exception e) {
        System.out.print("Problem parsing the file.");
      }
    }
}
```

In this case, rather than creating a DOMBuilder and DOMInputSource, create a DOMWriter and DOMOutputStream. Set the destination of the DOMOutputStream, and write out the node.

Summary

The Document Object Model provides ways to navigate a document using parent-child relationships, through the Core module and, more specifically, through the Traversal module.

NodeIterators process the nodes in a document in document order and have a flat view of the document. They can move only forward and backward within the nodes. TreeWalkers process the document in descendant order, and can move to parents, children, and siblings. You can control the output of either using NodeFilters.

The DOM Level 3.0 provides a standardized means for loading and saving DOM documents, using DOMBuilders and DOMWriters.

Review Questions

1. How does a `NodeIterator` traverse a document?

2. How does a `TreeWalker` traverse a document?

3. What does a `NodeFilter` do?

4. What's the difference between the way a `NodeFilter` acts on a `NodeIterator` and the way it acts on a `TreeWalker`?

5. What does normalization do?

6. What's the purpose of canonicalization?

7. What's the purpose of the Load and Save portion of the DOM Level 3.0?

Programming Exercises

These exercises use the following source file:

```
<pets>
    <dog display="hidden"><name>Razzle</name><type>Yorkshire Terrier</type></dog>
    <dog display="hidden"><name>Sabre</name><type>German Shepherd Dog</type></dog>
    <cat display="hidden"><name>Tiger</name><type>Domestic Shorthair</type></cat>
    <bird display="hidden"><name>Frazzle</name><type>Quaker Parrot</type></bird>
    <fish><name display="hidden">Clark</name><type>goldfish</type></fish>
    <fish><name display="hidden">Lois</name><type>goldfish</type></fish>
</pets>
```

1. Write an application that uses a `NodeIterator` to display the text of a document.

2. Write a `NodeFilter` or `TreeWalker` that displays the text nodes of a document, but doesn't display "hidden" elements or their children.

3. Write an application that uses the DOM Level 3.0 to load a remotely located document.

CHAPTER 5

XML STREAMS:
THE SIMPLE API FOR XML (SAX)

You will learn about the following in this chapter:

- Event-based APIs versus object-based APIs

- Parsing a document using SAX

- Creating content and error handlers

- Handling data from a SAX parser

- Using filters to chain handlers together

S o far, we've looked at XML as a collection of objects with relationships to each other, which makes sense from the hierarchical view of XML that is normally emphasized. In this chapter, however, we're going to take a look at XML from a completely different perspective. Rather than viewing XML as a structure of objects, as the Document Object Model (DOM) does, the Simple API for XML (SAX) looks at it as a series of characters, some of which represent elements or other constructs.

What Is SAX?

The Simple API for XML (SAX) is an XML processing method that was created by the members of the XML-DEV mailing list to solve problems that DOM just didn't solve. Rather than looking at an XML file as one giant lump of data that must be digested all at once, SAX looks at it as a stream of events, each of which carries information.

Once this stream starts flowing, an application can examine it as it goes by and react accordingly, eliminating the need to store a huge amount of data that may never be needed.

Event-Based Versus Object-Based APIs

The major difference between object-based systems such as DOM and event-based systems such as SAX is in their perspectives on the world at large. Take for example a simple task such as picking up a friend at the airport. Using the object-based approach, you would need to know what airline your friend was using, what flight, the terminal at which that flight was coming in, and the gate within the terminal. Once you had that information, however, you could go directly to the gate and meet your friend.

On the other hand, that's a lot of information that isn't necessarily relevant to actually giving your friend a ride home. Using the event-based approach, you could just sit at the entrance to the baggage claim area and watch each person go by, then grab your friend as he went to pick up his luggage.

In both cases, you met up with your friend. Using the object-based approach, you went directly to him; using the event-based approach, you didn't have to keep a lot of extraneous information in your head.

Let's look at how this applies to XML.

A Simple Stream

In our example, we had only a single type of event: a person passing through the doors into the baggage claim area. When dealing with XML, we have several different types of events, such as the start of an element or a set of characters that are not part of markup.

Let's look at a snippet of XML:

```
<votes totalVotes="5">
    <voter personid="1" status="primary">
        <vote>Sparkle</vote>
        <comments>It's about time we had this vote!</comments>
    </voter>
</votes>
```

A DOM parser looks at this snippet as an element with three children (two text and one element) and five grandchildren (three text and two element). Within that structure, there are three elements and seven text nodes.

A SAX parser looks at this snippet as a series of events:

```
Start element (votes)
Ignorable whitespace
Start element (voter)
Ignorable whitespace
Start element (vote)
Characters (Sparkle)
End element (vote)
Ignorable whitespace
Start element (comments)
Characters (It's about time we had this vote!)
End element (comments)
Ignorable whitespace
End element (voter)
Ignorable whitespace
End element (votes)
```

This may seem like a lot of work for such a small document, but it helps to remember that you're only using the information that you actually need.

Pros and Cons

So which is better, DOM or SAX?

The answer depends on what you're doing with the information. In some cases, it will make more sense to use SAX, and in others, DOM will be a much more reasonable choice.

For example, SAX is a "read-only" method of accessing the information. You can change the information, but the changes aren't applied to the original document. Likewise, SAX is a "one-way" method. Once you pass by an element, you won't see it again without parsing the document a second time.

On the other hand, SAX has its advantages, particularly when dealing with large files. Because you're simply looking at the information as it goes by, there's no need to take up large portions of memory with information that may or may not ever be used.

SAX also has the advantage of allowing you to stop parsing before visiting the entire document once you have the information you need.

Creating the Parser

Now that you've got an idea of how SAX works, let's start building an application to use it.

In this case, we'll build an application to tally the votes in the election for the Vanguard Space Resort's Grand Major High Command Voilex, between Feldmar Sparkle and Dregraal the Enchreenomalpolymorph.

The application checks to make sure that all votes are valid based on the regulations—symbionts can only vote through their host to prevent double-voting—and stops counting when either Sparkle or Dregraal has a lead larger than the number of remaining votes.

Let's start by looking at all the pieces and how they fit together.

The Lay of the Land

A SAX parser is a puzzle that involves several pieces.

The main application creates the parser, or `XMLReader`. The `XMLReader` takes the input and sends specific events to another application designed to handle them. This application is known as a *handler*. SAX defines several types of handlers, including `ContentHandler`s and `ErrorHandler`s, but how you create them depends on your implementation.

SAX was created for Java, and in fact is included in the Java 2 SDK version 1.4. It has been incorporated into other languages and environments, but because it is only a de facto standard—no one is officially responsible for it—there are differences between implementations in different languages. In this chapter, we'll look at several different variations.

Creating the XMLReader

The first thing that we need to do is create the parser, or `XMLReader`.

Java

To build in flexibility, SAX uses a factory to create the `XMLReader`. This means that you can specify the driver, or parser class, when you actually run the application, allowing you to change classes if necessary.

Let's take a look at a simple example in Listings 5.1a–c.

LISTING 5.1a   Creating the `XMLReader` Using Java

```java
import org.xml.sax.helpers.XMLReaderFactory;
import org.xml.sax.XMLReader;
import org.xml.sax.SAXException;

public class MainSaxApp {

    public static void main (String[] args){

        try {

            String parserClass = "org.apache.crimson.parser.XMLReaderImpl";
            XMLReader reader = XMLReaderFactory.createXMLReader(parserClass);

        } catch (SAXException se) {
            System.out.println("SAX Exception: "+se.getMessage());
        }

    }

}
```

Here we use the static `createXMLReader()` method to create the `XMLReader` using the `org.apache.crimson.parser.XMLReaderImpl` driver.

Which driver you choose will depend in large part on what's available in the environment in which you work. The Crimson driver used in Listing 5.1a comes with the Java 2 SDK version 1.4.0. Other common drivers are listed here:

- `org.apache.crimson.parser.XMLReaderImpl`

- `org.apache.xerces.parsers.SAXParser` (likely to be included in future versions of Java)

- `gnu.xml.aelfred2.XmlReader`

- `oracle.xml.parser.v2.SAXParser`

In Java, you can set the driver in several different ways:

- **Specify the classname within the application, as shown in Listing 5.1a.** This works best in situations where you don't want users to have to enter the driver name, and you're absolutely certain the class will be available.

- **Compile in a default class.** In some environments, a default class has been provided within the factory, so if you don't specify one, that's what it will use.

- **Specify a system property at runtime.** Java allows you to specify the value of a system property at runtime using the `-D` switch. For example:

```
java -Dorg.xml.sax.driver=org.apache.crimson.parser.XMLReaderImpl MainSaxApp
```

    This command tells the Java runtime environment to set the system property `org.xml.sax.driver` to `org.apache.crimson.parser.XMLReaderImpl`.

In the last two cases, you can simply create the `XMLReader` without an argument, like this:

```
XMLReader reader = XMLReaderFactory.createXMLReader();
```

C++

Creating the `XMLReader` in C++ is similar to creating it in Java. Support for the `XMLReader` class is found in the Microsoft COM implementation of SAX2 located in `MSXML3.DLL` or higher. Open a Win32 project and select the Console check box under the Application Settings tab and then click the Finish button. Enter the code in Listing 5.1b into the project's `.cpp` file that was created by the wizard.

LISTING 5.1b   Creating the `XMLReader` Using C++

```cpp
#include "stdafx.h"

int _tmain(int argc, _TCHAR* argv[])
{
    ::CoInitialize(NULL);
    try
    {
        ISAXXMLReader* pReader = NULL;
        HRESULT hr = CoCreateInstance( __uuidof(SAXXMLReader), NULL, CLSCTX_ALL,
                                       uuidof(ISAXXMLReader),
                                       (void **)&pReader);
    }
    catch(...)
    {
        wprintf(L"Caught the exception");
    }
    ::CoUninitialize();
    return 0;
}
```

Add the following code to the `stdafx.h` file:

```cpp
#import <msxml3.dll> raw_interfaces_only
using namespace MSXML2;
```

You can create an **XMLReader** by creating a pointer of the type **ISAXXMLReader** and then calling **CoCreateInstance** to instantiate the **SAXXMLReader** class.

Visual Basic .NET

To create a SAX application using Visual Basic .NET, create a new Windows Application project. Select the form in the Design view and in the Properties window change the **Name** property to **SAXMainForm**. Right-click **Form1.vb** in the Solution Explorer, select Rename, and change its **Name** property to **SAXMainForm.vb**.

In the Design view, add controls to the form so that it looks like Figure 5.1. You'll need two Label, two Button, and two TextBox controls.

FIGURE 5.1
SAX API sample main form.

Now change the properties for the controls as shown in the following table:

Control	Property	Change To...
Label1	Name	lblOutput
	Text	Output Window:
Label2	Name	lblFileName
	Text	File Name:
Button1	Name	btnParse
	Text	Parse XML
Button2	Name	btnClose
	Text	Close

Control	Property	Change To...
TextBox1	Name	txtOutput
	AcceptsReturn	True
	Multiline	True
	ScrollBars	Vertical
	Text	(none—clear the Text property)
TextBox2	Name	txtFileName
	Text	(none—clear the Text property)

Add a reference for the project to MSXML2. Do this by selecting Project, Add Reference. Click on the COM tab, double-click on Microsoft XML, v4.0, and then click OK.

Go to the Design view for the form and double-click the Parse XML button. Enter the following code in the **btnParse_Click** subroutine:

```
Private Sub btnParse_Click(ByVal sender As System.Object, _
                      ByVal e As System.EventArgs) Handles btnParse.Click
    Dim Reader As New MSXML2.SAXXMLReader()
    txtOutput.Text = ""
End Sub
```

Double-click on the Close button and type End in the **btnClose_Click** subroutine as shown here:

```
Private Sub btnClose_Click(ByVal sender As System.Object, _
                      ByVal e As System.EventArgs) Handles btnClose.Click
    End
End Sub
```

PHP

PHP lacks a full-fledged object-oriented SAX interface, but luckily, constructing one based on PHP's built-in Expat-based XML parsing abilities is not difficult. Listing 5.1c shows the parser object, defined in a file called **sax.inc**.

LISTING 5.1c   Creating a SAX Application Using PHP

```php
<?php

 class SAXParser {

    var $parser;

    function SAXParser ($args=array( 'encoding'  => false,
                                     'handler'   => null,
                                     'case_fold' => 0 ))
```

LISTING 5.1c Continued

```
    {
        $this->parser = xml_parser_create($args['encoding']);
        xml_set_object($this->parser,$this);

    }

}
?>
```

Instantiating the class involves including the file that defines it, then creating a new instance, like so:

```
<?php

 require_once("sax.inc");

 $parser =& new SAXParser();

?>
```

Perl

You can find a very good, complete, and stable SAX interface for Perl on the Comprehensive Perl Archive Network (CPAN); install the `XML::SAX` module, then the `XML::SAX::Expat` module to use Expat as your base parser. If you don't have a C compiler or can't install Expat for some other reason, you can use the pure-Perl parser that comes with the `XML::SAX` distribution; but be warned, it's very, very slow.

```
use XML::SAX;

$XML::SAX::ParserPackage = 'XML::SAX::Expat';

my $factory = XML::SAX::ParserFactory->new();
my $parser  = $factory->parser();
```

If you don't know what parsers might be available for use on your system, you can find out by querying `XML::SAX` using the following snippet:

```
use XML::SAX;

my $parsers = XML::SAX->parsers();
foreach my $p (@$parsers) {
    print "Name: $p->{Name}\n";
    print "Features:\n";
    foreach my $f ( keys %{ $p->{Features} } ) {
        print "  $f: ";
        if ( $p->{Features}->{$f} ) {
            print "YES\n";
        } else {
            print "NO\n";
```

```
        }
    }
    print "\n";
}
```

The `ContentHandler`

We've created a parser that will send notification of specific events, so the next step is creating a class that will react to those events. These classes are called *handlers*.

The SAX API defines several different types of handlers, such as `ContentHandlers` and `ErrorHandlers`. Each of these interfaces has its own set of event methods. For example, the `ErrorHandler` interface specifies three potential events (`warning`, `error`, and `fatalError`), whereas the `ContentHandler` interface specifies almost a dozen (including `startElement` and `endDocument`).

We could write a class that implements the `ContentHandler` interface, but then we'd have to write an implementation method for every single one of the events. Fortunately, SAX provides a helper class, `DefaultHandler`, that we can use instead, as shown in Listing 5.2.

LISTING 5.2   Creating the Content Handler

```
import org.xml.sax.helpers.DefaultHandler;

public class DataProcessor extends DefaultHandler
{

    public DataProcessor ()
    {
        super();
    }

}
```

`DefaultHandler` and Consolidation

One nice thing about using the `DefaultHandler` class is that we can use a single class as both content and error handler by including implementations for all the appropriate methods. (We won't do that here, but we could.)

What we've created here is a class that accepts all of the events that the `XMLReader` throws at it (based on the methods in `DefaultHandler`) but won't do anything with them. In the next section, we'll start creating new methods that override `DefaultHandler` and react to the events, but first we have to tell the `XMLReader` where to send them, as shown in Listings 5.3a–e.

Java

Setting the handler for the content in Java is simply a matter of calling an `XMLReader` method, as shown in Listing 5.3a.

LISTING 5.3a   Setting the Content Handler in Java

```
...
        XMLReader reader = XMLReaderFactory.createXMLReader(parserClass);

        reader.setContentHandler(new DataProcessor());

    } catch (SAXException se) {
...
```

Here we've done two things. First, we've created a new instance of the **DataProcessor** class, and second, we've told the **XMLReader** that that's where we want it to send its events when it actually does parse the XML input.

C++

C++ also uses handlers, but unlike Java, there is no **DefaultHandler** class, so you must implement the classes yourself based on the virtual classes provided by MSXML. In this section, we will implement the content handler.

Content generated by the **XMLReader** is handled by the content handler, which must be registered with the **XMLReader** using the **putContentHandler** method. First, declare your own derived class of **ISAXContentHandler** and implement the methods. Create a new file called **MySAXContentHandler.h** and add the code shown in Listing 5.3b to the file.

LISTING 5.3b   Setting the Content Handler in C++

```
class MySAXContentHandler : public ISAXContentHandler
{
public:
    MySAXContentHandler();
    virtual ~MySAXContentHandler();

        long __stdcall QueryInterface(const struct _GUID &,void ** );
        unsigned long __stdcall AddRef(void);
        unsigned long __stdcall Release(void);

        virtual HRESULT STDMETHODCALLTYPE putDocumentLocator(
            /* [in] */ ISAXLocator_RPC_FAR *pLocator);

        virtual HRESULT STDMETHODCALLTYPE startDocument( void);

        virtual HRESULT STDMETHODCALLTYPE endDocument( void);

        virtual HRESULT STDMETHODCALLTYPE startPrefixMapping(
            /* [in] */ wchar_t_RPC_FAR *pwchPrefix,
            /* [in] */ int cchPrefix,
            /* [in] */ wchar_t RPC_FAR *pwchUri,
            /* [in] */ int cchUri);

        virtual HRESULT STDMETHODCALLTYPE endPrefixMapping(
            /* [in] */ wchar_t RPC_FAR *pwchPrefix,
            /* [in] */ int cchPrefix);
```

LISTING 5.3b   *Continued*

```
        virtual HRESULT STDMETHODCALLTYPE startElement(
            /* [in] */ wchar_t RPC_FAR *pwchNamespaceUri,
            /* [in] */ int cchNamespaceUri,
            /* [in] */ wchar_t RPC_FAR *pwchLocalName,
            /* [in] */ int cchLocalName,
            /* [in] */ wchar_t RPC_FAR *pwchQualifiedName,
            /* [in] */ int cchQualifiedName,
            /* [in] */ ISAXAttributes RPC_FAR *pAttributes);

        virtual HRESULT STDMETHODCALLTYPE endElement(
            /* [in] */ wchar_t RPC_FAR *pwchNamespaceUri,
            /* [in] */ int cchNamespaceUri,
            /* [in] */ wchar_t RPC_FAR *pwchLocalName,
            /* [in] */ int cchLocalName,
            /* [in] */ wchar_t RPC_FAR *pwchQualifiedName,
            /* [in] */ int cchQualifiedName);

        virtual HRESULT STDMETHODCALLTYPE characters(
            /* [in] */ wchar_t RPC_FAR *pwchChars,
            /* [in] */ int cchChars);

        virtual HRESULT STDMETHODCALLTYPE ignorableWhitespace(
            /* [in] */ wchar_t RPC_FAR *pwchChars,
            /* [in] */ int cchChars);

        virtual HRESULT STDMETHODCALLTYPE processingInstruction(
            /* [in] */ wchar_t RPC_FAR *pwchTarget,
            /* [in] */ int cchTarget,
            /* [in] */ wchar_t RPC_FAR *pwchData,
            /* [in] */ int cchData);

        virtual HRESULT STDMETHODCALLTYPE skippedEntity(
            /* [in] */ wchar_t RPC_FAR *pwchName,
            /* [in] */ int cchName);
};
```

Now create a new file named `MySAXContentHandler.cpp` and add the following code. (We'll talk about what each section means as we begin to use it.)

```
#include "stdafx.h"
#include "MySAXContentHandler.h"

MySAXContentHandler::MySAXContentHandler()
{
}

MySAXContentHandler::~MySAXContentHandler()
{
}

HRESULT STDMETHODCALLTYPE MySAXContentHandler::putDocumentLocator(
            /* [in] */ ISAXLocator RPC_FAR *pLocator)
```

```
{
    return S_OK;
}

HRESULT STDMETHODCALLTYPE MySAXContentHandler::startDocument()
{
    return S_OK;
}

HRESULT STDMETHODCALLTYPE MySAXContentHandler::endDocument(void)
{
    return S_OK;
}

HRESULT STDMETHODCALLTYPE MySAXContentHandler::startPrefixMapping(
            /* [in] */ wchar_t RPC_FAR *pwchPrefix,
            /* [in] */ int cchPrefix,
            /* [in] */ wchar_t RPC_FAR *pwchUri,
            /* [in] */ int cchUri)
{
    return S_OK;
}

HRESULT STDMETHODCALLTYPE MySAXContentHandler::endPrefixMapping(
            /* [in] */ wchar_t RPC_FAR *pwchPrefix,
            /* [in] */ int cchPrefix)
{
    return S_OK;
}

HRESULT STDMETHODCALLTYPE MySAXContentHandler::startElement(
            /* [in] */ wchar_t RPC_FAR *pwchNamespaceUri,
            /* [in] */ int cchNamespaceUri,
            /* [in] */ wchar_t RPC_FAR *pwchLocalName,
            /* [in] */ int cchLocalName,
            /* [in] */ wchar_t RPC_FAR *pwchQualifiedName,
            /* [in] */ int cchQualifiedName,
            /* [in] */ ISAXAttributes RPC_FAR *pAttributes)
{
    return S_OK;
}

HRESULT STDMETHODCALLTYPE MySAXContentHandler::endElement(
            /* [in] */ wchar_t RPC_FAR *pwchNamespaceUri,
            /* [in] */ int cchNamespaceUri,
            /* [in] */ wchar_t RPC_FAR *pwchLocalName,
            /* [in] */ int cchLocalName,
            /* [in] */ wchar_t RPC_FAR *pwchQualifiedName,
            /* [in] */ int cchQualifiedName)
{
    return S_OK;
}
```

```
HRESULT STDMETHODCALLTYPE MySAXContentHandler::characters(
            /* [in] */ wchar_t RPC_FAR *pwchChars,
            /* [in] */ int cchChars)
{
    return S_OK;
}

HRESULT STDMETHODCALLTYPE MySAXContentHandler::ignorableWhitespace(
            /* [in] */ wchar_t RPC_FAR *pwchChars,
            /* [in] */ int cchChars)
{
    return S_OK;
}

HRESULT STDMETHODCALLTYPE MySAXContentHandler::processingInstruction(
            /* [in] */ wchar_t RPC_FAR *pwchTarget,
            /* [in] */ int cchTarget,
            /* [in] */ wchar_t RPC_FAR *pwchData,
            /* [in] */ int cchData)
{
    return S_OK;
}

HRESULT STDMETHODCALLTYPE MySAXContentHandler::skippedEntity(
            /* [in] */ wchar_t RPC_FAR *pwchVal,
            /* [in] */ int cchVal)
{
    return S_OK;
}

long __stdcall MySAXContentHandler::QueryInterface(const struct _GUID &riid,
                                                   void ** ppvObject)
{
    return 0;
}

unsigned long __stdcall MySAXContentHandler::AddRef()
{
    return 0;
}

unsigned long __stdcall MySAXContentHandler::Release()
{
    return 0;
}
```

For the purposes of this sample, not all the class methods have been fully implemented. If you were creating a real application that required this to be a COM DLL, it would be necessary to fully implement the **QueryInterface**, **AddRef**, and **Release** methods and also to customize the other methods to the needs of your application.

To complete the changes, we need to add the following to the main **.cpp** file:

```
#include "stdafx.h"
#include "MySAXContentHandler.h"
...
        HRESULT hr = CoCreateInstance( __uuidof(SAXXMLReader), NULL, CLSCTX_ALL,
                                       uuidof(ISAXXMLReader),
                                       (void **)&pReader);

        if(hr==S_OK)
        {
            //Register the content handler for the XMLReader
              MySAXContentHandler* pContent = new MySAXContentHandler();
              hr = pReader->putContentHandler(pContent);
        }
...
```

Visual Basic .NET

In Visual Basic .NET, you must implement the `ContentHandler` class. Create the `ContentHandler` class by selecting Project, Add Class. Name the class `MyContentHandler`. Enter this code following the class declaration:

```
Public Class MyContentHandler
    Implements MSXML2.IVBSAXContentHandler
```

This addition gives the class the ability to override the event handlers of the `IVBSAXContentHandler` class.

To override the event handlers, first select the Class Name drop-down box and select `IVBSAXContentHander` (MSXML) and then select `startDocument` in the Method Name drop-down box. This action places the skeleton of the event handler method into the class. Do this with all remaining methods so that the content handler looks like Listing 5.3c. (Again, we'll discuss the specifics of each event as we get to it.)

LISTING 5.3c   Creating the Content Handler in Visual Basic .NET

```
Public Sub startDocument() Implements MSXML2.IVBSAXContentHandler.startDocument
End Sub

Public Sub endDocument() Implements MSXML2.IVBSAXContentHandler.endDocument
End Sub

Public Sub startElement(ByRef strNamespaceURI As String, _
                        ByRef strLocalName As String, _
                        ByRef strQName As String, _
                        ByVal oAttributes As MSXML2.IVBSAXAttributes) _
                            Implements MSXML2.IVBSAXContentHandler.startElement
End Sub

Public Sub endElement(ByRef strNamespaceURI As String, _
                      ByRef strLocalName As String, _
                      ByRef strQName As String) _
                            Implements MSXML2.IVBSAXContentHandler.endElement
End Sub
```

LISTING 5.3c   Continued

```
Public Sub characters(ByRef strChars As String) _
                            Implements MSXML2.IVBSAXContentHandler.characters
End Sub

Public Sub ignorableWhitespace(ByRef strChars As String) _
                    Implements MSXML2.IVBSAXContentHandler.ignorableWhitespace
End Sub

Public Sub startPrefixMapping(ByRef strPrefix As String, _
                        ByRef strURI As String) _
                    Implements MSXML2.IVBSAXContentHandler.startPrefixMapping
End Sub

Public Sub endPrefixMapping(ByRef strPrefix As String) _
                        Implements MSXML2.IVBSAXContentHandler.endPrefixMapping
End Sub

Public WriteOnly Property documentLocator() As MSXML2.IVBSAXLocator _
                        Implements MSXML2.IVBSAXContentHandler.documentLocator
    Set(ByVal Value As MSXML2.IVBSAXLocator)
    End Set
End Property

Public Sub processingInstruction(ByRef strTarget As String, _
                        ByRef strData As String) _
                    Implements MSXML2.IVBSAXContentHandler.processingInstruction
End Sub

Public Sub skippedEntity(ByRef strName As String) _
                        Implements MSXML2.IVBSAXContentHandler.skippedEntity
End Sub
```

Finally, select **MyContentHandler** in the Class Name drop-down and then select New in the Method Name drop-down. Modify the **New** method to read as follows:

```
Dim myForm As New SAXMainForm()
Public Sub New(ByVal FormInst As SAXMainForm)
    myForm = FormInst
End Sub
```

This function allows us to get an instance reference to the main form so that the methods of the **MyContentHandler** class can access the controls of the main form during processing.

PHP

While PHP supports the passing of events in a SAX-like way, it doesn't exactly use SAX. This fact has two implications. First, there is no object or interface on which we can base the content handler, and second, we'll have to pass the events to it manually. We'll use the **SAXParser** object that we started in Listing 5.1c to adapt PHP's quirks to the standard.

Strictly speaking, we don't need to create a new class. We could process the events directly from the parser instead, but to make the PHP version more closely match the Java version, we'll create a separate class, SAXHandler, then forward events to it from the SAXParser object, as shown in Listing 5.3d. To do this, we need to create "hooks" for each of the events we'll be using.

LISTING 5.3d   Creating the Content Handler in PHP

```php
<?php

class SAXParser {

    var $file;
    var $handler;
    var $parser;

    function SAXParser ($args=array( 'encoding'  => false,
                                     'handler'   => null,
                                     'case_fold' => 0 ))
    {
        $this->parser = xml_parser_create($args['encoding']);
        xml_set_object($this->parser,$this);
    }

    function parse ($file)
    {
        xml_set_element_handler($this->parser,
                            "start_element", "end_element");
        xml_set_character_data_handler($this->parser, "characters");
        xml_set_default_handler($this->parser, "default_handler");

        if (!($fh = fopen($file, "r")))
            return false;

        $this->start_document();
        while ($ch = fread($fh, 4096)) {
            ...

        }
        xml_parser_free($this->parser);
        fclose($fh);

        $this->end_document();

        return true;
    }

    function set_handler (&$handler)
    {
        $this->handler =& $handler;
    }

    function start_document ()
    {
```

LISTING 5.3d   Continued

```php
        $this->handler->start_document();
    }

    function end_document ()
    {
        $this->handler->end_document();
    }

    function start_element ()
    {
        $this->handler->start_element();
    }

    function end_element ()
    {
        $this->handler->end_element();
    }

    function characters ()
    {
        $this->handler->characters();
    }

    function ignorable_whitespace ()
    {
        $this->handler->ignorable_whitespace();
    }

}

class SAXHandler {

    var $handler;

    function set_handler (&$handler)
    {
        $this->handler =& $handler;
    }

    function start_document ()
    {
        if (isset($this->handler))
            $this->handler->start_document();
    }

    function end_document ()
    {
        if (isset($this->handler))
            $this->handler->end_document();
    }

    function start_element ()
```

LISTING 5.3d   Continued

```php
    {
        if (isset($this->handler))
            $this->handler->start_element();
    }

    function end_element ()
    {
        if (isset($this->handler))
            $this->handler->end_element();
    }

    function characters ()
    {
        if (isset($this->handler))
            $this->handler->characters();
    }

    function ignorable_whitespace ()
    {
        if (isset($this->handler))
            $this->handler->ignorable_whitespace();
    }
}
?>
```

To make this work, we have to instantiate the content handler to create the `DataProcessor` object, then set that object as the handler for the parser. The following code shows the creation of the `DataProcessor` object as a subclass of `SAXHandler`, and its registration as the handler:

```php
<?php

  require_once("sax.inc");

  class DataProcessor extends SAXHandler
  {
      function DataProcessor () { }
  }

  $parser  =& new SAXParser();

  $handler =& new DataProcessor();
  $parser->set_handler($handler);

  ?>
```

Perl

In a Perl application, you set the content handler when you create the parser, as shown in Listing 5.3e.

LISTING 5.3e   Creating the Handler in Perl

```perl
package MyContentHandler;

use base qw(XML::SAX::Base);

package main;

use XML::SAX;

$XML::SAX::ParserPackage = 'XML::SAX::Expat';

my $factory = XML::SAX::ParserFactory->new();
my $parser  = $factory->parser( Handler => MyContentHandler->new() );
```

Parsing the Document

Once we've determined the content handler, actually parsing the file is a simple matter of determining the source of the data and feeding it to the **parse()** method, as shown in Listings 5.4a–e.

Java

LISTING 5.4a   Parsing the Input in Java

```java
...
import org.xml.sax.InputSource;
import java.io.IOException;

public class MainSaxApp {
    public static void main (String[] args){
        try {

            String parserClass = "org.apache.crimson.parser.XMLReaderImpl";
            XMLReader reader = XMLReaderFactory.createXMLReader(parserClass);

            reader.setContentHandler(new DataProcessor());

            InputSource file = new InputSource("votes.xml");
            reader.parse(file);

        } catch (IOException ioe) {
            System.out.println("IO Exception: "+ioe.getMessage());
        } catch (SAXException se) {
            System.out.println("SAX Exception: "+se.getMessage());
        }
    }
}
```

A SAX **InputSource** doesn't have to be a file. It can be a Java **InputStream** (bytes), a Java **Reader** (characters), or a **String**. The **String** represents the system ID of an XML file, so that file can be local or remote, as long as the URL is fully resolved (in other words, do not use a relative URL).

When the application runs, the XMLReader will send each event to the new DataProcessor object, but that object won't do anything until we override the event methods. We'll do that in the "Handling Events" section.

C++

In our C++ sample, the XML filename is a command-line argument that the user passes to us while executing the application. C++ uses the parseURL method to accept fully qualified URLs to give to the XMLReader (see Listing 5.4b).

LISTING 5.4b   Parsing the Input in C++

```
#include "stdafx.h"
#include <WinInet.h>
...

int _tmain(int argc, _TCHAR* argv[])
{
    static wchar_t XMLURL[INTERNET_MAX_URL_LENGTH];
...
                hr = pReader->putContentHandler(pContent);

        mbstowcs(XMLURL, argv[1], (INTERNET_MAX_URL_LENGTH-1));
        hr = pReader->parseURL(XMLURL);

        //Clean up the XMLReader
            pReader->Release();
...
```

Visual Basic .NET

The Visual Basic sample retrieves the filename of the XML file from the text box that is next to the Parse XML button. The file specified in that text box is then passed to the Reader via the parseURL method. Modify the code in the SAXMainForm as show in Listing 5.4c.

LISTING 5.4c   Parsing the Input in Visual Basic .NET

```
Private Sub btnParse_Click(ByVal sender As System.Object, _
                           ByVal e As System.EventArgs) Handles btnParse.Click
    Dim Reader As New MSXML2.SAXXMLReader()
    Dim ContentHandler As New MyContentHandler(Me)

    txtOutput.Text = ""
    Reader.contentHandler = ContentHandler

    On Error GoTo ErrorSub
    Reader.parseURL(txtFileName.Text)
    Exit Sub
```

LISTING 5.4c   Continued

```
ErrorSub:
    txtOutput.Text = txtOutput.Text & "* Error * " & " : " & Err.Description
End Sub
```

PHP

The PHP version can take a relative URL, as shown in Listing 5.4d.

LISTING 5.4d   Parsing the Input in PHP

```php
<?php

require_once("sax.inc");

class DataProcessor extends SAXHandler
{
    function DataProcessor () { }
}

$parser  =& new SAXParser();
$handler =& new DataProcessor();

$parser->set_handler($handler);
$parser->parse("votes.xml") or die("Parse failed");

?>
```

Perl

When passing a filename to an `XML::SAX` parser, you'll be tempted to use the `$parser->parse_file()` method. Don't! That method takes an open filehandle, not a filename. Use `$parser->parse_uri()` instead, as shown in Listing 5.4e.

LISTING 5.4e   Parsing the Input in Perl

```perl
package MyContentHandler;

use base qw(XML::SAX::Base);

package main;

use XML::SAX;

$XML::SAX::ParserPackage = 'XML::SAX::Expat';

my $factory = XML::SAX::ParserFactory->new();
my $parser  = $factory->parser( Handler => MyContentHandler->new() );

eval { $parser->parse_uri('votes.xml'); };

print "Error parsing file: $@" if $@;
```

The `ErrorHandler`

In addition to handling content-related events, the application should be prepared to handle problems such as malformed documents or validation errors (assuming that the parser is validating).

The `DefaultHandler` class contains the methods necessary to implement the `ErrorHandler` interface, so we can also use it to create the error handler, as shown in Listing 5.5a.

Java

LISTING 5.5a   Creating the Error Handler in Java

```
import org.xml.sax.helpers.DefaultHandler;
import org.xml.sax.SAXParseException;

public class ErrorProcessor extends DefaultHandler
{

    public ErrorProcessor ()
    {
        super();
    }

    public void error (SAXParseException e) {
        System.out.println("Error: "+e.getMessage());
    }

    public void fatalError (SAXParseException e) {
        System.out.println("Fatal Error: "+e.getMessage());
    }

    public void warning (SAXParseException e) {
        System.out.println("Warning: "+e.getMessage());
    }

}
```

In this case, we've overridden the error event handlers so that we can find out what's gone wrong:

- A `warning` is a problem that doesn't qualify as an error, but that you will probably want to know about. In most cases, you'll want the parser to keep going after a warning, but you can use this event to throw an exception. A warning might be triggered by a condition that's not defined as an actual error by the XML 1.0 Recommendation. This event can by used by filters (discussed later in the chapter) to report situations that are not related to the structure of the file itself.

- An `error` is a condition that is defined within the XML 1.0 specification as an error, but which doesn't keep the parser from continuing. For example, when you're validating a document, the presence of an element that hasn't been defined yet will cause an error. Again, you can choose to throw an exception here, but in most cases you'll want the application to keep going.

- If the parser can't keep going, it will send a `fatalError` event. This is an error, such as malformed XML, that makes it impossible to continue parsing the document.

Like the content handler, the error handler must be associated with the parser in order to receive events, as shown in Listing 5.6a–c.

LISTING 5.6a   Associating the Error Handler with the Parser in Java

```
...
        XMLReader reader = XMLReaderFactory.createXMLReader(parserClass);

        reader.setContentHandler(new DataProcessor());
        reader.setErrorHandler(new ErrorProcessor());

        InputSource file = new InputSource("votes.xml");
        reader.parse(file);

    } catch (IOException ioe) {
...
```

C++

In C++, errors generated by the `XMLReader` are handled by the error handler registered with the `XMLReader` using the `putErrorHander()` method. First, declare your own derived class of `ISAXErrorHandler` and implement the methods, as shown in Listing 5.6b. Create a new file called `MySAXErrorHandler.h` and add the code to it.

LISTING 5.6b   Creating the Error Handler in C++

```
class MySAXErrorHandler : public ISAXErrorHandler
{
public:
    MySAXErrorHandler();
    virtual ~MySAXErrorHandler();

        long __stdcall QueryInterface(const struct _GUID &,void ** );
        unsigned long __stdcall AddRef(void);
        unsigned long __stdcall Release(void);

        // Method for future support. All errors are currently fatalError.
        virtual HRESULT STDMETHODCALLTYPE error(
            /* [in] */ ISAXLocator __RPC_FAR *pLocator,
            /* [in] */ unsigned short * pwchErrorMessage,
            /* [in] */ HRESULT errCode);

        virtual HRESULT STDMETHODCALLTYPE fatalError(
            /* [in] */ ISAXLocator __RPC_FAR *pLocator,
```

LISTING 5.6b   *Continued*

```
                    /* [in] */ unsigned short * pwchErrorMessage,
                    /* [in] */ HRESULT errCode);

            // Method for future support. All errors are currently fatalError.
            virtual HRESULT STDMETHODCALLTYPE ignorableWarning(
                    /* [in] */ ISAXLocator __RPC_FAR *pLocator,
                    /* [in] */ unsigned short * pwchErrorMessage,
                    /* [in] */ HRESULT errCode);
};
```

Now create a new file named `MySAXErrorHandler.cpp` and add the following code:

```
#include "stdafx.h"
#include "MySAXErrorHandler.h"
#include <stdio.h>

MySAXErrorHandler::MySAXErrorHandler()
{
}

MySAXErrorHandler::~MySAXErrorHandler()
{
}

HRESULT STDMETHODCALLTYPE MySAXErrorHandler::error(
    /* [in] */ ISAXLocator RPC_FAR *pLocator,
    /* [in] */ unsigned short * pwchErrorMessage,
    /* [in] */ HRESULT errCode)
{
    return S_OK;
}

HRESULT STDMETHODCALLTYPE MySAXErrorHandler::fatalError(
    /* [in] */ ISAXLocator RPC_FAR *pLocator,
    /* [in] */ unsigned short * pwchErrorMessage,
    /* [in] */ HRESULT errCode)
{
    return S_OK;
}

HRESULT STDMETHODCALLTYPE MySAXErrorHandler::ignorableWarning(
    /* [in] */ ISAXLocator RPC_FAR *pLocator,
    /* [in] */ unsigned short * pwchErrorMessage,
    /* [in] */ HRESULT errCode)
{
    return S_OK;
}

long __stdcall MySAXErrorHandler::QueryInterface(const struct GUID &,void **)
{
    return 0;
}
```

```
unsigned long __stdcall MySAXErrorHandler::AddRef()
{
    return 0;
}

unsigned long __stdcall MySAXErrorHandler::Release()
{
    return 0;
}
```

Currently, all errors generated will call the `fatalError()` method. The other methods are for future implementation and should be included into your class for future compatibility. For the purposes of this sample, the class methods have not been fully implemented. If you were creating a real application that required this to be a COM DLL, it would be necessary to fully implement the `QueryInterface`, `AddRef`, and `Release` methods and also to customize the other methods to the needs of your application.

Finally, in Listing 5.6b, we make some changes to the main `.cpp` file of the application to associate the class that we have created with the content handler of the `XMLReader`.

LISTING 5.6b   Associating the Error Handler with the Parser in C++

```
#include "stdafx.h"
#include "MySAXErrorHandler.h"
...
            hr = pReader->putContentHandler(pContent);
        //Register the error handler for the XMLReader
        MySAXErrorHandler* pError = new MySAXErrorHandler();
        hr = pReader->putErrorHandler(pError);
...
```

Visual Basic .NET

Creating an error handler for Visual Basic is very similar to creating the content handler. First, create a new class called `MyErrorHandler.vb` and add the `Implements` statement to specify that you are implementing the `IVBSAXErrorHandler` class. You can then select the Class and Method Name drop-downs and add the methods that you will be implementing to the class.

One important thing to note is that one of the methods is called `error`, which is a reserved keyword in Visual Basic .NET. You will need to rename the subroutine in order to compile the project. Listing 5.5c uses `parseError` for the subroutine name.

LISTING 5.5c   Creating the Error Handler in Visual Basic .NET

```
Public Class MyErrorHandler
    Implements MSXML2.IVBSAXErrorHandler

    Dim myForm As New SAXMainForm()
    Public Sub New(ByVal FormInst As SAXMainForm)
        myForm = FormInst
    End Sub
```

LISTING 5.5c   *Continued*

```
Public Sub parseError(ByVal oLocator As MSXML2.IVBSAXLocator, _
                      ByRef strErrorMessage As String, _
                      ByVal nErrorCode As Integer) _
                          Implements MSXML2.IVBSAXErrorHandler.error
   End Sub

Public Sub fatalError(ByVal oLocator As MSXML2.IVBSAXLocator, _
                      ByRef strErrorMessage As String, _
                      ByVal nErrorCode As Integer) _
                        Implements MSXML2.IVBSAXErrorHandler.fatalError
   End Sub

Public Sub ignorableWarning(ByVal oLocator As MSXML2.IVBSAXLocator, _
                      ByRef strErrorMessage As String, _
                      ByVal nErrorCode As Integer) _
                  Implements MSXML2.IVBSAXErrorHandler.ignorableWarning
   End Sub
End Class
```

To finish wiring the class to the `Reader`, register the error handler just as you registered the content handler by making changes to the `btnParse_Click` subroutine, as shown in Listing 5.6c.

LISTING 5.6c   Associating the Error Handler with the Parser in Visual Basic .NET

```
...
      Dim ContentHandler As New MyContentHandler(Me)
      Dim ErrorHandler As New MyErrorHandler(Me)
...
      Reader.contentHandler = ContentHandler
      Reader.errorHandler = ErrorHandler
...
```

Other Handlers

The content and error handlers are far from the only handlers SAX has defined. Let's take a quick look at some other handlers:

- `DTDHandler`—This handler receives notifications for notations and unparsed entities that may be included in an internal DTD.

- `DeclHandler`—This handler receives notification of other events related to the `DOCTYPE` declaration.

- `LexicalHandler`—This handler receives notification of events such as `startDTD` and `endCDATA`.

These handlers are rarely used for SAX applications, but it's good to know they're available if you find that you need them. A complete list is available with the main SAX documentation at `http://sax.sourceforge.net`.

Handling Events

Okay, now that we've got the skeleton of the application, let's start putting some meat on the bones. First we'll consider the different types of events that we can look for using a content handler, and how to use them to retrieve information from the document.

In the next section, we'll use that information to tally the votes.

The Source Document

The source document is a small selection of votes and comments, as shown in Listing 5.7.

LISTING 5.7   The Source Document

```
<?xml version="1.0"?>
<votes totalVotes="5">
    <voter personid="Emp1" status="primary">
        <vote>Dregraal</vote>
        <extra:comments xmlns:extra="http://www.vanguardreport.com/extra">
            I would like to request that the date of voting be changed.
            Any klybrtan youth would realize that it falls on the 334th
            of Meeps, the Holiest of days for Squreenks.  It is totally
            unacceptable for us to vote then, since we have to spend the
            entire day in the positronic chamber of worship.
        </extra:comments>
    </voter>
    <voter personid="Emp2" status="symbiont">
        <vote>Sparkle</vote>
        <extra:comments xmlns:extra="http://www.vanguardreport.com/extra">
            Sfgrtng dwesvers melpy ypinee!
        </extra:comments>
    </voter>
    <voter personid="Emp3" status="symbiont">
        <vote>Dregraal</vote>
        <extra:comments xmlns:extra="http://www.vanguardreport.com/extra">
            As the leader of Symbiont Union 4*6^33, I would like to
            officially register a complaint against the rule that
            bans symbiotns from voting. We are a separate entity from
            our hosts mentally, and should be recognized as such.
        </extra:comments>
    </voter>
    <voter personid="Emp4" status="primary">
        <vote>Dregraal</vote>
        <extra:comments xmlns:extra="http://www.vanguardreport.com/extra">
```

LISTING 5.7 Continued

```
            We of the Claxx are agreeable, but we ask that next time we
            be allowed to vote before the Nreeks.
         </extra:comments>
      </voter>
      <voter personid="Emp5" status="primary">
         <vote>Sparkle</vote>
         <extra:comments xmlns:extra="http://www.vanguardreport.com/extra">
         </extra:comments>
      </voter>
   </votes>
```

Document Events

Probably the simplest events to capture are the `startDocument` and `endDocument` events. Together, they act as bookends for all other events. Listings 5.8a–e show the `DataProcessor` class (the content handler) with the new methods.

Java

LISTING 5.8a Adding Events in Java

```java
import org.xml.sax.helpers.DefaultHandler;

public class DataProcessor extends DefaultHandler
{
   public DataProcessor ()
   {
      super();
   }

   //----------------
   //UTILITY METHODS
   //----------------
   public static void println(String arg) {
      System.out.println(arg);
   }

   //-------------
   //EVENT METHODS
   //-------------
   public void startDocument() {
      println("Document START");
   }

   public void endDocument() {
      println("Document END");
   }
}
```

After we compile this class, a call to `MainSaxApp` produces the following output:

```
Document START
Document END
```

The reason is this: `XMLReader` sends all events to the `DataProcessor` class, but all but two of those events call the methods in the `DefaultHandler` class, which do nothing. The last two are `startDocument()` and `endDocument()`, which override their `DefaultHandler` counterparts and output text to the screen.

Notice that we have also added the `println()` method we used in the last chapter. You can add any methods that you need to the handler classes, as long as you also implement the required methods.

C++

In C++, we are required to implement all the methods in our own implementation of the `SAXContentHandler` class, so we can easily modify the `startDocument` and `endDocument` methods in `MySAXContentHandler.cpp`, as shown in Listing 5.8b.

LISTING 5.8b   Adding Events in C++

```cpp
HRESULT STDMETHODCALLTYPE MySAXContentHandler::startDocument()
{
    printf("Document START\n");
    return S_OK;
}

HRESULT STDMETHODCALLTYPE MySAXContentHandler::endDocument()
{
    printf("Document END\n");
    return S_OK;
}
```

Visual Basic .NET

In order to output text to the `txtOutPut` text box in Visual Basic .NET, we will need to create a class property that accepts strings passed to it and then sends them to the Output window. Place the `OutputText` property just before the `End Class` statement in the Code view of `SAXMainForm`, as shown in Listing 5.8c.

LISTING 5.8c   Adding Events in Visual Basic .NET

```vbnet
...
    Public Property OutputText() As String
        Get
            Return txtOutput.Text
        End Get
        Set(ByVal Value As String)
            txtOutput.Text = txtOutput.Text & Value
        End Set
```

LISTING 5.8c   Continued

```
      End Property
End Class
```

Now modify the `startDocument()` and `endDocument()` methods in the `MySAXContentHandler` class:

```
...
Public Sub startDocument() Implements MSXML2.IVBSAXContentHandler.startDocument
    myForm.OutputText = "Document START" & vbCrLf
End Sub

Public Sub endDocument() Implements MSXML2.IVBSAXContentHandler.endDocument
    myForm.OutputText = "Document END" & vbCrLf
End Sub
...
```

PHP

In PHP, simply override the appropriate functions by implementing them in the `DataProcessor` class, as shown in Listing 5.8d.

LISTING 5.8d   Adding Events in PHP

```
<?php

require_once("sax.inc");

class DataProcessor extends SAXHandler
{
    function DataProcessor () { }

    function start_document ()
    {
      echo "Document START<br>\n";
    }

    function end_document ()
    {
      echo "Document END<br>\n";
    }

}

...

?>
```

Perl

In Perl, override the `start_document()` and `end_document()` methods as shown in Listing 5.8e.

LISTING 5.8e   Adding Events in Perl

```perl
package MyContentHandler;

use base qw(XML::SAX::Base);

sub start_document {
    print "Document START\n";
}

sub end_document {
    print "Document END\n";
}

package main;
...
```

Element Events

The start and end points of a document are useful for seeing events in action, but they don't really provide much information. Elements provide information in several ways; through their names and namespaces, through their attributes, and through the text they contain. In this section we'll look at names, namespaces, and attributes; we'll tackle text later.

Elements

First let's take a look at the basic information that's passed along with the element events, as shown in Listing 5.9.

LISTING 5.9   Getting Basic Element Information

```java
import org.xml.sax.helpers.DefaultHandler;
import org.xml.sax.Attributes;

public class DataProcessor extends DefaultHandler
{
...
   public void endDocument() {
      println("Document END");
   }

   public void startElement (String namespaceUri, String localName,
                     String qualifiedName, Attributes attributes)
   {
      println("Element START:");
      println("   Namespace: " + namespaceUri);
      println("   Local name: " + localName);
      println("   Qualified name: " + qualifiedName);
      println("-----------------");

   }
```

LISTING 5.9 Continued

```
public void endElement (String namespaceUri, String localName,
                String qualifiedName)
{
    println("Element END:");
    println("    Namespace: " + namespaceUri);
    println("    Local name: " + localName);
    println("    Qualified name: " + qualifiedName);
    println("-----------------");
}

}
```

In each case, we're outputting text that tells us what kind of event has occurred, and then some of the information that was passed in with the event. Let's look at Listing 5.10, which shows a segment of the results.

LISTING 5.10 Element Information

```
Document START
Element START:
    Namespace:
    Local name: votes
    Qualified name: votes
-----------------
Element START:
    Namespace:
    Local name: voter
    Qualified name: voter
-----------------
Element START:
    Namespace:
    Local name: vote
    Qualified name: vote
-----------------
Element END:
    Namespace:
    Local name: vote
    Qualified name: vote
-----------------
Element START:
    Namespace: http://www.vanguardreport.com/extra
    Local name: comments
    Qualified name: extra:comments
-----------------
Element END:
    Namespace: http://www.vanguardreport.com/extra
    Local name: comments
    Qualified name: extra:comments
-----------------
Element END:
    Namespace:
```

LISTING 5.10   Continued

```
      Local name: voter
      Qualified name: voter
- - - - - - - - - - - - - - - - -
...
- - - - - - - - - - - - - - - - -
Element END:
    Namespace:
    Local name: votes
    Qualified name: votes
- - - - - - - - - - - - - - - - -
Document END
```

I've pulled out all but the first voter, but the pattern should still be visible; start and end element events correspond to the start and end tags in the original document, and the presence or absence of text within them makes absolutely no difference to the application.

Notice also the namespace information. First, even though the namespace itself is only defined in the root element, the entire URI is available as part of each of the relevant element events. Remember, the alias is just a convenience; it's the URI that actually determines the namespace. Second, notice that if a namespace alias is present, it makes up the difference between the local name and the qualified name.

Help! My `localNames` Are Blank!

Not all SAX parsers are namespace-aware. The SAX specification states that the feature `http://xml.org/sax/features/namespaces` should be set to `true` by default, but some implementations—most notably JAXP—set it to `false`. To correct this problem, set the feature on the `XMLReader` object, like this:

```
reader.setFeature("http://xml.org/sax/features/namespaces", true);
```

Attributes

Keep in mind that at this point, the application has no idea what the contents of the element are. The only other information that's available during the `startElement` event is the content of the attributes, as shown in Listing 5.11.

Java

LISTING 5.11   Getting Attribute Information in Java

```java
import org.xml.sax.helpers.DefaultHandler;
import org.xml.sax.Attributes;

public class DataProcessor extends DefaultHandler
{
...
    public void startElement (String namespaceUri, String localName,
                    String qualifiedName, Attributes attributes)
```

LISTING 5.11 Continued

```
    {
        println("Element START: " + localName);

        int numAttributes = attributes.getLength();
        for (int i = 0; i < numAttributes; i++) {

            String localAttName = attributes.getLocalName(i);
            String qualAttName = attributes.getQName(i);
            String attValue = attributes.getValue(qualAttName);

            println("   Attribute: " + qualAttName + "=\"" + attValue + "\"");
        }

        println("-----------------");

    }

    public void endElement (String namespaceUri, String localName,
                            String qualifiedName)
    {
        println("Element END: " + localName);
        println("-----------------");
    }

}
```

The attributes are collectively passed to the event handler as an **Attributes** object, which acts much like a DOM **NamedNodeMap**. You can iterate through the collection to find each name, and then use the name to get the information. (Note that attributes are like elements in that they have local and qualified names.) The results are shown in Listings 5.12a–e.

Java

LISTING 5.12a Attribute Information in Java

```
Document START
Element START: votes
   Attribute: totalVotes="5"
-----------------
Element START: voter
   Attribute: personid="Emp1"
   Attribute: status="primary"
-----------------
Element START: vote
-----------------
Element END: vote
-----------------
Element START: comments
-----------------
Element END: comments
```

LISTING 5.12a   Continued

```
------------------
Element END: voter
------------------
...
------------------
Element END: votes
------------------
Document END
```

Namespace Declarations as Attributes

Some parsers will also show the namespace declarations, such as those on the `comments` elements, as attributes.

C++

To add this functionality to our C++ sample, we will implement the `startElement()` and `endElement()` methods. In C++, the implementations of the `Attributes` class methods have a `buffer` and a `length` variable assigned to each attribute. The `buffer` contains the string and the `length` value defines how much of the buffer is the name or value. Therefore, to have the same output as the Java sample, we need to write a helper function that will help us to print the information, as shown in Listing 5.12b. Make these changes in the `MySAXContentHandler.cpp` file.

LISTING 5.12b   Getting Attribute Information in C++

```cpp
HRESULT STDMETHODCALLTYPE MySAXContentHandler::startElement(
            /* [in] */ wchar_t __RPC_FAR *pwchNamespaceUri,
            /* [in] */ int cchNamespaceUri,
            /* [in] */ wchar_t __RPC_FAR *pwchLocalName,
            /* [in] */ int cchLocalName,
            /* [in] */ wchar_t __RPC_FAR *pwchQualifiedName,
            /* [in] */ int cchQualifiedName,
            /* [in] */ ISAXAttributes __RPC_FAR *pAttributes)
{
    int numAttributes, cchLocalAttName, cchQAttName, cchLocalAttValue;
    wchar_t *pwchLocalAttName, *pwchQAttName, *pwchLocalAttValue;

    PrintVarStr(L"Element START: %s\n", pwchLocalName, cchLocalName);
    pAttributes->getLength(&numAttributes);
    for (int i = 0; i < numAttributes; i++)
        {
        pAttributes->getLocalName(i, &pwchLocalAttName, &cchLocalAttName);
        pAttributes->getQName(i, &pwchQAttName, &cchQAttName);
        pAttributes->getValueFromQName(pwchQAttName, cchQAttName,
                                &pwchLocalAttValue, &cchLocalAttValue);
        PrintVarStr(L"  Attribute: %s=", pwchQAttName, cchQAttName);
        PrintVarStr(L"\"%s\"\n", pwchLocalAttValue, cchLocalAttValue);
        }
```

LISTING 5.12b   *Continued*

```
        printf("------------------\n");
        return S_OK;
    }

    HRESULT STDMETHODCALLTYPE MySAXContentHandler::endElement(
                /* [in] */ wchar_t __RPC_FAR *pwchNamespaceUri,
                /* [in] */ int cchNamespaceUri,
                /* [in] */ wchar_t __RPC_FAR *pwchLocalName,
                /* [in] */ int cchLocalName,
                /* [in] */ wchar_t __RPC_FAR *pwchQualifiedName,
                /* [in] */ int cchQualifiedName)
    {
        PrintVarStr(L"Element END: %s\n", pwchLocalName, cchLocalName);
        printf("------------------\n");
        return S_OK;
    }
```

In addition, we need the `PrintVarStr` function. This function will be part of the `MySAXContentHandler` class and needs to be added to the class definition. Open the `MySAXContentHandler.h` file and insert the following just before the end of the class:

```
private:
        void PrintVarStr(
            /* [in] */ const wchar_t * pwchFmt,
            /* [in] */ const wchar_t __RPC_FAR *pwchElement,
            /* [in] */ int cchElement);
```

Now switch to the `MySAXContentHandler.cpp` file and add the following:

```
void MySAXContentHandler::PrintVarStr(
                /* [in] */ const wchar_t * pwchFmt,
                /* [in] */ const wchar_t __RPC_FAR *pwchElement,
                /* [in] */ int cchElement)
{
    static wchar_t buffer[500];
        cchElement = cchElement > 499 ? 499 : cchElement;
    wcsncpy(buffer, pwchElement, cchElement);
    buffer[cchElement] = 0;
    wprintf(pwchFmt, buffer);
}
```

For the purposes of this example, we will assume that no element name or value will be longer than 499 characters. This may need to be changed for actual production code to meet the needs of your XML Schema.

Visual Basic .NET

To show the element information in Visual Basic .NET, select the `MySAXContentHandler` class and modify the `startElement()` and `endElement()` methods as shown in Listing 5.12c.

LISTING 5.12c   Getting Attribute Information in Visual Basic .NET

```vbnet
Public Sub startElement(ByRef strNamespaceURI As String, _
                        ByRef strLocalName As String, _
                        ByRef strQName As String, _
                        ByVal oAttributes As MSXML2.IVBSAXAttributes) _
                               Implements MSXML2.IVBSAXContentHandler.startElement
    Dim i As Short

    myForm.OutputText = "Element START: " & strLocalName & vbCrLf
    For i = 0 To (oAttributes.length - 1)
        myForm.OutputText = "   Attribute: " + oAttributes.getQName(i) + "=""" _
                                    + oAttributes.getValue(i) + """" & vbCrLf
    Next
    myForm.OutputText = "-----------------" & vbCrLf
End Sub

Public Sub endElement(ByRef strNamespaceURI As String, _
                      ByRef strLocalName As String, _
                      ByRef strQName As String) _
                             Implements MSXML2.IVBSAXContentHandler.endElement
    myForm.OutputText = "Element END: " & strLocalName & vbCrLf
    myForm.OutputText = "-----------------" & vbCrLf
End Sub
```

PHP

To show the information in PHP, implement the new methods in the **DataProcessor** class as shown in Listing 5.12d.

LISTING 5.12d   Attribute Information in PHP

```php
<?php

require_once("sax.inc");

class DataProcessor extends SAXHandler
{
    function DataProcessor () { }

    ...

    function start_element ($name, $attr)
    {
        echo "Element START: $name<br><ul>\n";
        foreach ($attr as $attr_name => $attr_value)
        {
            echo "<li>$attr_name = \"$attr_value\"</li>\n";
        }
        echo "</ul><hr>\n";
    }

    function end_element ($name)
```

LISTING 5.12d   Continued

```
        {
               echo "Element END: $name<br><hr>\n";
        }

    }

    ...

?>
```

Perl

To show the information in Perl, implement the new methods as shown in Listing 5.12e.

LISTING 5.12e   Attribute Information in Perl

```perl
package MyContentHandler;

use base qw(XML::SAX::Base);

sub start_document {
    print "Document START\n";
}

sub end_document {
    print "Document END\n";
}

sub start_element {
    my $self = shift;
    my $el   = shift;

    print "Element START:\n";
    print "  Namespace: $el->{NamespaceURI}\n";
    print "  Local name: $el->{LocalName}\n";

    foreach my $ak ( keys %{ $el->{Attributes} } ) {
        my $at = $el->{Attributes}->{$ak};

        print qq(  Attribute: $at->{Name} = "$at->{Value}"\n);
    }
    print "-" x 20, "\n";
}

sub end_element {
    my $self = shift;
    my $el   = shift;

    print "Element END:\n";
    print "  Namespace: $el->{NamespaceURI}\n";
    print "  Local name: $el->{LocalName}\n";
```

LISTING 5.12e   Continued

```
    print "-" x 20, "\n";

}

package main;
...
```

Text Events

Now let's look at text content for elements.

The first thing it's important to understand is that the actual text is sent to the `characters` event, but not necessarily in the form you might expect.

Rather than simply sending the characters that make up the content of the element, the parser actually sends a string that represents all the characters in the document, along with the position of the first character in this particular set, and the number of characters in this particular set.

Complicating things further, there is no guarantee that all the text for a particular element will be sent in a single event. This forces us to compromise, as you can see in Listings 5.13a–c.

LISTING 5.13a   Getting Element Text in Java

```java
import org.xml.sax.helpers.DefaultHandler;
import org.xml.sax.Attributes;

public class DataProcessor extends DefaultHandler
{
    public DataProcessor ()
    {
        super();
    }

    StringBuffer thisText = new StringBuffer();

    //----------------
    //UTILITY METHODS
    //----------------
    public static void println(String arg) {
        System.out.println(arg);
    }

    public void displayText() {
        if (thisText.length() > 0) {
            println("   TEXT: [" + thisText.toString() + "]");
            thisText.delete(0, thisText.length());
        }
    }
```

LISTING 5.13a Continued

```
//-------------
//EVENT METHODS
//-------------
public void startDocument() {
    println("Document START");
}

public void endDocument() {
    println("Document END");
}

 public void startElement (String namespaceUri, String localName,
                     String qualifiedName, Attributes attributes)
    {

       displayText();

       println("Element START: " + localName);

       int numAttributes = attributes.getLength();
       for (int i = 0; i < numAttributes; i++) {

          String localAttName = attributes.getLocalName(i);
          String qualAttName = attributes.getQName(i);
          String attValue = attributes.getValue(qualAttName);

          println("   Attribute: " + qualAttName + "=\"" + attValue + "\"");
       }

       println("-----------------");

    }

    public void endElement (String namespaceUri, String localName,
                     String qualifiedName)
    {
       displayText();

       println("Element END: " + localName);
       println("-----------------");
    }

    public void characters (char[] ch, int start, int length)
    {
       thisText.append(ch, start, length);
    }

}
```

In this case, we're creating a new method, `characters()`, to receive the `characters` events. When it does, it appends them to the end of the `thisText` `StringBuffer`. This way, text is added to `thisText` until it reaches either the end of the element or the beginning of another element. At that point, the text is displayed and `thisText` is cleared out to prepare for the next string. The results are shown in Listing 5.14a.

Java

LISTING 5.14a   Character Strings in Java

```
Document START
Element START: votes
   Attribute: totalVotes="5"
- - - - - - - - - - - - - - - - -
   TEXT: [
   ]
Element START: voter
   Attribute: personid="Emp1"
   Attribute: status="primary"
- - - - - - - - - - - - - - - - -
   TEXT: [
       ]
Element START: vote
- - - - - - - - - - - - - - - - -
   TEXT: [Dregraal]
Element END: vote
- - - - - - - - - - - - - - - - -
   TEXT: [
       ]
Element START: comments
- - - - - - - - - - - - - - - - -
   TEXT: [
           I would like to request that the date of voting be changed.
           Any klybrtan youth would realize that it falls on the 334th
           of Meeps, the Holiest of days for Squreenks.  It is totally
           unacceptable for us to vote then, since we have to spend the
           entire day in the positronic chamber of worship.
       ]
Element END: comments
- - - - - - - - - - - - - - - - -
   TEXT: [
   ]
Element END: voter
- - - - - - - - - - - - - - - - -
   ...
- - - - - - - - - - - - - - - - -
   TEXT: [
]
Element END: votes
- - - - - - - - - - - - - - - - -
Document END
```

Notice that `characters()` events are also called for the whitespace between elements, which is why we have to check for text at the beginning of elements as well as at the end.

C++

In order to receive the `characters()` events in our C++ sample, we need to add the code in Listing 5.13b to the `private:` section of the `MySAXContentHandler.h` file.

LISTING 5.13b   Getting Element Text in C++

```
private:
        wchar_t wchText[1000];
        void MySAXContentHandler::displayText(void);
```

We need to add the following code to the bottom of the `MySAXContentHandler.cpp` file:

```
...
void MySAXContentHandler::displayText()
{
    int len = wcslen(wchText);
    if (len > 0)
    {
        wprintf(L"   TEXT: [%s]\n", wchText);
        wchText[0] = 0;
    }
}
```

Now, make the following changes to the `startDocument()`, `startElement()`, `endElement()`, and `characters()` functions as shown here:

```
HRESULT STDMETHODCALLTYPE MySAXContentHandler::startDocument()
{
    wchText[0] = 0;
...

HRESULT STDMETHODCALLTYPE MySAXContentHandler::startElement(
....
    displayText();
    PrintVarStr(L"Element START: %s\n", pwchLocalName, cchLocalName);
...

HRESULT STDMETHODCALLTYPE MySAXContentHandler::endElement(
...
    displayText();
    PrintVarStr(L"Element END: %s\n", pwchLocalName, cchLocalName);
...

HRESULT STDMETHODCALLTYPE MySAXContentHandler::characters(
            /* [in] */ wchar_t __RPC_FAR *pwchChars,
            /* [in] */ int cchChars)
{
    wcsncat(&*wchText, pwchChars, cchChars);
    return S_OK;
}
```

Visual Basic .NET

In Visual Basic .NET, place the declaration of the `thisText` variable at the top of the `MyContentHandler` class:

```
Dim thisText As String
```

Now we need to add the `displayText()` subroutine to the class:

```
Public Sub displayText()
    If Len(thisText) > 0 Then
        myForm.OutputText = "    TEXT: [" & thisText & "]" & vbCrLf
        thisText = Nothing
    End If
End Sub
```

Place a call to `displayText()` at the beginning of both the `startElement()` and `endElement()` subroutines and make changes to the `characters()` subroutine as shown in Listing 5.13c.

LISTING 5.13c   Getting Element Text in Visual Basic .NET

```
...
Public Sub startElement(ByRef strNamespaceURI As String, _
                        ByRef strLocalName As String, _
                        ByRef strQName As String, _
                        ByVal oAttributes As MSXML2.IVBSAXAttributes) _
                            Implements MSXML2.IVBSAXContentHandler.startElement
    Dim i As Short

    displayText()

    myForm.OutputText = "Element START: " & strLocalName & vbCrLf
    For i = 0 To (oAttributes.length - 1)
        myForm.OutputText = "    Attribute: " + oAttributes.getQName(i) + "=""" _
                                    + oAttributes.getValue(i) + """" & vbCrLf
    Next
    myForm.OutputText = "-----------------" & vbCrLf
End Sub

Public Sub endElement(ByRef strNamespaceURI As String, _
                      ByRef strLocalName As String, _
                      ByRef strQName As String) _
                            Implements MSXML2.IVBSAXContentHandler.endElement

    displayText()

    myForm.OutputText = "Element END: " & strLocalName & vbCrLf
    myForm.OutputText = "-----------------" & vbCrLf
End Sub
...
Public Sub characters(ByRef strChars As String)_
                            Implements MSXML2.IVBSAXContentHandler.characters
    strChars = Replace(strChars, vbLf, vbCrLf)
```

LISTING 5.13c Continued

```
    thisText = thisText & strChars
End Sub
...
```

PHP

The changes are straightforward in PHP, as shown in Listing 5.14b.

LISTING 5.14b Character Strings in PHP

```php
<?php

require_once("sax.inc");

class DataProcessor extends SAXHandler
{

    var $text = '';

    function DataProcessor () { }

    ...

    function display_text ()
    {
        if ($this->text != "")
            echo "TEXT: [$this->text]<br>\n";

        $this->text = '';
    }


    function start_element ($name, $attr)
    {
        $this->display_text();

        echo "Element START: $name<br><ul>\n";
        foreach ($attr as $attr_name => $attr_value)
        {
            echo "<li>$attr_name = \"$attr_value\"</li>\n";
        }
        echo "</ul><hr>\n";
    }

    function end_element ($name)
    {
        $this->display_text();

        echo "Element END: $name<br><hr>\n";
    }
```

LISTING 5.14b   Continued

```
        function characters ($data)
        {
            $this->text .= $data;
        }

    }

    ...

    ?>
```

Perl

The changes are also straightforward in Perl, as shown in Listing 5.14c.

LISTING 5.14c   Character Strings in Perl

```perl
package MyContentHandler;

use base qw(XML::SAX::Base);

sub start_document {
    my $self = shift;

    print "Document START\n";

    $self->{text} = '';
}

sub end_document {
    my $self = shift;
    print "Document END\n";
}

sub start_element {
    my $self = shift;
    my $el   = shift;

    $self->display_text();
...
    print "-" x 20, "\n";
}

sub end_element {
    my $self = shift;
    my $el   = shift;

    $self->display_text();
...
    print "-" x 20, "\n";
```

LISTING 5.14c   Continued

```
    }

    sub display_text {
        my $self = shift;
        if ( defined( $self->{text} )
            && $self->{text} ne "" )
        {
            print "  Text: [$self->{text}]\n";
            $self->{text} = '';
        }
    }

    sub characters {
        my $self = shift;
        my $text = shift;

        $self->{text} .= $text->{Data};
    }
    ...
```

ignorableWhitespace()

In some cases, whitespace is not reported with the **characters** event, but rather with the **ignorableWhitespace** event.

Just overriding the **ignoreableWhitespace()** method isn't enough to see these events, though. The parser must be able to distinguish between normal characters and ignorable whitespace. One way to do this is by providing a DTD or a reference to a DTD, as in

```
<?xml version="1.0"?>
<!DOCTYPE votes SYSTEM "votes.dtd">
<votes totalVotes="5" xmlns:extra="http://www.vanguardreport.com/extra">
...
```

Listing 5.15 shows the new event handler and associated methods.

LISTING 5.15   The **ignorableWhitespace** Event

```
    ...
    public void characters (char[] ch, int start, int length)
    {
        thisText.append(ch, start, length);
    }

    public void ignorableWhitespace (char[] ch, int start, int length)
    {
     println("---- Ignorable: [" + new String(ch, start, length) + "]");
    }
}
```

With these measures in place, the output changes slightly, as shown in Listing 5.16.

LISTING 5.16   Ignorable Whitespace

```
Document START
Element START: votes
    Attribute: totalVotes="5"
-------------------
---- Ignorable: []
---- Ignorable: [
]
---- Ignorable: [    ]
Element START: voter
    Attribute: personid="Emp1"
    Attribute: status="primary"
-------------------
---- Ignorable: []
---- Ignorable: [
]
---- Ignorable: [        ]
Element START: vote
-------------------
    TEXT: [Dregraal]
Element END: vote
-------------------
---- Ignorable: []
---- Ignorable: [
]
---- Ignorable: [        ]
Element START: comments
...
```

Notice that the normal element text is still shown as part of the `characters()` event. Notice also that because we're not aggregating the whitespace as we did with the characters, a single block of whitespace may be reported as a series of events.

Other Events

These are not the only events that the parser might trigger, of course. Others include

- `startPrefixMapping(String prefix, String uri)`--This event occurs when a namespace is in scope.

- `endPrefixMapping(String prefix)`—This event occurs when the namespace goes out of scope.

- `processingInstruction(String target, String data)`—This event occurs when the parser encounters a processing instruction.

- `skippedEntity(String name)`—This event occurs when the parser encounters an externally defined entity that is not expanded. (We'll talk more about entities in Chapter 7, "Document Type Definitions [DTDs].")

Creating the Application

Now we have the means to access all the information we need, so it's time to start using it. In this section, we'll tally the votes for each candidate, stopping when the winner is clear.

Detecting Votes

In the previous section, "Handling Events," we looked at gathering text. Now we need to weed out everything but the text that belongs to the **vote** element.

With a DOM application, this would be a simple matter, because we could just retrieve the **vote** element and get the text node, or if we had the text node, check the name of the parent element. With SAX, neither of these options is available to us, because SAX handles only one event at a time. By the time it's gotten to the characters, it's well past the name of the element.

Our only option, then, is to use what we know about the flow of these events, as shown in Listing 5.17.

LISTING 5.17   Detecting Votes

```
import org.xml.sax.helpers.DefaultHandler;
import org.xml.sax.Attributes;

public class DataProcessor extends DefaultHandler
{
   public DataProcessor ()
   {
      super();
   }

   StringBuffer thisText = new StringBuffer();
   int sTally = 0;
   int dTally = 0;

   //----------------
   //UTILITY METHODS
   //--------------
   public static void println(String arg) {
      System.out.println(arg);
   }

   //-------------
   //EVENT METHODS
   //-------------
   public void startDocument() { }
   public void endDocument() { }
   public void ignorableWhitespace (char[] ch, int start, int length) { }

   public void startElement (String namespaceUri, String localName,
                   String qualifiedName, Attributes attributes) {
      thisText.delete(0, thisText.length());
```

LISTING 5.17   Continued

```
        }

        public void endElement (String namespaceUri, String localName,
                        String qualifiedName)
        {
            if (localName.equals("vote")){
                if (thisText.toString().equals("Sparkle")){
                    sTally = sTally + 1;
                } else if (thisText.toString().equals("Dregraal")){
                    dTally = dTally + 1;
                }
            }
            thisText.delete(0, thisText.length());
        }

        public void characters (char[] ch, int start, int length)
        {
            thisText.append(ch, start, length);
        }

    }
```

We've made some major changes for this portion of the application. First of all, the methods we're not using now have empty implementations. We also have the option of removing them altogether. We've also stripped out the output statements.

As for the votes themselves, we know that they consist of the text between the start of a **vote** element and the end of a **vote** element. So the easiest way to record a vote is simply to clear out **thisText** at the start of every element and check the name of each element when it ends to see whether it's a **vote** element. If it is, the **thisText** variable contains the text of the vote.

From there, we're simply adding up the votes as they come in.

Determining the Winner

We've detected and added up the votes, so determining the winner is simply a matter of comparing tallies when all is said and done. Fortunately, we have an event for just such a situation: **endDocument()**. The new class is shown in Listing 5.18.

LISTING 5.18   Determining the Winner

```
import org.xml.sax.helpers.DefaultHandler;
import org.xml.sax.Attributes;

public class DataProcessor extends DefaultHandler
{
...
    public static void println(String arg) {
        System.out.println(arg);
    }
```

LISTING 5.18   Continued

```
        public void outputResults(){
            if (sTally > dTally) {
                println("SPARKLE is the winner!");
            } else if (dTally > sTally) {
                println("DREGRAAL is the winner!");
            } else {
                println("It's a TIE!");
            }
        }

        //------------
        //EVENT METHODS
        //------------
        public void startDocument() { }

        public void endDocument() {
            outputResults();
        }

        public void ignorableWhitespace (char[] ch, int start, int length) { }
    ...
```

This method simply compares the two tallies and outputs the winner. Keeping the logic in a separate method will make our lives easier later, when we want to stop parsing arbitrarily.

Given the sample file, the application shows that Dregraal is the winner.

```
DREGRAAL is the winner!
```

Stopping When You've Had Enough

One of the major advantages of SAX is the ability to stop parsing when you have all the information you need. In this section, we'll talk about how to do this.

In our case, we only want the application to keep counting if it needs to; if Dregraal is 150 votes ahead of Sparkle and there are only 149 uncounted votes, there's no way Sparkle can catch up, so we know Dregraal is the winner. Listings 5.19a–e show how to keep track of the margin and the potential votes.

Java

LISTING 5.19a   Interrupting a Parse in Java

```
    ...
    import org.xml.sax.SAXException;

    public class DataProcessor extends DefaultHandler
    {
    ...
        int dTally = 0;
```

LISTING 5.19a *Continued*

```
    int totalVotes = 0;
    int votesLeft = 0;

    //---------------
...

    public void startElement (String namespaceUri, String localName,
                    String qualifiedName, Attributes attributes) {
      thisText.delete(0, thisText.length());

      if (localName.equals("votes")) {
        totalVotes = Integer.parseInt(attributes.getValue("totalVotes"));
        votesLeft = totalVotes;
      }
    }

    public void endElement (String namespaceUri, String localName,
                    String qualifiedName) throws SAXException
    {
      if (localName.equals("vote")){
        if (thisText.toString().equals("Sparkle")){
          sTally = sTally + 1;
        } else if (thisText.toString().equals("Dregraal")){
          dTally = dTally + 1;
        }

        int spread = sTally - dTally;
        if (spread < 0) {
          spread = spread * -1;
        }

        votesLeft = votesLeft - 1;
        if (votesLeft > 0) {
          if (spread > votesLeft) {
            outputResults();
            throw new SAXException("Definitive answer after "+
                            (totalVotes - votesLeft)+" votes.");
          }
        }
      }
      thisText.delete(0, thisText.length());
    }

    public void characters (char[] ch, int start, int length)
    {
        thisText.append(ch, start, length);
    }
  }
}
```

Let's take this step by step. First we make note of how many votes there are in total so that we can determine how many votes are left at any given time, from the **totalVotes** attribute of the **votes** element. After we tally the current vote, we check the spread (margin) between the two candidates, making sure that the number is positive. Next, we update the number of votes left and if there are any, we compare that number to the spread.

If the spread is greater than the number of votes left, there's no way for the candidate with fewer votes to catch up, so we want to display the results and stop parsing. We do this by throwing a `SAXException`. The results are shown here:

```
DREGRAAL is the winner!
SAX Exception: Definitive answer after 4 votes.
```

Notice that the output text "SAX Exception" is nowhere to be found in `DataProcessor`. So where did it come from?

To find the answer, we have to go back to `MainSaxApp`:

```
...
    try {

...

        reader.parse(file);

    } catch (IOException ioe) {
        System.out.println("IO Exception: "+ioe.getMessage());
    } catch (SAXException se) {
        System.out.println("SAX Exception: "+se.getMessage());
    }
...
```

The flow goes like this: The parser sends the events to the `DataProcessor` class, which handles them. When the `endElement()` method throws the exception—notice that we had to alter the signature to specify that it could—there's nothing in `DataProcessor` to catch it, so it bubbles up to the calling object, `MainSaxApp`, where it's caught.

You could also use this method to create and catch your own custom exceptions based on business logic, which would allow you to take various actions based on the type of exception or the message it carries. The important thing is that by throwing an exception, you can stop parsing at any time without killing the application.

C++

Before we discuss stopping the parser, note that there have been many changes to the `MySAXContentHandler.cpp` and `.h` files. Listing 5.19b shows the complete listing of these files. Make the necessary changes to your code.

LISTING 5.19b   The C++ Application So Far

```
class MySAXContentHandler : public ISAXContentHandler
{
public:
    MySAXContentHandler();
    virtual ~MySAXContentHandler();
```

LISTING 5.19b   *Continued*

```
long __stdcall QueryInterface(const struct _GUID &,void ** );
unsigned long __stdcall AddRef(void);
unsigned long __stdcall Release(void);

virtual HRESULT STDMETHODCALLTYPE putDocumentLocator(
    /* [in] */ ISAXLocator __RPC_FAR *pLocator);

virtual HRESULT STDMETHODCALLTYPE startDocument(void);

virtual HRESULT STDMETHODCALLTYPE endDocument(void);

virtual HRESULT STDMETHODCALLTYPE startPrefixMapping(
    /* [in] */ wchar_t __RPC_FAR *pwchPrefix,
    /* [in] */ int cchPrefix,
    /* [in] */ wchar_t __RPC_FAR *pwchUri,
    /* [in] */ int cchUri);

virtual HRESULT STDMETHODCALLTYPE endPrefixMapping(
    /* [in] */ wchar_t __RPC_FAR *pwchPrefix,
    /* [in] */ int cchPrefix);

virtual HRESULT STDMETHODCALLTYPE startElement(
    /* [in] */ wchar_t __RPC_FAR *pwchNamespaceUri,
    /* [in] */ int cchNamespaceUri,
    /* [in] */ wchar_t __RPC_FAR *pwchLocalName,
    /* [in] */ int cchLocalName,
    /* [in] */ wchar_t __RPC_FAR *pwchQualifiedName,
    /* [in] */ int cchQualifiedName,
    /* [in] */ ISAXAttributes __RPC_FAR *pAttributes);

virtual HRESULT STDMETHODCALLTYPE endElement(
    /* [in] */ wchar_t __RPC_FAR *pwchNamespaceUri,
    /* [in] */ int cchNamespaceUri,
    /* [in] */ wchar_t __RPC_FAR *pwchLocalName,
    /* [in] */ int cchLocalName,
    /* [in] */ wchar_t __RPC_FAR *pwchQualifiedName,
    /* [in] */ int cchQualifiedName);

virtual HRESULT STDMETHODCALLTYPE characters(
    /* [in] */ wchar_t __RPC_FAR *pwchChars,
    /* [in] */ int cchChars);

virtual HRESULT STDMETHODCALLTYPE ignorableWhitespace(
    /* [in] */ wchar_t __RPC_FAR *pwchChars,
    /* [in] */ int cchChars);

virtual HRESULT STDMETHODCALLTYPE processingInstruction(
    /* [in] */ wchar_t __RPC_FAR *pwchTarget,
    /* [in] */ int cchTarget,
    /* [in] */ wchar_t __RPC_FAR *pwchData,
    /* [in] */ int cchData);
```

LISTING 5.19b Continued

```cpp
            virtual HRESULT STDMETHODCALLTYPE skippedEntity(
                /* [in] */ wchar_t __RPC_FAR *pwchName,
                /* [in] */ int cchName);

    private:
            wchar_t wchText[1000];
            int sTally,
                dTally,
                totalVotes,
                votesLeft;

            void MySAXContentHandler::PrintVarStr(
                /* [in] */ const wchar_t * pwchFmt,
                /* [in] */ const wchar_t __RPC_FAR *pwchElement,
                /* [in] */ int cchElement);

            void MySAXContentHandler::outputResults(void);
    };
    #include "stdafx.h"
    #include "MySAXContentHandler.h"

    MySAXContentHandler::MySAXContentHandler()
    {
    }

    MySAXContentHandler::~MySAXContentHandler()
    {
    }

    HRESULT STDMETHODCALLTYPE MySAXContentHandler::putDocumentLocator(
                /* [in] */ ISAXLocator __RPC_FAR *pLocator
                )
    {
        return S_OK;
    }

    HRESULT STDMETHODCALLTYPE MySAXContentHandler::startDocument()
    {
        wchText[0] = 0;
        sTally = 0;
        dTally = 0;
        totalVotes = 0;
        votesLeft = 0;
        return S_OK;
    }

    HRESULT STDMETHODCALLTYPE MySAXContentHandler::endDocument()
    {
        outputResults();
        return S_OK;
    }
```

LISTING 5.19b   *Continued*

```
HRESULT STDMETHODCALLTYPE MySAXContentHandler::startPrefixMapping(
            /* [in] */ wchar_t __RPC_FAR *pwchPrefix,
            /* [in] */ int cchPrefix,
            /* [in] */ wchar_t __RPC_FAR *pwchUri,
            /* [in] */ int cchUri)
{
    return S_OK;
}

HRESULT STDMETHODCALLTYPE MySAXContentHandler::endPrefixMapping(
            /* [in] */ wchar_t __RPC_FAR *pwchPrefix,
            /* [in] */ int cchPrefix)
{
    return S_OK;
}

HRESULT STDMETHODCALLTYPE MySAXContentHandler::startElement(
            /* [in] */ wchar_t __RPC_FAR *pwchNamespaceUri,
            /* [in] */ int cchNamespaceUri,
            /* [in] */ wchar_t __RPC_FAR *pwchLocalName,
            /* [in] */ int cchLocalName,
            /* [in] */ wchar_t __RPC_FAR *pwchQualifiedName,
            /* [in] */ int cchQualifiedName,
            /* [in] */ ISAXAttributes __RPC_FAR *pAttributes)
{
    int numAttributes, cchLocalAttName, cchLocalAttValue;
    wchar_t *pwchLocalAttName, *pwchLocalAttValue, buffer[10];

    wchText[0] = 0;
    buffer[0] = 0;
    if (wcsncmp(L"votes", pwchLocalName, cchLocalName) == 0)
    {
        pAttributes->getLength(&numAttributes);
        for (int i = 0; i < numAttributes; i++)
        {
            pAttributes->getLocalName(i, &pwchLocalAttName, &cchLocalAttName);
            if(wcsncmp(L"totalVotes", pwchLocalAttName, cchLocalAttName) == 0)
            {
                pAttributes->getValue(i, &pwchLocalAttValue, &cchLocalAttValue);
                wcsncat(&*buffer, pwchLocalAttValue, cchLocalAttValue);
                totalVotes = _wtoi(buffer);
                votesLeft = totalVotes;
            }
        }
    }
    return S_OK;
}

HRESULT STDMETHODCALLTYPE MySAXContentHandler::endElement(
            /* [in] */ wchar_t __RPC_FAR *pwchNamespaceUri,
            /* [in] */ int cchNamespaceUri,
            /* [in] */ wchar_t __RPC_FAR *pwchLocalName,
```

LISTING 5.19b Continued

```
                    /* [in] */ int cchLocalName,
                    /* [in] */ wchar_t __RPC_FAR *pwchQualifiedName,
                    /* [in] */ int cchQualifiedName)
    {
        if (wcsncmp(L"vote", pwchLocalName, cchLocalName) == 0)
        {
            if (wcsncmp(L"Sparkle", wchText, wcslen(wchText)) == 0)
                sTally++;
            else if (wcsncmp(L"Dregraal", wchText, wcslen(wchText)) == 0)
                dTally++;
            votesLeft--;
        }
        int spread = sTally - dTally;
        if (spread < 0)
            spread = abs(spread);
        if (votesLeft > 0)
        {
            if (spread > votesLeft)
            {
                outputResults();
                printf("Definitive answer after %i votes.\n", totalVotes - votesLeft);
                return E_FAIL;
            }
        }
        wchText[0] = 0;
        return S_OK;
    }

    HRESULT STDMETHODCALLTYPE MySAXContentHandler::characters(
                    /* [in] */ wchar_t __RPC_FAR *pwchChars,
                    /* [in] */ int cchChars)
    {
        wcsncat(&*wchText, pwchChars, cchChars);
        return S_OK;
    }

    HRESULT STDMETHODCALLTYPE MySAXContentHandler::ignorableWhitespace(
                    /* [in] */ wchar_t __RPC_FAR *pwchChars,
                    /* [in] */ int cchChars)
    {
        return S_OK;
    }

    HRESULT STDMETHODCALLTYPE MySAXContentHandler::processingInstruction(
                    /* [in] */ wchar_t __RPC_FAR *pwchTarget,
                    /* [in] */ int cchTarget,
                    /* [in] */ wchar_t __RPC_FAR *pwchData,
                    /* [in] */ int cchData)
    {
        return S_OK;
    }
```

LISTING 5.19b   *Continued*

```c
HRESULT STDMETHODCALLTYPE MySAXContentHandler::skippedEntity(
            /* [in] */ wchar_t __RPC_FAR *pwchVal,
            /* [in] */ int cchVal)
{
    return S_OK;
}

long __stdcall MySAXContentHandler::QueryInterface(const struct _GUID &riid,
                                            void ** ppvObject)
{
    return 0;
}

unsigned long __stdcall MySAXContentHandler::AddRef()
{
    return 0;
}

unsigned long __stdcall MySAXContentHandler::Release()
{
    return 0;
}

void MySAXContentHandler::PrintVarStr(
            /* [in] */ const wchar_t * pwchFmt,
            /* [in] */ const wchar_t __RPC_FAR *pwchElement,
            /* [in] */ int cchElement)
{
    static wchar_t buffer[500];
  cchElement = cchElement > 499 ? 499 : cchElement;
    wcsncpy(buffer, pwchElement, cchElement);
    buffer[cchElement] = 0;
    wprintf(pwchFmt, buffer);
}

void MySAXContentHandler::outputResults()
{
    if (sTally > dTally)
        printf("SPARKLE is the winner!\n");
    else if (dTally > sTally)
        printf("DREGRAAL is the winner!\n");
    else
        printf("It's a TIE!\n");
}
```

Unlike Java, MSXML does not support the **SAXException** object. All the parser exceptions are handled as COM calls to the **ISAXErrorHandler** methods. Currently, only the **fatalError()** method is called and this means that any error encountered will terminate parsing. You can force an error to occur by returning a non **S_OK** return value from any **ISAXContentHandler** method. For example, the following **if** clause appears in the **endElement()** method:

```
...
if (spread > votesLeft)
{
    outputResults();
    printf("Definitive answer after %i votes.\n", totalVotes - votesLeft);
    return E_FAIL;
...
```

This is similar to the Java code, but after printing the results, the application prints the message that was part of the `SAXException` in the Java sample and then returns `E_FAIL`. The `E_FAIL` return value causes the invocation of the `fatalError()` method of the `MySAXErrorHandler`, which in turn terminates the parser.

Visual Basic .NET

There have also been many changes to the `MyContentHandler.vb` file, shown in Listing 5.19c.

LISTING 5.19c   The Visual Basic .NET Application So Far

```
Public Class MyContentHandler
    Implements MSXML2.IVBSAXContentHandler

    Dim myForm As New SAXMainForm()
    Dim thisText As String
    Dim sTally As Integer = 0
    Dim dTally As Integer = 0
    Dim totalVotes As Integer = 0
    Dim votesLeft As Integer = 0

    Public Sub New(ByVal FormInst As SAXMainForm)
        myForm = FormInst
    End Sub

    Public Sub startDocument() _
                        Implements MSXML2.IVBSAXContentHandler.startDocument

    End Sub

    Public Sub endDocument() Implements MSXML2.IVBSAXContentHandler.endDocument
        outputResults()
    End Sub

    Public Sub startElement(ByRef strNamespaceURI As String, _
                        ByRef strLocalName As String, _
                        ByRef strQName As String, _
                        ByVal oAttributes As MSXML2.IVBSAXAttributes) _
                        Implements MSXML2.IVBSAXContentHandler.startElement
        Dim i As Short

        thisText = Nothing
        If strLocalName.Equals("votes") Then
            For i = 0 To (oAttributes.length - 1)
```

LISTING 5.19c   Continued

```
                If oAttributes.getQName(i) = "totalVotes" Then
                    totalVotes = Val(oAttributes.getValue(i))
                End If
            Next
            votesLeft = totalVotes
        End If
    End Sub

    Public Sub endElement(ByRef strNamespaceURI As String, _
                        ByRef strLocalName As String, _
                        ByRef strQName As String) _
                        Implements MSXML2.IVBSAXContentHandler.endElement
        Dim spread As Short

        If strLocalName.Equals("vote") Then
            If thisText.Equals("Sparkle") Then
                sTally = sTally + 1
            ElseIf thisText.Equals("Dregraal") Then
                dTally = dTally + 1
            End If
            votesLeft = votesLeft - 1
        End If
        spread = sTally - dTally
        If spread < 0 Then
            spread = spread * -1
        End If
        If votesLeft > 0 Then
            If spread > votesLeft Then
                outputResults()
                Err.Raise(vbObjectError + 1, "ContentHandler.endElement", _
                        "Definitive answer after " & (totalVotes - votesLeft) _
                                        & " votes." & vbCrLf)
            End If
        End If
        thisText = Nothing
    End Sub

    Public Sub characters(ByRef strChars As String) _
                            Implements MSXML2.IVBSAXContentHandler.characters
        strChars = Replace(strChars, vbLf, vbCrLf)
        thisText = thisText & strChars
    End Sub

    Public Sub ignorableWhitespace(ByRef strChars As String) Implements
MSXML2.IVBSAXContentHandler.ignorableWhitespace

    End Sub

    Public Sub startPrefixMapping(ByRef strPrefix As String, _
                            ByRef strURI As String) _
                        Implements MSXML2.IVBSAXContentHandler.startPrefixMapping
```

LISTING 5.19c   Continued

```
        End Sub

        Public Sub endPrefixMapping(ByRef strPrefix As String) _
                    Implements MSXML2.IVBSAXContentHandler.endPrefixMapping

        End Sub

        Public WriteOnly Property documentLocator() As MSXML2.IVBSAXLocator _
                    Implements MSXML2.IVBSAXContentHandler.documentLocator
            Set(ByVal Value As MSXML2.IVBSAXLocator)

            End Set
        End Property

        Public Sub processingInstruction(ByRef strTarget As String, _
                            ByRef strData As String) _
                    Implements MSXML2.IVBSAXContentHandler.processingInstruction

        End Sub

        Public Sub skippedEntity(ByRef strName As String) _
                    Implements MSXML2.IVBSAXContentHandler.skippedEntity

        End Sub

        Public Sub displayText()
            If Len(thisText) > 0 Then
                myForm.OutputText = "    TEXT: [" & thisText & "]" & vbCrLf
                thisText = Nothing
            End If
        End Sub

        Public Sub outputResults()
            If (sTally > dTally) Then
                myForm.OutputText = "SPARKLE is the winner!" & vbCrLf
            ElseIf (dTally > sTally) Then
                myForm.OutputText = "DREGRAAL is the winner!" & vbCrLf
            Else
                myForm.OutputText = "It's a TIE!" & vbCrLf
            End If
        End Sub
    End Class
```

PHP

Our mini-SAX class doesn't use any fancy error reporting or handling, so it will just die() if it encounters an exception (see Listing 5.19d).

LISTING 5.19d   Interrupting a Parse in PHP

```php
<?php

require_once("sax.inc");

class DataProcessor extends SAXHandler
{
    ...

    var $d_tally     = 0;
    var $total_votes = 0;
    var $votes_left  = 0;

    ...

    function start_element ($name, $attr)
    {
        $this->text = '';

        if ($name == "votes") {
            $this->total_votes = $attr['totalVotes'];
            $this->votes_left  = $this->total_votes;
        }

    }

    function end_element ($name)
    {

        if ($name == "vote") {

            switch ($this->text) {
                case "Sparkle":
                    $this->s_tally++;
                    break;
                case "Dregraal":
                    $this->d_tally++;
                    break;
            }

            $this->votes_left--;
            $spread = abs($this->s_tally - $this->d_tally);

            if (($this->votes_left > 0) &&
                ($spread > $this->votes_left))
                {
                    $this->output_results();
                    die("Definitive answer after " .
                        ($this->total_votes - $this->votes_left) .
                        " votes");
                }
        }

    }
```

LISTING 5.19d   Continued

```
        $this->text = '';
    }

    function characters ($data)
    {
        $this->text .= $data;
    }

}

...

?>
```

Perl

In Perl, `XML::SAX` stores element attributes in a hash keyed by "James Clark" notation: The namespace of the attribute is bundled in with its local name—even when it's in the default namespace. The namespace comes before the local name, in braces. So to find an attribute called `totalVotes`, as in Listing 5.19e, you'll have to look it up like this:

```
$el->{Attributes}->{'{}totalVotes'}
```

You'll see this notation in several other places in the examples that follow.

Also note that `XML::SAX` defines its own exception class, `XML::SAX::Exception`, which we're using in Listing 5.19e in place of `die()`. This is what `XML::SAX` uses internally to report exceptions; it winds up calling `die()` anyway, so we can catch it with an `eval {}` block just like `die()`.

LISTING 5.19e   Interrupting a Parse in Perl

```perl
package MyContentHandler;

use base qw(XML::SAX::Base);

use XML::SAX::Exception;

sub start_document {
    my $self = shift;

    $self->{text} = '';

    $self->{s_tally}     = 0;
    $self->{d_tally}     = 0;
    $self->{total_votes} = 0;
    $self->{votes_left}  = 0;
}

sub end_document {
```

LISTING 5.19e   *Continued*

```perl
    my $self = shift;

    $self->output_results();
}

sub start_element {
    my $self = shift;
    my $el   = shift;

    $self->{text} = 0;

    if ( $el->{LocalName} eq 'votes' ) {
        $self->{total_votes} =
          $el->{Attributes}->{'{}totalVotes'}->{Value};
        $self->{votes_left} = $self->{total_votes};
    }
}

sub end_element {
    my $self = shift;
    my $el   = shift;

    if ( $el->{LocalName} eq 'vote' ) {

        if ( $self->{text} =~ /Sparkle/ ) {
            $self->{s_tally}++;
        } elsif ( $self->{text} =~ /Dregraal/ ) {
            $self->{d_tally}++;
        }
        $self->{votes_left}--;

        my $spread = abs( $self->{s_tally} - $self->{d_tally} );

        if (   ( $self->{votes_left} > 0 )
            && ( $spread > $self->{votes_left} ) )
        {

            $self->output_results();
            throw XML::SAX::Exception(
                Message => "Definitive answer after "
                  . ( $self->{total_votes} - $self->{votes_left} )
                  . " votes.\n" );
        }
    }
    $self->{text} = '';
}

sub output_results {
    my $self = shift;

    if ( $self->{s_tally} > $self->{d_tally} ) {
        print "SPARKLE is the winner!\n";
```

LISTING 5.19e Continued

```
      } elsif ( $self->{d_tally} > $self->{s_tally} ) {
         print "DREGRAAL is the winner!\n";
      } else {
         print "It's a TIE!\n";
      }
   }

   ...
```

Filters and Chains

Based on the output of the current application, Dregraal the Enchreenomalpolymorph appears to have won the election. But did he really?

At this point, the application is counting all votes, whether they come from primary voters or symbionts. Because the symbionts aren't supposed to vote for themselves, we need a way to filter out votes that don't come from primaries.

To do that, we'll create an XMLFilter.

What Does a Filter Do?

Normally, SAX events flow directly from the parser to the content handler to the application, as shown in Figure 5.2.

FIGURE 5.2
The normal flow of events.

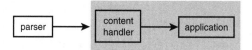

In our case, the content handler actually performs all the application logic, so there is no separate application, but that's not a requirement.

When we create a filter, we insert it into the flow between the parser and the content handler. We can then use the filter to alter the data before it's ever processed, as shown in Figure 5.3. In this case, we want to create a filter that will look for votes from non-primary voters and disable them.

FIGURE 5.3
A filter sits between the XMLReader and the content handler.

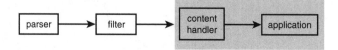

Creating the Filter

There are a number of ways to create an XMLFilter, but the most straightforward is to simply extend the XMLFilterImpl class, as shown in Listings 5.20a–e.

Java

LISTING 5.20a   Creating the Filter in Java

```
import org.xml.sax.XMLReader;
import org.xml.sax.helpers.XMLFilterImpl;

public class DataFilter extends XMLFilterImpl
{

    public DataFilter ()
    {
    }

    public DataFilter (XMLReader parent)
    {
        super(parent);
    }

}
```

The XMLFilterImpl implements all the methods in the XMLReader class as well as all the methods in the DefaultHandler class. This means that it is capable of performing the roles of both classes.

C++

In C++, the situation is a bit more complex. The ISAXXMLFilter class is an abstract base class derived from ISAXXMLReader. This means that you have to implement the functionality of your filter class and override the methods of the reader class as well. You also have to derive your filter class from any SAX handlers whose events you want to filter and implement that functionality as well, as shown in Listing 5.20b.

LISTING 5.20b   Creating the Filter in C++

Create a header file named MySAXFilter.h and add this code to the file:

```
class MySAXFilter : public ISAXXMLFilter, ISAXContentHandler
{
public:
    MySAXFilter();
    virtual ~MySAXFilter();

        long STDMETHODCALLTYPE QueryInterface(const struct _GUID &,void **);
        unsigned long STDMETHODCALLTYPE AddRef(void);
        unsigned long STDMETHODCALLTYPE Release(void);
```

LISTING 5.20b   *Continued*

```
//ISAXXMLFilter methods
virtual HRESULT STDMETHODCALLTYPE getParent(
    /* [out, retval] */ ISAXXMLReader ** ppReader);

virtual HRESULT STDMETHODCALLTYPE putParent(
    /* [in] */ ISAXXMLReader * pReader);

virtual HRESULT STDMETHODCALLTYPE getFeature(
    /*[in]*/ unsigned short * pwchName,
    /*[out,retval]*/ VARIANT_BOOL * pvfValue);

virtual HRESULT STDMETHODCALLTYPE putFeature(
    /*[in]*/ unsigned short * pwchName,
    /*[in]*/ VARIANT_BOOL vfValue);

virtual HRESULT STDMETHODCALLTYPE getProperty(
    /*[in]*/ unsigned short * pwchName,
    /*[out,retval]*/ VARIANT * pvarValue);

virtual HRESULT STDMETHODCALLTYPE putProperty(
    /*[in]*/ unsigned short * pwchName,
    /*[in]*/ VARIANT varValue);

virtual HRESULT STDMETHODCALLTYPE getEntityResolver(
    /*[out,retval]*/ struct ISAXEntityResolver * * ppResolver);

virtual HRESULT STDMETHODCALLTYPE putEntityResolver(
    /*[in]*/ struct ISAXEntityResolver * pResolver);

virtual HRESULT STDMETHODCALLTYPE getContentHandler(
    /*[out,retval]*/ struct ISAXContentHandler * * ppHandler);

virtual HRESULT STDMETHODCALLTYPE putContentHandler(
    /*[in]*/ struct ISAXContentHandler * pHandler);

virtual HRESULT STDMETHODCALLTYPE getDTDHandler(
    /*[out,retval]*/ struct ISAXDTDHandler * * ppHandler);

virtual HRESULT STDMETHODCALLTYPE putDTDHandler(
    /*[in]*/ struct ISAXDTDHandler * pHandler);

virtual HRESULT STDMETHODCALLTYPE getErrorHandler(
    /*[out,retval]*/ struct ISAXErrorHandler * * ppHandler);

virtual HRESULT STDMETHODCALLTYPE putErrorHandler(
    /*[in]*/ struct ISAXErrorHandler * pHandler);

virtual HRESULT STDMETHODCALLTYPE getBaseURL(
    /*[out,retval]*/ unsigned short * * ppwchBaseUrl);

virtual HRESULT STDMETHODCALLTYPE putBaseURL(
    /*[in]*/ unsigned short * pwchBaseUrl);
```

LISTING 5.20b   Continued

```
virtual HRESULT STDMETHODCALLTYPE getSecureBaseURL(
    /*[out,retval]*/ unsigned short * * ppwchSecureBaseUrl);

virtual HRESULT STDMETHODCALLTYPE putSecureBaseURL(
    /*[in]*/ unsigned short * pwchSecureBaseUrl);

virtual HRESULT STDMETHODCALLTYPE parse(
    /*[in]*/ VARIANT varInput);

virtual HRESULT STDMETHODCALLTYPE parseURL(
    /*[in]*/ unsigned short * pwchUrl);

//ISAXContentHandler methods
virtual HRESULT STDMETHODCALLTYPE putDocumentLocator(
    /*[in]*/ struct ISAXLocator * pLocator);

virtual HRESULT STDMETHODCALLTYPE startDocument();

virtual HRESULT STDMETHODCALLTYPE endDocument();

virtual HRESULT STDMETHODCALLTYPE startPrefixMapping(
    /*[in]*/ unsigned short * pwchPrefix,
    /*[in]*/ int cchPrefix,
    /*[in]*/ unsigned short * pwchUri,
    /*[in]*/ int cchUri);

virtual HRESULT STDMETHODCALLTYPE endPrefixMapping(
    /*[in]*/ unsigned short * pwchPrefix,
    /*[in]*/ int cchPrefix);

virtual HRESULT STDMETHODCALLTYPE startElement(
    /*[in]*/ unsigned short * pwchNamespaceUri,
    /*[in]*/ int cchNamespaceUri,
    /*[in]*/ unsigned short * pwchLocalName,
    /*[in]*/ int cchLocalName,
    /*[in]*/ unsigned short * pwchQName,
    /*[in]*/ int cchQName,
    /*[in]*/ struct ISAXAttributes * pAttributes);

virtual HRESULT STDMETHODCALLTYPE endElement(
    /*[in]*/ unsigned short * pwchNamespaceUri,
    /*[in]*/ int cchNamespaceUri,
    /*[in]*/ unsigned short * pwchLocalName,
    /*[in]*/ int cchLocalName,
    /*[in]*/ unsigned short * pwchQName,
    /*[in]*/ int cchQName);

virtual HRESULT STDMETHODCALLTYPE characters(
    /*[in]*/ unsigned short * pwchChars,
    /*[in]*/ int cchChars);
```

LISTING 5.20b   Continued

```
            virtual HRESULT STDMETHODCALLTYPE ignorableWhitespace(
                /*[in]*/ unsigned short * pwchChars,
                /*[in]*/ int cchChars);

            virtual HRESULT STDMETHODCALLTYPE processingInstruction(
                /*[in]*/ unsigned short * pwchTarget,
                /*[in]*/ int cchTarget,
                /*[in]*/ unsigned short * pwchData,
                /*[in]*/ int cchData);

            virtual HRESULT STDMETHODCALLTYPE skippedEntity(
                /*[in]*/ unsigned short * pwchName,
                /*[in]*/ int cchName);

    private:
        ISAXXMLReader* pSAXReader;
        struct ISAXContentHandler* pbaseContentHandler;
        HRESULT hr;

    };
```

Now create a C++ file called **MySAXFilter.cpp** and enter the following code:

```
#include "stdafx.h"
#include "MySAXFilter.h"

extern bool isValidVote;
wchar_t wchText[];

MySAXFilter::MySAXFilter()
{

}

MySAXFilter::~MySAXFilter()
{

}

HRESULT STDMETHODCALLTYPE MySAXFilter::getParent(
            /* [out, retval] */ ISAXXMLReader ** ppReader)
{
        *ppReader = pSAXReader;
    return hr;
}

HRESULT STDMETHODCALLTYPE MySAXFilter::putParent(
            /* [in] */ ISAXXMLReader * pReader)
{
        pSAXReader = pReader;
    return hr;
}
```

LISTING 5.20b   Continued

```
HRESULT STDMETHODCALLTYPE MySAXFilter::getFeature(
            /*[in]*/ unsigned short * pwchName,
            /*[out,retval]*/ VARIANT_BOOL * pvfValue)
{
    hr = pSAXReader->getFeature(pwchName, pvfValue);
    return hr;
}

HRESULT STDMETHODCALLTYPE MySAXFilter::putFeature(
            /*[in]*/ unsigned short * pwchName,
            /*[in]*/ VARIANT_BOOL vfValue)
{
    hr = pSAXReader->putFeature(pwchName, vfValue);
    return hr;
}

HRESULT STDMETHODCALLTYPE MySAXFilter::getProperty(
            /*[in]*/ unsigned short * pwchName,
            /*[out,retval]*/ VARIANT * pvarValue)
{
    hr = pSAXReader->getProperty(pwchName, pvarValue);
    return hr;
}

HRESULT STDMETHODCALLTYPE MySAXFilter::putProperty(
            /*[in]*/ unsigned short * pwchName,
            /*[in]*/ VARIANT varValue)
{
    hr = pSAXReader->putProperty(pwchName, varValue);
    return hr;
}

HRESULT STDMETHODCALLTYPE MySAXFilter::getEntityResolver(
            /*[out,retval]*/ struct ISAXEntityResolver * * ppResolver)
{
    hr = pSAXReader->getEntityResolver(ppResolver);
    return hr;
}

HRESULT STDMETHODCALLTYPE MySAXFilter::putEntityResolver(
            /*[in]*/ struct ISAXEntityResolver * pResolver)
{
    hr = pSAXReader->putEntityResolver(pResolver);
    return hr;
}

HRESULT STDMETHODCALLTYPE MySAXFilter::getContentHandler(
            /*[out,retval]*/ struct ISAXContentHandler * * ppHandler)
{
    hr = pSAXReader->getContentHandler(ppHandler);
    return hr;
}
```

LISTING 5.20b Continued

```
HRESULT STDMETHODCALLTYPE MySAXFilter::putContentHandler(
          /*[in]*/ struct ISAXContentHandler * pHandler)
{
    hr = pSAXReader->putContentHandler(pHandler);
    return hr;
}

HRESULT STDMETHODCALLTYPE MySAXFilter::getDTDHandler(
          /*[out,retval]*/ struct ISAXDTDHandler * * ppHandler)
{
    hr = pSAXReader->getDTDHandler(ppHandler);
    return hr;
}

HRESULT STDMETHODCALLTYPE MySAXFilter::putDTDHandler(
          /*[in]*/ struct ISAXDTDHandler * pHandler)
{
    hr = pSAXReader->putDTDHandler(pHandler);
    return hr;
}

HRESULT STDMETHODCALLTYPE MySAXFilter::getErrorHandler(
          /*[out,retval]*/ struct ISAXErrorHandler * * ppHandler)
{
    hr = pSAXReader->getErrorHandler(ppHandler);
    return hr;
}

HRESULT STDMETHODCALLTYPE MySAXFilter::putErrorHandler(
          /*[in]*/ struct ISAXErrorHandler * pHandler)
{
    hr = pSAXReader->putErrorHandler(pHandler);
    return hr;
}

HRESULT STDMETHODCALLTYPE MySAXFilter::getBaseURL(
          /*[out,retval]*/ unsigned short * * ppwchBaseUrl)
{
    hr = pSAXReader->getBaseURL(ppwchBaseUrl);
    return hr;
}

HRESULT STDMETHODCALLTYPE MySAXFilter::putBaseURL(
          /*[in]*/ unsigned short * pwchBaseUrl)
{
    hr = pSAXReader->putBaseURL(pwchBaseUrl);
    return hr;
}

HRESULT STDMETHODCALLTYPE MySAXFilter::getSecureBaseURL(
          /*[out,retval]*/ unsigned short * * ppwchSecureBaseUrl)
{
```

LISTING 5.20b   Continued

```
      hr = pSAXReader->getSecureBaseURL(ppwchSecureBaseUrl);
      return hr;
}

HRESULT STDMETHODCALLTYPE MySAXFilter::putSecureBaseURL(
            /*[in]*/ unsigned short * pwchSecureBaseUrl)
{
      hr = pSAXReader->putSecureBaseURL(pwchSecureBaseUrl);
      return hr;
}

HRESULT STDMETHODCALLTYPE MySAXFilter::parse(
            /*[in]*/ VARIANT varInput)
{
      hr = pSAXReader->parse(varInput);
      return hr;
}

HRESULT STDMETHODCALLTYPE MySAXFilter::parseURL(
            /*[in]*/ unsigned short * pwchUrl)
{
      hr = pSAXReader->parseURL(pwchUrl);
      return hr;
}

HRESULT STDMETHODCALLTYPE MySAXFilter::startElement(
            /* [in] */ wchar_t __RPC_FAR *pwchNamespaceUri,
            /* [in] */ int cchNamespaceUri,
            /* [in] */ wchar_t __RPC_FAR *pwchLocalName,
            /* [in] */ int cchLocalName,
            /* [in] */ wchar_t __RPC_FAR *pwchQualifiedName,
            /* [in] */ int cchQualifiedName,
            /* [in] */ ISAXAttributes __RPC_FAR *pAttributes)
{
      hr = pbaseContentHandler->startElement(pwchNamespaceUri, cchNamespaceUri,
                                    pwchLocalName, cchLocalName,
                                    pwchQualifiedName, cchQualifiedName,
                                    pAttributes);
      return hr;
}

HRESULT STDMETHODCALLTYPE MySAXFilter::characters(
            /* [in] */ wchar_t __RPC_FAR *pwchChars,
            /* [in] */ int cchChars)
{
      hr = pbaseContentHandler->characters(pwchChars, cchChars);
      return hr;
}

HRESULT STDMETHODCALLTYPE MySAXFilter::putDocumentLocator(
            /*[in]*/ struct ISAXLocator * pLocator)
{
```

LISTING 5.20b Continued

```
    hr = pbaseContentHandler->putDocumentLocator(pLocator);
    return hr;
}

HRESULT STDMETHODCALLTYPE MySAXFilter::startDocument()
{
    hr = pbaseContentHandler->startDocument();
    return hr;
}

HRESULT STDMETHODCALLTYPE MySAXFilter::endDocument()
{
    hr = pbaseContentHandler->endDocument();
    return hr;
}

HRESULT STDMETHODCALLTYPE MySAXFilter::startPrefixMapping(
            /*[in]*/ unsigned short * pwchPrefix,
            /*[in]*/ int cchPrefix,
            /*[in]*/ unsigned short * pwchUri,
            /*[in]*/ int cchUri)
{
    hr = pbaseContentHandler->startPrefixMapping(pwchPrefix, cchPrefix,
                                                     pwchUri, cchUri);
    return hr;
}

HRESULT STDMETHODCALLTYPE MySAXFilter::endPrefixMapping(
            /*[in]*/ unsigned short * pwchPrefix,
            /*[in]*/ int cchPrefix)
{
    hr = pbaseContentHandler->endPrefixMapping(pwchPrefix, cchPrefix);
    return hr;
}

HRESULT STDMETHODCALLTYPE MySAXFilter::endElement(
            /*[in]*/ unsigned short * pwchNamespaceUri,
            /*[in]*/ int cchNamespaceUri,
            /*[in]*/ unsigned short * pwchLocalName,
            /*[in]*/ int cchLocalName,
            /*[in]*/ unsigned short * pwchQName,
            /*[in]*/ int cchQName)
{
    hr = pbaseContentHandler->endElement(pwchNamespaceUri, cchNamespaceUri,
                                         pwchLocalName, cchLocalName,
                                         pwchQName, cchQName);
    return hr;
}

HRESULT STDMETHODCALLTYPE MySAXFilter::ignorableWhitespace(
            /*[in]*/ unsigned short * pwchChars,
            /*[in]*/ int cchChars)
```

LISTING 5.20b *Continued*

```
{
    hr = pbaseContentHandler->ignorableWhitespace(pwchChars, cchChars);
    return hr;
}

HRESULT STDMETHODCALLTYPE MySAXFilter::processingInstruction(
            /*[in]*/ unsigned short * pwchTarget,
            /*[in]*/ int cchTarget,
            /*[in]*/ unsigned short * pwchData,
            /*[in]*/ int cchData)
{
    hr = pbaseContentHandler->processingInstruction(pwchTarget, cchTarget,
                                            pwchData, cchData);
    return hr;
}

HRESULT STDMETHODCALLTYPE MySAXFilter::skippedEntity(
            /*[in]*/ unsigned short * pwchName,
            /*[in]*/ int cchName)
{
    hr = pbaseContentHandler->skippedEntity(pwchName, cchName);
    return hr;
}

long __stdcall MySAXFilter::QueryInterface(const struct _GUID &,void ** )
{
        return 0;
}

unsigned long __stdcall MySAXFilter::AddRef()
{
        return 0;
}

unsigned long __stdcall MySAXFilter::Release()
{
        return 0;
}
```

Visual Basic .NET

In Visual Basic .NET, the **IVBSAXXMLFilter** class is an abstract base class that is derived from **IDispatch**. This means that you have to implement the functionality of this filter class. All Visual Basic classes must either be derived from **IUnknown** or **IDispatch**, so it's also necessary to derive your filter class from **IVBSAXXMLReader** and any SAX handlers whose events you want to filter and implement that functionality as well. Create a new class file named **MyFilter.vb** and enter the code as shown in Listing 5.20c.

LISTING 5.20c   Creating the Filter in Visual Basic .NET

```
Public Class MyFilter
    Implements MSXML2.IVBSAXContentHandler
    Implements MSXML2.IVBSAXXMLReader
    Implements MSXML2.IVBSAXXMLFilter

    Private parentReader As MSXML2.SAXXMLReader
    Private cHandler As MyContentHandler
    Dim myForm As New SAXMainForm()

    'Implementation of the parent property for IVBSAXXMLFilter
    Public Property parent() As MSXML2.IVBSAXXMLReader _
                            Implements MSXML2.IVBSAXXMLFilter.parent
        Get
            Return parentReader
        End Get
        Set(ByVal Value As MSXML2.IVBSAXXMLReader)
            parentReader = Value
        End Set
    End Property

    'Implementation of the IVBSAXContentHandler methods for IVBSAXXMLFilter
    Public Sub startElement(ByRef strNamespaceURI As String,_
                        ByRef strLocalName As String,_
                        ByRef strQName As String,_
                        ByVal oAttributes As MSXML2.IVBSAXAttributes)_
                            Implements MSXML2.IVBSAXContentHandler.startElement
        cHandler.startElement(strNamespaceURI, strLocalName,
    strQName, oAttributes)
    End Sub

    Public Sub characters(ByRef strChars As String)_
                            Implements MSXML2.IVBSAXContentHandler.characters
            cHandler.characters(strChars)
    End Sub

    Public WriteOnly Property documentLocator() As MSXML2.IVBSAXLocator_
                            Implements MSXML2.IVBSAXContentHandler.
documentLocator
        Set(ByVal Value As MSXML2.IVBSAXLocator)
            cHandler.documentLocator = Value
        End Set
    End Property

    Public Sub endDocument() Implements MSXML2.IVBSAXContentHandler.endDocument
        cHandler.endDocument()
    End Sub

    Public Sub endElement(ByRef strNamespaceURI As String,_
                        ByRef strLocalName As String, ByRef strQName As String)_
                            Implements MSXML2.IVBSAXContentHandler.endElement
        cHandler.endElement(strNamespaceURI, strLocalName, strQName)
    End Sub
```

LISTING 5.20c   Continued

```
      Public Sub endPrefixMapping(ByRef strPrefix As String)_
                              Implements MSXML2.IVBSAXContentHandler.
➥endPrefixMapping
          cHandler.endPrefixMapping(strPrefix)
      End Sub

      Public Sub ignorableWhitespace(ByRef strChars As String)_
                              Implements MSXML2.IVBSAXContentHandler.
➥ignorableWhitespace
          cHandler.ignorableWhitespace(strChars)
      End Sub

      Public Sub processingInstruction(ByRef strTarget As String,_
                                  ByRef strData As String)_
                              Implements MSXML2.IVBSAXContentHandler.
➥processingInstruction
          cHandler.processingInstruction(strTarget, strData)
      End Sub

      Public Sub skippedEntity(ByRef strName As String)_
                              Implements MSXML2.IVBSAXContentHandler.skippedEntity
          cHandler.skippedEntity(strName)
      End Sub

      Public Sub startDocument()_
                              Implements MSXML2.IVBSAXContentHandler.startDocument
          cHandler.startDocument()
      End Sub

      Public Sub startPrefixMapping(ByRef strPrefix As String,_
                                  ByRef strURI As String)_
                              Implements MSXML2.IVBSAXContentHandler.
➥startPrefixMapping
          cHandler.startPrefixMapping(strPrefix, strURI)
      End Sub

      'Implementation of the IVBSAXXMLReader methods for IVBSAXXMLFilter
      Public Property baseURL() As String Implements MSXML2.IVBSAXXMLReader.baseURL
          Get
              Return parentReader.baseURL
          End Get
          Set(ByVal Value As String)
              parentReader.baseURL = Value
          End Set
      End Property

      Public Property contentHandler() As MSXML2.IVBSAXContentHandler_
                              Implements MSXML2.IVBSAXXMLReader.contentHandler
          Get
              Return cHandler
          End Get
          Set(ByVal Value As MSXML2.IVBSAXContentHandler)
```

LISTING 5.20c   Continued

```
            cHandler = Value
        End Set
    End Property

    Public Property dtdHandler() As MSXML2.IVBSAXDTDHandler_
                            Implements MSXML2.IVBSAXXMLReader.dtdHandler
        Get
            Return parentReader.dtdHandler
        End Get
        Set(ByVal Value As MSXML2.IVBSAXDTDHandler)
            parentReader.dtdHandler = Value
        End Set
    End Property

    Public Property entityResolver() As MSXML2.IVBSAXEntityResolver_
                            Implements MSXML2.IVBSAXXMLReader.entityResolver
        Get
            Return parentReader.entityResolver
        End Get
        Set(ByVal Value As MSXML2.IVBSAXEntityResolver)
            parentReader.entityResolver = Value
        End Set
    End Property

    Public Property errorHandler() As MSXML2.IVBSAXErrorHandler_
                            Implements MSXML2.IVBSAXXMLReader.errorHandler
        Get
            Return parentReader.errorHandler
        End Get
        Set(ByVal Value As MSXML2.IVBSAXErrorHandler)
            parentReader.errorHandler = Value
        End Set
    End Property

    Public Function getFeature(ByVal strName As String) As Boolean_
                            Implements MSXML2.IVBSAXXMLReader.getFeature
        parentReader.getFeature(strName)
    End Function

    Public Function getProperty(ByVal strName As String) As Object_
                            Implements MSXML2.IVBSAXXMLReader.getProperty
        parentReader.getProperty(strName)
    End Function

    Public Sub parse(ByVal varInput As Object)_
                            Implements MSXML2.IVBSAXXMLReader.parse
        parentReader.parse(varInput)
    End Sub

    Public Sub parseURL(ByVal strURL As String)_
                            Implements MSXML2.IVBSAXXMLReader.parseURL
        parentReader.parseURL(strURL)
    End Sub
```

LISTING 5.20c   Continued

```
    Public Sub putFeature(ByVal strName As String, ByVal fValue As Boolean)_
                        Implements MSXML2.IVBSAXXMLReader.putFeature
        parentReader.putFeature(strName, fValue)
    End Sub

    Public Sub putProperty(ByVal strName As String, ByVal varValue As Object)_
                        Implements MSXML2.IVBSAXXMLReader.putProperty
        parentReader.putProperty(strName, varValue)
    End Sub

    Public Property secureBaseURL() As String_
                        Implements MSXML2.IVBSAXXMLReader.secureBaseURL
        Get
            Return parentReader.secureBaseURL
        End Get
        Set(ByVal Value As String)
            parentReader.secureBaseURL = Value
        End Set
    End Property
End Class
```

PHP

Our mini-SAX class makes no distinction between content filters and content handlers; both are subclasses of `SAXHandler` (see Listing 5.20d).

LISTING 5.20d   Creating the Filter in PHP

```
<?php

require_once("sax.inc");

class DataFilter extends SAXHandler
{
    function DataFilter () { }
}

?>
```

Perl

`XML::SAX` doesn't define a distinct filter class. Like content handlers, filters are subclasses of `XML::SAX::Base` (see Listing 5.20e).

LISTING 5.20e   Creating the Filter in Perl

```
package MyFilter;

use base qw(XML::SAX::Base);

...
```

Inserting the Filter into the Stream

Of course, the filter won't do anything until we insert it into the stream.

Here's what we want to happen: When the parser sends events, we want them to go to the filter, but if the filter doesn't do anything with them, we want them to automatically pass on to our original content handler, the `DataProcessor` object. On the other hand, if the filter *does* do something with the events, we want the modified events to pass on to the `DataProcessor` object.

We'll set this up in Listing 5.21.

LISTING 5.21   Setting the Filter as the Content Handler

```
...
import java.io.IOException;
import org.xml.sax.XMLFilter;

public class MainSaxApp {

    public static void main (String[] args){

        try {

            String parserClass = "org.apache.crimson.parser.XMLReaderImpl";
            XMLReader reader = XMLReaderFactory.createXMLReader(parserClass);

            XMLFilter filter = new DataFilter();
            filter.setParent(reader);

            filter.setContentHandler(new DataProcessor());
            filter.setErrorHandler(new ErrorProcessor());

            InputSource file = new InputSource("votes.xml");
            filter.parse(file);

        } catch (IOException ioe) {
            System.out.println("IO Exception: "+ioe.getMessage());
...
    }
}
```

For the filter to work, we need to take care of both sides of the equation. First, we'll set the `XMLReader` to be the filter's parent. We don't have any methods defined for reading the file, so we'll use the `XMLReader` methods. That takes care of the left side of the equation.

When the `XMLFilter` encounters an event, it can handle the event itself (because it has content handler methods as part of `XMLFilterImpl`) or it can pass it on to another content handler. To put that content handler in place, we'll use `setContentHandler()` on the filter and assign it a new `DataProcessor` method, just as we did for the `XMLReader`.

Finally, we use the `filter` object to parse the file, rather than the `reader` object.

At this point, the filter passes all events on to its content handler, the `DataProcessor`, so executing the application this way produces no changes from before.

Affecting the Data

Now it's time to start actually affecting the data. What we want to do is check each voter, and if the voter is the primary, pass its information on unchanged. If it's not the primary, we want to eliminate its vote. In Listings 5.22a–e, we clear the text for non-primary voters.

Java

LISTING 5.22a   Filtering the Data in Java

```java
import org.xml.sax.XMLReader;
import org.xml.sax.helpers.XMLFilterImpl;
import org.xml.sax.Attributes;
import org.xml.sax.SAXException;

public class DataFilter extends XMLFilterImpl
{

    public DataFilter ()
    {
    }

    public DataFilter (XMLReader parent)
    {
        super(parent);
    }

    boolean isValidVote = false;
    public void startElement (String namespaceUri, String localName,
                    String qualifiedName, Attributes attributes)
                        throws SAXException
    {
        if (localName.equals("voter")) {
            if (attributes.getValue("status").equals("primary")){
                isValidVote = true;
            } else {
                isValidVote = false;
            }
        }
        super.startElement(namespaceUri, localName, qualifiedName, attributes);
    }

    public void characters (char[] ch, int start, int length) throws SAXException
    {

        if (isValidVote) {
            super.characters(ch, start, length);
        } else {
```

LISTING 5.22a   Continued

```
            super.characters(ch, start, 0);
        }
    }
}
```

We only need to override two methods to accomplish the filtering we need. In `startElement()`, we check each voter, and if it's a primary, we set a flag indicating that its vote is valid. In any case, we then pass the unchanged `startElement` event on to the `DataProcessor` object for processing.

The difference comes in the `characters()` method. Here we check the flag and if we're in the midst of the information from a valid voter, we pass it on unchanged. If not, we pass it on without the actual text (using a length of zero). We can take this simplistic approach because the votes are the only text we're actually checking in the content handler. If we were, say, outputting comments, we'd have to be a lot more careful, checking for the current element before determining what to pass on.

Note also that passing events to another handler carries with it the possibility of a `SAXException`, so we need to indicate that our methods might throw this exception.

C++

Listing 5.22b shows the changes to the `MySAXContentHandler.cpp` file.

LISTING 5.22b   Filtering in C++

```
#include "stdafx.h"
#include "MySAXContentHandler.h"

extern bool isValidVote;
extern wchar_t wchText[];

MySAXContentHandler::MySAXContentHandler()
{
}
...
HRESULT STDMETHODCALLTYPE MySAXContentHandler::startDocument()
{
    wchText[0] = 0;
    sTally = 0;
    dTally = 0;
    totalVotes = 0;
    votesLeft = 0;
    votesDropped = 0;
    isValidVote = false;
    return S_OK;
}
...
HRESULT STDMETHODCALLTYPE MySAXContentHandler::startElement(
```

LISTING 5.22b   *Continued*

```
              /* [in] */ wchar_t __RPC_FAR *pwchNamespaceUri,
              /* [in] */ int cchNamespaceUri,
              /* [in] */ wchar_t __RPC_FAR *pwchLocalName,
              /* [in] */ int cchLocalName,
              /* [in] */ wchar_t __RPC_FAR *pwchQualifiedName,
              /* [in] */ int cchQualifiedName,
              /* [in] */ ISAXAttributes __RPC_FAR *pAttributes)
{
    int numAttributes, cchLocalAttName, cchLocalAttValue;
    wchar_t *pwchLocalAttName, *pwchLocalAttValue, buffer[10];

    wchText[0] = 0;
    buffer[0] = 0;

    if (wcsncmp(L"votes", pwchLocalName, cchLocalName) == 0)
    {
        pAttributes->getLength(&numAttributes);
        for (int i = 0; i < numAttributes; i++)
        {
            pAttributes->getLocalName(i, &pwchLocalAttName, &cchLocalAttName);
            if(wcsncmp(L"totalVotes", pwchLocalAttName, cchLocalAttName) == 0)
            {
                pAttributes->getValue(i, &pwchLocalAttValue, &cchLocalAttValue);
                wcsncat(&*buffer, pwchLocalAttValue, cchLocalAttValue);
                totalVotes = _wtoi(buffer);
                votesLeft = totalVotes;
            }
        }
    }
    return S_OK;
}
...
}
```

We also need to make changes to the `MySAXContentHandler.h` file:

```
class MySAXContentHandler : public ISAXContentHandler
{
public:
    MySAXContentHandler();
...
private:
        int sTally,
            dTally,
            totalVotes,
            votesLeft,
            votesDropped;

        void MySAXContentHandler::outputResults(void);
};
```

Now we need to make some changes to the implementation of the `MySAXFilter.cpp` file:

```cpp
#include "stdafx.h"
#include "MySAXFilter.h"
...
HRESULT STDMETHODCALLTYPE MySAXFilter::parseURL(
            /*[in]*/ unsigned short * pwchUrl)
{
    this->getContentHandler(&pbaseContentHandler);
    hr = pSAXReader->putContentHandler(this);
    hr = pSAXReader->parseURL(pwchUrl);
    return hr;
}

HRESULT STDMETHODCALLTYPE MySAXFilter::startElement(
            /* [in] */ wchar_t __RPC_FAR *pwchNamespaceUri,
            /* [in] */ int cchNamespaceUri,
            /* [in] */ wchar_t __RPC_FAR *pwchLocalName,
            /* [in] */ int cchLocalName,
            /* [in] */ wchar_t __RPC_FAR *pwchQualifiedName,
            /* [in] */ int cchQualifiedName,
            /* [in] */ ISAXAttributes __RPC_FAR *pAttributes)
{
    int numAttributes, cchLocalAttName, cchLocalAttValue;
    wchar_t *pwchLocalAttName, *pwchLocalAttValue;

    wchText[0] = 0;

    if(wcsncmp(L"voter", pwchLocalName, cchLocalName) == 0)
    {
        pAttributes->getLength(&numAttributes);
        for (int i = 0; i < numAttributes; i++)
        {
            pAttributes->getLocalName(i, &pwchLocalAttName, &cchLocalAttName);
            if(wcsncmp(L"status", pwchLocalAttName, cchLocalAttName) == 0)
            {
                pAttributes->getValue(i, &pwchLocalAttValue, &cchLocalAttValue);
                if(wcsncmp(L"primary", pwchLocalAttValue, cchLocalAttValue) == 0)
                    isValidVote = true;
                else
                    isValidVote = false;
            }
        }
    }
    hr = pbaseContentHandler->startElement(pwchNamespaceUri, cchNamespaceUri,
                                    pwchLocalName, cchLocalName,
                                    pwchQualifiedName, cchQualifiedName,
                                    pAttributes);

    return hr;
}

HRESULT STDMETHODCALLTYPE MySAXFilter::characters(
            /* [in] */ wchar_t __RPC_FAR *pwchChars,
            /* [in] */ int cchChars)
```

```
{
    if(isValidVote)
        hr = pbaseContentHandler->characters(pwchChars, cchChars);
    return hr;
}
...
}
```

Finally, we make some changes to the main application .cpp file:

```
#include "stdafx.h"
...
#include "MySAXFilter.h"

wchar_t wchText[1000];
bool isValidVote;

int _tmain(int argc, _TCHAR* argv[])
{
...
        if(hr==S_OK)
          {
            MySAXFilter* pFilter = new MySAXFilter();
            hr = pFilter->putParent(pReader);
            //Register the content handler for the XMLReader
                MySAXContentHandler* pContent = new MySAXContentHandler();
                hr = pFilter->putContentHandler(pContent);
...

            mbstowcs(XMLURL, argv[1], (INTERNET_MAX_URL_LENGTH-1));
            hr = pFilter->parseURL(XMLURL);

            //Clean up the XMLReader
                pFilter->Release();
            pReader->Release();
          }
    }
    catch(...)  // For catching standard exceptions.
...
}
```

Visual Basic .NET

Listing 5.22c shows how to implement the functionality of the Java sample in Visual Basic
.NET. We begin by making changes in the MySAXContentHandler.vb file.

LISTING 5.22c   Filtering in Visual Basic .NET

```
Public Class MyContentHandler
    Implements MSXML2.IVBSAXContentHandler

    Dim myForm As New SAXMainForm()
    Dim thisText As String
```

LISTING 5.22c Continued

```
            Dim sTally As Integer = 0
            Dim dTally As Integer = 0
            Dim totalVotes As Integer = 0
            Dim votesLeft As Integer = 0
            Dim votesDropped As Integer = 0
            Private isValidVote As Boolean = False
    ...
            Public Sub startElement(ByRef strNamespaceURI As String,_
                                    ByRef strLocalName As String,_
                                    ByRef strQName As String,_
                                    ByVal oAttributes As MSXML2.IVBSAXAttributes)_
                                        Implements MSXML2.IVBSAXContentHandler.startElement
                Dim i As Short

                thisText = Nothing
                If strLocalName.Equals("votes") Then
                    For i = 0 To (oAttributes.length - 1)
                        If oAttributes.getQName(i) = "totalVotes" Then
                            totalVotes = Val(oAttributes.getValue(i))
                        End If
                    Next
                    votesLeft = totalVotes
                End If
            End Sub

            Public Sub endElement(ByRef strNamespaceURI As String,_
                                  ByRef strLocalName As String, ByRef strQName As String)_
                                      Implements MSXML2.IVBSAXContentHandler.endElement
                Dim spread As Short

                If strLocalName.Equals("vote") Then
                    If isValidVote Then
                        If thisText.Equals("Sparkle") Then
                            sTally = sTally + 1
                        ElseIf thisText.Equals("Dregraal") Then
                            dTally = dTally + 1
                        End If
                    Else
                        thisText = Nothing
                        votesDropped = votesDropped + 1
                    End If
                    votesLeft = votesLeft - 1
                Else
                    thisText = Nothing
                End If

                spread = sTally - dTally
                If spread < 0 Then
                    spread = spread * -1
                End If
                If votesLeft > 0 Then
                    If spread > votesLeft Then
```

LISTING 5.22c   *Continued*

```
                outputResults()
                Err.Raise(vbObjectError + 1, "ContentHandler.endElement",_
                        "Definitive answer after " &_
                        (totalVotes - votesLeft - votesDropped)_
                        & " votes." & vbCrLf)
            End If
        End If
        thisText = Nothing
    End Sub

    Public Sub characters(ByRef strChars As String)_
                    Implements MSXML2.IVBSAXContentHandler.characters
        strChars = Replace(strChars, vbLf, vbCrLf)
        thisText = thisText & strChars
    End Sub
...
    Public Property ValidVote() As Boolean
        Get
            Return isValidVote
        End Get
        Set(ByVal Value As Boolean)
            isValidVote = Value
        End Set
    End Property
End Class
```

Next, we need to add additional functionality to the **MyFilter** class:

```
Public Class MyFilter
...
    Public Sub startElement(ByRef strNamespaceURI As String,_
                        ByRef strLocalName As String,_
                        ByRef strQName As String,_
                        ByVal oAttributes As MSXML2.IVBSAXAttributes)_
                            Implements MSXML2.IVBSAXContentHandler.startElement

        Dim i As Short

        If strLocalName.Equals("voter") Then
            For i = 0 To (oAttributes.length - 1)
                If oAttributes.getQName(i) = "status" Then
                    If oAttributes.getValue(i) = "primary" Then
                        cHandler.ValidVote = True
                    Else
                        cHandler.ValidVote = False
                    End If
                End If
            Next
        End If
        cHandler.startElement(strNamespaceURI, strLocalName,_
                        strQName, oAttributes)
    End Sub
```

```
    Public Sub characters(ByRef strChars As String)_
                        Implements MSXML2.IVBSAXContentHandler.characters
        If cHandler.ValidVote Then
            cHandler.characters(strChars)
        Else
            cHandler.characters("")
        End If
    End Sub
...
    Public Property contentHandler() As MSXML2.IVBSAXContentHandler_
                        Implements MSXML2.IVBSAXXMLReader.contentHandler
        Get
            Return cHandler
        End Get
        Set(ByVal Value As MSXML2.IVBSAXContentHandler)
            cHandler = Value
        End Set
    End Property
...
    Public Sub parseURL(ByVal strURL As String)_
                        Implements MSXML2.IVBSAXXMLReader.parseURL
        parentReader.contentHandler = Me
        parentReader.parseURL(strURL)
    End Sub
...
End Class
```

Finally, we change the main form's code so that it uses the filter instead of the reader to parse the XML:

```
Public Class SAXMainForm
...
    Private Sub btnParse_Click(ByVal sender As System.Object,_
                        ByVal e As System.EventArgs) Handles btnParse.Click
        Dim Reader As New MSXML2.SAXXMLReader()
        Dim Filter As New MyFilter()
...
        txtOutput.Text = ""
        Filter.parent = Reader
        Filter.contentHandler = ContentHandler
        Filter.errorHandler = ErrorHandler

        On Error GoTo ErrorSub
        Filter.parseURL(txtFileName.Text)
        Exit Sub
...
End Class
```

PHP

In PHP, we can just add the functionality to the **DataFilter** and insert it into the stream between the **SAXParser** and the **DataProcessor**, as shown in Listing 5.22d.

LISTING 5.22d   *Filtering the Data in PHP*

```php
<?php

require_once("sax.inc");

class DataFilter extends SAXHandler
{
    function DataFilter () { }

    var $is_valid_vote = false;

    function start_element ($name, $attr)
    {
        if ($name == "voter") {
            if ($attr['status'] == "primary") {
                $this->is_valid_vote = true;
            } else {
                $this->is_valid_vote = false;
            }
        }

        $this->handler->start_element($name,$attr);
    }

    function characters ($data)
    {
        if ($this->is_valid_vote) {
            $this->handler->characters($data);
        } else {
            $this->handler->characters('');
        }
    }
}

class DataProcessor extends SAXHandler
{
    var $text         = '';
    var $s_tally      = 0;
    var $d_tally      = 0;
    var $total_votes  = 0;
    var $votes_left   = 0;
    var $votes_dropped = 0;

    ...

    function end_element ($name)
    {
        if ($name == "vote") {

            switch ($this->text) {
```

LISTING 5.22d   Continued

```
                    case "Sparkle":
                        $this->s_tally++;
                        break;
                    case "Dregraal":
                        $this->d_tally++;
                        break;
                    case "":
                        $this->votes_dropped++;
                        break;
                }
                ...

                if (($this->votes_left > 0) &&
                    ($spread > $this->votes_left))
                    {
                        $this->output_results();
                        die("Definitive answer after " .
                            ($this->total_votes -
                             $this->votes_left -
                             $this->votes_dropped) .
                            " votes");
                    }
            }

            $this->text = '';
        }

        ...

    }

    $parser  =& new SAXParser();
    $handler =& new DataProcessor();
    $filter  =& new DataFilter();
    $filter->set_handler($handler);
    $parser->set_handler($filter);

    $parser->parse("votes.xml") or die("Parse failed");

    ?>
```

Perl

When filtering in Perl, watch out for the "James Clark" notation in the `Attributes` hash. And note that because the character handler is expecting a hash, we can't send an invalid vote through as `undef`; instead, we'll pass in a character data hash with an empty `Data` element, as shown in Listing 5.22e.

LISTING 5.22e   *Filtering the Data in Perl*

```perl
package MyFilter;

use base qw(XML::SAX::Base);

sub start_element {
    my $self = shift;
    my $el   = shift;

    if ( $el->{LocalName} eq "voter" ) {

        if ( $el->{Attributes}->{'{}status'}->{Value} eq 'primary' ) {
            $self->{valid_vote} = 1;
        } else {
            $self->{valid_vote} = 0;
        }
    }

    $self->SUPER::start_element($el);
}

sub characters {
    my $self = shift;
    my $text = shift;

    if ( $self->{valid_vote}') {
        $self->SUPER::characters($text);
    } else {
        $self->SUPER::characters( { Data => '' } );
    }
}

package MyContentHandler;

use base qw(XML::SAX::Base);

use XML::SAX::Exception;

sub start_document {
    my $self = shift;

    $self->{text} = '';

    $self->{s_tally}       = 0;
    $self->{d_tally}       = 0;
    $self->{total_votes}   = 0;
    $self->{votes_left}    = 0;
    $self->{votes_dropped} = 0;
}

sub end_document {
    my $self = shift;
```

LISTING 5.22e Continued

```perl
        $self->output_results();
    }

    sub start_element {
        my $self = shift;
        my $el   = shift;

        $self->{text} = '';

        if ( $el->{LocalName} eq 'votes' ) {
            $self->{total_votes} =
              $el->{Attributes}->{'{}totalVotes'}->{Value};
            $self->{votes_left} = $self->{total_votes};
        }
    }

    sub end_element {
        my $self = shift;
        my $el   = shift;

        if ( $el->{LocalName} eq 'vote' ) {

            if ( $self->{text} =~ /Sparkle/ ) {
                $self->{s_tally}++;
            } elsif ( $self->{text} =~ /Dregraal/ ) {
                $self->{d_tally}++;
            } elsif ( !$self->{text} ) {
                $self->{votes_dropped}++;
            }
            $self->{votes_left}--;

            my $spread = abs( $self->{s_tally} - $self->{d_tally} );

            if (   ( $self->{votes_left} > 0 )
                && ( $spread > $self->{votes_left} ) )
            {

                $self->output_results();
                throw XML::SAX::Exception(
                    Message => "Definitive answer after "
                      . (
                        $self->{total_votes} - $self->{votes_left} -
                          $self->{votes_dropped}
                      )
                      . " votes.\n"
                );
            }
        }
        $self->{text} = '';
    }

    sub output_results {
```

LISTING 5.22e   Continued

```perl
        my $self = shift;

        if ( $self->{s_tally} > $self->{d_tally} ) {
            print "SPARKLE is the winner!\n";
        } elsif ( $self->{d_tally} > $self->{s_tally} ) {
            print "DREGRAAL is the winner!\n";
        } else {
            print "It's a TIE!\n";
        }
    }
}

...


package main;

use XML::SAX;

$XML::SAX::ParserPackage = 'XML::SAX::Expat';

my $factory = XML::SAX::ParserFactory->new();
my $filter = MyFilter->new();
$filter->set_content_handler( MyContentHandler->new() );
my $parser = $factory->parser(
    Handler => $filter
);
eval { $parser->parse_uri('votes.xml'); };

print "Error parsing file: $@" if $@;
```

The Final Step

The final step is to account for the missing votes so that our vote totals aren't off, as shown in Listing 5.23.

LISTING 5.23   Accounting for Missing Votes

```java
...
public class DataProcessor extends DefaultHandler
{
...
   int totalVotes = 0;
   int votesLeft = 0;
   int votesDropped = 0;

...
   public void endElement (String namespaceUri, String localName,
                    String qualifiedName) throws SAXException
   {
       if (localName.equals("vote")){
```

LISTING 5.23   Continued

```
            if (thisText.toString().equals("Sparkle")){
               sTally = sTally + 1;
            } else if (thisText.toString().equals("Dregraal")){
               dTally = dTally + 1;
            } else if (thisText.toString().equals("")) {
               votesDropped = votesDropped + 1;
            }
   ...
            if (votesLeft > 0) {
               if (spread > votesLeft) {
                  outputResults();
                  throw new SAXException("Definitive answer after "+(totalVotes -
                                          votesLeft - votesDropped)+" votes.");
               }
            }
         }
         thisText.delete(0, thisText.length());
      }
   ...
```

With the filter in place and our changes made, the final results are as follows:

```
DREGRAAL is the winner!
SAX Exception: Definitive answer after 2 votes.
```

The ultimate result didn't change because the eliminated votes were split between the two candidates, but the dropped votes indicate that the filter was in place.

Summary

The Simple API for XML (SAX) provides an event-based means for parsing XML information. Rather than looking at the data as a tree, it views it as a series of events, such as `startElement()` and `characters()`. This allows you to deal with only the information that you need, and to stop parsing when you've got the appropriate information.

On the downside, SAX is a read-only API. You can only analyze the information; you can't use it to change the original data. You also need to build in your own logic for determining context, as the parser only knows about one event at a time and has no concept of parent and child nodes.

SAX works by creating an `XMLReader`, which sends events to a content handler. The content handler has methods for each of the standard events, and these methods are executed when the events occur. You can also create an `XMLFilter`, which sits between the `XMLReader` and the content handler and has the ability to alter information as it goes by. `XMLFilter`s can be chained together, linking the input of one to the output of the next. We'll see some examples of this in Chapter 10, "Transformation and Applications."

Review Questions

1. What is an event-based API?

2. Under what conditions would an event-based API be preferable to an object-based API?

3. Under what conditions would an object-based API be preferable to an event-based API?

4. What are the two main event handlers defined for SAX?

5. What does an `XMLReader` do?

6. What does an `XMLFilter` do?

Programming Exercises

1. Write an application that takes the simple XML document from this chapter, parses it using SAX, and outputs it to the screen. Whitespace is optional. If possible in your programming language, do this with a single class. Be sure to include the XML declaration and namespace definitions.

2. Create a filter that appends `_test` to the end of every element name. Use it with the solution to exercise 1.

3. Alter the sample program in this chapter to output voter comments and complete vote tallies. (Don't stop parsing when the winner is clear.)

CHAPTER 6

VALIDATION

You will learn about the following in this chapter:

- The purpose of validation
- Document Type Definitions
- XML Schemas

- Activating a validating parser
- Working with validation errors

V*alidation* is the act of comparing an XML document against a predetermined structure. This means that at this point in the book, we have a choice: We can talk about building the predetermined structure (in the form of Document Type Definitions and XML schemas) or we can talk about the applications that do the comparison.

Unfortunately, this is sort of a "chicken and egg" dilemma. We can't talk about validating documents without something to validate against, but if we discuss the details without talking about the applications, you won't have any way to test your DTDs and schemas to make sure you're creating them properly.

I decided on a compromise. This chapter will discuss the bare essentials of DTDs and schemas, but will go into the details of creating programs that use them. In Chapter 7, "Document Type Definitions (DTDs)," we'll go into detail regarding all the structures you can create, and in Chapter 8, "XML Schemas," we'll discuss the use of schemas for validation.

What Is Validation?

The creation of an XML file is a fairly straightforward process. You create tags and content, and go on from there. This provides you with a tremendous amount of flexibility. Unfortunately, it also provides everyone else with a tremendous amount of flexibility.

The problem is that if you need your data to be in a particular form, whether for display or for programmatic analysis, this flexibility, which includes the flexibility to make mistakes, can be deadly.

Hence the need for validation. Validation is the process of making sure that a document contains the expected XML, in the expected form, with the expected pieces in the expected order. A document that has been validated is said to be *valid*.

Note the difference between a valid document and a well-formed document. A well-formed document conforms to the rules of the XML 1.0 Recommendation—opening and closing tags, quotes around attributes, and so on—but may contain any data in any order in any place. A valid document is always well-formed, but a well-formed document might not be valid.

A Basic DOCTYPE

The most basic way to specify the information that must be contained in an XML file is to use a DOCTYPE definition. This is a special construct at the top of the file that specifies the elements, attributes, and other objects that must be part of the file. DOCTYPE definitions can be present right there on the page or in another file.

Listing 6.1 shows the beginning of a DOCTYPE definition for the sample XML file in Chapter 5, "XML Streams: The Simple API for XML (SAX)."

LISTING 6.1   A Simple DOCTYPE Definition

```
<?xml version="1.0"?>
<!DOCTYPE votes [
   <! - Definitions will go here  - >
]>
<votes totalVotes="5">
    <voter personid="Emp1" status="primary">
       <vote>Dregraal</vote>
...
```

This construct, the DOCTYPE definition, specifies the root element for the document (in this case, votes) and the structure, which we haven't defined yet. A DTD, as you'll see in Chapter 7, can have internal and external subsets. Here we're showing just the internal subset, which means that all the data is included within this file.

Defining the Elements

DTDs specify content models for elements. A content model defines what components an element must contain, the order in which these components must appear, and the number of times each may appear. The elements from the preceding chapter can be defined as shown in Listing 6.2.

LISTING 6.2   Defining Elements

```
<?xml version="1.0"?>
<!DOCTYPE votes [
   <!ELEMENT votes (voter*)>
   <!ELEMENT voter (vote, comments)>
```

LISTING 6.2   Continued

```
      <!ELEMENT vote (#PCDATA)>
      <!ELEMENT comments (#PCDATA)>
]>
<votes totalVotes="5">
   <voter personid="Emp1" status="primary">
...
```

In this case, the **votes** element can contain zero or more **voter** elements, as shown by the asterisk (*) modifier in the content model. A **voter** element, on the other hand, must contain exactly one **vote** element, followed by exactly one **comments** element. Order counts. Finally, the **vote** and **comments** elements can contain general text, or parsed character data.

Changing Namespaces

To make things simple, I've moved the **comments** element back into the default namespace.

Defining the Attributes

The DTD can also specify attributes. Attributes are added to the DTD by means of an attribute list (or **ATTLIST** construct) that associates them with an element, as shown in Listing 6.3.

LISTING 6.3   Adding Attributes

```
<?xml version="1.0"?>
<!DOCTYPE votes [
   <!ELEMENT votes (voter*)>
   <!ELEMENT voter (vote, comments)>
   <!ELEMENT vote (#PCDATA)>
   <!ELEMENT comments (#PCDATA)>
   <!ATTLIST voter personid CDATA #REQUIRED
                   status CDATA "symbiont">
   <!ATTLIST votes totalVotes CDATA #REQUIRED>
]>
<votes totalVotes="5">
   <voter personid="Emp1" status="primary">
...
```

Here the **personid**, **status**, and **totalVotes** attributes are specified for their respective elements. In this case, all three attributes consist of character data, or **CDATA**. The **personid** and **totalVotes** attributes must be present on their respective elements, but the **status** attribute can be omitted, in which case it is assumed to have a value of **symbiont**.

Attribute Data Types

DTDs allow for a number of different data types, which are detailed in Chapter 7.

External DTDs

Chapter 7 includes a complete discussion of internal versus external DTDs, but for now understand that all of this information can be represented in a separate file, accessible by either a **SYSTEM** or a **PUBLIC** identifier, as shown in Listing 6.4.

LISTING 6.4   Moving the DTD to Another File

```
<?xml version="1.0"?>
<!DOCTYPE votes PUBLIC "-//Vanguard Resort IT//DTD Voting System 2.0//EN"
                                                        "votes.dtd">
<votes totalVotes="5">
    <voter personid="Emp1" status="primary">
...
```

Here we've included both a **SYSTEM** and a **PUBLIC** identifier. The formal public identifier

```
-//Vanguard Resort IT//DTD Voting System 2.0//EN
```

is meant as a "lookup" value. (We'll discuss the details of its construction in Chapter 7.) The system is meant to resolve this string to a specific location, usually using a repository of addresses. Just in case the system can't do this and doesn't know what the public identifier represents, however, it's common to include a system identifier as a fallback option. The system identifier is typically a URI, such as the relative URI **votes.dtd** in Listing 6.4.

Now that we've got something to validate against, let's start building our applications.

Validating Documents

Nowhere in the XML 1.0 Recommendation will you find any explanation of how a parser should determine whether it's supposed to validate the content. As a result, almost every implementation performs this function differently, which makes it difficult to give a general overview.

Although we talked about DOM parsers first when it came to parsing, we need to talk about SAX parsers first when it comes to validation. The reason for this is very simple: Many DOM parsers are actually built on top of SAX parsers and use the SAX events to build the DOM representation of the document. For this reason, you may find that you need to use SAX-related methods to turn on validation in your particular DOM parser.

SAX Features

SAX provides a very specific means of turning on validation. Validation is a "feature" that can be turned on or off, or rather set to **true** or **false**.

Version 2 of SAX (which we've been using up to now) defines 12 standard features, only 2 of which are actually required for a parser implementation. The most commonly used are

- `http://xml.org/sax/features/validation`

- `http://xml.org/sax/features/namespaces` (required)

- `http://xml.org/sax/features/namespace-prefixes` (required)

- `http://xml.org/sax/features/external-general-entities`

- `http://xml.org/sax/features/external-parameter-entities`

Notice that these are all specified as URIs. The reason for this is that anybody who is implementing a parser can come up with features. By specifying a URI unique to them, parser implementers decrease the likelihood that programmers will accidentally choose the wrong feature. As with namespace URIs, feature URIs don't have to represent an actual Web address (and in fact, these don't).

The `true`/`false` value for a feature is set using the `setFeature()` method. If the application attempts to set a feature that the implementation doesn't recognize, it will cause a `SAXNotRecognizedException`, which we can then deal with appropriately.

Let's turn on validation so we can see these features in action.

Turning on Validation in SAX

We'll start by creating the main application, as shown in Listing 6.5.

LISTING 6.5   Turning on Validation

```
import org.xml.sax.helpers.XMLReaderFactory;
import org.xml.sax.XMLReader;
import org.xml.sax.SAXException;
import org.xml.sax.InputSource;
import java.io.IOException;

public class MainSaxApp {

    public static void main (String[] args){

        try {

            String parserClass = "org.apache.crimson.parser.XMLReaderImpl";
            XMLReader reader = XMLReaderFactory.createXMLReader(parserClass);

            String featureId = "http://xml.org/sax/features/validation";
            reader.setFeature(featureId, true);

            reader.setContentHandler(new DataProcessor());

            InputSource file = new InputSource("votes.xml");
            reader.parse(file);

        } catch (IOException ioe) {
```

LISTING 6.5   *Continued*

```
        System.out.println("IO Exception: "+ioe.getMessage());
    } catch (SAXException se) {
        System.out.println("SAX Exception: "+se.getMessage());
    }

    }
}
```

Notice that we've set the validation feature on the **reader** to **true**. Otherwise, this is virtually the same application we used in Chapter 5.

In this case, we've created a content handler that doesn't actually do anything but announce the start and end of the document, as shown in Listings 6.6a and b.

Java

LISTING 6.6a   The Java Content Handler

```
import org.xml.sax.helpers.DefaultHandler;

public class DataProcessor extends DefaultHandler
{
    public DataProcessor ()
    {
        super();
    }

    public void startDocument() {
        System.out.println("Document start");
    }

    public void endDocument() {
        System.out.println("Document end");
    }

}
```

C++ and Visual Basic .NET

The SAX parser in Microsoft's MSXML version 4.0 doesn't support DTDs for validation. We can perform validation with a SAX-based parser using XSD schemas. XSD schemas are discussed later in this chapter and a sample for C++ and Visual Basic is provided there.

PHP

PHP currently has no internal support for XML validation using DTDs or XML schemas. The only option at this time, if you need to do validation inside PHP, is to build PHP with the sablotron extension, and use Luis Argerich's schematron class. You can find more information on schematron validation in PHP at
http://phpxmlclasses.sourceforge.net/show_doc.php?class=class_schematron.html.

Perl

The XML::Xerces package that we used in Chapter 3, "Manipulating Documents: The Document Object Model (DOM)," and Chapter 4, "Advanced DOM Techniques," includes a fast validating SAX parser whose interface conforms very well to the standard set by the XML::SAX package. It also tracks the emerging standards in the Java world closely. The main practical difference between the base class used here for the content handler (XML::Xerces::PerlContentHandler) and that used in the last chapter (XML::Base) is that XML::Base automatically takes care of chaining handlers and filters for you, but XML::Xerces::PerlContentHandler doesn't.

Listing 6.6b shows the main application and content handler.

LISTING 6.6b   The Perl Content Handler

```perl
package MyContentHandler;

@ISA = qw(XML::Xerces::PerlContentHandler);

sub start_document {
    print "Document START\n";
}

sub end_document {
    print "Document END\n";
}

package main;

use XML::Xerces;

my $file = XML::Xerces::LocalFileInputSource->new("votes.xml");
my $reader = XML::Xerces::XMLReaderFactory::createXMLReader();
my $handler = MyContentHandler->new();

eval {
    $reader->setFeature( "http://xml.org/sax/features/validation", 1 );
    $reader->setContentHandler($handler);
    $reader->parse($file);
};
die XML::Xerces::error($@) if ($@);
```

Running the SAX Application

Now let's remove the DTD, as shown in Listing 6.7.

LISTING 6.7   The Document, Sans DTD

```xml
<?xml version="1.0"?>
<votes totalVotes="5">
    <voter personid="Emp1" status="primary">
```

LISTING 6.7   Continued

```
...
    </voter>
</votes>
```

If we execute the application, we see a simple result:

```
Document start
Document end
```

Notice that there are no errors, even though we set the parser to validate and then left out something to validate against. In fact, errors are being generated, but there's nowhere for them to go.

Creating an Error Handler

Because we haven't created an error handler, our application doesn't show us the many errors generated. Listing 6.8 shows a simple error handler that returns information on each problem the XMLReader encounters.

LISTING 6.8   A Simple Error Handler

```java
import org.xml.sax.helpers.DefaultHandler;
import org.xml.sax.SAXParseException;

public class ErrorProcessor extends DefaultHandler
{

    public ErrorProcessor ()
    {
      super();
    }

    public void error (SAXParseException e) {
        System.out.println("Error: "+e.getMessage());
    }

    public void fatalError (SAXParseException e) {
        System.out.println("Fatal Error: "+e.getMessage());
    }

    public void warning (SAXParseException e) {
        System.out.println("Warning: "+e.getMessage());
    }

}
```

We need to set the error handler on the XMLReader, as in Listings 6.9a and b.

Java

LISTING 6.9a   Setting the Java Error Handler

```
    ...
            String featureId = "http://xml.org/sax/features/validation";
            reader.setFeature(featureId, true);

            reader.setContentHandler(new DataProcessor());
            reader.setErrorHandler(new ErrorProcessor());

            InputSource file = new InputSource("votes.xml");
            reader.parse(file);
    ...
```

Now when we parse the document, we'll see the errors.

Perl

In Perl, if you don't set an error handler, errors will be transparently thrown away. The default error handler included with `XML::Xerces` calls `croak()` on fatal errors, with a message indicating where the parse stopped and why.

Even with an error handler set, as in Listing 6.9b, however, the output is different from the Java version.

LISTING 6.9b   Setting a Perl Error Handler

```
    ...

my $file    = XML::Xerces::LocalFileInputSource->new("votes.xml");
my $reader  = XML::Xerces::XMLReaderFactory::createXMLReader();
my $handler = MyContentHandler->new();

my $error_handler = XML::Xerces::PerlErrorHandler->new();

eval {
    $reader->setFeature( "http://xml.org/sax/features/validation", 1 );
    $reader->setErrorHandler($error_handler);
    $reader->setContentHandler($handler);
    $reader->parse($file);
};
die XML::Xerces::error($@) if ($@);
```

If a Perl application encounters an error in parsing, such as an undeclared element, it simply sends back a message and then dies. Running this application might give us output similar to the following:

```
Document START
Error in eval: ERROR:
FILE:    /home/vanguard/ne_votes.xml
```

LISTING 6.9b   Continued

```
LINE:     3
COLUMN:   23
MESSAGE: Unknown element 'votes'
 at listing_6.9.pl line 38
 at listing_6.9.pl line 40
```

This is the same problem encountered by the Java application ("Hey, I don't know what to do with a **votes** element!"), but in Perl, processing just stops.

Types of Problems

Let's look at the results of parsing the document in Java, as shown in Listing 6.10.

LISTING 6.10   Parsing the Document: Results

```
Document start
Warning: Valid documents must have a <!DOCTYPE declaration.
Error: Element type "votes" is not declared.
Error: Attribute "totalVotes" is not declared for element "votes".
Error: Element type "voter" is not declared.
Error: Attribute "personid" is not declared for element "voter".
Error: Attribute "status" is not declared for element "voter".
Error: Element type "vote" is not declared.
Error: Element type "comments" is not declared.
Error: Attribute "personid" is not declared for element "voter".
Error: Attribute "status" is not declared for element "voter".
Error: Attribute "personid" is not declared for element "voter".
Error: Attribute "status" is not declared for element "voter".
Error: Attribute "personid" is not declared for element "voter".
Error: Attribute "status" is not declared for element "voter".
Error: Attribute "personid" is not declared for element "voter".
Error: Attribute "status" is not declared for element "voter".
Document end
```

Notice that there are two types of problems here: warnings and errors. Neither of these problems with the document keeps the parser from continuing. A fatal error, on the other hand, *does* keep the parser from continuing. Let's change the document so that it's not well-formed, as in Listing 6.11.

LISTING 6.11   A Fatally Flawed Document

```
<?xml version="1.0"?>
<votes totalVotes="5">
    <voter personid="Emp2" status="symbiont">
        <vote>Sparkle</vote>
        <comments>
            Sfgrtng dwesvers melpy ypinee!
        </comments>
</votes>
```

This document is not well-formed because the **voter** element isn't closed. Attempting to parse the document produces the results in Listing 6.12.

LISTING 6.12   Parsing the Fatally Flawed Document

```
Document start
Warning: Valid documents must have a <!DOCTYPE declaration.
Error: Element type "votes" is not declared.
Error: Attribute "totalVotes" is not declared for element "votes".
Error: Element type "voter" is not declared.
Error: Attribute "personid" is not declared for element "voter".
Error: Attribute "status" is not declared for element "voter".
Error: Element type "vote" is not declared.
Error: Element type "comments" is not declared.
Fatal Error: Expected "</voter>" to terminate element starting on line 3.
SAX Exception: Expected "</voter>" to terminate element starting on line 3.
```

Notice that parsing continues after the warnings and errors, but stops after the fatal error, which also causes a **SAXException** that propagates back to the main application.

DOM and Validation

Now let's talk about the DOM parser. Depending on your implementation, your task may be as easy as setting a simple attribute on the parser, or it may be considerably more complicated.

Many parsers allow you to determine whether the parser is validating by simply setting a property, as in Listing 6.13.

LISTING 6.13   Turning On Validation

```
import javax.xml.parsers.DocumentBuilder;
import javax.xml.parsers.DocumentBuilderFactory;
import org.w3c.dom.Document;
import java.io.File;

public class DocumentListing {

   public static void main (String args[]) {
      File docFile = new File("votes.xml");

      Document doc = null;
      try {
         DocumentBuilderFactory dbf = DocumentBuilderFactory.newInstance();
         dbf.setValidating(true);

         DocumentBuilder db = dbf.newDocumentBuilder();

         doc = db.parse(docFile);

      } catch (Exception e) {
         System.out.print("Problem parsing the file.");
```

LISTING 6.13 Continued

```
        }

    }
}
```

Notice that in this case, we're setting validation not on the parser (or `DocumentBuilder` object) but rather on the `DocumentBuilderFactory` that creates the parser. Any parser the factory creates will have validation turned on.

If we run this application on the fatally flawed file, we get the results shown in Listing 6.14.

LISTING 6.14 DOM Parsing Results

```
Warning: validation was turned on but an org.xml.sax.ErrorHandler was not
set, which is probably not what is desired.  Parser will use a default
ErrorHandler to print the first 10 errors.  Please call
the 'setErrorHandler' method to fix this.
Error: URI=file:H:/PrimerPlusXML/ppxmlch6/votes.xml Line=2: Document root
element "votes", must match DOCTYPE root "null".
Error: URI=file:H:/PrimerPlusXML/ppxmlch6/votes.xml Line=2: Document is
invalid: no grammar found.
Problem parsing the file.
```

First, notice that all three problem types are represented. A warning notifies us about the error handler (which we'll discuss shortly), two errors are encountered with respect to validation, and one fatal error occurs because of the malformed document. This fatal error propagates up to the main application, where it is caught as an exception and our text is output.

In this case, we don't have to use the default error handler. Even though this is a DOM document, we can set a SAX error handler on it using `setErrorHandler()`, as shown in Listing 6.15.

LISTING 6.15 Setting an Error Handler on a DOM Parser

```
    ...
        DocumentBuilderFactory dbf = DocumentBuilderFactory.newInstance();
        dbf.setValidating(true);

        DocumentBuilder db = dbf.newDocumentBuilder();
        db.setErrorHandler(new ErrorProcessor());

        doc = db.parse(docFile);
    ...
```

Notice that this is the same class we used for the SAX parser, but we're using it with the DOM parser.

Now if we run the application, we see the results shown in Listing 6.16.

LISTING 6.16   DOM Errors

```
Error: Document root element "votes", must match DOCTYPE root "null".
Error: Document is invalid: no grammar found.
Fatal Error: The element type "voter" must be terminated by the matching
end-tag "</voter>".
Problem parsing the file.
```

Notice that the same document processed by the same error handler generates errors that are similar, but not quite the same. The XML 1.0 Recommendation determines what conditions should cause errors, but in many cases it's up to the implementer to decide whether the problem should be a warning, error, or fatal error, and what to say about it at the time.

Schema Validation

DTDs are not the only means for providing a structure against which the parser can validate. Several proposals for XML schemas are currently jockeying for position in the marketplace, and we'll look at the most promising in Chapter 8.

In the meantime, understand that the general idea is to provide a means for validation that's easier to understand, more flexible, and more powerful. While the goals are the same for DTD validation, we need to make slight changes to applications to enable them to validate against schemas.

Schema Overview

The basic purpose of XML schemas is to provide a means for specifying the structure of an XML document using XML, rather than DTDs. In this chapter, we'll use the W3C's XML Schema Recommendation as an example.

Listing 6.17 shows a schema document that describes the structure we've been using up to this point.

LISTING 6.17   An XML Schema for the Document

```
<?xml version="1.0"?>
<xsd:schema xmlns:xsd="http://www.w3.org/2001/XMLSchema">

    <xsd:element name="votes" type="voteType"/>

    <xsd:complexType name="voteType">
        <xsd:sequence>
            <xsd:element name="voter" type="voterType"
                        minOccurs="0" maxOccurs="unbounded"/>
        </xsd:sequence>
        <xsd:attribute name="totalVotes" type="xsd:integer"/>
    </xsd:complexType>

    <xsd:complexType name="voterType">
```

LISTING 6.17   Continued

```
        <xsd:sequence>
            <xsd:element name="vote" type="xsd:string"/>
            <xsd:element name="comments" type="xsd:string"/>
        </xsd:sequence>
        <xsd:attribute name="personid" type="xsd:string"/>
        <xsd:attribute name="status" type="xsd:string"/>
    </xsd:complexType>

</xsd:schema>
```

We'll discuss schemas in detail in Chapter 8, but for now understand that we've defined a main element, **votes**, which is of type **voteType**. We've defined **voteType** to be an unlimited number of **voter** elements, all of the type **voterType**. Finally, we've defined **voterType** to be just two elements, **vote** and **comments**, both of which are simple strings. We've also added the appropriate attributes to each type.

Specifying a Schema

Now that we have a schema document, we need to associate it with the data, or instance document. We do so using an attribute that's part of a special namespace, as shown in Listing 6.18.

LISTING 6.18   Specifying a Schema

```
<?xml version="1.0"?>
<votes totalVotes="5" xmlns:xsi="http://www.w3.org/2001/XMLSchema-instance"
    xsi:noNamespaceSchemaLocation="votes.xsd">
    <voter personid="Emp1" status="primary">
        <vote>Dregraal</vote>
        <comments>
...
```

Here we've defined the **XMLSchema-instance** namespace and provided the **noNamespaceSchemaLocation** attribute, which gives the processor a hint as to where to find the schema for elements and attributes that are not part of a namespace, like those in our document.

The application doesn't have to use this hint, but ours will.

Turning on Schema Validation

Like creating a parser, turning on schema validation is highly implementation-dependent. In most cases, it hinges on setting a feature (as in a SAX parser) or on specifically setting the schema "language" for a validator.

Although we typically use the word *schema* (with a small *s*) to refer to structures like the one in the preceding section, it can refer to any type of document that defines a grammar for data; a DTD can be considered a schema, albeit in a different schema language.

In Java's default parser, turning on XML schema validation involves setting an attribute on the parser, telling it what schema language to use, and setting that language to point to the W3C's XML Schema Recommendation language, as in Listings 6.19a–d.

Java

LISTING 6.19a   Schema Validation in DOM

```java
import javax.xml.parsers.DocumentBuilder;
import javax.xml.parsers.DocumentBuilderFactory;
import org.w3c.dom.Document;
import java.io.File;

public class DocumentListing {

    public static void main (String args[]) {

        File docFile = new File("votes.xml");
        Document doc = null;

        try {

            DocumentBuilderFactory dbf = DocumentBuilderFactory.newInstance();

            dbf.setValidating(true);
            dbf.setNamespaceAware(true);

            try {
                dbf.setAttribute(
                        "http://java.sun.com/xml/jaxp/properties/schemaLanguage",
                        "http://www.w3.org/2001/XMLSchema");
            } catch (IllegalArgumentException e) {
                System.out.println(e.getMessage());
            }

            DocumentBuilder db = dbf.newDocumentBuilder();
            db.setErrorHandler(new ErrorProcessor());

            doc = db.parse(docFile);

        } catch (Exception e) {
            System.out.print("Problem parsing the file:"+e.getMessage());
        }

    }
}
```

First, note how flexible this method is. As other schema-type languages are created, the parser can be expanded to support them, and applications can use them simply by setting the appropriate value for the schema language attribute.

Why java.sun.com?

The attribute set in this example is referenced by a unique URI. Because this is Sun's parser, Sun chose a URI it controls for the unique name of its schemaLanguage attribute.

Notice also that we have to make sure that the parser is looking at namespaces, because it needs to be able to both perceive the location of the schema document from the noNamespaceSchemaLocation attribute and decipher the schema document itself.

C++

As you can see in Listing 6.19b, using a schema in C++ is fairly straightforward, except that unlike the error or content handlers, we pass the pointer of the schema declaration handler as a variant type. This is because ISAXContentHandler is derived from IDispatch and that automation interface uses variants to package information. We also have some rudimentary COM implementation in the MySAXSchemaDeclHandler class so that the call to QueryInterface() made by the reader will succeed. You wouldn't want to do this in your actual application, but it helps to simplify the example for our purposes.

LISTING 6.19b   Using a Schema in C++

```
#include "stdafx.h"
#include <WinInet.h>
#include "MySAXContentHandler.h"
#include "MySAXSchemaDeclHandler.h"

int _tmain(int argc, _TCHAR* argv[])
{
    static wchar_t XMLURL[INTERNET_MAX_URL_LENGTH];
    ::CoInitialize(NULL);
    try
    {
        ISAXXMLReader* pReader = NULL;
        HRESULT hr = CoCreateInstance( __uuidof(SAXXMLReader40), NULL,
                                       CLSCTX_ALL, __uuidof(ISAXXMLReader),
                                       (void **)&pReader);
        if(hr==S_OK)
          {
            //Register the content handler for the XMLReader
                MySAXContentHandler* pContent = new MySAXContentHandler();
                hr = pReader->putContentHandler(pContent);

            //Create and configure the SchemaCache
            IXMLDOMSchemaCollectionPtr pSchemaCache = NULL;
            hr = pSchemaCache.CreateInstance(__uuidof(XMLSchemaCache40));
            _variant_t vSchemaCache(new IXMLDOMSchemaCollectionPtr);
            V_VT(&vSchemaCache) = VT_DISPATCH;
            V_DISPATCH(&vSchemaCache) = pSchemaCache;

            //Create and configure the SchemaDeclHandler
```

LISTING 6.19b   Continued

```
                MySAXSchemaDeclHandler* pMySAXSchemaDeclHandler =
                                new MySAXSchemaDeclHandler();
                _variant_t vSchemaDecl(new MySAXSchemaDeclHandler());
                V_VT(&vSchemaDecl) = VT_DISPATCH;
                V_DISPATCH(&vSchemaDecl) = pMySAXSchemaDeclHandler;

                //Configure the SAX reader and load schema cache and decl handler
                hr = pReader->putFeature(L"schema-validation", TRUE);
                hr = pReader->putProperty(L"schemas", vSchemaCache);
                hr = pReader->putProperty(L"schema-declaration-handler",
                                vSchemaDecl);

                mbstowcs(XMLURL, argv[1], (INTERNET_MAX_URL_LENGTH-1));
                hr = pReader->parseURL(XMLURL);

                //Clean up the XMLReader
                    pReader->Release();
        }
    }
    catch(...)  // For catching standard exceptions.
    {
        printf("Caught the exception");
    }
    ::CoUninitialize();
    return 0;
}
```

Our application needs a content handler like our original SAX application. Create a new file called `MySAXContentHandler.h` and enter the following code:

```
class MySAXContentHandler : public ISAXContentHandler
{
public:
    MySAXContentHandler();
    virtual ~MySAXContentHandler();

        long __stdcall QueryInterface(const struct _GUID &,void ** );
        unsigned long __stdcall AddRef(void);
        unsigned long __stdcall Release(void);

        virtual HRESULT STDMETHODCALLTYPE putDocumentLocator(
            /* [in] */ ISAXLocator __RPC_FAR *pLocator);

        virtual HRESULT STDMETHODCALLTYPE startDocument(void);

        virtual HRESULT STDMETHODCALLTYPE endDocument(void);

        virtual HRESULT STDMETHODCALLTYPE startPrefixMapping(
            /* [in] */ wchar_t __RPC_FAR *pwchPrefix,
            /* [in] */ int cchPrefix,
            /* [in] */ wchar_t __RPC_FAR *pwchUri,
            /* [in] */ int cchUri);
```

```
            virtual HRESULT STDMETHODCALLTYPE endPrefixMapping(
                /* [in] */ wchar_t __RPC_FAR *pwchPrefix,
                /* [in] */ int cchPrefix);

            virtual HRESULT STDMETHODCALLTYPE startElement(
                /* [in] */ wchar_t __RPC_FAR *pwchNamespaceUri,
                /* [in] */ int cchNamespaceUri,
                /* [in] */ wchar_t __RPC_FAR *pwchLocalName,
                /* [in] */ int cchLocalName,
                /* [in] */ wchar_t __RPC_FAR *pwchQualifiedName,
                /* [in] */ int cchQualifiedName,
                /* [in] */ ISAXAttributes __RPC_FAR *pAttributes);

            virtual HRESULT STDMETHODCALLTYPE endElement(
                /* [in] */ wchar_t __RPC_FAR *pwchNamespaceUri,
                /* [in] */ int cchNamespaceUri,
                /* [in] */ wchar_t __RPC_FAR *pwchLocalName,
                /* [in] */ int cchLocalName,
                /* [in] */ wchar_t __RPC_FAR *pwchQualifiedName,
                /* [in] */ int cchQualifiedName);

            virtual HRESULT STDMETHODCALLTYPE characters(
                /* [in] */ wchar_t __RPC_FAR *pwchChars,
                /* [in] */ int cchChars);

            virtual HRESULT STDMETHODCALLTYPE ignorableWhitespace(
                /* [in] */ wchar_t __RPC_FAR *pwchChars,
                /* [in] */ int cchChars);

            virtual HRESULT STDMETHODCALLTYPE processingInstruction(
                /* [in] */ wchar_t __RPC_FAR *pwchTarget,
                /* [in] */ int cchTarget,
                /* [in] */ wchar_t __RPC_FAR *pwchData,
                /* [in] */ int cchData);

            virtual HRESULT STDMETHODCALLTYPE skippedEntity(
                /* [in] */ wchar_t __RPC_FAR *pwchName,
                /* [in] */ int cchName);
};
```

Now let's implement the content handler functions. In this sample, we basically stub out all the methods of `MySAXContentHandler`. Create a new file called `MySAXContentHandler.cpp` and enter the following code:

```
#include "stdafx.h"
#include "MySAXContentHandler.h"

MySAXContentHandler::MySAXContentHandler()
{
}

MySAXContentHandler::~MySAXContentHandler()
{
}
```

```
HRESULT STDMETHODCALLTYPE MySAXContentHandler::putDocumentLocator(
          /* [in] */ ISAXLocator __RPC_FAR *pLocator
          )
{
    return S_OK;
}


HRESULT STDMETHODCALLTYPE MySAXContentHandler::startDocument()
{
    return S_OK;
}


HRESULT STDMETHODCALLTYPE MySAXContentHandler::endDocument()
{
    return S_OK;
}


HRESULT STDMETHODCALLTYPE MySAXContentHandler::startPrefixMapping(
          /* [in] */ wchar_t __RPC_FAR *pwchPrefix,
          /* [in] */ int cchPrefix,
          /* [in] */ wchar_t __RPC_FAR *pwchUri,
          /* [in] */ int cchUri)
{
    return S_OK;
}


HRESULT STDMETHODCALLTYPE MySAXContentHandler::endPrefixMapping(
          /* [in] */ wchar_t __RPC_FAR *pwchPrefix,
          /* [in] */ int cchPrefix)
{
    return S_OK;
}


HRESULT STDMETHODCALLTYPE MySAXContentHandler::startElement(
          /* [in] */ wchar_t __RPC_FAR *pwchNamespaceUri,
          /* [in] */ int cchNamespaceUri,
          /* [in] */ wchar_t __RPC_FAR *pwchLocalName,
          /* [in] */ int cchLocalName,
          /* [in] */ wchar_t __RPC_FAR *pwchQualifiedName,
          /* [in] */ int cchQualifiedName,
          /* [in] */ ISAXAttributes __RPC_FAR *pAttributes)
{
    return S_OK;
}


HRESULT STDMETHODCALLTYPE MySAXContentHandler::endElement(
          /* [in] */ wchar_t __RPC_FAR *pwchNamespaceUri,
          /* [in] */ int cchNamespaceUri,
          /* [in] */ wchar_t __RPC_FAR *pwchLocalName,
          /* [in] */ int cchLocalName,
          /* [in] */ wchar_t __RPC_FAR *pwchQualifiedName,
          /* [in] */ int cchQualifiedName)
```

```
{
    return S_OK;
}

HRESULT STDMETHODCALLTYPE MySAXContentHandler::characters(
        /* [in] */ wchar_t __RPC_FAR *pwchChars,
        /* [in] */ int cchChars)
{
    return S_OK;
}

HRESULT STDMETHODCALLTYPE MySAXContentHandler::ignorableWhitespace(
        /* [in] */ wchar_t __RPC_FAR *pwchChars,
        /* [in] */ int cchChars)
{
    return S_OK;
}

HRESULT STDMETHODCALLTYPE MySAXContentHandler::processingInstruction(
        /* [in] */ wchar_t __RPC_FAR *pwchTarget,
        /* [in] */ int cchTarget,
        /* [in] */ wchar_t __RPC_FAR *pwchData,
        /* [in] */ int cchData)
{
    return S_OK;
}

HRESULT STDMETHODCALLTYPE MySAXContentHandler::skippedEntity(
        /* [in] */ wchar_t __RPC_FAR *pwchVal,
        /* [in] */ int cchVal)
{
    return S_OK;
}

long __stdcall MySAXContentHandler::QueryInterface (
                            const struct _GUID &riid,
                            void ** ppvObject)
{
    return 0;
}

unsigned long __stdcall MySAXContentHandler::AddRef()
{
    return 0;
}

unsigned long __stdcall MySAXContentHandler::Release()
{
    return 0;
}
```

Finally, we need to implement the `MySAXSchemaDeclHandler`, which helps handle the SAX event associated with schema validation. Create a `MySAXSchemaDeclHander.h` file and enter the following code:

```
class MySAXSchemaDeclHandler : public IMXSchemaDeclHandler
{
    public:
        MySAXSchemaDeclHandler();
            virtual ~MySAXSchemaDeclHandler();

            // If your handler must be a COM Object (in this example it does not)
            long __stdcall QueryInterface(const struct _GUID &,void ** );
            unsigned long __stdcall AddRef(void);
            unsigned long __stdcall Release(void);

        virtual HRESULT STDMETHODCALLTYPE schemaElementDecl(
            /* [in] */ ISchemaElement *pSchemaElement);

        virtual HRESULT STDMETHODCALLTYPE GetTypeInfoCount(
            /* [out] */ UINT *pctinfo);

        virtual HRESULT STDMETHODCALLTYPE GetTypeInfo(
            /* [in] */ UINT iTInfo,
            /* [in] */ LCID lcid,
            /* [out] */ ITypeInfo **ppTInfo);

        virtual HRESULT STDMETHODCALLTYPE GetIDsOfNames(
            /* [in] */ REFIID riid,
            /* [in] */ LPOLESTR *rgszNames,
            /* [in] */ UINT cNames,
            /* [in] */ LCID lcid,
            /* [out] */ DISPID *rgDispId);

        virtual HRESULT STDMETHODCALLTYPE Invoke(
            /* [in] */ DISPID dispIdMember,
            /* [in] */ REFIID riid,
            /* [in] */ LCID lcid,
            /* [in] */ WORD wFlags,
            /* [out][in] */ DISPPARAMS *pDispParams,
            /* [out] */ VARIANT *pVarResult,
            /* [out] */ EXCEPINFO *pExcepInfo,
            /* [out] */ UINT *puArgErr);
};
```

Now let's implement the functions of the `MySAXSchemaDeclHandler` class. Create a new file called `MySAXSchemaDeclHandler.cpp` and enter the following code:

```
#include "stdafx.h"
#include "MySAXSchemaDeclHandler.h"
#include <stdio.h>

MySAXSchemaDeclHandler::MySAXSchemaDeclHandler()
{
}
```

```cpp
MySAXSchemaDeclHandler::~MySAXSchemaDeclHandler()
{
}

HRESULT STDMETHODCALLTYPE MySAXSchemaDeclHandler::schemaElementDecl(
            /* [in] */ ISchemaElement *pSchemaElement)
{
    return S_OK;
}

HRESULT STDMETHODCALLTYPE MySAXSchemaDeclHandler::GetTypeInfoCount(
            /* [out] */ UINT *pctinfo)
{
    return S_OK;
}

HRESULT STDMETHODCALLTYPE MySAXSchemaDeclHandler::GetTypeInfo(
            /* [in] */ UINT iTInfo,
            /* [in] */ LCID lcid,
            /* [out] */ ITypeInfo **ppTInfo)
{
    return S_OK;
}

HRESULT STDMETHODCALLTYPE MySAXSchemaDeclHandler::GetIDsOfNames(
            /* [in] */ REFIID riid,
            /* [in] */ LPOLESTR *rgszNames,
            /* [in] */ UINT cNames,
            /* [in] */ LCID lcid,
            /* [out] */ DISPID *rgDispId)
{
    return S_OK;
}

HRESULT STDMETHODCALLTYPE MySAXSchemaDeclHandler::Invoke(
            /* [in] */ DISPID dispIdMember,
            /* [in] */ REFIID riid,
            /* [in] */ LCID lcid,
            /* [in] */ WORD wFlags,
            /* [out][in] */ DISPPARAMS *pDispParams,
            /* [out] */ VARIANT *pVarResult,
            /* [out] */ EXCEPINFO *pExcepInfo,
            /* [out] */ UINT *puArgErr)
{
    return S_OK;
}

long __stdcall MySAXSchemaDeclHandler::QueryInterface (
                              const struct _GUID &riid,
                              void ** ppvObject)
{
    if (riid == __uuidof(IMXSchemaDeclHandler))
        *ppvObject = reinterpret_cast<IMXSchemaDeclHandler*>(this);
    return 0;
```

```
}

unsigned long __stdcall MySAXSchemaDeclHandler::AddRef()
{
    return 0;
}

unsigned long __stdcall MySAXSchemaDeclHandler::Release()
{
    return 0;
}
```

Visual Basic .NET

Create a new Windows Application project. Select the form in the Design view; in the Properties window, change the `Name` property to `SAXMainForm` and change the `Text` property to `SAX Validation Sample`. Right-click `Form1.vb` in the Solution Explorer, select Rename, and change its `Name` property to `SAXMainForm.vb`.

In the Design view, add controls to the form so that it looks like Figure 6.1. You will need three Label, two Button, and three TextBox controls.

FIGURE 6.1

SAX validation sample main form.

Now change the properties for the controls as shown in the following table:

Control	Property	Change To...
Label1	Name	lblOutput
	Text	Output Window:
Label2	Name	lblXMLFileName
	Text	XML File Name:
Label3	Name	lblSchemaFileName
	Text	Schema File Name:

Control	Property	Change To...
Button1	Name	btnValidate
	Text	Validate XML
Button2	Name	btnClose
	Text	Close
TextBox1	Name	txtOutput
	AcceptsReturn	True
	Multiline	True
	ScrollBars	Vertical
	Text	(none—clear the Text property)
TextBox2	Name	txtXMLFile
	Text	(none—clear the Text property)
TextBox3	Name	txtSchemaFile
Text	(none—clear the Text property)	

Add a reference for the project to MSXML2. Do this by selecting Project, Add Reference. Click the COM tab, double-click Microsoft XML, v4.0, and then click OK.

Once your form is created, open the code view of the form and modify the **SAXMainForm** class as shown in Listing 6.19c. It is important to note that we are using the explicit instantiation of the 4.0 version of the **SAXXMLReader**. Validation using schemas is only supported starting with this version of MSXML. While namespace support is on by default, there is currently no support for setting the schema language; W3C Schemas, as described in Chapter 8, are all that is currently available.

Listing 6.19c shows the main application.

LISTING 6.19c The Main Visual Basic.NET Application

```
Public Class SAXMainForm
    Inherits System.Windows.Forms.Form

    Public Property OutputText() As String
        Get
            Return txtOutput.Text
        End Get
        Set(ByVal Value As String)
            txtOutput.Text = txtOutput.Text & Value
        End Set
    End Property
End Property
```

```
    Private Sub btnValidate_Click(ByVal sender As System.Object,
                               ByVal e As System.EventArgs)
                                        Handles btnValidate.Click
        Dim Reader As New MSXML2.SAXXMLReader40()
        Dim SchemaCache As New MSXML2.XMLSchemaCache40()
        Dim ContentHandler As New MyContentHandler(Me)
        Dim SchemaDeclHandler As New MySchemaDeclHandler()

        SchemaCache.add("", txtSchemaFile.Text)
        Reader.putFeature("schema-validation", True)
        Reader.putProperty("schemas", SchemaCache)
        Reader.putProperty("schema-declaration-handler", SchemaDeclHandler)

        txtOutput.Text = ""
        Reader.contentHandler = ContentHandler

        On Error Resume Next
        Reader.parseURL(txtXMLFile.Text)
        On Error GoTo 0
    End Sub

    Private Sub btnClose_Click(ByVal sender As System.Object,
                            ByVal e As System.EventArgs)
                                        Handles btnClose.Click

        End
    End Sub
End Class
```

Select Project, Add Class and create a new class named **MyContentHandler.vb**. Open the class file and change it to match this class definition:

```
Public Class MyContentHandler
    Implements MSXML2.IVBSAXContentHandler

    Dim myForm As New SAXMainForm()

    Public Sub New(ByVal FormInst As SAXMainForm)
        myForm = FormInst
    End Sub

    Public Sub startDocument()
                Implements MSXML2.IVBSAXContentHandler.startDocument
        myForm.OutputText = "Beginning XML document validation" & vbCrLf
    End Sub

    Public Sub endDocument() Implements MSXML2.IVBSAXContentHandler.endDocument
        myForm.OutputText = "XML document validation is complete. " &
                                        "Document is valid." & vbCrLf
    End Sub

    Public Sub startElement(ByRef strNamespaceURI As String,
                        ByRef strLocalName As String,
```

```
                               ByRef strQName As String,
                               ByVal oAttributes As MSXML2.IVBSAXAttributes)
                               Implements MSXML2.IVBSAXContentHandler.startElement

        End Sub

        Public Sub endElement(ByRef strNamespaceURI As String,
                              ByRef strLocalName As String,
                              ByRef strQName As String)
                                 Implements MSXML2.IVBSAXContentHandler.endElement

        End Sub

        Public Sub characters(ByRef strChars As String)
                                 Implements MSXML2.IVBSAXContentHandler.characters

        End Sub

        Public Sub ignorableWhitespace(ByRef strChars As String)
                        Implements MSXML2.IVBSAXContentHandler.ignorableWhitespace

        End Sub

        Public Sub startPrefixMapping(ByRef strPrefix As String,
                              ByRef strURI As String)
                        Implements MSXML2.IVBSAXContentHandler.startPrefixMapping

        End Sub

        Public Sub endPrefixMapping(ByRef strPrefix As String)
                          Implements MSXML2.IVBSAXContentHandler.endPrefixMapping

        End Sub

        Public WriteOnly Property documentLocator() As MSXML2.IVBSAXLocator
                            Implements MSXML2.IVBSAXContentHandler.documentLocator
            Set(ByVal Value As MSXML2.IVBSAXLocator)

            End Set
        End Property

        Public Sub processingInstruction(ByRef strTarget As String,
                                    ByRef strData As String)
                      Implements MSXML2.IVBSAXContentHandler.processingInstruction

        End Sub

        Public Sub skippedEntity(ByRef strName As String)
                              Implements MSXML2.IVBSAXContentHandler.skippedEntity

        End Sub
    End Class
```

Create another class named **MySchemaDeclHandler.vb** and enter the following code:

```
Public Class MySchemaDeclHandler
    Implements MSXML2.IMXSchemaDeclHandler

    Public Sub schemaElementDecl(ByVal oSchemaElement As MSXML2.ISchemaElement)
                        Implements MSXML2.IMXSchemaDeclHandler.schemaElementDecl

    End Sub
End Class
```

Perl

For schema validation in the DOM parser, **XML::Xerces** doesn't use the URL-style feature activation. Listing 6.19d shows how to set the parser to use schemas.

LISTING 6.19d   Using Schemas in Perl

```
use XML::Xerces;
use XML::Xerces::DOMParse;

my $file         = XML::Xerces::LocalFileInputSource->new("votes.xml");
my $parser       = XML::Xerces::DOMParser->new();
my $error_handler = XML::Xerces::PerlErrorHandler->new();

$parser->setDoSchema(1);
$parser->setDoNamespaces(1);
$parser->setErrorHandler($error_handler);

eval { $parser->parse($file); };
XML::Xerces::error($@) if $@;
```

Working with Errors

In some cases, all you want to know is whether the document is valid. In a fully functional application, however, you're going to have to do something with that information. How you work with it depends on your application. In some cases you'll merely signal the error, in others you'll take action according to the type of error.

Errors and SAX

Because even DOM parsers typically throw SAX-related exceptions, it makes sense to look at errors from the SAX point of view.

You can handle the errors within the error handler, or send the information back to the main application by throwing an exception. For example, in Listings 6.20a–d, we report warnings using the error handler, but propagate errors and fatal errors back up to the application.

Java

LISTING 6.20a   Propagating Errors in Java

```
import org.xml.sax.helpers.DefaultHandler;
import org.xml.sax.SAXParseException;

public class ErrorProcessor extends DefaultHandler
{

    public ErrorProcessor ()
    {
        super();
    }

    public void error (SAXParseException e) throws SAXParseException {
        throw e;
    }

    public void fatalError (SAXParseException e) throws SAXParseException {
        throw e;
    }

    public void warning (SAXParseException e) {
        System.out.println("Warning: "+e.getMessage());
    }

}
```

C++

Because MSXML doesn't support **SAXException**-style errors but instead implements them as COM exceptions, some of the rich error reporting you see in Java is not available in C++. However, by using the error information that is available and the location of the error, it's possible to locate and fix validation errors. The MSXML **Reader** also terminates parsing anytime it encounters an error, so only the first error is reported and then the application stops parsing the document. Unlike the Java sample, error handling and reporting are done in the error handler class.

To add error handling to the sample, we need to create an error handler and associate it with the **SAXXMLReader**. We do this by creating two new files called **MySAXErrorHander.h** and **MySAXErrorHandler.cpp** and then modifying our existing code to match the code in Listing 6.20b.

LISTING 6.20b   Creating the Error Handler Class in C++

```
...
#include <WinInet.h>
#include "MySAXErrorHandler.h"
...
            //Register the content handler for the XMLReader
```

LISTING 6.20b *Continued*

```
            MySAXContentHandler* pContent = new MySAXContentHandler();
            hr = pReader->putContentHandler(pContent);
        //Register the error handler for the XMLReader
        MySAXErrorHandler* pError = new MySAXErrorHandler();
        hr = pReader->putErrorHandler(pError);
...
}
```

Next, add a `MySAXErrorHander.h` file and enter the following code:

```
class MySAXErrorHandler : public ISAXErrorHandler
{
public:
    MySAXErrorHandler();
    virtual ~MySAXErrorHandler();

        // If your handler must be a COM Object (in this example it does not)
        long __stdcall QueryInterface(const struct _GUID &,void ** );
        unsigned long __stdcall AddRef(void);
        unsigned long __stdcall Release(void);

        // Method for future support. All errors are currently fatalError.
            virtual HRESULT STDMETHODCALLTYPE error(
            /* [in] */ ISAXLocator __RPC_FAR *pLocator,
            /* [in] */ unsigned short * pwchErrorMessage,
            /* [in] */ HRESULT errCode);

        virtual HRESULT STDMETHODCALLTYPE fatalError(
            /* [in] */ ISAXLocator __RPC_FAR *pLocator,
            /* [in] */ unsigned short * pwchErrorMessage,
            /* [in] */ HRESULT errCode);

        // Method for future support. All errors are currently fatalError.
        virtual HRESULT STDMETHODCALLTYPE ignorableWarning(
            /* [in] */ ISAXLocator __RPC_FAR *pLocator,
            /* [in] */ unsigned short * pwchErrorMessage,
            /* [in] */ HRESULT errCode);

};
```

Now create a new class file called `MySAXErrorHandler.cpp` and add the following code:

```
#include "stdafx.h"
#include "MySAXErrorHandler.h"
#include <stdio.h>

MySAXErrorHandler::MySAXErrorHandler()
{

}

MySAXErrorHandler::~MySAXErrorHandler()
{
```

```
}

HRESULT STDMETHODCALLTYPE MySAXErrorHandler::error(
            /* [in] */ ISAXLocator __RPC_FAR *pLocator,
            /* [in] */ unsigned short * pwchErrorMessage,
            /* [in] */ HRESULT errCode)
{
    int nLine;
    int nColumn;
    pLocator->getLineNumber(&nLine);
    pLocator->getColumnNumber(&nColumn);
    wprintf(L"Error: %s at line %i, column %i\n", pwchErrorMessage,
                                            nLine, nColumn);

    return S_OK;
}

HRESULT STDMETHODCALLTYPE MySAXErrorHandler::fatalError(
            /* [in] */ ISAXLocator __RPC_FAR *pLocator,
            /* [in] */ unsigned short * pwchErrorMessage,
            /* [in] */ HRESULT errCode)
{
    int nLine;
    int nColumn;
    pLocator->getLineNumber(&nLine);
    pLocator->getColumnNumber(&nColumn);
    wprintf(L"Fatal Error: %s at line %i, column %i\n", pwchErrorMessage,
                                            nLine, nColumn);

    return S_OK;
}

HRESULT STDMETHODCALLTYPE MySAXErrorHandler::ignorableWarning(
            /* [in] */ ISAXLocator __RPC_FAR *pLocator,
            /* [in] */ unsigned short * pwchErrorMessage,
            /* [in] */ HRESULT errCode)
{
    int nLine;
    int nColumn;
    pLocator->getLineNumber(&nLine);
    pLocator->getColumnNumber(&nColumn);
    wprintf(L"Ignorable Warning: %s at line %i, column %i\n", pwchErrorMessage,
                                            nLine, nColumn);

    return S_OK;
}

long __stdcall MySAXErrorHandler::QueryInterface(const struct _GUID &,void ** )
{
    return 0;
}

unsigned long __stdcall MySAXErrorHandler::AddRef()
{
    return 0;
}
```

```
unsigned long __stdcall MySAXErrorHandler::Release()
{
    return 0;
}
```

Visual Basic .NET

The situation in Visual Basic .NET is the same as in C++. To add error handling to the sample, we need to create an error handler and associate it with the **SAXXMLReader**. We do this by creating a new class file called **MyErrorHandler.vb** and then entering the code in Listing 6.20c.

LISTING 6.20c Creating the Error Handler Class in Visual Basic .NET

```
Public Class MyErrorHandler
    Implements MSXML2.IVBSAXErrorHandler

    Dim myForm As New SAXMainForm()
    Public Sub New(ByVal FormInst As SAXMainForm)
        myForm = FormInst
    End Sub

    Public Sub parseError(ByVal oLocator As MSXML2.IVBSAXLocator,
                      ByRef strErrorMessage As String,
                      ByVal nErrorCode As Integer)
                                Implements MSXML2.IVBSAXErrorHandler.error
        OutputError("Error", strErrorMessage,
                    oLocator.lineNumber, oLocator.columnNumber)
    End Sub

    Public Sub fatalError(ByVal oLocator As MSXML2.IVBSAXLocator,
                      ByRef strErrorMessage As String,
                      ByVal nErrorCode As Integer)
                                Implements MSXML2.IVBSAXErrorHandler.fatalError
        OutputError("Fatal Error", strErrorMessage,
                    oLocator.lineNumber, oLocator.columnNumber)
    End Sub

    Public Sub ignorableWarning(ByVal oLocator As MSXML2.IVBSAXLocator,
                      ByRef strErrorMessage As String,
                      ByVal nErrorCode As Integer)
                      Implements MSXML2.IVBSAXErrorHandler.ignorableWarning
        OutputError("Ignorable Warning", strErrorMessage,
                    oLocator.lineNumber, oLocator.columnNumber)
    End Sub

    Private Function OutputError(ByVal strLabel As String,
                                 ByVal strDescription As String,
                                 ByVal Line As Long,
                                 ByVal Column As Long)
        myForm.OutputText = strLabel & ": " & strDescription & "at line " &
                                Str(Line) & ", column " & Str(Column) & vbCrLf
    End Function
End Class
```

Make the following changes to the `SAXMainForm.vb` code in order to associate the new error handler with the `Reader` object:

```
Public Class SAXMainForm
    Inherits System.Windows.Forms.Form
...

    Private Sub btnValidate_Click(ByVal sender As System.Object,
                                  ByVal e As System.EventArgs)
                                                 Handles btnValidate.Click
...

        Dim ContentHandler As New MyContentHandler(Me)
        Dim ErrorHandler As New MyErrorHandler(Me)
...

        Reader.contentHandler = ContentHandler
        Reader.errorHandler = ErrorHandler
...
End Class
```

Perl

If we want to change the default error behavior of either the `XML::Xerces` DOM parser or the SAX parser, we can subclass `XML::Xerces::PerlErrorHandler` and override the `error()`, `fatal_error()`, and `warning()` methods. Here, for `error()` and `fatal_error()`, we store the object reference from `XML::Xerces`' error system (avoiding `die()`'s automatic "stringification"), and then `die()` with a concise error message, as shown in Listing 6.20d.

LISTING 6.20d   Changing Error Behavior in Perl

```
package MyErrorHandler;

@ISA = (XML::Xerces::PerlErrorHandler);

sub error {
    my $self = shift;
    $self->{error} = shift;

    die "Error: " . $self->{error}->getMessage();
}

sub fatal_error {
    my $self = shift;
    $self->{error} = shift;

    die "Error: " . $self->{error}->getMessage();
}

sub warning {
    my $self = shift;
    my $err  = shift;

    warn "Warning: " . $err->getMessage() . "\n";
}
```

LISTING 6.20d   Continued

```
...

my $error_handler = MyErrorHandler->new();

eval {
    $reader->setFeature( "http://xml.org/sax/features/validation", 1 );
    $reader->setErrorHandler($error_handler);
    $reader->setContentHandler($handler);
    $reader->parse($file);
};
warn $@ if $@;
```

Handling the Errors

In this case, the exception is handled by the main application, as shown in Listings 6.21a and b.

Java

LISTING 6.21a   Handling the Exception in Java

```
...
            DocumentBuilder db = dbf.newDocumentBuilder();
            db.setErrorHandler(new ErrorProcessor());

            doc = db.parse(docFile);

        } catch (Exception e) {
            SAXParseException saxException = (SAXParseException)e;
            System.out.println("Problem parsing the file:" +
                                            saxException.getMessage());
            System.out.println();
            System.out.println("File: "+saxException.getSystemId());
            System.out.println("Line number: "+saxException.getLineNumber());
            System.out.println("Column number: "+saxException.getColumnNumber());
            System.out.println();
        }

    }
}
```

Here we're not only displaying the message, we're also displaying specific information provided by the SAXParseException. If we were to misspell a voter tag in votes.xml and run this application, we would see the following results:

```
Problem parsing the file:cvc-complex-type.2.4.a: Invalid content starting with
element 'votr'. The content must match '("":voter){0-UNBOUNDED}'.

File: file:H:/PrimerPlusXML/ppxmlch6/votes.xml
Line number: 4
Column number: 45
```

When it's finished, version 2.1 of SAX will also provide specific exception IDs that relate directly back to the XML Recommendations.

C++ and Visual Basic .NET

Because SAX `Exceptions` are thrown as COM exceptions, we handled the errors thrown by the SAX `Reader` in the error handler that we defined in the application. The main application class does not handle exceptions generated by the SAX `Reader`.

Perl

In Perl, we'll pick up the `XML::Xerces` error object from our error handler in order to differentiate the types of errors. As a last resort, if we don't know what the error is, we'll just pass back the message from `die()`, as shown in Listing 6.21b.

LISTING 6.21b   Differentiating Errors in Perl

```perl
...

my $error_handler = MyErrorHandler->new();

eval {
    $reader->setFeature( "http://xml.org/sax/features/validation", 1 );
    $reader->setErrorHandler($error_handler);
    $reader->setContentHandler($handler);
    $reader->parse($file);
};

if ($@) {

    if ( ref( $error_handler->{error} ) ) {
        my $error = $error_handler->{error};

        if ( $error->isa('XML::Xerces::SAXNotSupportedException') ) {
            die "Feature not supported: " . $error->getMessage() . "\n";
        } elsif (
            $error->isa('XML::Xerces::SAXNotRecognizedException') )
        {
            die "Feature not recognized: "
                . $error->getMessage() . "\n";
        } elsif ( $error->isa('XML::Xerces::SAXParseException') ) {
            die "Parse error: " . $error->getMessage() . "\n";
        } else {
            die "Unknown error: " . $error->getMessage() . "\n";
        }

    } else {
        die "Untyped error: $@";
    }
}
```

Changes After the Fact

It might seem that validation would be handy for making sure that a document stays in its proper form as we add to it, but this isn't the case. At the time of this writing, validation has no effect on an existing **Document** object. For example, even though we've created a schema and validated **votes.xml**, we can still add invalid information to the **Document** object, as shown in Listing 6.22.

LISTING 6.22   Adding Invalid Information to a Valid Document

```
import javax.xml.parsers.DocumentBuilder;
import javax.xml.parsers.DocumentBuilderFactory;
import org.w3c.dom.Document;
import org.w3c.dom.Element;
import java.io.File;

public class DocumentListing {

    public static void main (String args[]) {

        File docFile = new File("votes.xml");
        Document doc = null;

        try {

            DocumentBuilderFactory dbf = DocumentBuilderFactory.newInstance();

            dbf.setValidating(true);
            dbf.setNamespaceAware(true);

            try {
               dbf.setAttribute(
                     "http://java.sun.com/xml/jaxp/properties/schemaLanguage",
                     "http://www.w3.org/2001/XMLSchema");
            } catch (IllegalArgumentException e) {
               System.out.println(e.getMessage());
            }

            DocumentBuilder db = dbf.newDocumentBuilder();
            db.setErrorHandler(new ErrorProcessor());

            doc = db.parse(docFile);

            Element root = doc.getDocumentElement();
            root.appendChild(doc.createTextNode("This node doesn't belong here."));

            System.out.println(root.getLastChild());

        } catch (Exception e) {
           System.out.print("Problem parsing the file:"+e.getMessage());
        }

    }
}
```

Here we're adding a text node after the last **voter** element, which is not permitted under the schema currently in effect for this document. Nevertheless, the application will proceed without a problem, because there is not yet a way to validate the **Document** object on the fly.

Summary

Validation is the process of making sure that a parsed document takes the proper form. This includes allowable and required elements and attributes, as well as element order and content.

Specifying that a parser should validate is a highly implementation-specific task. It may involve setting an attribute on a DOM parser, or setting a feature or features on a SAX parser.

When errors are uncovered, they're typically handled by a SAX error handler. These errors may be dealt with specifically by the error handler, or they may be thrown back to the application, which can handle them appropriately.

Review Questions

1. What is validation?

2. Why is validation important?

3. What are the two main validation languages?

4. Can validation control the structure of a **Document** object after it's created?

5. What do SAX features do?

Programming Exercises

1. Create an application that ignores warnings, but stops completely upon encountering any error.

2. Create an application that displays the line and column number for warnings.

3. Using documentation, create a SAX parser that validates against an XML schema.

CHAPTER 7

DOCUMENT TYPE DEFINITIONS (DTDS)

You will learn about the following in this chapter:

- Types of DTDs
- Creating elements and content models
- Creating attributes

- Default values
- General entities
- Parameter entities

*I*n Chapter 6, "Validation," we looked at the code and methods necessary to make sure that an XML document conforms to a particular predefined structure, or *grammar*. In this chapter, we'll look at defining that grammar in more detail.

Document Type Definitions, or *DTDs*, have been around much longer than XML has. They were first defined as an integral part of the Standard Generalized Markup Language (SGML). XML is a subset of SGML, and when it was first developed, DTDs were brought along as a means for defining what can and cannot be present within an XML document, as part of the validation process.

These days, various flavors of XML Schemas and other options provide even more capabilities, but DTDs are still the foundation of XML, and still provide valuable capabilities, even if the document is not being validated. Also, many industry-standard grammars are implemented as DTDs, so you'll need to understand how to read and use them effectively.

In this chapter, we'll discuss creating both internal and external DTDs, from basic structures such as elements and attributes to more advanced features such as parameter entities and conditional sections.

Types of DTDs

DTDs are most often used to ensure that collections of documents all adhere to the same structure. Because of this, DTDs frequently exist in individual files separate from the actual content.

On the other hand, an internal subset of DTD information is not unusual, for two reasons:

- An application may require a "standalone" document, in which case all definitions must reside within the document.

- An internal subset allows an author to override certain sections of an external DTD, as you'll see when we discuss parameter entities later in this chapter.

External DTDs

In the case of external DTDs, the DTD file contains all the definitions, and the XML file simply references the DTD file. Let's start by creating a small DTD in Listing 7.1. We'll go over the actual syntax in the section titled "Creating Elements and Content Models," but for now understand that we're simply creating a definition of three elements.

LISTING 7.1   A Simple DTD

```
<!ELEMENT orchestra (instruments)>
<!ELEMENT instruments (woodwind)>
<!ELEMENT woodwind (#PCDATA)>
```

These three elements define a document such as the one shown in Listing 7.2.

LISTING 7.2   A Simple Document Referencing the DTD

```
<?xml version="1.0" encoding="ISO-8859-1" ?>
<!DOCTYPE orchestra SYSTEM "orchestra.dtd">
<orchestra>
    <instruments>
        <woodwind>Oboe, clarinet, and so on.</woodwind>
    </instruments>
</orchestra>
```

If you run this file through a validating parser, it should parse correctly.

You can make sure the parser is actually reading the DTD by changing one of the elements and checking for a validation error. If no error occurs, the parser isn't validating, and you need to check the documentation to find out why.

At the moment, we're more concerned with the **DOCTYPE** than the actual document. This is the markup (shown in bold in Listing 7.2) that tells the parser where to find the information needed to validate the included XML content.

Let's take a look at it piece by piece.

DOCTYPE Definitions

The <!DOCTYPE markup simply alerts the processor to the fact that the following content up to the matching > is the document type declaration.

Next comes the definition of the root element. In Listing 7.2, I've chosen to use the `orchestra` element, but I could just as easily have chosen the `instruments` element. Of course, in that case, `instruments` would have to be the root element, as shown in Listing 7.3.

LISTING 7.3 Changing the Root Element

```
<?xml version="1.0" encoding="ISO-8859-1" ?>
<!DOCTYPE instruments SYSTEM "orchestra.dtd">
<instruments>
    <woodwind>Oboe, clarinet, and so on.</woodwind>
</instruments>
```

You can change the root element in situations where you only want a document to contain a subset of the actual grammar. For example, you might have an XML structure that defines an entire accounting system, but if you just want a report of clients, it might be prudent to use `clients` as the root element, rather than including the entire complex accounting structure.

System Identifiers

Next, Listing 7.2 specifies the actual DTD document. You can do this in two ways. The first, as shown in the listing, is to use a *system identifier*. This identifier is literally some notation that the system understands. In this case, we're looking at a file called `orchestra.dtd` in the same directory as the XML file. You might also reference a file using a URI, like this:

```
<!DOCTYPE html SYSTEM
        "http://www.w3.org/TR/xhtml1/DTD/xhtml1-transitional.dtd">
```

Other operating systems and applications might respond to other `SYSTEM` identifiers. The main thing is that the system on which the file is being processed (and thus the application that's processing the file) knows how to retrieve the file directly.

Formal Public Identifiers

Another option is to use a *formal public identifier*. Such identifiers are not locations, but rather official "names" of resources such as DTDs. For example, the public identifier for the XHTML DTD in the previous example is

```
-//W3C//DTD XHTML 1.0 Transitional//EN
```

Public identifiers are used as a way to tell the processor what grammar to use, without having to specify a specific file. For example, I could have written this:

```
<!DOCTYPE html PUBLIC "-//W3C//DTD XHTML 1.0 Transitional//EN">
```

SGML systems, where the formal public identifier originated, typically have a lookup system where an administrator can maintain an "official" location for the DTD. This way, the file can be changed or moved, and authors don't have to be aware of its location, making maintenance much easier.

In XML, however, it is common to list both the public identifier and a system identifier as a backup, in case the processor doesn't recognize the public identifier. When we employ this technique, the document type declaration looks like this:

```
<!DOCTYPE html PUBLIC "-//W3C//DTD XHTML 1.0 Transitional//EN"
        "http://www.w3.org/TR/xhtml1/DTD/xhtml1-transitional.dtd">
```

The formal public identifier itself has several sections, each of which has a specific meaning. These sections are as follows:

{standards indicator}//{organization name}//{DTD name}//{language}

- The first section, the standards indicator, shows whether the document has been approved by a standards body, such as the ISO. If it has, the first notation is either a plus sign (+) or the standard's designation, and if not, the indicator is a minus sign (-).

- The second section indicates the organization or company that is responsible for the DTD.

- The third section is the name of the DTD. If you're making up your own, it's a good idea to include both a meaningful name and a version number.

- The fourth and final section indicates the language in which this particular document is written, using the ISO 639 list of language codes. For example, American English is indicated by the code `EN-US` and French is `FR`.

Note

In this and other examples, placeholders appear in italics and are enclosed in braces. When you replace such placeholders with actual code, do not include the braces.

Language Codes

A complete list of language codes is available at `http://www.w3.org/WAI/ER/IG/ert/iso639.htm`.

Given all of this, we can translate the formal public identifier

`-//W3C//DTD XHTML 1.0 Transitional//EN`

as follows:

> *A DTD created by the W3C, called DTD XHTML 1.0 Transitional, written in English, and not submitted to a standards body.*

Standard Versus Recommendation

Contrary to popular belief, work that comes out of the World Wide Web Consortium is not a standard, but a recommendation, because the W3C is not a standards body. On the other hand, if a recommendation is widely adopted, it may be considered a "de facto standard," as are most W3C recommendations.

Internal DTDs

In some situations, you may want to include the DTD information directly within the document. For example, you may want to create a standalone document. In this case, the actual DTD information replaces the reference to an external file, as in Listing 7.4.

LISTING 7.4   An Internal DTD

```
<?xml version="1.0" encoding="ISO-8859-1" ?>
<!DOCTYPE orchestra [

<!ELEMENT orchestra (instruments)>
<!ELEMENT instruments (woodwind)>
<!ELEMENT woodwind (#PCDATA)>

]>
<orchestra>
    <instruments>
        <woodwind>Oboe, clarinet, and so on.</woodwind>
    </instruments>
</orchestra>
```

Notice that the definitions are contained between brackets (`[ ]`).

Internal subsets are handy for two reasons. The first, as mentioned previously, has to do with standalone documents. If a document is marked as `standalone="yes"`, all of its definitions, including not only elements and attributes but also custom entities (described later), must exist within the document itself. If a document is marked as `standalone="no"` (or is not marked at all, as `"no"` is the default value), this requirement loosens up somewhat, but a non-validating parser is not required to look outside the document for entities, so you'll still want to include entity references in the internal subset.

Notice that I said *subset*. This is because you can have both external and internal definitions as part of the `DOCTYPE`. We'll cover this in more detail when we talk about entities, but including both an external and an internal subset involves including the system and/or public identifier, then the internal subset in brackets, as shown in Listing 7.5.

LISTING 7.5   Internal and External DTD Subsets

```
<?xml version="1.0" encoding="ISO-8859-1" ?>
<!DOCTYPE orchestra SYSTEM "orchestra.dtd" [
    <!ENTITY specific "Oboe, clarinet">
]>
<orchestra>
    <instruments>
        <woodwind>&specific;, and so on.</woodwind>
    </instruments>
</orchestra>
```

Creating Elements and Content Models

Now that we've got the basic syntax down, let's start actually creating a DTD to control data used in orchestra call sheets. This data indicates who should be present and when, and what he or she should be prepared to play.

First you'll need a document, of course. Listing 7.6 shows the document, along with a reference to an external DTD.

LISTING 7.6 The Basic Document

```
<?xml version="1.0" encoding="ISO-8859-1" ?>
<!DOCTYPE orchestra SYSTEM "orchestra.dtd">
<orchestra>
    <performance>
        <piece>Pachelbel's Canon in D</piece>
    </performance>
    <instruments>
        <violin>Joel Borgnine</violin>
        <glockenspiel>Marie Andrassy</glockenspiel>
    </instruments>
</orchestra>
```

To make this document valid, create a second file, `orchestra.dtd`, to define the elements. An element declaration takes the form

```
<!ELEMENT {name} ({content model})>
```

Remember, the braces (`{}`) are not part of the declaration.

Add element definitions to the file, as in Listing 7.7.

LISTING 7.7 Defining Elements

```
<!ELEMENT orchestra (performance, instruments)>
<!ELEMENT performance (piece)>
<!ELEMENT piece (#PCDATA)>
<!ELEMENT instruments (violin, glockenspiel)>
<!ELEMENT violin (#PCDATA)>
<!ELEMENT glockenspiel (#PCDATA)>
```

Each element declaration contains the name of the element and the content model, such as `piece`, `instruments`, or `#PCDATA`. The content model defines what the element can contain. For example, the `violin` element can contain only `PCDATA`, or *parsed character data*, whereas the `performance` element can contain only a `piece` element.

Element order matters when building DTDs. For example, the element declaration

```
<!ELEMENT instruments (violin, glockenspiel)>
```

allows this content:

```
<instruments>
    <violin>Joel Borgnine</violin>
    <glockenspiel>Marie Andrassy</glockenspiel>
</instruments>
```

But it does not allow this:

```
<instruments>
    <glockenspiel>Marie Andrassy</glockenspiel>
    <violin>Joel Borgnine</violin>
</instruments>
```

More flexibility is possible, however, using modifiers and combinations of elements, as discussed next.

Content Modifiers

When a content model cites an element without a modifier, the element must appear once and only once, which rather limits what you can do with a document. Fortunately, modifiers exist that give you some control over how many times an element can or must appear, as shown in Table 7.1.

TABLE 7.1   Content Model Modifiers

Modifier	Description
?	Indicates an optional element. If the element appears, it can appear only once.
+	Indicates an element that's mandatory, but can be repeated any number of times.
*	Indicates an optional element. Unlike elements specified with the ? modifier, however, this element can be repeated any number of times.

Listing 7.8 demonstrates these modifiers.

LISTING 7.8   Modifiers in Action

```
<!ELEMENT orchestra (performance, instruments)>
<!ELEMENT performance (piece+)>
<!ELEMENT piece (#PCDATA)>
<!ELEMENT instruments (violin*, glockenspiel?)>
<!ELEMENT violin (#PCDATA)>
<!ELEMENT glockenspiel (#PCDATA)>
```

With these modifiers, the **performance** element can include one or more **piece**s (but must include at least one). Both elements within the **instruments** element are optional; you can include as many **violin**s as you want, but just one **glockenspiel**.

Element Choices

Content modifiers make the model somewhat more flexible, but you may still need to allow authors to add elements in different orders, or to choose between different options. These capabilities are tied together in the "or" operator, the pipe (|).

To allow the author to make a choice between elements in a content model, separate them with a pipe rather than a comma, as shown in Listing 7.9.

LISTING 7.9   Allowing the Author to Make a Choice

```
<!ELEMENT orchestra (performance, instruments)>
<!ELEMENT performance (piece+ | improv)>
<!ELEMENT piece (#PCDATA)>
<!ELEMENT improv (#PCDATA)>
<!ELEMENT instruments (violin*, glockenspiel?)>
<!ELEMENT violin (#PCDATA)>
<!ELEMENT glockenspiel (#PCDATA)>
```

Notice that the `performance` element can contain either a single `improv` element or one or more `piece` elements.

You can also group choices within a content model by using parentheses, as shown in Listing 7.10.

LISTING 7.10   Grouping Choices

```
<!ELEMENT orchestra (performance, instruments)>
<!ELEMENT performance (piece+ | improv)>
<!ELEMENT piece (#PCDATA)>
<!ELEMENT improv (#PCDATA)>
<!ELEMENT instruments ((violin*, glockenspiel?) | (piano?, clarinet+))>
<!ELEMENT violin (#PCDATA)>
<!ELEMENT glockenspiel (#PCDATA)>
<!ELEMENT piano (#PCDATA)>
<!ELEMENT clarinet (#PCDATA)>
```

Each set of elements within parentheses is a single choice. Here, the `instruments` element can contain either `violins` and a `glockenspiel` or a `piano` and `clarinets`.

You can also add modifiers to groups of choices, which allows an author to add elements in any order, as shown in Listing 7.11.

LISTING 7.11   Allowing Different Element Order

```
<!ELEMENT orchestra (performance, instruments)>
<!ELEMENT performance (piece | improv)+>
<!ELEMENT piece (#PCDATA)>
<!ELEMENT improv (#PCDATA)>
...
```

This flexibility allows you to create the document in Listing 7.12.

LISTING 7.12   Multiple Choices

```
<?xml version="1.0" encoding="ISO-8859-1" ?>
<!DOCTYPE orchestra SYSTEM "orchestra.dtd">
<orchestra>
    <performance>
        <piece>Pachelbel's Canon in D</piece>
        <improv>Jazz on the Shore</improv>
        <piece>Beethoven's Ode to Joy</piece>
    </performance>
    <instruments>
        <violin>Joel Borgnine</violin>
        <glockenspiel>Marie Andrassy</glockenspiel>
    </instruments>
</orchestra>
```

Here is where we run into a limitation of DTDs. While modifiers and choices allow an author to select any order for elements, there is no way to control the number of times an element appears. For example, there is no way, with a DTD, to specify that you must have at least one **piece** within the **performance** element, and that it may appear in any order with any number (including zero) of **improv** elements.

To allow different orders in a DTD, you need to build a content model that allows multiple occurrences of a single choice, which may include any of the allowed elements. When you use such a model, there is no way to limit the number of occurrences of a particular element. In many cases, however, this tradeoff is acceptable.

Filling in the Gaps

Controlling both order and frequency of elements is one area where XML Schemas, such as the W3C XML Schema Recommendation, give designers more control over the structure of the data. Some programmers also use an application to perform final validation of data for requirements that can't be written into a DTD.

Mixed Content

One common situation involves an element that may contain a mixture of element and text content, as shown in Listing 7.13.

LISTING 7.13   Mixed Content

```
<?xml version="1.0" encoding="ISO-8859-1" ?>
<!DOCTYPE orchestra SYSTEM "orchestra.dtd">
<orchestra>
    <performance>
        <piece>Pachelbel's Canon in D</piece>
```

LISTING 7.13 Continued

```
            <improv>Jazz on the Shore</improv>
            <piece>Beethoven's Ode to Joy</piece>
        </performance>
        <description>
            This rehearsal will showcase <violin>Joel
            Borgnine</violin> and his brilliant improvisation,
            <improv>Jazz on the Shore</improv>. We will also
            be rehearsing <piece>Pachelbel's Canon in D</piece>
            and <piece>Beethoven's Ode to Joy</piece>.
        </description>
        <instruments>
                <violin>Joel Borgnine</violin>
                <glockenspiel>Marie Andrassy</glockenspiel>
        </instruments>
    </orchestra>
```

The use of both elements and text within a single element produces *mixed content*, which must be specified in the DTD. For example, to make Listing 7.13 valid, make changes to the DTD as shown in Listing 7.14.

LISTING 7.14 Defining Mixed Content

```
<!ELEMENT orchestra (performance, description, instruments)>
<!ELEMENT performance (piece | improv)+>
<!ELEMENT piece (#PCDATA)>
<!ELEMENT improv (#PCDATA)>
<!ELEMENT description ( #PCDATA | violin | improv | piece )*>
<!ELEMENT instruments ((violin*, glockenspiel?) | (piano?, clarinet+))>
<!ELEMENT violin (#PCDATA)>
<!ELEMENT glockenspiel (#PCDATA)>
<!ELEMENT piano (#PCDATA)>
<!ELEMENT clarinet (#PCDATA)>
```

When building the `description` element, you can include any number of choices, where each choice may be a `violin`, `improv`, `piece`, or string of text.

Whitespace, Mixed Content, and DOM

The Document Object Model (DOM) considers the whitespace between elements to be text nodes, but as far as DTDs are concerned, non-whitespace (characters other than spaces, tabs, line feeds, and so on) is needed to create mixed content.

You still have to specify the elements you're including; they're not considered simple text. Note also that because you're once again using choices and modifiers, you won't be able to control how many times each element appears, or in what order.

Order

#PCDATA must be listed first in a mixed-content declaration.

Normally, in a mixed-content situation, the biggest hassle is specifying all the elements that can appear within an element. For example, to be truly useful, the `description` element's content model would also have to include all the different instrument elements, such as `piano` and `clarinet`. Fortunately, XML offers us an easier way.

ANY Elements

One aspect of XML DTDs that isn't used as frequently as you might expect is an element that can, by definition, contain any of the elements that have already been defined. For example, the previous example might be defined as shown in Listing 7.15.

LISTING 7.15   Using the ANY Keyword

```
<!ELEMENT orchestra (performance, description, instruments)>
<!ELEMENT performance (piece | improv)+>
<!ELEMENT piece (#PCDATA)>
<!ELEMENT improv (#PCDATA)>
<!ELEMENT description ANY>
<!ELEMENT instruments ((violin*, glockenspiel?) | (piano?, clarinet+))>
<!ELEMENT violin (#PCDATA)>
<!ELEMENT glockenspiel (#PCDATA)>
<!ELEMENT piano (#PCDATA)>
<!ELEMENT clarinet (#PCDATA)>
```

Notice that the keyword ANY is not enclosed in parentheses. Parentheses would indicate that the element could contain an element called ANY, rather than any element.

In this case, any of the predefined elements could be included in the `description` element.

While the ANY keyword is convenient, it's not used as often as you might think because in many ways it defeats the purpose of validation by being overly generous in the content that it allows. For example, in a situation like the one we've been discussing, you probably wouldn't want the `instruments` element within the `description` element, because it wouldn't make organizational sense. The ANY keyword, however, would allow it.

Empty Elements

Sometimes an element's content model is the ultimate in simplicity: The element can't contain anything else. Such elements are known as *empty elements*.

An empty element typically contains all of its information in attributes. For example, the HTML image tag is an empty element:

```
<img src="images/logo.gif" alt="Logo"/>
```

Similarly, we can define the `intermission` element as empty, as in Listing 7.16.

LISTING 7.16   Defining an Empty Element

```
<!ELEMENT orchestra (performance, description, instruments)>
<!ELEMENT performance (piece | improv | intermission)+>
<!ELEMENT piece (#PCDATA)>
<!ELEMENT intermission EMPTY>
<!ELEMENT improv (#PCDATA)>
<!ELEMENT description ANY>
...
```

Note that we don't have to use the abbreviated notation shown in the `img` example. Listing 7.17 shows two valid versions of the empty elements.

LISTING 7.17   Empty Elements

```
<?xml version="1.0" encoding="ISO-8859-1" ?>
<!DOCTYPE orchestra SYSTEM "orchestra.dtd">
<orchestra>
    <performance>
        <piece>Pachelbel's Canon in D</piece>
        <intermission/>
        <improv>Jazz on the Shore</improv>
        <intermission></intermission>
        <piece>Beethoven's Ode to Joy</piece>
    </performance>
    <description>
        This rehearsal will showcase <violin>Joel
        Borgnine</violin> and his brilliant improvisation,
        <improv>Jazz on the Shore</improv>. We will also
        be rehearsing <piece>Pachelbel's Canon in D</piece>
        and <piece>Beethoven's Ode to Joy</piece>.
    </description>
    <instruments>
         <violin>Joel Borgnine</violin>
         <glockenspiel>Marie Andrassy</glockenspiel>
    </instruments>
</orchestra>
```

Keep in mind, however, that this is one situation where whitespace matters. For example, the following element is not empty:

```
<intermission> </intermission>
```

Empty Elements and Browsers

The process of translating HTML into XML and transforming it into XHTML created empty elements such as `<img />` and `<br />`. While it's technically correct to write them with an end tag (`<br></br>`, for example), most current browsers won't interpret them properly. Some, for example, interpret this code as two `<br>` tags. Similarly, browsers might not understand the meaning of the slash within the tag, interpreting <br/> as a **br/** tag. To solve these problems, don't use a separate closing tag and include a space before the slash, like this:

```
<br />
```

If no browsers are involved, the space is not necessary, but can make the document more readable.

Creating Attributes

Now that we have elements, it's time to add attributes to them. To do so, add attribute lists to the DTD. Each attribute list takes the form

```
<!ATTLIST {element name} {attribute name} {type} {default option}>
```

and can specify one or more attributes, as shown in Listing 7.18.

LISTING 7.18   Defining Attributes

```
<!ELEMENT orchestra (performance, description, instruments)>
<!ELEMENT performance (piece | improv | intermission)+>
<!ELEMENT piece (#PCDATA)>
<!ELEMENT intermission EMPTY>
<!ATTLIST intermission setup  CDATA #IMPLIED
                       length CDATA #IMPLIED>
<!ELEMENT improv (#PCDATA)>
...
<!ELEMENT piano (#PCDATA)>
<!ELEMENT clarinet (#PCDATA)>

<!ATTLIST violin seat CDATA #IMPLIED>
```

Implied Attributes

We'll discuss attribute default values in the next section, but for now understand that an *implied* attribute is one that is optional.

Keep in mind that the attribute definition doesn't need to directly follow the element to which it applies, and the order in which attributes are specified doesn't necessarily correspond to the order in which they will appear in the document.

Default Values

The simplest attribute definition is one that declares an optional text attribute, as shown in the **violin** element's **seat** attribute in Listing 7.18.

In Listing 7.18, we've defined attributes for the **intermission** and **violin** elements. These attributes may consist of character data, or they may be left out entirely, and the document will still be valid, as shown in Listing 7.19.

LISTING 7.19 Implied Attributes

```
<?xml version="1.0" encoding="ISO-8859-1" ?>
<!DOCTYPE orchestra SYSTEM "orchestra.dtd">
<orchestra>
    <performance>
        <piece>Pachelbel's Canon in D</piece>
        <intermission length="15 minutes" setup="minimal"/>
        <improv>Jazz on the Shore</improv>
        <intermission length="20 minutes"></intermission>
        <piece>Beethoven's Ode to Joy</piece>
    </performance>
    <description>
        This rehearsal will showcase <violin>Joel
        Borgnine</violin> and his brilliant improvisation,
        <improv>Jazz on the Shore</improv>. We will also
        be rehearsing <piece>Pachelbel's Canon in D</piece>
        and <piece>Beethoven's Ode to Joy</piece>.
    </description>
    <instruments>
        <violin seat="first">Joel Borgnine</violin>
        <glockenspiel>Marie Andrassy</glockenspiel>
    </instruments>
</orchestra>
```

Similarly, you can require that the attribute be present by changing the default value from #IMPLIED to #REQUIRED, as shown in Listing 7.20.

LISTING 7.20 A Required Attribute

```
...
<!ELEMENT clarinet (#PCDATA)>
<!ATTLIST violin seat CDATA #REQUIRED>
```

Note that if a required attribute isn't present in an element, the document is invalid, but it is still well-formed and will be processed without a problem by a nonvalidating parser.

All of this raises the question, "Why are #IMPLIED and #REQUIRED called default values?"

The reason is that #IMPLIED and #REQUIRED are just two of the possible values. You could, for example, add an actual default value using the DTD, as shown in Listing 7.21.

LISTING 7.21 Using a Default Value

```
...
<!ELEMENT intermission EMPTY>
<!ATTLIST intermission setup  CDATA "full"
                       length CDATA #IMPLIED>
<!ELEMENT improv (#PCDATA)>
...
```

Processing the document adds the default value to the element, as shown in Figure 7.1.

FIGURE 7.1

Default values are automatically added to a document, as evidenced by the `setup="full"` attribute of the second intermission element.

```
<?xml version="1.0" encoding="ISO-8859-1" ?>
<!DOCTYPE orchestra (View Source for full doctype...)>
- <orchestra>
  - <performance>
      <piece>Pachelbel's Canon in D</piece>
      <intermission length="15 minutes" setup="minimal" />
      <improv>Jazz on the Shore</improv>
      <intermission length="20 minutes" setup="full" />
      <piece>Beethoven's Ode to Joy</piece>
    </performance>
  - <description>
      This rehearsal will showcase
      <violin seat="first">Joel Borgnine</violin>
      and his brilliant improvisation,
      <improv>Jazz on the Shore</improv>
      . We will also be rehearsing
      <piece>Pachelbel's Canon in D</piece>
      and
      <piece>Beethoven's Ode to Joy</piece>
      .
    </description>
  - <instruments>
      <violin seat="first">Joel Borgnine</violin>
      <glockenspiel>Marie Andrassy</glockenspiel>
    </instruments>
  </orchestra>
```

This process is known as *infoset augmentation*, and occurs with any XML 1.0–compliant parser, even if it is nonvalidating.

Notice that if no value is provided, the default value is used, but an author can override the default by specifying a value for the element, as evidenced by the first intermission value in the example. On the other hand, if you don't want an author to override these values, you can designate them as *fixed*, as shown in Listing 7.22.

LISTING 7.22   Fixed Attribute Values

```
<!ELEMENT intermission EMPTY>
<!ATTLIST intermission setup  CDATA "full"
                       length CDATA #FIXED "15 minutes">
<!ELEMENT improv (#PCDATA)>
...
```

In this case, if the author leaves out the attribute, the fixed value will be used, as in Figure 7.2, where I haven't supplied a `length` attribute in either `intermission` element, and yet it still appears in the final document.

The difference between `#IMPLIED` and `#FIXED` values is that if the value of a `#FIXED` attribute is specified, it must match the fixed value or the document is invalid, even though it's well-formed.

Enumerated Attributes

Fortunately, restriction is not an all-or-nothing game. In an enumerated attribute, the value must come from a predetermined list, as in Listing 7.23.

FIGURE 7.2
Fixed values are automatically added to a document.

```
C:\WINNT\Profiles\nchase\Desktop\Projects\PrimerPlus\XML\PPXMLCh...
File   Edit   View   Favorites   Tools   Help

<?xml version="1.0" encoding="ISO-8859-1" ?>
<!DOCTYPE orchestra (View Source for full doctype...)>
- <orchestra>
  - <performance>
      <piece>Pachelbel's Canon in D</piece>
      <intermission setup="minimal" length="15 minutes" />
      <improv>Jazz on the Shore</improv>
      <intermission setup="full" length="15 minutes" />
      <piece>Beethoven's Ode to Joy</piece>
    </performance>
  - <description>
      This rehearsal will showcase
      <violin seat="first">Joel Borgnine</violin>
      and his brilliant improvisation,
      <improv>Jazz on the Shore</improv>
      . We will also be rehearsing
      <piece>Pachelbel's Canon in D</piece>
      and
      <piece>Beethoven's Ode to Joy</piece>
      .
    </description>
  - <instruments>
      <violin seat="first">Joel Borgnine</violin>
      <glockenspiel>Marie Andrassy</glockenspiel>
    </instruments>
  </orchestra>
```

LISTING 7.23   Enumerated Attributes

```
...
<!ELEMENT intermission EMPTY>
<!ATTLIST intermission setup   (full | partial | minimal) "full"
                       length CDATA #FIXED "15 minutes">
<!ELEMENT improv (#PCDATA)>
...
```

Notice that the enumerated values are not enclosed in quotes, and that the pipe symbol (|) acts as an "or" operator, just as it did in the element content models. If the author chooses a value that's not in the list, the document is invalid.

Enumeration Restrictions

Enumerated values must be **NMTOKEN** values. We'll discuss **NMTOKEN**s in the section titled "NMTOKEN Attributes," but basically this restriction means that they must be single words, without punctuation or spaces.

All four types of default values can coexist with enumerated values, as shown in Listing 7.24.

LISTING 7.24   Default Types and Enumerated Attributes

```
...
<!ELEMENT intermission EMPTY>
<!ATTLIST intermission setup   (full | partial | minimal) "full"
                       length (15 | 30 | 45 | 60) #FIXED "15">
```

LISTING 7.24   Continued

```
<!ELEMENT improv (#PCDATA)>
...
<!ELEMENT piano (#PCDATA)>
<!ATTLIST piano type (accoustic | electronic) #IMPLIED>
<!ELEMENT clarinet (#PCDATA)>
<!ATTLIST violin seat (first | second | other) #REQUIRED>
```

ID and IDREF Attributes

When using XML as a means for storing data, you will often need to emulate some of the functionality (or at least the thought patterns) behind storage of data in a database. One specific area where this comes into play is in using foreign keys, where the value of one information item must refer to an identical value in another information item.

In DTDs, you can accomplish this (to some extent) by using ID and IDREF attributes.

An ID is an attribute that has as its type ID rather than CDATA, and an IDREF is an attribute that has as its type IDREF rather than CDATA, as in Listing 7.25.

LISTING 7.25   ID and IDREF Attributes

```
<!ELEMENT orchestra (performance, description, instruments, concertpieces)>
<!ELEMENT performance (piece | improv | intermission)+>
<!ELEMENT piece EMPTY>
<!ATTLIST piece pid IDREF #REQUIRED>
<!ELEMENT intermission EMPTY>
<!ATTLIST intermission setup  (full | partial | minimal) "full"
                       length (15 | 30 | 45 | 60) #FIXED "15">
<!ELEMENT improv EMPTY>
<!ATTLIST improv iid IDREF #REQUIRED>
<!ELEMENT description ANY>
...
<!ATTLIST violin seat (first | second | other) #REQUIRED>
<!ELEMENT concertpieces (concertpiece*)>
<!ELEMENT concertpiece (#PCDATA)>
<!ATTLIST concertpiece pieceid ID #REQUIRED>
```

Structuring attributes this way brings certain restrictions into play:

- ID attributes must take a certain form. For one thing, they cannot start with a number. This restriction can be jarring to database programmers who are used to numeric keys. Many authors get around this restriction by starting an ID with the underscore character (_), as shown in Listing 7.26. IDs also cannot contain spaces or other punctuation, and each ID attribute value must be unique.

- IDREF attributes have the same format restrictions as ID attributes, because while they don't need to be unique, they need to match an existing ID attribute. Take Listing 7.26, for example.

LISTING 7.26 Valid and Invalid `IDREF` Attributes

```
<?xml version="1.0" encoding="ISO-8859-1" ?>
<!DOCTYPE orchestra SYSTEM "orchestra.dtd">
<orchestra>
    <performance>
        <piece pid="_1"/>
        <intermission setup="minimal"/>
        <improv iid="_3"/>
        <intermission></intermission>
        <piece pid="_2"/>
        <piece pid="_4"/>
    </performance>
    <description>
        This rehearsal will showcase <violin seat="first">Joel
        Borgnine</violin> and his brilliant improvisation,
        <improv iid="_3"/>. We will also be rehearsing
        <piece pid="_1"/> and <piece pid="_2"/>.
    </description>
    <instruments>
        <violin seat="first">Joel Borgnine</violin>
        <glockenspiel>Marie Andrassy</glockenspiel>
    </instruments>
    <concertpieces>
        <concertpiece pieceid="_1">Pachelbel's Canon in D</concertpiece>
        <concertpiece pieceid="_2">Beethoven's Ode to Joy</concertpiece>
        <concertpiece pieceid="_3">Jazz on the Shore</concertpiece>
    </concertpieces>
</orchestra>
```

The first two `pid` attributes and the `iid` attribute are fine, but the third `pid` attribute will cause a validation error because there is no corresponding `pieceid` ID value. (There is no concert-piece element with a `pieceid` attribute of `4`.)

Notice also that two different `IDREF`s are defined, but they both point back to the same `ID` attribute. Each document has only one `ID` "pool" from which all `ID`s are drawn, so even if you have two `ID` attributes with different names, on different elements, they can't share values.

Schema Improvements

IDs and IDREFs are areas where XML Schemas attempt to make improvements in functionality, and generally succeed.

One extension of the `IDREF` attribute is the `IDREFS` attribute. This attribute can carry several `IDREF` values, separated by spaces, as shown in Listings 7.27 and 7.28.

LISTING 7.27 Defining `IDREFS` Attributes

```
<!ELEMENT orchestra (performance, description, instruments, concertpieces)>
<!ELEMENT performance (piece | improv | intermission)+>
```

LISTING 7.27   Continued

```
<!ELEMENT piece EMPTY>
<!ATTLIST piece pid IDREFS #REQUIRED>
<!ELEMENT intermission EMPTY>
<!ATTLIST intermission setup  (full | partial | minimal) "full"
                       length (15 | 30 | 45 | 60) #FIXED "15">
<!ELEMENT improv EMPTY>
<!ATTLIST improv iid IDREFS #REQUIRED>
<!ELEMENT description ANY>
...
```

LISTING 7.28   Using IDREFS Attributes

```
<?xml version="1.0" encoding="ISO-8859-1" ?>
<!DOCTYPE orchestra SYSTEM "orchestra.dtd">
<orchestra>
    <performance>
        <piece pid="_1"/>
        <intermission setup="minimal"/>
        <improv iid="_3"/>
        <intermission></intermission>
        <piece pid="_2 _4"/>
    </performance>
...
    <concertpieces>
        <concertpiece pieceid="_1">Pachelbel's Canon in D</concertpiece>
        <concertpiece pieceid="_2">Beethoven's Ode to Joy</concertpiece>
        <concertpiece pieceid="_3">Jazz on the Shore</concertpiece>
        <concertpiece pieceid="_4">Bach's Brandenburg Concerto</concertpiece>
    </concertpieces>
</orchestra>
```

Each value specified in an IDREFS attribute must satisfy the same requirements as an IDREF value; it must exist as an ID within the document.

NMTOKEN **Attributes**

Another specialized type of attribute value is the NMTOKEN. Like IDs, NMTOKENs cannot contain spaces, but unlike IDs, they can start with a number.

> **NMTOKEN**
>
> NMTOKEN is short for *name token*. NMTOKEN values have no spaces; they have been broken down as far as possible, into "tokens."

Typically, you define a NMTOKEN attribute in order to force users to limit their values to those suitable as keywords. You can also create a NMTOKENS attribute, which enables an author to specify multiple keywords such as jazz and modern, as shown in Listings 7.29 and 7.30.

LISTING 7.29   NMTOKEN and NMTOKENS Attributes

```
...
<!ELEMENT concertpiece (#PCDATA)>
<!ATTLIST concertpiece pieceid ID #REQUIRED
                       genre NMTOKENS #IMPLIED>
```

LISTING 7.30   NMTOKENS Attributes

```
...
    <concertpieces>
        <concertpiece pieceid="_1" genre="classical">Pachelbel's Canon in D
                                                     </concertpiece>
        <concertpiece pieceid="_2" genre="classical">Beethoven's Ode to Joy
                                                     </concertpiece>
        <concertpiece pieceid="_3" genre="jazz modern">Jazz on the Shore
                                                     < /concertpiece>
        <concertpiece pieceid="_4" genre="classical">Bach's Brandenburg Concerto
                                                     </concertpiece>
    </concertpieces>
</orchestra>
```

NMTOKEN and NMTOKENS attributes don't have to refer to other resources or attributes; they simply have to satisfy the format constraints.

ENTITY Attributes

An attribute can also be defined as an ENTITY, but this is rarely used in XML applications, which typically concern themselves with text. There is a place for ENTITY attributes, however, when dealing with XML-unfriendly data. We'll talk more about ENTITY and ENTITIES attributes after we define entities in the next section.

General Entities

Another type of content that appears in XML documents is the *general entity*. An *entity* is a reference to other content, in the form of an ampersand (&), a numeric or alphabetical code, and a semicolon (;). For example, many HTML authors are familiar with using some of XML's predefined entities, shown in bold in Listing 7.31.

LISTING 7.31   Using Predefined Entities

```
<html>
<head><title>Entity demonstration</title></head>
<body>
    <p>&quot;To levitate a human being would take a magnet
    more powerful than anything currently available,&quot;
    said the scientist from the &lt;EMPIRE&gt; institute.</p>
</body>
</html>
```

When the browser encounters entities such as <, >, and ", it replaces them with the appropriate text, such as <, >, and ", as shown in Figure 7.3. (The *lt* in < stands for *less than*, the *gt* in > stands for *greater than*, and *quot* is short for *quotation mark*.)

FIGURE 7.3
Entities are replaced with the appropriate text.

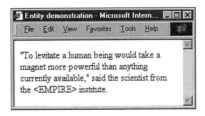

XML enables you to define your own entities for use within an XML document.

Custom Entities

One problem with XML data is that unless it's dynamically generated, it can be a nightmare to maintain. For example, if you have thousands of pages with masthead information, adding or removing an individual name from all of those pages is not only difficult, it's impractical.

DTD designers can head off this problem by creating general entities that represent replacement text. For example, Listing 7.32 shows the creation of an entity that, when the document is processed, is replaced by specific text, as shown in Figure 7.4.

LISTING 7.32   General Entities

```
<?xml version="1.0" encoding="ISO-8859-1" ?>
<!DOCTYPE orchestra SYSTEM "orchestra.dtd" [
    <!ENTITY callwarning "Please arrive prepared to play!">
]>
<orchestra>
    <performance>
        <piece pid="_1"/>
        <intermission setup="minimal"/>
        <improv iid="_3"/>
        <intermission></intermission>
        <piece pid="_2 _4"/>
    </performance>
    <description>
        &callwarning;
        This rehearsal will showcase <violin seat="first">Joel
        Borgnine</violin> and his brilliant improvisation,
        <improv iid="_3"/>. We will also be rehearsing
        <piece pid="_1"/> and <piece pid="_2"/>.
    </description>
    ...
</orchestra>
```

FIGURE 7.4

General entities in action.

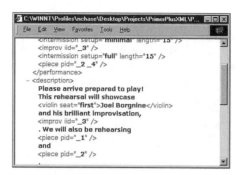

The entity definition specifies the name of the entity, such as `callwarning`, and the replacement text. To use the entity within the document, surround the name with the ampersand (`&`) and semicolon (`;`), as in `&callwarning;`.

When creating the content for these parsed entities, keep in mind that the replacement text can't create a document that is not well-formed. Listing 7.33 shows an example of a non-well-formed document.

LISTING 7.33   Incorrect Entity Text

```
<?xml version="1.0" encoding="ISO-8859-1" ?>
<!DOCTYPE orchestra SYSTEM "orchestra.dtd" [
    <!ENTITY callwarning "Please arrive prepared to <play>!">
]>
<orchestra>
...
    <description>
        &callwarning;
        This rehearsal will showcase <violin seat="first">Joel
        Borgnine</violin> and his brilliant improvisation,
        <improv iid="_3"/>. We will also be rehearsing
        <piece pid="_1"/> and <piece pid="_2"/>.
    </description>
...
</orchestra>
```

If the processor were to use the replacement text for the `callwarning` entity, it would result in a single `<play>` tag without a closing tag:

```
...
    <description>
        Please arrive prepared to <play>!
        This rehearsal will showcase <violin seat="first">Joel
        Borgnine</violin> and his brilliant improvisation,
        <improv iid="_3"/>. We will also be rehearsing
        <piece pid="_1"/> and <piece pid="_2"/>.
    </description>
...
```

For this reason, the document would not be well-formed.

This is not to say that entities can't be used to include problem information. See the next section for details.

Named Entities Versus Numerical Entities

Another common use for entities is to allow authors to add information that would otherwise be difficult for them to type, or would create well-formedness problems.

For example, if I want to indicate that a piece is to be played in the key of B-flat, I have a problem, because there's no key on my keyboard for the flat symbol. I do know, however, that this character has a Unicode number of 9837, so I can add it as a numeric entity, as in Listing 7.34.

LISTING 7.34   Adding a Numeric Entity

```
<?xml version="1.0" encoding="ISO-8859-1" ?>
<!DOCTYPE orchestra SYSTEM "orchestra.dtd" [
    <!ENTITY flat "&#9837;">
]>
<orchestra>
...
    <description>
        This rehearsal will showcase <violin seat="first">Joel
        Borgnine</violin> and his brilliant improvisation in B&flat;,
        <improv iid="_3"/>. We will also be rehearsing
        <piece pid="_1"/> and <piece pid="_2"/>.
    </description>
...
</orchestra>
```

The processor can then replace the entity with the appropriate character, as shown in Figure 7.5.

FIGURE 7.5

Entities can reference characters by number.

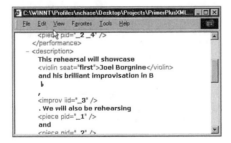

Any character can be referenced this way. You can reference these characters either by their decimal number or by their hexadecimal number. To specify that an entity is referencing a hexadecimal number, follow the number sign (#) with an **x**. For example, you can specify the flat symbol using its hexadecimal number, 266D:

```
<!ENTITY flat "&#x266D">
```

Entity definitions can create general entities that map to numerical entities. For example, the five "predefined" entities are actually general entities that have as their replacement text numerical entities. You can also create your own, as I've done here:

```
<!ENTITY lt       "&#38;#60;">
<!ENTITY gt       "&#62;">
<!ENTITY amp      "&#38;#38;">
<!ENTITY apos     "&#39;">
<!ENTITY quot     "&#34;">
<!ENTITY flat     "&#9837;">
<!ENTITY natural  "&#x266E;">
<!ENTITY sharp    "&#x266F;">
```

Note that **amp** in the third line is short for *ampersand* (**&**) and **apos** in the fourth line is short for *apostrophe* (').

External Entities

Entities can also be used to gather information from different sources and documents. An *external entity* is an entity that references an external resource such as a file. Web programmers may be familiar with the concept of external entities, which are also called *include files*.

Parsed Entities

The creation of an external parsed entity is similar to the creation of a general entity, but instead of referencing specific characters, you specify a system or public identifier. You can then pull this information into the file by referencing the entity.

For example, you might have a file that contains external content that is referenced from multiple locations. For example, all call sheets will use the same list of standard pieces, so you can store them in a separate file called **musicalnumbers.xml**. You can then create an external parsed entity to refer to the file, and reference it rather than listing all the content explicitly. Listing 7.35 demonstrates this.

LISTING 7.35   *Content Used in Multiple Places*

```
<?xml version="1.0" encoding="ISO-8859-1" ?>
<!DOCTYPE orchestra SYSTEM "orchestra.dtd" [
    <!ENTITY flat "&#9837;">
    <!ENTITY sharp "&#x266F;">
    <!ENTITY natural "&#x266E;">

    <!ENTITY concertpieces SYSTEM "musicalnumbers.xml">
]>
<orchestra>
...
```

LISTING 7.35 *Continued*

```
        <instruments>
            <violin seat="first">Joel Borgnine</violin>
            <glockenspiel>Marie Andrassy</glockenspiel>
        </instruments>
        &concertpieces;
</orchestra>
```

The contents of the file become part of the document where you reference the entity, as shown in Figure 7.6.

FIGURE 7.6
External parsed entities are added to the document wherever they are referenced.

It's tempting to use this technique to add commonly used DTD definitions to the document, but general entities can only be referenced within the document itself. To use entities within the actual DTD, you need a different type of entity—the *parameter entity* (described later).

Keep two very important factors in mind when using external parsed entities:

- As with general entities specified within the document, because these entities are parsed, the replacement text must not cause the XML document to be non-well-formed.

- If a document is specified as `standalone="yes"`, a nonvalidating processor is not required to retrieve the contents of an external entity, so if your document depends on such content, you may have a problem. If you'll only be using your document with validating parsers, this isn't an issue, as validating parsers must always retrieve external entities.

In addition to specifying local resources, you can build entities based on `SYSTEM` identifiers categorized by URI. This capability enables you to insert into the document not only remote information, but also information that's dynamically generated. For example, I could have specified the `concertpieces` entity as follows:

```
<!ENTITY concertpieces SYSTEM
    "http://www.nicholaschase.com/musicapp/getmusic.asp?date=4.23.04">
```

The processor would then retrieve the contents of the URI and insert them into the document.

You can also use public identifiers to specify your entities, though you'll probably want to include a system identifier for them as well. For example:

```
<!ENTITY greek PUBLIC "ISO 8879:1986//ENTITIES Greek Symbols//EN"
 "http://www.nicholaschase.com/resources/greek.ent">
```

Unparsed Entities

Not all entities are parsed. Some are *unparsed entities*, which makes it possible to pull in information that is not, by nature, well-formed. One example is binary files, such as images.

To create an unparsed entity, first create a *notation*, which defines a type of file. Then create the entity as an external entity, adding a reference to the notation as shown in Listing 7.36.

LISTING 7.36   Creating Unparsed Entities

```
<?xml version="1.0" encoding="ISO-8859-1" ?>
<!DOCTYPE orchestra SYSTEM "orchestra.dtd" [
...

    <!ENTITY concertpieces SYSTEM "musicalnumbers.xml">

    <!NOTATION gif SYSTEM "c:\winnt\system32\mspaint.exe ">
    <!ENTITY logo SYSTEM "logo.gif" NDATA gif >
]>
<orchestra>
...
</orchestra>
```

The difference between parsed and unparsed entities lies in how they can be used. While a parsed entity can be referenced within the text, in XML an unparsed entity is generally referenced as the content of an attribute. For example, you might have a series of images that you want to link into your data so that they can be referenced by an application. To do this, you must create an attribute that uses either the **ENTITY** or **ENTITIES** data type, then create the entities themselves, and then reference the entities within the document, as shown in Listing 7.37.

LISTING 7.37   Using Unparsed Entities

```
<?xml version="1.0" encoding="ISO-8859-1" ?>
<!DOCTYPE orchestra SYSTEM "orchestra.dtd" [
...

    <!NOTATION gif SYSTEM "c:\winnt\system32\mspaint.exe ">
    <!ENTITY logo SYSTEM "logo.gif" NDATA gif >

    <!ENTITY violinimg SYSTEM "violin.gif" NDATA gif >
    <!ENTITY firstseatimg SYSTEM "firstseat.gif" NDATA gif >
    <!ENTITY glockenspielimg SYSTEM "glockenspiel.gif" NDATA gif >

    <!ATTLIST violin graphics ENTITIES #IMPLIED>
```

LISTING 7.37   Continued

```
    <!ATTLIST glockenspiel graphics ENTITY #IMPLIED>
]>
<orchestra>
...
    <instruments>
        <violin seat="first" graphics="violinimg firstseatimg">Joel Borgnine
                                                            </violin>
        <glockenspiel graphics="glockenspielimg">Marie Andrassy</glockenspiel>
    </instruments>
    &concertpieces;
</orchestra>
```

Notice that when calling an entity in this way, you list only the name, rather than the ampersand, name, and semicolon.

Current browsers will allow you to build such a document, but won't actually do anything with the data, so this technique is of limited use in the browser environment. In building your own applications, however, you'll have the information necessary for retrieving the external resource for further processing. You may choose, for example, to attach a particular data file to an element, and use your overall application to process it.

Referencing External Resources from a Browser

Browsers don't have the ability to reference unparsed entities. HTML authors instead add the location of the resource directly, like this:

```
<img src="images/logo.gif" />
```

Parameter Entities

General entities have uses, but only in the construction of the document itself. *Parameter entities*, on the other hand, are useful in the creation of the DTD. A parameter entity is created in the same way as a general entity, except that the name is preceded by a percent sign (%) and a space, and the reference uses a percent sign rather than an ampersand, as in Listing 7.38.

LISTING 7.38   Parameter Entities

```
<?xml version="1.0" encoding="ISO-8859-1" ?>
<!DOCTYPE orchestra SYSTEM "orchestra.dtd" [

    <!ENTITY % flatEnt "<!ENTITY flat &#34;&#x266F;&#34;>">
    %flatEnt;

    <!ENTITY sharp "&#x266F;">
    <!ENTITY natural "&#x266E;">
...
]>
```

```
<orchestra>
...
</orchestra>
```

Parameter entities are most useful for specifications that are used over and over again, such as common attributes or groups of elements, but when used as part of markup—as opposed to directly, as in the previous example—they can only appear in the external subset, as shown in Listing 7.39.

LISTING 7.39   Using Parameter Entities as Part of Markup

```
...
<!ELEMENT clarinet (#PCDATA)>

<!ENTITY % seatAtt "first | second | other">

<!ATTLIST violin seat (%seatAtt;) #REQUIRED>
<!ELEMENT concertpieces (concertpiece*)>
<!ELEMENT concertpiece (#PCDATA)>
<!ATTLIST concertpiece pieceid ID #REQUIRED
                       genre NMTOKENS #IMPLIED>
```

Note that a parameter entity can't be recursive; it can't reference itself, either directly or indirectly.

Parameter entities can be one of the most powerful features of DTDs.

Making Decisions

One way that parameter entities provide flexibility is in helping to determine which sections of a DTD should be "active" at any given time. The specification enables you to indicate which sections to include or ignore, allowing you to have several different versions of a DTD for different applications. For example, Listing 7.40 shows a DTD with woodwind section and piano information included, but string section and glockenspiel information excluded.

LISTING 7.40   Conditional DTD Sections

```
...
<!ELEMENT improv EMPTY>
<!ATTLIST improv iid IDREFS #REQUIRED>
<!ELEMENT description ANY>

<![INCLUDE[
    <!ELEMENT instruments (piano?, clarinet+)>
]]>
<![IGNORE[
    <!ELEMENT instruments (violin*, glockenspiel?)>
]]>
<!ELEMENT violin (#PCDATA)>
<!ELEMENT glockenspiel (#PCDATA)>
```

```
...
<!ATTLIST concertpiece pieceid ID #REQUIRED
                       genre NMTOKENS #IMPLIED>
```

When the document is processed, only the first section will be included, so the document as we've been using it will be invalid.

Parameter entities can assist in this process by giving you an easy way to determine which sections are active. Consider Listing 7.41.

LISTING 7.41   Using Parameter Entities with Conditional Sections

```
<!ENTITY % woodwind "INCLUDE">
<!ENTITY % string "IGNORE">

<!ELEMENT orchestra (performance, description, instruments, concertpieces)>
...
<!ELEMENT description ANY>

<![%woodwind;[
    <!ELEMENT instruments (piano?, clarinet+)>
]]>
<![%string;[
    <!ELEMENT instruments (violin*, glockenspiel?)>
]]>
<!ELEMENT violin (#PCDATA)>
<!ELEMENT glockenspiel (#PCDATA)>
...
```

By changing the values of `string` and `woodwind`, you can control which sections of the DTD are effective at any given time. This way, if you are building a call sheet for the woodwind instruments and the piano, you can activate the `woodwind` section, whereas if you are building a call sheet for the string instruments and the glockenspiel, you can activate the `string` section.

You can also pass this power on to your users.

Customization

Perhaps the most useful aspect of parameter entities comes from a technicality regarding DTDs. You might remember that earlier in the chapter we mentioned that a document can have both an external DTD subset and an internal DTD subset. Well, it turns out that while the first definition in a DTD will generally take precedence, all definitions in the internal subset will take precedence over definitions in the external subset.

This means that you can create a *parameterized DTD*, where certain pieces of information, such as key phrases or conditional switches, have been encoded as parameter entities. When an author uses this DTD, he or she can change the values and the new values will be carried into the processing of the document.

Consider the DTD in Listing 7.42.

LISTING 7.42   A Parameterized DTD

```
<!ENTITY % woodwind "INCLUDE">
<!ENTITY % string "IGNORE">
<!ENTITY % custom "IGNORE">
<!ENTITY % customSet "">

<!ELEMENT orchestra (performance, description, instruments, concertpieces)>
<!ELEMENT performance (piece | improv | intermission)+>
...
<![%woodwind;[
    <!ELEMENT instruments (piano?, clarinet+)>
]]>
<![%string;[
    <!ELEMENT instruments (violin*, glockenspiel?)>
]]>
<![%custom;[
    <!ELEMENT instruments (%customSet;)>
]]>
<!ELEMENT violin (#PCDATA)>
...
```

This DTD has several parameter entities that the author can control. The author can choose between the woodwind, string, and custom versions of the instruments element, and, if choosing the custom version, can determine what the actual content model should be. Listing 7.43 shows the use of this DTD and the customization of these values.

LISTING 7.43   Using Parameter Entities

```
<?xml version="1.0" encoding="ISO-8859-1" ?>
<!DOCTYPE orchestra SYSTEM "orchestra.dtd" [
...
    <!ATTLIST violin graphics ENTITIES #IMPLIED>
    <!ATTLIST glockenspiel graphics ENTITY #IMPLIED>

    <!ENTITY % woodwind "IGNORE">
    <!ENTITY % string "IGNORE">
    <!ENTITY % custom "INCLUDE">
    <!ENTITY % customSet "piano, glockenspiel">
]>
<orchestra>
...
    <instruments>
        <piano>Joel Borgnine</piano>
        <glockenspiel graphics="glockenspielimg">Marie Andrassy</glockenspiel>
    </instruments>
    &concertpieces;
</orchestra>
```

Here we have "turned off" the **string** and **woodwind** versions of the **instruments** element, and "turned on" the **custom** version, for which we have provided a content model.

By using parameterized DTDs, you have the ability to control what authors can and cannot change about the structure. Thus, you can prevent them from changing the actual DTD and defeating the whole purpose of validation.

Summary

Creating a Document Type Definition, or DTD, for an XML document involves defining the elements and attributes and what they can contain.

For an element, this means defining the content model. A content model may include a list of mandatory elements in a specific order, a choice of elements, or a combination thereof. The modifiers +, ?, and * affect whether an element is optional, and whether it can appear more than once. You can also define an element as containing only text, or a combination of text and elements. Some elements are defined as **EMPTY**, in which case all information is conveyed through the use of attributes.

For an attribute, a definition determines the type of data to some extent. Data types for attributes include character data (**CDATA**), **ID**s and **IDREF**s, **NMTOKEN**s (useful for keywords), and **ENTITIES**. Attribute definitions also include information pertaining to whether an attribute is required, and whether a default value is used if the attribute is not specified. Attributes can also have their values drawn from an enumerated list, or can be fixed at a single value.

DTDs also contain the definitions of both general entities and parameter entities. General entities are created and defined within the DTD and used within the document. They begin with an ampersand and end with a semicolon (such as **>**) and are replaced with their defined text by the processor. These entities can refer to data within the document or in an external resource. Entities can also be defined as nonparsed, if they refer to data that is not XML-friendly. In this case, their use is limited to attribute values. External resources may be referenced by system or public identifiers.

Parameter entities are defined within the DTD, and can only be used within the DTD. Because a definition in the internal subset of a DTD takes precedence over a definition in the external subset, parameter entities can be used to give an author some control over the contents of the DTD. For example, they can be used, along with **INCLUDE** and **IGNORE** sections, to turn sections of the DTD on and off.

Review Questions

1. What is a DTD used for?

2. Can a document have both an internal and an external DTD subset?

3. What are the possible data types for an attribute?

4. Is it possible to create an element declaration that does not require elements to be present in a particular order?

5. What is a content model?

6. What is a content model called if it includes both element and text content?

7. What is the difference between a general entity and a parameter entity?

8. What is a numeric entity?

9. If a DTD specifies default values for an attribute and the document is processed by a nonvalidating parser, what happens to those values?

10. How does the value of the `standalone` attribute affect DTDs (specifically entity declarations)?

11. What is the difference between a system identifier and a public identifier?

Programming Exercises

1. Create a DTD that includes a hierarchy of at least three elements, at least one of which has an enumerated attribute.

2. Create a DTD that includes a mixed-content element that cannot contain itself.

3. Create a DTD that includes an attribute that is optional, but if present must contain a value present within another defined attribute.

4. Create a DTD that includes a section the author can turn on or off, and create a document that utilizes it.

CHAPTER 8

XML SCHEMAS

You will learn about the following in this chapter:

- Schema structure
- Simple and complex elements
- Referencing predefined elements
- Adding attributes
- Creating new types

- Deriving custom types
- Data integrity
- Namespaces
- Other schema proposals

M uch has been made of XML Schema as a "replacement" for DTDs, but the fact is that each has its place. In some situations, particularly with regard to user control through the use of parameter entities, DTDs are still an appropriate choice, while in others, particularly with regard to data types and namespaces, XML Schema will serve you much better.

In this chapter, we'll study the creation of schemas and discuss their strengths and weaknesses. We'll concentrate on the W3C's XML Schema Recommendation, but we'll also take a quick look at RELAX NG, a competing schema proposal, and Schematron, a different way of looking at schemas.

Schema Structure

One of the main complaints about Document Type Definitions (DTDs) is that their syntax is somewhat alien to new XML developers. XML Schema, on the other hand, uses XML to describe XML structures. Let's lay the groundwork for understanding schemas by creating a basic schema document.

Basic Structure

In its most basic form, a *schema document* is an XML document with a `schema` root element and appropriate namespace declarations, as shown in Listing 8.1.

LISTING 8.1 A Basic Schema Document

```
<?xml version="1.0" encoding="UTF-8"?>
<xs:schema xmlns:xs="http://www.w3.org/2001/XMLSchema">
</xs:schema>
```

In the section titled "Namespaces," we'll look at the process of creating documents for specific target namespaces, but for now we'll assume that the data that will ultimately be validated against this schema will not belong to any namespace. Let's consider that assumption for a moment. We have two sets of information items here: those that are part of the schema, and those that are part of the document being defined. It's crucial that the processor be able to tell them apart, and using different namespaces is one way to accomplish that goal.

The XML Schema Recommendation defines the "Schema namespace" as `http://www.w3.org/2001/XMLSchema`, but the choice of alias is up to you. The `xs:` and `xsd:` prefixes are customary. All information preceded by the `xs:` alias is part of the schema itself, and any information that doesn't have an alias is part of the structure being defined.

Documenting the System

As long as we're making decisions (such as the one concerning the namespace issue), we should document them. XML Schema provides a standard means for documenting information about the schema, and even for providing information to an application processing the schema, as shown in Listing 8.2.

Schema or *schema*?

There's no hard-and-fast rule about when to capitalize *schema*. In general, we'll capitalize it when referring to the W3C XML Schema Recommendation or other recommendations, but not when we're talking about the actual schema document.

LISTING 8.2 Documenting the Schema

```
<?xml version="1.0" encoding="UTF-8"?>
<xs:schema xmlns:xs="http://www.w3.org/2001/XMLSchema">
    <xs:annotation>

        <xs:documentation>
            This document describes the schema for the
            collectibles inventory. In phase one of the
            project, no namespaces are used for the data.
        </xs:documentation>

        <xs:appinfo>
            <config xmlns="http://www.example.com/externalapp">
                <customertype>pop culture</customertype>
                <destination id="I43"/>
            </config>
        </xs:appinfo>
```

LISTING 8.2   Continued

```
    </xs:annotation>

</xs:schema>
```

Annotations can reside at several places within the schema document, but they are most common at the root level, as in this listing.

The `documentation` element contains human-readable information about the document and its intended use, while the `appinfo` element contains information intended for an application, and can consist of any well-formed XML. For example, Listing 8.2 shows configuration information (in its own namespace) that can be passed to an application validating the document, as long as the application knows to look for it.

Using the Schema Document

After you create the basic schema document, you need to link it to the instance document. An *instance document* is just what it sounds like: an instance of the structure defined within the schema.

Validating parsers look for "hints" about the location of the schema document in the root element of the instance document, as in Listing 8.3.

LISTING 8.3   Linking to a Schema Document

```
<?xml version="1.0" encoding="UTF-8"?>
<collection xmlns:xsi="http://www.w3.org/2001/XMLSchema-instance"
        xsi:noNamespaceSchemaLocation="collectibles.xsd">

</collection>
```

In order for the parser to recognize its instructions, they must belong to the schema instance namespace, `http://www.w3.org/2001/XMLSchema-instance`. Again, it's the namespace itself that's important, but it's customary to alias it with `xsi:`. As mentioned earlier, the data in our example will not belong to a namespace, so here we've pointed to the schema using the `noNamespaceSchemaLocation` attribute (described later).

Simple Elements

The basic building block of a document is, of course, the element, and the ways in which elements can be defined within an XML schema document depend on their ultimate structure. Some can be defined with a single empty element, and others require a more complex nested structure.

We'll start by looking at elements that can be considered simple types. These are elements that have no attributes and that contain no element content. The most basic of these use one of the predefined data types that are built into XML Schema. Consider Listing 8.4.

LISTING 8.4   Simple Elements

```
<?xml version="1.0" encoding="UTF-8"?>
<xs:schema xmlns:xs="http://www.w3.org/2001/XMLSchema">
    <xs:annotation>
...
    </xs:annotation>

    <xs:element name="description" type="xs:string"/>
    <xs:element name="originDate" type="xs:date"/>
    <xs:element name="numOwners" type="xs:positiveInteger"/>
</xs:schema>
```

Elements are declared using the `element` element, which itself uses attributes to specify the name of the intended element and the type of data it can contain. So the declaration

```
<xs:element name="numOwners" type="xs:positiveInteger"/>
```

describes an element named `numOwners` that can take as its content any positive integer value. Already this is an improvement over DTDs. With a DTD, all you can specify is that an element can contain text, elements, both, or neither. This declaration, on the other hand, limits `numOwners` to integers greater than zero, so this element is valid:

```
<numOwners>2</numOwners>
```

But these are not:

```
<numOwners>-5</numOwners>
```

```
<numOwners>one</numOwners>
```

Similarly, you no longer have to worry about making sure that date values are actually date values, because the `date` data type causes the parser to signal an error if the value doesn't conform to one of the available date formats. XML Schema defines 44 "ready-to-use" data types.

Built-in Data Types

As you'll see in the section "Creating New Types," XML Schema allows you to create your own data types, but it also provides several dozen of the most common types, ready for use. Some types even cause the parser to perform cleanup actions on the data before further processing. Built-in types include

- **Text types**—For plain text, you have the basic `string` type, but you can also specify `normalizedString`, which converts all whitespace characters (such as newlines and tabs) to spaces before processing, and `token`, which does the `normalizedString` conversion and then collapses multiple spaces into one and trims the leading and trailing spaces.

- **Integer values**—XML Schema defines several versions of integers, as shown in the following table:

Type	Values
byte	−128 to 127
unsignedByte	0 to 255
integer	negative infinity to infinity
positiveInteger	1 to infinity
negativeInteger	negative infinity to −1
nonNegativeInteger	0 to infinity
nonPositiveInteger	negative infinity to 0
int	−2,147,483,648 to 2,147,483,647
unsignedInt	0 to 4,294,967,295
long	−9,223,372,036,854,775,808 to 9,223,372,036,854,775,807
unsignedLong	0 to 18,446,744,073,709,551,615
short	−32,768 to 32,767
unsignedShort	0 to 65,535

- **Decimal types**—XML Schema also provides several non-integer numeric types, including `decimal`, in which the number of digits supported must be at least 18 and is determined by the specific processor; `float`, a standard single-precision 32-bit floating point value; and `double`, a standard double-precision 64-bit floating point value.

- **Boolean types**—Values using the `boolean` type may be specified as `true` or `false`, or as 1 (representing `true`) or 0 (representing `false`).

- **Date and time values**—Several date formats are available, including those based on the Gregorian calendar (`gMonth`, `gYear`, `gYearMonth`, `gDay`, and `gMonthDay`), `duration`, `time`, `dateTime`, and `date`.

- **Binary types**—The `base64Binary` and `hexBinary` types allow you to add binary data with their respective encodings.

- **DTD compatibility types**—These types are included mostly to preserve compatibility with DTDs, and should only be used for attributes. They include `ID`, `IDREF`, `IDREFS`, `ENTITY`, `ENTITIES`, `NOTATION`, `NMTOKEN`, and `NMTOKENS`. Their definitions are the same as in DTDs.

- **Namespace-related types**—These types come from the namespaces in the XML Recommendation. A `QName` is a *qualified name*, which is written as *{namespace alias}:{local name}*. When processed by an application, however, it's translated into a pair of values: the actual namespace name and the local part of the name. An NCName is the local part of a Qname, and can't contain a colon. (NCName is short for "non-colon name.")

- **Other types**—These types include the anyURI type, which must contain a URI; the language type, which must contain language codes (like those for xml:lang); and the Name type, which must start with a letter, an underscore (_), or a colon (:).

You can use any of these types in the creation of your elements. Later, we'll see how to extend these types even further.

Fixed and Default Values

In DTDs, you can define a default value for an attribute, or give it a fixed value to which users must adhere. XML Schema gives you the same capabilities for elements. For example, you can create an obtainable element that must be set to yes (on the theory that you won't list anything you can't reasonably get your hands on). You can also provide a default value for the originalOwner element, as in Listing 8.5.

LISTING 8.5   Using Default and Fixed Element Values

```
<?xml version="1.0" encoding="UTF-8"?>
<xs:schema xmlns:xs="http://www.w3.org/2001/XMLSchema">
...
    <xs:element name="numOwners" type="xs:integer"/>

    <xs:element name="obtainable" type="xs:string" fixed="yes"/>
    <xs:element name="originalOwner" type="xs:string" default="unknown"/>

</xs:schema>
```

Because of these values, the elements

```
<obtainable></obtainable>
<originalOwner/>
<originalOwner></orginalOwner>
```

are converted to

```
<obtainable>yes</obtainable>
<originalOwner>unknown</originalOwner>
<originalOwner>unknown</orginalOwner>
```

before further processing by the parser.

Note that unlike defaulted attribute values, defaulted and fixed element values are only added to the document if the element itself is actually present. For fixed values, the element can be empty, but if it does have a value, the value must match the fixed attribute. So the following is not valid:

```
<obtainable>maybe</obtainable>
```

Elements with fixed values can also help to replace general entities, in some ways. For example, if you define an element such as

```
<xs:element name="copy" fixed="©"/>
```

you can use it throughout the document. For example:

```
<rights>Copyright <copy/>2003</rights>
```

Complex Elements

This is all well and good, but to create a useful XML document you need more than just a simple element with text content. You need the ability to nest elements, creating the parent-child relationships that define an XML hierarchy.

If an element contains element content, it's considered a complex type. In the section titled "Creating New Types," we'll look at creating complex types as independent, referenceable components, but first let's look at creating these types anonymously, or *inlining* them.

Defining Child Elements

Let's start with a simple hierarchy of elements. We'll use the basic categories of collectibles. Listing 8.6 shows the definition of the root element, `collection`, and the elements it can contain.

LISTING 8.6 Creating Child Elements

```
<?xml version="1.0" encoding="UTF-8"?>
<xs:schema xmlns:xs="http://www.w3.org/2001/XMLSchema">
...
    <xs:element name="obtainable" type="xs:string" fixed="yes"/>
    <xs:element name="originalOwner" type="xs:string" default="unknown"/>

    <xs:element name="collection">
        <xs:complexType>
            <xs:sequence>
                <xs:element name="toys" type="xs:string"/>
                <xs:element name="furniture" type="xs:string"/>
                <xs:element name="pottery" type="xs:string"/>
                <xs:element name="autographs" type="xs:string"/>
                <xs:element name="advertising" type="xs:string"/>
            </xs:sequence>
        </xs:complexType>
    </xs:element>

</xs:schema>
```

Because this definition uses the `sequence` element, these elements must occur in the order in which they are specified, as shown in Listing 8.7.

LISTING 8.7   The Basic Document

```
<?xml version="1.0" encoding="UTF-8"?>
<collection xmlns:xsi="http://www.w3.org/2001/XMLSchema-instance"
        xsi:noNamespaceSchemaLocation="collectibles.xsd">

    <toys></toys>
    <furniture></furniture>
    <pottery></pottery>
    <autographs></autographs>
    <advertising></advertising>

</collection>
```

Two other options exist for creating child elements.

The first is to simply specify that you want all the elements, but you don't care what order they're in, as in Listing 8.8.

LISTING 8.8   Child Elements That Can Appear in Any Order

```
<?xml version="1.0" encoding="UTF-8"?>
<xs:schema xmlns:xs="http://www.w3.org/2001/XMLSchema">
...
    <xs:element name="collection">
        <xs:complexType>
            <xs:all>
                <xs:element name="toys" type="xs:string"/>
                <xs:element name="furniture" type="xs:string"/>
                <xs:element name="pottery" type="xs:string"/>
                <xs:element name="autographs" type="xs:string"/>
                <xs:element name="advertising" type="xs:string"/>
            </xs:all>
        </xs:complexType>
    </xs:element>

</xs:schema>
```

In this way, you're telling the processor that all these elements must appear, but the order is unimportant. You also have the option to allow the user to choose one or more elements from such a list, as shown in Listing 8.9.

LISTING 8.9   Choosing Child Elements

```
<?xml version="1.0" encoding="UTF-8"?>
<xs:schema xmlns:xs="http://www.w3.org/2001/XMLSchema">
...
    <xs:element name="collection">
        <xs:complexType>
            <xs:choice>
                <xs:element name="toys" type="xs:string"/>
                <xs:element name="furniture" type="xs:string"/>
```

LISTING 8.9   Continued

```
                    <xs:element name="pottery" type="xs:string"/>
                    <xs:element name="autographs" type="xs:string"/>
                    <xs:element name="advertising" type="xs:string"/>
                </xs:choice>
            </xs:complexType>
        </xs:element>

</xs:schema>
```

In this example, you can (and in fact must) choose exactly one element from the list, so you can't specify **toys** and **pottery**, for example. This is not a limitation of XML Schema, but of this particular example. Not only can you allow more than one choice in XML Schema, you can control precisely how many choices there should be.

Number of Occurrences

XML Schema improves on the modifiers that exist in DTDs by giving you explicit control over the number of times a particular element can appear in any given context using the **minOccurs** and **maxOccurs** attributes. For example, Listing 8.9 allows you to specify that a **toy** can have up to five **previousOwners**.

LISTING 8.9   Controlling the Number of Occurrences

```
<?xml version="1.0" encoding="UTF-8"?>
<xs:schema xmlns:xs="http://www.w3.org/2001/XMLSchema">
...
    <xs:element name="collection">
        <xs:complexType>
            <xs:choice>
                <xs:element name="toys">
                    <xs:complexType>
                        <xs:sequence>
                            <xs:element name="previousOwner"
                                        type="xs:string"
                                        minOccurs="0" maxOccurs="5"/>
                            <xs:element name="description"
                                        type="xs:string"/>
                            <xs:element name="originDate"
                                        type="xs:date"/>
                            <xs:element name="numOwners"
                                        type="xs:integer"/>
                            <xs:element name="obtainable"
                                        type="xs:string"
                                        fixed="yes"/>
                            <xs:element name="originalOwner"
                                        type="xs:string"
                                        default="unknown"/>
                        </xs:sequence>
                    </xs:complexType>
```

LISTING 8.9   Continued

```
        </xs:element>
        <xs:element name="furniture" type="xs:string"/>
        <xs:element name="pottery" type="xs:string"/>
        <xs:element name="autographs" type="xs:string"/>
        <xs:element name="advertising" type="xs:string"/>
      </xs:choice>
    </xs:complexType>
  </xs:element>

</xs:schema>
```

A few things are going on here. First, we've nested the inline definition of the **toys** element, which no longer has a type of **xs:string**. Second, we've created a subelement called **previousOwner** for **toys**. Because we've set the **minOccurs** attribute to **0**, the element is optional, but if it appears, it may appear up to five times, as specified by **maxOccurs**.

You can also use these attributes for elements in a **choice** element, as shown in Listing 8.10.

LISTING 8.10   Determining the Number of Choices

```
<?xml version="1.0" encoding="UTF-8"?>
<xs:schema xmlns:xs="http://www.w3.org/2001/XMLSchema">
...
  <xs:element name="collection">
    <xs:complexType>
      <xs:choice minOccurs="1" maxOccurs="unbounded">
        <xs:element name="toys">
...
        </xs:element>
        <xs:element name="furniture" type="xs:string"/>
        <xs:element name="pottery" type="xs:string"/>
        <xs:element name="autographs" type="xs:string"/>
        <xs:element name="advertising" type="xs:string"/>
      </xs:choice>
    </xs:complexType>
  </xs:element>

</xs:schema>
```

Here you can explicitly set how many of a specific element the user is allowed to choose, creating a schema that allows the elements to appear in any order, but potentially controls how many of them will appear.

In this case, **maxOccurs** is unbounded, so the collection can contain as many children as the author desires.

By combining **sequence**, **choice**, and **all** elements, and by placing **minOccurs** and **maxOccurs** attributes carefully, you can create virtually any structure.

Mixed Content

Inevitably, we run up against the same problem that we had with DTDs: How do we represent mixed content? Fortunately, XML Schema makes this easy. The `complexType` element has an available attribute, `mixed`, that you can set to a Boolean value, as shown in Listing 8.11.

LISTING 8.11   Mixed Content

```
<?xml version="1.0" encoding="UTF-8"?>
<xs:schema xmlns:xs="http://www.w3.org/2001/XMLSchema">
...

    <xs:element name="collection">
        <xs:complexType mixed="false">
            <xs:choice minOccurs="1" maxOccurs="unbounded">
                <xs:element name="toys">
                    <xs:complexType>
                        <xs:sequence>
                            <xs:element name="previousOwner"
                                        type="xs:string"
                                        minOccurs="0" maxOccurs="5"/>
                            <xs:element name="description">
                                <xs:complexType mixed="true">
                                    <xs:choice maxOccurs="unbounded">
                                        <xs:element name="condition"
                                                    type="xs:string"/>
                                        <xs:element name="brand"
                                                    type="xs:string"/>
                                        <xs:element name="tradeName"
                                                    type="xs:string"/>
                                    </xs:choice>
                                </xs:complexType>
                            </xs:element>
...

                        </xs:sequence>
                    </xs:complexType>
                </xs:element>
...

            </xs:choice>
        </xs:complexType>
    </xs:element>

</xs:schema>
```

According to this schema document, the `collection` element can contain only elements, which is the default behavior, but the `description` element can contain text within its description, as shown in Listing 8.12.

LISTING 8.12   Using Mixed Content

```
<?xml version="1.0" encoding="UTF-8"?>
<collection xmlns:xsi="http://www.w3.org/2001/XMLSchema-instance"
        xsi:noNamespaceSchemaLocation="collectibles.xsd">
```

LISTING 8.12   Continued

```
<toys>
    <previousOwner>John Sorhed</previousOwner>
    <description>
        This piece is a genuine wooden <brand>Silhaven</brand>
        <tradeName>Volunteer Firetruck</tradeName>. It is in
        <condition>excellent</condition> condition and just waiting
        for the right collector.
    </description>
    <originDate>1940</originDate>
    <numOwners>1</numOwners>
    <obtainable>yes</obtainable>
    <originalOwner>John Sorhed</originalOwner>
</toys>
<autographs></autographs>
<advertising></advertising>
<furniture></furniture>
<pottery></pottery>
</collection>
```

Catchall Elements

Mixed content is also useful for sections that will contain HTML, but as it was for DTDs, specifying each and every permissible element can be tiresome. XML Schema provides one more type for this purpose: `anyType`. An element declared as `anyType` (or, because this is the default, declared without a type attribute) can contain any text and any defined elements as long as they're well-formed, as shown in Listing 8.13.

LISTING 8.13   An Unconstrained Element

```
<?xml version="1.0" encoding="UTF-8"?>
<xs:schema xmlns:xs="http://www.w3.org/2001/XMLSchema">
    <xs:annotation>
...
    </xs:annotation>

    <xs:element name="condition" type="xs:string"/>
    <xs:element name="brand" type="xs:string"/>
    <xs:element name="tradeName" type="xs:string"/>

    <xs:element name="collection">
        <xs:complexType mixed="false">
            <xs:choice minOccurs="1" maxOccurs="unbounded">
                <xs:element name="toys">
                    <xs:complexType>
                        <xs:sequence>
                            <xs:element name="previousOwner"
                                        type="xs:string"
                                        minOccurs="0" maxOccurs="5"/>
                            <xs:element name="description"
                                        type="xs:anyType"/>
                            <xs:element name="originDate"
                                        type="xs:gYear"/>
...
```

LISTING 8.13   Continued

```
                    </xs:sequence>
                </xs:complexType>
            </xs:element>
...
            </xs:choice>
        </xs:complexType>
    </xs:element>

</xs:schema>
```

Notice that the `condition`, `brand`, and `tradeName` elements are declared independently of their implied use within the `description` element. You can use this capability to clean up the document somewhat (see the next section for details).

Referencing Predefined Elements

At this point the schema does everything that's required of it, but it's getting harder and harder to read, with multiple levels of nested definitions and declarations.

You can clean this up somewhat by creating global elements, then referencing them within the definition. This also allows you to reuse definitions. Listing 8.14 shows a variation on the existing structure, and cleans it up a bit.

LISTING 8.14   Referencing Named Elements

```
<?xml version="1.0" encoding="UTF-8"?>
<xs:schema xmlns:xs="http://www.w3.org/2001/XMLSchema">
    <xs:annotation>
...
    </xs:annotation>

    <xs:element name="condition" type="xs:string"/>
    <xs:element name="brand" type="xs:string"/>
    <xs:element name="tradeName" type="xs:string"/>
    <xs:element name="previousOwner" type="xs:string"/>
    <xs:element name="description" type="xs:anyType"/>
    <xs:element name="originDate" type="xs:gYear"/>
    <xs:element name="numOwners" type="xs:integer"/>
    <xs:element name="obtainable" type="xs:string" fixed="yes"/>
    <xs:element name="originalOwner" type="xs:string"
                                    default="unknown"/>

    <xs:element name="item">
        <xs:complexType>
            <xs:sequence>
                <xs:element ref="previousOwner"
                        minOccurs="0" maxOccurs="5"/>
```

LISTING 8.14 Continued

```xml
                    <xs:element ref="description"/>
                    <xs:element ref="originDate"/>
                    <xs:element ref="numOwners"/>
                    <xs:element ref="obtainable"/>
                    <xs:element ref="originalOwner"/>
                </xs:sequence>
            </xs:complexType>
        </xs:element>

        <xs:element name="collection">
            <xs:complexType mixed="false">
                <xs:choice minOccurs="1" maxOccurs="unbounded">
                    <xs:element name="toys">
                        <xs:complexType>
                            <xs:sequence>
                                <xs:element ref="item" minOccurs="0"
                                            maxOccurs="unbounded"/>
                            </xs:sequence>
                        </xs:complexType>
                    </xs:element>
                    <xs:element name="furniture">
                        <xs:complexType>
                            <xs:sequence>
                                <xs:element ref="item" minOccurs="0"
                                            maxOccurs="unbounded"/>
                            </xs:sequence>
                        </xs:complexType>
                    </xs:element>
                    <xs:element name="pottery">
                        <xs:complexType>
                            <xs:sequence>
                                <xs:element ref="item" minOccurs="0"
                                            maxOccurs="unbounded"/>
                            </xs:sequence>
                        </xs:complexType>
                    </xs:element>
                    <xs:element name="autographs">
                        <xs:complexType>
                            <xs:sequence>
                                <xs:element ref="item" minOccurs="0"
                                            maxOccurs="unbounded"/>
                            </xs:sequence>
                        </xs:complexType>
                    </xs:element>
                    <xs:element name="advertising">
                        <xs:complexType>
                            <xs:sequence>
                                <xs:element ref="item" minOccurs="0"
                                            maxOccurs="unbounded"/>
                            </xs:sequence>
                        </xs:complexType>
                    </xs:element>
```

LISTING 8.14   Continued

```
            </xs:choice>
        </xs:complexType>
    </xs:element>

</xs:schema>
```

At first glance, this doesn't look much better—one might even argue that it's worse—but we've gained a significant advantage here.

Notice the definition of the **item** element, which contains references to all the elements that were formerly under **toys**. The actual elements are defined separately, then referenced using the **ref** attribute. Any attributes such as **fixed** or **default** that are intrinsic to the element itself are defined in the element declaration, but any attributes such as **minOccurs** and **maxOccurs** that pertain to how it's used are defined when the element is referenced.

The advantage here is that a globally defined element can be reused in several places. For example, notice that all the main elements (**toys**, **furniture**, and so on) can now contain zero or more **item** elements. Using inline definitions in this situation would push the limits of maintainability.

Scope

One of the strengths of schemas is the ability to define several different elements with the same name, as long as they're used in different contexts.

For example, suppose you want to add a **material** element to **pottery items**. Listing 8.15 demonstrates the creation of a new **item** element containing a new **material** element just for **pottery**.

LISTING 8.15   Element Definitions and Scope

```
<?xml version="1.0" encoding="UTF-8"?>
<xs:schema xmlns:xs="http://www.w3.org/2001/XMLSchema">
...
    <xs:element name="item">
        <xs:complexType>
            <xs:sequence>
                <xs:element ref="previousOwner"
                            minOccurs="0" maxOccurs="5"/>
                <xs:element ref="description"/>
                <xs:element ref="originDate"/>
                <xs:element ref="numOwners"/>
                <xs:element ref="obtainable"/>
                <xs:element ref="originalOwner"/>
            </xs:sequence>
        </xs:complexType>
    </xs:element>
```

LISTING 8.15   *Continued*

```
<xs:element name="collection">
    <xs:complexType mixed="false">
        <xs:choice minOccurs="1" maxOccurs="unbounded">
...

            <xs:element name="pottery">
                <xs:complexType>
                    <xs:sequence>
                        <xs:element name="item" minOccurs="0"
                                    maxOccurs="unbounded">
                            <xs:complexType>
                                <xs:sequence>
                                    <xs:element ref="previousOwner"
                                                minOccurs="0"
                                                maxOccurs="5"/>
                                    <xs:element ref="description"/>
                                    <xs:element ref="originDate"/>
                                    <xs:element ref="numOwners"/>
                                    <xs:element ref="obtainable"/>
                                    <xs:element ref="originalOwner"/>
                                    <xs:element name="material"
                                                type="xs:string"/>
                                </xs:sequence>
                            </xs:complexType>
                        </xs:element>
                    </xs:sequence>
                </xs:complexType>
            </xs:element>
...

        </xs:choice>
    </xs:complexType>
</xs:element>

</xs:schema>
```

In this case, the definitions are fairly similar, but you could create two entirely different elements with the same name, as long as they're used in different places. How you define them determines their scope. For example, the `item` element defined within the `pottery` element is local to the `pottery` element; you can't reference it anywhere else.

To make a definition available for reference within other definitions, you must make it global. In other words, it must be the child of the `schema` element. That way, it's in scope for all other elements.

Backward Compatibility

Keep in mind that using the ability to create different elements with the same name makes it difficult, if not impossible, to keep the structure intact if you ever need to covert your schema back to a DTD. You'll need to do so if you want to transfer your data to an application or system that relies on DTDs rather than schemas.

Element Groups

In the previous example, both versions of the `item` element used the same group of elements. In a DTD, you might accomplish this using a parameter entity, which prevents you from having to add the elements manually both times, but you don't have that option with a schema. What you do have, however, is the ability to create a grouping of elements to which you can then refer as a unit, as in Listing 8.16.

LISTING 8.16   *Using Group Elements*

```
<?xml version="1.0" encoding="UTF-8"?>
<xs:schema xmlns:xs="http://www.w3.org/2001/XMLSchema">
...
    <xs:element name="originalOwner" type="xs:string"
                                     default="unknown"/>

    <xs:group name="itemCommon">
        <xs:sequence>
            <xs:element ref="previousOwner"
                        minOccurs="0" maxOccurs="5"/>
            <xs:element ref="description"/>
            <xs:element ref="originDate"/>
            <xs:element ref="numOwners"/>
            <xs:element ref="obtainable"/>
            <xs:element ref="originalOwner"/>
        </xs:sequence>
    </xs:group>

    <xs:element name="item">
        <xs:complexType>
            <xs:sequence>
                <xs:group ref="itemCommon"/>
            </xs:sequence>
        </xs:complexType>
    </xs:element>

    <xs:element name="collection">
        <xs:complexType mixed="false">
            <xs:choice minOccurs="1" maxOccurs="unbounded">
...
                <xs:element name="pottery">
                    <xs:complexType>
                        <xs:sequence>
                            <xs:element name="item" minOccurs="0"
                                        maxOccurs="unbounded">
                                <xs:complexType>
                                    <xs:sequence>
                                        <xs:group ref="itemCommon"/>
                                        <xs:element name="material"
                                                    type="xs:string"/>
```

LISTING 8.16   Continued

```
                                                </xs:sequence>
                                          </xs:complexType>
                                     </xs:element>
                                </xs:sequence>
                           </xs:complexType>
                      </xs:element>
        ...

                      </xs:choice>
                 </xs:complexType>
            </xs:element>

</xs:schema>
```

Groups can also be used within choices to enable you to require one group or another. For example, if you want to require **pottery** items to contain either the main **item** elements or the **material** element (an admittedly questionable choice), you can write that portion of the schema as follows:

```
...
<xs:element name="item" minOccurs="0"
            maxOccurs="unbounded">
    <xs:complexType>
        <xs:choice>
            <xs:group ref="itemCommon"/>
            <xs:element name="material"
                        type="xs:string"/>
        </xs:choice>
    </xs:complexType>
</xs:element>
...
```

In this case, the group is considered a choice in and of itself.

Adding Attributes

Now that you're familiar with elements, it's time to start adding attributes. Overall, the process is similar to adding elements.

First of all, if an element has any attributes, it's automatically a complex type, just as it would be if it had any child elements. Second, an attribute is declared via an **attribute** element that's similar to the **element** element.

In Listing 8.17, we'll add an attribute to the **item** element.

LISTING 8.17   Adding Attributes

```
<?xml version="1.0" encoding="UTF-8"?>
<xs:schema xmlns:xs="http://www.w3.org/2001/XMLSchema">
    ...
```

LISTING 8.17 Continued

```
<xs:element name="item">
    <xs:complexType>
        <xs:sequence>
            <xs:group ref="itemCommon"/>
        </xs:sequence>
        <xs:attribute name="itemid" type="xs:integer"/>
        <xs:attribute name="keeper" type="xs:string"/>
        <xs:attribute name="demand" type="xs:string"/>
        <xs:attribute name="legal" type="xs:string"/>
    </xs:complexType>
</xs:element>

<xs:element name="collection">
    <xs:complexType mixed="false">
        <xs:choice minOccurs="1" maxOccurs="unbounded">
            <xs:element name="toys">
                <xs:complexType>
                    <xs:sequence>
                        <xs:element ref="item" minOccurs="0"
                                    maxOccurs="unbounded"/>
                    </xs:sequence>
                </xs:complexType>
            </xs:element>
...
            <xs:element name="pottery">
                <xs:complexType>
                    <xs:sequence>
                        <xs:element name="item" minOccurs="0"
                                    maxOccurs="unbounded">
                            <xs:complexType>
                                <xs:choice>
                                    <xs:group ref="itemCommon"/>
                                    <xs:element name="material"
                                                type="xs:string"/>
                                </xs:choice>
                                <xs:attribute name="itemid"
                                              type="xs:integer"/>
                                <xs:attribute name="keeper"
                                              type="xs:string"/>
                                <xs:attribute name="demand"
                                              type="xs:string"/>
                                <xs:attribute name="legal"
                                              type="xs:string"/>
                            </xs:complexType>
                        </xs:element>
                    </xs:sequence>
                </xs:complexType>
            </xs:element>
...
        </xs:choice>
    </xs:complexType>
```

LISTING 8.17   Continued

```
    </xs:element>

</xs:schema>
```

Attributes can use all the built-in types we discussed in the "Built-in Data Types" section, including those that are reserved just for attributes, such as `ID` and `NMTOKEN`.

Note that the attribute definition must come last within an element, *after* the definition of child elements. Note also that because the XML 1.0 specification prohibits an attribute from appearing more than once, the `minOccurs` and `maxOccurs` attributes don't appear within an `attribute` element. But you can control whether the attribute should appear.

Complex Type, Simple Content

To create an element with a simple type, such as `string`, but also allow attributes, extend the simple type. We'll discuss this procedure in the section titled "Adding Attributes to Simple Types by Extension."

Optional and Default Attribute Values

Just as a DTD can specify that a particular attribute is `#REQUIRED`, `#IMPLIED`, or `#FIXED`, a schema controls the use of an attribute through the `use`, `fixed`, and `default` attributes. For example, Listing 8.18 shows four possible scenarios.

LISTING 8.18   Required, Optional, and Fixed Attributes

```
...
    <xs:element name="item">
        <xs:complexType>
            <xs:sequence>
                <xs:group ref="itemCommon"/>
            </xs:sequence>
            <xs:attribute name="itemid" type="xs:integer"
                          use="required"/>
            <xs:attribute name="keeper" type="xs:string"
                          default="yes"/>
            <xs:attribute name="demand" type="xs:string"
                          use="optional"/>
            <xs:attribute name="legal" type="xs:string"
                          fixed="yes"/>
        </xs:complexType>
    </xs:element>
...
```

Typically, the `use`, `default`, and `fixed` attributes will not be used together. A little bit of investigation shows why:

- The `keeper` attribute has a default value of `yes`. Even if the attribute isn't included, the processor will add the default value, so it will always be present in the element. There is no need to mark it as `required`, and marking it as `optional` is incorrect.

- The `legal` attribute has a fixed value of `yes`. The processor will add it if it is missing, and it will always be present in the element, so there is no need to mark it as `required` or `optional`.

- The `itemid` attribute is `required`, so the user has to provide a value. The `demand` attribute is `optional`, so if no value is provided, it will not be part of the document. In both of these cases, providing a default or fixed value is contrary to the intent of the attribute.

Prohibiting Attributes

There is one situation where the `use` element will be used with a `default` or `fixed` attribute: the case in which the `use` attribute takes its third permissible value, `prohibited`. While it may not seem to make any sense to create an attribute and prohibit its use, one situation in which this might be valuable is the substitution of one element for another. In this case, it may make sense to specifically prohibit an attribute that was declared in a related element.

Named Attributes and Attribute Groups

Just as you can with elements, you can declare attributes at the global level and reference them within the definition of an element, as in Listing 8.19.

LISTING 8.19   Referencing Predefined Attributes

```
<?xml version="1.0" encoding="UTF-8"?>
<xs:schema xmlns:xs="http://www.w3.org/2001/XMLSchema">
...
    <xs:group name="itemCommon">
...
    </xs:group>

    <xs:attribute name="itemid" type="xs:integer"/>
    <xs:attribute name="keeper" type="xs:string"/>
    <xs:attribute name="demand" type="xs:string"/>
    <xs:attribute name="legal" type="xs:string"/>

    <xs:element name="item">
        <xs:complexType>
            <xs:sequence>
```

LISTING 8.19 Continued

```
                    <xs:group ref="itemCommon"/>
                </xs:sequence>
                <xs:attribute ref="itemid" use="required"/>
                <xs:attribute ref="keeper" default="yes"/>
                <xs:attribute ref="demand" use="optional"/>
                <xs:attribute ref="legal" fixed="yes"/>
            </xs:complexType>
        </xs:element>

        <xs:element name="collection">
            <xs:complexType mixed="false">
                <xs:choice minOccurs="1" maxOccurs="unbounded">
...

                    <xs:element name="pottery">
                        <xs:complexType>
                            <xs:sequence>
                                <xs:element name="item" minOccurs="0"
                                            maxOccurs="unbounded">
                                    <xs:complexType>
                                        <xs:choice>
                                            <xs:group ref="itemCommon"/>
                                            <xs:element name="material"
                                                        type="xs:string"/>
                                        </xs:choice>
                                        <xs:attribute ref="itemid"
                                                      use="required"/>
                                        <xs:attribute ref="keeper"
                                                      default="no"/>
                                        <xs:attribute ref="demand"
                                                      default="low"/>
                                        <xs:attribute ref="legal"
                                                      fixed="yes"/>
                                    </xs:complexType>
                                </xs:element>
                            </xs:sequence>
                        </xs:complexType>
                    </xs:element>
...
                </xs:choice>
            </xs:complexType>
        </xs:element>

</xs:schema>
```

Notice that while the syntax is similar to that of named elements, it's the reference that specifies the **default**, **use**, and **fixed** attributes. This gives us the ability to use different values in different situations.

An exception to this rule occurs when you want to define the attributes as a group (similar to an element group), as shown in Listing 8.20.

LISTING 8.20   *Using Attribute Groups*

```
<?xml version="1.0" encoding="UTF-8"?>
<xs:schema xmlns:xs="http://www.w3.org/2001/XMLSchema">
...
    <xs:attribute name="itemid" type="xs:integer"/>
    <xs:attribute name="keeper" type="xs:string"/>
    <xs:attribute name="demand" type="xs:string"/>
    <xs:attribute name="legal" type="xs:string"/>

    <xs:attributeGroup name="itemAtts">
        <xs:attribute ref="itemid" use="required"/>
        <xs:attribute ref="keeper" default="yes"/>
        <xs:attribute ref="demand" use="optional"/>
        <xs:attribute ref="legal" fixed="yes"/>
    </xs:attributeGroup>

    <xs:element name="item">
        <xs:complexType>
            <xs:sequence>
                <xs:group ref="itemCommon"/>
            </xs:sequence>
            <xs:attributeGroup ref="itemAtts"/>
        </xs:complexType>
    </xs:element>

    <xs:element name="collection">
...
    </xs:element>

</xs:schema>
```

Note that the attribute group references the predefined attributes, and that it includes settings such as `default` and `use`. You can create multiple groupings with different settings and use them in the appropriate places.

Empty Elements

We will discuss the creation of empty elements in the upcoming section titled "Restriction."

Creating New Types

We could stop at this point, and you'd likely have just about all the functionality that you need to create schemas to describe your documents. But we're far from the end of the story.

Much of the strength of XML Schema lies in its ability to define new data types. These types can be simple, such as a particular range of numbers, or they can be much more complex, such as a hierarchy of elements and attributes.

Once you define these types, you can reference them in much the same way that you referenced the built-in data types.

Named Types

Ironically, the simplest way to create a new type is to start with a complex type and give it a name, as shown in Listing 8.21.

LISTING 8.21   Naming a Complex Type

```xml
<?xml version="1.0" encoding="UTF-8"?>
<xs:schema xmlns:xs="http://www.w3.org/2001/XMLSchema">
...
    <xs:attributeGroup name="itemAtts">
...
    </xs:attributeGroup>

    <xs:complexType name="itemType">
        <xs:sequence>
            <xs:group ref="itemCommon"/>
        </xs:sequence>
        <xs:attributeGroup ref="itemAtts"/>
    </xs:complexType>

    <xs:element name="collection">
        <xs:complexType mixed="false">
            <xs:choice minOccurs="1" maxOccurs="unbounded">
                <xs:element name="toys">
                    <xs:complexType>
                        <xs:sequence>
                            <xs:element name="item" type="itemType"
                                        minOccurs="0"
                                        maxOccurs="unbounded"/>
                        </xs:sequence>
                    </xs:complexType>
                </xs:element>
                <xs:element name="furniture">
                    <xs:complexType>
                        <xs:sequence>
                            <xs:element name="item" type="itemType"
                                        minOccurs="0"
                                        maxOccurs="unbounded"/>
                        </xs:sequence>
                    </xs:complexType>
                </xs:element>
                <xs:element name="pottery">
                    <xs:complexType>
                        <xs:sequence>
                            <xs:element name="item" minOccurs="0"
                                        maxOccurs="unbounded">
                                <xs:complexType>
                                    <xs:choice>
```

LISTING 8.21   *Continued*

```
                                    <xs:group ref="itemCommon"/>
                                    <xs:element name="material"
                                                type="xs:string"/>
                            </xs:choice>
                            <xs:attributeGroup
                                            ref="itemAtts"/>
                        </xs:complexType>
                    </xs:element>
                </xs:sequence>
            </xs:complexType>
        </xs:element>
        <xs:element name="autographs">
            <xs:complexType>
                <xs:sequence>
                    <xs:element name="item" type="itemType"
                                minOccurs="0"
                                maxOccurs="unbounded"/>
                </xs:sequence>
            </xs:complexType>
        </xs:element>
        <xs:element name="advertising">
            <xs:complexType>
                <xs:sequence>
                    <xs:element name="item" type="itemType"
                                minOccurs="0"
                                maxOccurs="unbounded"/>
                </xs:sequence>
            </xs:complexType>
        </xs:element>
        </xs:choice>
    </xs:complexType>
</xs:element>

</xs:schema>
```

Here we've removed the global definition of the item element and replaced it with a global definition of the itemType. We can use that type on each of the item elements that are now declared inline rather than referenced. Notice that whereas earlier we were prefixing the type definitions with xs:, here we're not. This is because earlier we were referencing types that were in the Schema namespace, and now we're referencing types that are not.

Right about now you're probably wondering why we bothered. After all, the document isn't very much different than it was when we created the element and referenced it, rather than the type. The value lies in our ability to take these types and use them as a base for creating new ones.

Restriction

The simplest way to create a new type out of one that already exists is to add conditions to one of XML Schema's built-in types. For example, the document we created in Listing 8.21 will likely need to specify several types of prices, so it would be convenient to have a data type representing currency. For U.S. currency, we need a decimal number with two places to the right of the decimal point. To create one, we can create a new type, based on the built-in `decimal`, that limits acceptable values to those with two decimal places, or `fractionDigits`, as in Listing 8.22.

LISTING 8.22   Creating a New Simple Type

```
<?xml version="1.0" encoding="UTF-8"?>
<xs:schema xmlns:xs="http://www.w3.org/2001/XMLSchema">
...
    <xs:attributeGroup name="itemAtts">
...
    </xs:attributeGroup>

    <xs:simpleType name="USCurrency">
        <xs:restriction base="xs:decimal">
            <xs:fractionDigits value="2"/>
        </xs:restriction>
    </xs:simpleType>

    <xs:complexType name="itemType">
        <xs:sequence>
            <xs:group ref="itemCommon"/>
            <xs:element name="originalPrice" type="USCurrency"/>
            <xs:element name="lastPrice" type="USCurrency"/>
            <xs:element name="desiredPrice" type="USCurrency"/>
        </xs:sequence>
        <xs:attributeGroup ref="itemAtts"/>
    </xs:complexType>
...
</xs:schema>
```

Let's take this one step at a time. First, we create a new simple type and give it a name, `USCurrency`. From there, the `restriction` element tells the processor that we're creating a subset of an existing `base` type, `decimal`. We define the subtype as those numbers that have two fractional digits, or digits after the decimal point.

Finally, we add three new elements that use the `USCurrency` type. Because we're adding them to the `itemCommon` group, they're added not only to the `itemType`, but also to the item `element` under `pottery`.

Simple types can be restricted on the basis of one or more facets (requirements). These facets include

- `minInclusive`—The minimum value of the number (or other ordered quantity). If the `minInclusive` value is **5**, the value can be 5 or greater.

- `minExclusive`—The minimum value that the number (or other ordered quantity) must exceed. If the `minExclusive` value is **5**, the value can be any number greater than 5.

- **maxInclusive**—The maximum value for the number (or other ordered quantity). If the maxInclusive value is **5**, the value can be any number up to and including **5**.

- **maxExclusive**—The maximum value that the number (or other ordered quantity) must be less than. If the maxExclusive value is **5**, the value must be less than 5.

- **totalDigits**—the number of digits, both before and after the decimal point, that a numeric value must have.

- **fractionDigits**—The number of digits after the decimal point that a numeric value must have.

- **length**—The number of units for a value. For most types, the length facet refers to characters, but for lists (discussed in the upcoming "Lists" section), it refers to the number of items, and for binary items it refers to the number of octets.

- **minLength** and **maxLength**—Minimum and maximum values for the length facet.

- **pattern**—The format of the required value, as specified by a traditional regular expression.

- **enumeration**—A set of potential values from which the data may be chosen.

- **whiteSpace**—This facet controls not so much what may be allowed as a value, but the form of the content after the document has been processed. If the value is set to **preserve**, the data is untouched. If it's set to **replace**, tabs, line feeds, and carriage returns are replaced with spaces. If it's set to **collapse**, the **replace** action is performed, followed by the replacement of multiple spaces with a single space.

You can use these facets in combination, and within inline definitions as well as named types.

Enumeration

One particularly useful way to utilize facets is to create an enumerated type to restrict choices for an element or attribute, as in Listing 8.23.

LISTING 8.23   Enumerated Types

```
...
    <xs:attribute name="keeper" type="xs:string"/>
    <xs:attribute name="demand">
        <xs:simpleType>
            <xs:restriction base="xs:string">
                <xs:enumeration value="low"/>
                <xs:enumeration value="medium"/>
                <xs:enumeration value="high"/>
                <xs:enumeration value="money is no object"/>
            </xs:restriction>
        </xs:simpleType>
    </xs:attribute>
    <xs:attribute name="legal" type="xs:string"/>
...
```

Often, it's convenient to create an enumerated type and reference it within elements and attributes.

Lists

One handy simple type is the list. Similar to the `enumeration` facet, it allows the inclusion of multiple values separated by spaces. Lists allow you to choose the type of data that make up the items, including custom types. You can apply other facets, such as `length`, as seen in Listing 8.24.

LISTING 8.24   Using Lists

```
<?xml version="1.0" encoding="UTF-8"?>
<xs:schema xmlns:xs="http://www.w3.org/2001/XMLSchema">
...
    <xs:attributeGroup name="itemAtts">
...
    </xs:attributeGroup>

    <xs:simpleType name="possibleOutlets">
        <xs:restriction base="xs:string">
            <xs:enumeration value="oBoy"/>
            <xs:enumeration value="Yoohoo!"/>
            <xs:enumeration value="ConJunction"/>
            <xs:enumeration value="Anazone"/>
        </xs:restriction>
    </xs:simpleType>

    <xs:simpleType name="outletList">
        <xs:list itemType="possibleOutlets"/>
    </xs:simpleType>

    <xs:simpleType name="outlets">
        <xs:restriction base="outletList">
            <xs:maxLength value="3"/>
        </xs:restriction>
    </xs:simpleType>

    <xs:simpleType name="USCurrency">
        <xs:restriction base="xs:decimal">
            <xs:fractionDigits value="2"/>
        </xs:restriction>
    </xs:simpleType>

    <xs:complexType name="itemType">
        <xs:sequence>
            <xs:group ref="itemCommon"/>
            <xs:element name="originalPrice" type="USCurrency"/>
            <xs:element name="lastPrice" type="USCurrency"/>
            <xs:element name="desiredPrice" type="USCurrency"/>
            <xs:element name="outlets" type="outlets"/>
        </xs:sequence>
```

```
            <xs:attributeGroup ref="itemAtts"/>
        </xs:complexType>

        <xs:element name="collection">
...
        </xs:element>

</xs:schema>
```

Here we have an element type, **outlets**, that uses the type **outlets**. Although this is confusing, giving elements and types the same names is permitted.

The type **outlets** is defined as a restriction of type **outletList** where the **length** can be no greater than **3**. The type **outletList** is defined as a list where the items are of type **possibleOutlets**. Finally, **possibleOutlets** is defined as an **enumeration**. So an instance document might look like Listing 8.25.

LISTING 8.25   Lists Within the Document

```
<?xml version="1.0" encoding="UTF-8"?>
<collection xmlns:xsi="http://www.w3.org/2001/XMLSchema-instance"
        xsi:noNamespaceSchemaLocation="collectibles.xsd">

    <toys>
        <item itemid="1">
            <previousOwner>John Sorhed</previousOwner>
            <description>
                This piece is a genuine wooden <brand>Silhaven</brand>
                <tradeName>Volunteer Firetruck</tradeName>. It is in
                <condition>excellent</condition> condition and just waiting
                for the right collector.
            </description>
            <originDate>1940</originDate>
            <numOwners>1</numOwners>
            <obtainable>yes</obtainable>
            <originalOwner>John Sorhed</originalOwner>
            <originalPrice>2.00</originalPrice>
            <lastPrice>49.00</lastPrice>
            <desiredPrice>79.99</desiredPrice>
            <outlets>oBoy Yoohoo!</outlets>
        </item>
    </toys>
...
</collection>
```

Adding Attributes to Simple Types by Extension

Just as we can create new classes by restricting existing ones, we can create new classes by extending the model. The most commonly used type of extension adds attributes to a simple type.

Suppose you want to add an attribute to the `originalOwner` element to specify whether this information has been confirmed. You can't just specify the `string` type, as before, because that's a simple type, and simple types can't have attributes. On the other hand, if you define it as a complex type, you'll be able to add attributes, but the only way to add content will be to add a child element.

To get around this problem, you can extend the simple type and add attributes to its model, as in Listing 8.26.

LISTING 8.26   Extending a Simple Type

```
...
    <xs:element name="obtainable" type="xs:string" fixed="yes"/>

    <xs:element name="originalOwner">
        <xs:complexType>
            <xs:simpleContent>
                <xs:extension base="xs:string">
                    <xs:attribute name="confirmed" default="no"/>
                </xs:extension>
            </xs:simpleContent>
        </xs:complexType>
    </xs:element>

    <xs:group name="itemCommon">
...
    </xs:group>
...
```

Because it has an attribute, you must declare `originalOwner` as a `complexType`, but you can tell it that you only want simple content (in other words, no elements, just text) using the `simpleContent` element. *Simple content* is defined as a type that's derived from the base type `string`, but extended to include the `confirmed` attribute.

Deriving Custom Types

You can also extend custom types. For example, the `pottery` item type is the same as the generic item type, except for the extra `material` element. Rather than redefining the item type for the `pottery` element, you can create a generic item type, then extend it for each category, as in Listing 8.27.

LISTING 8.27   Extending Custom Types

```
<?xml version="1.0" encoding="UTF-8"?>
<xs:schema xmlns:xs="http://www.w3.org/2001/XMLSchema">
...
    <xs:complexType name="itemType">
```

LISTING 8.27   Continued

```xml
        <xs:sequence>
            <xs:element ref="previousOwner"
                        minOccurs="0" maxOccurs="5"/>
            <xs:element ref="description"/>
            <xs:element ref="originDate"/>
            <xs:element ref="numOwners"/>
            <xs:element ref="obtainable"/>
            <xs:element ref="originalOwner"/>
            <xs:element name="originalPrice" type="USCurrency"/>
            <xs:element name="lastPrice" type="USCurrency"/>
            <xs:element name="desiredPrice" type="USCurrency"/>
            <xs:element name="outlets" type="outlets"/>
        </xs:sequence>
        <xs:attributeGroup ref="itemAtts"/>
    </xs:complexType>

    <xs:complexType name="potteryItemType">
        <xs:complexContent>
            <xs:extension base="itemType">
                <xs:sequence>
                    <xs:element name="material" type="xs:string"/>
                </xs:sequence>
            </xs:extension>
        </xs:complexContent>
    </xs:complexType>

    <xs:element name="collection">
        <xs:complexType mixed="false">
            <xs:choice minOccurs="1" maxOccurs="unbounded">
                <xs:element name="toys">
                    <xs:complexType>
                        <xs:sequence>
                            <xs:element name="item" type="itemType"
                                        minOccurs="0"
                                        maxOccurs="unbounded"/>
                        </xs:sequence>
                    </xs:complexType>
                </xs:element>
...
                <xs:element name="pottery">
                    <xs:complexType>
                        <xs:sequence>
                            <xs:element name="item"
                                        type="potteryItemType"
                                        minOccurs="0"
                                        maxOccurs="unbounded"/>
                        </xs:sequence>
                    </xs:complexType>
                </xs:element>
...
            </xs:choice>
```

LISTING 8.27   Continued

```
        </xs:complexType>
    </xs:element>

</xs:schema>
```

To aid in reading the schema, we've removed the `element` group and added the elements to the original item type directly, then created a new `complexType` called `potteryItemType`. That type has `complexContent`, which consists of an extension of the `itemType`. That extension adds a new element, `material`.

Once the new type has been created, you can use it directly on the `item` element under the `pottery` element, rather than redefining the item type. The result is an element that looks like the original `item`, but adds the `material` element, as shown in Listing 8.28.

LISTING 8.28   Using an Extended Type

```
<?xml version="1.0" encoding="UTF-8"?>
<collection xmlns:xsi="http://www.w3.org/2001/XMLSchema-instance"
        xsi:noNamespaceSchemaLocation="collectibles.xsd">
...
    <pottery>
        <item itemid="2" demand="low">
            <previousOwner>John Sorhed</previousOwner>
            <description>
                This piece is <brand>Rommbel</brand> figurine from the
                <tradeName>Everyday Instants</tradeName> collection. It is in
                <condition>good</condition> condition and just needs a good
                cleaning.
            </description>
            <originDate>1925</originDate>
            <numOwners>1</numOwners>
            <obtainable>yes</obtainable>
            <originalOwner>John Sorhed</originalOwner>
            <originalPrice>20.00</originalPrice>
            <lastPrice>500.00</lastPrice>
            <desiredPrice>700.00</desiredPrice>
            <outlets>oBoy Yoohoo!</outlets>
            <material>Porcelain</material>
        </item>
    </pottery>
</collection>
```

Deriving via Restriction

Earlier, we discussed the process of creating a new data type by restricting the values for a simple type. Deriving a new type via the restriction of complex data types is a bit more cumbersome than extension, but follows the same basic principles.

In extension, you indicate the base type and then simply specify the additions. Restriction of the model requires you to re-specify the parts of the original model that you're keeping. For example, suppose you want to remove `originalPrice` from the content model for `advertising` items. You would need to create the restriction by listing all the other elements, as shown in Listing 8.29.

LISTING 8.29   Restricting Complex Types

```
<?xml version="1.0" encoding="UTF-8"?>
<xs:schema xmlns:xs="http://www.w3.org/2001/XMLSchema">
...
    <xs:complexType name="itemType">
        <xs:sequence>
            <xs:element ref="previousOwner"
                        minOccurs="0" maxOccurs="5"/>
            <xs:element ref="description"/>
            <xs:element ref="originDate"/>
            <xs:element ref="numOwners"/>
            <xs:element ref="obtainable"/>
            <xs:element ref="originalOwner"/>
            <xs:element name="originalPrice" type="USCurrency"/>
            <xs:element name="lastPrice" type="USCurrency"/>
            <xs:element name="desiredPrice" type="USCurrency"/>
            <xs:element name="outlets" type="outlets"/>
        </xs:sequence>
        <xs:attributeGroup ref="itemAtts"/>
    </xs:complexType>

    <xs:complexType name="advertisingItemType">
        <xs:complexContent>
            <xs:restriction base="itemType">
                <xs:sequence>
                    <xs:element ref="previousOwner"
                                minOccurs="0" maxOccurs="5"/>
                    <xs:element ref="description"/>
                    <xs:element ref="originDate"/>
                    <xs:element ref="numOwners"/>
                    <xs:element ref="obtainable"/>
                    <xs:element ref="originalOwner"/>
                    <xs:element name="lastPrice" type="USCurrency"/>
                    <xs:element name="desiredPrice" type="USCurrency"/>
                    <xs:element name="outlets" type="outlets"/>
                </xs:sequence>
            </xs:restriction>
        </xs:complexContent>
    </xs:complexType>

    <xs:complexType name="potteryItemType">
        <xs:complexContent>
            <xs:extension base="itemType">
```

LISTING 8.29 Continued

```
                        <xs:sequence>
                            <xs:element name="material" type="xs:string"/>
                        </xs:sequence>
                    </xs:extension>
                </xs:complexContent>
            </xs:complexType>

    <xs:element name="collection">
        <xs:complexType mixed="false">
            <xs:choice minOccurs="1" maxOccurs="unbounded">
    ...
                <xs:element name="advertising">
                    <xs:complexType>
                        <xs:sequence>
                            <xs:element name="item"
                                        type="advertisingItemType"
                                        minOccurs="0"
                                        maxOccurs="unbounded"/>
                        </xs:sequence>
                    </xs:complexType>
                </xs:element>
            </xs:choice>
        </xs:complexType>
    </xs:element>

</xs:schema>
```

Notice that because the attribute specification is unchanged, you don't specify it as part of the restriction.

In some situations, you may want to both restrict and extend a type. For example, an autographed item typically doesn't have an "original" price, and the brand and trade name don't belong in the description. On the other hand, you should probably include information about the person whose autograph is on the item. Listing 8.30 shows a restriction of the `itemType`, with a subsequent extension of the new type.

LISTING 8.30 Restriction and Extension

```
<?xml version="1.0" encoding="UTF-8"?>
<xs:schema xmlns:xs="http://www.w3.org/2001/XMLSchema">
...
    <xs:complexType name="autographRestrictType">
        <xs:complexContent>
            <xs:restriction base="itemType">
                <xs:sequence>
                    <xs:element ref="previousOwner"
                                minOccurs="0" maxOccurs="5"/>
                    <xs:element ref="originDate"/>
                    <xs:element ref="numOwners"/>
                    <xs:element ref="obtainable"/>
```

LISTING 8.30   Continued

```
                        <xs:element ref="originalOwner"/>
                        <xs:element name="lastPrice" type="USCurrency"/>
                        <xs:element name="desiredPrice" type="USCurrency"/>
                        <xs:element name="outlets" type="outlets"/>
                    </xs:sequence>
                </xs:restriction>
            </xs:complexContent>
        </xs:complexType>

        <xs:complexType name="autographItemType">
            <xs:complexContent>
                <xs:extension base="autographRestrictType">
                    <xs:sequence>
                        <xs:element name="description" type="xs:string"/>
                        <xs:element name="personFirst" type="xs:string"/>
                        <xs:element name="personLast" type="xs:string"/>
                        <xs:element name="medium" type="xs:string"/>
                        <xs:element name="legible" type="xs:string"/>
                    </xs:sequence>
                </xs:extension>
            </xs:complexContent>
        </xs:complexType>
...
    <xs:element name="collection">
        <xs:complexType mixed="false">
            <xs:choice minOccurs="1" maxOccurs="unbounded">
...
                <xs:element name="autographs">
                    <xs:complexType>
                        <xs:sequence>
                            <xs:element name="item"
                                        type="autographItemType"
                                        minOccurs="0"
                                        maxOccurs="unbounded"/>
                        </xs:sequence>
                    </xs:complexType>
                </xs:element>
...
            </xs:choice>
        </xs:complexType>
    </xs:element>

</xs:schema>
```

The end result is the instance document shown in Listing 8.31.

LISTING 8.31   The Extended Restricted Data

```
...
    <autographs>
        <item itemid="4" demand="high">
```

LISTING 8.31   Continued

```
            <previousOwner>John Sorhed</previousOwner>
            <originDate>1903</originDate>
            <numOwners>1</numOwners>
            <obtainable>yes</obtainable>
            <originalOwner>John Sorhed</originalOwner>
            <lastPrice>255.50</lastPrice>
            <desiredPrice>350.00</desiredPrice>
            <outlets>oBoy Yoohoo!</outlets>
            <description>
                This autograph comes at the bottom of a cancelled check
                from Smythe to his landlady dated January 5, 1903.
            </description>
            <personFirst>John</personFirst>
            <personLast>Smythe</personLast>
            <medium>paper</medium>
            <legible>yes</legible>
        </item>
    </autographs>
    ...
```

Data Integrity

One place where XML Schema shines over DTDs is in the area of data integrity. DTDs give you
the ability to create `ID` and `IDREF` attributes that mimic, in some ways, the primary and foreign
keys available in some relational databases, but they're severely limited. XML Schema improves
on DTDs in terms of data integrity by allowing unique keys and multiple foreign key relationships.

Unique Keys

The simplest type of key is one that requires that each value within it be unique. A document
can carry any number of unique keys, because the definition of the key specifies what, exactly,
must be unique. For example, Listing 8.32 demonstrates the creation of a unique key for the
`itemid` attribute.

LISTING 8.32   Creating a Unique Key

```
<?xml version="1.0" encoding="UTF-8"?>
<xs:schema xmlns:xs="http://www.w3.org/2001/XMLSchema">
...
    <xs:element name="collection">
        <xs:complexType mixed="false">
            <xs:choice minOccurs="1" maxOccurs="unbounded">
                <xs:element name="toys">
...

                </xs:element>
                <xs:element name="furniture">
...
```

LISTING 8.32   *Continued*

```
            </xs:element>
            <xs:element name="pottery">
...

            </xs:element>
            <xs:element name="autographs">
...

            </xs:element>
            <xs:element name="advertising">
...

            </xs:element>
        </xs:choice>
    </xs:complexType>
    <xs:unique name="itemIdKey">
        <xs:selector xpath=".//item"/>
        <xs:field xpath="@itemid"/>
    </xs:unique>
</xs:element>

</xs:schema>
```

First, create the unique key and name it. Here the `unique` element is placed within the definition of the `collection` element to give it a context node. Next, the `field` and the `selector` use XPath expressions to tell the processor exactly what must be unique, and where to find it. In this case, the `itemid` attribute of any `item` descendant of the context node (that's the `collection` element, as you might remember) must be unique. With this restriction in place, no two `item` elements can have the same `itemid` attribute, no matter where they are in the structure of the document.

XPath

XPath expressions are covered in detail in Chapter 11, "Selecting Data: XPath," but here's a very quick overview. Elements are shown in hierarchies using slashes, so the `item` element in the structure

```
<collection>
    <autograph itemid="...">
        <item>...</item>
    </autograph>
</collection>
```

can be represented as `/collection/autograph/item`. A single slash represents a child, and two slashes represent any descendant, so the expressions `/collection//item` and `//item` also refer to the `item` element. We represent an attribute by preceding the name with the @ symbol, as in `@itemid`.

On the other hand, because you can specify the keys using XPath expressions, you can just as easily create a unique key that is limited to each of the collection's child elements. You might have an `autograph` item and an `advertising` item that have identical `itemid` attributes, but within each of these elements the `itemid`s are unique.

Keys and Keyrefs

Database designers moving to XML and those working with data from a database are usually most interested in the ability to duplicate foreign keys. In a foreign key, one field acts as the primary key; each value must be present and unique. The second field references the first; if a value is present, it must match an existing value from the primary key.

For example, if we add an `onSale` element that lists the items that are currently for sale, we need to make sure that the items referenced actually exist. This requirement is shown in Listing 8.33.

LISTING 8.33   Key and Keyref Elements

```xml
<?xml version="1.0" encoding="UTF-8"?>
<xs:schema xmlns:xs="http://www.w3.org/2001/XMLSchema">
...
    <xs:element name="collection">
        <xs:complexType mixed="false">
            <xs:choice minOccurs="1" maxOccurs="unbounded">
...
                <xs:element name="onSale">
                    <xs:complexType>
                        <xs:sequence>
                            <xs:element name="itemForSale" minOccurs="0"
                                                           maxOccurs="unbounded">
                                <xs:complexType>
                                    <xs:sequence>
                                        <xs:element name="outlet" type="outlets"/>
                                        <xs:element name="itemid"
                                                            type="xs:integer"/>
                                    </xs:sequence>
                                </xs:complexType>
                                <xs:keyref name="onSaleItems"
                                                    refer="existingItems">
                                    <xs:selector xpath="."/>
                                    <xs:field xpath="itemid"/>
                                </xs:keyref>
                            </xs:element>
                        </xs:sequence>
                    </xs:complexType>
                </xs:element>
            </xs:choice>
        </xs:complexType>

        <xs:unique name="itemIdKey">
            <xs:selector xpath=".//item"/>
            <xs:field xpath="@itemid"/>
        </xs:unique>

        <xs:key name="existingItems">
            <xs:selector xpath=".//item"/>
            <xs:field xpath="@itemid"/>
```

LISTING 8.33   Continued

```
        </xs:key>

    </xs:element>

</xs:schema>
```

This example demonstrates a few different concepts. First, the `onSale` element is defined inline, with `complexType`s nested within one another and within `element` definitions.

Second, the `key` is defined at the bottom of the listing, with the `collection` element again serving as the context node. Notice that the structure is identical to that of the `unique` element. Once the `key` is defined, create a `keyref` that defines the data that must refer back to it. In this case, that definition is within the `itemForSale` element, but it could appear anywhere within the `collection` element, as long as the XPath expressions are correct.

The end result is that the `itemid` element within `itemForSale` must contain a value that matches an existing `itemid` attribute from elsewhere within the document.

Namespaces

Because XML Schema was designed with XML namespaces in mind, it provides a number of useful features. For example, a particular schema can target data from a particular namespace, allowing you to add data to another namespace without invalidating the document. You can also specify different schemas for data from different namespaces, thus allowing all of your content to be validated.

To do this, it's important to document the namespaces properly.

noNamespaceSchemaLocation

Let's review the setup that we have now. The current schema document contains this definition:

```
<xs:schema xmlns:xs="http://www.w3.org/2001/XMLSchema">
...
```

Notice that the only namespace defined is that for the schema itself, and that all schema elements and attributes are preceded by the `xs:` alias, indicating that they're part of that namespace.

The definitions, on the other hand, don't have a namespace alias, which means that the elements that are being defined have no namespace. Because of this, when we created the instance document, we indicated the schema location with the element

```
<collection xmlns:xsi="http://www.w3.org/2001/XMLSchema-instance"
        xsi:noNamespaceSchemaLocation="collectibles.xsd">
...
```

The first definition creates the `xsi:` alias and links it to the `XMLSchema-instance` namespace, so the processor understands that anything prefixed with `xsi:` is an instruction for the processor. The first of these instructions is the `noNamespaceSchemaLocation` attribute, which points back to the schema document. In short, the schema defines elements with no namespace, so the schema for them is listed as the `noNamespaceSchemaLocation` attribute. That schema validates any elements or attributes that are not part of a namespace.

This is just the tip of the iceberg when it comes to namespaces, however.

The `targetnamespace`

In many cases, we want to create a schema for data that belongs to a particular namespace. For example, the data might belong to a namespace representing the overall collection data, such as `http://www.example.com/collection`. The schema will therefore designate this as the target namespace, because it's the target of the definitions being created. Listing 8.34 shows the creation of the target namespace and makes the Schema namespace the default namespace.

LISTING 8.34   A Schema with a Target Namespace

```
<?xml version="1.0" encoding="UTF-8"?>
<schema xmlns="http://www.w3.org/2001/XMLSchema"
        xmlns:col="http://www.example.com/collection"
        targetNamespace="http://www.example.com/collection"
        elementFormDefault="qualified"
        attributeFormDefault="qualified"
>
...
    <attribute name="itemid" type="integer"/>
    <attribute name="keeper" type="string"/>
    <attribute name="demand">
        <simpleType>
            <restriction base="string">
                <enumeration value="low"/>
                <enumeration value="medium"/>
                <enumeration value="high"/>
                <enumeration value="money is no object"/>
            </restriction>
        </simpleType>
    </attribute>
    <attribute name="legal" type="string"/>
    <attributeGroup name="itemAtts">
        <attribute ref="col:itemid" use="required"/>
        <attribute ref="col:keeper" default="yes"/>
        <attribute ref="col:demand" use="optional"/>
        <attribute ref="col:legal" fixed="yes"/>
    </attributeGroup>

    <simpleType name="possibleOutlets">
        <restriction base="string">
            <enumeration value="oBoy"/>
```

LISTING 8.34   Continued

```
                <enumeration value="Yoohoo!"/>
                <enumeration value="ConJunction"/>
                <enumeration value="Anazone"/>
        </restriction>
</simpleType>

<simpleType name="outletList">
    <list itemType="col:possibleOutlets"/>
</simpleType>

<simpleType name="outlets">
    <restriction base="col:outletList">
        <maxLength value="3"/>
    </restriction>
</simpleType>

<simpleType name="USCurrency">
    <restriction base="decimal">
        <fractionDigits value="2"/>
    </restriction>
</simpleType>

<complexType name="itemType">
    <sequence>
        <element ref="col:previousOwner"
                    minOccurs="0" maxOccurs="5"/>
        <element ref="col:description"/>
        <element ref="col:originDate"/>
        <element ref="col:numOwners"/>
        <element ref="col:obtainable"/>
        <element ref="col:originalOwner"/>
        <element name="originalPrice" type="col:USCurrency"/>
        <element name="lastPrice" type="col:USCurrency"/>
        <element name="desiredPrice" type="col:USCurrency"/>
        <element name="outlets" type="col:outlets"/>
    </sequence>
    <attributeGroup ref="col:itemAtts"/>

</complexType>

<complexType name="autographRestrictType">
    <complexContent>
        <restriction base="col:itemType">
            <sequence>
                <element ref="col:previousOwner"
                            minOccurs="0" maxOccurs="5"/>
                <element ref="col:originDate"/>
                <element ref="col:numOwners"/>
                <element ref="col:obtainable"/>
                <element ref="col:originalOwner"/>
                <element name="lastPrice" type="col:USCurrency"/>
                <element name="desiredPrice" type="col:USCurrency"/>
```

LISTING 8.34 Continued

```
                            <element name="outlets" type="col:outlets"/>
                        </sequence>
                    </restriction>
                </complexContent>
            </complexType>

            <complexType name="autographItemType">
                <complexContent>
                    <extension base="col:autographRestrictType">
                        <sequence>
...
                        </sequence>
                    </extension>
                </complexContent>
            </complexType>

            <complexType name="advertisingItemType">
                <complexContent>
                    <restriction base="col:itemType">
                        <sequence>
                            <element ref="col:previousOwner"
                                        minOccurs="0" maxOccurs="5"/>
                            <element ref="col:description"/>
                            <element ref="col:originDate"/>
                            <element ref="col:numOwners"/>
                            <element ref="col:obtainable"/>
                            <element ref="col:originalOwner"/>
                            <element name="lastPrice" type="col:USCurrency"/>
                            <element name="desiredPrice" type="col:USCurrency"/>
                            <element name="outlets" type="col:outlets"/>
                        </sequence>
                    </restriction>
                </complexContent>
            </complexType>

            <complexType name="potteryItemType">
                <complexContent>
                    <extension base="col:itemType">
                        <sequence>
                            <element name="material" type="string"/>
                        </sequence>
                    </extension>
                </complexContent>
            </complexType>

            <element name="collection">
                <complexType mixed="false">
                    <choice minOccurs="1" maxOccurs="unbounded">
                        <element name="toys">
                            <complexType>
                                <sequence>
                                    <element name="item" type="col:itemType"
```

LISTING 8.34   Continued

```
                                minOccurs="0"
                                maxOccurs="unbounded"/>
                </sequence>
            </complexType>
        </element>
        <element name="furniture">
            <complexType>
                <sequence>
                    <element name="item" type="col:itemType"
                                minOccurs="0"
                                maxOccurs="unbounded"/>
                </sequence>
            </complexType>
        </element>
        <element name="pottery">
            <complexType>
                <sequence>
                    <element name="item"
                                type="col:potteryItemType"
                                minOccurs="0"
                                maxOccurs="unbounded"/>
                </sequence>
            </complexType>
        </element>
        <element name="autographs">
            <complexType>
                <sequence>
                    <element name="item"
                                type="col:autographItemType"
                                minOccurs="0"
                                maxOccurs="unbounded"/>
                </sequence>
            </complexType>
        </element>
        <element name="advertising">
            <complexType>
                <sequence>
                    <element name="item"
                                type="col:advertisingItemType"
                                minOccurs="0"
                                maxOccurs="unbounded"/>
                </sequence>
            </complexType>
        </element>
        <element name="onSale">
            <complexType>
                <sequence>
                    <element name="itemForSale" minOccurs="0"
                                                maxOccurs="unbounded">
                        <complexType>
                            <sequence>
                                <element name="outlet"
```

LISTING 8.34   Continued

```
                                            type="col:outlets"/>
                    <element name="itemid" type="integer"/>
                  </sequence>
                </complexType>
                <keyref name="onSaleItems"
                                   refer="col:existingItems">
                  <selector xpath="."/>
                  <field xpath="col:itemid"/>
                </keyref>
              </element>
            </sequence>
          </complexType>
        </element>
      </choice>
    </complexType>
    <unique name="itemIdKey">
      <selector xpath=".//col:item"/>
      <field xpath="@col:itemid"/>
    </unique>

    <key name="existingItems">
      <selector xpath=".//col:item"/>
      <field xpath="@col:itemid"/>
    </key>

  </element>

</schema>
```

We'll deal with `elementFormDefault` and `attributeFormDefault` in a moment, but notice that the situation has now reversed itself in some ways. Earlier, the Schema namespace was specified with an alias, and the data itself was not part of a namespace, so whenever we referred to built-in schema elements and types we used the **xs:** prefix, and when we referred to custom elements and types we didn't use a prefix.

Now, the Schema namespace is the default namespace, and we have an alias for the namespace that represents the `targetNamespace`, so we've removed all the **xs:** aliases and prefixed all references to elements or types that were previously defined with **col:**.

On the instance document side, the data now has to be part of a namespace, as shown in Listing 8.35.

LISTING 8.35   Referencing Elements in the Target Namespace

```
<?xml version="1.0" encoding="UTF-8"?>
<c:collection xmlns:xsi="http://www.w3.org/2001/XMLSchema-instance"
          xmlns:c="http://www.example.com/collection"
          xsi:schemaLocation=
              "http://www.example.com/collection collectibles.xsd">
```

LISTING 8.35   Continued

```
<c:toys>
    <c:item c:itemid="1" c:demand="money is no object">
        <c:previousOwner>John Sorhed</c:previousOwner>
        <c:description>
            This piece is a genuine wooden <c:brand>Silhaven</c:brand>
            <c:tradeName>Volunteer Firetruck</c:tradeName>. It is in
            <c:condition>excellent</c:condition> condition and just waiting
            for the right collector.
        </c:description>
        <c:originDate>1940</c:originDate>
        <c:numOwners>1</c:numOwners>
        <c:obtainable>yes</c:obtainable>
        <c:originalOwner>John Sorhed</c:originalOwner>
        <c:originalPrice>2.00</c:originalPrice>
        <c:lastPrice>49.00</c:lastPrice>
        <c:desiredPrice>79.99</c:desiredPrice>
        <c:outlets>oBoy Yoohoo!</c:outlets>
    </c:item>
</c:toys>
...
</c:collection>
```

The namespace for the data must match the `targetNamespace` in the schema document. Here it's aliased to `c:`, and all the data is explicitly qualified. Because of this, the schema document specifies that `elementFormDefault` and `attributeFormDefault` are `qualified`.

To give the processor an idea where to find the schema document, the `schemaLocation` attribute designates both the namespace and the corresponding schema document, separated by a space. This format allows you to specify different schema documents for different namespaces.

Multiple Namespaces

Suppose you want to include an optional `specifications` element to enhance the description, but it belongs to a different namespace. You can declare the namespace and reference it within the schema, as in Listing 8.36.

LISTING 8.36   Using Definitions from Another Namespace

```
<?xml version="1.0" encoding="UTF-8"?>
<schema xmlns="http://www.w3.org/2001/XMLSchema"
        xmlns:col="http://www.example.com/collection"
        xmlns:spec="http://www.example.com/spec"
        targetNamespace="http://www.example.com/collection"
        elementFormDefault="qualified"
        attributeFormDefault="qualified"
>
...
    <complexType name="itemType">
```

LISTING 8.36   Continued

```
            <sequence>
                <element ref="col:previousOwner"
                            minOccurs="0" maxOccurs="5"/>
                <element ref="col:description"/>
                <element ref="spec:specifications" minOccurs="0"/>
                <element ref="col:originDate"/>
    ...
            </sequence>
            <attributeGroup ref="col:itemAtts"/>

        </complexType>
    ...
</schema>
```

The instance document can now reference the data, with the extra namespace and schema listed as part of `schemaLocation`, as in Listing 8.37.

LISTING 8.37   Referencing Multiple Namespaces

```
<?xml version="1.0" encoding="UTF-8"?>
<c:collection xmlns:xsi="http://www.w3.org/2001/XMLSchema-instance"
            xmlns:c="http://www.example.com/collection"
            xmlns:s="http://www.example.com/spec"
            xsi:schemaLocation=
                    "http://www.example.com/collection collectibles.xsd
                    http://www.example.com/spec specs.xsd">

    <c:toys>
        <c:item c:itemid="1" c:demand="money is no object">
            <c:previousOwner>John Sorhed</c:previousOwner>
            <c:description>
                This piece is a genuine wooden <c:brand>Silhaven</c:brand>
                <c:tradeName>Volunteer Firetruck</c:tradeName>. It is in
                <c:condition>excellent</c:condition> condition and just waiting
                for the right collector.
            </c:description>
            <s:specifications>The specifications are...</s:specifications>
            <c:originDate>1940</c:originDate>
    ...
        </c:item>
    </c:toys>
    ...
</c:collection>
```

Other Schema Proposals

The idea of defining the structure of an XML document using XML was natural once XML entered into common usage, and the W3C's XML Schema Recommendation is not the only proposal that does so. Other schema proposals resemble XML Schema to varying degrees, but the goal of all of them is the same: to make the specification of an XML grammar easier.

Abstract Schema and Load and Save

If you've followed this book through from the beginning, you've already seen how to use an in-memory representation of XML data in the form of a Document Object Model (DOM) document. It may also have occurred to you that because XML Schema documents are simple XML documents, there should be no reason that they can't be represented as DOM documents.

Technically, that's true, but until recently there was no standard way for a parser to handle this information. At the time of this writing, the Document Object Model Level 3 Abstract Schemas and Load and Save Specification is at the Working Draft stage. Eventually, Abstract Schema implementations will provide a means for creating an in-memory representation of a DTD, XML Schema, or other means for defining an XML grammar.

An overview of Abstract Schema (which is subject to change in the final version) is as follows: First a model is created, usually by parsing a document, and set as the abstract schema for the parser. From there, the parser can validate any number of documents without having to reload the schema. The specification also allows you to change the "active" schema for a document, should requirements change during processing.

Listing 8.38 shows the creation and use of an abstract schema using an early implementation in Java as part of Apache's Xerces-Java 2. (Remember, this is subject to change in the final draft!)

> **Note**
>
> As this book goes to press, the DOM Level 3.0 Abstract Schemas and Load and Save module have been split into the Load and Save, Validation, and Abstract Schemas modules, with the Abstract Schemas module removed from DOM Level 3.0 altogether.

LISTING 8.38   Using an Abstract Schema

```
import org.xml.sax.helpers.DefaultHandler;
import org.apache.xerces.dom.DOMImplementationImpl;
import org.apache.xerces.dom3.as.DOMImplementationAS;
import org.apache.xerces.dom3.as.DOMASBuilder;
import org.apache.xerces.dom3.as.ASModel;
import org.apache.xerces.dom3.DOMError;
import org.apache.xerces.dom3.DOMErrorHandler;

public class AbstractDemo implements DOMErrorHandler {

    public static void main(String argv[]) {

        //Create the parser
```

LISTING 8.38   Continued

```
DOMImplementationAS domImpl =
                (DOMImplementationAS)DOMImplementationImpl
                                    .getDOMImplementation();
DOMASBuilder parser = domImpl.createDOMASBuilder();
parser.setErrorHandler(new AbstractDemo());

//Set the necessary features
parser.setFeature("http://xml.org/sax/features/validation", true);
parser.setFeature("http://apache.org/xml/features/validation/schema",
                    true);

//Parse the schema to create the ASModel
try {
    ASModel asmodel = parser.parseASURI("myschema.xsd");
    parser.setAbstractSchema(asmodel);
} catch (Exception e) {
    System.out.print("Cannot create schema: ");
    System.out.println(e.getMessage());
}

//Parse the instance document
try {
    parser.parseURI("mydocument.xml");
} catch (Exception e) {
    System.out.print("Cannot parse file: ");
    System.out.println(e.getMessage());
}
}

public boolean handleError(DOMError domerror) {
    if (domerror.getSeverity() == domerror.SEVERITY_WARNING){
        System.out.println("Warning: "+domerror.getMessage());
        return true;
    } else if (domerror.getSeverity() == domerror.SEVERITY_ERROR){
        System.out.println("Error: "+domerror.getMessage());
        return true;
    } else { //domerror.getSeverity() == domerror.SEVERITY_FATAL_ERROR
        System.out.println("Fatal error: "+domerror.getMessage());
        return false;
    }
}
}
```

Basically, the parser is created from the DOM object. The parser parses the schema document to create an ASModel, which is set as the abstract schema. This schema comes into play when the parser parses an instance document.

As long as the implementation understands the schema language in use, it doesn't matter what that language is. It might be an XML Schema like those we've been discussing, a database schema, or one of the alternate schemas discussed in the following sections.

RELAX NG

RELAX NG, pronounced *relaxing*, is short for REgular LAnguage description for XML Next Generation, and represents the unification of RELAX and the Tree Regular Expressions for XML (TREX). The idea is to provide a means for creating XML schemas (note the small *s*) without having to get into the complexities of the W3C XML Schema Recommendation. Consider the example shown in Listing 8.39.

LISTING 8.39   Sample XML Data

```
<class>
    <students>
        <student>John</student>
        <student>Mary</student>
    </students>
    <classroom>3G</classroom>
    <subject>Landscape painting</subject>
</class>
```

Listing 8.40 shows the RELAX NG schema representation of this structure.

LISTING 8.40   RELAX NG Schema

```
<element name="class" xmlns="http://relaxng.org/ns/structure/1.0">
    <element name="students">
        <zeroOrMore>
            <element name="student">
                <text/>
            </element>
        </zeroOrMore>
    </element>
    <element name="classroom">
        <text/>
    </element>
    <element name="subject">
        <text/>
    </element>
</element>
```

The RELAX NG standard will eventually be submitted to the ISO standards body.

Schematron

The Schematron takes a completely different tack. Rather than creating a structure that mimics the document, as XML Schema and RELAX NG do, it instead indicates elements and attributes that must exist by specifying XPath statements. We'll cover XPath in Chapter 11, but a simple Schematron document representing the data from Listing 8.39 is shown in Listing 8.41.

LISTING 8.41   A Simple Schematron Document

```
<schema xmlns="http://www.ascc.net/xml/schematron">
    <title>The classroom data structure</title>
    <ns prefix="c" uri="http://www.example.com/classes"/>
    <pattern>
        <rule context="c:class">
            <assert test="c:students">A class has a "students"
                                      element.</assert>
            <assert test="c:students/c:student">The students element
                        contains the student elements.</assert>
            <assert test="c:classroom">You must specify a
                                       classroom</assert>
            <assert test="c:subject">You must specify a
                                     subject</assert>
        </rule>
    </pattern>
</schema>
```

A Schematron schema consists of patterns and rules, with assertions that specifically designate XPath expressions and the explanations of what they mean, in plain language.

Summary

XML Schema, as maintained by the World Wide Web Consortium, is a means for specifying a grammar to which an XML instance document must conform while still using XML rather than the additional syntax of a DTD.

XML Schema offers the convenience of greater type control, with dozens of built-in types such as `string`, `integer`, and `date`, and the ability to define your own types. These custom types can be variations of simple types, such as a range of dates, or they can be entire hierarchies of elements and attributes. You can create new types by extending or restricting existing types. Schemas also enable you to create keys to facilitate data integrity.

In contrast to the "0, 1, or unlimited" nature of element models in a DTD, schemas allow you to specify exactly how many times an element can appear.

XML Schema makes use of namespaces. This allows you to combine information from multiple namespaces and still maintain the integrity of validation.

Several competing schema proposals are in current use, such as RELAX NG and Schematron.

Review Questions

1. List three advantages that XML Schema offers over Document Type Definitions.

2. What is a facet?

3. What does restriction do?

4. What does extension do?

5. What is the difference between a simple type and a complex type?

6. What attribute or attributes specify how many times an element can appear in a document?

7. What is a default value, and can it be applied to an element?

8. What does *inlining* mean?

Programming Exercises

1. Define a simple element that can take only integer values.

2. Create an element that can contain at least two child elements, one of which is optional but can appear an unlimited number of times, and one of which must appear between 5 and 10 times.

3. Create an element that can contain only date values and carries at least one attribute.

4. Create an element that can contain its child elements in any order.

5. Create an element that can contain mixed content.

6. Create an element that contains child elements and attributes that have been previously defined.

7. Create a simple type that represents a specific set of numeric values.

8. Create a simple type that uses two or more facets. Create an element of that type.

9. Create a complex type and an element that references it.

10. Create a new type by extending it.

11. Create a new type by restricting it.

12. Create the same element with an inline, or anonymous, definition.

13. Create an instance document that references your schema. The data must not belong to a namespace.

14. Create an instance document that references your schema. The data must belong to a namespace.

CHAPTER 9

EXTENSIBLE STYLESHEET LANGUAGE TRANSFORMATIONS (XSLT)

You will learn about the following in this chapter:

- Style sheets
- XPath basics
- Templates
- Output format
- Dynamic elements and attributes

- Looping and sorting
- Variables and parameters
- If-then statements
- Modes

*I*f you've done any Web page design, you may be familiar with cascading style sheets, which tell a browser to perform a particular action on a particular type of element, such as applying a particular style to all content enclosed in an <h1> element. Extensible Stylesheet Language (XSL) performs much the same function for XML, but goes well beyond simple presentation.

XSL Transformations (XSLT) is half of the XSL equation. They allow you to create "rules" by which data is transformed, allowing it to move from one system to another. For example, one common use for XSLT is to transform XML data into an HTML page for display in a browser. XSLT can also transform data from one XML structure into another, or from XML into plain text. In fact, XSLT can accomplish virtually any text-based transformation, and extensions allow even more functionality.

The other half of the equation, XSL Formatting Objects (XSL-FO), enables you to create files that can be accurately formatted in any compliant system. A sort of "hyper-CSS," XSL-FO is commonly used to create PDF files.

XSL, XSLT, and XSL-FO

PDF Files

Portable Document Format (PDF) files are viewable on virtually any platform via the Adobe Acrobat Reader, free from `http://www.adobe.com/products/acrobat/readstep2.html`.

The distinction between XSLT and XSL-FO is important, but the two are often confused. Part of the confusion stems from the fact that while the term *style sheets* implies the functionality that comes with XSL-FO, XSLT is currently much more commonly used. Muddying the waters even further is the fact that XSLT is even used to generate XSL-FO files!

Chapter 16, "XML and Publishing," covers XSL Formatting Objects in detail, but let's quickly compare XSLT and XSL-FO to give you an idea of what we're dealing with.

Suppose you have an XML file of news stories, as in Listing 9.1.

LISTING 9.1 The Source Document

```
<?xml version="1.0"?>
<!DOCTYPE news SYSTEM "source.dtd">
<news>
    <newsitem itemnum="1">
        <newsdate>6.18.3425</newsdate>
        <title>End Of The Line For The Incumbent?</title>
        <body>
            The Universal News Network is reporting that <person>His
            Magnificence The Supreme Leader For Life</person>
            announced today that he has decided not to be cloned for
            a 14th term.
        </body>
    </newsitem>

    <newsitem itemnum="2">
        <newsdate>6.19.3425</newsdate>
        <title>New Fall Lineup</title>
        <body>
            The Omega Channel has announced two new shows for its new
            fall lineup. <program>Who's Running the Galaxy?</program>
            features a team of government scientists who accidentally
            clone two Supreme Leaders. If you think you're confused,
            imagine what the first family must be going through.
            <program>Trading Species</program> follows two teams of
            aliens who trade species and have only 48 hours to adjust
            and fool their neighbors.
        </body>
    </newsitem>
</news>
```

Using XSL Transformations, you can convert this file into a number of different formats. For example, you can create an XSLT style sheet to convert the document to XHTML, as in Listing 9.2.

LISTING 9.2   The XSLT Style Sheet

```
<?xml version="1.0"?>
<xsl:transform xmlns:xsl="http://www.w3.org/1999/XSL/Transform"
               version="1.0">

<xsl:template match="/">
    <html>
        <head><title>Today's headlines</title></head>
        <body>
            <h2 align="center">Today's UNN Headlines</h2>
            <h3 align="center">You give us 22 standard
                millirotations, we'll give you the universe</h3>

            <xsl:apply-templates/>

        </body>
    </html>
</xsl:template>

<xsl:template match="newsitem">
    <p>
        <b><i><xsl:value-of select="title"/></i></b>
        (<xsl:value-of select="newsdate"/>)<br />

        <xsl:apply-templates select="body"/>

    </p>
</xsl:template>

<xsl:template match="person">
    <b><xsl:value-of select="."/></b>
</xsl:template>

<xsl:template match="program">
    <i><xsl:value-of select="."/></i>
</xsl:template>

</xsl:transform>
```

Notice that none of the actual content is in this file. Instead, the file contains some elements (such as the main headline) and instructions for dealing with the XML content. Listing 9.3 shows the resulting document.

LISTING 9.3   The Resulting XHTML

```
<?xml version="1.0" encoding="UTF-8"?>
<html>
    <head>
        <title>Today's headlines</title>
    </head>
    <body>
        <h2 align="center">Today's UNN Headlines</h2>
        <h3 align="center">You give us 22 standard
            millirotations, we'll give you the universe</h3>
        <p>
            <b><i>End Of The Line For The Incumbent?</i></b>
            (6.18.3425)
            <br />

            The Universal News Network is reporting that
            <b>His Magnificence The Supreme Leader For Life</b>
            announced today that he has decided not to be cloned for
            a 14th term.
        </p>
        <p>
            <b><i>New Fall Lineup</i></b>
            (6.19.3425)
            <br />

            The Omega Channel has announced two new shows for its new
            fall lineup. <i>Who's Running the Galaxy?</i>
            features a team of government scientists who accidentally
            clone two Supreme Leaders. If you think you're confused,
            imagine what the first family must be going through.
            <i>Trading Species</i> follows two teams of aliens who
            trade species and have only 48 hours to adjust and fool
            their neighbors.
        </p>
    </body>
</html>
```

Viewing the file in the browser results in output similar to Figure 9.1.

You can also use XSLT to generate an XSL-FO file. Again, we'll cover XSL-FO in Chapter 16, but a simple example might involve taking the same news stories and creating a document where each appears on a separate page, with each page 14 centimeters long. The XSLT file might look like Listing 9.4.

FIGURE 9.1
XSLT can be used to
transform XML data into
an XHTML file for dis-
play controlled by a
browser.

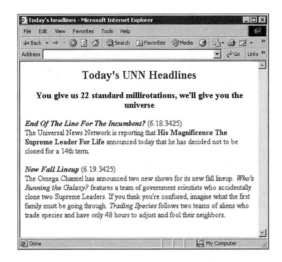

LISTING 9.4   XSLT Creating XSL-FO

```
<?xml version="1.0"?>
<xsl:transform xmlns:xsl="http://www.w3.org/1999/XSL/Transform"
xmlns:fo="http://www.w3.org/1999/XSL/Format"
                    version="1.0">

<xsl:template match="/">
<fo:root >

    <fo:layout-master-set>
        <fo:simple-page-master master-name="mainpages"
                page-height="14cm" page-width="21cm" margin-top="1cm"
                margin-bottom="2cm" margin-left="2.5cm"
                margin-right="2.5cm">
                    <fo:region-body margin-top="2.5cm"/>
                    <fo:region-before extent="3.75cm"/>
                    <fo:region-after extent="1.5cm"/>
        </fo:simple-page-master>

        <fo:page-sequence-master master-name="pageMaster">
            <fo:repeatable-page-master-alternatives>
                <fo:conditional-page-master-reference
                                    master-name="mainpages" />
            </fo:repeatable-page-master-alternatives>
        </fo:page-sequence-master>
    </fo:layout-master-set>

    <fo:page-sequence master-name="pageMaster">

        <fo:static-content flow-name="xsl-region-before">
            <fo:block font-size="24pt" font-family="sans-serif"
```

LISTING 9.4   Continued

```
                    font-weight="bold" line-height="24pt"
                    space-after.optimum="15pt" background-color="blue"
                    color="white" text-align="center" padding-top="3pt">
                        Today's UNN Headlines
                </fo:block>
                <fo:block font-size="18pt" font-family="sans-serif"
                    font-weight="bold" line-height="18pt"
                    space-after.optimum="15pt" background-color="blue"
                    color="white" text-align="center" padding-top="3pt">
                        You give us 22 standard millirotations, we'll
                        give you the universe
                </fo:block>
            </fo:static-content>


            <fo:flow flow-name="xsl-region-body">
                <xsl:apply-templates/>
            </fo:flow>
        </fo:page-sequence>

    </fo:root>

</xsl:template>

<xsl:template match="newsitem">
    <fo:block font-size="24pt" font-family="serif"
        line-height="20pt" space-before.optimum="20pt"
        space-after.optimum="14pt" >
            <xsl:value-of select="title"/>
            (<xsl:value-of select="newsdate"/>)
    </fo:block>
    <fo:block font-size="18pt" break-after="page"
        space-after.optimum="3pt" font-family="serif">

            <xsl:apply-templates select="body"/>

    </fo:block>
</xsl:template>

<xsl:template match="person">
    <fo:inline font-weight="bold">
        <xsl:value-of select="."/>
    </fo:inline>
</xsl:template>

<xsl:template match="program">
    <fo:inline font-style="italic">
        <xsl:value-of select="."/>
    </fo:inline>
</xsl:template>

</xsl:transform>
```

Again, the XSLT style sheet contains not the data, but instructions for transforming the data. The result of running the transformation is the XSL Formatting Objects document shown in Listing 9.5.

LISTING 9.5   XSL Formatting Objects

```
<?xml version="1.0" encoding="utf-8"?>
<fo:root xmlns:fo="http://www.w3.org/1999/XSL/Format">

    <fo:layout-master-set>
        <fo:simple-page-master master-name="mainpages"
              page-height="14cm" page-width="21cm" margin-top="1cm"
              margin-bottom="2cm" margin-left="2.5cm"
              margin-right="2.5cm">
                  <fo:region-body margin-top="2.5cm"/>
                  <fo:region-before extent="3.75cm"/>
                  <fo:region-after extent="1.5cm"/>
        </fo:simple-page-master>

        <fo:page-sequence-master master-name="pageMaster">
            <fo:repeatable-page-master-alternatives>
                <fo:conditional-page-master-reference
                                        master-name="mainpages" />
            </fo:repeatable-page-master-alternatives>
        </fo:page-sequence-master>
    </fo:layout-master-set>

    <fo:page-sequence master-name="pageMaster">

        <fo:static-content flow-name="xsl-region-before">
            <fo:block font-size="24pt" font-family="sans-serif"
                font-weight="bold" line-height="24pt"
                space-after.optimum="15pt" background-color="blue"
                color="white" text-align="center" padding-top="3pt">
                    Today's UNN Headlines
            </fo:block>
            <fo:block font-size="18pt" font-family="sans-serif"
                font-weight="bold" line-height="18pt"
                space-after.optimum="15pt" background-color="blue"
                color="white" text-align="center" padding-top="3pt">
                    You give us 22 standard millirotations, we'll
                    give you the universe
            </fo:block>
        </fo:static-content>


        <fo:flow flow-name="xsl-region-body">
            <fo:block font-size="24pt" font-family="serif"
                line-height="20pt" space-before.optimum="20pt"
                space-after.optimum="14pt" >
                    End Of The Line For The Incumbent? (6.18.3425)
            </fo:block>
            <fo:block font-size="18pt" break-after="page"
```

LISTING 9.5   *Continued*

```
          space-after.optimum="3pt" font-family="serif">

          The Universal News Network is reporting that
          <fo:inline font-weight="bold">His Magnificence The
          Supreme Leader For Life</fo:inline> announced today
          that he has decided not to be cloned for a 14th term.

      </fo:block>

      <fo:block font-size="24pt" font-family="serif"
          line-height="20pt" space-before.optimum="20pt"
          space-after.optimum="14pt">
              New Fall Lineup (6.19.3425)
      </fo:block>
      <fo:block font-size="18pt" space-after.optimum="3pt"
          font-family="serif">

          The Omega Channel has announced two new shows for its
          new fall lineup. <fo:inline font-style="italic">Who's
          Running the Galaxy?</fo:inline> features a team of
          government scientists who accidentally clone two
          Supreme Leaders. If you think you're confused,
          imagine what the first family must be going through.
          <fo:inline font-style="italic">Trading
          Species</fo:inline> follows two teams of aliens who
          trade species and have only 48 hours to adjust and
          fool their neighbors.

      </fo:block>
    </fo:flow>
  </fo:page-sequence>

</fo:root>
```

At the time of this writing, few browsers support XSL-FO directly, but a browser such as X-Smiles, available at `http://www.x-smiles.org` (see Figure 9.2), shows the control that formatting objects can give. XSL-FO files are often used to generate PDF files.

In short, you can use XSL Transformations to create different outputs from the same XML data, allowing you to use the data in many different contexts without having to write a new application each time.

FIGURE 9.2
Because of the control they give, formatting objects are often used as an intermediate step between XML and PDF files.

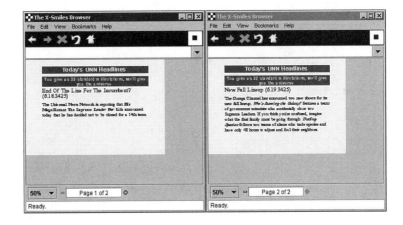

Basic Style Sheet Transformations

Although a style sheet contains all the information about a transformation, it doesn't actually perform the transformation itself. Instead, it provides instructions for a transformation engine (processor). The processor consists of an application that takes the style sheet and follows the instructions within it to transform the source document into the resulting form.

Before getting into the details of building the style sheets themselves, let's put together a pair of basic documents so you can set up a test environment.

The Style Sheet Document

A single `transform` element specifies all the functionality within a style sheet. This element designates the XSL namespace and contains at least one template, as shown in Listing 9.6.

LISTING 9.6 The Basic Style Sheet

```
<?xml version="1.0"?>
<xsl:transform xmlns:xsl="http://www.w3.org/1999/XSL/Transform"
    version="1.0">

<xsl:template match="/">

    <html>
        <head><title>Thank you letter</title></head>
        <body>
            <p>Dear valued customer,</p>
            <p>Thank you for staying with us through this difficult
                time,</p>
```

LISTING 9.6   Continued

```
                <p>Sincerely, the staff</p>
            </body>
        </html>

</xsl:template>

</xsl:transform>
```

stylesheet or transform?

Although **stylesheet** is traditionally used as the root element for an XSLT style sheet, the XSLT 1.0 Recommendation specifies that **transform** can be used instead. Because **transform** more accurately describes what's going on, many companies are adopting this terminology.

The **transform** element carries a namespace declaration creating the **xsl:** alias, which maps to the official namespace URL, http://www.w3.org/1999/XSL/Transform. As usual, the use of **xsl:** as an alias is purely traditional. The transformation engine uses namespaces to distinguish between style sheet–related elements, such as **template**, and elements that are part of the result, such as **html** and **body**.

Outputting a Value

You can use the **value-of** element to tell the processor to output a specific information item. For example, Listing 9.7 shows a sample XML file (**test.xml**) to transform as a test, and Listing 9.8 shows the style sheet (**test.xsl**) with an additional element instructing the processor to output the value of the **custName** element.

LISTING 9.7   The Source Document

```
<?xml version="1.0" encoding="UTF-8"?>
<customer>
    <custName>John Livingston</custName>
</customer>
```

LISTING 9.8   Outputting a Value

```
<?xml version="1.0"?>
<xsl:transform xmlns:xsl="http://www.w3.org/1999/XSL/Transform"
    version="1.0">

<xsl:template match="customer">

    <html>
        <head><title>Thank you letter</title></head>
        <body>
            <p>Dear <xsl:value-of select="custName"/>,</p>
```

LISTING 9.8 Continued

```
                <p>Thank you for staying with us through this difficult
                    time,</p>
                <p>Sincerely, the staff</p>
            </body>
        </html>

</xsl:template>

</xsl:transform>
```

The `value-of` element tells the processor to output a value in that spot, and the `select` attribute gives the processor information on what value to output. The `select` attribute takes an XPath expression, which we'll discuss in a moment. First, though, let's set up a test environment.

Testing the Style Sheet

If you're really determined, you can go through this chapter without trying the examples, but you'll get much more out of it if you take a few minutes to set up a test environment. Besides, you'll need these applications for the next chapter, "Transformation and Applications."

Many, many, many transformation engines exist, and for virtually any programming language and environment. A number of them are listed in Appendix A, "Resources," and the Apache project maintains Java and C++ versions of the Xalan processor at `http://xml.apache.org`.

Typically, the transformation engine that you choose will have a command-line option that allows you to directly specify a document to transform, the style sheet to transform it with, and the output to transform it to. For example, to transform the sample files to a third file called `test.html` using Xalan-Java, you can go to the command line and type something like this:

```
java org.apache.xalan.xslt.Process -IN test.xml -XSL test.xsl -OUT test.html
```

Once you've installed your transformation engine, check the documentation for the particular commands it expects, and for any additional steps (for instance, setting environment variables such as `CLASSPATH`) you need to take.

Executing the transformation should result in the output shown in Listing 9.9 and Figure 9.3.

LISTING 9.9 The Final Document

```
<html>
<head>
<title>Thank you letter</title>
</head>
<body>
<p>Dear John Livingston,</p>
<p>Thank you for staying with us through this difficult
            time,</p>
```

LISTING 9.9   Continued

```
<p>Sincerely, the staff</p>
</body>
</html>
```

FIGURE 9.3
The final test output.

If your results differ, make sure that you followed the instructions for your tool exactly, and that it recognizes the Recommendation namespace. Early versions of Microsoft's MSXML (included with some versions of Internet Explorer) and other early implementations of XSLT used the Working Draft of the Recommendation, which included some differences from the final standard. Some of these changes were major, some minor, but the namespace tells the processor which implementation the style sheet conforms to. If the processor doesn't recognize the implementation, it will not transform the document properly, even if all the other information is the same.

An Overview of XPath

In the previous example, we created a style sheet that outputs a value using the `value-of` element. That element carries a `select` attribute that specifies what information to output, in the form of an XPath statement. We will cover XPath in detail in Chapter 11, "Selecting Data: XPath," but in order to create an effective style sheet you need at least a basic grasp of XPath concepts. In this section you'll get an overview, and in the next section you'll see how to apply the concepts on a practical basis.

Children and Descendants

At its most basic level, XPath provides a "road map" to the desired node from the current node, called the *context node*. Consider the source document for this chapter (`content.xml`), shown in Listing 9.10.

LISTING 9.10   The Source Document

```
<?xml version="1.0"?>
<content>
```

LISTING 9.10   *Continued*

```
<events>
    <eventitem eventid="A335">
        <eventdate>6.20.3425</eventdate>
        <title>Making Friends With The Venusian Flu Virus</title>
        <description>Dr. Biff Mercury discusses his theory on
        coexisting with this useful organism.</description>
    </eventitem>

    <eventitem eventid="B963" optional="no">
        <eventdate>6.21.3425</eventdate>
        <title>Putting the Manners in Bedside Manner</title>
        <description>Dr. Zingzowpowie, the famous xenoneurosurgeon
        lectures on Bedside Manner and the benefits of using cold
        tentacles during a physical.</description>
    </eventitem>

    <eventitem eventid="C934" optional="yes">
        <eventdate>6.25.3425</eventdate>
        <title>An Evening of Fun</title>
        <description>This evening join us for the monthly "Identify
        that Food" contest.</description>
    </eventitem>

</events>
<news>
    <newsitem itemnum="1">
        <newsdate>6.18.3425</newsdate>
        <title>End Of The Line For The Incumbent?</title>
        <body>
            The Universal News Network is reporting that <person>His
            Magnificence The Supreme Leader For Life</person>
            announced today that he has decided not to be cloned for
            a 14th term.
        </body>
    </newsitem>

    <newsitem itemnum="2">
        <newsdate>6.19.3425</newsdate>
        <title>New Fall Lineup</title>
        <body>
            The Omega Channel has announced two new shows for its new
            fall lineup. <program>Who's Running the Galaxy?</program>
            features a team of government scientists who accidentally
            clone two Supreme Leaders. If you think you're confused,
            imagine what the first family must be going through.
            <program>Trading Species</program> follows two teams of
            aliens who trade species and have only 48 hours to adjust
            and fool their neighbors.
        </body>
    </newsitem>
</news>
</content>
```

We'll discuss context nodes in more detail in the next section, but for now understand that the context node is the node currently being processed, so if we are currently working with the news element, that is the context node.

Once you establish the context node, navigating to another node is similar to navigating a file system or URL; slashes separate the different elements you encounter while walking the tree from parent to child. For example, to get to the newsdate element from the content element, use this XPath expression:

```
news/newsitem/newsdate
```

To get there from the news element, use this XPath expression:

```
newsitem/newsdate
```

Note that these XPath expressions are not limited to a single element. Assuming that content is the context element, the following expression applies to all eventdate elements:

```
events/eventitem/eventdate
```

You can abbreviate these paths using two slashes, rather than one, to indicate that you're looking for any descendant, and not just a child. For example, assuming that the content element is the context node, the XPath expression

```
content//title
```

selects all the title elements, whether they are children of the eventitem elements or the newsitem elements.

The descendant notation can be useful when you are looking for a particular type of node anywhere in the document. In that case, you're looking for any descendant of the document root.

The Document Root

The one difficulty of the relative approach is that it can make constructing expressions difficult if you don't know where they're going to be used. XPath provides a way to create absolute paths by referencing the document root, represented by a leading slash. For example, the newsdate element can be represented by the expression

```
/content/news/newsitem/newsdate
```

without any concern for the context element, because the leading slash always represents the document root.

URI Similarity

Those with experience in Web design and programming may notice a correlation between absolute XPath expressions and absolute URIs, which also use a leading slash to indicate the server's document root. In absolute URIs, however, the slash indicates the root directory for all documents, whereas in XPath expressions, it refers to a single document.

The document root is easily confused with the root element of the document, but they're not the same. The root element (in this case, **content**) is the child of the document root.

As mentioned earlier, you can use the document root in combination with the descendant notation to find an element anywhere in the document. For example, the expression

```
//title
```

finds any **title** element anywhere in the document, because wherever it is, it's a descendant of the document root.

Attributes

Now that you have mastered the basics of navigating to an element, what about attributes? You may remember from the discussion of the Document Object Model that attributes are not, strictly speaking, children of the elements that carry them. This is the case in XPath expressions, as well.

Use the **@** symbol rather than the slash to indicate an attribute. For example, assuming that **news** is the context element, the following expressions all reference attributes:

```
/content/events/eventitem@eventid
```

```
/content//newsitem@newsid
```

```
newsitem@newsid
```

Testing Criteria

Occasionally, you'll need to filter a group of elements based on certain criteria. For example, you might want only an element with a specific attribute value, or only those with a specific type of attribute.

To add criteria to an XPath expression, enclose it within brackets (**[ ]**) following the element to which it applies. In other words, to select only the **eventitem** with an **eventid** attribute equal to **C934**, you can use this expression:

```
/content/events/eventitem[@eventid='C934']
```

Note that this expression returns the **eventitem** element, *not* the attribute. The text between the brackets is a condition that the expression to the left of the brackets must fulfill. To see this in action, you can create a basic style sheet, as shown in Listing 9.11, and use it to transform the sample document.

LISTING 9.11   A Basic Style Sheet

```
<?xml version="1.0"?>
<xsl:transform xmlns:xsl="http://www.w3.org/1999/XSL/Transform"
    version="1.0">

<xsl:template match="/">
```

LISTING 9.11   Continued

```
The selected value is
<xsl:value-of select="/content/events/eventitem[@eventid='C934']"/>

</xsl:template>
</xsl:transform>
```

You can use the same command you used to test your installation (with appropriate filenames, of course). We'll get into the mechanics in the following sections, but for now understand that the `template` sets the context node as the document root, and the `value-of` element outputs the results of the XPath expression.

The result should be all the text in the appropriate `eventitem` element, as shown in Listing 9.12.

LISTING 9.12   The Resulting Text

```
<?xml version="1.0" encoding="UTF-8"?>

The selected value is

        6.25.3425
        An Evening of Fun
        This evening join us for the monthly "Identify
        that Food" contest.
```

XML Declaration Outputs

Note that your processor may include the XML declaration by default, as Xalan does, even if the resulting text is not well-formed XML, as this is not.

It's important to understand exactly what an expression returns, particularly when testing for the existence of an attribute (or other information) rather than a specific value. For example, Listing 9.13 shows the same style sheet, but instead of looking for a specific value, it's looking for an element that actually carries an attribute, in this case the `optional` attribute.

LISTING 9.13   Testing for the Existence of Information

```
<?xml version="1.0"?>
<xsl:transform xmlns:xsl="http://www.w3.org/1999/XSL/Transform"
    version="1.0">

<xsl:template match="/">

  The selected value is
  <xsl:value-of select="/content/events/eventitem[@optional]"/>
```

LISTING 9.13   Continued

```
</xsl:template>

</xsl:transform>
```

The results should exclude the first `eventitem` and should look like Listing 9.14.

LISTING 9.14   The Resulting Text

```
<?xml version="1.0" encoding="UTF-8"?>

  The selected value is

        6.21.3425
        Putting the Manners in Bedside Manner
        Dr. Zingzowpowie, the famous xenoneurosurgeon
        lectures on Bedside Manner and the benefits of using cold
        tentacles during a physical.
```

Templates

In an XSLT style sheet, all work is done within *templates* of one sort or another. The template selects the portions of the source document to work on, determines the form the output will take, and in most cases sends the data off to any other relevant templates for processing.

Creating a Template

Let's start with the two basic functions of a template element: selecting and outputting. Take, for example, Listing 9.15.

LISTING 9.15   Selecting and Outputting Data

```
<?xml version="1.0"?>
<xsl:transform xmlns:xsl="http://www.w3.org/1999/XSL/Transform"
               version="1.0">

<xsl:template match="/content/events/eventitem">

    <h2>An event title</h2>
    <h3>(Date)</h3>
    <p>An event description</p>

    <hr />

</xsl:template>

<xsl:template match="/content/news">
```

LISTING 9.15   Continued

```
</xsl:template>

</xsl:transform>
```

The `match` attribute determines the node or nodes that the template will process. In this case, the first template processes all the `eventitem` nodes, outputting the enclosed content for each one. (The second template processes the `news` element, outputting nothing for it. We'll discuss why in the section titled "Built-in Templates".) In this case, the template contains only static (unchanging) content, so the output is the same for each element. You can see this by processing the source document with the style sheet, as shown in Listing 9.16 and Figure 9.4.

LISTING 9.16   The Resulting Text

```
<?xml version="1.0" encoding="UTF-8"?>


    <h2>An event title</h2><h3>(Date)</h3><p>An event description</p><hr/>

    <h2>An event title</h2><h3>(Date)</h3><p>An event description</p><hr/>

    <h2>An event title</h2><h3>(Date)</h3><p>An event description</p><hr/>
```

FIGURE 9.4

The static template is repeated for each item in the node-set selected by the XPath expression.

We'll discuss HTML in detail in Chapter 12, "Browser-Based XML: Cascading Style Sheets (CSS)," but for now note that `<h2>` and `<h3>` tags are headings, a `<p>` element contains a paragraph, and an `<hr>` element creates a horizontal line on the page.

To recap, for each node in the node-set that a template matches, the processor outputs the contents of the template. A corollary to this fact is that each time the template is output, the node being processed becomes the context node. This has an effect on any XPath statements within the template. For example, you can now add output from the actual XML document, as shown in Listing 9.17.

LISTING 9.17   Adding Dynamic Information

```
<?xml version="1.0"?>
<xsl:transform xmlns:xsl="http://www.w3.org/1999/XSL/Transform"
               version="1.0">

<xsl:template match="/content/events/eventitem">

    <h2><xsl:value-of select="title"/></h2>
    <h3>(<xsl:value-of select="eventdate"/>)</h3>
    <p><xsl:value-of select="description"/></p>

    <hr />

</xsl:template>

<xsl:template match="/content/news">
</xsl:template>

</xsl:transform>
```

Transforming the document produces the output shown in Listing 9.18 and Figure 9.5.

LISTING 9.18   The Result Text

```
<?xml version="1.0" encoding="UTF-8"?>

    <h2>Making Friends With The Venusian Flu Virus</h2>
    <h3>(6.20.3425)</h3><p>Dr. Biff Mercury discusses his theory on
        coexisting with this useful organism.</p><hr/>

    <h2>Putting the Manners in Bedside Manner</h2>
    <h3>(6.21.3425)</h3><p>Dr. Zingzowpowie, the famous
...
```

Applying Templates

A single template can be useful, but doesn't even begin to scratch the surface of what XSLT can do. Its real strength lies in the ability it gives you to cascade information through several templates. As a node passes through each template, changes are made to the resulting node-set. Consider Listing 9.19.

FIGURE 9.5
A style sheet can add dynamic information to each template.

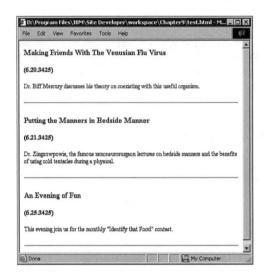

LISTING 9.19   Applying Templates to All Children

```
<?xml version="1.0"?>
<xsl:transform xmlns:xsl="http://www.w3.org/1999/XSL/Transform"
               version="1.0">

<xsl:template match="/">

    <xsl:apply-templates />

</xsl:template>

<xsl:template match="/content/events/eventitem/title">
    <h2><xsl:value-of select="."/></h2>
</xsl:template>

<xsl:template match="/content/events/eventitem/eventdate">
    <h3>(<xsl:value-of select="."/>)</h3>
</xsl:template>

<xsl:template match="/content/events/eventitem/description">
    <p><xsl:value-of select="."/></p>
    <hr />
</xsl:template>

<xsl:template match="/content/news">
</xsl:template>

</xsl:transform>
```

In this case, the means are different, but the ends are almost the same. Like many style sheets, this one starts with a template that selects the document root. The nodes processed are the same as in the last example, but instead of formatting and outputting the values, the style sheet uses the `apply-templates` element to send the text off in search of other appropriate templates.

When the transformation engine goes off in search of other templates, it finds them later in the style sheet file, and adds tags (such as `<h2></h2>`) and other content (such as (and)) as those templates dictate. This kind of modularization offers its own advantages, such as the ability to quickly change the template that is applied to a particular item.

Applying the transformation, however, exposes a problem, as shown in Listing 9.20.

LISTING 9.20   Applying Templates to All Children—The Result Text

```
<?xml version="1.0" encoding="UTF-8"?>

        <h3>(6.20.3425)</h3>
        <h2>Making Friends With The Venusian Flu Virus</h2>
        <p>Dr. Biff Mercury discusses his theory on
        coexisting with this useful organism.</p><hr/>

        <h3>(6.21.3425)</h3>
        <h2>Putting the Manners in Bedside Manner</h2>
...
```

Because you're no longer controlling the order in which the nodes are processed, the engine outputs them in the order in which they appeared in the original document, which is not the intended effect (see Figure 9.6).

FIGURE 9.6

Turning complete control over to `apply-templates` can have unexpected results. In this case, the nodes are output in the wrong order.

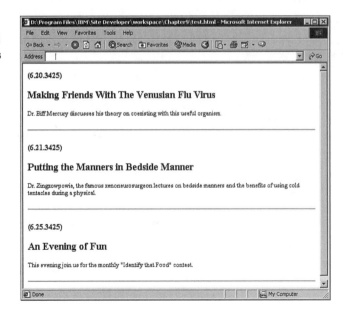

What we actually want is for the processor to look at each **eventitem** node in turn, then apply templates to the children in the order in which we want it, not the order in which they appear in the source document. To do this, have the overall template process the **newsitem** nodes, then send the individual children off to find additional templates, as shown in Listing 9.21.

LISTING 9.21   Selectively Applying Templates

```xml
<?xml version="1.0"?>
<xsl:transform xmlns:xsl="http://www.w3.org/1999/XSL/Transform"
               version="1.0">

<xsl:template match="/content/events/eventitem">

    <xsl:apply-templates select="title"/>
    <xsl:apply-templates select="eventdate"/>
    <xsl:apply-templates select="description"/>

    <hr />

</xsl:template>

<xsl:template match="title">
    <h2><xsl:value-of select="."/></h2>
</xsl:template>

<xsl:template match="eventdate">
    <h3>(<xsl:value-of select="."/>)</h3>
</xsl:template>

<xsl:template match="description">
    <p><xsl:value-of select="."/></p>
</xsl:template>
...
</xsl:transform>
```

The resulting document puts everything back in order. Before looking at the result text, let's look quickly at what's happening here. Because we changed the **match** attribute, the style sheet is explicitly processing each **eventitem** element. Each time it encounters another one, that element becomes the context node.

Within the template, the **apply-templates** element selects a node to send off based on the **select** attribute and the current context node. For this reason, the **match** attributes in the subsequent templates are no longer absolute; they're relative to the **eventitem** node currently being processed. When the child node is selected to have templates applied, it becomes the context node until the subtemplate is complete and control is returned to the main template, where the **eventitem** once again becomes the context node.

The end result is a page that's once again in the proper order, as shown in Listing 9.22.

LISTING 9.22   Selectively Applying Templates—The Result Text

```
<?xml version="1.0" encoding="UTF-8"?>


    <h2>Making Friends With The Venusian Flu Virus</h2>
<h3>(6.20.3425)</h3><p>Dr. Biff Mercury discusses his theory on
coexisting with this useful organism.</p><hr/>
...
```

The style sheet is once again working properly, but one issue remains: the template that currently processes the news elements.

Built-in Templates

If we comment out the news template from the style sheet as shown in Listing 9.23, something interesting happens.

LISTING 9.23   Removing the Temporary Template

```
...
<xsl:template match="description">
    <p><xsl:value-of select="."/></p>
</xsl:template>

<!-- <xsl:template match="/content/news">
</xsl:template> -->

</xsl:transform>
```

The resulting text is a hybrid of processed and unprocessed text, as shown in Listing 9.24.

LISTING 9.24   Removing the Temporary Template—The Result Text

```
...
    <h2>An Evening of Fun</h2><h3>(6.25.3425)</h3><p>This evening
join us for the monthly "Identify that Food" contest.</p><hr/>

        6.18.3425
        <h2>End Of The Line For The Incumbent?</h2>

            The Universal News Network is reporting that His
            Magnificence The Supreme Leader For Life
            announced today that he has decided not to be cloned for
            a 14th term.

        6.19.3425
        <h2>New Fall Lineup</h2>

            The Omega Channel has announced two new shows for its new
            fall lineup. Who's Running the Galaxy?
```

LISTING 9.24 *Continued*

```
            features a team of government scientists who accidentally
            clone two Supreme Leaders. If you think you're confused,
            imagine what the first family must be going through.
            Trading Species follows two teams of
            aliens who trade species and have only 48 hours to adjust
            and fool their neighbors.
```

Every processor assumes a series of templates designed to make a developer's life a little easier. There are two such templates that are particularly relevant right now. One is designed to make sure that all nodes are processed:

```
<xsl:template match="*|/">
    <xsl:apply-templates/>
</xsl:template>
```

The other is designed to make sure that all content is eventually output unless the style sheet specifies otherwise:

```
<xsl:template match="text()|@*">
    <xsl:value-of select="."/>
</xsl:template>
```

The end result is that the **news** element and its children are processed, and the text is output. The exception is the **title** element, which is processed according to the **title** template designed for the **eventitems** because they share the name.

This template "captures" these nodes, so to speak:

```
<xsl:template match="/content/news">
</xsl:template>
```

It takes precedence over the built-in templates, but it doesn't do anything. The result is that the nodes are not sent off looking for other templates, and thus don't appear in the results.

Creating Content

The examples so far have shown a fairly simple conversion from XML to HTML, but elements and attributes lie at the heart of the matter. Up to now, we've been able to get away with simply adding start and end tags to the output, but often the situation makes this impossible. For example, suppose you want to create an HTML link that used the **itemnum** attribute as part of the **href** attribute. The target output will be something similar to this:

```
<a href="newspage.php?itemnum=2"> New Fall Lineup</a>
```

But there's no way to create such a link using just text tags. The reason for this lies in the definition of a well-formed document. To create the preceding code, you would need a template similar to this:

```
<a href="newspage.php?itemnum=<xsl:value-of select="@itemnum"/>">
<xsl:value-of select="title"/></a>
```

But according to the definition of a well-formed XML document, you can't have an element (such as `value-of`) as part of the value of an attribute (such as `href`).

To solve this problem, the Recommendation provides a way to create elements explicitly, rather than simply adding tags to the content of a template.

Dynamic Elements

Let's start by adapting the current style sheet. For example, Listing 9.25 shows the explicit creation of the `h2` element using the `element` element, with the name of the new element specified using the `name` attribute.

LISTING 9.25   Creating Elements

```
...
    <xsl:apply-templates select="description"/>

    <hr />

</xsl:template>

<xsl:template match="title">

    <xsl:element name="h2">
        <xsl:value-of select="."/>
    </xsl:element>

</xsl:template>

<xsl:template match="eventdate">
    <h3>(<xsl:value-of select="."/>)</h3>
</xsl:template>
...
```

Running this transformation produces the same output as before, as shown in Listing 9.26.

LISTING 9.26   Creating Elements—The Result Text

```
<?xml version="1.0" encoding="UTF-8"?>

    <h2>Making Friends With The Venusian Flu Virus</h2>
<h3>(6.20.3425)</h3><p>Dr. Biff Mercury discusses his theory on
coexisting with this useful organism.</p><hr/>
...
```

Notice that the `element` element creates an element in the output. The `name` attribute determines the name of the new element, and any content between the element tags becomes the content of the element.

Adding attributes involves a similar process.

Dynamic Attributes

To add an attribute to a dynamically created element, use the **attribute** element, as shown in Listing 9.27.

LISTING 9.27 Creating an Attribute

```
...
<xsl:template match="title">

    <xsl:element name="h2">
        <xsl:element name="a">
            <xsl:attribute name="href">register.php?event=<xsl:value-of
                                   select="../@eventid"/></xsl:attribute>
            <xsl:value-of select="."/>
        </xsl:element>
    </xsl:element>

</xsl:template>
...
```

The attribute is part of the content of the **element** element. The **name** attribute determines the name of the attribute, and the content of the **attribute** element determines the value of the new attribute. Note that this means you must remove any extraneous spaces from the **attribute** element, as they will be added to the value if present. (Even though spaces within the **attribute** element might be collapsed, they still exist. A line feed might be converted to a single space, but that might be all it takes to create a problem.)

Parents

We will discuss the .. notation in the XPath expression at length in Chapter 11, but for now understand that it refers to the parent of the context node. The **title** element is the context node, so the parent is **eventitem**, and **../@eventid** is the **eventid** attribute of the **eventitem** element.

Processing this style sheet produces the text shown in Listing 9.28 and Figure 9.7.

LISTING 9.28 The Created Element and Attribute

```
<?xml version="1.0" encoding="UTF-8"?>

    <h2><a href="register.php?event=A335">Making Friends With The
Venusian Flu Virus</a></h2><h3>(6.20.3425)</h3><p>Dr. Biff Mercury
discusses his theory on coexisting with this useful organism.</p>
<hr/>
...
```

FIGURE 9.7
Dynamic elements and
attributes.

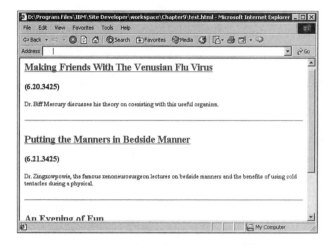

XML-to-XML Conversion

Throughout the chapter we've been creating HTML elements, but XML-to-XML mappings are a big part of XSLT, and these techniques for creating new elements and attributes are a big part of that process. Listing 9.29 shows a style sheet that creates a new mapping for the source data.

LISTING 9.29   Creating an Alternate Structure

```
<?xml version="1.0"?>
<xsl:transform xmlns:xsl="http://www.w3.org/1999/XSL/Transform" version="1.0">

<xsl:template match="/">
    <schedule>
        <xsl:apply-templates/>
    </schedule>
</xsl:template>

<xsl:template match="content/events/eventitem">
    <xsl:element name="action">
        <xsl:attribute name="optional"><xsl:value-of
                            select="@optional"/></xsl:attribute>
        <xsl:attribute name="date"><xsl:value-of
                            select="eventdate"/></xsl:attribute>

        <title><xsl:value-of select="title"/></title>
        <details><xsl:value-of select="description"/></details>
    </xsl:element>
</xsl:template>

<xsl:template match="/content/news">
</xsl:template>

</xsl:transform>
```

Notice that you can mix elements created with the **element** element and elements created with tags. Performing the transformation results in the output shown in Listing 9.30.

LISTING 9.30   Creating an Alternate Structure—The Result Text

```
<?xml version="1.0" encoding="UTF-8"?>
<schedule>

    <action optional="" date="6.20.3425">
        <title>Making Friends With The Venusian Flu Virus</title>
        <details>Dr. Biff Mercury discusses his theory on coexisting
                 with this useful organism.</details>
    </action>

    <action optional="no" date="6.21.3425">
        <title>Putting the Manners in Bedside Manner</title>
        <details>Dr. Zingzowpowie, the famous xenoneurosurgeon
                 lectures on Bedside Manner and the benefits of
                 using cold tentacles during a physical.</details>
    </action>
...
</schedule>
```

Adding Comments

Other types of nodes often present their own challenges to inclusion in a style sheet. For example, you can add comments to a style sheet, but they serve to document the style sheet, and not the output. For example, Listing 9.31 adds comments to the event template.

LISTING 9.31   Adding Comments to the Style Sheet

```
<?xml version="1.0"?>
<xsl:transform xmlns:xsl="http://www.w3.org/1999/XSL/Transform" version="1.0">

<xsl:template match="/">
    <schedule>

        <!-- If an event is not explicitly marked
             as "optional", then it's mandatory -->
        <xsl:apply-templates/>

    </schedule>
</xsl:template>

<xsl:template match="content/events/eventitem">
    <xsl:element name="action">
        <xsl:attribute name="optional"><xsl:value-of
                            select="@optional"/></xsl:attribute>
```

LISTING 9.31   Continued

```
        <xsl:attribute name="date"><xsl:value-of
                            select="eventdate"/></xsl:attribute>

        <title><xsl:value-of select="title"/></title>
    <!--<details><xsl:value-of select="description"/></details> -->
    </xsl:element>
</xsl:template>

<xsl:template match="/content/news">
</xsl:template>

</xsl:transform>
```

Here we see two uses of the comment. The first provides commentary that probably belongs in the output, and the second serves to temporarily remove the **description** element from the output. When this style sheet is processed, neither comment appears in the output, as shown in Listing 9.32.

LISTING 9.32   Disappearing Comments

```
<?xml version="1.0" encoding="UTF-8"?>
<schedule>

    <action optional="" date="6.20.3425">
        <title>Making Friends With The Venusian Flu Virus</title>
    </action>
...
</schedule>
```

Given the example of the **description** element, this behavior makes sense. But what if you want to include comments in the output, as in the case of the first comment? Listing 9.33 demonstrates the use of the **comment** element, which makes this possible.

LISTING 9.33   Creating Comments

```
...
<xsl:template match="/">
    <schedule>

        <xsl:comment> If an event is not explicitly marked
            as "optional", then it's mandatory </xsl:comment>
        <xsl:apply-templates/>

    </schedule>
</xsl:template>
...
```

Now, when you process the document, the comment comes through, as in Listing 9.34.

LISTING 9.34 Comments in the Output

```
<?xml version="1.0" encoding="UTF-8"?>
<schedule>
    <!-- If an event is not explicitly marked
             as "optional", then it's mandatory -->

    <action optional="" date="6.20.3425">
        <title>Making Friends With The Venusian Flu Virus</title>
    </action>
...
```

Processing Instructions

Processing instructions present a similar challenge. Because the application performing the transformation might also be looking for processing instructions, you can't add them directly to the templates. Instead, you must create them explicitly, as in Listing 9.35.

LISTING 9.35 Creating Processing Instructions

```
...
<xsl:template match="content/events/eventitem">
    <xsl:processing-instruction name="updateSched">id="<xsl:value-of
                   select="@eventid"/>"</xsl:processing-instruction>

    <xsl:element name="action">
...
    </xsl:element>
</xsl:template>
...
```

Processing the style sheet creates the processing instructions, as shown in Listing 9.36.

LISTING 9.36 Generated Processing Instructions

```
<?xml version="1.0" encoding="UTF-8"?>
<schedule>
    <!-- If an event is not explicitly marked
             as "optional", then it's mandatory -->

    <?updateSched id="A335"?>
    <action optional="" date="6.20.3425">
        <title>Making Friends With The Venusian Flu Virus</title>
    </action>
...
```

Sorting Data

Although the processor normally outputs data in the order in which it appeared in the original document, you can control the order of output with the **sort** element, as shown in Listing 9.37.

LISTING 9.37   Sorting the Data

```
...
<xsl:template match="/">
    <schedule>

        <xsl:comment> If an event is not explicitly marked
              as "optional", then it's mandatory </xsl:comment>
        <xsl:apply-templates select="content/events/eventitem">
          <xsl:sort select="eventdate" order="descending"/>
        </xsl:apply-templates>


    </schedule>
</xsl:template>
...
```

Here you're applying templates to the `eventitem` elements, which are then sorted by `eventdate`. Acceptable orders are `ascending` and `descending`.

You can also sort by multiple levels by adding additional `sort` elements.

Creating a Loop

While applying templates gives the impression of a loop (because it does the same thing over and over), XSLT provides a way to explicitly create and control a loop with the `for-each` element. As shown in Listing 9.38, the `select` attribute determines a set of nodes for which the loop executes.

LISTING 9.38   Creating a Loop

```
...
<xsl:template match="/">

    <xsl:for-each select="eventitem">
        <xsl:apply-templates select="title"/>
        <xsl:apply-templates select="eventdate"/>
        <xsl:apply-templates select="description"/>

        <hr />
    </xsl:for-each>

</xsl:template>
...
```

Processing the style sheet produces the same results as before, but it does so through repetition, which will come in handy for named templates in the next section.

copy-of **Versus** value-of

So far, every time we've wanted to output something, it's been just a value, such as the text node of an element. That's the purpose of the `value-of` element. If you created a simple style sheet that just output the value of the document root, you would get just the text of the source document. For example, processing the style sheet in Listing 9.39 produces the output in Listing 9.40.

LISTING 9.39   Outputting the Value of the Document Root

```
<?xml version="1.0"?>
<xsl:transform xmlns:xsl="http://www.w3.org/1999/XSL/Transform" version="1.0">

<xsl:template match="/">
    <xsl:value-of select="."/>
</xsl:template>

</xsl:transform>
```

LISTING 9.40   The Value of the Document Root

```
<?xml version="1.0" encoding="UTF-8"?>
        6.20.3425
        Making Friends With The Venusian Flu Virus
        Dr. Biff Mercury discusses his theory on
        coexisting with this useful organism.

        6.21.3425
        Putting the Manners in Bedside Manner
        Dr. Zingzowpowie, the famous xenoneurosurgeon
        lectures on Bedside Manner and the benefits of using cold
        tentacles during a physical.

        6.25.3425
        An Evening of Fun
        This evening join us for the monthly "Identify
        that Food" contest.

        6.18.3425
        End Of The Line For The Incumbent?
            The Universal News Network is reporting that His
            Magnificence The Supreme Leader For Life
            announced today that he has decided not to be cloned for
            a 14th term.

        6.19.3425
        New Fall Lineup
            The Omega Channel has announced two new shows for its new
            fall lineup. Who's Running the Galaxy?
            features a team of government scientists who accidentally
            clone two Supreme Leaders. If you think you're confused,
            imagine what the first family must be going through.
            Trading Species follows two teams of
            aliens who trade species and have only 48 hours to adjust
            and fool their neighbors.
```

Often, particularly when working with XSLT programmatically, we want not just the text nodes, but the entire structure of a node-set, including elements and attributes. To achieve this, you will need the `copy-of` element. For example, to return to the XML version of the style sheet (as opposed to the HTML version) we could easily output each event element in its entirety, as shown in Listing 9.41.

LISTING 9.41   *Copying a Node*

```
<?xml version="1.0"?>
<xsl:transform xmlns:xsl="http://www.w3.org/1999/XSL/Transform"
               version="1.0">

<xsl:template match="content/events/eventitem">
    <xsl:copy-of select="."/>
</xsl:template>

<xsl:template match="content/news">
</xsl:template>

</xsl:transform>
```

In this case, rather than the entire document, the style sheet outputs each `eventitem` element, as shown in Listing 9.42.

LISTING 9.42   *The Output Elements*

```
<?xml version="1.0" encoding="UTF-8"?>

    <eventitem eventid="A335">
        <eventdate>6.20.3425</eventdate>
        <title>Making Friends With The Venusian Flu Virus</title>
        <description>Dr. Biff Mercury discusses his theory on
        coexisting with this useful organism.</description>
    </eventitem>

    <eventitem eventid="B963" optional="no">
        <eventdate>6.21.3425</eventdate>
        <title>Putting the Manners in Bedside Manner</title>
        <description>Dr. Zingzowpowie, the famous xenoneurosurgeon
        lectures on Bedside Manner and the benefits of using cold
        tentacles during a physical.</description>
    </eventitem>

    <eventitem eventid="C934" optional="yes">
        <eventdate>6.25.3425</eventdate>
        <title>An Evening of Fun</title>
        <description>This evening join us for the monthly "Identify
        that Food" contest.</description>
    </eventitem>
```

This ability is particularly useful when building documents dynamically within an application.

Variables and Parameters

One of XSLT's strengths is the ability to emulate many programming constructs from within the style sheet. In this section, we'll discuss parallels to subroutines, parameters, and variables.

The first of these is *named templates*, which allow you to explicitly execute a set of instructions. These templates can also take parameters, which can affect the actions of the template, and can be specified at runtime. Finally, we'll talk about variables, which expand on the functionality provided by parameters.

Named Templates

You construct a named template the same way you construct any other template, except that instead of specifying nodes for it to match, you give it a name. From within the template, you can then select the appropriate nodes, as shown in Listing 9.43. The `call-template` element then invokes the template directly.

LISTING 9.43   Creating a Named Template

```
<?xml version="1.0"?>
<xsl:transform xmlns:xsl="http://www.w3.org/1999/XSL/Transform"
               version="1.0">

<xsl:template match="/content/events">

    <xsl:call-template name="eventTemplate"/>

</xsl:template>

<xsl:template name="eventTemplate">
  <xsl:for-each select="eventitem">
    <xsl:apply-templates select="title"/>
    <xsl:apply-templates select="eventdate"/>
    <xsl:apply-templates select="description"/>
  </xsl:for-each>
</xsl:template>

<xsl:template match="title">
<xsl:element name="h2">
    <xsl:element name="a">
        <xsl:attribute name="href">register.php?event=<xsl:value-of
                                    select="../@eventid"/></xsl:attribute>
        <xsl:value-of select="."/>
    </xsl:element>
</xsl:element>
</xsl:template>
...
</xsl:transform>
```

Let's look at what's happening here. The main template matches the **events** element, which calls the **eventTemplate** template. At that point, the **events** element is still the context node, so that template can loop through each **eventitem** element, processing the child elements exactly as they were processed before, with the same templates.

Parameters

You can use parameters in an XSLT style sheet in much the same way you can use them in a procedural programming language. Specifically, you can set a value and reference it later. For example, you can set a parameter that allows you to choose specific values for the **optional** attribute, as in Listing 9.44.

LISTING 9.44   Creating a Parameter

```
<?xml version="1.0"?>
<xsl:transform xmlns:xsl="http://www.w3.org/1999/XSL/Transform"
               version="1.0">

<xsl:param name="optionalChoice" select="'no'"/>

<xsl:template match="/content/events">
    <xsl:call-template name="eventTemplate"/>
</xsl:template>

<xsl:template name="eventTemplate">
  <xsl:for-each select="eventitem[@optional=$optionalChoice]">
    <xsl:apply-templates select="title"/>
    <xsl:apply-templates select="eventdate"/>
    <xsl:apply-templates select="description"/>
  </xsl:for-each>
</xsl:template>
...
```

First, create the parameter using the **param** element. To reference it, precede the name with a dollar sign (**$**). Here, the parameter is used as a condition for the value of the optional element.

Notice the construction of the parameter value. If you were to write it as simply

```
<xsl:param name="optionalChoice" select="no"/>
```

when the style sheet references it, it would create the expression as

```
<xsl:for-each select="eventitem[@optional=no]">
```

In this case, the processor assumes that you were referencing an element named **no**, which of course it wouldn't find. When you reference literal values in a parameter (or later, in a variable), be sure to enclose them in quotes, as in the listing. The end result is that only the events that have the specified value for the optional attribute appear, as shown in Listing 9.45.

LISTING 9.45 *Only Mandatory Events*

```
<?xml version="1.0" encoding="UTF-8"?>

<h2><a href="register.php?event=">Putting the Manners in Bedside Manner</a></h2>
<h3>(6.21.3425)</h3><p>Dr. Zingzowpowie, the famous
xenoneurosurgeon lectures on Bedside Manner and the benefits of
using cold tentacles during a physical.</p>
```

Possibly the best part of using parameters is that you can specify them from outside the style sheet. For example, in this case the default value of `optionalChoice` is `no`, but most processors will allow you to add a parameter value in some way. For example, Xalan-Java looks for parameters as an input argument, as in

```
java org.apache.xalan.xslt.Process -IN source.xml -XSL style.xsl
-OUT test.html -PARAM optionalChoice yes
```

The new value overrides the default on the `param` element, and only the optional events appear, as in Listing 9.46.

LISTING 9.46 *Only Optional Events*

```
<?xml version="1.0" encoding="UTF-8"?>

<h2><a href="register.php?event=C934">An Evening of Fun</a></h2>
<h3>(6.25.3425)</h3><p>This evening join us for the monthly "Identify
that Food" contest.</p>
```

It's important to note that the value of a parameter cannot be reset once it has been set.

Parameters and Named Templates

You also have the option of including parameters within a named template itself, then specifying a value when you call the template. For example, Listing 9.47 adds a layer of abstraction to the solution in Listing 9.46.

LISTING 9.47 *Calling a Parameter Within a Template*

```
<?xml version="1.0"?>
<xsl:transform xmlns:xsl="http://www.w3.org/1999/XSL/Transform"
               version="1.0">

<xsl:param name="optionalChoice" select="'no'"/>

<xsl:template match="/content/events">

    <xsl:call-template name="eventTemplate">
        <xsl:with-param name="isOptional"><xsl:value-of
                                select="$optionalChoice"/></xsl:with-param>
    </xsl:call-template>
    <xsl:call-template name="eventTemplate">
```

LISTING 9.47   Continued

```
        <xsl:with-param name="isOptional"><xsl:value-of
                                select="$optionalChoice"/>x</xsl:with-param>
    </xsl:call-template>

</xsl:template>

<xsl:template name="eventTemplate">
  <xsl:param name="isOptional" select="'no'"/>
  <xsl:for-each select="eventitem[@optional=$isOptional]">
    <xsl:apply-templates select="title"/>
    <xsl:apply-templates select="eventdate"/>
    <xsl:apply-templates select="description"/>
  </xsl:for-each>
</xsl:template>
...
</xsl:transform>
```

Here we've added a new parameter to the template itself, providing a value for it when the template is referenced. Notice that the second time you call the template, the value of the parameter is different. We'll see a much more elegant way to do this in the next section, but for now the effect is to output the desired events the first time, then nothing the second time, as shown in Listing 9.48.

LISTING 9.48   Using Parameters Within Templates

```
<?xml version="1.0" encoding="UTF-8"?>

<h2><a href="register.php?event=B963">Putting the Manners in Bedside
Manner</a></h2>
<h3>(6.21.3425)</h3><p>Dr. Zingzowpowie, the famous
xenoneurosurgeon lectures on Bedside Manner and the benefits of
using cold tentacles during a physical.</p>
```

Variables

Variables are in some respects more useful than parameters and in other respects less useful. They're less useful in that you can't specify a value for them from outside the style sheet, but this difficulty is offset by the fact that, unlike parameters, variables can get new values after they're already in use. This makes them more flexible within the body of the style sheet, as shown in Listing 9.49.

LISTING 9.49   Using a Variable

```
<?xml version="1.0"?>


<xsl:transform xmlns:xsl="http://www.w3.org/1999/XSL/Transform" version="1.0">
```

LISTING 9.49   Continued

```
<xsl:param name="optionalChoice" select="'no'"/>

<xsl:template match="/content/events">

    <xsl:variable name="optionalChoiceValue" select="$optionalChoice"/>
    <xsl:call-template name="eventTemplate">
        <xsl:with-param name="isOptional"><xsl:value-of
                          select="$optionalChoiceValue"/></xsl:with-param>
    </xsl:call-template>
    <xsl:variable name="optionalChoiceValue"><xsl:value-of
                          select="$optionalChoice"/>x</xsl:variable>
    <xsl:call-template name="eventTemplate">
        <xsl:with-param name="isOptional"><xsl:value-of
                          select="$optionalChoiceValue"/></xsl:with-param>
    </xsl:call-template>

</xsl:template>
...
</xsl:transform>
```

The effect is the same as in Listing 9.48. Although it doesn't look any cleaner, it prepares the way for setting this value more conveniently using an if-then construction in the next section.

Notice that variables (and parameters) can be set using two different syntaxes. In the first, the value is set directly, using the **select** attribute. In the second, the value is set as the contents of the **variable** element. This method allows you to specify a node-set, including elements, as the value of the variable.

Flow Control

One requirement for a programming language is the ability to control the flow of operations based on various criteria. XSLT provides this ability in several ways, from if-then and if-then-else functionality to the ability to specify a particular condition under which the transformation engine will process a specific template.

If-Then

Aside from just applying templates, the simplest form of flow control involves an if-then statement, or rather an **if** element, as shown in Listing 9.50.

LISTING 9.50   Using an **if** Element

```
...
<xsl:template name="eventTemplate">
  <xsl:param name="isOptional" select="'no'"/>
  <xsl:element name="div">
      <xsl:if test="$isOptional='no'">
```

LISTING 9.50   Continued

```
              <xsl:attribute name="style">color:red</xsl:attribute>
          </xsl:if>
          <xsl:for-each select="eventitem[@optional=$isOptional]">
            <xsl:apply-templates select="title"/>
            <xsl:apply-templates select="eventdate"/>
            <xsl:apply-templates select="description"/>
          </xsl:for-each>
      </xsl:element>

</xsl:template>
...
</xsl:transform>
```

In this case, we're enclosing each set of events in a `div` element, with the intention of displaying the mandatory events in red.

The `if` element includes a `test` attribute that contains the condition in the form of an expression. If the `test` evaluates to `true`, the contents of the `if` element are processed. If not, the contents of the `if` element are ignored.

Choose

The `if` element is good for basic conditions, but doesn't leave any room for an "else" to be processed if the condition is `false`. To fill in this gap, XSLT provides a `choose` element.

The `choose` element provides a container for a set of conditions, as each condition must be a well-formed element. It can contain one or more `when` elements, which act in a manner similar to `if` elements, and a final `otherwise` element that's processed if all the preceding `when` statement tests evaluated as `false`. Consider Listing 9.51.

LISTING 9.51   Using the `choose` Element

```
<?xml version="1.0"?>
<xsl:transform xmlns:xsl="http://www.w3.org/1999/XSL/Transform"
               version="1.0">

<xsl:param name="optionalChoice" select="'no'"/>

<xsl:template match="/content/events">

    <xsl:call-template name="eventTemplate">
        <xsl:with-param name="isOptional"><xsl:value-of
                                  select="$optionalChoice"/></xsl:with-param>
    </xsl:call-template>

    <xsl:choose>
        <xsl:when test="$optionalChoice='yes'">
            <xsl:call-template name="eventTemplate">
                <xsl:with-param name="isOptional">no</xsl:with-param>
            </xsl:call-template>
```

LISTING 9.51   Continued

```
            </xsl:when>
            <xsl:when test="$optionalChoice='no'">
                <xsl:call-template name="eventTemplate">
                    <xsl:with-param name="isOptional">yes</xsl:with-param>
                </xsl:call-template>
            </xsl:when>
            <xsl:otherwise>
                <!-- If a yes or no value was not originally specified, assume
                     it should have been no.  That means the opposite is yes. -->
                <xsl:call-template name="eventTemplate">
                    <xsl:with-param name="isOptional">yes</xsl:with-param>
                </xsl:call-template>
            </xsl:otherwise>
        </xsl:choose>

</xsl:template>
...
</xsl:transform>
```

Overall, you're looking at more lines of code, but from a business logic standpoint, this is a bit cleaner. First, we output the template with the original value. Next, the **choose** container determines what the second value should be. It first toggles the **yes** and **no** values, and then provides a value of **yes** if the original value was neither **yes** nor **no**. The result is that events marked as nonoptional are displayed in red, as in Figure 9.8. (Obviously you can't see the color red in this black-and-white image. The first date and item in the figure are red.)

FIGURE 9.8
Conditional elements give you control over how content is treated.

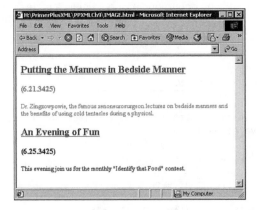

Modes

At this point, we've looked at two different versions of the events listing document: an XHTML version and an XML version. This is a situation for which XSLT is particularly well suited: customized content.

One of the great strengths of XML is its ability to provide content customized for different media. For example, say you want to provide the same content to a traditional browser, such as Netscape Navigator or Microsoft Internet Explorer, and to a mobile phone, as well as outputting it to your printer. All these media have different requirements. XSLT allows you to store your content in XML, then use XSLT to provide the appropriate version.

To facilitate this process, XSLT templates can carry a **mode** attribute so that once the transformation engine determines the environment in which it is running, it can choose the appropriate templates.

As it turns out, however, you also have the ability to specify a mode from within the style sheet, so you can use this capability for a wide range of logical applications.

For example, rather than using a parameter to determine how the event template will behave, you can use the **mode** attribute, as shown in Listing 9.52.

LISTING 9.52   Using the mode Attribute

```
<?xml version="1.0"?>
<xsl:transform xmlns:xsl="http://www.w3.org/1999/XSL/Transform"
               version="1.0">

<xsl:param name="optionalChoice" select="'no'"/>

<xsl:template match="/content/events">

    <xsl:choose>
        <xsl:when test="$optionalChoice='yes'">
            <xsl:apply-templates select="eventitem[@optional='yes']" mode="yes"/>
        </xsl:when>
        <xsl:when test="$optionalChoice='no'">
            <xsl:apply-templates select="eventitem[@optional='no']" mode="no"/>
        </xsl:when>
        <xsl:otherwise>
            <!-- If a yes or no value was not original specified, assume
                 it should have been no.  -->
            <xsl:apply-templates select="eventitem[@optional='no']" mode="no"/>
        </xsl:otherwise>
    </xsl:choose>

    <xsl:choose>
        <xsl:when test="$optionalChoice='yes'">
            <xsl:apply-templates select="eventitem[@optional='no']" mode="no"/>
        </xsl:when>
        <xsl:when test="$optionalChoice='no'">
            <xsl:apply-templates select="eventitem[@optional='yes']" mode="yes"/>
        </xsl:when>
        <xsl:otherwise>
            <!-- If a yes or no value was not original specified, assume
                 it should have been no.  That means the opposite is yes. -->
            <xsl:apply-templates select="eventitem[@optional='yes']" mode="yes"/>
```

LISTING 9.52   Continued

```
            </xsl:otherwise>
        </xsl:choose>

</xsl:template>

<xsl:template match="eventitem" mode="yes">
  <xsl:element name="div">
        <xsl:apply-templates select="title"/>
        <xsl:apply-templates select="eventdate"/>
        <xsl:apply-templates select="description"/>
  </xsl:element>
</xsl:template>

<xsl:template match="eventitem" mode="no">
  <xsl:element name="div">
      <xsl:attribute name="style">color:red</xsl:attribute>
        <xsl:apply-templates select="title"/>
        <xsl:apply-templates select="eventdate"/>
        <xsl:apply-templates select="description"/>
      </xsl:element>
</xsl:template>
...
</xsl:transform>
```

In this case, you're still applying templates, but the `mode` allows you to have different templates for different purposes without having to take such explicit control over the propagation.

Summary

Extensible Stylesheet Language Transformations (XSLT) provides some of the most useful functionality in XML. XSLT allows you to transform XML from one structure into another, whether XML to XML, XML to HTML, or XML to text.

Using a system of templates, an XSLT style sheet transforms the data, using it to create new elements and attributes using the original source information. XSLT retrieves this source information through the use of XPath expressions.

An XPath expression symbolizes the parent-child relationship using a URI-like notation; the `sedan` child of the `car` element is expressed as `car/sedan`. The `model` attribute of the `sedan` element is expressed as `car/sedan@model`.

XSLT allows source data to be processed by multiple templates, either implicitly (through `apply-templates`) or explicitly (through `call-template`). Parameters can be specified at run-time, and variables can be used in conjunction with control structures such as `if` and `choose`.

XSLT has many more capabilities than one chapter can possibly cover. Look for more information in Chapter 10, "Transformation and Applications," Chapter 11, "Selecting Data: XML Path Language (XPath)," Chapter 12, "Browser-Based XML: Cascading Style Sheets," and Chapter 16, "XML and Publishing: Formatting Objects with XSL."

Review Questions

1. What is the difference between XSLT and XSL-FO?

2. What is the main purpose of XSLT?

3. What is the difference between the document root and the root element?

4. What is the basic building block of an XSLT style sheet?

5. What is the "current" node called?

6. How can you add information to the style sheet at runtime?

7. How do nodes propagate through different templates?

8. What happens if no template applies to a particular node?

9. What is the difference between a parameter and a variable?

10. What is the difference between `value-of` and `copy-of`?

11. How can you prevent information from appearing in the resultset?

Programming Exercises

1. Create a simple style sheet that outputs the text of an XML document.

The remaining exercises refer to the following document:

```xml
<?xml version="1.0"?>
<orders>
    <order>
        <customerid>2384</customerid>
        <status>pending</status>
        <item instock="Y" itemid="SD93">
            <name>Flying By Roller Skates</name>
            <price>25.00</price>
            <qty>25</qty>
        </item>
        <item instock="N" itemid="B12">
            <name>Bounce-o Ball</name>
            <price>.35</price>
            <qty>150</qty>
        </item>
    </order>
    <order>
        <customerid>5268</customerid>
        <status>complete</status>
        <item instock="Y" itemid="Q52">
            <name>Crash N Burn Skis</name>
            <price>20</price>
            <qty>10</qty>
        </item>
```

```
    </order>
</orders>
```

2. Create a style sheet that outputs a list of `customerid` values.

3. Create a style sheet that transforms the document to the following form:

```
<html>
<head>
<title>Order Status</title>
</head>
<body>
    <h2>Order Status</h2>

    <p>Customer number: 2384</p>
    <ul>
        <li>SD93: Flying By Roller Skates</li>
        <li>B12: Bounce-o Ball</li>
    </ul>

    <p>Customer number: 5268</p>
    <ul>
        <li>Q52: Crash N Burn Skis</li>
    </ul>

</body>
</html>
```

4. Alter the style sheet in exercise 2 to show only pending orders.

5. Alter the style sheet in exercise 2 to show only items that are in stock.

6. Alter the style sheet in exercise 2 to show backordered items in this form:

```
<li><i>B12: Bounce-o Ball</i></li>
```

7. Convert the document to this form:

```
<?xml version="1.0" encoding="UTF-8"?>
<currentorders>
    <order custid="2384" status="pending">
        <inventory stocknumber="SD93" prodname="Flying By Roller Skates"
                                      quantity="25"/>
        <inventory stocknumber="B12" prodname="Bounce-o Ball"
                                     quantity="150"/>
    </order>
    <order custid="5268" status="complete">
        <inventory stocknumber="Q52" prodname="Crash N Burn Skis"
                                     quantity="10"/>
    </order>
</currentorders>
```

CHAPTER 10

TRANSFORMATION AND APPLICATIONS

You will learn about the following in this chapter:

- Transforming documents
- Transformation sources, results, and style sheets

- Using SAX with XSL transformations
- Extension elements and functions

*I*n the grand scheme of things, there are plenty of reasons you might want to use XSL to transform data. The most common revolves around XML's ability to separate content from presentation; XSL transformations (XSLT) allow you to have a single XML file for your content, but provide different presentations for Web pages, paper reports, cell phones, and so on.

XSL transformations can also be used to massage data into a different form. For example, you could build an application that transforms XML from one format to another using a style sheet, then let users create the style sheet. In this way, they can control the final output and you don't have to alter the application.

XSL transformations can be carried out on the client side—in a browser, for example—but they are most useful when they're performed as part of an application.

In this chapter, we'll create applications that perform transformations using the style sheets created in Chapter 9, "Extensible Stylesheet Language Transformations (XSLT)." We'll look at the different sources and outputs, as well as different ways to make transformations more efficient and to control them programmatically, such as by choosing a style sheet based on the XML file, or adding parameters. We'll also look at the relationship between SAX and transformations.

Finally, we'll go in the other direction, adding programming to a style sheet itself, creating extension functions and elements using first JavaScript, then Java.

Transformation Methodologies

Before we actually start programming, let's consider several different ways to look at performing transformations. The XSLT Recommendation provides no guidance on how the actual transformation is to be implemented, only on what it should do when it is implemented.

Getting Ready

Before starting the examples in this chapter, be sure that you have an XSL transformation engine installed. (If you did the examples in Chapter 9, you've likely taken care of this already.) You may also need to consult your documentation for specific classnames.

The Java examples in this chapter use the implementation of XSLT that comes with Java 1.4.

Transformation API for XML (TrAX)

Currently, the most common way to perform a transformation is to use the Transformation API for XML (TrAX). The TrAX methodology was originally intended for Java programmers, but its utility is evidenced by the fact that it has been adopted by implementers in most other languages. Using TrAX involves three steps:

1. Create a transformer factory. This allows you to choose an implementation other than the standard one for the factory, if necessary.

2. Create the transformer, giving it a style sheet as input. The transformer is particular to the style sheet with which it was created. Any file it transforms will use that style sheet.

3. Use the `transform()` method of the `Transformer` object (or something similar) to transform a particular supplied source into a particular supplied result. For example:

```
transformerObj.transform(source, result);
```

Language-Specific Issues

In some languages and implementations, such as C++ and Visual Basic .NET, the situation is slightly altered. In these languages, the source object itself performs the transformation, using the style sheet and result as inputs. The following sections show some examples.

C++ and Visual Basic .NET

MSXML 4.0 provides two methods to invoke transformations from C++ and Visual Basic .NET. The only difference between the two methods is the way the transformed data is returned. To receive the data as a `BSTR`, use `transformNode();`. To receive the data as an `IXMLDOMDocument` or `IStream` object, use `transformNodeToObject()`, as shown in these C++ examples:

```
// This call will produce a string for output
bstrXMLStr = pXMLDoc->transformNode(pXSLTDoc);

// This call will produce an object for output
pXMLDoc->transformNodeToObject(pXSLTDoc, vOutput);
```

Implementation Note

The Apache Project also provides a C++ version of the Xalan transformation engine, which uses a TrAX-like means for transforming documents much like the Java version, rather than the object-based method used by MSXML. You can find more information at `http://xml.apache.org/xalan-c/index.html`.

PHP

Sablotron, produced by the Ginger Alliance (`http://www.gingerall.cz`), is the most mature XSLT processor available for use directly by PHP. Using XSLT in PHP with Sablotron is quite straightforward and relies on the TrAX methodology shown earlier in the Java example, though I should note that many of the features of TrAX are not supported. Building Sablotron for use in PHP is not at all easy, however; both the PHP and Sablotron source code must be patched, and PHP must be built with options that vary depending on whether you plan to use JavaScript extensions in your style sheets. In other words, if you can find a prebuilt PHP+Sablotron package for your operating system or distribution, use it.

Perl

There are three major XSLT packages for Perl in active use and development: `XML::Sablotron`, based on the Sablotron library produced by the Ginger Alliance (`http://www.gingerall.cz`); `XML::LibXSLT`, based on the GNOME XSLT library (`http://xmlsoft.org/XSLT`); and `XML::Xalan`, based on the Xalan XSLT processor, a part of the Apache project (`http://xml.apache.org/xalan-c`). Of these, `XML::Sablotron` is the most mature and widely packaged, so we'll use `XML::Sablotron` for our Perl examples. Though based on the same library as PHP's XSLT functions, `XML::Sablotron` exposes much more of the underlying library's abilities than does PHP's library. Unlike Sablotron for PHP, no patching is required to build Sablotron for use by Perl. However, if you plan to use JavaScript extensions in your style sheets, you must first install the Mozilla JavaScript library and build `XML::Sablotron` with JavaScript support. Once you've installed it, the usage patterns vary from Java, but not by much.

Transforming Streams

In the case of a SAX stream, there is no object to transform, but this doesn't mean that SAX streams can't use XSLT. In such cases, the transformer acts like the `ContentHandler`, making changes as it goes along. In this way, transformations can even be chained together, with the results of one transformation serving as the source of another, just as SAX streams can be chained together.

In this chapter, we'll examine the transformation of both objects and streams in the appropriate languages.

Transforming Data

Let's start by taking a look at the specifics of putting together an application that simply uses a style sheet to transform a source document into a particular result document. In this case, we're using the term *document* loosely.

Sources

One of the advantages of TrAX is that it's designed to be able to handle XML from a variety of sources. Data may come from a file on the system or in a remote location, or it may come from an in-memory object, such as a DOM `Node`. It could even be a stream of data, in the sense of a character stream or a SAX stream.

All of these cases are handled by implementations of the `Source` interface. Listing 10.1a shows the `StreamSource` used to designate a file on the local system.

LISTING 10.1a   Creating the Source in Java

```java
import javax.xml.transform.stream.StreamSource;

public class TransformFile extends Object {
    public static void main (String args[]) throws Exception
    {
        String XMLFileName = "events.xml";
        StreamSource source = new StreamSource(XMLFileName);
    }
}
```

In this case, we created the `StreamSource` with the system identifier for the file, but we can also create it with a `File` object, or with the output from a bytestream or character reader.

We could have used a `DOMSource` with a DOM `Node` object as the argument, or a `SAXSource` with an `InputSource` and potentially an `XMLReader` as arguments. We'll see how to do this in detail in the "Transformations and SAX" section.

C++

In C++, preparing for the transformation involves loading the XML file into a `DOMDocument` object. This is the same procedure as you would use when working with an XML using DOM normally. Listing 10.1b gets the document ready to work with.

LISTING 10.1b   Creating the Source in C++

```cpp
#include "stdafx.h"
#import "C:\windows\system32\msxml2.dll"
using namespace MSXML2;

int _tmain(int argc, _TCHAR* argv[])
{
    ::CoInitialize(NULL);
```

LISTING 10.1b   Continued

```
    try
    {
        CComPtr<MSXML2::IXMLDOMDocument> pXMLDoc;
        pXMLDoc.CoCreateInstance(__uuidof(MSXML2::DOMDocument));
        pXMLDoc->load("events.xml");
    }
    catch(...)
    {
        wprintf(L"Caught the exception");
    }
    ::CoUninitialize();
    return 0;
}
```

Visual Basic .NET

In Visual Basic .NET, preparing for the transformation involves loading the XML file into a
`DOMDocument40` object, just as you would when working with DOM under other circumstances, as shown in Listing 10.1c.

LISTING 10.1c   Creating the Source in Visual Basic .NET

```
Private Sub Button1_Click(ByVal sender As System.Object, ByVal e As _
    System.EventArgs) Handles Button1.Click
        Dim XMLDoc As New MSXML2.DOMDocument40()
        XMLDoc.async = False
        XMLDoc.load("events.xml")
    End Sub
```

PHP

PHP merely requires the filename, so the basic code is simple, as shown in Listing 10.1d.

LISTING 10.1d   Creating the Source in PHP

```
<?php
 $xml = 'source.xml';
?>
```

Perl

Like PHP, Perl requires just the name, but we also have to import the Sablotron package, as
shown in Listing 10.1e.

LISTING 10.1e   Creating the Source in Visual Basic .NET

```
use XML::Sablotron;

my $source = 'source.xml';
```

Results

Transformation results can also take multiple forms similar to those for transformation sources. In this case, we're referring to implementations of the `Result` interface. Listing 10.2a shows the most common form.

LISTING 10.2a   Creating the Result in Java

```
import javax.xml.transform.stream.StreamSource;
import javax.xml.transform.stream.StreamResult;

public class TransformFile extends Object {
   public static void main (String args[]) throws Exception
   {
      String XMLFileName = "events.xml";
      String OutputFileName = "transform.html";

      StreamSource source = new StreamSource(XMLFileName);
      StreamResult result = new StreamResult(OutputFileName);
   }
}
```

As with the `StreamSource`, we could have created the `StreamResult` in a variety of ways. Here we provide a relative URL as the system ID for a file. We could also provide a `File` object, or a `Writer` or `OutputStream`.

Like the `Source` interface, the `Result` interface has a `DOMResult` implementation that takes a `Node` as its argument, and a `SAXResult` implementation that takes a `ContentHandler` as its argument. Again, we'll see the `SAXResult` in detail in a later section.

C++

The result stream for MSXML can be one of two types. The first occurs when you use the `transformNode()` method. This creates a `BSTR` that contains the text that is the output of the transformation. The other output is as a `DOMDocument` object and is generated by the `transformNodeToObject()` method. We'll use the `transformNode()` method in this example, so Listing 10.2b simply creates a new variable to hold the result.

LISTING 10.2b   Creating the Result in C++

```
...
        CComPtr<MSXML2::IXMLDOMDocument>  pXMLDoc;
        _bstr_t bstrXMLStr;
        pXMLDoc.CoCreateInstance(__uuidof(MSXML2::DOMDocument));
...
```

Visual Basic .NET

Similarly, in Visual Basic .NET, we'll simply create a variable to hold the result string, as shown in Listing 10.2c.

LISTING 10.2c   Creating the Result in Visual Basic .NET

```
...
        Dim XSLTDoc As New MSXML2.DOMDocument40()
        Dim myString As String

        'Load XMLDoc
        XMLDoc.async = False
        XMLDoc.load("events.xml")
...
```

PHP and Perl

PHP and Perl simply need a string for the resulting filename, as you'll see when we perform the transformation.

The `TransformerFactory`

Before we can create the actual `Transformer` object, we'll need a `TransformerFactory`. Listing 10.3 shows the creation of a `TransformerFactory` object that will create `Transformers` from the standard classes, whatever they happen to be for this particular implementation.

LISTING 10.3   Creating the `TransformerFactory`

```
import javax.xml.transform.stream.StreamSource;
import javax.xml.transform.stream.StreamResult;
import javax.xml.transform.TransformerFactory;

public class TransformFile extends Object {
   public static void main (String args[]) throws Exception
   {
       String XMLFileName = "events.xml";
       String OutputFileName = "transform.html";

       StreamSource source = new StreamSource(XMLFileName);
       StreamResult result = new StreamResult(OutputFileName);

       TransformerFactory transFactory = TransformerFactory.newInstance();
   }
}
```

It would seem that the next logical step would be to create the `Transformer`, but there's one task we need to accomplish first.

Plugging In Another Transformation Engine

The advantage of this architecture is that it allows you to choose a different implementation of the transformation engine, if that's what you want. For example, we could substitute the SAXON transformation for the reference implementation:

```
...
System.setProperty("javax.xml.parsers.TransformerFactory",
            "com.icl.saxon.om.TransformerFactoryImpl");
TransformerFactory transFactory = TransformerFactory.newInstance();
...
```

Determining the Style Sheet

The `Transformer` object is based on a particular style sheet, so before we can create the `Transformer` we need to determine the style sheet.

As far as TrAX is concerned, a style sheet is just another `Source` implementation, so it can be a file, a DOM `Node`, or a stream, just as the source itself can be any of these. In most cases, the style sheet will be a file, as shown in Listing 10.4.

LISTING 10.4   Specifying a Style Sheet in Java

```
import javax.xml.transform.stream.StreamSource;
import javax.xml.transform.stream.StreamResult;
import javax.xml.transform.TransformerFactory;

public class TransformFile extends Object {
    public static void main (String args[]) throws Exception
    {
        String XMLFileName = "events.xml";
        String XSLFileName = "style.xml";
        String OutputFileName = "transform.html";

        StreamSource source = new StreamSource(XMLFileName);
        StreamSource style = new StreamSource(XSLFileName);
        StreamResult result = new StreamResult(OutputFileName);

        TransformerFactory transFactory = TransformerFactory.newInstance();
    }
}
```

If it's this simple, why didn't we just specify the style sheet when we specified the source? It just so happens that we have another, much more powerful option for determining the style sheet. Rather than simply specifying it within the application, we can instruct the application to read the style sheet processing instruction in the document to determine the appropriate style sheet. For example, Listing 10.5 shows the XML document with two possible style sheets specified.

LISTING 10.5   Specifying the Style Sheet within an XML document

```
<?xml version="1.0"?>
<?xml-style sheet href="events.xsl" type="text/xsl" ?>
<?xml-style sheet href="events_print.xsl" type="text/xsl" media="cellphone" ?>
<content>
```

LISTING 10.5   Continued

```
<events>
    <eventitem eventid="A335">
...
```

The `TransformerFactory` object can read these processing instructions, as shown in Listing 10.6a.

LISTING 10.6a   Determining the Style Sheet

```
import javax.xml.transform.stream.StreamSource;
import javax.xml.transform.stream.StreamResult;
import javax.xml.transform.TransformerFactory;
import javax.xml.transform.Source;

public class TransformFile extends Object {
    public static void main (String args[]) throws Exception
    {
        String XMLFileName = "events.xml";
        String OutputFileName = "transform.html";

        StreamSource source = new StreamSource(XMLFileName);
        StreamResult result = new StreamResult(OutputFileName);

        TransformerFactory transFactory = TransformerFactory.newInstance();
        Source style = transFactory.getAssociatedStylesheet(source,
                                             null, null, null);

    }
}
```

The `getAssociatedStylesheet()` method allows you to choose a style sheet based on the `media`, `title`, and `charset` attributes in the processing instruction (in that order). For example, to choose the `cellphone` style sheet, you would use the following instruction:

```
Source style = transFactory.getAssociatedStylesheet(source, "cellphone",
                                             null, null);
```

Once we have the style sheet `Source`, we're ready to create the `Transformer`.

C++

As with Java, the style sheet in C++ is a `DOMDocument` object that we load into the application just as we created the original XML document. Listing 10.6b shows the creation of the style sheet document.

LISTING 10.6b   Specifying a Style Sheet in C++

```
...
        CComPtr<MSXML2::IXMLDOMDocument>  pXMLDoc;
        CComPtr<MSXML2::IXMLDOMDocument>  pXSLTDoc;
        _bstr_t bstrXMLStr;
```

LISTING 10.6b   Continued

```
    pXMLDoc.CoCreateInstance(__uuidof(MSXML2::DOMDocument));
    pXSLTDoc.CoCreateInstance(__uuidof(MSXML2::DOMDocument));

    pXMLDoc->load("events.xml");
    pXSLTDoc->load("style.xsl");
...
```

Visual Basic .NET

In Visual Basic .NET, we also have to load the style sheet as a DOMDocument40 object, as shown in Listing 10.6c.

LISTING 10.6c   Specifying a Style Sheet in Visual Basic .NET

```
...
    Dim XMLDoc As New MSXML2.DOMDocument40()
    Dim XSLTDoc As New MSXML2.DOMDocument40()
    Dim myString As String

    'Load XMLDoc
    XMLDoc.async = False
    XMLDoc.load("events.xml")

    'Load XSLTDoc
    XSLTDoc.async = False
    XSLTDoc.load("style.xsl")
...
```

PHP

PHP has no equivalent to the built-in getAssociatedStyleSheet() function, but fortunately it's not hard to replicate. We've chosen to be "correct" and parse the source XML with an XML parser; if you want a faster but sloppier method, you can just use regular expressions to do the whole job. Listing 10.6d shows the function that parses the document and retrieves the style sheet information.

LISTING 10.6d   Parsing the Document and Retrieving the Style Sheet

```
<?php

$styles = array();

$xh  = xslt_create();
$xml = join('',file('events.xml'));
$xsl = get_associated_stylesheet($xml,'cellphone');

$args = array ( '/_xml' => $xml );

...
```

LISTING 10.6d   Continued

```php
function get_associated_stylesheet ($xml, $media="default")
{
    global $styles;

    if (preg_match("/^(.*?)<[^?]/s", $xml, $matches)) {
        $xml = $matches[1];
    }

    $xp = xml_parser_create();
    xml_set_processing_instruction_handler($xp,'get_style');

    if (xml_parse($xp,$xml)) {

        if (isset($styles[$media])) {
            xml_parser_free($xp);
            return $styles[$media];
        }

        xml_parser_free($xp);
        die("No style sheet for media '$media' found");

    } else {

        xml_parser_free($xp);
        die("Error getting associated style sheet: " .
            xml_error_string($xp));

    }
}

function get_style ($parser, $target, $data)
{
    global $styles;

    $matches = array();
    $media   = 'default';
    if ($target == 'xml-style') {
        if (preg_match('/media="([^"]+)"/',$data,$matches))
            $media =  $matches[1];

        if (preg_match('/href="([^"]+)"/',$data,$matches))
            $styles[$media] = $matches[1];
    }
}
?>
```

Perl

Using XML::Sablotron::DOM, you can pre-parse the source document to find the desired style sheet, without wasting a parse: You can pass the pre-parsed DOM structure to the XSLT processor, so the source document doesn't have to be parsed twice. You can also use this functionality to implement something like the templates provided by TrAX, which we'll discuss in the section titled "Templates and Parameters." You can pre-parse a style sheet and apply it to many source documents without reparsing it, or pre-parse a source document and transform it with many style sheets, without re-parsing the source document. (See Listing 10.10b in the section titled "Transforming Multiple Files" for an example.)

In Listing 10.6e, once we've parsed the source document into a DOM object, we use an XPATH query to find all the XML-style processing instructions and extract the style sheet name and media type for each.

LISTING 10.6e   Specifying a Style Sheet in Perl

```perl
use XML::Sablotron;
use XML::Sablotron::DOM;

my $source = 'events.xml';
my $xsl    = new XML::Sablotron;

my $sit = new XML::Sablotron::Situation;

my ( $media, $doc, $sheet, $style );
eval {
    $media = 'cellphone';
    $doc   = XML::Sablotron::DOM::parse( $sit, $source );
    $sheet = get_associated_stylesheet( $sit, $doc, $media );
    $style = XML::Sablotron::DOM::parseStylesheet( $sit, $sheet );
};

if ($@) {
    die "Error loading stylesheet for media type '$media': $@\n";
}
eval {

    $xsl->addArgTree( $sit, 'source', $doc );
    $xsl->addArgTree( $sit, 'sheet',  $style );
    $xsl->process( $sit, 'arg:/sheet', 'arg:/source', 'arg:/result' );
    my $result = $xsl->getResultArg('arg:/result');
    print $result;
};

if ($@) {
    die "Error processing $source with $style: $@";
}

sub get_associated_stylesheet {
    my ( $sit, $doc, $media ) = @_;

    $media ||= 'default';

    my $doc_style_el =
      $doc->xql( "/processing-instruction('xml-style')", $sit );
    my %styles;
```

LISTING 10.6e   Continued

```perl
    foreach my $ds (@$doc_style_el) {
        my $data = $ds->getNodeValue($sit);
        my $mt   = 'default';

        if ( $data =~ /media="([^"]+)"/ ) {
            $mt = $1;
        }

        if ( $data =~ /href="([^"]+)"/ ) {
            $styles{$mt} = $1;
        }
    }

    die "No style sheet found for '$media'\n"
      unless $styles{$media};

    return $styles{$media};
}
```

Creating the Transformer and Transforming the Data

We've created the `TransformerFactory` object, we've determined the style sheet, and now we're ready to create the `Transformer`.

When we create the `Transformer` from the `TransformerFactory`, we feed it a style sheet that provides the instructions for all transformations it subsequently performs. We can create it without a style sheet, in which case it will perform an "identity transformation," essentially passing the information on unchanged. This ability can be useful in situations where we simply want to serialize XML data, sending it to a file or to an output stream such as a Web page.

In Listing 10.7a, we'll create the `Transformer` with the style sheet specified on the XML document, and then use it to actually perform the transformation.

LISTING 10.7a   Transforming the Source in Java

```java
...
import javax.xml.transform.Transformer;

public class TransformFile extends Object {
  public static void main (String args[]) throws Exception
  {
    String XMLFileName = "events.xml";
    String OutputFileName = "transform.html";

    StreamSource source = new StreamSource(XMLFileName);
    StreamResult result = new StreamResult(OutputFileName);

    TransformerFactory transFactory = TransformerFactory.newInstance();
    Source style=transFactory.getAssociatedStylesheet(source, null, null, null);
```

LISTING 10.7a   Continued

```
        Transformer trans = transFactory.newTransformer(style);
        trans.transform(source, result);
    }
}
```

The `Transformer` object transforms the source (the list of events) into the result (an HTML file, in this case) using the instructions in the style sheet specified by the document. In this case, the `result` is a simple HTML page, as shown in Figure 10.1.

FIGURE 10.1
A transformation can create a traditional HTML file to be opened in the browser, among other things.

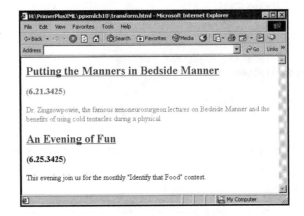

C++

In C++, to begin the transformation of the XML document, we only need to make a call to the `transformNode()` or `transformNodeToObject()` method, as shown in Listing 10.7b.

LISTING 10.7b   Transforming the Source in C++

```
    ...
        CComPtr<MSXML2::IXMLDOMDocument>  pXMLDoc;
        CComPtr<MSXML2::IXMLDOMDocument>  pXSLTDoc;
        _bstr_t bstrXMLStr;

        pXMLDoc.CoCreateInstance(__uuidof(MSXML2::DOMDocument));
        pXSLTDoc.CoCreateInstance(__uuidof(MSXML2::DOMDocument));

        pXMLDoc->load("events.xml");
        pXSLTDoc->load("style.xsl");

        // This call will produce a string for output
        bstrXMLStr = pXMLDoc->transformNode(pXSLTDoc);
    }
    ...
```

Visual Basic .NET

In Visual Basic .NET, to begin the transformation of the XML document, we simply need to make a call to either the `transformNode()` method or the `transformNodeToObject()` method, as shown in Listing 10.7c.

LISTING 10.7c   Transforming the Source in Visual Basic .NET

```
...
            Dim XMLDoc As New MSXML2.DOMDocument40()
            Dim XSLTDoc As New MSXML2.DOMDocument40()
            Dim myString As String

            'Load XMLDoc
            XMLDoc.async = False
            XMLDoc.load("events.xml")

            'Load XSLTDoc
            XSLTDoc.async = False
            XSLTDoc.load("style.xsl")

            'Do the transformation
            myString = XMLDoc.transformNode(XSLTDoc)
        End Sub
```

Templates and Parameters

If you're going to transform multiple files, it's often better to precompile the `Transformer` in order to improve performance. One way of doing this is through the use of the `Templates` object.

Creating a Template

In TrAX, creating a template is an intermediate step between the `TransformerFactory` and the `Transformer`. As shown in Listing 10.8a, the `Templates` object actually creates the `Transformer`, rather than the `TransformerFactory`.

LISTING 10.8a   Using Templates in Java

```
import javax.xml.transform.stream.StreamSource;
import javax.xml.transform.stream.StreamResult;
import javax.xml.transform.TransformerFactory;
import javax.xml.transform.Source;
import javax.xml.transform.Transformer;
import javax.xml.transform.Templates;

public class TransformFile extends Object {
   public static void main (String args[]) throws Exception
   {
      String XMLFileName = "events.xml";
```

LISTING 10.8a Continued

```
            String OutputFileName = "transform.html";

            StreamSource source = new StreamSource(XMLFileName);
            StreamResult result = new StreamResult(OutputFileName);

            TransformerFactory transFactory = TransformerFactory.newInstance();
            Source style=transFactory.getAssociatedStylesheet(source, null, null, null);

            Templates template = transFactory.newTemplates(style);
            Transformer trans = template.newTransformer();
            trans.transform(source, result);

    }
}
```

Templates are most helpful when you intend to do more than one transformation using the same style sheet. Often this involves the use of a parameter, as described in the next section.

C++

Templates are easy to use in C++. In order to use a template, you must declare the XSLT style sheet as a `FreeThreadedDOMDocument` object. You must also create an `IXSLProcessor` object that will perform the actual transformation of the XML document. To complete the transformation, load the XML document into the processor and then use the transform method to complete the transformation. The `get_output` method will retrieve the resulting HTML string, as shown in Listing 10.8b.

LISTING 10.8b Using Templates in C++

```
    ...
            CComPtr<MSXML2::IXMLDOMDocument> pXSLTDoc;
            CComPtr<MSXML2::IXSLTemplate> pXSLTTemplate;
            CComPtr<MSXML2::IXSLProcessor> pXSLTProcessor;
            CComVariant varOutput;

            pXMLDoc.CoCreateInstance(__uuidof(MSXML2::DOMDocument));
            pXSLTDoc.CoCreateInstance(__uuidof(MSXML2::FreeThreadedDOMDocument));
            pXSLTTemplate.CoCreateInstance(__uuidof(MSXML2::XSLTemplate));

            pXMLDoc->load("events.xml");
            pXSLTDoc->load("style.xsl");
            pXSLTTemplate->putref_stylesheet(pXSLTDoc);

            pXSLTProcessor = pXSLTTemplate->createProcessor();
            pXSLTProcessor->put_input(CComVariant(pXMLDoc));
            pXSLTProcessor->transform();
            pXSLTProcessor->get_output(&varOutput);

            wprintf(L"%s", V_BSTR(&varOutput));
    }
    ...
```

Visual Basic .NET

Templates are also easy to use in Visual Basic. In order to use a template, you must declare the XSLT style sheet as a `FreeThreadedDOMDocument40` object. You must also create an `IXSLProcessor` object that will perform the actual transformation of the XML document. To complete the transformation, load the XML document into the processor and then use the `transform` method to complete the transformation, as shown in Listing 10.8c. The `output` property contains the resulting HTML.

LISTING 10.8c   Using Templates in Visual Basic .NET

```
...
        Dim XMLDoc As New MSXML2.DOMDocument40()
        Dim XSLTDoc As New MSXML2.FreeThreadedDOMDocument40()
        Dim XSLTTemplate As New MSXML2.XSLTemplate40()
        Dim XSLTProcessor As MSXML2.IXSLProcessor

        'Load XMLDoc
        XMLDoc.async = False
        XMLDoc.load("events.xml")

        'Load XSLTDoc
        XSLTDoc.async = False
        XSLTDoc.load("style.xsl")

        'Load XSLTTemplate with stylesheet
        XSLTTemplate.stylesheet = XSLTDoc

        'Create processor and then perform transformation
        XSLTProcessor = XSLTTemplate.createProcessor()
        XSLTProcessor.input = XMLDoc
        XSLTProcessor.transform()
        MsgBox(XSLTProcessor.output)
    End Sub
```

PHP

There's no means of reusing a style sheet without reparsing it in PHP's Sablotron interface.

Perl

As discussed in the text that introduced Listing 10.6e, you can use `XML::Sablotron::DOM` and `XML::Sablotron`'s `addAgrTree()` method to obtain the same function result as you'd get by using TrAX-style templates. (See Listing 10.10c in the section titled "Transforming Multiple Files" for an example.)

Using a Parameter

As mentioned in Chapter 9, *parameters* are values you can pass in when executing the transformation. These values can then affect the output. In Listing 9.43, we had a parameter, `optionalChoice`, that determined what information would be displayed and how.

We can also pass parameters into the transformation programmatically (as opposed to passing parameters from the command line) using the `setParameter()` method on the `Transformer` object, as shown in Listing 10.9a.

LISTING 10.9a Setting a Parameter in Java

```
...

        Templates template = transFactory.newTemplates(style);
        Transformer trans = template.newTransformer();

        trans.setParameter("optionalChoice", "yes");

        trans.transform(source, result);

    }
}
```

With the parameter set, the output is affected accordingly, as shown in Figure 10.2.

FIGURE 10.2
Adding the parameter affects the final output.

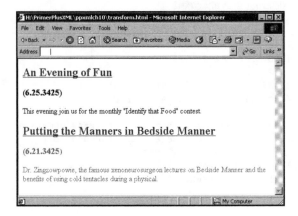

C++ and Visual Basic .NET

In Visual Basic .NET MSXML's implementation, parameters are embedded into the XSLT style sheet using the `<xsl: param>` tag. For example, if we wanted to implement the `optionalChoice` parameter, it would look like this:

```
<xsl:param name="optionalChoice">yes</xsl:param>
...
optionalChoice = <xsl:value-of select="$optionalChoice"/>
```

There is no mechanism for passing parameters programmatically.

PHP

You can pass parameters to the XSLT processor with PHP's `xslt_process()` command as a hash, as shown in Listing 10.9b.

LISTING 10.9b   Setting a Parameter in PHP

```php
<?php
 ...

$args = array ( '/_xml' => $xml );
$params = array ( 'optionalChoice' => 'yes' );
$transformed = xslt_process($xh, 'arg:/_xml', $xsl,
                            NULL, $args, $params);

 ...

?>
```

Perl

As with PHP's Sablotron interface, you can pass parameters directly to the process command. But using XML::Sablotron, you can also add parameters before processing using the addParam() method, as shown in Listing 10.9c.

LISTING 10.9c   Setting a Parameter in Perl

```perl
...

eval {
    $xsl->addArgTree( $sit, 'source', $doc );
    $xsl->addArgTree( $sit, 'sheet',  $style );

    $xsl->addParam( $sit, 'optionalChoice', 'yes' );

    $xsl->process( $sit, 'arg:/sheet', 'arg:/source', 'arg:/result' );

    my $result = $xsl->getResultArg('arg:/result');
    print $result;
};

...
```

Transforming Multiple Files

With templates and parameters, we can efficiently transform multiple files or transform the same file multiple times, as shown in Listing 10.10a.

LISTING 10.10a   Multiple Transformations in Java

```java
...
public class TransformFile extends Object {
   public static void main (String args[]) throws Exception
   {
      String XMLFileName = "events.xml";
      String OutputFileName_opt = "transform_opt.html";
      String OutputFileName_mand = "transform_mand.html";
```

LISTING 10.10a   Continued

```
    StreamSource source = new StreamSource(XMLFileName);
    StreamResult result_opt = new StreamResult(OutputFileName_opt);
    StreamResult result_mand = new StreamResult(OutputFileName_mand);

    TransformerFactory transFactory = TransformerFactory.newInstance();
    Source style=transFactory.getAssociatedStylesheet(source, null, null, null);

    Templates template = transFactory.newTemplates(style);
    Transformer trans = template.newTransformer();

    trans.setParameter("optionalChoice", "yes");
    trans.transform(source, result_opt);

    trans.setParameter("optionalChoice", "no");
    trans.transform(source, result_mand);

    }
}
```

You can transform as many files as you like. As long as you're using the same transformer, they'll all use the same style sheet. However, you can change the source, or in this case, the result.

Perl

Processing the same file multiple times without re-parsing it is easy. The only caveat is that the argument list is flushed each time you execute the **process()** method; you have to add all arguments each time you process, even if they haven't changed. In Listing 10.10b, the only change will be the parameter **optionalChoice**, but we could just as easily apply a new style sheet to the source document, or parse a new source with the same style sheet, by inserting the appropriate **addArgTree()** calls.

LISTING 10.10b   Multiple Transformations in Perl

```
    ...

eval {
    $xsl->addArgTree( $sit, 'source',        $doc );
    $xsl->addArgTree( $sit, 'style',         $style );
    $xsl->addParam( $sit,   'optionalChoice', 'yes' );
    $xsl->process( $sit, 'arg:/style', 'arg:/source', 'arg:/result' );
    my $result = $xsl->getResultArg('arg:/result');
    print $result;

    $xsl->addArgTree( $sit, 'source',        $doc );
    $xsl->addArgTree( $sit, 'style',         $style );
    $xsl->addParam( $sit,   'optionalChoice', 'no' );
    $xsl->process( $sit, 'arg:/style', 'arg:/source', 'arg:/result2' );
    my $result2 = $xsl->getResultArg('arg:/result2');
```

LISTING 10.10b   Continued

```
    print $result2;
};

...
```

Transformations and SAX

Now that you've got an idea of how transformations work, it's time to throw a wrench into the works.

TrAX is pretty straightforward when we're dealing with objects such as files and DOM `Node`s, but what happens when we throw SAX into the mix? With SAX, we have a stream of events, such as `startElement` and `endDocument`, so how can we incorporate this into a transformation?

It turns out that we have several options, each of which we'll discuss in the sections that follow:

- Use TrAX as before, but with `SAXSource`s and/or `SAXResult`s.

- Create a content handler that performs the transformation, and then parse the document as usual.

- Chain transformations together, with or without `XMLFilter`s.

Source and Style Sheet

In this section, we'll be taking a closer look at the results, so let's make sure we know what we're dealing with. As the source document, we'll use the votes from Chapter 5, "XML Streams: The Simple API for XML (SAX)," as shown in Listing 10.11.

LISTING 10.11   The Source Data

```
<?xml version="1.0"?>
<?xml-style sheet href="votes.xsl" type="text/xsl" ?>
<votes totalVotes="5">
    <voter personid="Emp1" status="primary">
        <vote>Dregraal</vote>
        <extra:comments xmlns:extra="http://www.vanguardreport.com/extra">
            I would like to request that the date of voting be changed.
            Any klybrtan youth would realize that it falls on the 334th
            of Meeps, the Holiest of days for Squreenks.  It is totally
            unacceptable for us to vote then, since we have to spend the
            entire day in the positronic chamber of worship.
        </extra:comments>
    </voter>
    <voter personid="Emp2" status="symbiont">
        <vote>Sparkle</vote>
        <extra:comments xmlns:extra="http://www.vanguardreport.com/extra">
            Sfgrtng dwesvers melpy ypinee!
        </extra:comments>
```

LISTING 10.11 Continued

```
    </voter>
...
</votes>
```

The style sheet is straightforward; it changes the structure of the data to contain only the personid and vote, as shown in Listing 10.12.

LISTING 10.12 The Style Sheet

```
<?xml version="1.0"?>
<xsl:stylesheet xmlns:xsl="http://www.w3.org/1999/XSL/Transform" version="1.0">

<xsl:template match="/">
  <finalVotes>
    <xsl:apply-templates />
  </finalVotes>
</xsl:template>

<xsl:template match="votes/voter">
    <vote>
        <person><xsl:value-of select="@personid"/></person>
        <candidate><xsl:value-of select="vote"/></candidate>
    </vote>
</xsl:template>

</xsl:stylesheet>
```

The results of this simple transformation are shown in Listing 10.13.

LISTING 10.13 The Transformed Data

```
<?xml version="1.0" encoding="UTF-8"?>
<finalVotes>
    <vote><person>Emp1</person><candidate>Dregraal</candidate></vote>
    <vote><person>Emp2</person><candidate>Sparkle</candidate></vote>
    <vote><person>Emp3</person><candidate>Dregraal</candidate></vote>
    <vote><person>Emp4</person><candidate>Dregraal</candidate></vote>
    <vote><person>Emp5</person><candidate>Sparkle</candidate></vote>
</finalVotes>
```

SAX as Input

Let's start simple, with a SAXSource as input for a transformation. In Listing 10.14, we'll create a source of SAX events, and we'll use it as the input for the transformation.

LISTING 10.14 Using a SAX Source in Java

```
import javax.xml.transform.Source;
import javax.xml.transform.sax.SAXSource;
```

LISTING 10.14   *Continued*

```
import javax.xml.transform.stream.StreamResult;
import javax.xml.transform.TransformerFactory;
import javax.xml.transform.Transformer;

import org.xml.sax.helpers.XMLReaderFactory;
import org.xml.sax.XMLReader;
import org.xml.sax.InputSource;
import org.xml.sax.SAXException;

public class TransformFile extends Object {
   public static void main (String args[]) throws Exception
   {

      try {
         String XMLFileName = "votes.xml";
         String OutputFileName = "finalvotes.xml";

         String parserClass = "org.apache.crimson.parser.XMLReaderImpl";
         XMLReader reader = XMLReaderFactory.createXMLReader(parserClass);
         SAXSource source = new SAXSource(reader, new InputSource(XMLFileName));

         StreamResult result = new StreamResult(OutputFileName);

         TransformerFactory transFactory = TransformerFactory.newInstance();
         Source style =
                  transFactory.getAssociatedStylesheet(source, null, null, null);

         Transformer trans = transFactory.newTransformer(style);

         trans.transform(source, result);

      } catch (SAXException e) {
         System.out.println(e.getMessage());
      }

   }
}
```

To create SAX events, we need an **XMLReader**, so first we'll create that, just as we did when building an ordinary SAX application. We'll then use that **XMLReader**, along with a SAX **InputSource** for the original document, to create a **SAXSource**.

The rest of the application proceeds normally, as if we had specified a simple file as the input, but behind the scenes, the transformer sets itself as the **ContentHandler** for the **XMLReader**, then calls the **parse()** method. In this way, the events generated by parsing the document go to the **Transformer**, which transforms them into the new structure.

But what did we actually gain here, besides the necessity of specifying the classname for the **XMLReader**? Well, for one thing, because we're dealing with an **XMLReader**, we can set features on it. For example, we can set up the application so that in addition to transforming the document, the application validates it, as shown in Listing 10.15a.

LISTING 10.15a   Validating the Document

```
        ...
                String parserClass = "org.apache.crimson.parser.XMLReaderImpl";
                XMLReader reader = XMLReaderFactory.createXMLReader(parserClass);

                String featureId = "http://xml.org/sax/features/validation";
                reader.setFeature(featureId, true);

                SAXSource source = new SAXSource(reader, new InputSource(XMLFileName));
                StreamResult result = new StreamResult(OutputFileName);
        ...
```

Now if we run the application, we'll see validation errors because we haven't specified a DTD or XML Schema.

C++ and Visual Basic .NET

The XSLT processor in these examples, MSXSL, has no means of using SAX events as direct input.

PHP

PHP has no way to use SAX events as direct input for an XSLT processor.

Perl

You can use SAX events to build a Sablotron DOM tree with the `XML::Sablotron::SAXBuilder` module, and then pass that DOM tree to `XML::Sablotron` for processing using `addArgTree()`. In effect, then, you can use SAX events as input for the XSLT processor, though somewhat indirectly. `XML::Sablotron::SAXBuilder` conforms to the Perl SAX 2 standard set by `XML::SAX`, so you should be able to use it with any source of Perl-standard SAX events. Here we use it with `XML::SAX` and `XML::SAX::Expat`.

One major drawback to using `XML::Sablotron::SAXBuilder` is that the source XML document cannot contain any elements outside of the default XML namespace; the processor will exit with an error if it encounters any such elements. To execute the remaining examples using `XML::Sablotron`, copy the `votes.xml` file to a new file called `ne_votes.xml`, and edit the `<extra:comments>` tags to remove the namespace.

This:

```
<extra:comments xmlns:extra="http://www.vanguardreport.com/extra">
...
</extra:comments>
```

becomes this:

```
<comments>
...
</comments>
```

Use this file as the source document for the remaining examples in this chapter.

Listing 10.15b shows the transformation using the SAX stream representing the new document as the source.

LISTING 10.15b   Using a SAX Source in Perl

```
use XML::Sablotron;
use XML::Sablotron::SAXBuilder;
use XML::SAX;

$XML::SAX::ParserPackage = 'XML::SAX::Expat';

my $xsl = new XML::Sablotron;
my $sit = new XML::Sablotron::Situation;

eval {
    my $builder = new XML::Sablotron::SAXBuilder;
    my $factory = XML::SAX::ParserFactory->new();
    my $parser  = $factory->parser( Handler => $builder );
    my $doc     = $parser->parse_uri('ne_votes.xml');
    my $sheet   = get_associated_stylesheet( $sit, $doc );
    my $style   = XML::Sablotron::DOM::parseStylesheet( $sit, $sheet );

    $xsl->addArgTree( $sit, 'source', $doc );
    $xsl->addArgTree( $sit, 'style',  $style );
    $xsl->process( $sit, 'arg:/style', 'arg:/source', 'arg:/result' );
    my $result = $xsl->getResultArg('arg:/result');
    print $result;
};

...
```

Sablotron is based on `XML::Parser`, which is a nonvalidating parser. If you need validation and transformation, look into using `XML::LibXSLT`. `XML:LibXSLT` requires `XML::LibXML`, and is based on the GNOME XSLT library; see `http://xmlsoft.org` for more information.

The Transformer as `ContentHandler`

In the previous example, we used a SAX stream as the input for the transformation. Now let's look at using SAX for the middle piece of the puzzle, the style sheet. Listing 10.16 shows the explicit creation of a `Transformer` as a `ContentHandler` (as opposed to the implicit creation in the previous example).

LISTING 10.16   The `Transformer` as `ContentHandler`

```
import javax.xml.transform.Source;
import javax.xml.transform.stream.StreamSource;
import javax.xml.transform.stream.StreamResult;
import javax.xml.transform.TransformerFactory;
import javax.xml.transform.Transformer;
```

LISTING 10.16 *Continued*

```
import org.xml.sax.helpers.XMLReaderFactory;
import org.xml.sax.XMLReader;
import org.xml.sax.InputSource;
import org.xml.sax.SAXException;
import javax.xml.transform.sax.SAXTransformerFactory;
import javax.xml.transform.sax.TransformerHandler;

public class TransformFile extends Object {
    public static void main (String args[]) throws Exception
    {

        try {
            String XMLFileName = "votes.xml";
            String OutputFileName = "finalvotes.xml";

            StreamSource source = new StreamSource(XMLFileName);
            StreamResult result = new StreamResult(OutputFileName);

            TransformerFactory transFactory = TransformerFactory.newInstance();
            Source style =
                    transFactory.getAssociatedStylesheet(source, null, null, null);

            SAXTransformerFactory saxTransFactory =
                                        (SAXTransformerFactory)transFactory;
            TransformerHandler trans = saxTransFactory.newTransformerHandler(style);
            trans.setResult(result);

            String parserClass = "org.apache.crimson.parser.XMLReaderImpl";
            XMLReader reader = XMLReaderFactory.createXMLReader(parserClass);

            reader.setContentHandler(trans);

            reader.parse(XMLFileName);

        } catch (SAXException e) {
            System.out.println(e.getMessage());
        }

    }
}
```

In this case, we create the `result` as usual, and we create the `source` object just so we can extract the style sheet information. Next, we cast the `TransformerFactory` to a `SAXTransformerFactory`, and use it to create a `TransformerHandler`. The `TransformerHandler` is similar to a `Transformer`, but will be used as the `ContentHandler`. The `TransformerHandler` is also where we'll determine the destination of the transformation using the `setResult()` method.

Finally, we create the `XMLReader`, set the `TransformerHandler` as the `ContentHandler`, and parse the file. The `TransformerHandler` transforms the data, sending it to the `result`.

SAX as a Result

Okay, we've looked at SAX in the first two positions; now we'll look at a transformation where a stream of SAX events is the result.

For the SAX stream to make any sense, we've got to send it to a `ContentHandler`. In this case, we'll create one that totals the votes and outputs the results. (We won't get as detailed as we did in Chapter 5; we'll just total the votes.) The code for the `ContentHandler` is shown in Listing 10.17.

LISTING 10.17   The `ContentHandler`

```
import org.xml.sax.helpers.DefaultHandler;
import org.xml.sax.Attributes;
import org.xml.sax.SAXException;

public class DataProcessor extends DefaultHandler
{
   public DataProcessor ()
   {
      super();
   }

   StringBuffer thisText = new StringBuffer();
   int sTally = 0;
   int dTally = 0;

   public static void println(String arg) {
      System.out.println(arg);
   }

   public void outputResults(){
      println("Sparkle: "+sTally+"   Dregraal: "+dTally);
   }

   public void endDocument() {
      outputResults();
   }

   public void startElement (String namespaceUri, String localName,
                        String qualifiedName, Attributes attributes) {
      thisText.delete(0, thisText.length());
   }

   public void endElement (String namespaceUri, String localName,
                        String qualifiedName) throws SAXException
   {
      if (localName.equals("candidate")){
         if (thisText.toString().equals("Sparkle")){
            sTally = sTally + 1;
         } else if (thisText.toString().equals("Dregraal")){
            dTally = dTally + 1;
```

LISTING 10.17   Continued

```
            }
        }
        thisText.delete(0, thisText.length());
    }

    public void characters (char[] ch, int start, int length)
    {
        thisText.append(ch, start, length);
    }

}
```

There's nothing new here; this is simply a version of the **DataProcessor** class from Chapter 5.

Now we want to create a **SAXResult** that sends events to this **ContentHandler**, as shown in Listing 10.18a.

LISTING 10.18a   Using a SAXResult

```
import javax.xml.transform.Source;
import javax.xml.transform.stream.StreamSource;
import javax.xml.transform.sax.SAXResult;
import javax.xml.transform.TransformerFactory;
import javax.xml.transform.Transformer;

public class TransformFile extends Object {
    public static void main (String args[]) throws Exception
    {

        String XMLFileName = "votes.xml";
        String OutputFileName = "finalvotes.xml";

        StreamSource source = new StreamSource(XMLFileName);
        SAXResult result = new SAXResult(new DataProcessor());

        TransformerFactory transFactory = TransformerFactory.newInstance();
        Source style =
                transFactory.getAssociatedStylesheet(source, null, null, null);

        Transformer trans = transFactory.newTransformer(style);
        trans.transform(source, result);

    }
}
```

In many ways, this is the simplest of the SAX-related transformations. It's a normal TrAX transformation, but the result is a **SAXResult** that sends a SAX stream to the **ContentHandler** with which it's created.

When you execute the transformation, the **personid** attribute and **vote** element are converted to the **person** and **candidate** elements, as expected. These elements are then forwarded to

DataProcessor, which acts on them. The result is the output specified in the endDocument() method:

Sparkle: 2   Dregraal: 3

C++

In C++, you can cause SAX events to be generated by the IXSLProcessor object by assigning a class to the IXSLProcessor put_output property that implements the methods of the ISAXContentHandler interface. If you need to handle other events, you will need to implement the appropriate interface(s) and implement the methods for those interfaces in the same class. Additionally, you must implement either the IStream interface or the IPersistStream interface to support the output of the final transformation. Building the application this way enables you to handle the SAX events as usual, but to have the process initiated by a transformation.

This is difficult to do in vanilla C++. It is much easier to implement in either MFC or ATL, where the handling of the interfaces and vtables and so on is managed for you, but unfortunately, such an implementation is well beyond the scope of this book. If you're curious, Listing 10.18b shows the basic application skeleton. I leave it to you to implement the appropriate interfaces.

LISTING 10.18b Transforming to a SAX Stream in C++

```cpp
#include "stdafx.h"
#include "MySAXContentHandler.h"

int _tmain(int argc, _TCHAR* argv[])
{
    ::CoInitialize(NULL);
    try
    {
        HRESULT hr = S_OK;

        if(hr==S_OK)
        {
            //Create the pointers for the XML, XSL, Template and Processor
            CComPtr<MSXML2::IXMLDOMDocument> pXMLDoc;
            CComPtr<MSXML2::IXMLDOMDocument> pXSLTDoc;
            CComPtr<MSXML2::IXSLTemplate> pXSLTTemplate;
            CComPtr<MSXML2::IXSLProcessor> pXSLTProcessor;
            VARIANT_BOOL vSuccess;
            vSuccess = VARIANT_TRUE;

            //Load pointers
            MySAXContentHandler* pContent = new MySAXContentHandler();
            hr = pXMLDoc.CoCreateInstance(__uuidof(MSXML2::DOMDocument));
            hr = pXSLTDoc.CoCreateInstance(
                             __uuidof(MSXML2::FreeThreadedDOMDocument));
            hr = pXSLTTemplate.CoCreateInstance(__uuidof(MSXML2::XSLTemplate));
```

LISTING 10.18b   Continued

```
                //Load the XML, XSL and then set the Template to the XSL
                hr = pXMLDoc->load(CComVariant("c:\\sales.xml"), &vSuccess);
                hr = pXSLTDoc->load(CComVariant("c:\\transform.xsl"), &vSuccess);
                hr = pXSLTTemplate->putref_stylesheet(pXSLTDoc);

                //Create and configure the processor
                hr = pXSLTTemplate->createProcessor(&pXSLTProcessor);
                hr = pXSLTProcessor->put_input(CComVariant(pXMLDoc));
                hr = pXSLTProcessor->put_output(_variant_t(pContent, true));

                //Begin the transformation
                hr = pXSLTProcessor->transform(&vSuccess);

                //This is where you would output the result that was provided by
                //IStream or IPersistStream interface that you implemented in the
                //MySAXContentHandler class that was registered as the in
                //the put_output method of the pXSLTProcessor object.
                ...
                //End output
        }
    }
    catch(...)      // For catching standard exceptions.
    {
        printf("Caught the exception");
    }
    ::CoUninitialize();
    return 0;
}
```

Make the following changes to the MySAXContentHandler.h file:

```
class MySAXContentHandler : public ISAXContentHandler
{
...
private:
        wchar_t wchText[1000];
        int sTally,
            dTally;

        void MySAXContentHandler::outputResults(void);
};
```

Finally, update the MySAXContentHandler.cpp file:

```
#include "stdafx.h"
#include "MySAXContentHandler.h"
...
HRESULT STDMETHODCALLTYPE MySAXContentHandler::startDocument()
{
    wchText[0] = 0;
    sTally = 0;
    dTally = 0;
    return S_OK;
}
```

```
HRESULT STDMETHODCALLTYPE MySAXContentHandler::endDocument()
{
    outputResults();
    return S_OK;
}
...
HRESULT STDMETHODCALLTYPE MySAXContentHandler::startElement(
            /* [in] */ wchar_t __RPC_FAR *pwchNamespaceUri,
            /* [in] */ int cchNamespaceUri,
            /* [in] */ wchar_t __RPC_FAR *pwchLocalName,
            /* [in] */ int cchLocalName,
            /* [in] */ wchar_t __RPC_FAR *pwchQualifiedName,
            /* [in] */ int cchQualifiedName,
            /* [in] */ ISAXAttributes __RPC_FAR *pAttributes)
{
    wchText[0] = 0;
    return S_OK;
}

HRESULT STDMETHODCALLTYPE MySAXContentHandler::endElement(
            /* [in] */ wchar_t __RPC_FAR *pwchNamespaceUri,
            /* [in] */ int cchNamespaceUri,
            /* [in] */ wchar_t __RPC_FAR *pwchLocalName,
            /* [in] */ int cchLocalName,
            /* [in] */ wchar_t __RPC_FAR *pwchQualifiedName,
            /* [in] */ int cchQualifiedName)
{
    if (wcsncmp(L"candidate", pwchLocalName, cchLocalName) == 0)
    {
        if (wcsncmp(L"Sparkle", wchText, wcslen(wchText)) == 0)
            sTally++;
        else if (wcsncmp(L"Dregraal", wchText, wcslen(wchText)) == 0)
            dTally++;
    }
    else
        wchText[0] = 0;
    return S_OK;
}

HRESULT STDMETHODCALLTYPE MySAXContentHandler::characters(
            /* [in] */ wchar_t __RPC_FAR *pwchChars,
            /* [in] */ int cchChars)
{
    wcsncat(&*wchText, pwchChars, cchChars);
    return S_OK;
}
...
void MySAXContentHandler::outputResults()
{
    printf("Sparkle: %s   Dregraal: %s\n", sTally, dTally);
}
```

Visual Basic .NET

In Visual Basic .NET, you can cause SAX events to be generated by the `IXSLProcessor` object by assigning a class to the `IXSLProcessor output` property that implements the methods of the `IVBSAXContentHandler` interface. If you also need error handling, you can implement those methods in the same class. This allows you to handle the SAX events as usual but to have the process initiated by a transformation.

To demonstrate this, you can make the following changes to the project that we used in Chapter 5 when we implemented a SAX parser. In this project, change the button's `Text` property to `Transform XML` and its `Name` property to `btnTransform`. Add new Label and TextBox controls to the main form, and set the text box's `Name` property to `txtXSLFileName`. Change the existing text box's `Name` property to `txtXMLFileName` and modify the label controls as appropriate so that the main form resembles the form in Figure 10.3.

FIGURE 10.3

The main form for the SAX Transformation example.

You should make the changes to the main form shown in Listing 10.18b in the code view.

LISTING 10.18c   Transforming to a SAX Stream in Visual Basic .NET

```
...
    Private Sub btnTransform_Click(ByVal sender As System.Object,
                              ByVal e As System.EventArgs)
                                        Handles btnTransform.Click
        Dim ContentHandler As New MyContentHandler(Me)
        Dim XMLDoc As New MSXML2.DOMDocument40()
        Dim XSLTDoc As New MSXML2.FreeThreadedDOMDocument40()
        Dim XSLTTemplate As New MSXML2.XSLTemplate40()
        Dim XSLTProcessor As MSXML2.IXSLProcessor

        On Error GoTo ErrorSub
        XMLDoc.async = False
        XMLDoc.load(txtXMLFileName.Text)
        XSLTDoc.async = False
        XSLTDoc.load(txtXSLFileName.Text)
```

LISTING 10.18c   *Continued*

```
XSLTTemplate.stylesheet = XSLTDoc
XSLTProcessor = XSLTTemplate.createProcessor()
XSLTProcessor.input = XMLDoc

'Assign ContentHandler to processor output to receive SAX events
XSLTProcessor.output = ContentHandler

'Perform the transformation
XSLTProcessor.transform()
Exit Sub
```
...

The changes in Listing 10.18c should be made to the `MyContentHandler.vb` class file.

...
```
Dim myForm As New SAXMainForm()
Dim thisText As String
Dim sTally As Integer = 0
Dim dTally As Integer = 0
```
...
```
Public Sub endDocument() Implements MSXML2.IVBSAXContentHandler.endDocument
    outputResults()
End Sub

Public Sub startElement(ByRef strNamespaceURI As String,
                        ByRef strLocalName As String,
                        ByRef strQName As String,
                        ByVal oAttributes As MSXML2.IVBSAXAttributes)
                            Implements MSXML2.IVBSAXContentHandler.startElement
    thisText = Nothing
End Sub

Public Sub endElement(ByRef strNamespaceURI As String,
                      ByRef strLocalName As String,
                      ByRef strQName As String)
                            Implements MSXML2.IVBSAXContentHandler.endElement
    If strLocalName.Equals("candidate") Then
        If thisText.Equals("Sparkle") Then
            sTally = sTally + 1
        ElseIf thisText.Equals("Dregraal") Then
            dTally = dTally + 1
        End If
    End If
    thisText = Nothing
End Sub
```
...
```
Public Sub outputResults()
    myForm.OutputText="Sparkle: " & sTally & "    Dregraal: " _
                                            & dTally & vbCrLf
End Sub
```

PHP

Use the `xslt_set_sax_handlers()` function to register functions that the XSLT processor can use as handlers for SAX events. One caveat is that if you define one handler in a group (document, element, and so on), you must define all the handlers in that group, or the transformation will fail. (You can see in Listing 10.18d that we've defined a `start_document()` handler that does nothing.)

A further caveat is that `xslt_set_sax_handlers()` doesn't support the object-oriented processing approach that you can use with the "normal" XML parser with `xml_set_object()`. Your XSLT SAX handlers must be global functions, and if you want to pass any data between them or get data back from them, you must use global variables, as shown in Listing 10.18d.

LISTING 10.18d   Transforming to a SAX Stream in PHP

```php
<?php

$styles = array();

$xh  = xslt_create();
$xml = join('',file('votes.xml'));
$xsl = get_associated_stylesheet($xml,'default');

$args = array ( '/_xml' => $xml );
$handlers = array ( 'document' =>
                      array ( 'start_document',
                              'end_document' ),
                    'element' =>
                      array ( 'start_element',
                              'end_element' ),
                    'character' => 'characters'
                  );

$result = array ( 'text'  => '',
                  'stally' => 0,
                  'dtally' => 0 );

xslt_set_sax_handlers($xh, $handlers);
...

function output_results ()
{
    global $result;
    echo "Sparkle: {$result['stally']} Dregraal: {$result['dtally']}<br>\n";
}

function start_document ()
{
    // NOP
}
```

LISTING 10.18d   Continued

```
function end_document ()
{
    output_results();
}

function start_element ($parser, $name, $data)
{
    global $result;
    $result['text'] = '';
}

function end_element ($parser, $name)
{
    global $result;

    if ($name == 'candidate') {
        switch ($result['text']) {
          case 'Sparkle':
              $result['stally']++;
              break;
          case 'Dregraal':
              $result['dtally']++;
              break;
        }
        $result['text'] = '';
    }
}

function characters ($parser, $data)
{
    global $result;
    $result['text'] .= $data;
}
...

?>
```

Perl

The complement to `XML::Sablotron::SAXBuilder` is `XML::SAXDriver::Sablotron`, which hooks into `XML::Sablotron`'s native near-SAX handler support to provide a source of Perl SAX 2 standard SAX events. The content handler used here is unchanged from the one we used in earlier chapters. Listing 10.18e demonstrates a transformation that creates a SAX stream, which is then handled by the content handler.

LISTING 10.18e   Transforming to a SAX Stream in Perl

```
package MyContentHandler;
use base qw(XML::SAX::Base);
```

LISTING 10.18e Continued

```perl
sub output_results {
    my $self = shift;
    print "Sparkle: $self->{s_tally} Dregraal: $self->{d_tally}\n";
}

sub start_document {
    my $self = shift;

    $self->{text}    = '';
    $self->{s_tally} = 0;
    $self->{d_tally} = 0;
}

sub end_document {
    my $self = shift;
    $self->output_results();
}

sub start_element {
    my $self = shift;
    $self->{text} = '';
}

sub end_element {
    my $self = shift;
    my $el   = shift;

    if ( $el->{LocalName} eq 'candidate' ) {
        if ( $self->{text} =~ /Sparkle/ ) {
            $self->{s_tally}++;
        } elsif ( $self->{text} =~ /Dregraal/ ) {
            $self->{d_tally}++;
        }
    }
}

sub characters {
    my $self = shift;
    my $text = shift;

    $self->{text} .= $text->{Data};
}

package main;

use XML::SAXDriver::Sablotron;

my $source  = 'ne_votes.xml';
my $style   = 'votes.xsl';
my $handler = MyContentHandler->new();

eval {
```

LISTING 10.18e   Continued

```
    my $xsl = new XML::SAXDriver::Sablotron(
        Stylesheet => $style,
        Handler    => $handler
    );
    $xsl->parse_uri($source);
};
if ($@) {
    die "Error processing $source with $style: $@";
}
```

Chaining Transformations

In some situations, you'll want one transformation to feed into another. For example, we've narrowed the vote data down to just the **person** and the **candidate**. We might want to perform a second transformation to strip out everything but the candidate's name using a style sheet like the one in Listing 10.19.

LISTING 10.19   The Second Style Sheet

```
<?xml version="1.0"?>
<xsl:stylesheet xmlns:xsl="http://www.w3.org/1999/XSL/Transform" version="1.0">

<xsl:template match="/">
    <xsl:apply-templates />
</xsl:template>

<xsl:template match="finalVote/vote">
    <xsl:value-of select="candidate"/><xsl:text>
    </xsl:text>
</xsl:template>

<xsl:template match="person">
</xsl:template>

</xsl:stylesheet>
```

This style sheet works on the output of the first transformation.

To chain together these transformations, we want to set the result of the first transformation to be the source of the second transformation, as shown in Listing 10.20a.

LISTING 10.20a   Chaining Transformations in Java

```
import javax.xml.transform.stream.StreamSource;
import javax.xml.transform.stream.StreamResult;
import javax.xml.transform.sax.SAXResult;
import javax.xml.transform.TransformerFactory;

import org.xml.sax.helpers.XMLReaderFactory;
import org.xml.sax.XMLReader;
```

LISTING 10.20a   *Continued*

```
import org.xml.sax.InputSource;
import org.xml.sax.SAXException;
import javax.xml.transform.sax.SAXTransformerFactory;
import javax.xml.transform.sax.TransformerHandler;

public class TransformFile extends Object {
   public static void main (String args[]) throws Exception
   {

      try {
         String XMLFileName = "votes.xml";
         String OutputFileName = "finalvotes.xml";

         StreamSource source = new StreamSource(XMLFileName);
         StreamSource style1 = new StreamSource("votes.xsl");
         StreamSource style2 = new StreamSource("votesOnly.xsl");

         StreamResult result = new StreamResult(OutputFileName);

         TransformerFactory transFactory = TransformerFactory.newInstance();

         SAXTransformerFactory saxTransFactory =
                                    (SAXTransformerFactory)transFactory;
         TransformerHandler trans1 =
                       saxTransFactory.newTransformerHandler(style1);
         TransformerHandler trans2 =
                       saxTransFactory.newTransformerHandler(style2);

         trans1.setResult(new SAXResult(trans2));
         trans2.setResult(result);

         String parserClass = "org.apache.crimson.parser.XMLReaderImpl";
         XMLReader reader = XMLReaderFactory.createXMLReader(parserClass);

         reader.setContentHandler(trans1);

         reader.parse(XMLFileName);

      } catch (SAXException e) {
         System.out.println(e.getMessage());
      }

   }
}
```

To keep things simple, we're specifying both style sheets directly and using them to create two
different TransformerHandler objects. We set the result of trans1 to be a SAXResult that
sends the output events to trans2. The output of trans2 is the original result file.

We're setting the ContentHandler for the reader to be trans1, so as the original file is parsed,
its data is sent to trans1. The trans1 object performs the first transformation and sends the

results to `trans2`, which performs the second transformation and sends its results to the `finalvotes.xml` file. The final result is simply the names of the candidates:

```
<?xml version="1.0" encoding="UTF-8"?>

    Dregraal
    Sparkle
    Dregraal
    Dregraal
    Sparkle
```

Perl

You can accomplish something like the transformation chaining possible with TrAX by using `XML::Sablotron::SAXBuilder` as the SAX handler for an `XML::SAXDriver::Sablotron` object. But since `XML::Sablotron::SAXBuilder` produces an `XML::Sablotron::DOM` object, not a stream of SAX events, you can't chain them together indefinitely. The last step in the chain must be an `XML::Sablotron` object to process the DOM document, as shown in Listing 10.20b.

LISTING 10.20b   Chaining Transformations in Perl

```
use XML::SAXDriver::Sablotron;
use XML::Sablotron::SAXBuilder;

my $source  = 'ne_votes.xml';
my $sheet1  = 'votes.xsl';
my $sheet2  = 'votesOnly.xsl';
my $sit     = new XML::Sablotron::Situation;
my $xsl     = new XML::Sablotron;
my $builder = new XML::Sablotron::SAXBuilder;
my $parser  = new XML::SAXDriver::Sablotron(
    Stylesheet => $sheet1,
    Handler    => $builder
);
my $doc    = $parser->parse_uri($source);
my $style2 = XML::Sablotron::DOM::parseStylesheet( $sit, $sheet2 );

$xsl->addArgTree( $sit, 'source',    $doc );
$xsl->addArgTree( $sit, 'style',     $style2 );
$xsl->process( $sit,    'arg:/style', 'arg:/source', 'arg:/result' );
my $result = $xsl->getResultArg('arg:/result');
print $result;
```

SAX and `XMLFilters`

We can accomplish the same thing using `XMLFilters`, but we'll need to turn the order around a bit. Listing 10.21 shows the same transformation using `XMLFilters`.

LISTING 10.21 Using XMLFilters in Java

```java
import javax.xml.transform.stream.StreamSource;
import javax.xml.transform.stream.StreamResult;
import javax.xml.transform.sax.SAXResult;
import javax.xml.transform.TransformerFactory;

import org.xml.sax.helpers.XMLReaderFactory;
import org.xml.sax.XMLReader;
import org.xml.sax.XMLFilter;
import org.xml.sax.InputSource;
import org.xml.sax.SAXException;
import javax.xml.transform.sax.SAXTransformerFactory;
import javax.xml.transform.sax.TransformerHandler;

public class TransformFile extends Object {
    public static void main (String args[]) throws Exception
    {

      try {
         String XMLFileName = "votes.xml";
         String OutputFileName = "finalvotes.xml";

         StreamSource source = new StreamSource(XMLFileName);
         StreamSource style1 = new StreamSource("votes.xsl");
         StreamSource style2 = new StreamSource("votesOnly.xsl");

         StreamResult result = new StreamResult(OutputFileName);

         TransformerFactory transFactory = TransformerFactory.newInstance();

         SAXTransformerFactory saxTransFactory =
                              (SAXTransformerFactory)transFactory;
         XMLFilter trans1 = saxTransFactory.newXMLFilter(style1);
         XMLFilter trans2 = saxTransFactory.newXMLFilter(style2);

         TransformerHandler output = saxTransFactory.newTransformerHandler();
         output.setResult(result);

         String parserClass = "org.apache.crimson.parser.XMLReaderImpl";
         XMLReader reader = XMLReaderFactory.createXMLReader(parserClass);

         trans1.setParent(reader);
         trans2.setParent(trans1);
         trans2.setContentHandler(output);

         trans2.parse(XMLFileName);

      } catch (SAXException e) {
         System.out.println(e.getMessage());
      }

    }
}
```

In this case, rather than creating `TransformerHandler` objects for the style sheets, we're creating `XMLFilters` using the `SAXTransformerFactory`. These `XMLFilters` include the instructions for carrying out each transformation as the filter gets its turn with the data.

We do need one `TransformerHandler` to act as the main `ContentHandler`, however, so we'll create one without a style sheet—so it will pass the data through unchanged—and set its result to be the output file.

As before, we set the parent for each filter, set the `ContentHandler` for the last filter, and use it to actually parse the document.

In this case, that means we ask `trans2` to parse the file. It passes the request to its parent, `trans1`, which sends the request to its parent, `reader`. The `reader` object parses the file and sends its events to `trans1`, which acts on them and sends them to `trans2`, which acts on them and sends the results to its `ContentHandler`, `output`.

Programming Within a Style Sheet

In this section, we're going to leave the application alone and look at the style sheet itself.

The XSLT 1.0 Recommendation allows developers to create extension functions and elements that perform sophisticated programming. For example, we could duplicate the vote counting . programming from Chapter 5 using just extensions built into the style sheet itself. Rather than creating an application to count the votes, we could simply transform the file.

Extensions can be handy because they allow sophisticated programming that can be carried out anywhere an appropriate transformation engine is available, rather than requiring a number of different applications. For example, IBM's developerWorks site (`http://www.ibm.com/developerworks/`) receives tutorials from authors in XML. A single transformation (spanning several XSLT style sheets) not only converts the single XML document into individual HTML pages for each tutorial panel, it also moves images into their proper folder, creates PDF files (in two sizes) and makes a ZIP file of all the HTML pages and graphics.

Before going any further, check the documentation for your XSL transformation engine to see whether any additional setup is required. For example, Java's transformation engine requires that `bsf.jar` be part of the `CLASSPATH` if any language other than Java is used for the extensions. We're going to start with JavaScript, so we'll need not only `bsf.jar` (which is part of the Java distribution), but also `js.jar`, downloadable from

`http://www.mozilla.org/rhino/`

Although extension elements and functions are defined within the XSLT 1.0 Recommendation, there is no guidance on how to actually implement them; different vendors may choose different approaches.

Extension Functions

When we talked about XPath in Chapter 9, we discussed XPath functions. These functions provide a way to perform an action on data. For example, Listing 10.22 shows a style sheet that simply outputs the first letter of each vote.

	A Fortunate Choice

Fortunately, our candidates have names that start with different letters. We wouldn't get any useful information if Dregraal's opponent were named D'nx'w!

LISTING 10.22 Using a Function

```
<?xml version="1.0"?>
<xsl:stylesheet xmlns:xsl="http://www.w3.org/1999/XSL/Transform" version="1.0">

<xsl:template match="/">
   <xsl:apply-templates select="votes/voter" />
</xsl:template>

<xsl:template match="voter">
   <xsl:value-of select="substring(vote, 1, 1)"/>
</xsl:template>

</xsl:stylesheet>
```

When we request the value of this built-in function, it executes the appropriate operations and outputs any data returned by the function.

We can use this same principle to define and use custom functions, or extension functions.

In this case, we simply want to transform the **votes.xml** file using a single XSL file, **votes.xsl**. Update **TransformFile.java** to look like Listing 10.7, but with the appropriate filenames.

To use the functions, we'll need to create a new namespace for them so that the processor knows they're extensions, and not mistakes. We'll also create a component that not only explicitly lists the functions we'll be creating, but will eventually hold the appropriate code as well. Listing 10.23 shows the basic form, including references to the soon-to-be-built functions.

LISTING 10.23 Creating the Functions

```
<?xml version="1.0"?>
<xsl:stylesheet xmlns:xsl="http://www.w3.org/1999/XSL/Transform"
                xmlns:lxslt="http://xml.apache.org/xslt"
                xmlns:results="http://www.example.com/results"
                extension-element-prefixes="results"
                version="1.0">
```

LISTING 10.23 Continued

```
<lxslt:component prefix="results" functions="addVote, getResults">
</lxslt:component>

<xsl:template match="/">

    <xsl:apply-templates select="votes/voter"/>
    <xsl:value-of select="results:getResults()"/>

</xsl:template>

<xsl:template match="voter">
    <xsl:value-of select="results:addVote(string(vote))"/>
</xsl:template>

</xsl:stylesheet>
```

Here we've created an overall extension namespace, aliased with `lxslt`, to house the elements necessary for actually creating the extension elements and functions. The second new namespace, `results`, differentiates the extension elements and functions and points back to the component via the `prefix` attribute. We'll also explicitly list the prefix for extension elements so the processor knows how to handle them.

The `component` element specifies the functions that are defined within (we'll get to that next).

The functions themselves are called just as an XPath function might be called, using data from the document as any necessary arguments. The first, `getResults()`, takes no argument, but returns a string to be output to the page—in this case, with the election results. The second, `addVote()`, takes the value of the `vote` element and passes it to a function.

The functions themselves are shown in Listing 10.24a.

LISTING 10.24a Adding the Functions for a Java Implementation

```
...
   <lxslt:component prefix="results" functions="addVote, getResults">
     <lxslt:script lang="javascript">

       var sparkle, dregraal;
       sparkle = 0;
       dregraal = 0;

       function addVote (thisVote) {
         if (thisVote.equals("Sparkle")) {
           sparkle = sparkle + 1;
         } else {
           dregraal = dregraal + 1;
         }
         return null;
       }
```

LISTING 10.24a   *Continued*

```
        function getResults(){
            return "Sparkle: "+sparkle+"  Dregraal: "+dregraal;
        }
    </lxslt:script>
  </lxslt:component>

<xsl:template match="/">

    <xsl:apply-templates select="votes/voter"/>
    <xsl:value-of select="results:getResults()"/>

</xsl:template>

<xsl:template match="voter">
    <xsl:value-of select="results:addVote(string(vote))"/>
</xsl:template>

</xsl:stylesheet>
```

In this case, we're using JavaScript and embedding the code right in the page. Notice that the functions share names with their extension counterparts, so finding the right function to use is simple.

When we call for the value of `addVote`, the `addVote()` function adds the appropriate value and returns `null`, so nothing is output. When the document is complete, the `getResults()` function, which simply outputs the appropriate value, is called.

In this way, we can perform actions on data that we can explicitly pass as an argument. Extension elements give us even more power.

C++ and Visual Basic .NET

Prior to version 4.0, MSXML did not include support for XSLT extensions at all. MSXML 4.0 supports extension functions (but not extension elements, which are discussed next) via the `msxsl:script` element. Listing 10.24b shows an example.

LISTING 10.24b   Implementing XSLT Extensions Using MSXML

```
<?xml version="1.0"?>
<xsl:stylesheet xmlns:xsl="http://www.w3.org/1999/XSL/Transform"
                xmlns:msxsl="urn:schemas-microsoft-com:xslt"
                xmlns:results="http://www.example.com/results"
                version="1.0">

<msxsl:script implements-prefix="results" language="JScript"><![CDATA[

    var sparkle, dregraal;
    sparkle = 0;
    dregraal = 0;
```

LISTING 10.24b   Continued

```
    function addVote (thisVote) {
        if (thisVote == "Sparkle") {
            sparkle = sparkle + 1;
        } else {
            dregraal = dregraal + 1;
        }
        return '';
    }

    function getResults() {
        return "Sparkle: "+sparkle+"  Dregraal: "+dregraal;
    }
]]></msxsl:script>

<xsl:template match="/">
    <xsl:apply-templates select="votes/voter"/>
    <xsl:value-of select="results:getResults()"/>
</xsl:template>

<xsl:template match="voter">
    <xsl:value-of select="results:addVote(string(vote))"/>
</xsl:template>

</xsl:stylesheet>
```

For documentation on the `msxsl:script` element, see the MSXML XSLT Reference Guide at `http://msdn.microsoft.com/library/default.asp?url=/library/en-us/xmlsdk/htm/xsl_ref_overview_1vad.asp`.

PHP and Perl

Sablotron can support JavaScript extensions, but it uses a different function namespace and format than that used in the preceding Java example. JavaScript extension functionality in Sablotron is also not built in by default; you must first install the Mozilla JavaScript library. (This is true even if you have Mozilla itself installed; the browser installation lacks the headers required to build against the library.) Then you must build both PHP and the Perl Sablotron wrapper module `XML::Sablotron` to explicitly link against the Mozilla JavaScript library as well as against Sablotron itself. It's not a process for the faint of heart; again, if you can find prebuilt binaries of Perl or PHP and Sablotron+JavaScript, you'll probably save yourself much frustration by using them.

Listing 10.24c shows a version of the XSL document in Listing 10.24b that will work with Sablotron.

LISTING 10.24c   Adding the Functions for Sablotron in PHP or Perl

```
<?xml version="1.0"?>
<xsl:stylesheet version="1.0"
            xmlns:xsl="http://www.w3.org/1999/XSL/Transform"
```

LISTING 10.24c *Continued*

```
            xmlns:func="http://www.exslt.org/functions"
            xmlns:results="http://www.example.com/results"
            extension-element-prefixes="func"
            exclude-result-prefixes="results">

<func:script implements-prefix="results" language="javascript"><![CDATA[

    var sparkle, dregraal;
    sparkle = 0;
    dregraal = 0;

    function addVote (thisVote) {
        if (thisVote == "Sparkle") {
            sparkle = sparkle + 1;
        } else {
            dregraal = dregraal + 1;
        }
        return '';
    }

     function getResults() {
         return "Sparkle: "+sparkle+"  Dregraal: "+dregraal;
     }
]]>
<xsl:fallback>
  <xsl:text>Javscript extensions not supported</xsl:text>
</xsl:fallback>
</func:script>

<xsl:template match="/">
    <xsl:apply-templates select="votes/voter"/>
    <xsl:value-of select="results:getResults()"/>
</xsl:template>

<xsl:template match="voter">
    <xsl:value-of select="results:addVote(string(vote))"/>
</xsl:template>

</xsl:stylesheet>
```

The actual transformation is performed as usual.

Extension Elements

In the next section, we'll take a look at how extension elements enable us to use information about the context node, but first let's look at the elements themselves.

In Listing 10.25, we're turning the **addVote** function into an **addVote** element.

LISTING 10.25   *Creating an Extension Element*

```xml
<?xml version="1.0"?>
<xsl:stylesheet xmlns:xsl="http://www.w3.org/1999/XSL/Transform"
                xmlns:lxslt="http://xml.apache.org/xslt"
                xmlns:results="http://www.example.com/results"
                extension-element-prefixes="results"
                version="1.0">


  <lxslt:component prefix="results" functions="getResults" elements="addVote">
    <lxslt:script lang="javascript">
      var sparkle, dregraal;
      sparkle = 0;
      dregraal = 0;

      function addVote(ctx, elem) {
          if (elem.getAttribute("enforced") == "no") {
              return ("Voting restrictions not enforced.");
          } else {
              return ("Voting restrictions enforced.");
          }

          if (thisVote.equals("Sparkle")) {
             sparkle = sparkle + 1;
          } else {
             dregraal = dregraal + 1;
          }
          return null;
      }

      function getResults(){
          return "Sparkle: "+sparkle+"  Dregraal: "+dregraal;
      }
    </lxslt:script>
  </lxslt:component>

<xsl:template match="/">

    <xsl:apply-templates select="votes/voter/vote"/>
    <xsl:value-of select="results:getResults()"/>

</xsl:template>

<xsl:template match="vote">
    <results:addVote enforced="yes"/>
</xsl:template>

</xsl:stylesheet>
```

We've made several changes here. First, we've told the component to treat `addVote` as an element rather than as a function, so we've changed the signature of `addVote()` to match that of a function linked to an extension element. We'll talk about the parameters in a moment.

The actual function itself has been changed to an extension element. No attributes are required for an extension element, but we're adding one: `enforced`. This attribute tells the script whether we're enforcing the rule that says only single beings and hosts can vote; symbionts are not allowed to vote.

In the script itself, the extension element is represented by the second parameter, in this case called `elem`. To get the value of the enforced attribute, we can use the `getAttribute()` method. This should look familiar; we're calling the same DOM `Element getAttribute()` method as before, but in JavaScript instead of Java or the other languages we've been looking at. The `elem` argument represents a plain old DOM `Element` object.

Finally, we made a slight change to the XPath expressions, for reasons we'll discuss after the next example.

If we were to execute this transformation, the results would look like this:

```
Voting restrictions enforced.Voting restrictions enforced.Voting restrictions
enforced.Voting restrictions enforced.Voting restrictions enforced.Sparkle: 0
Dregraal: 0
```

For every vote, the `addVote` element was accessed, so the `addVote()` function was called. It output the results of the element test, but no votes were actually added, so the tally is inaccurate.

Next, let's look at that tally.

Element Context

Upon first reflection, you may be wondering how we're going to pass in the vote information if there's no parameter for it, as there was when we were creating custom functions. In fact, there is a way to pass this information to the script: the context node.

At any point during the transformation of a document, a single node acts as the context node. When the style sheet asks for text, it's looking for the text of the context node. When it asks for a child element, it's referring to a child of that node.

We'll pass this context node into the extension element's function, as shown in Listing 10.26.

LISTING 10.26   Using Context

```
<?xml version="1.0"?>
<xsl:stylesheet xmlns:xsl="http://www.w3.org/1999/XSL/Transform"
                xmlns:lxslt="http://xml.apache.org/xslt"
                xmlns:results="http://www.example.com/results"
                extension-element-prefixes="results"
                version="1.0">

  <lxslt:component prefix="results" functions="getResults" elements="addVote">
    <lxslt:script lang="javascript">

      var sparkle, dregraal;
```

LISTING 10.26   Continued

```
        sparkle = 0;
        dregraal = 0;

        function addVote(ctx, elem) {
          ctxNode = ctx.getContextNode();
          vote = ctxNode.getFirstChild().getNodeValue();
          if (elem.getAttribute("enforced") == "no") {
              //Just add votes
              if (vote.equals("Sparkle")) {
                  sparkle = sparkle + 1;
              } else {
                  dregraal = dregraal + 1;
              }
          } else {
              voter = ctxNode.parentNode;
              voterStatus = voter.getAttribute("status");
              if (voterStatus.equals("primary")) {
                  if (vote.equals("Sparkle")) {
                      sparkle = sparkle + 1;
                  } else {
                      dregraal = dregraal + 1;
                  }
              }
          }
          return null;
      }

      function getResults(){
          return "Sparkle: "+sparkle+"  Dregraal: "+dregraal;
      }
    </lxslt:script>
  </lxslt:component>
...
<xsl:template match="vote">
    <results:addVote enforced="yes"/>
</xsl:template>

</xsl:stylesheet>
```

The first parameter of an extension element's function represents the context of the request. We can get the actual context node, vote, using the getContextNode() method. From here, vote is just a simple DOM Node object, so we can get its value by getting the value of the first child, its text node.

From there, we're checking to see whether voting restrictions are being enforced. If they're not, we're simply updating totals, as before. If voting restrictions are being enforced, we'll need to check the voter's status.

Because the context node is just a DOM Node object, we can get its parent, voter, from the parentNode attribute of the object. (This is comparable to getParentNode() in Java.) The voter's status is represented by the **status** attribute, so again, we can use a traditional DOM method to get it. If the voter is the primary, we count the vote. If not, we do nothing.

Now when we run the transformation, the voting restrictions will be taken into account:

```
Sparkle: 1  Dregraal: 2
```

C++ and Visual Basic .NET

MSXML doesn't currently support extension elements.

PHP and Perl

Sablotron doesn't currently support extension elements.

External Classes

All this is well and good, but what if you don't want to do your extensions in JavaScript? Maybe you want to keep them separate and private. In that case, you'll want to use an external class to hold your functions.

An *external class* is a single class that holds all the functions that extension elements or functions in use may need to execute. For example, Listing 10.27 shows all of our functions converted to a single Java class, **VoteSystem**.

LISTING 10.27   The **VoteSystem** Functions

```java
import org.apache.xalan.extensions.XSLProcessorContext;
import org.w3c.dom.Element;
import org.w3c.dom.Node;

public class VoteSystem {

    int sparkle = 0;
    int dregraal = 0;

    public String getResults(){
       return "Sparkle: "+sparkle+"  Dregraal: "+dregraal;
    }

    public void addVote( XSLProcessorContext ctx, Element elem)
    {
        Node ctxNode = ctx.getContextNode();
        String vote = ctxNode.getFirstChild().getNodeValue();
        if (elem.getAttribute("enforced").equals("no")) {
            //Just add votes
            if (vote.equals("Sparkle")) {
                sparkle = sparkle + 1;
            } else {
                dregraal = dregraal + 1;
            }
        } else {
```

LISTING 10.27   Continued

```
            Element voter = (Element)ctxNode.getParentNode();
            String voterStatus = voter.getAttribute("status");
             if (voterStatus.equals("primary")) {
                 if (vote.equals("Sparkle")) {
                     sparkle = sparkle + 1;
                 } else {
                     dregraal = dregraal + 1;
                 }
             }
        }
    }
}
```

Note that these are straight conversions from JavaScript. With the exception of a few variable casting and typing issues, the class is identical to what we had. Now we need to tell the style sheet where to find the functions, as shown in Listing 10.28.

LISTING 10.28   Using an External Class

```
<?xml version="1.0"?>
<xsl:stylesheet xmlns:xsl="http://www.w3.org/1999/XSL/Transform"
xmlns:lxslt="http://xml.apache.org/xslt"
                xmlns:results="http://www.example.com/results"
                extension-element-prefixes="results"
                version="1.0">


  <lxslt:component prefix="results" functions="getResults" elements="addVote">
      <lxslt:script lang="javaclass" src="VoteSystem"/>
  </lxslt:component>

<xsl:template match="/">

    <xsl:apply-templates select="votes/voter/vote"/>
    <xsl:value-of select="results:getResults()"/>

</xsl:template>

<xsl:template match="vote">
    <results:addVote enforced="yes"/>
</xsl:template>

</xsl:stylesheet>
```

In this case, the only thing that changes is where the processor looks for the functions.

PHP

There is currently no way to write XSL extensions in PHP.

Perl

Sablotron doesn't support writing XSL extensions in Perl, but the Perl wrapper for the Xalan project from the Apache group does provide such support. I've chosen not to use it for examples here for various reasons, but if you need support for Perl extension functions, it's your only option at present. You can find more information about Xalan at `http://xml.apache.org/xalan-c`, and about `XML::Xalan`, the Perl wrapper for Xalan, at `http://search.cpan.org`.

Summary

XSL transformations can be carried out from the command line of most XLST processors, but their real power comes when you add them to an application.

The most common way to carry out transformations within an application is to use some variation of TrAX (Transformation API for XML). Using this method, a source, style sheet, and result are designated; a `Transformer` object is created using the style sheet object; and this `Transformer` object transforms the source into the result. In some languages, a similar approach is used, where the object itself carries out the transformation using the style information.

Transformations can be integrated with SAX applications. A SAX stream can serve as the source or the result of the transformation, and a reader can use a transformer as the `ContentHandler` to perform the transformation as part of the natural parsing process. Transformations can be chained together with or without `XMLFilter`s.

Programming can also take place within the spreadsheet itself. We looked at JavaScript and Java, but most other languages can also be added to a style sheet as long as the processor supports them. XSLT 1.0 allows extension through functions, which can have a parameter passed in, and elements, which can pass in attribute values and can access the context of the request to pull information directly from the original document.

Review Questions

1. What are the three main components of an XSL transformation?

2. What kind of object can act as the source of a transformation?

3. What are the major steps involved in a transformation in your software?

4. What should you do if you're going to perform several transformations with the same style sheet?

5. How can transformations be used with SAX?

Programming Exercises

1. Create an application that transforms several source documents using a single style sheet.

2. Create an application that transforms a DOM `Node`.

3. Create a transformer as a serializer for a SAX stream.

4. Create an application that chains three transformations together.

CHAPTER 11

SELECTING DATA: XML PATH LANGUAGE (XPATH)

You will learn about the following in this chapter:

- Axes
- Node tests
- Location paths
- XPath abbreviations

- Context nodes
- Predicates
- Built-in XPath functions

*I*n Chapter 9, "Extensible Stylesheet Language Transformations (XSLT)," we talked briefly about XPath as a means for selecting information in the document in order to transform it. In this chapter, we'll go into detail about XPath and how it works.

What Is XPath?

XPath actually serves two purposes. The first is as an addressing mechanism. It provides a way to "point" specifically to a part of an XML document, whether that part is as small as a single character or as large and complex as an entire node-set. This is how we used it in our style sheets in Chapter 9, "Extensible Stylesheet Language Transformations (XSLT)": to select a node such as the `event` element or `newsid` attribute. XPath is used for this purpose not only for XSL Transformations, but also for XLink and XPointer, which we will discuss in Chapter 14, "XML Linking Language (XLink)."

The second use for XPath is as a means for manipulating data. Once an XPath expression locates a particular information item, it has built-in functions that allow actions such as string manipulation and mathematical operations. These functions can be used to output altered data or to locate specific data. For example, we might want to search for all events that fall within a specific month, which would require us to use an XPath expression capable of looking at just the data that precedes the first / character.

In this chapter, we'll take an in-depth look at XPath and how to use it for both of these purposes.

How XPath Works

At its simplest level, XPath works by specifying a progressive series of filtering instructions for a processor. For example, the XPath expression

```
/universe/galaxy/starSystem
```

starts with the entire document, then filters out everything that isn't a **universe** element. It then takes all the children of the **universe** element and eliminates everything that isn't a **galaxy** element, including the **universe** element itself. It then takes the children of those nodes and eliminates everything that isn't a **starSystem** element. The result is a set of nodes, as shown in Figure 11.1.

FIGURE 11.1
XPath progressively narrows the available information until it comes to a final result.

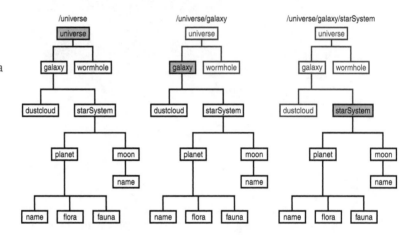

This is a simple example, of course. It uses the "abbreviated" notation for XPath. In this section, we'll look at the full notation, which provides more clarity and flexibility, but first let's set up the test system.

Testing the Results

To demonstrate the examples, we'll use variations on a simple XSL style sheet, as shown in Listing 11.1.

LISTING 11.1   The Demonstration Style Sheet

```
<?xml version="1.0"?>
<xsl:stylesheet xmlns:xsl="http://www.w3.org/1999/XSL/Transform" version="1.0">

<xsl:template match="/">
    The XPath expression: "/"
    evaluates to:
    <xsl:copy-of select="/" />
</xsl:template>

</xsl:stylesheet>
```

In most cases, we'll use `copy-of` instead of `value-of` so we can see the structure of any returned node-sets. This style sheet will pull data from a sample document, shown in Listing 11.2.

LISTING 11.2   The Sample Document

```xml
<?xml version="1.0"?>
<universe>
  <galaxy gid="g3999">
    <dustCloud did="D32" size="6345432"/>
    <dustCloud did="X84" size="9249357213"/>
    <starSystem sid="_22">
      <planet pid="P_22_2">
        <name>Troy 2</name><flora>yes</flora><fauna>no</fauna>
      </planet>
      <planet pid="P_22_7">
        <name>Troy 7</name><flora>yes</flora><fauna>yes</fauna>
      </planet>
      <moon orbits="P_22_7"><name>Unnamed</name></moon>
    </starSystem>
  </galaxy>
  <galaxy gid="g7283">
    <starSystem sid="_95">
      <planet pid="P_95_3">
        <name>Violetta 3</name><flora>yes</flora><fauna>yes</fauna>
      </planet>
      <planet pid="P_95_4">
        <name>Violetta 4</name><flora>yes</flora><fauna>yes</fauna>
      </planet>
    </starSystem>
  </galaxy>
  <wormhole wid="WFRSA" stable="no" start="g7283"/>
  <wormhole wid="WFRSB" stable="yes" start="g3999" destination="g7283"/>
</universe>
```

Just as you did in Chapter 9, check the documentation for your XSLT processor to determine how to process the style sheet. For Xalan-Java 2, type this:

```
java org.apache.xalan.xslt.Process -IN input.xml -XSL style.xsl -OUT output.txt
```

To see the result of the text expression, alter the style sheet as shown in Listing 11.3.

LISTING 11.3   Testing the Expression

```xml
<?xml version="1.0"?>
<xsl:stylesheet xmlns:xsl="http://www.w3.org/1999/XSL/Transform" version="1.0">

<xsl:template match="/">
    The XPath expression: "/universe/galaxy/starSystem"
    evaluates to:
    <xsl:copy-of select="/universe/galaxy/starSystem" />
</xsl:template>

</xsl:stylesheet>
```

The results (see Listing 11.4) have the structure shown in Figure 11.1.

LISTING 11.4   The Resulting Node-Set

```
<?xml version="1.0" encoding="UTF-8"?>

The XPath expression: "/universe/galaxy/starSystem"
evaluates to:
<starSystem sid="_22">
   <planet pid="P_22_2">
     <name>Troy 2</name><flora>yes</flora><fauna>no</fauna>
   </planet>
   <planet pid="P_22_7">
     <name>Troy 7</name><flora>yes</flora><fauna>yes</fauna>
   </planet>
   <moon orbits="P_22_7"><name>Unnamed</name></moon>
 </starSystem><starSystem sid="_95">
   <planet pid="P_95_3">
     <name>Violetta 3</name><flora>yes</flora><fauna>yes</fauna>
   </planet>
   <planet pid="P_95_4">
     <name>Violetta 4</name><flora>yes</flora><fauna>yes</fauna>
   </planet>
   <moon orbits="P_22_7"><name>Unnamed</name></moon>
 </starSystem>
```

As we go through the chapter, we'll test expressions by plugging them into the style sheet and processing the transformation.

Location Steps

An XPath expression is built out of one or more location steps, each of which can consist of three parts: an axis, a node test, and an optional predicate. Let's look first at the axes and the node test.

In nonabbreviated form, the `/universe/galaxy/starSystem` example we used earlier looks like this:

`/child::universe/child::galaxy/child::starSystem`

This expression represents three location steps, each of which has an axis and a node test. In the case of the first step, the context node is the document root. The first step is

`child::universe`

Because the axis is `child`, the processor first selects the children of the context element (the document root). Of these elements, it looks for any that are named `universe` and thus passes the node test.

This isn't much of a test, of course, because there is only one child of the document root, and it is called `universe`. Nevertheless, this node-set of one node is the result of this location step. It becomes the context node for the next location step:

```
child::galaxy
```

First the processor selects all the children of the context node. Of those, it chooses only the ones named `galaxy`.

None of this is very different from the abbreviated version, except that `child` is the default axis. As we'll see in the upcoming section titled "Axes," there are many different kinds of axes, such as `parent`, `sibling`, and `descendant`. For example, we could have written the XPath expression as

```
/descendant::starSystem
```

and skipped the first two steps. Here again, the context element is the document root, as evidenced by the leading slash (`/`). The `descendant` axis first selects all the descendants of the document root (every node in the document) and then narrows its selection down to just those named `starSystem`.

The third portion of a location step, the predicate, narrows the choice even more. For example, the location step

```
/descendant::starSystem[@sid='_95']
```

takes the two `starSystem` elements and filters them, keeping only the ones that have a `sid` attribute of `_95`.

Abbreviations

Strictly speaking, the unabbreviated versions of the location step in this example is

```
/descendant::starSystem[attribute::sid='_95']
```

Predicates allow more precise filtering, and also allow the application of functions, discussed later in this section.

Context

The results of an XPath expression depend on the context node as the starting place. The overall context, however, is more than just the context node. Instead, it's any information that might influence the final result, including

- **Context node**—The node currently being analyzed.
- **Context size**—The number of nodes in the node-set currently being analyzed.
- **Context position**—The position of the context node within the current node-set.
- **Namespaces in scope**—Namespaces that exist within the scope of the context node.
- **Functions in scope**—Functions, either built-in or added by the application, that exist within the scope of the context node.

Each of these items becomes important under a particular set of circumstances. As we discuss those circumstances, we'll cover each item in greater detail.

Types of Returned Data

An XPath expression (or location step, for that matter) can return one of four types of data, which may or may not be filtered or analyzed further:

- `string`—A string value, such as `'Troy 7'`, or `'yes'`, or even `'2'`, is a series of characters that may or may not include whitespace.

- `number`—A number such as `2` or `50` or `-2342`, to which mathematical operations such as addition and multiplication can be applied.

Strictly Speaking

The XPath definition of a number is any 64-bit floating point number, as specified in IEEE 754.

- `boolean`—One of two possible values: `true` or `false`. A `boolean` value is typically returned by a function or similar expression, as opposed to an actual location step.

- `node-set`—A set of nodes, such as an element and its children. A node-set may include attributes carried by an element, text within an element, or even namespaces and processing instructions.

Different types of operations produce different result types.

Functions

XPath has a number of built-in functions. All functions return a value, but some also manipulate the data in some way. For example, the `position()` function simply returns the position of the context node within the current set, whereas the `concat()` function concatenates any number of strings into a single value. Each data type has a set of functions associated with it.

We will discuss functions in detail in the "Functions" section.

Axes

Now that you've gotten an overview of XPath, let's start to get specific. The first step in understanding XPath is to understand axes and how they affect the nodes that can potentially end up in the result.

In this section, we'll take a look at each axis type by setting a context (using the template's `match` attribute in the style sheet) and then using the * node test, which selects all nodes that are part of the axis.

Child

The `child` axis is probably the easiest to understand, and is certainly the most commonly used. It includes the child elements of the context node. For example, Listing 11.5 shows the style sheet edited so that the context node is the first **starSystem** element. (Don't worry about the expression we used to set the context; it will become clear as we go along. For now, just understand that **starSystem _22** is the context node.) It selects all nodes within the **child** axis.

LISTING 11.5   The child Axis

```
<?xml version="1.0"?>
<xsl:stylesheet xmlns:xsl="http://www.w3.org/1999/XSL/Transform"
                version="1.0">

<xsl:template match="/">
    <xsl:apply-templates select="/universe/galaxy/starSystem[@sid='_22']"/>
</xsl:template>

<xsl:template match="*">
    The XPath expression: "child::*"
    evaluates to:
    <xsl:copy-of select="child::*" />
</xsl:template>

</xsl:stylesheet>
```

Let's take a careful look at the style sheet before we move on to the results. The first template selects the document root for processing. This will keep nodes from being processed by the default templates within the processor, so we can see only the nodes we specifically ask for.

The template then selects a specific node that we want as the context node and sends it off looking for other templates.

The only other template is the second template, which, because it uses *****, will match any node that comes to it. Fortunately, because of the first template, the only nodes that come to it are those that are sent off by the **apply-templates** element. In this way, we can control the context node for our XPath expression, selected in the second template.

In this case, the context node is **starSystem _22**, and the XPath expression being tested is **child::***. The resulting node-set is shown in Listing 11.6.

LISTING 11.6   The child Axis Results

```
<?xml version="1.0" encoding="UTF-8"?>
    The XPath expression: "child::*"
    evaluates to:
    <planet pid="P_22_2">
        <name>Troy 2</name><flora>yes</flora><fauna>no</fauna>
      </planet><planet pid="P_22_7">
        <name>Troy 7</name><flora>yes</flora><fauna>yes</fauna>
      </planet><moon orbits="P_22_7"><name>Unnamed</name></moon>
```

This node-set includes all the children of the specific `starSystem` node. Notice that the result doesn't include the `starSystem` element itself.

It's important to note that the `name`, `flora`, and `fauna` elements appear in the resultset only because they are part of the node-set that includes the `planet` and `moon` elements. The actual child nodes are shown in Figure 11.2.

FIGURE 11.2
The `child` axis includes only the direct children of the context node.

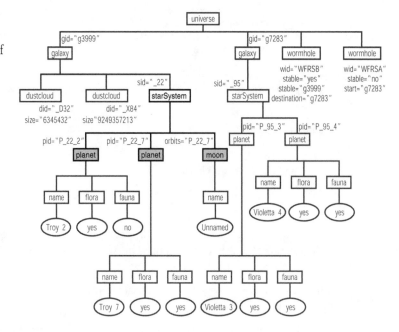

Self

To include the context node in the result, you will need to use the `self` axis or one of its variations. As the name implies, the `self` axis selects only the context node itself, as demonstrated by Listing 11.7.

LISTING 11.7 The `self` Axis

```
<?xml version="1.0"?>
<xsl:stylesheet xmlns:xsl="http://www.w3.org/1999/XSL/Transform"
                version="1.0">

<xsl:template match="/">
    <xsl:apply-templates select="/universe/galaxy/starSystem[@sid='_22']"/>
</xsl:template>

<xsl:template match="*">
    The XPath expression: "self::*"
    evaluates to:
    <xsl:copy-of select="self::*" />
```

LISTING 11.7   Continued

```
</xsl:template>

</xsl:stylesheet>
```

The resulting node-set includes only the context node, as shown in Listing 11.8 and Figure 11.3.

LISTING 11.8   The Context Node

```
<?xml version="1.0" encoding="UTF-8"?>

The XPath expression: "self::*"
evaluates to:
<starSystem sid="_22">
   <planet pid="P_22_2">
     <name>Troy 2</name><flora>yes</flora><fauna>no</fauna>
   </planet>
   <planet pid="P_22_7">
     <name>Troy 7</name><flora>yes</flora><fauna>yes</fauna>
   </planet>
   <moon orbits="P_22_7"><name>Unnamed</name></moon>
 </starSystem>
```

FIGURE 11.3

The `self` axis includes only the context node.

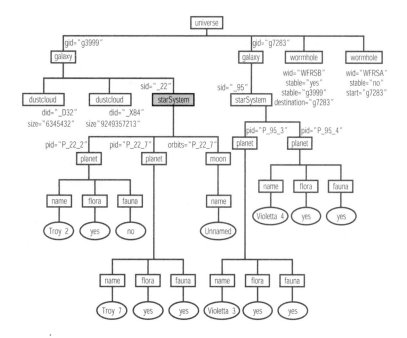

Parents

The `parent` axis selects the parent of the context node. For example, we can alter the style sheet to look for the parent of the context node, as in Listing 11.9.

LISTING 11.9 The parent Axis

```
...
<xsl:template match="*">
    The XPath expression: "parent::*"
    evaluates to:
    <xsl:copy-of select="parent::*" />
</xsl:template>
...
```

This shows the `galaxy` element that contains `starSystem _22`, as in Listing 11.10 and Figure 11.4.

LISTING 11.10 The Parent Node

```
<?xml version="1.0" encoding="UTF-8"?>

    The XPath expression: "parent::*"
    evaluates to:
    <galaxy gid="g3999">
    <dustCloud did="D32" size="6345432"/>
    <dustCloud did="X84" size="9249357213"/>
    <starSystem sid="_22">
        <planet pid="P_22_2">
          <name>Troy 2</name><flora>yes</flora><fauna>no</fauna>
        </planet>
        <planet pid="P_22_7">
          <name>Troy 7</name><flora>yes</flora><fauna>yes</fauna>
        </planet>
        <moon orbits="P_22_7"><name>Unnamed</name></moon>
      </starSystem>
    </galaxy>
```

It's important to note that elements are not the only nodes that have parents. All nodes, with the exception of the document root, have parents. For text nodes, comments, and processing instructions, it's the element that contains them (or the document root, in the case of comments and processing instructions that are not part of any element).

Attributes also have parents. The parent of an attribute is the element that carries it, but strangely enough, the attribute is not considered the child of the element, and is not selected by the `child` axis. (It's sort of like having a teenager!)

FIGURE 11.4

The parent axis.

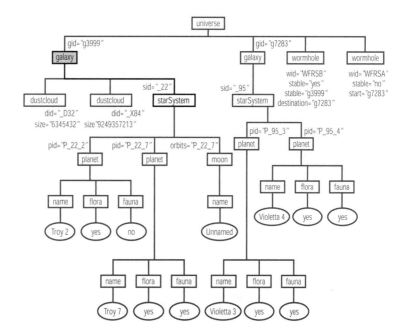

Siblings

Just as in real life, the siblings of a node are the nodes that have the same parents. Note that this description doesn't mention anything about the name or type of the node. Any node that has the same parent node as the context node is a sibling.

Siblings come in two varieties: `preceding-siblings` (those that come before the context node in the document) and `following-siblings` (those that come after it).

Listing 11.11 shows a change so that the context node is `planet P_22_7`. The style sheet selects first the `preceding-siblings`, then the `following-siblings`.

LISTING 11.11   Siblings of a Node

```
<?xml version="1.0"?>
<xsl:stylesheet xmlns:xsl="http://www.w3.org/1999/XSL/Transform"
                version="1.0">

<xsl:template match="/">
    <xsl:apply-templates
        select="/universe/galaxy/starSystem/planet[@pid='P_22_7']"/>
</xsl:template>

<xsl:template match="*">
    The XPath expression: "preceding-sibling::*"
    evaluates to:
    <xsl:copy-of select="preceding-sibling::*" />

- - - - - - - - - - - - - - - - - - - - - - - - -
```

LISTING 11.11   Continued

```
      The XPath expression: "following-sibling::*"
      evaluates to:
      <xsl:copy-of select="following-sibling::*" />

  </xsl:template>

  </xsl:stylesheet>
```

The resulting document shows a **planet** as the **preceding-sibling**, and a **moon** as the **following-sibling**. Note that if more elements were present in the document, they would also be selected by these expressions. Listing 11.12 and Figure 11.5 show the results.

LISTING 11.12   Sibling Nodes

```
      <?xml version="1.0" encoding="UTF-8"?>

      The XPath expression: "preceding-sibling::*"
      evaluates to:
      <planet pid="P_22_2">
          <name>Troy 2</name><flora>yes</flora><fauna>no</fauna>
      </planet>


      - - - - - - - - - - - - - - - - - - - - - - - - - -

      The XPath expression: "following-sibling::*"
      evaluates to:
      <moon orbits="P_22_7"><name>Unnamed</name></moon>
```

FIGURE 11.5

Preceding and following siblings.

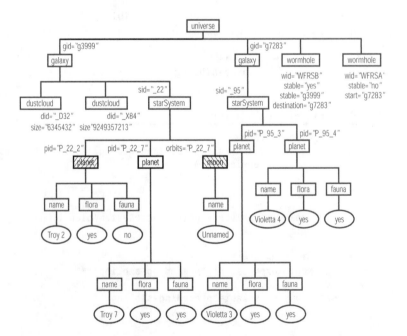

Descendants

Descendants are a node's children, and children's children, and children's children's children, and so on. Listing 11.13 shows the style sheet once again using **starSystem _22** as the context node, and selecting all of its descendants.

LISTING 11.13   Descendant Nodes

```
<?xml version="1.0"?>
<xsl:stylesheet xmlns:xsl="http://www.w3.org/1999/XSL/Transform"
                version="1.0">

<xsl:template match="/">
    <xsl:apply-templates
        select="/universe/galaxy/starSystem[@sid='_22']"/>
</xsl:template>

<xsl:template match="*">
    The XPath expression: "descendant::*"
    evaluates to:
    <xsl:copy-of select="descendant::*" />
</xsl:template>

</xsl:stylesheet>
```

From the context, you might assume that the resultset here would consist of the two **planet**s and the **moon** and their children, and you'd be right. But you might not realize how right. Listing 11.14 shows the resulting node-set. (I've adjusted the formatting on it to make it a bit more clear.) Figure 11.6 also shows the relevant nodes.

LISTING 11.14   The Descendant Nodes

```
<?xml version="1.0" encoding="UTF-8"?>

    The XPath expression: "descendant::*"
    evaluates to:
    <planet pid="P_22_2">
        <name>Troy 2</name><flora>yes</flora><fauna>no</fauna>
    </planet>
    <name>Troy 2</name>
    <flora>yes</flora>
    <fauna>no</fauna>

    <planet pid="P_22_7">
        <name>Troy 7</name><flora>yes</flora><fauna>yes</fauna>
    </planet>
    <name>Troy 7</name>
    <flora>yes</flora>
    <fauna>yes</fauna>

    <moon orbits="P_22_7">
```

LISTING 11.14   Continued

```
            <name>Unnamed</name>
        </moon>
        <name>Unnamed</name>
```

FIGURE 11.6
The descendant nodes.

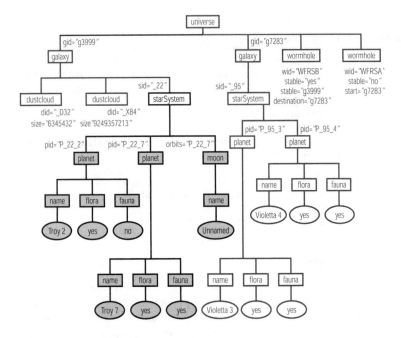

Notice that the children are output along with all of their children, because the "grandchildren" are part of the child nodes. These grandchild nodes are then output themselves, because they are also descendants of the context node.

What About the Text Nodes?

You might have noticed that the text nodes are highlighted in the figure, but don't appear in the output. This is because of the way the * node test handles things, as you'll see in the next section. The text nodes are part of the `descendant` axis.

A similar effect takes place with the `ancestor` axis, as shown in Listings 11.15 and 11.16.

LISTING 11.15   The ancestor Axis

```
<?xml version="1.0"?>
<xsl:stylesheet xmlns:xsl="http://www.w3.org/1999/XSL/Transform"
                version="1.0">

<xsl:template match="/">
    <xsl:apply-templates
```

LISTING 11.15   Continued

```
            select="/universe/galaxy/starSystem[@sid='_22']"/>
</xsl:template>

<xsl:template match="*">
    The XPath expression: "ancestor::*"
    evaluates to:
    <xsl:copy-of select="ancestor::*" />
</xsl:template>

</xsl:stylesheet>
```

LISTING 11.16   The Ancestor Nodes

```
<?xml version="1.0" encoding="UTF-8"?>

    The XPath expression: "ancestor::*"
    evaluates to:
    <universe>
  <galaxy gid="g3999">
    <dustCloud did="D32" size="6345432"/>
    <dustCloud did="X84" size="9249357213"/>
    <starSystem sid="_22">
        <planet pid="P_22_2">
          <name>Troy 2</name><flora>yes</flora><fauna>no</fauna>
        </planet>
        <planet pid="P_22_7">
          <name>Troy 7</name><flora>yes</flora><fauna>yes</fauna>
        </planet>
        <moon orbits="P_22_7"><name>Unnamed</name></moon>
     </starSystem>
  </galaxy>
  <galaxy gid="g7283">
    <starSystem sid="_95">
        <planet pid="P_95_3">
          <name>Violetta 3</name><flora>yes</flora><fauna>yes</fauna>
        </planet>
        <planet pid="P_95_4">
          <name>Violetta 4</name><flora>yes</flora><fauna>yes</fauna>
        </planet>
        <moon orbits="P_22_7"><name>Unnamed</name></moon>
     </starSystem>
  </galaxy>
  <wormhole wid="WFRSA" stable="no" start="g7283"/>
  <wormhole wid="WFRSB" stable="yes" start="g3999" destination="g7283"/>
</universe>
<galaxy gid="g3999">
    <dustCloud did="D32" size="6345432"/>
    <dustCloud did="X84" size="9249357213"/>
    <starSystem sid="_22">
        <planet pid="P_22_2">
          <name>Troy 2</name><flora>yes</flora><fauna>no</fauna>
```

LISTING 11.16   Continued

```
        </planet>
        <planet pid="P_22_7">
          <name>Troy 7</name><flora>yes</flora><fauna>yes</fauna>
        </planet>
        <moon orbits="P_22_7"><name>Unnamed</name></moon>
      </starSystem>
    </galaxy>
```

The node's parent, `galaxy`, is output by itself, and as part of `galaxy`'s parent, `universe` (see Figure 11.7). Both are part of the `ancestor` axis.

In each case, however, it's important to remember that while entire structures are being output, only the single nodes are actually part of the axis. Their content is only along for the ride.

FIGURE 11.7

The `ancestor` axis.

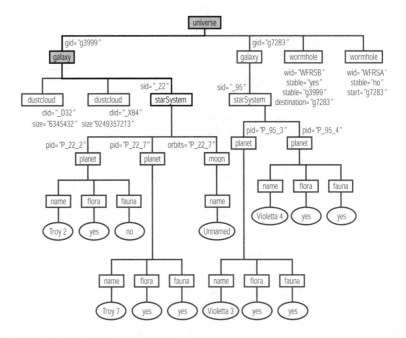

Both `descendant` and `ancestor` allow you to include the context node by using the `descendant-or-self` or `ancestor-or-self` axis.

Preceding and Following

The `preceding` and `following` axes are to `preceding-sibling` and `following-sibling` what `ancestor` and `descendant` are to `parent` and `child`. While `preceding-sibling` and `following-sibling` select only the nodes that share parents with the context node, `preceding` and `following` select those nodes and all their descendants, as shown in Figures 11.8 and 11.9.

FIGURE 11.8

The `preceding` axis.

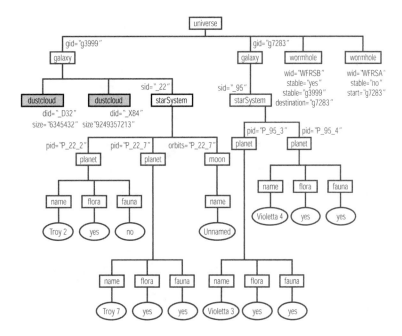

FIGURE 11.9

The `following` axis.

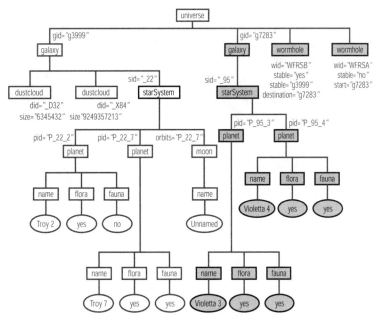

Note that the `following` and `preceding` axes don't include the context node itself, nor do they include any of its `descendant`s or `ancestor`s. In fact, these five axes—`ancestor`, `descendant`, `self`, `preceding`, and `following`—cover the entire document, as shown in Figure 11.10.

FIGURE 11.10

The combination of ancestor, descendant, self, preceding, and following.

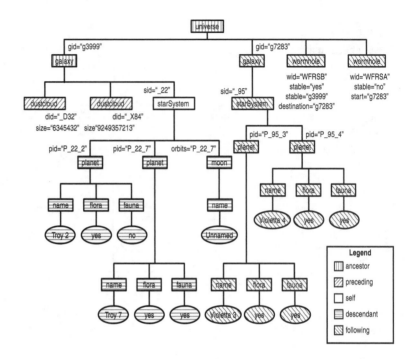

Attribute

You may have noticed that none of the axes discussed so far includes attributes. Attributes have their own axis, `attribute`. The `attribute` axis includes only the attribute nodes that belong to the context node, which must, of course, be an element.

For example, Listing 11.17 shows the style sheet altered to output the attributes of the worm-hole designated WFRSB.

LISTING 11.17   The `attribute` Axis

```
<?xml version="1.0"?>
<xsl:stylesheet xmlns:xsl="http://www.w3.org/1999/XSL/Transform"
                version="1.0">

<xsl:template match="/">
    <xsl:apply-templates
        select="/universe/wormhole[@wid='WFRSB']" />
</xsl:template>

<xsl:template match="*">
    The XPath expression: "attribute::"
    evaluates to:
    <xsl:for-each select="attribute::*">
    -|- <xsl:value-of select="." /> -|-
    </xsl:for-each>
</xsl:template>

</xsl:stylesheet>
```

The `attribute` axis must be used from the context of an element, which is sent off to the bottom template by the top template. Because of the way XSLT works, the attributes must be explicitly called using a `for-each` loop. Also, because of the structure of an attribute node, you must use `value-of` rather than `copy-of`.

Executing the transaction gives the results shown in Listing 11.18 and Figure 11.11.

LISTING 11.18   The Attribute Nodes

```
<?xml version="1.0" encoding="UTF-8"?>

The XPath expression: "attribute::"
evaluates to:

- | - WFRSB - | -

- | - yes - | -

- | - g3999 - | -

- | - g7283 - | -
```

FIGURE 11.11

The attribute nodes.

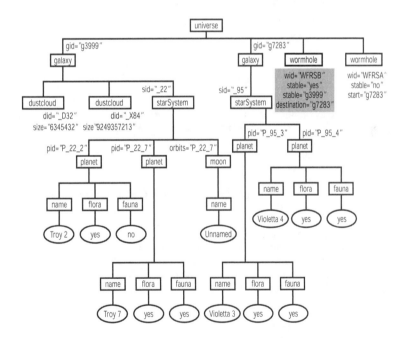

Namespace

Namespace nodes are not part of the main structure of parents and children, but every node is associated with a namespace node for every namespace in scope, whether or not the node is part of the namespace.

For example, we can add two namespaces to the source document, as in Listing 11.19.

LISTING 11.19   Adding Namespaces to the Document

```
<?xml version="1.0"?>
<universe xmlns="http://www.example.com/default"
          xmlns:tourist="http://www.example.com/tourist" >
  <galaxy gid="g3999">
...
  </galaxy>
  <galaxy gid="g7283">
...
  </galaxy>
  <wormhole wid="WFRSA" stable="no" start="g7283"/>
  <wormhole wid="WFRSB" stable="yes" start="g3999" destination="g7283"/>
</universe>
```

`http://www.example.com/default` is the default namespace, so all elements belong to that namespace, but we won't add any nodes to the `tourist` namespace.

We also need to make changes to the style sheet. Although there are no prefixes on any of the elements, they all belong to the `http://www.example.com/default` namespace, so in order for the style sheet to find them, it must declare that namespace and use it in the XPath expression, as shown in Listing 11.20.

LISTING 11.20   The `namespace` Axis

```
<?xml version="1.0"?>
<xsl:stylesheet xmlns:xsl="http://www.w3.org/1999/XSL/Transform"
                xmlns:info="http://www.example.com/default"
                version="1.0">

<xsl:template match="/">
    <xsl:apply-templates
        select="/info:universe/info:wormhole[@wid='WFRSB']"/>
</xsl:template>

<xsl:template match="*">
    The XPath expression: "namespace::*"
    evaluates to:
    <xsl:for-each select="namespace::*">
    -|- <xsl:value-of select="." /> -|-
    </xsl:for-each>
</xsl:template>

</xsl:stylesheet>
```

The style sheet will output all namespace nodes associated with the `wormhole` element, as shown in Listing 11.21.

LISTING 11.21   Namespace Nodes

```
<?xml version="1.0" encoding="UTF-8"?>

    The XPath expression: "namespace::*"
    evaluates to:

    -|- http://www.example.com/default -|-

    -|- http://www.example.com/tourist -|-
```

Notice that both namespaces are represented, even though the `wormhole` element has nothing to do with the `tourist` namespace.

Searching for Namespaces

Unfortunately, XSLT doesn't allow the `namespace` axis in a `select` attribute, so although it's possible to examine the in-scope namespaces for a node, it's impossible to select all nodes for a specific namespace.

Node Tests

Axes are just the first part of a location step, and by themselves can't accomplish anything. At a minimum, they must be coupled with a node test.

The examples in the previous section used the `*` node test to complete the expression, which selects all nodes returned by the axis. Part of what determines the makeup of this node-set is the principal node type.

Each axis has a principal node type that determines its initial makeup. For example, the primary node type for the `attribute` axis is, of course, the attribute, so the `*` node test returns only attribute nodes. Similarly, the principal node type for the `namespace` axis is the namespace, so the `*` node test returns only namespace nodes.

For all other axes, the principal node type is the element. That doesn't mean that we can't get at other node types, such as text, but it does mean that we'll need node tests other than `*` to do it.

Names

The most common node test is the name test. A name node test looks at the nodes returned by the axis and returns only those whose names match the test. For example, Listing 11.22 shows a change to the style sheet so that the context node is `starSystem _22`.

LISTING 11.22   The Name Node Test

```
<?xml version="1.0"?>
<xsl:stylesheet xmlns:xsl="http://www.w3.org/1999/XSL/Transform"
                version="1.0">

<xsl:template match="/">
    <xsl:apply-templates
        select="/universe/galaxy/starSystem[@sid='_22']"/>
</xsl:template>

<xsl:template match="*">
    The XPath expression: "child::planet"
    evaluates to:
        <xsl:copy-of select="child::planet" />
</xsl:template>

</xsl:stylesheet>
```

The XPath expression `child::planet` uses the `child` axis, so all children of the `starSystem` element are selected to start with. This includes two `planet`s and a `moon`, but only the `planet`s match the name node test, so only they are returned, as shown in Listing 11.23 and Figure 11.12.

LISTING 11.23   Name Node Test Results

```
<?xml version="1.0" encoding="UTF-8"?>

    The XPath expression: "child::planet"
    evaluates to:
        <planet pid="P_22_2">
          <name>Troy 2</name><flora>yes</flora><fauna>no</fauna>
        </planet><planet pid="P_22_7">
          <name>Troy 7</name><flora>yes</flora><fauna>yes</fauna>
        </planet>
```

We have, in fact, been using the name node test all along, though it may not be obvious because of its abbreviated form. Remember, the expression

```
/universe/galaxy/starSystem[@sid='_22']
```

is the abbreviated form of

```
/child::universe/child::galaxy/child::starSystem[attribute::sid='_22']
```

Both the abbreviated form and multiple steps are covered in the upcoming section "Location Paths."

FIGURE 11.12

The name node test.

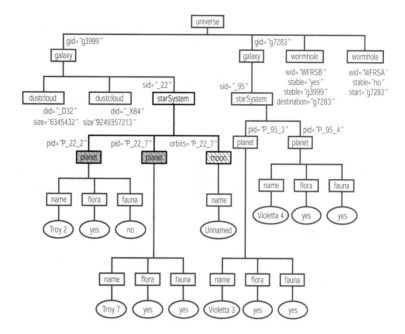

Text Nodes

So far we've dealt with elements and attributes, but nowhere have we returned text nodes, unless they were part of another element being returned. As you can see in several of the figures, however, they were often part of the axis. For example, the descendants of an element include the text node children of any of its children or other descendants.

By using the * node test, we have only returned the principal node type, which is never text. To get to a text node, you need to use the `text()` node test.

The `text()` node test selects any members of the axis that are also text nodes. For example, Listing 11.24 shows the style sheet selecting all the text node descendants of `planet p_22_7`.

LISTING 11.24   The `text()` Node Test

```
<?xml version="1.0"?>
<xsl:stylesheet xmlns:xsl="http://www.w3.org/1999/XSL/Transform"
                version="1.0">

<xsl:template match="/">
    <xsl:apply-templates
        select="/universe/galaxy/starSystem/planet[@pid='P_22_7']"/>
</xsl:template>

<xsl:template match="*">
    The XPath expression: "descendant::text()"
    evaluates to:
```

LISTING 11.24   Continued

```
            <xsl:copy-of select="descendant::text()" />
    </xsl:template>

</xsl:stylesheet>
```

The result is all the text nodes that descend from the `planet`, as in Listing 11.25. (I've refor-matted slightly for clarity.)

LISTING 11.25   The Descendant Text Nodes

```
<?xml version="1.0" encoding="UTF-8"?>

    The XPath expression: "descendant::text()"
    evaluates to:

        Troy 7
        yes
        yes
```

As shown in Figure 11.13, all the descendant nodes are part of the `descendant` axis, but the expression only returns the text nodes.

FIGURE 11.13

The descendant text nodes.

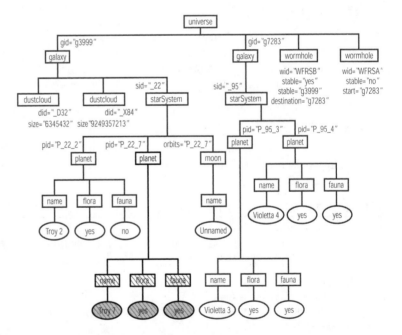

Comment and Processing Instruction Nodes

Just as text nodes need their own node test, so do comments and processing instructions. We can add a comment and a processing instruction to the input data, as in Listing 11.26.

LISTING 11.26   Adding Comments and Processing Instructions

```
<?xml version="1.0"?>
<universe>
  <galaxy gid="g3999">
    <dustCloud did="D32" size="6345432"/>
    <dustCloud did="X84" size="9249357213"/>
    <starSystem sid="_22">
      <?updateData ref="3/30/56"?>
      <planet pid="P_22_2">
        <name>Troy 2</name><flora>yes</flora><fauna>no</fauna>
      </planet>
      <planet pid="P_22_7">
        <name>Troy 7</name><flora>yes</flora><fauna>yes</fauna>
      </planet>
      <!-- Moons without an official designation should be listed
          as "unnamed". -->
      <moon orbits="P_22_7"><name>Unnamed</name></moon>
    </starSystem>
  </galaxy>
...
</universe>
```

If we set the context node to be `starSystem _22`, as in Listing 11.27, we can select comments and processing instructions using the `comment()` and `processing-instruction()` node tests.

LISTING 11.27   The `comment()` and `processing-instruction()` Node Tests

```
<?xml version="1.0"?>
<xsl:stylesheet xmlns:xsl="http://www.w3.org/1999/XSL/Transform"
                version="1.0">

<xsl:template match="/">
    <xsl:apply-templates select="/universe/galaxy/starSystem[@sid='_22']"/>
</xsl:template>

<xsl:template match="*">
    The XPath expression: "descendant::comment()"
    evaluates to:
       <xsl:value-of select="descendant::comment()" />

    The XPath expression: "descendant::processing-instruction()"
    evaluates to:
       <xsl:value-of select="descendant::processing-instruction()" />
</xsl:template>

</xsl:stylesheet>
```

The result is the content of these two information items, as shown in Listing 11.28.

LISTING 11.28   The Comment and Processing Instruction Nodes

```
<?xml version="1.0" encoding="UTF-8"?>

    The XPath expression: "descendant::comment()"
    evaluates to:
        Moons without an official designation should be listed
            as "unnamed".

    The XPath expression: "descendant::processing-instruction()"
    evaluates to:
        ref="3/30/56"
```

Note that we could have produced duplicates of the information items themselves, rather than just the content, by using `copy-of` rather than `value-of`.

All Nodes

Because the * node test only selects information items that fit the principal node test of the axis, it will never select the comment, processing instruction, and text nodes present in the structure. The `node()` node test, however, selects all nodes, no matter what their type. For example, Listing 11.29 shows the style sheet modified to output all children of `starSystem _22`, no matter their type.

LISTING 11.29   The `node()` Node Test

```
<?xml version="1.0"?>
<xsl:stylesheet xmlns:xsl="http://www.w3.org/1999/XSL/Transform"
                version="1.0">

<xsl:template match="/">
    <xsl:apply-templates select="/universe/galaxy/starSystem[@sid='_22']"/>
</xsl:template>

<xsl:template match="*">
    The XPath expression: "child::node()"
    evaluates to:
        <xsl:value-of select="child::node()" />
</xsl:template>

</xsl:stylesheet>
```

The result is that all the child nodes are output, including the comment and processing instruction, as shown in Listing 11.30.

LISTING 11.30   All Child Nodes

```
<?xml version="1.0" encoding="UTF-8"?>

    The XPath expression: "child::node()"
    evaluates to:

        <?updateData ref="3/30/56"?>
```

LISTING 11.30   Continued

```
<planet pid="P_22_2">
  <name>Troy 2</name><flora>yes</flora><fauna>no</fauna>
</planet>
<planet pid="P_22_7">
  <name>Troy 7</name><flora>yes</flora><fauna>yes</fauna>
</planet>
<!-Moons without an official designation should be listed
    as "unnamed".->
<moon orbits="P_22_7"><name>Unnamed</name></moon>
```

Notice that while the comment and processing instruction nodes are returned, the attribute nodes are not. Remember, the element is the parent of the attributes it holds, but they're not its children.

Location Paths

Now that you're familiar with the basic units of a location step, it's time to start combining them into location paths. Each step takes the previous context node and generates its own resultset.

In this section, we'll look at how these steps are combined, and we'll start using abbreviated forms where possible.

Combining Steps and the Context Node

Throughout the chapter, we've been combining location steps as we set the context node for each transaction. For example, at the start of the chapter, when we wrote

```
/universe/galaxy/starSystem
```

we really meant

```
/child::universe/child::galaxy/child::starSystem
```

which is three location steps combined into a location path, with a slash (/) separating each step. On its own, each step should now make sense. Each consists of the `child` axis and a named node test.

While you may have an instinctual understanding of how this works as a "filtering" of nodes, it's important to understand how it works at a deeper level.

The first step

```
/child::universe
```

looks at all the children of the document root, and selects only those named `universe`. The single `universe` element node becomes the context node for the next step:

```
child::galaxy
```

This step selects all the child nodes of the `universe` node, and returns only those that pass the `galaxy` name test. At this point, the resultset consists of two nodes, as shown in Figure 11.14.

FIGURE 11.14
The result of the second location step.

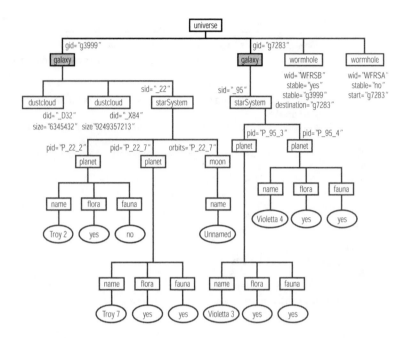

From here, one more location step remains, but processing it is not a single operation. Instead, the location step is evaluated twice—once for each of the nodes in the previous resulting node-set. Each time, a different `galaxy` node becomes the context node, and the location step is evaluated. The overall result is the union of the two resulting node-sets, as shown in Figure 11.15.

FIGURE 11.15
The overall resultset.

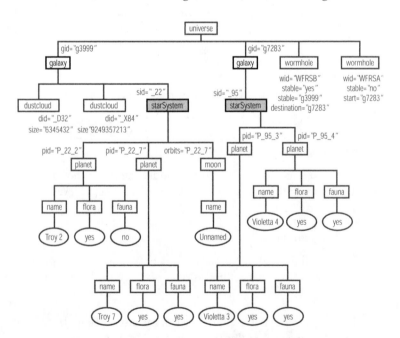

Some Examples

A location path can contain as many location steps as necessary, as long as at each step the previous resulting nodes each become the context node. Take, for example, the expression

```
/descendant::planet/child::name
```

The first step selects all descendants of the document root—which is to say, every single element and text node in the document—and returns those named `planet`. Each of those nodes then becomes the context node for the second location step, which selects all child nodes with the name `name`. The results are shown in Figure 11.16.

FIGURE 11.16

The `name` children of `planet`s.

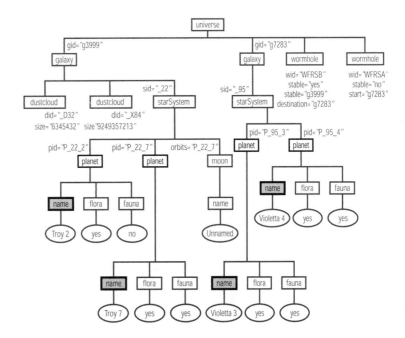

There is no rule that says that a location path must progress smoothly in one direction or another. Figure 11.17 shows the result of the expression

```
/descendant::name/parent::*
```

In this case, the first step selects all `name` descendants of the document root. Each of these nodes then becomes the context node for the expression

```
parent::*
```

The resulting node-set contains four `planet`s and a `moon`.

As a third example, consider an expression that selects the names of `planet`s that come before a `starSystem` in the document:

```
/descendant::starSystem/preceding::planet/child::name
```

FIGURE 11.17
A location path can move in more than one direction.

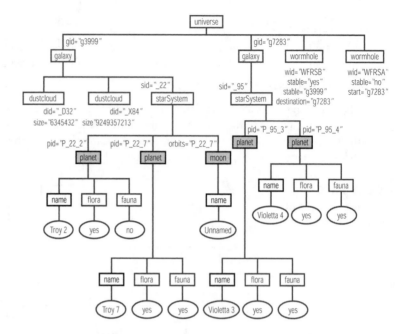

The first step is familiar by now: It simply selects all the **starSystem** elements in the document, as shown in Figure 11.18.

FIGURE 11.18
The **starSystem** nodes.

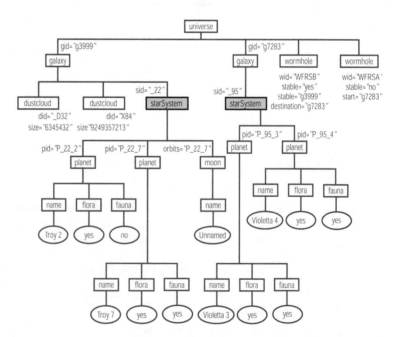

The second step takes a little bit more thought. Remember, each of the two `starSystem` nodes gets its turn as the context node. The first `starSystem` node has two preceding nodes, but they are both `dustclouds`; neither satisfies the expression

```
preceding::planet
```

Figure 11.19 shows the result of the same location step applied with the second `starSystem` as the context node.

FIGURE 11.19

The preceding `planet` nodes.

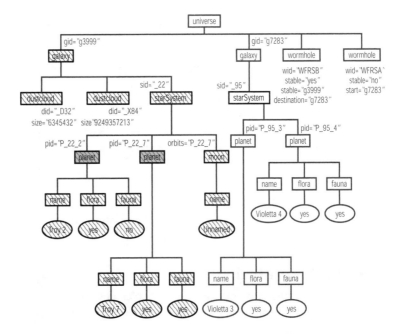

The two `planet` nodes are selected. Each of these then becomes the context node for the third location step

```
child::name
```

as shown in Figure 11.20.

FIGURE 11.20

The `name` child nodes.

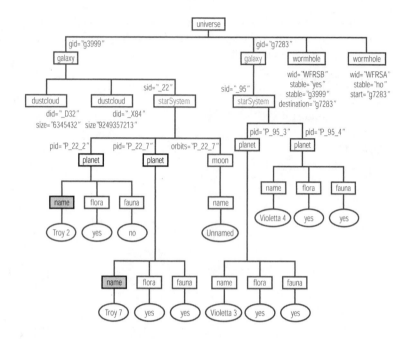

In practice, you will rarely see location steps written out in long form. Instead, they're typically expressed using abbreviations where possible.

The Abbreviated Form

In most cases, the appropriate location step can be written using abbreviations for the axes. For example, the `child` axis is the default, so it's usually left out altogether. This changes the expression

```
/child::universe/child::wormhole
```

to

```
/universe/wormhole
```

Similarly, the `attribute` axis is almost never written out, and instead its abbreviation, `@`, is used. So the expression

```
/universe/wormhole[attribute::wid='WFRSB']
```

is written

```
/universe/wormhole[@wid='WFRSB']
```

Not all axes have abbreviations, but those that do are mostly intuitive.

Some abbreviations don't replace an axis, but instead replace an entire location step:

- `descendant-or-self:node()`—Note first that this is the `descendant-or-self` axis, and not the `descendant` axis. We abbreviate it by using two slashes (`//`). This means that

```
/descendant-or-self::node()/child::planet/child:name
```

becomes

```
//planet/name
```

- `parent::*`—The abbreviation for this location step is `..`, like the parent directory in most file systems. So the location path

```
/descendant-or-self::node()/child::moon/parent::*/child::planet
```

becomes

```
//moon/../planet
```

- `self::node()`—The context node can be selected with a single period (`.`). So the location path

```
self::node()/child:planet
```

becomes

```
./planet
```

and selects the `planet` children of the context node.

Sometimes the best way to understand a complex XPath expression is to write it out in long form and look at the axes explicitly.

Relative Versus Absolute Paths

Like URIs, XPath expressions can be absolute or relative. A relative expression works from the current context node, and the results may change if the context node changes. An absolute expression always starts with the document root as the original context node, and will return the same results no matter what the current context node is.

An absolute expression starts with a leading slash (`/`), so the expression

```
/starSystem/planet
```

is absolute (and returns an empty set, in this case) whereas the expression

```
starSystem/planet
```

is relative and may or may not return any results, depending on the current context node. If the context node were a `galaxy` element, it would return two `planet` nodes. If the context node were any other node in the document, the expression would return an empty node-set.

Relative expressions are much more common than absolute expressions. They're the foundation of XSLT (in that different templates use relative expressions based on the current context node). Also, any location path with more than one location step uses relative expressions, at least for the second location step and all that follow it.

Predicates

In many cases, an axis and a node test are enough to specify the set of nodes that you want, but sometimes you want to be even more specific. In this chapter, for example, we've frequently wanted to specify a particular node to use as the context node. In order to do that, we've used predicates. A *predicate* is an expression that filters the results of the axis and node test. Written in brackets ([ ]), it's evaluated with each node in the resultset as the context node. Nodes for which the expression is not true are removed from the resultset.

The expressions can test the existence of various nodes, their value, or their position in the current resultset, among other things. Predicates are one way in which the built-in XPath functions are applied to a resultset.

Simply put, the complete process is as follows:

1. The axis adds nodes to the resultset.

2. The node test removes nodes from the set based on type or name.

3. The predicate removes nodes from the set based on an arbitrary expression.

Note that all of this happens within a single location step; there's no rule that says a predicate can only happen at the end of a location path.

Existence

The simplest predicate is one that simply checks for the existence of a particular node. For example, the expression

```
/descendant-or-self::galaxy/child::starSytem[child::moon]
```

or

```
//galaxy/starSytem[moon]
```

returns only those **starSystem**s that have a **moon** child.

The resultset consists of both **galaxy** elements, which are descendants of the document root, as shown in Figure 11.21.

FIGURE 11.21

The `galaxy` descendants of the root.

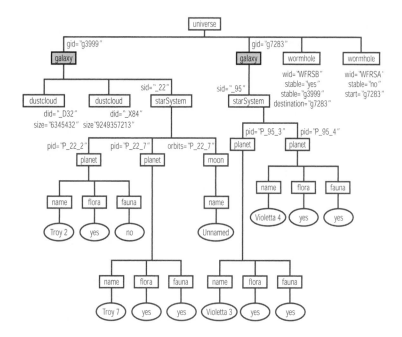

These elements act as the context nodes for the `child::starSystem` location step, yielding both `starSystem` elements, as shown in Figure 11.22.

FIGURE 11.22

The `starSystem` children of `galaxy`.

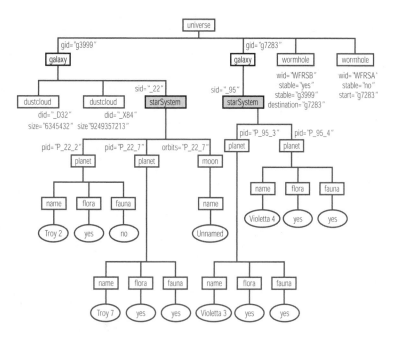

The predicate is evaluated *for the current resultset*. The first `starSystem` becomes the context node for the expression `child::moon`, as in Figure 11.23.

FIGURE 11.23

The first `starSystem`.

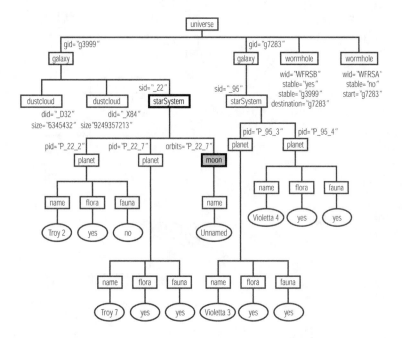

The result is a nonempty node-set, which is considered to be "true," so the first `starSystem` node (*not* the `moon` node) is kept in the resultset.

Finally, the second `starSystem` node becomes the context node for the expression `child::moon`, as shown in Figure 11.24.

FIGURE 11.24

The second `starSystem`.

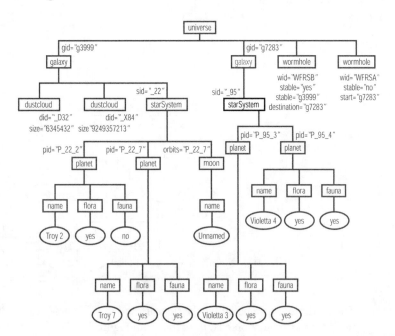

Because the second **starSystem** has no **moon** children, the result of the **child::moon** location step is an empty set, which is considered to be "false." Because the predicate evaluates to **false** for this node, it's removed from the resultset, leaving only the first **starSystem**, as shown in Figure 11.25.

FIGURE 11.25
The final resultset.

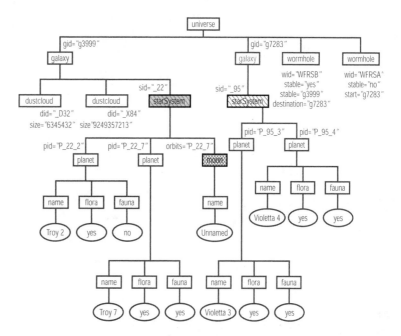

Equality

Another common type of predicate is one that checks for a specific value for an element or attribute. We've used these extensively throughout the chapter for attribute values, but we can also use them for element values. For example, we can select only those **planet**s that have animals using

```
//planet[fauna='yes']
```

All **planet**s are selected initially, but only those that have a child named **fauna** with a value of **yes** will be kept, as shown in Figure 11.26.

Element Values

According to the Document Object Model (DOM), an element node actually has no value; it's the text node descendant that contains a value. When testing for the value of an element, XPath actually converts it to a string, as discussed in the "Functions" section a bit later in the chapter. Put simply, the descendant text nodes become the element's value.

FIGURE 11.26
The final resultset.

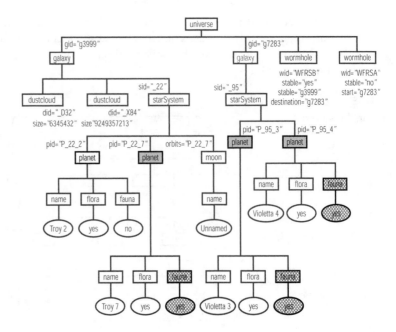

We can take this a step further, selecting the **starSystem**s that have **planet**s with life on them, using

```
//planet[fauna='yes']/parent::starSystem
```

The first location step selects the three **planet** nodes. The second step selects all of their parent nodes, and keeps only those that are named **starSystem** (in this case, all of them) as shown in Figure 11.27.

FIGURE 11.27
A location step after a predicate selects nodes based on the first resultset.

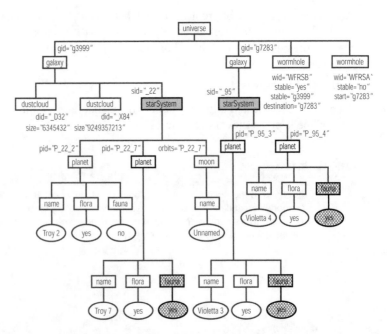

Context Size and Position

We've talked about the context node, but that's only part of the context for an expression. Two other factors are the context size and position. The context size is the size of the current result-set, and the context position is the node's position within that set.

For example, the expression

```
//planet
```

returns four nodes, so the context size is **4**. Each node within the set has a context position. To select the third `planet`, `Violetta 3`, you can use the expression

```
//planet[position()=3]
```

or its abbreviation

```
//planet[3]
```

Note that the first item in the resultset has a position of **1**, and not **0**.

Functions

Predicates are most often used with XPath functions, but functions also stand on their own in many cases, and are evaluated with regard to the current context. For example, the style sheet in Listing 11.31 outputs the position and value of the `name` child of each `planet`.

LISTING 11.31   Outputting Position

```
<?xml version="1.0"?>
<xsl:stylesheet xmlns:xsl="http://www.w3.org/1999/XSL/Transform"
                version="1.0">

<xsl:template match="/">
    <xsl:apply-templates select="//planet"/>
</xsl:template>

<xsl:template match="*">
    (<xsl:value-of select="position()"/>) <xsl:value-of select="name"/>
</xsl:template>

</xsl:stylesheet>
```

The result is a numbered list of `planet` names, as shown in Listing 11.32.

LISTING 11.32   Numbered `planets`

```
<?xml version="1.0" encoding="UTF-8"?>

    (1) Troy 2
    (2) Troy 7
    (3) Violetta 3
    (4) Violetta 4
```

Boolean Functions

At their heart, most XPath expressions hinge on a Boolean evaluation: A node is included in or excluded from a resultset based on whether a certain condition is `true` or `false`.

In fact, all the predicates discussed in the previous section are implicitly processed by the `boolean()` function to determine whether a result should be output. For an equality test, such as

```
@sid='_95'
```

the Boolean nature is obvious. The expression is either `true`, or it's `false`. But what about the existence tests? How do you convert

```
child::moon
```

to a Boolean? The `boolean()` function takes an argument, such as a node-set or number, and converts it to a `true` or `false` value as follows:

- `boolean(node-set)`—If the node-set is empty (meaning it has zero nodes) the function returns `false`. If it's not empty, it returns `true`.

- `boolean(number)`—The function returns `true` for any nonzero number. For `0` or `NaN` (Not a Number), it returns `false`.

- `boolean(string)`—The function returns `false` if the length of the string is zero. Otherwise, it returns `true`.

XPath also defines a number of other Boolean functions:

- `not(arg)`—Toggles the Boolean value. If `arg` is `true`, it returns `false`, and vice versa. So the expression

  ```
  //starSystem[not(@sid='_95')]
  ```

  returns only `starSystem _22`.

- `true()`—This function doesn't take an argument, and always returns `true`. So the expression

  ```
  //starSystem[true()]
  ```

  returns every `starSystem` element.

- `false()`—This function doesn't take an argument, and always returns `false`. So the expression

  ```
  //starSystem[false()]
  ```

  returns nothing, because every node returned by the axis and node test will fail the predicate test.

- `lang(arg)`—This function takes a language code and compares it to the language in scope for the context node, returning **true** if it matches. For example, if the context node is

  ```
  <name xml:lang='en-us'>Troy 7</name>
  ```

  then the functions `lang('en')` and `lang('en-us')` return **true**.

  Note that the `xml:lang` attribute doesn't have to be set on the actual node, as long as it's set on one of the context node's ancestors. If it isn't set at all, or if it doesn't match the argument, `lang()` returns **false**.

Node Functions

XPath defines a set of functions specifically for node-sets. Each of them acts on the current node-set, whatever that may be, or on a node-set provided as an argument. They are listed here:

- `position()`—This function returns the context position of the current context node, as discussed earlier in the "Predicates" section.

- `last()`—This function returns the context position of the last node in the node-set, as opposed to the actual last node. So to select the last **planet**, we can use the expression

  ```
  /descendant::planet[position()=last()]
  ```

  Note that this is different from the expression

  ```
  //planet[position()=last()]
  ```

  which expands to

  ```
  /descendant-or-self::node()/child::planet[position()=last()]
  ```

  In this case, there are two initial resultsets: the **planet** children of **starSystem _22**, and the **planet** children of **starSystem _95**. Each of these sets has a context size of two, so the last **planet** in *each* set is returned.

- `count(arg)`—In this case, **arg** represents a node-set, and `count()` returns the number of nodes in it. For example, if the style sheet outputs

  ```
  There are <xsl:value-of select="count(//planet)"/> planets in this document.
  ```

  the result is

  ```
  There are 4 planets in this document.
  ```

- `id(arg)`—In this case, `arg` is meant to be a string (and is converted to one if necessary) and the function returns the element represented by an `id` equal to `arg`. For example, we could select the `planet` children of any element with an ID of `_95` using

  `/descendant::node[id('_95')]/planet`

  In this case, the `planet` could be the descendant of a `starSystem`, `nebula`, or any other element, as long as the element has an attribute that has been declared to be of type `ID` in a DTD, with a value of `_95`.

  This function is also useful for simply selecting an individual node for further processing.

- `name()` or `name(arg)`—This function returns the entire name of either the context node or the node-set provided as an argument, including namespace information.

- `local-name()` or `local-name(arg)`—This function returns just the local part of the context node or node-set argument.

- `namespace-uri()` or `namespace-uri(arg)`—This function returns the full namespace of the context node or the node-set provided as an argument, if there is one.

String Functions

String functions are used implicitly every time an XSLT style sheet uses a `value-of` element, and every time an expression compares a node to a string. Specifically, the `string()` function takes an argument and converts it to a string.

Numbers are converted in the obvious way: both positive zero and negative zero become `0`, and NaN, negative infinity, and positive infinity become `'NaN'`, `'-Infinity'`, and `'Infinity'`, respectively.

For Boolean values, a value of `true` is converted to `'true'` and a value of `false` is converted to `'false'`.

Finally, a node-set is converted to a string by concatenating all descendant text nodes of the initial node. Attributes are ignored. So the expression

`string(//planet[@pid='P_22_7'])`

returns

`Troy 7yesyes`

Other string functions include

- `concat(arg, arg, arg*)`—This function can take any number of arguments and concatenate them into a single string. If an argument is a node or node-set, it's first converted to a string, as shown in Listing 11.33.

LISTING 11.33   Concatenation

```
<?xml version="1.0"?>
<xsl:stylesheet xmlns:xsl="http://www.w3.org/1999/XSL/Transform"
                version="1.0">

<xsl:template match="/">
    <xsl:apply-templates select="//planet"/>
</xsl:template>

<xsl:template match="*">
    -+- <xsl:value-of select="concat(@pid, ' : ', name)"/> -+-
</xsl:template>

</xsl:stylesheet>
```

The results are shown in Listing 11.34.

LISTING 11.34   Concatenated Values

```
<?xml version="1.0" encoding="UTF-8"?>

    -+- P_22_2 : Troy 2 -+-

    -+- P_22_7 : Troy 7 -+-

    -+- P_95_3 : Violetta 3 -+-

    -+- P_95_4 : Violetta 4 -+-
```

- starts-with(*arg1*, *arg2*)—This function returns **true** if the first argument starts with the second argument. So the expression

  ```
  //planet[starts-with(@pid, 'P_95')]
  ```

  selects only the **planet**s with **pid** attributes that start with **P_95**.

- contains(*arg1*, *arg2*)—Similar to **starts-with()**, **contains()** returns **true** if the first string contains the second string, as in

  ```
  //planet[contains(@pid, '95')]
  ```

- substring-before(*arg1*, *arg2*)—This function splits the first argument into two pieces at the location of the first occurrence of the second argument and returns the first piece. So the expression

  ```
  substring-before('Violetta 4', ' ');
  ```

  returns

  ```
  Violetta
  ```

  If the second argument is not present in the first, the result is an empty string.

- substring-after(*arg1*, *arg2*)—This function acts like substring-before(), but selects the part of the first argument after the second argument. So the expression

```
substring-after('P_95_4', '_')
```

returns

```
95_4
```

- substring(*arg1*, *num1*) or substring(*arg1*, *num1*, *num2*)—This function returns the portion of the first argument that starts at the position specified by *num1* (assuming that the first character is numbered 1) and continues for the number of characters specified in *num2*. (If *num2* is not specified, the substring continues to the end of the string.) So the expressions

```
substring('P_95_4', 3)
substring('P_95_4', 3, 2)
```

and

```
substring('P_95_4', -2, 6)
```

return

```
95_4
95
```

and

```
P_95
```

Note that the second argument merely specifies the offset of the start position. In this last example, that offset is two characters before the beginning of the string, so the six positions evaluated include two with no characters, then four with characters. In this way, we return the first four characters of the string.

- string-length() or string-length(*arg*)—This function returns the number of characters in the argument provided, or in the context node. In the case of a node-set rather than a string, the argument is converted using the string() function before evaluation.

- normalize-space() or normalize-space(*arg*)—This function removes leading and trailing whitespace and converts multiple whitespace characters to a single whitespace character. So the expression

```
normalize-space('     Troy 7
                 yes
                 yes')
```

returns

```
Troy 7 yes yes
```

- translate(*arg1*, *arg2*, *arg3*)—This function is most often used to convert text from uppercase to lowercase (or vice versa), though it's not well suited to this purpose for all languages. In any case, translate() acts as a global search and replace function. For each character in the first argument, the processor checks the second argument for that character. If found, it's replaced with the character in the corresponding position in the third argument, like a child's code. So the expression

```
translate('Troy 7', 'abcedefghijklmnopqrstuvwzyz',
                     'ABCDEFGHIJKLMNOPQRSTUVWXYZ')
```

returns

```
TROY 7
```

Note that because neither the space nor the number is represented in either the second or third argument, they are left unchanged. If they had been listed in the second argument but not the third, they would have been removed. So the expression

```
translate('Troy 7', 'abcedefghijklmnopqrstuvwzyz 7',
                     'ABCDEFGHIJKLMNOPQRSTUVWXYZ')
```

returns

```
TROY
```

Number Functions

The example in this chapter doesn't lend itself to much in the way of mathematics, but XPath does have a number of mathematics-related functions:

- `number()` or `number(arg)`—Just as the `boolean()` and `string()` functions convert other types to their base types, `number()` converts an argument or the context node to a number. A string that represents a positive or negative number is converted to that number. If it doesn't represent a number, it's converted to `NaN` (Not a Number). A Boolean value of `true` is converted to `1`, and `false` is converted to `0`. A node-set is first converted to a string using the `string()` function, then is converted just as strings are.

- `sum(arg)`—This function takes a node-set as an argument. It figures the sum by converting each node to a string, then converting those strings to numbers and adding them.

- `floor(num)`—For an integer, this function returns the original number. For a non-integer, it returns the next lowest integer. The expressions `floor(3)`, `floor(3.2)`, and `floor(3.9)` all return `3`.

- `ceiling(arg)`—This function is the opposite of `floor()`, returning the next highest integer. So the expression `ceiling(3)` returns `3`, but `ceiling(3.2)` and `ceiling(3.9)` both return `4`.

- `round(arg)`—The XPath Recommendation describes this function as one that "returns the number that is closest to the argument that is an integer." The expressions `round(3.2)` and `round(3.9)` return `3` and `4`, respectively, but what about `round(3.5)`?

The Recommendation says that in this case, the number "closest to positive infinity" is returned. This seems obvious with positive numbers; `round(3.5)` returns `4`. But for negative numbers, the situation is reversed, so `round(-3.5)` returns `-3`.

Summary

XPath provides a means for selecting a specific node or nodes within an XML document. It does this through a series of location steps, each of which consists of an axis (such as `child`, `ancestor`, or `attribute`), a node test (such as the name of the element or a node type such as `text()`), and an optional predicate (such as an existence or equality test).

In evaluating a location step, a processor starts with a context node and adds the codes specified by the axis, then removes any nodes that don't match the node test or predicate. If there is more than one location step in a location path, each node in the resultset is used as the context node for the next location step in line.

XPath also has built-in functions that can identify information about a node or its environment, or can manipulate the data within it.

Review Questions

1. What are the three parts of a location step?

2. Name three axes.

3. What does a node test do?

4. What does a predicate do?

5. What's the difference between an absolute and a relative expression?

6. How does an element get converted to a text value?

7. Which axis is used in two location steps in the expression

   `/horse/race`

8. What axis selects all of a node's children and their children?

Programming Exercises

The following exercises use the source document from Chapter 9:

```
<?xml version="1.0"?>
<content>
<events>
    <eventitem eventid="A335">
        <eventdate>6.20.3425</eventdate>
        <title>Making Friends With The Venusian Flu Virus</title>
        <description>Dr. Biff Mercury discusses his theory on
        coexisting with this useful organism.</description>
    </eventitem>

    <eventitem eventid="B963" optional="no">
        <eventdate>6.21.3425</eventdate>
```

```
        <title>Putting the Manners in Bedside Manner</title>
        <description>Dr. Zingzowpowie, the famous xenoneurosurgeon
        lectures on Bedside Manner and the benefits of using cold
        tentacles during a physical.</description>
    </eventitem>

    <eventitem eventid="C934" optional="yes">
        <eventdate>6.25.3425</eventdate>
        <title>An Evening of Fun</title>
        <description>This evening join us for the monthly "Identify
        that Food" contest.</description>
    </eventitem>

</events>
<news>
    <newsitem itemnum="1">
        <newsdate>6.18.3425</newsdate>
        <title>End Of The Line For The Incumbent?</title>
        <body>
            The Universal News Network is reporting that <person>His
            Magnificence The Supreme Leader For Life</person>
            announced today that he has decided not to be cloned for
            a 14th term.
        </body>
    </newsitem>

    <newsitem itemnum="2">
        <newsdate>6.19.3425</newsdate>
        <title>New Fall Lineup</title>
        <body>
            The Omega Channel has announced two new shows for its new
            fall lineup. <program>Who's Running the Galaxy?</program>
            features a team of government scientists who accidentally
            clone two Supreme Leaders. If you think you're confused,
            imagine what the first family must be going through.
            <program>Trading Species</program> follows two teams of
            aliens who trade species and have only 48 hours to adjust
            and fool their neighbors.
        </body>
    </newsitem>
</news>
</content>
```

1. Write an absolute expression that selects only the event title nodes.

2. Write a relative expression that selects the body of news item number 1, assuming that the news element is the context node.

3. Write an expression that returns the **eventitem** element for any event that mentions Dr. Zingzowpowie in the description.

4. Write an expression that assumes that the news element is the context node, and returns the title of any news item that has a program element in the description.

PART II

USING XML

12   Browser-Based XML: Cascading Style Sheets (CSS)

13   Browser-Based XML: XHTML

14   XML Linking Language (XLink)

15   XForms

16   XML and Publishing: Formatting Objects with XSL

17   XML and Web Services

18   Data Binding

19   XML and Databases: Relational Databases

20   XML and Databases: Native XML Databases

21   Where We Go from Here

BROWSER-BASED XML: CASCADING STYLE SHEETS (CSS)

You will learn about the following in this chapter:

- Selectors
- Properties
- Controlling text format

- Linking to external style sheets
- Page layout flow
- Positioning items on the page

W e're going to cover a lot of ground in this chapter and the next, but you probably have at least a passing familiarity with some of the topics.

In Chapter 13, "Browser-Based XML: XHTML," we're going to look at HTML, the original language of the Web. HTML is an XML-like language in which the browser understands that certain tags have certain meanings. If you include the element

```
<h1>Chapter 12</h1>
```

the browser knows that it's a major heading for the page. Moreover, it knows that it should display the text large, and bold, and on a line by itself. These are *properties* of the h1 element.

On the other hand, if you were to include the element

```
<chapternumber>Chapter 12</chapternumber>
```

in the page, the browser wouldn't have a clue what to do with it, and would display it as generic text.

Cascading Style Sheets, or CSS, allow us to specifically set the properties that control how the browser (or other client application) displays information. This means that we have a way to tell the browser to display the content of any chapternumber element as large, and bold, and on a line by itself.

In this chapter, we're going to use CSS to create a Web page out of XML data. We'll look at selecting content to style, and at the properties that we can use to style it. Along the way, we'll take a good look at how the browser lays out a page, so you can take control of that process.

In Chapter 13, we'll look at applying this process to HTML.

Gathering the Pieces

CSS allows you to control the appearance, presence, and even position of information in a browser or other user-agent. Some user-agents support more of the CSS recommendation than others, particularly when it comes to XML. In our examples, we'll use Microsoft Internet Explorer 6.0 and Netscape Navigator 7.0.

In this section, we're going to take a look at how a browser handles XML, both with and without a style sheet attached.

Keeping Tabs

The W3C maintains the Cascading Style Sheets Recommendation. CSS2 is supported to varying degrees by current browsers, and CSS3 is in the works.

The Source File

The subject of this chapter is the Vanguard Station Resort's annual comet hunting contest. The results are stored as an XML file, as shown in Listing 12.1.

LISTING 12.1 The Source File, `comets.xml`

```
<?xml-stylesheet href="comet_styles.css" type="text/css"?>
<comets>
  <comet class="confirmed" id="DF1">
    <discovery>
        <date>4.28.2356</date>
        <hunter>Mack</hunter>
        <description>Sungrazing comet, tail visible</description>
        <brightness>Magnitude 2.1</brightness>
        <vantage>Deck 4, Aperture DF</vantage>
    </discovery>
    <positions>
        <datapoint>
            <date>4.25.2356</date>
            <time>27:03</time>
            <position>495, 3443</position>
        </datapoint>
        <datapoint>
            <date>4.25.2356</date>
            <time>27:33</time>
            <position>615, 3465</position>
        </datapoint>
        <datapoint>
```

LISTING 12.1 Continued

```
            <date>4.26.2356</date>
            <time>00:03</time>
            <position>735, 3487</position>
        </datapoint>
        <datapoint>
            <date>4.26.2356</date>
            <time>00:33</time>
            <position>855, 3509</position>
        </datapoint>
    </positions>
  </comet>
  <comet class="pending" id="DF2">
    <discovery>
        <date>5.1.2356</date>
        <hunter>Vega</hunter>
        <description>Possible Kreutz comet</description>
        <brightness>Magnitude: faint</brightness>
        <vantage>Deck 4, Aperture DF</vantage>
    </discovery>
    <positions>
        <datapoint>
            <date>4.30.2356</date>
            <time>09:03</time>
            <position>2934, 1003</position>
        </datapoint>
        <datapoint>
            <date>4.30.2356</date>
            <time>09:33</time>
            <position>2709, 1070</position>
        </datapoint>
        <datapoint>
            <date>4.30.2356</date>
            <time>10:03</time>
            <position>2484, 1137</position>
        </datapoint>
        <datapoint>
            <date>4.30.2356</date>
            <time>10:33</time>
            <position>2229, 1204</position>
        </datapoint>
    </positions>
  </comet>
</comets>
```

If we open this file in the browser as is, the results are going to depend on the browser, as shown in Figures 12.1 and 12.2.

The HTML Recommendation on which browsers are built state that if a browser encounters a tag that it doesn't recognize, it should just display the contents without taking any further action, and as you can see in Figure 12.2, that's exactly what Navigator is doing.

FIGURE 12.1

The raw XML file in Microsoft Internet Explorer 6.0.

FIGURE 12.2

The raw XML file in Netscape Navigator 7.0.

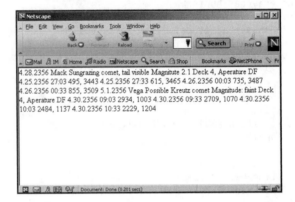

But if that's the way it's supposed to be handled, why does IE show the data in a nice hierarchical fashion, as seen in Figure 12.1? It's because IE has a built-in CSS style sheet for XML files that creates the effect that you see when you load the file.

Now let's create a style sheet of our own.

Creating a Style Sheet

We'll start by creating the very simplest of style sheets: a blank file. Create a new text file and save it as `comet_styles.css` in the same directory as `comets.xml`.

To get the browser to use the new style sheet in displaying `comets.xml`, we can use a familiar processing instruction, as shown in Listing 12.2.

LISTING 12.2   Adding the Style Sheet

```
<?xml version="1.0"?>
<?xml-stylesheet href="comet_styles.css" type="text/css"?>
<comets>
```

LISTING 12.2   Continued

```
<comet class="confirmed" id="DF1">
  <discovery>
      <date>4.28.2356</date>
      <hunter>Mack</hunter>
...
```

This is exactly the same as the processing instruction we used to associate an XSLT style sheet with a file in Chapter 10, "Transformation and Applications," but we've changed the type from `text/xsl` to `text/css` to let the browser know how to handle it.

Adding the new style sheet to the document overrides the default style sheet, so IE, like Netscape Navigator, displays just text, as shown in Figure 12.3.

FIGURE 12.3
Without the default style sheet, IE displays just text.

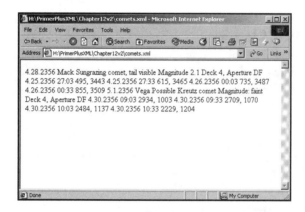

It's important to notice also that the browser doesn't display attribute values. In Chapter 13, we'll look at using XSLT to get those values onto the page.

Selectors

Now we'll start building the basic style sheet. Each style sheet rule consists of a selector and a declaration or declarations. A declaration consists of a property and a value. The most basic selector is the asterisk (*), which selects all elements, as shown in Listing 12.3.

LISTING 12.3   The Most Basic Style Sheet

```
* { display: block }
```

Let's take a look at the structure here. The declaration follows the selector in brackets, with the property name and value separated by a colon (:). (The declaration `display: block` simply outputs an item on a line by itself.) Figure 12.4 shows what happens when we declare every element as a block element.

FIGURE 12.4
The * selector affects all elements.

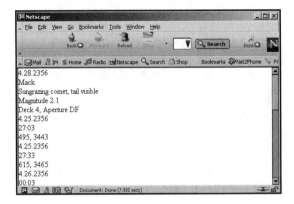

Element Selectors

Of course, while this may be useful in some situations, we need to be a little more selective here. For example, perhaps we only want the `date`, `hunter`, `description`, and `datapoint`s to appear on their own lines. Fortunately, we can use element selectors to chose specific elements to display as blocks, as shown in Listing 12.4.

LISTING 12.4   Choosing Elements

```
date          { display: block;
                font-weight: bold; }
hunter        { display: block }
description   { display: block }
datapoint     { display: block }
```

We've done a couple of things here. First, we've added several different rules, each on its own line. We can add as many as we want, generally with no concern for their order.

Conflicting Rules

When two different rules can apply to the same element, CSS specifies that the "most restrictive" rule should be used. If we have a rule for hunters, and a rule for hunters with a particular attribute, the latter will be used.

We've also added a second property to the `date` rule, separating it from the first with a semi-colon (`;`). A single rule can contain as many declarations as you want, as long as they're all delimited this way, so they can also be on a single line. Figure 12.5 shows the results.

Descendant Selectors

Looking at the results in Figure 12.5, you can see a couple of things. First, the `brightness` and `vantage` are now on the same line, as are the `time` and `position` elements. Unfortunately, the `date` elements for each `datapoint` are also on their own lines, which is not what we want. Fortunately, we can get a little more specific with our selectors, as shown in Listing 12.5.

FIGURE 12.5
Selectors can target specific elements.

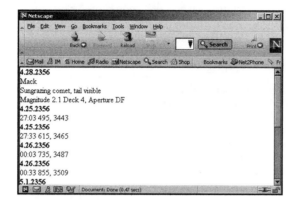

LISTING 12.5   Choosing Elements by Structure

```
discovery date { display: block;
                 font-weight: bold; }
hunter          { display: block }
description     { display: block }
datapoint       { display: block }
```

In this case, the selector chooses only those `date` elements that are descendants of a `discovery` element, as shown in Figure 12.6.

FIGURE 12.6
Selectors can target specific element descendants.

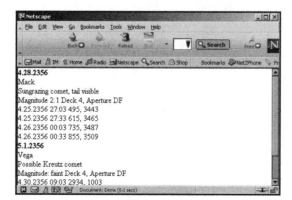

Children, Rather Than Descendants

You can also restrict choices to children, like this:

```
discovery > date { display: block;
                   font-weight: bold; }
```

Unfortunately, this doesn't work reliably in most browsers.

Sibling Selectors

Another way we can use the structure of the document to choose content is to look at following siblings. In other words, we can also choose only elements that follow a particular element, as shown in Listing 12.6.

LISTING 12.6   Following Siblings

```
discovery date { display: block;
                 font-weight: bold; }
hunter          { display: block }
description     { display: block }
datapoint       { display: block;
                 font-style: italic; font-weight:bold; }
datapoint + datapoint { font-style: normal; font-weight: normal; }
```

In this case, our goal is to display only the first `datapoint` in bold and italic, as shown in Figure 12.7.

FIGURE 12.7

Putting the cascade in Cascading Style Sheets.

Let's take this step by step. First, we set all `datapoint`s to be blocks, and to be displayed as italic and bold. We then create a rule that applies only to `datapoint`s that are the following sibling of a `datapoint`, as specified by the plus sign (+). This rule applies to all but the first `datapoint`.

Notice that although we have a specific rule for these `datapoint`s, only the properties we explicitly add to it take effect. We set them to be neither italic nor bold, but the block designation carries through just the same, because any existing properties will still be in effect unless we explicitly override them, as we're doing with the style and weight.

Classes and IDs

The last two selectors we're going to look at are normally used only for HTML, but we're going to cheat a little. They are the `class` and `id` selectors, and they're based on attributes of those names. Because we named our attributes `class` and `id`, we can use them.

Listing 12.7 selects all elements in the class `pending`. In this case, we're talking about the second `comet`, which the browser displays just a little bit smaller. The second new rule selects the element with an ID of `DF1`—the first `comet`—and renders it in green.

LISTING 12.7 Classes and IDs

```
discovery date { display: block;
                 font-weight: bold; }
hunter          { display: block }
description     { display: block }
datapoint       { display: block;
                 font-style: italic; font-weight:bold; }
datapoint + datapoint    { font-style: normal; font-weight: normal; }
.pending { font-size: smaller }
#DF1 { color: green }
```

Because these selectors are meant for HTML, they're not always well supported in XML. Figure 12.8 shows the results in IE.

FIGURE 12.8

Using `classes` and `ids`.

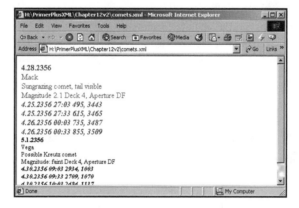

In HTML documents, classes are useful because they allow you to determine the type of styling an item should have, allowing you to control an entire site using style sheets. You can get even more specific. For example, if we had multiple elements with `class="pending"`, we could choose just the `comet` with

```
comet.pending { font-size: smaller }
```

Pseudoclasses

CSS also provides selectors called *pseudoclasses*, which we'll discuss in the next chapter.

Properties

Before we begin using the actual properties themselves, let's get a feel for the lay of the land.

Types of Properties

There are over 100 different properties defined in CSS, and they generally fall into the following categories:

- **Formatting and layout**—These properties involve where and how items are placed on the page, allowing control over position, size, and other aspects of layout.

- **Text and fonts**—These properties control the fonts used for various text items, as well as size, weight, style, and other text-related aspects.

- **Colors and backgrounds**—These properties allow you to choose colors for foregrounds and backgrounds of items, and to choose background images.

- **Generated content**—These properties allow you to add items such as line numbers or other content, but are not well supported by current browsers.

- **Alternative media**—These properties take into account that content may be viewed on alternative systems, such as an audio system that reads a page or a paged system (such as a printout) rather than continuous pages (such as a Web browser).

In many cases, you'll use these properties directly, as we did in earlier examples with `display` and `font-weight`. That's not always the case, however.

Shorthand Properties

Even within these groups, properties generally also fall into subgroups. For example, the style

```
margin: 5px;
```

sets the margin all around an item at 5 pixels, but it's actually shorthand for

```
margin-top: 5px;
margin-bottom: 5px;
margin-left: 5px;
margin-right: 5px;
```

This degree of specificity allows you to choose different values. For example, we could set a margin, but override it for the top:

```
margin: 5px;
margin-top: 10px;
```

Combining Properties

In some cases, styles are also combined. For example, we can set several font-related properties at the same time, like this:

```
datapoint        { display: block;
                   font: italic bold 16px Arial; }
datapoint + datapoint      { font-style: normal; font-weight: normal; }
```

Here, `font` is a different type of shorthand property, setting `font-style`, `font-weight`, `font-size`, and `font-family` all at once. The subsequent style only overrides `font-style` and `font-weight`, leaving `font-size` and `font-family` intact, as shown in Figure 12.9.

FIGURE 12.9

Using shorthand properties.

Controlling Appearance

Now let's consider how to actually control the way our data looks. As far as individual items such as comet hunters' names or data items, we can control their color and size, whether they're rendered as bold or italic, the font in which they're rendered, and other aspects of their appearance.

Color

Because this book is printed in black and white, it's difficult to demonstrate slight changes in color, but color is an important part of Web design, so let's talk about where we can use it and how to determine what the actual color should be.

There are five major properties that allow you to set color:

- `background-color` applies to the page, sections of the page, or even sections of text.

- `border-color` controls the color of the border. It's used with `border-right-color`, `border-top-color`, and so on.

- `color` controls the color of text or other objects that don't have a specific color property.

- `outline-color` and `text-shadow` apply to text but are not well supported in current browsers.

Aside from the earlier example of setting the color for a specifically identified `comet` element, color setting doesn't work well for XML in today's browsers; we'll see more of it in the next chapter when we work with HTML, but for now let's look at color choices.

We can set colors using either names or hex values based on RGB values.

The first method allows you to choose from sixteen "official" colors: aqua, black, blue, fuchsia, gray, green, lime, maroon, navy, olive, purple, red, silver, teal, white, and yellow.

A list of additional colors the browser likely supports is referenced in Appendix A, "Resources."

The second method allows you to expand these choices by using a variation of the RGB, or red-green-blue values, each of which ranges from 0 to 255. These values govern all the colors you see on your computer monitor, with black represented by `0,0,0` and white by `255,255,255`. The colors that are created in between depend on the ratio of the three values. Table 12.1 shows some common colors, along with their RGB values and the hex values that represent them in a style sheet.

TABLE 12.1   Sample Colors

Color Name	RGB Value	Hex Value
Red	255,0,0	#FF0000
Green	0,255,0	#00FF00
Blue	0,0,255	#0000FF
Bright yellow	255,255,0	#FFFF00
Bright purple	255,0,255	#FF00FF
Muted purple	153,0,153	#990099
Light green	153,238,153	#99EE99
Dark gray	85,85,85	#555555
Blue gray	85,102,153	#556699

To turn the `DF1` comet to muted purple, we could change the style sheet to

`#DF1 { color: #990099 }`

Notice that the colors listed here use "double" values. In other words, rather than using `#970097`, which would have given a very similar purple, we used `#990099`. These are known as "browser safe" colors, because they should render reliably on most systems even though different platforms and color-depths have different palettes of colors available.

Hex Values

The hex value of a number is that number in "base 16," where digits run from 0 to 9, then from A to F. The decimal number 9 is the same as hexadecimal 9, but the decimal number 14 is hexadecimal E. The decimal number 20 is represented as 14 in hexadecimal. See Appendix A for more information on conversion.

Text Size

Some of the most commonly manipulated properties are those revolving around text, such as `font-size`, `font-family`, and `font-weight`. We saw `font-weight` earlier, when we set the discovery dates to be bold. Let's take a look at font sizes and families.

One commonly used technique is to set text size, usually using a fixed size, as in Listing 12.8.

LISTING 12.8   Setting a Fixed Text Size

```
discovery date { display: block;
                 font-weight: bold;
                 font-size: 16pt;  }
hunter        { display: block }
description   { display: block }
datapoint     { display: block; }
.pending      { font-size: smaller }
#DF1          { color: green }
```

Absolute text sizes can be set in points, as they are in Listing 12.8, or in pixels, using `px`. You can also use keywords such as `small`, `large`, `x-large`, `xx-small`, and `medium`.

As you can see in Figure 12.10, however, absolute sizes aren't always a good idea.

FIGURE 12.10

Absolute font sizes aren't always the best idea.

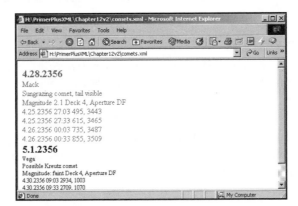

Notice that the font size doesn't take into account the fact that the second `comet`'s text is smaller, so the date should be smaller too. Instead, both discovery dates are the same size. To solve the problem, we can use relative sizes, as in Listing 12.9.

LISTING 12.9   Relative Font Sizes

```
discovery date { display: block;
                 font-weight: bold;
                 font-size: larger;  }
hunter        { display: block }
description   { display: block }
```

LISTING 12.9   Continued

```
datapoint      { display: block; }
.pending       { font-size: smaller }
#DF1           { color: green }
```

As you can see in Figure 12.11, the dates are now larger than the rest of the text, but proportionately so. Other ways to set relative sizes include using percentages and measurements based on ems and exes, which refer to the size of the existing font.

FIGURE 12.11
Setting relative text sizes is usually a better idea.

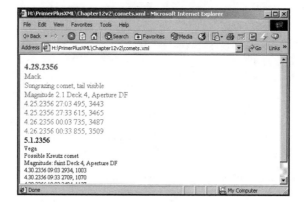

Font Appearance

Another commonly used font property is the `font-family`. This property allows you to choose a specific font or set of fonts, and to set a default font to be used if none of them are available.

For example, Listing 12.10 sets a made-up font called `Borgia` as the font for the page. If `Borgia` is not available (either it is not available at all, or it can't represent a particular character) the page will use `Arial`. If `Arial` isn't available, it'll use `Helvetica`, and if that's not available, it will pick a sans-serif font and use that.

LISTING 12.10   Choosing a `font-family`

```
discovery date { display: block;
                 font-weight: bold;
                 font-size: larger;  }
hunter         { display: block; }
description    { display: block;
                 font-style: italic; }
datapoint      { display: block; }
.pending       { font-size: smaller }
#DF1           { color: green }
*              { font-family: Borgia, Arial, Helvetica, sans-serif; }
```

The available generic font families are

- `serif` (such as Times New Roman)

- `sans-serif` (such as Arial and Helvetica)

- `cursive` (fonts in which letters join, such as Caflisch Script or Zaph-Chancery)

- `fantasy` (primarily decorative fonts, such as Alpha Geometrique and Critter)

- `monospace` (such as Courier)

Figure 12.12 shows the font family change.

FIGURE 12.12
Setting font family, font style, and font weight.

The figure also shows the `font-style` and `font-weight` changes. The `font-style` property can be set to `normal`, `italic`, or `oblique` (similar to `italic`). The `font-weight` property can be set to an absolute value from `100` to `900` (in multiples of 100) or to a relative value such as `bolder` or `lighter`, or simply to `bold` or `normal`.

Layout and Flow

Now we have some idea how to control the appearance of our content, so it's time to start looking at the overall layout of the page.

CSS enables control in small ways, such as using borders and margins, and large ways, such as moving content around the page. The key is in understanding what the browser does under normal circumstances and using that to your advantage.

Borders

We mentioned earlier that some styles are simply shorthand for a collection of other styles, and nowhere is that more true than for the `border` style. The `border` style encompasses `border-width`, `border-style`, and `border-color`, and each side of the border can be controlled individually (for instance, `border-right-color`). In Listing 12.11, we'll set the border for a comet.

LISTING 12.11   Setting a Border

```
discovery date { display: block;
                 font-weight: bold;
                 font-size: larger;  }
hunter          { display: block }
description     { display: block;
                 font-style: italic; }
datapoint       { display: block; }
.pending { font-size: smaller }
#DF1 { color: green }
* { font-family: Borgia, Arial, Helvetica, sans-serif; }
comet { border: 2px solid green };
```

As you can see in Figure 12.13, however, this doesn't give us quite the effect we expected.

FIGURE 12.13

Borders rely on having a `display` option set.

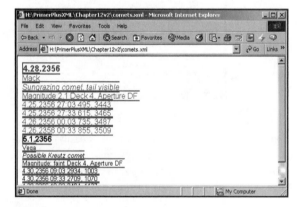

In order to determine how to add a border, the browser depends on the `display` property. Because the `comet` element doesn't have the `display` property set, the borders propagate down to the child elements. We can fix that by setting `comet` to be displayed as a block, as in Listing 12.12.

LISTING 12.12   The `comet` as a Block

```
discovery date { display: block;
                 font-weight: bold;
                 font-size: larger;  }
hunter          { display: block }
description     { display: block;
                 font-style: italic; }
datapoint       { display: block; }
.pending { font-size: smaller }
```

LISTING 12.12   Continued

```
#DF1 { color: green }
* { font-family: Borgia, Arial, Helvetica, sans-serif; }
comet { display: block;
        border: 2px solid green; };
```

This means that we have blocks within blocks, because the `comet` contains the other blocks we created earlier, but this isn't a problem; the browser depends on these relationships, in fact. Setting the property solves the problem, as shown in Figure 12.14.

FIGURE 12.14

With the `display` property set, the `comet` can take a border.

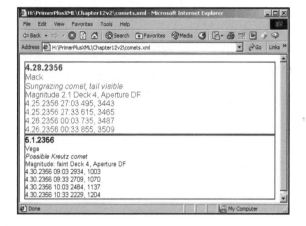

Borders can be simple, as they are here, or they can be a bit more fancy. Available border types are `none`, `hidden`, `dotted`, `dashed`, `solid`, `double`, `groove`, `ridge`, `inset`, and `outset`. If a browser doesn't support a `border-style`, it generally renders the border as solid.

Margins and Padding

The page is starting to shape up a bit, but the data's still pretty crowded together. We can take care of that by setting the `margin` and `padding` for each `comet`.

The `margin` specifies space around the outside of the element, and the `padding` specifies space between the content of the element and the inside of the box containing it, as shown in Listing 12.13.

LISTING 12.13   Setting the Margin and Padding

```
discovery date { display: block;
                 font-weight: bold;
                 font-size: larger;  }
hunter         { display: block }
description    { display: block;
                 font-style: italic; }
datapoint      { display: block; }
```

LISTING 12.13   Continued

```
.pending { font-size: smaller }
#DF1 { color: green }
* { font-family: Borgia, Arial, Helvetica, sans-serif; }
comet { display: block;
        border: 2px solid green;
        margin: 20px;
        padding: 10px;
        padding-bottom: 40px; }
```

As you can see in Figure 12.15, the `padding-bottom` value overrides the `padding` value, leaving room for someone to write notes on a printout.

FIGURE 12.15

`margin` and `padding` settings space out the content.

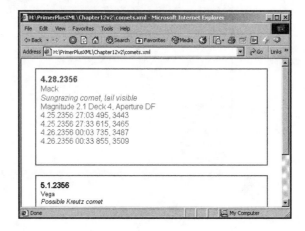

Notice that the border takes the width of the overall window. This is not necessarily what we want. We'll fix that next.

Size

Using CSS, we can set the size of an object's **bounding box**, or the area in which it's enclosed. This is the area surrounded by the border.

In Listing 12.14, we set the width of the `comet` to be exactly 300 pixels, no matter how wide or narrow the browser window gets. Figure 12.16 shows the page with this setting in effect in two browser windows.

LISTING 12.14   Setting a Width

```
discovery date { display: block;
                 font-weight: bold;
                 font-size: larger;  }
```

LISTING 12.14   Setting a Width

```
hunter          { display: block }
description     { display: block;
                  font-style: italic; }
datapoint       { display: block; }
.pending { font-size: smaller }
#DF1 { color: green }
* { font-family: Borgia, Arial, Helvetica, sans-serif; }
comet { display: block;
        border: 2px solid green;
        margin: 20px;
        padding: 10px;
        padding-bottom: 40px;
        width: 300px; }
```

FIGURE 12.16

When we set the `width` property, the width of the box is constant even if the window size changes.

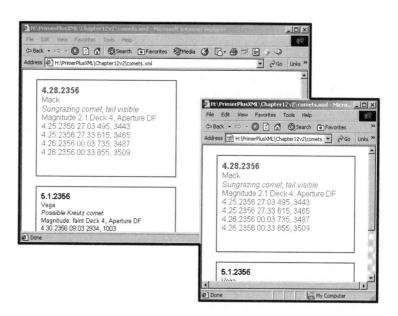

Size considerations

If you're going to set an absolute size, make sure that it's small enough to accommodate your audience. Remember, not everyone works on huge screens! There are still users with 640×480 monitors, and laptops frequently limit the available screen size.

You can also set the `length` property. Both `width` and `length` can be set in pixels, percentages, `em`s, and `ex`es.

Position

CSS also allows us to move items around on the page, but the `position` property doesn't set the actual location. Instead, it designates the method used to determine the location. It has four properties:

- `static`—The location where the object would have been if you hadn't adjusted it.
- `relative`—Changes will be made relative to the `static` position.
- `fixed`—The object is positioned relative to the browser window itself (in the case of Web pages).
- `absolute`—We'll discuss this property shortly.

Of these four, `relative` and `absolute` are the most commonly used, because `static` is the default for all objects, and `fixed` isn't well supported in today's browsers.

Relatively positioned values, as I said, are positioned relative to the spot they would have been in if no other changes had been made. These changes are made using the `left`, `right`, `top`, and `bottom` properties. In Listing 12.15, we'll use these properties to shift the `comets` themselves, and the `description` within each `comet`.

LISTING 12.15 Setting Position and Location Properties

```
discovery date { display: block;
                 font-weight: bold;
                 font-size: larger;  }
hunter         { display: block }
description    { display: block;
                 font-style: italic;
                 position: relative;
                 left: 75px;}
datapoint      { display: block; }
.pending       { font-size: smaller }
#DF1           { color: green }
*              { font-family: Borgia, Arial, Helvetica, sans-serif; }
comet          { display: block;
                 border: 2px solid green;
                 margin: 20px;
                 padding: 10px;
                 padding-bottom: 40px;
                 width: 300px;
                 top: 50px;
                 right: 50px;
                 position: relative; }
```

The results can sometimes be counterintuitive, as shown in Figure 12.17.

Based on the names `left` and `right`, you might assume that we are moving the `description` 75 pixels to the left, and the `comet` 50 pixels to the right, but you can see that this is not, in fact, the case.

FIGURE 12.17

Positions are based on margins, not directions.

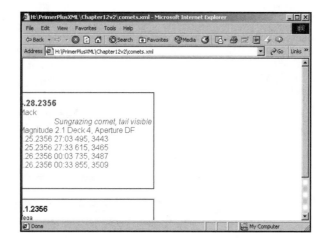

Instead, these properties work by creating a space between the reference point (in this case, where the object would have been) and the new location. That margin is set on the side specified.

In other words, we set the property **top** to 50 pixels, so a 50-pixel space is created between where the top of the **comet** would have been and where it eventually ends up. That makes sense. Then we set the **right** property, and a space is created between where the right side would have been and where it ends up, pushing the object to the *left*. Similarly, by setting the **left** property, we create a 75-pixel margin between where the left side of the **description** would have been and where it ends up, pushing it to the *right*.

All of this is for relative positioning. Let's look at what happens if we change the **position** property to **absolute**, as in Listing 12.16.

LISTING 12.16   Absolute Positioning

```
discovery date { display: block;
                 font-weight: bold;
                 font-size: larger;  }
hunter         { display: block }
description    { display: block;
                 font-style: italic;
             position: relative;
             left: 75px;}
datapoint      { display: block; }
.pending { font-size: smaller }
#DF1 { color: green }
* { font-family: Borgia, Arial, Helvetica, sans-serif; }
comet { display: block;
        border: 2px solid green;
        margin: 20px;
        padding: 10px;
```

LISTING 12.16   Continued

```
        padding-bottom: 40px;
        width: 300px;
        top: 50px;
        right: 50px;
        position: absolute;  }
```

If we look at the results, as shown in Figure 12.18, we see that the two `comet` boxes are now piled on top of one another, which is definitely not what we wanted. But why would this happen?

FIGURE 12.18

Absolute positioning disturbs the flow of the page.

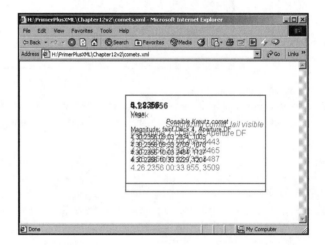

The reason for this is that absolute positioning removes an object from the normal "flow" of laying out the page, so the reference point becomes the overall bounding box—in this case, the browser window. We set only the `top` and `right` values, so those are what take effect.

For absolute positioning, the reference point is with respect to the "containing object." This is the closest ancestor that is also a block object. For example, the `description`'s containing object is the `comet`. If we make a temporary change to the style sheet to hide the first `comet` and make the `description` bold, as in Listing 12.17, we can see that the `description` is positioned relative to the `comet`'s box, whereas the `comet`, which doesn't have a block ancestor, is positioned relative to the window, as shown in Figure 12.19.

LISTING 12.17   Examining Absolute Positioning

```
discovery date { display: block;
                 font-weight: bold;
                 font-size: larger;  }
hunter         { display: block }
description    { display: block;
                 font-style: italic;
               position: absolute;
```

LISTING 12.17   *Continued*

```
                  left: 75px;
                  color: red;
                  font-weight: 900;}
datapoint        { display: block; }
.pending { font-size: smaller }
#DF1 { color: green;
        display: none; }
* { font-family: Borgia, Arial, Helvetica, sans-serif; }
comet { display: block;
        border: 2px solid green;
        margin: 20px;
        padding: 10px;
        padding-bottom: 40px;
        width: 300px;
        top: 50px;
        right: 50px;
        position: absolute;  }
```

FIGURE 12.19

The description is positioned relative to the `comet`.

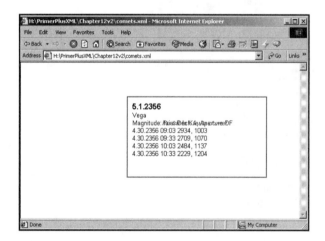

Remove these changes before moving on.

Flow

In order to understand where items should be on the page, it helps to understand how a page is laid out under normal circumstances. This is known as the *page flow*.

A page is laid out in terms of lines. Each item is added to the current line unless one of the following events occurs:

- **The line is full**—If there is no room for the object on the current line, the browser starts a new line and keeps going.

- **The object is a block object**—In this case, the browser ends the current line, starts a new one for the current object, places it, then starts a third line for subsequent objects.

- **An object is removed from the flow**—Absolutely positioned objects are removed from the flow and placed in a specific position, so they don't affect any objects that come after them. Similarly, objects with a `display` value of `none` are removed from the flow, as we'll see in a moment.

- **An object is floated**—Some objects may be floated to the left or to the right, in which case they're placed at the appropriate end of the line and the lines are shortened to accommodate them.

Let's take a look at floated objects. In Listing 12.18, we'll float both `comet`s to the right side of the window.

LISTING 12.18   Floating Objects

```
discovery date { display: block;
                 font-weight: bold;
                 font-size: larger;  }
hunter         { display: block }
description    { display: block;
                 font-style: italic;
               position: relative;
               left: 75px;}
datapoint      { display: block; }
.pending { font-size: smaller }
#DF1 { color: green }
* { font-family: Borgia, Arial, Helvetica, sans-serif; }
comet { display: block;
        border: 2px solid green;
        margin: 20px;
        padding: 10px;
        padding-bottom: 40px;
        width: 300px;
        float: right;  }
```

We've removed the `position` property of the `comet`, instead using the `float` property to move it to the right, as shown in Figure 12.20.

FIGURE 12.20

Floating objects allows them to appear next to each other.

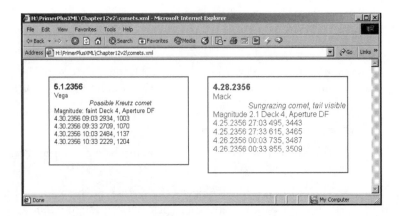

Notice that the objects seem to have switched places, with the second comet appearing before the first. This is because the first comet is floated to the right, leaving the second comet on the original line. The second comet is then floated to the right, up against the first one.

Remember, the flow line is shortened to accommodate the first comet; if it weren't long enough to accommodate the second, the second would have been moved to a new line. We can guarantee that an item appears on a new line using the clear property, as shown in Listing 12.19.

LISTING 12.19   Using the clear Property

```
discovery date { display: block;
                 font-weight: bold;
                 font-size: larger;  }
hunter         { display: block }
description    { display: block;
                 font-style: italic;
               position: relative;
               left: 75px;}
datapoint      { display: block; }
.pending { font-size: smaller }
#DF1 { color: green }
* { font-family: Borgia, Arial, Helvetica, sans-serif; }
comet { display: block;
        border: 2px solid green;
        margin: 20px;
        padding: 10px;
        padding-bottom: 40px;
        width: 300px;
        float: right;
        clear: right;  }
```

With the clear property in place, the object moves down to the first line where there is nothing floated to the right (or the left, if that's the value of the clear property), as shown in Figure 12.21, on the next page.

Removing Objects from the Flow

Many Web designers use the visibility property to "hide" objects such as menus, which they later make visible when a user rolls the mouse over a particular object. It's important to understand that there is a distinction between an object that is hidden and one that uses display: none. In Listing 12.20 we'll use the visibility property to hide the first comet.

LISTING 12.20   Hiding an Object

```
discovery date { display: block;
                 font-weight: bold;
                 font-size: larger;  }
hunter         { display: block }
description    { display: block;
                 font-style: italic;
```

LISTING 12.20   Continued

```
                position: relative;
                left: 75px;}
datapoint       { display: block; }
.pending { font-size: smaller }
#DF1 { color: green }
* { font-family: Borgia, Arial, Helvetica, sans-serif; }
comet { display: block;
        border: 2px solid green;
        margin: 20px;
        padding: 10px;
        padding-bottom: 40px;
        width: 300px;
        float: right;
        clear: right;   }
.confirmed { visibility: hidden }
```

FIGURE 12.21

The clear property
moves items down to the
next clear line.

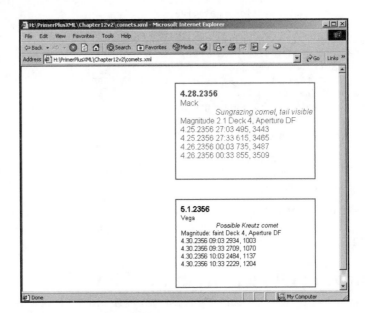

If you look at the results in Figure 12.22, you can see that even though the comet is hidden, it still takes up the same amount of space, affecting subsequent items in the flow.

FIGURE 12.22
Just because an object is hidden doesn't mean it's removed from the flow.

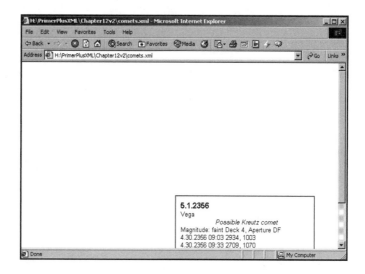

On the other hand, we can remove an item completely using `display: none`, as in Listing 12.21.

LISTING 12.21 Removing an Item from the Flow

```
discovery date { display: block;
                 font-weight: bold;
                 font-size: larger;  }
hunter         { display: block }
description    { display: block;
                 font-style: italic;
               position: relative;
               left: 75px;}
datapoint      { display: block; }
.pending { font-size: smaller }
#DF1 { color: green }
* { font-family: Borgia, Arial, Helvetica, sans-serif; }
comet { display: block;
        border: 2px solid green;
        margin: 20px;
        padding: 10px;
        padding-bottom: 40px;
        width: 300px;
        float: right;
        clear: right;  }
.confirmed { display: none; }
```

As you can see in Figure 12.23, the browser lays out the page as though the first `comet` didn't exist

Using `display: none` removes an item from the flow altogether.

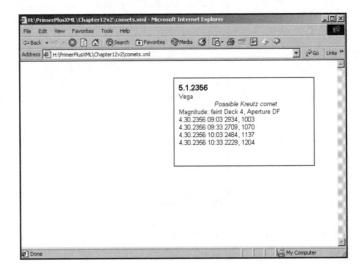

Other Media

One good thing about CSS is the fact that it's designed to be used in a variety of media. For example, the same content displayed in the browser might be read aloud for the visually impaired or for someone using a voice system to browse while they drive a car. Similarly, content that's displayed on the Web might be reused for a paper-based presentation or a slide show. Each of these purposes has properties that don't necessarily apply to the everyday browser experience.

Aural properties include `azimuth` and `elevation`, which determine where the sound seems to be coming from, `pause`, `pitch`, `speech-rate`, `stress`, `volume`, and `voice-family`. These properts allow for a range of different voices in much the same way that text can have different fonts, and other properties that make sense only in the context of material being presented aurally.

Paged media such as print or slides have their own unique issues as well, including `size` (`landscape` or `portrait`), `page-break-before` and `page-break-after`, and `orphans`, which controls the minimum number of lines that must appear on the next page.

Summary

On its own, a browser doesn't know how to display XML content and will simply display the text, unstyled. Fortunately, Cascading Style Sheets (CSS) allow you to control the presentation of content, setting properties such as font, size, color, and position.

Cascading Style Sheets are implemented as rules, each of which consists of a *selector*, which determines the content to which the rule applies, and a *declaration*, which specifies a property to apply and the appropriate value.

Pages are laid out according to the page flow, and objects can be manipulated within that flow or removed from it altogether.

Review Questions

1. What do Cascading Style Sheets do?

2. How can a style sheet be associated with an XML document?

3. How many declarations can a rule contain?

4. What happens if a particular property isn't specified for an element?

5. What happens if more than one rule applies to an element?

6. What is the difference between relative and absolute positioning?

7. Why is it a good idea to specify more than one font family choice?

Programming Exercises

1. Create an XML file and a style sheet that sets all of its text to a cursive font.

2. Modify the style sheet so that only the text of a particular element is light blue, bold, and italic.

3. Add a dotted pink border 3 pixels wide to the text that is now light blue.

4. Set the style sheet so that the content occupies a box that is 200 pixels wide, with the upper-right corner 50 pixels to the left of the right-hand edge of the window, no matter what the window size is.

CHAPTER 13

BROWSER-BASED XML: XHTML

You will learn about the following in this chapter:

- Basic XHTML
- XHTML forms
- Converting XML to XHTML with XSLT
- HTML DOM in the browser

*I*n Chapter 12, "Browser-Based XML: Cascading Style Sheets (CSS)," we took a look at properties that control the way a browser presents content. For years, however, the Web community got along without CSS, because browsers already knew how to display content marked up with an XML-like language called *Hypertext Markup Language (HTML)*. In this chapter, we're going to look at the details of that language, and how it interoperates with XML.

Notice that I said an *XML-like* language. HTML is not exactly XML; the differences are significant, but are all related to syntax. In that light, we'll discuss XHTML, which is what you get when you cross HTML 4.01 with XML 1.0, and how to put XHTML pages together.

Next, we'll talk about converting XML into XHTML using XSLT style sheets and the issues you need to consider while making the transformation.

Finally, we'll look at scripting the page. Most of today's browsers allow developers to manipulate data on the page using JavaScript or other languages, based on the idea that HTML is, in many ways, a DOM-like structure. We'll look at using JavaScript to access data within that structure.

With all of this ground to cover, it should be obvious by now that we're talking about a brief overview, rather than an in-depth discussion. When you've finished this chapter, you'll understand the concepts behind these topics, and you'll be ready to dive into the relevant specifications for details on accomplishing your particular task.

XHTML Overview

Now that you've got a feel for the types of things that you can do with a page in a browser, it's time to look at making things a little easier on you.

As you probably know, the Web didn't start out with XML and Cascading Style Sheets to control the way it looked. Instead, it started out with HTML, or Hypertext Markup Language. HTML is a tagged language, similar (but not identical) to XML, with elements and attributes that the browser interprets in order to lay out the page. It knows that an `<h1></h1>` tag is a heading, and should be displayed large and bold and on its own line. It knows how to display an image or link to another page.

In this section, we'll discuss HTML and its counterpart, XHTML. We'll look at building pages, and at the elements and attributes the browser understands.

What Is XHTML?

No, the *X* in XHTML is not a typo. HTML is similar to XML in that it uses elements and attributes, but it is a lot less strict than XML. For example, HTML is not case sensitive, while XML is. HTML also allows opening tags without closing tags in some circumstances, and doesn't require attribute values to be enclosed in quotes.

XHTML 1.0 is a reformulation of HTML 4.01 using the rules of XML. All the tags are exactly the same, but all aspects of HTML that violate the rules of XML (such as those mentioned in the preceding paragraph) are changed. For example, an image can be added to an HTML page as

```
<img src=/images/myimage.gif height=100 width=200 alt=Logo>
```

This is perfectly valid HTML, but in XML, it would cause the document to be non-well-formed for two reasons: First, the attribute values must be enclosed in quotes, and second, there's no closing tag. To solve the problem, such elements are converted to empty elements, like this:

```
<img src="/images/myimage.gif" height="100" width="200" alt="Logo" />
```

Empty Elements in the Browser

Notice the space before the ending slash in the empty element tag. This space is necessary to help older browsers interpret the tag properly.

In short, for all practical purposes, HTML and XHTML are the same, but XHTML is cleaner and is the preferred method for building pages.

Now let's look at the mechanics of building XHTML pages.

Basic Page Structure

A basic XHTML page has a simple structure. It has a single root element, `html`, which has as its children a `head` element and a `body` element, as shown in Listing 13.1.

LISTING 13.1   The Basic XHTML Page

```
<html>
<head><title>Comet Hunt Results</title></head>
```

LISTING 13.1   Continued

```
<body>
</body>
</html>
```

The **head** element includes information such as the title. It may also include client-side scripts or style information. The **body** includes the actual content of the page.

XHTML Versions

Because XHTML is XML, it's possible to validate it against a DTD. The XHTML 1.0 Recommendation defines three different "flavors" of XHTML:

- **XHTML Transitional**—This version of XHTML is virtually identical to HTML 4.01, in that it includes elements that are strictly presentational in nature, such as **center**. This version also excludes any elements related to *frames*, a way to divide up the browser window into multiple sections. This is the version that you will most likely use to convert legacy HTML documents to XHTML.

  The **DOCTYPE** declaration for XHTML Transitional documents is

  ```
  <!DOCTYPE html PUBLIC "-//W3C//DTD XHTML 1.0 Transitional//EN"
      "http://www.w3.org/TR/xhtml1/DTD/xhtml1-transitional.dtd">
  ```

- **XHTML Strict**—This version of XHTML excludes any elements or attributes that are related to presentation. This is the version that will conform most closely to future versions of XHTML, so if you can use it, you should.

  The **DOCTYPE** declaration for XHTML Strict documents is

  ```
  <!DOCTYPE html PUBLIC "-//W3C//DTD XHTML 1.0 Strict//EN"
      "http://www.w3.org/TR/xhtml1/DTD/xhtml1-strict.dtd">
  ```

- **XHTML Frameset**—This version of XHTML includes every single element and attribute currently defined in HTML 4.01, including those involving frames.

  The **DOCTYPE** declaration for XHTML Frameset documents is

  ```
  <!DOCTYPE html PUBLIC "-//W3C//DTD XHTML 1.0 Frameset//EN"
      "http://www.w3.org/TR/xhtml1/DTD/xhtml1-frameset.dtd">
  ```

Validating Documents

Strictly speaking, it's not absolutely crucial to validate an XHTML document, but it's still a good idea. Part of the purpose of XHTML is to close the loopholes left by HTML, and validating the document is the best way to make sure that you've actually succeeded in doing so.

As with any XML document, validation is a simple matter of adding a **DOCTYPE** declaration or a reference to an XML Schema or other grammar and running the document through a validating parser. For convenience, the W3C has a validation service at **http://validator.w3.org/**.

To use it, enter the URI (or URL) of the file to be validated, or use the service's upload capabilities.

In order to be considered a "strictly conforming" document, a document must include one of the three `DOCTYPE` declarations and must declare the default namespace as

`http://www.w3.org/1999/xhtml`

as shown in Listing 13.2.

LISTING 13.2 A Strictly Conforming Document

```
<!DOCTYPE html PUBLIC "-//W3C//DTD XHTML 1.0 Transitional//EN"
          "http://www.w3.org/TR/xhtml1/DTD/xhtml1-transitional.dtd">
<html xmlns="http://www.w3.org/1999/xhtml">
<head><title>Comet Hunt Results</title></head>
<body>
</body>
</html>
```

Basic XHTML

Now that we've got a document, we can start adding content to it. In this section, we'll look at creating basic XHTML pages that include text, manage whitespace appropriately, and include simple formatting. We'll then move on to discuss links, images, and using XHTML tables to format content.

Our goal is to create an XHTML page for the comet hunt data from Chapter 12.

Whitespace

One important aspect of XHTML is the way in which the browser handles whitespace. In general, it's not preserved. In other words, multiple spaces on a line, or blank spaces within the file, are treated as though they were just a single space.

We can see this if we add the basic information from the XML document to the XHTML document, as in Listing 13.3, and open it in the browser.

LISTING 13.3 Whitespace

```
<!DOCTYPE html PUBLIC "-//W3C//DTD XHTML 1.0 Transitional//EN"
          "http://www.w3.org/TR/xhtml1/DTD/xhtml1-transitional.dtd">
<html xmlns="http://www.w3.org/1999/xhtml">
<head><title>Comet Hunt Results</title></head>
<body>

        4.28.2356
        Mack
        Sungrazing comet, tail visible
        Magnitude 2.1
```

LISTING 13.3   Continued

```
Deck 4, Aperture DF

    4.25.2356
    27:03
    495, 3443

    4.25.2356
    27:33
    615, 3465

    4.26.2356
    00:03
    735, 3487

    4.26.2356
    00:33
    855, 3509

5.1.2356
Vega
Possible Kreutz comet
Magnitude: faint
Deck 4, Aperture DF

    4.30.2356
    09:03
    2934, 1003

    4.30.2356
    09:33
    2709, 1070

    4.30.2356
    10:03
    2484, 1137

    4.30.2356
    10:33
    2229, 1304

</body>
</html>
```

Even though all these items are on different lines, the browser renders them together, as shown in Figure 13.1.

Just as we created blocks for the XML page using style sheets, we can use the paragraph tag (`<p></p>`) to specify pieces of information that should be kept together and create blocks in an XHTML page, as shown in Listing 13.4.

FIGURE 13.1
The browser doesn't pre-serve whitespace.

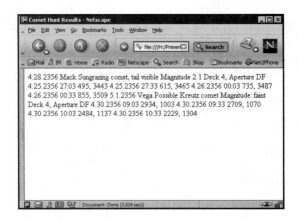

LISTING 13.4 Adding Block Formatting

```
<!DOCTYPE html PUBLIC "-//W3C//DTD XHTML 1.0 Transitional//EN"
           "http://www.w3.org/TR/xhtml1/DTD/xhtml1-transitional.dtd">
<html xmlns="http://www.w3.org/1999/xhtml">
<head><title>Comet Hunt Results</title></head>
<body>

        <p>4.28.2356</p>
        <p>Mack</p>
        <p>Sungrazing comet, tail visible</p>
        <p>Magnitude 2.1
Deck 4, Aperture DF</p>

        <p>4.25.2356
           27:03
           495, 3443</p>

        <p>4.25.2356
           27:33
           615, 3465</p>

        <p>4.26.2356
           00:03
           735, 3487</p>

        <p>4.26.2356
           00:33
           855, 3509</p>

        <p>5.1.2356</p>
        <p>Vega</p>
        <p>Possible Kreutz comet</p>
        <p>Magnitude: faint
```

LISTING 13.4   Continued

```
            Deck 4, Aperture DF</p>

            <p>4.30.2356
                09:03
                2934, 1003</p>

            <p>4.30.2356
                09:33
                2709, 1070</p>

            <p>4.30.2356
                10:03
                2484, 1137</p>

            <p>4.30.2356
                10:33
                2229, 1304</p>

    </body>
    </html>
```

The `<p>` element has built-in properties such as `display: block` and margins that set it off from the rest of the content, as shown in Figure 13.2.

FIGURE 13.2
Paragraph tags create
blocks of content.

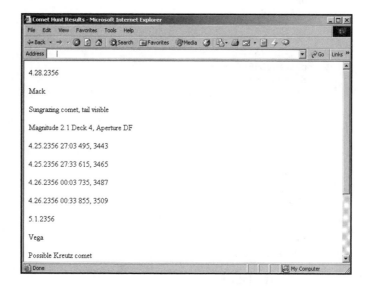

Notice that not only is every paragraph displayed on a separate line, but the paragraphs are also separated by blank lines. We can prevent the blank lines but still get the line feeds by using the line break element (`<br />`) instead of the paragraph tag, as in Listing 13.5.

LISTING 13.5 Using the Break Tag

```
<!DOCTYPE html PUBLIC "-//W3C//DTD XHTML 1.0 Transitional//EN"
          "http://www.w3.org/TR/xhtml1/DTD/xhtml1-transitional.dtd">
<html xmlns="http://www.w3.org/1999/xhtml">
<head><title>Comet Hunt Results</title></head>
<body>

        <p>4.28.2356</p>
        <p>Mack</p>
        <p>Sungrazing comet, tail visible</p>
        <p>Magnitude 2.1
        Deck 4, Aperture DF</p>

        <p>4.25.2356
            27:03
            495, 3443
        <br />
        4.25.2356
            27:33
            615, 3465
        <br />
        4.26.2356
            00:03
            735, 3487
        <br />
        4.26.2356
            00:33
            855, 3509</p>
    <br /><br /><br />
        <p>5.1.2356</p>
        <p>Vega</p>
        <p>Possible Kreutz comet</p>
        <p>Magnitude: faint
        Deck 4, Aperture DF</p>

        <p>4.30.2356
            09:03
            2934, 1003
        <br />
        4.30.2356
            09:33
            2709, 1070
        <br />
        4.30.2356
            10:03
            2484, 1137
        <br />
        4.30.2356
            10:33
            2229, 1304</p>

    </body>
    </html>
```

The break tag creates a new line, but doesn't create extra space in between lines, as shown in Figure 13.3.

FIGURE 13.3
Break tags add new lines without the extra space.

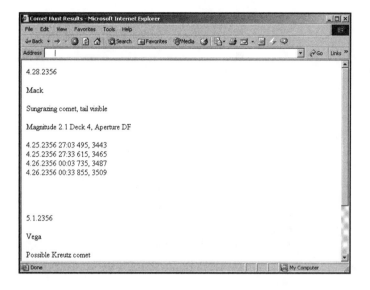

Notice also that the three successive break tags in between the two comet sightings create three new lines, even though they themselves are on a single line. Simply put, the browser ignores the whitespace in the document itself, paying attention only to the instructions it receives in the form of XHTML tags such as `<p></p>` and `<br />`.

Simple Formatting

Now let's look at some simple formatting, such as creating the date headlines and bold and italic sections (see Listing 13.6).

LISTING 13.6   Adding Formatting

```
<!DOCTYPE html PUBLIC "-//W3C//DTD XHTML 1.0 Transitional//EN"
            "http://www.w3.org/TR/xhtml1/DTD/xhtml1-transitional.dtd">
<html xmlns="http://www.w3.org/1999/xhtml">
<head><title>Comet Hunt Results</title></head>
<body>

        <h2 class="confirmed">4.28.2356</h2>
        <p><b>Mack</b></p>
        <p>Sungrazing comet, tail visible</p>
        <p>Magnitude 2.1
        <i>Deck 4, Aperture DF</i></p>

        <p>4.25.2356
```

LISTING 13.6   Continued

```
                27:03
                495, 3443
          <br />
          4.25.2356
                27:33
                615, 3465
          <br />
          4.26.2356
                00:03
                735, 3487
          <br />
          4.26.2356
                00:33
                855, 3509</p>
      <br /><br /><br />
          <h2 class="pending">5.1.2356</h2>
          <p><b>Vega</b></p>
          <p>Possible Kreutz comet</p>
          <p>Magnitude: faint
          <i>Deck 4, Aperture DF</i></p>

          <p>4.30.2356
                09:03
                2934, 1003
          <br />
          4.30.2356
                09:33
                2709, 1070
          <br />
          4.30.2356
                10:03
                2484, 1137
          <br />
          4.30.2356
                10:33
                2229, 1304</p>

</body>
</html>
```

In this listing, we're using h2, one of six headings. As shown in Figure 13.4, the text of the h2 heading is large and bold. Of the six headings, h1 is the largest, h6 the smallest. In fact, h6 is so small that you might wonder why we would even use it. The answer is that using structural tags such as these headings maintains at least some of the informational structure. A search engine reading a page to determine the relevance of a search query is going to rate text within an h1 tag as more important than text within an h3 tag, and certainly more important than information in a simple paragraph.

Content Versus Presentation

The notion of *content* versus *presentation* is an important one; we've spent a lot of time on cascading style sheets, which allow you to create the look you want without using structural tags such as headings. This is not good practice. Your content should maintain structure as much as possible, if for no other reason than to make it more transferable to other media and more readable by nontraditional browsers. In a future section, we'll look at adding style sheets to XHTML so you can still have complete control over the appearance of your content, allowing you to have your cake and eat it too.

FIGURE 13.4

Simple formatting.

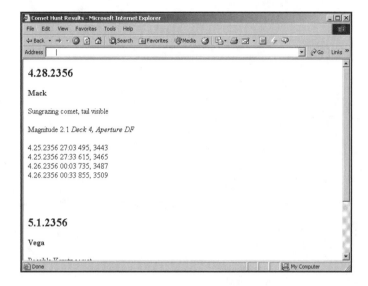

Formatting elements can be nested. For example, a headline might be italicized, or a section might be bold and italic. Just make sure that the tags are nested properly so the page is still well-formed.

Links

What would the Web be without links? A link can be a graphic or text. In Listing 13.7, we're going to link each comet hunter's name with a page of information about him or her (or it, for those whose species don't differentiate…).

LISTING 13.7   Adding Text Links

```
<!DOCTYPE html PUBLIC "-//W3C//DTD XHTML 1.0 Transitional//EN"
            "http://www.w3.org/TR/xhtml1/DTD/xhtml1-transitional.dtd">
<html xmlns="http://www.w3.org/1999/xhtml">
<head><title>Comet Hunt Results</title></head>
<body>
```

LISTING 13.7   Continued

```
        <h2 class="confirmed">4.28.2356</h2>
        <p><a href=" http://www.example.com/pages/Mack.html"><b>Mack</b></a></p>
        <p>Sungrazing comet, tail visible</p>
        <p>Magnitude 2.1
        <i>Deck 4, Aperture DF</i></p>

        <p>4.25.2356
            27:03
            495, 3443
        <br />
        4.25.2356
            27:33
            615, 3465
        <br />
        4.26.2356
            00:03
            735, 3487
        <br />
        4.26.2356
            00:33
            855, 3509</p>
    <br /><br /><br />
        <h2 class="pending">5.1.2356</h2>
        <p><a href="http://www.example.com/pages/Vega.html"><b>Vega</b></a></p>
        <p>Possible Kreutz comet</p>
        <p>Magnitude: faint
        <i>Deck 4, Aperture DF</i></p>

        <p>4.30.2356
            09:03
            2934, 1003
        <br />
        4.30.2356
            09:33
            2709, 1070
        <br />
        4.30.2356
            10:03
            2484, 1137
        <br />
        4.30.2356
            10:33
            2229, 1304</p>

</body>
</html>
```

The result is the familiar blue underlined text shown in Figure 13.5.

Links, which use the anchor tag (`<a></a>`), take a URI as the value for the `href` (or hypertext reference) attribute. This URI can take a number of forms.

FIGURE 13.5

Text links.

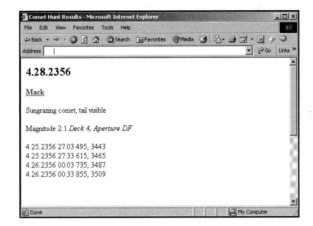

URI or URL?

You may refer to links as *URLs*, or *uniform resource locators*. This is technically correct, but it's more proper to refer to them as *URIs*, or *uniform resource identifiers*. A URL is a type of URI.

In this case, we're using the `http` protocol, which retrieves a file from another Web server. URIs can also take other protocols:

- `ftp:`—This protocol tells the browser to open a File Transfer Protocol connection, usually for downloading large files. For example:

  `ftp://www.example.com/pub/downloads/myFile.zip`

- `mailto:`—This protocol tells the browser to open a window in order to send a new email message. For example:

  `mailto:ppxml@nicholaschase.com`

- `file:///`—This protocol tells the browser to retrieve a file from the local file system. For example:

  `file:///D|/PPXML/Chapter13/comets.html`

- `https://`—This protocol tells the browser to open a secure, or encrypted, connection to the server.

  `https://www.example.com:443/orders.html`

Within the `http` protocol, you have a choice between an *absolute* URI, such as the one in the previous example, and a *relative* URI. An absolute URI includes the protocol and the server on which the material is housed. A relative URI doesn't include the protocol or the server name. It may or may not include directory information. The important thing to realize is that it uses the current document as a "base" when determining the reference point. For example, say the current document is

`http://www.example.com/comethunt/comets.html`

If, within this file, we have the link

```
<a href="hunt.html">The hunt</a>
```

it will link to

```
http://www.example.com/comethunt/hunt.html
```

because it's in the same directory as the base document. On the other hand, the link

```
<a href="images/cometDF1.gif">Image 1</a>
```

actually points to

```
http://www.example.com/comethunt/images/cometDF1.gif
```

We start out in the `comethunt` directory with the original document, then move to the `images` directory, where we find the file. Similarly, the link

```
<a href="../schedule.html">This week</a>
```

points to

```
http://www.example.com/schedule.html
```

We start out in the `comethunt` directory, but just as in the file system, we move up one level to the main root directory, where we'll find the `schedule.html` document.

URIs are also important in locating images.

Images

Of course, it's unthinkable in most situations today to write a Web page without images on it. In Listing 13.8, we'll add the images in which each comet was spotted.

LISTING 13.8   Adding Images

```
<!DOCTYPE html PUBLIC "-//W3C//DTD XHTML 1.0 Transitional//EN"
              "http://www.w3.org/TR/xhtml1/DTD/xhtml1-transitional.dtd">
<html xmlns="http://www.w3.org/1999/xhtml">
<head><title>Comet Hunt Results</title></head>
<body>

        <img src="images/cometDF1.gif" alt="Comet image DF1" />
        <h2 class="confirmed">4.28.2356</h2>
        <p><a href="/pages/Mack.html"><b>Mack</b></a></p>
        <p>Sungrazing comet, tail visible</p>
        <p>Magnitude 2.1
        <i>Deck 4, Aperture DF</i></p>

        <p>4.25.2356
            27:03
            495, 3443
        <br />
        4.25.2356
            27:33
```

LISTING 13.8   *Continued*

```
             615, 3465
          <br />
          4.26.2356
             00:03
             735, 3487
          <br />
          4.26.2356
             00:33
             855, 3509</p>
      <br /><br /><br />
          <img src="images/cometDF2.gif" alt="Comet image DF2" />
          <h2 class="pending">5.1.2356</h2>
          <p><a href="/pages/Vega.html"><b>Vega</b></a></p>
          <p>Possible Kreutz comet</p>
          <p>Magnitude: faint
          <i>Deck 4, Aperture DF</i></p>

          <p>4.30.2356
             09:03
             2934, 1003
          <br />
          4.30.2356
             09:33
             2709, 1070
          <br />
          4.30.2356
             10:03
             2484, 1137
          <br />
          4.30.2356
             10:33
             2229, 1304</p>

   </body>
   </html>
```

Note the relative URIs used for the images. We could just as easily have used absolute URIs. The `alt` attribute contains text that should be displayed if for some reason the image is not available, or if the browser doesn't support images. If we look at Figure 13.6, however, we see that the layout is far from optimal.

What we really want here is for the images to be significantly smaller, and for the text of the comet discovery to sit next to them on the page. In Listing 13.9, we'll do just that.

LISTING 13.9   *Adjusting the Images*

```
<!DOCTYPE html PUBLIC "-//W3C//DTD XHTML 1.0 Transitional//EN"
           "http://www.w3.org/TR/xhtml1/DTD/xhtml1-transitional.dtd">
<html xmlns="http://www.w3.org/1999/xhtml">
<head><title>Comet Hunt Results</title></head>
<body>
```

```
        <img src="images/cometDF1.gif" alt="Comet image DF1" width="200"
                                        height="200" align="left" />
        <h2 class="confirmed">4.28.2356</h2>
        <p><a href="/pages/Mack.html"><b>Mack</b></a></p>
        <p>Sungrazing comet, tail visible</p>
        <p>Magnitude 2.1
        <i>Deck 4, Aperture DF</i></p>

        <p>4.25.2356
            27:03
            495, 3443
        <br />
        4.25.2356
            27:33
            615, 3465
        <br />
        4.26.2356
            00:03
            735, 3487
        <br />
        4.26.2356
            00:33
            855, 3259</p>
    <br /><br /><br />
        <img src="images/cometDF2.gif" alt="Comet image DF2" width="200"
                                        height="200" align="left" />
        <h2 class="pending">5.1.2356</h2>
        <p><a href="/pages/Vega.html"><b>Vega</b></a></p>
        <p>Possible Kreutz comet</p>
        <p>Magnitude: faint
        <i>Deck 4, Aperture DF</i></p>

        <p>4.30.2356
            09:03
            2934, 1003
        <br />
        4.30.2356
            09:33
            2709, 1070
        <br />
        4.30.2356
            10:03
            2484, 1137
        <br />
        4.30.2356
            10:33
            2229, 1304</p>

    </body>
    </html>
```

FIGURE 13.6
Adding images.

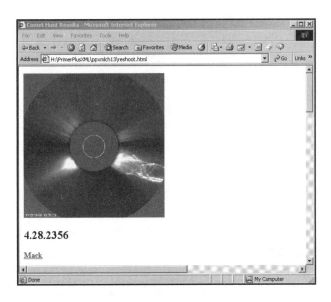

Here are some important things to note about images:

- Setting the height and/or width changes the way that the image is displayed on the page, but it doesn't change the size of the file that must be downloaded to the user's machine. Always make your files as small as possible.

- Using `align` values of `left` or `right` is similar to using the `float` property, as shown in Figure 13.7.

FIGURE 13.7
Aligning images.

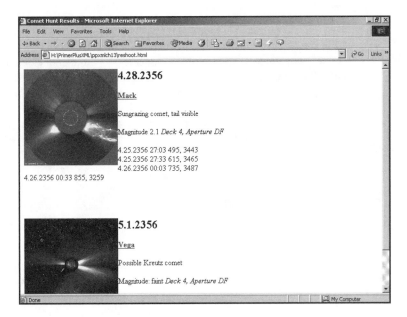

Tables

The page is definitely taking shape, but it could still use some adjustments, such as positioning the comets next to each other on the page.

In order to control page layout, designers often use *tables*, which allow you to arrange elements on the page in rows and columns, controlling their location with a good deal of precision. They can also be used as a means for structuring data in a tabular form.

Tables are useful for both purposes, but they should always be used for one or the other; use them either for layout, or for structure, but not for both at the same time.

Before we start creating tables on our page, let's look at tables in general. Listing 13.10 shows a simple table with three rows and three columns.

LISTING 13.10 A Simple Table

```
<!DOCTYPE html PUBLIC "-//W3C//DTD XHTML 1.0 Transitional//EN"
            "http://www.w3.org/TR/xhtml1/DTD/xhtml1-transitional.dtd">
<html xmlns="http://www.w3.org/1999/xhtml">
<head><title>Table</title></head>
<body>

<table border="2" width="75%">
    <tr><td>Row 1, Cell 1</td><td>Row 1, Cell 2</td><td>Row 1, Cell 3</td></tr>
    <tr><td>Row 2, Cell 1</td><td>Row 2, Cell 2</td><td>Row 2, Cell 3</td></tr>
    <tr><td>Row 3, Cell 1</td><td>Row 3, Cell 2</td><td>Row 3, Cell 3</td></tr>
</table>

</body>
</html>
```

As you can see in Figure 13.8, this table has a border of two pixels, and three rows (specified by table row elements) and columns (specified by table data elements) that span 75% of the width of the browser window. Table sizes can also be set absolutely using pixels rather than percentages. If you don't set the size at all, the table will be just large enough to hold its data.

FIGURE 13.8
A simple table.

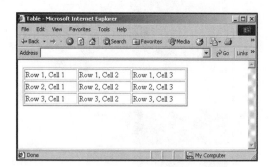

We can cause a single cell of a table to "span" multiple rows or columns, as in Listing 13.11. (A *cell* is the intersection of a row and a column.)

LISTING 13.11 Spanning Rows and Columns

```
<!DOCTYPE html PUBLIC "-//W3C//DTD XHTML 1.0 Transitional//EN"
              "http://www.w3.org/TR/xhtml1/DTD/xhtml1-transitional.dtd">
<html xmlns="http://www.w3.org/1999/xhtml">
<head><title>Table</title></head>
<body>

<table border="2" width="75%">
    <tr><td colspan="2">Row 1, Cell 1</td><td>Row 1, Cell 2</td></tr>
    <tr><td rowspan="2">Row 2, Cell 1</td><td>Row 2, Cell 2</td>
                                          <td>Row 2, Cell 3</td></tr>
    <tr><td>Row 3, Cell 1, now in position 2</td><td>Row 3, Cell 2</td></tr>
</table>

</body>
</html>
```

In this case, we set `Row 1, Cell 1` to span two columns, so it makes sense that we would remove the third cell in that row. In Figure 13.9, you can see how `Row 1, Cell 2` moves over into position 3. Perhaps less obviously, `Row 3, Cell 1` also moves, having been pushed to the right by the row spanning `Row 2, Cell 1`, so the third row also has to have its third cell removed. (Otherwise, it will move to the right to make a fourth column, even though there are no cells above it.)

FIGURE 13.9

Spanning rows and columns.

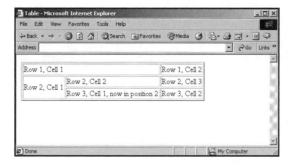

Notice also that adding the text makes the cell wider, and that the entire column becomes wider to accommodate this one cell. This is the strength of tables. Every cell in a column has the same width, and every cell in a row has the same height.

We can take these principles and apply them to our comet page, as shown in Listing 13.12.

LISTING 13.12 Using Tables to Lay Out the Page

```
<!DOCTYPE html PUBLIC "-//W3C//DTD XHTML 1.0 Transitional//EN"
            "http://www.w3.org/TR/xhtml1/DTD/xhtml1-transitional.dtd">
<html xmlns="http://www.w3.org/1999/xhtml">
<head><title>Comet Hunt Results</title></head>
<body>

<table width="100%" border="5">
  <tr><td>
      <table border="1">
        <tr>
          <td rowspan="5">
            <img src="images/cometDF1.gif" alt="Comet image DF1" width="180"
                                            height="180" align="left" />
          </td>
          <td><h2 class="confirmed">4.28.2356</h2></td>
        </tr>
        <tr><td><a href="/pages/Mack.html"><b>Mack</b></a></td></tr>
        <tr><td>Sungrazing comet, tail visible</td></tr>
        <tr><td>Magnitude 2.1
        <i>Deck 4, Aperture DF</i></td></tr>

        <tr><td>
            4.25.2356 27:03 495, 3443<br />
            4.25.2356 27:33 615, 3465<br />
            4.26.2356 00:03 735, 3487<br />
            4.26.2356 00:33 855, 3259
        </td></tr>
      </table>
  </td><td>
      <table border="1">
        <tr>
          <td rowspan="5">
            <img src="images/cometDF2.gif" alt="Comet image DF2" width="180"
                                            height="180" align="left" />
          </td>
          <td><h2 class="pending">5.1.2356</h2></td>
        </tr>
        <tr><td><a href="/pages/Vega.html"><b>Vega</b></a></td></tr>
        <tr><td>Possible Kreutz comet</td></tr>
        <tr><td>Magnitude: faint
        <i>Deck 4, Aperture DF</i></td></tr>

        <tr><td>
            4.30.2356 09:03 2934, 1003<br />
            4.30.2356 09:33 2709, 1070<br />
            4.30.2356 10:03 2484, 1137<br />
            4.30.2356 10:33 2229, 1304
        </td></tr>
      </table>
  </td></tr>
</table>
```

LISTING 13.12   Continued

```
</body>
</html>
```

I've turned the table borders on in Figure 13.10 so you can see that we have nested tables. Each comet table is the content for a table cell in the overall table.

FIGURE 13.10

Nested tables.

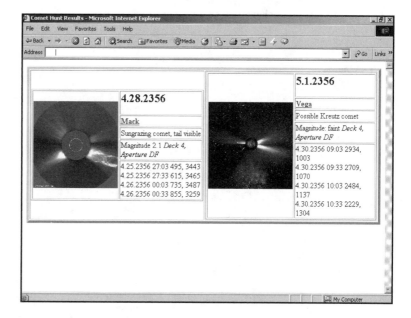

Setting the border attributes to 0 removes the borders and leaves us with a nice clean presentation, as shown in Figure 13.11.

Tables also allow formatting such as aligning the content in a cell horizontally (using the `align` attribute on a table cell) and vertically (using the `valign` attribute on a table cell), as well as setting the `height` and `width` of individual cells and rows.

CSS in XHTML

We can add style sheets to an XHTML page in a number of ways. First, we can include the information directly in the page, as in Listing 13.13.

LISTING 13.13   Including Style Information

```
<!DOCTYPE html PUBLIC "-//W3C//DTD XHTML 1.0 Transitional//EN"
            "http://www.w3.org/TR/xhtml1/DTD/xhtml1-transitional.dtd">
<html xmlns="http://www.w3.org/1999/xhtml">
<head><title>Comet Hunt Results</title>
```

LISTING 13.13   Continued

```
<style type="text/css">

    .pending { color: red }
    * { font-family: Arial, Helvetica, sans-serif;
        font-size: small; }
    a { text-decoration: none; }
    :hover { background-color: red; }

</style>

</head>
<body>

<table width="100%" border="0">
  <tr><td>
      <table border="0">
        <tr>
          <td rowspan="5">
            <img alt="Comet image DF1" src="images/cometDF1.gif" width="180"
                                       height="180" align="left" />
          </td>
          <td><h2 class="confirmed">4.28.2356</h2></td>
        </tr>
        <tr><td><a href="/pages/Mack.html"><b>Mack</b></a></td></tr>
        <tr><td>Sungrazing comet, tail visible</td></tr>
        <tr><td>Magnitude 2.1
        <i>Deck 4, Aperture DF</i></td></tr>

        <tr><td>
            4.25.2356 27:03 495, 3443<br />
            4.25.2356 27:33 615, 3465<br />
            4.26.2356 00:03 735, 3487<br />
            4.26.2356 00:33 855, 3259
        </td></tr>
      </table>
  </td><td>
      <table border="0">
        <tr>
          <td rowspan="5">
            <img alt="Comet image DF2" src="images/cometDF2.gif" width="180"
                                       height="180" align="left" />
          </td>
          <td><h2 class="pending">5.1.2356</h2></td>
        </tr>
        <tr><td><a href="/pages/Vega.html"><b>Vega</b></a></td></tr>
        <tr><td>Possible Kreutz comet</td></tr>
        <tr><td>Magnitude: faint
        <i>Deck 4, Aperture DF</i></td></tr>

        <tr><td>
            4.30.2356 09:03 2934, 1003<br />
            4.30.2356 09:33 2709, 1070<br />
            4.30.2356 10:03 2484, 1137<br />
```

LISTING 13.13   Continued

```
                4.30.2356 10:33 2229, 1304
        </td></tr>
      </table>
    </td></tr>
  </table>

  </body>
  </html>
```

FIGURE 13.11

Using tables for layout.

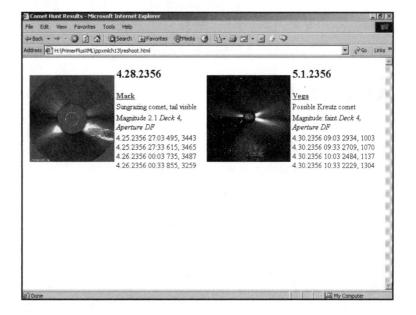

The **style** element contains exactly the same type of text that was in the external **comets_style.css** file we used in Chapter 12, but now it's directed at elements and attributes that exist in the HTML file.

In addition, we've added a new selector, **:hover**. This selector is known as a *pseudoclass*, and selects items, such as links, that currently have the mouse or other pointer over them, as shown in Figure 13.12.

You can also add a style sheet to an XHTML document using a **link** element, like this:

```
<link rel="stylesheet" href="comet_html.css" type="text/css" />
```

Style information can also be added "inline." This means that it's added directly to the appropriate element using the **style** attribute, like this:

```
<h2 style="color: red;">5.1.2356</h2>
```

For maintenance purposes, however, it's better to use style sheets and avoid inline declarations.

FIGURE 13.12
Style sheets can be
embedded in an
XHTML file.

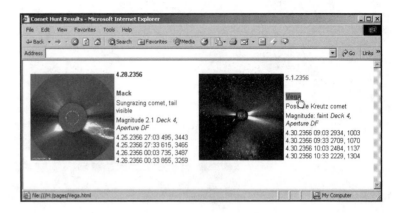

XHTML Forms

Most programmers are less interested in how a page looks than in what it can do. XHTML
enables programmers to create forms on a Web page that allow users to enter information.
This information may be incoming (such as information destined for a database) or it may simply be a request for information, such as a search query.

In this section, we're going to build a form through which comet hunters can enter their dis-
coveries. Later, we'll look at accessing the information in the form through JavaScript.

Form elements fall into three rough categories: text, choices, and buttons. We'll look at each,
and also at the way in which the information is sent to the server.

Text Elements

We'll start with the text-based elements. Listing 13.14 shows the basic form, which allows
comet hunters to enter their name, a description of the suspected comet, the brightness, and
their vantage point, along with the data points.

LISTING 13.14   The Basic Form

```
<!DOCTYPE html PUBLIC "-//W3C//DTD XHTML 1.0 Transitional//EN"
           "http://www.w3.org/TR/xhtml1/DTD/xhtml1-transitional.dtd">
<html xmlns="http://www.w3.org/1999/xhtml">
<head><title>Comet Report Form</title></head>
<body>

<h2>Report a new suspected comet</h2>
<form action="http://www.example.com/report.php" method="get">

<table>
<tr><td>Your name: </td><td><input type="text" name="hunter" /></td></tr>
<tr>
   <td>Description: </td>
   <td><textarea name="description" rows="5" cols="30"></textarea></td>
```

LISTING 13.14   Continued

```
    </tr>
    <tr>
      <td>Brightness: </td>
      <td><input type="text" name="bright" maxlength="15" /></td>
    </tr>
    <tr><td>Vantage: </td><td><input type="password" name="vantage" /></td></tr>
    <tr><td>
    Datapoints:</td><td>
                <input name="datapoint" type="text" /><br />
                <input name="datapoint" type="text" /><br />
                <input name="datapoint" type="text" /><br />
                <input name="datapoint" type="text" /><br />
                <input name="datapoint" type="text" /><br />
    </td></tr>
    </table>
    </form>

    </body>
    </html>
```

Here we have a basic **form** element that shows where the information is going (**action**) and how it's going to get there (**method**). We'll talk more about the **form** element itself in a later section.

In the meantime, we have three types of form fields on this page. The **input** element can take several different values for the **type** attribute. Here we see **text**, which just takes text, and **password**, which also takes text, but which visually replaces it with asterisks, as shown in Figure 13.13. You normally supply the **password** field when you don't want users to have to take a chance on someone seeing what they're typing (such as a good vantage point for spotting comets).

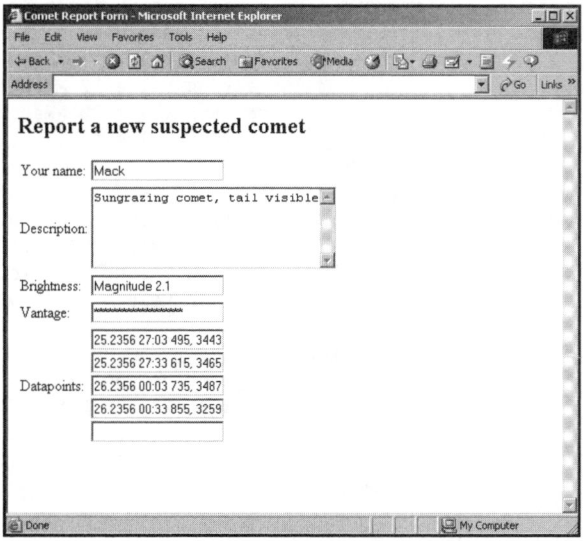

FIGURE 13.13

A simple form.

You can set the length of the box for a `text` or `password` field using the `size` attribute (not shown here). You can also set the maximum number of characters that may be entered into a field using the `maxlength` attribute.

The `<textarea>` element provides more control over appearance, in that you set both the height and width of the box (in terms of characters) but you can't limit the number of characters that can be submitted through one.

Notice that all these elements have a `name` attribute. This is the way each piece of information will be identified later, when the form is submitted.

Choice Elements

Sometimes you don't want to give your users the freedom to enter information into a text field. This may be because there are a limited number of choices, or because you want to avoid problems with misspellings, abbreviations, or other variations in the data. In these cases, you may want to use choices such as pull-down menus, check boxes, and radio groups (a set of radio elements that have the same `name` attribute), as shown in Listing 13.15.

LISTING 13.15 Adding Choice Elements

```
<!DOCTYPE html PUBLIC "-//W3C//DTD XHTML 1.0 Transitional//EN"
             "http://www.w3.org/TR/xhtml1/DTD/xhtml1-transitional.dtd">
<html xmlns="http://www.w3.org/1999/xhtml">
<head><title>Comet Report Form</title></head>
<body>

<h2>Report a new suspected comet</h2>
<form action="http://www.example.com/report.php" method="get">

<table>
<tr><td>Your name: </td><td><input type="text" name="hunter" /></td></tr>
<tr><td>Today's date:   </td><td> <select name="month">
                            <option value="1">January</option>
                            <option value="2">February</option>
                            <option value="3">March</option>
                            <option value="...">...</option>
                </select>
                <select name="day">
                            <option value="1">1</option>
                            <option value="2">2</option>
                            <option value="3">3</option>
                            <option value="...">...</option>
                </select>
                <select name="year">
                            <option value="2355">2355</option>
                            <option value="2356">2356</option>
                            <option value="2357">2357</option>
                            <option value="...">...</option>
                </select></td></tr>
```

LISTING 13.15   *Continued*

```
<tr>
   <td>Description: </td>
   <td><textarea name="description" rows="5" cols="30"></textarea></td>
</tr>
<tr>
   <td>Brightness: </td>
   <td><input type="text" name="bright" maxlength="15" /></td>
</tr>
<tr><td>Vantage: </td><td><input type="password" name="vantage" /></td></tr>
<tr><td>
Datapoints:</td><td>
            <input type="checkbox" name="point" value="0" />
            <input name="datapoint" type="text" /><br />

            <input type="checkbox" name="point" value="1" />
            <input name="datapoint" type="text" /><br />

            <input type="checkbox" name="point" value="2" />
            <input name="datapoint" type="text" /><br />

            <input type="checkbox" name="point" value="3" />
            <input name="datapoint" type="text" /><br />

            <input type="checkbox" name="point" value="4" />
            <input name="datapoint" type="text" /><br />
</td></tr>
<tr><td>
Status:    </td><td><input type="radio" name="status" value="conf" id="c" />
           <label for="c">Confirmed</label><br />

           <input type="radio" name="status" value="pend" id="p" />
           <label for="p">Pending</label><br />
</td></tr>
</table>
</form>

</body>
</html>
```

Here we have three different types of elements, as shown in Figure 13.14. The first, `select`, creates a pull-down menu, with `option` elements defining the choices. It's important to note that the information that's actually submitted depends on the `value` attribute. The text of the `option` element is ignored in favor of that value.

We can also make the `<select>` element into a list by giving it a size, and we can set it to accept multiple entries using the `multiple` attribute. For example, the code

```
<form>
<select name="vantage" size="3" multiple="multiple">
    <option value="DF">Deck 4, Aperture DF</option>
    <option value="C1">Deck 5, Aperture C1</option>
    <option value="TI">Deck 6, Aperture TI</option>
```

```
        <option value="FT">Deck 7, Aperture FT</option>
        <option value="PD">Deck 8, Aperture PD</option>
    </select>
    </form>
```

produces the results shown in Figure 13.15, with multiple options selected and a scrollbar to accommodate extra options.

FIGURE 13.14

Adding choice elements.

FIGURE 13.15

A variation on the select box.

We've also added check boxes and a radio group in Listing 13.15. These two input types are similar in that the user clicks on them to activate them, but they're different in that multiple check boxes can be active at any given time, whereas only one button in a radio group can be checked at any given time. In both these cases, the value submitted for a checked item is the `value` attribute. If a check box is not checked, nothing is submitted.

Finally, we've added a `label` for the comet's status. This is text that appears on the page, usually immediately after a form element such as a radio button or check box. It doesn't affect the data submitted in any way, but it emulates traditional applications more closely by allowing

the user to click the text in order to activate the button. For example, if we click the
`Confirmed` text, the `c` radio button will be checked.

Graceful Degradation

Not all browsers support the `label` element. Because it just provides convenience, users whose
browsers don't support it will be none the wiser, but those whose browsers do support it will have
the added functionality. This ability to add new features without disturbing users whose browsers
don't support them is known as *graceful degradation*.

Button Types

This is all well and good, but there's no way to actually submit the form. We can solve this
problem by adding buttons. In Listing 13.16, we add a Submit Report button, a Save and
Return button, and a Reset Form button.

LISTING 13.16   Adding Buttons

```
<!DOCTYPE html PUBLIC "-//W3C//DTD XHTML 1.0 Transitional//EN"
            "http://www.w3.org/TR/xhtml1/DTD/xhtml1-transitional.dtd">
<html xmlns="http://www.w3.org/1999/xhtml">
<head><title>Comet Report Form</title></head>
<body>

<h2>Report a new suspected comet</h2>
<form action="http://www.example.com/report.php" method="get">

<table>
<tr><td>Your name: </td><td><input type="text" name="hunter" /></td></tr>
<tr><td>Today's date:   </td><td> <select name="month">
                            <option value="1">January</option>
                            <option value="2">February</option>
                            <option value="3">March</option>
                            <option value="...">...</option>
                </select>
                <select name="day">
                            <option value="1">1</option>
                            <option value="2">2</option>
                            <option value="3">3</option>
                            <option value="...">...</option>
                </select>
                <select name="year">
                            <option value="2355">2355</option>
                            <option value="2356">2356</option>
                            <option value="2357">2357</option>
                            <option value="...">...</option>
                </select></td></tr>
<tr>
   <td>Description: </td>
```

LISTING 13.16 Continued

```
    <td><textarea name="description" rows="5" cols="30"></textarea></td>
</tr>
<tr>
    <td>Brightness: </td>
    <td><input type="text" name="bright" maxlength="15" /></td>
</tr>
<tr><td>Vantage: </td><td><input type="password" name="vantage" /></td></tr>
<tr><td>
Datapoints:</td><td>
            <input type="checkbox" name="point" value="0" />
            <input name="datapoint" type="text" /><br />

            <input type="checkbox" name="point" value="1" />
            <input name="datapoint" type="text" /><br />

            <input type="checkbox" name="point" value="2" />
            <input name="datapoint" type="text" /><br />

            <input type="checkbox" name="point" value="3" />
            <input name="datapoint" type="text" /><br />

            <input type="checkbox" name="point" value="4" />
            <input name="datapoint" type="text" /><br />
</td></tr>
<tr><td>
Status:   </td><td><input type="radio" name="status" value="conf" id="c" />
            <label for="c">Confirmed</label><br />

            <input type="radio" name="status" value="pend" id="p" />
            <label for="p">Pending</label><br />
</td></tr>
<tr><td colspan="2">
            <input type="submit" name="buttonname" value="Submit Report" />
            <input type="submit" name="buttonname" value="Save and Return" />
            <input type="reset"  value="Reset Form" />
</td></tr>
</table>
</form>

</body>
</html>
```

The `value` attribute determines what text is displayed on the button in the page, as shown in Figure 13.16. In most cases, it's not necessary to give a `name` attribute to `submit` buttons, but if you have more than one, the `name` provides the only way to know which one a user clicked. The name and value for the clicked button are submitted with the rest of the form. It's not necessary to put a `name` on a `reset` button, because it will never submit the form; it just returns the form to its original state.

FIGURE 13.16
Buttons allow users to submit the page.

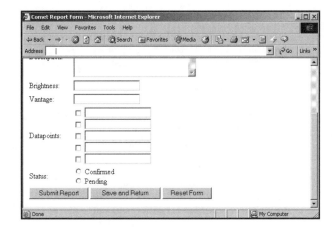

Presetting Form Information

Notice that I said a **reset** button returns the page to its original state; I didn't say it clears the form.

Forms don't have to start out blank. In browser-based applications, it's very common to provide users with a form that allows them to edit information that already exists, and it's convenient for them to have the form prefilled with information.

In Listing 13.17, we add the original information to the page.

LISTING 13.17   Adding the Original Information

```
<!DOCTYPE html PUBLIC "-//W3C//DTD XHTML 1.0 Transitional//EN"
              "http://www.w3.org/TR/xhtml1/DTD/xhtml1-transitional.dtd">
<html xmlns="http://www.w3.org/1999/xhtml">
<head><title>Comet Report Form</title></head>
<body>

<h2>Report a new suspected comet</h2>
<form action="http://www.example.com/report.php" method="get">

<table>
<tr>
   <td>Your name: </td>
   <td><input type="text" name="hunter" value="Mack" /></td>
</tr>
<tr>
   <td>Today's date:  </td>
   <td> <select name="month">
           <option value="1">January</option>
```

LISTING 13.17   Continued

```
                <option value="2" selected="selected">February</option>
                <option value="3">March</option>
                <option value="...">...</option>
            </select>
            <select name="day">
                <option value="1">1</option>
                <option value="2" selected="selected">2</option>
                <option value="3">3</option>
                <option value="...">...</option>
            </select>
            <select name="year">
                <option value="2355">2355</option>
                <option value="2356" selected="selected">2356</option>
                <option value="2357">2357</option>
                <option value="...">...</option>
            </select></td></tr>
    <tr><td>Description: </td><td>
        <textarea name="description" rows="5" cols="30">
            Sungrazing comet, tail visible
        </textarea></td></tr>
    <tr>
        <td>Brightness: </td>
        <td>
            <input type="text" name="bright" maxlength="15" value="Magnitude 2.1" />
        </td>
    </tr>
    <tr>
        <td>Vantage: </td>
        <td><input type="password" name="vantage" value="Deck 4, Aperture DF" /></td>
    </tr>
    <tr>
        <td>Datapoints:</td>
        <td>
            <input type="checkbox" name="point" value="0" checked="checked" />
            <input name="datapoint" type="text" value="4.25.2356 27:03 495, 3443" />
            <br />
            <input type="checkbox" name="point" value="1" checked="checked" />
            <input name="datapoint" type="text" value="4.25.2356 27:33 615, 3465" />
            <br />
            <input type="checkbox" name="point" value="2" />
            <input name="datapoint" type="text" />
            <br />
            <input type="checkbox" name="point" value="3" checked="checked" />
            <input name="datapoint" type="text" value="4.26.2356 00:03 735, 3487" />
            <br />
            <input type="checkbox" name="point" value="4" checked="checked" />
            <input name="datapoint" type="text" value="4.26.2356 00:33 855, 3259" />
            <br />
        </td>
    </tr>
    <tr>
        <td>Status: </td>
```

LISTING 13.17   Continued

```
        <td><input type="radio" name="status" value="conf" id="c" />
            <label for="c">Confirmed</label><br />

            <input type="radio" name="status" value="pend" id="p" checked="checked" />
            <label for="p">Pending</label><br />
        </td>
    </tr>
    <tr>
      <td colspan="2">
              <input type="submit" name="buttonname" value="Submit Report" />
              <input type="submit" name="buttonname" value="Save and Return" />
              <input type="reset"  value="Reset Form" />
      </td>
    </tr>
    </table>
    </form>

    </body>
    </html>
```

For text and password elements, it's simple to add the value using the `value` attribute. `textarea` takes as its value anything between the opening and closing tags; note that it's treated as preformatted text, and whitespace is preserved. For a `<select>` list, options are chosen as the default choice using the `selected` attribute. The reason for this odd syntax (`selected="selected"`) is that in HTML, you can add `selected` by itself, with no value. This syntax, known as *minimized attributes*, is not allowed in XHTML, so the rule was modified. The same situation led to the `checked="checked"` attributes for check boxes and radio groups.

The results are shown in Figure 13.17.

Submitting Form Information

It's certainly possible to produce a form without the user ever submitting the information, but that's only useful in a few cases. Most of the time, you want the user to actually submit the form so you can work with the information.

To understand what happens when they do, let's go back to the `form` tag:

```
<form action="http://www.example.com/report.php" method="get">
...
</form>
```

The `action` and `method` attributes determine where the information goes, and how it gets there.

The `action` attribute must be a relative or absolute URI, and is normally a traditional Web-based URI. In essence, it tells the browser where to "go" when the user submits the form. The `method` attribute tells the browser what to do with the form information. For the `get` method, as shown here, name-value pairs are appended to the URI. For example, the form in the previous example yields the following (all on one line, of course):

FIGURE 13.17

Form values can be pre-set.

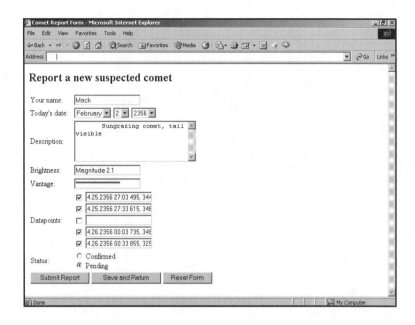

```
http://www.example.com/http://www.example.com/report.php?hunter=Mack&month=2&da
y=2&year=2356&description=+++++++Sungrazing+comet%2C+tail+visible%0D%0A+&bright
=Magnitude+2.1&vantage=Deck+4%2C+Aperture+DF&point=0&datapoint=4.25.2356+27%3A
03+495%2C+3443&point=1&datapoint=4.25.2356+27%3A33+615%2C+3465&datapoint=&point
=3&datapoint=4.26.2356+00%3A03+735%2C+3487&point=4&datapoint=4.26.2356+00%3A33+
855%2C+3259&status=pend&buttonname=Submit+Report
```

Looking at this bit by bit, we see that the URI starts with the action, followed by a question mark (**?**). The question mark signals that what follows is a list of parameters meant for the script at the URI. Each form value is presented as a name-value pair, with each pair separated by an ampersand.

Notice also that the data isn't presented exactly as it was in the form. Some characters, such as spaces, would create a URI that the browser couldn't process, so they're "escaped," or converted to safe characters such as plus signs (+). Typically, the application on the other end, such as PHP or ASP, automatically converts these values back into their original form so that you can use them.

As far as security is concerned, the **get** method is not ideal, for several reasons. For one, notice that the vantage point, which we so carefully hid with the **password** field, is displayed in plain sight. The same thing happens for hidden elements. Also, many Web servers have a problem with **get** requests that are too long—something you can't necessarily avoid if you're using a **<textarea>**.

Hidden Element

A *hidden element* is a form input with a **type** value of **hidden**. These values are not displayed on the Web page, but are submitted with the rest of the form. For example, we could use a hidden field to include a session identifier:

```
<input type="hidden" name="session_id" value="KEJWOSIOE3" />
```

Because of the **get** method's security limitations, you should use the **post** method instead. With **post**, values are sent as HTTP header values. These values are part of the request sent from the browser to the server, but typically are not accessible by the user, and don't appear on the URI line of the browser.

Converting XML to XHTML with XSLT

Now that you have a basic understanding of XHTML, let's look at transforming our XML document into XHTML using XSLT.

The process itself is straightforward; for the most part, you already have all the tools you need if you've read Chapter 9, "Extensible Stylesheet Language Transformations (XSLT)."

In this section, we'll look at a few aspects of XSLT that are specific to XHTML transformations, such as action in the browser and the HTML output method.

The Style Sheet

Creating a style sheet that converts the XML file we used in Chapter 12 to the HTML file we eventually wound up with in Listing 13.13 is fairly straightforward. The style sheet is shown in Listing 13.18.

LISTING 13.18   The XSLT Style Sheet

```
<?xml version="1.0"?>
<xsl:stylesheet xmlns:xsl="http://www.w3.org/1999/XSL/Transform" version="1.0">

<xsl:template match="/">
<!DOCTYPE html PUBLIC "-//W3C//DTD XHTML 1.0 Transitional//EN"
            "http://www.w3.org/TR/xhtml1/DTD/xhtml1-transitional.dtd">
<html xmlns="http://www.w3.org/1999/xhtml">
<head><title>Comet Hunt Results</title>

<style type="text/css">

    .pending { color: red }
    * { font-family: Arial, Helvetica, sans-serif;
        font-size: x-small;}
    a {text-decoration: none}
    :hover {background-color: red}
```

LISTING 13.18   Continued

```
    </style>

    </head>
    <body>
    <table>
        <tr><xsl:apply-templates select="comets/comet"/></tr>
    </table>
    </body>
    </html>
    </xsl:template>

    <xsl:template match="comet">
    <td>

    <table>
    <tr><td rowspan="5">
    <xsl:element name="img">
        <xsl:attribute name="src">images/comet<xsl:value-of
                                      select="@id"/>.gif</xsl:attribute>
        <xsl:attribute name="height">180</xsl:attribute>
        <xsl:attribute name="width">180</xsl:attribute>
        <xsl:attribute name="align">left</xsl:attribute>
        <xsl:attribute name="alt">Comet <xsl:value-of select="@id"/></xsl:attribute>
    </xsl:element>
    </td>
    <td>
        <xsl:element name="h2">
            <xsl:attribute name="class"><xsl:value-of
                                      select="@class" /></xsl:attribute>
            <xsl:value-of select="./discovery/date" />
        </xsl:element>
    </td></tr>
    <tr><td>
        <xsl:element name="a">
            <xsl:attribute name="href"><xsl:value-of
                                      select="hunter/@homepage"/></xsl:attribute>
            <b><xsl:value-of select="discovery/hunter"/></b>
        </xsl:element>
        </td></tr>
    <tr><td><xsl:value-of select="discovery/description"/></td></tr>
    <tr><td><xsl:value-of select="discovery/magnitude"/>
            <i><xsl:value-of select="discovery/vantage"/></i></td></tr>
    <tr><td>
    <xsl:apply-templates select="positions/datapoint"/>
    </td></tr>
    </table>

    </td>

    </xsl:template>

    <xsl:template match="datapoint">
```

LISTING 13.18   Continued

```
<xsl:value-of select="date"/><xsl:text> </xsl:text>
<xsl:value-of select="time"/><xsl:text> </xsl:text>
<xsl:value-of select="position"/>
<br />
</xsl:template>
</xsl:stylesheet>
```

We can use this style sheet for the transformation in one of two locations: in the browser or on the server.

XSLT in the Browser

Telling the browser to use an XSLT style sheet is as simple as adding the `stylesheet` processing instruction to the XML file, as in Listing 13.19.

LISTING 13.19   Adding the Style Sheet Processing Instruction

```
<?xml version="1.0"?>
<?xml-stylesheet href="comets.xsl" type="text/xsl"?>
<comets>
  <comet class="confirmed" id="DF1">
...
```

That's the easy part. The hard part is figuring out what the browser is going to do with it.

Not all browsers support XSLT, though such support is becoming more common. Older browsers, such as Netscape Navigator 4.x, may attempt to open the XML in another application, or may display it as text, depending on how they've been configured.

And just because a browser understands what it's supposed to do with an XSLT style sheet doesn't mean that it does it in the manner you'd expect. Some older browsers that do understand XSLT, such as Microsoft Internet Explorer 4.x and some versions of 5.x, use an older version of the XSLT recommendation, called the *working draft*. The style sheet as it appears in Listing 13.18 won't work; instead, you need to change the namespace, as in Listing 13.20.

LISTING 13.20   The Working Draft Namespace

```
<?xml version="1.0"?>
<xsl:stylesheet xmlns:xsl="http://www.w3.org/TR/WD-xsl/" version="1.0" >

<xsl:template match="/">
<!DOCTYPE html PUBLIC "-//W3C//DTD XHTML 1.0 Transitional//EN"
            "http://www.w3.org/TR/xhtml1/DTD/xhtml1-transitional.dtd">
<html xmlns="http://www.w3.org/1999/xhtml">
<head><title>Comet Hunt Results</title>
...
```

Slowly but surely, browsers are standardizing on the proper namespace, but until you're certain that your audience can read and understand browser-based XSLT, it's probably better to simply do the conversion on the server and stream the results to the browser as a regular HTML page, just as you would do any other XSL transformation.

XSLT Style Sheets on the Server

Outputting XML as HTML involves doing the transformation on the server and simply returning the XHTML or HTML. The browser doesn't know the difference between that and a static HTML file, so there are no compatibility issues. For example, Listing 13.21 shows a sample Java servlet that transforms the `comets.xml` file and returns the result to the browser.

LISTING 13.21   Transforming with a Servlet

```
import javax.xml.transform.stream.StreamSource;
import javax.xml.transform.stream.StreamResult;
import javax.xml.transform.TransformerFactory;
import javax.xml.transform.Source;
import javax.xml.transform.Transformer;
import javax.servlet.http.HttpServlet;

public class OutputFile extends HttpServlet {

    public void doGet(
            javax.servlet.http.HttpServletRequest request,
            javax.servlet.http.HttpServletResponse response)
            throws javax.servlet.ServletException, java.io.IOException {

        String XMLFileName = "comets.xml";

        StreamSource source = new StreamSource(XMLFileName);
        StreamResult result = response.out;

        TransformerFactory transFactory = TransformerFactory.newInstance();
        Source style = transFactory.getAssociatedStylesheet(source,
                                                    null,
                                                    null,
                                                    null);

        Transformer trans = transFactory.newTransformer();
        trans.transform(source, result);
    }
}
```

Outputting HTML

There's one more issue to consider when transforming XML into HTML or XHTML: HTML features that are not compatible with XML. Suppose, for example, that we want to add a script to the page that gives an alert if the contest deadline has already passed, as shown in Listing 13.22.

LISTING 13.22   Adding a Script

```
<?xml version="1.0"?>
<xsl:stylesheet xmlns:xsl="http://www.w3.org/1999/XSL/Transform" version="1.0">

<xsl:template match="/">
<!DOCTYPE html PUBLIC "-//W3C//DTD XHTML 1.0 Transitional//EN"
            "http://www.w3.org/TR/xhtml1/DTD/xhtml1-transitional.dtd">
<html xmlns="http://www.w3.org/1999/xhtml">
<head><title>Comet Hunt Results</title>

<style type="text/css">

    .pending { color: red }
    * { font-family: Arial, Helvetica, sans-serif;
        font-size: x-small;}
    a {text-decoration: none}
    :hover {background-color: red}

</style>

<script type="text/javascript">
<![CDATA[
    function getStatus() {
        var today = new Date();
        var contest_end = new Date("7/1/2358");
        if (contest_end < today) {
            alert("The contest is over.  No more entries will be accepted."); }
        };
    }
]]>
</script>

</head>
<body onload="getStatus()">
<table>
    <tr><xsl:apply-templates select="comets/comet"/></tr>
</table>
</body>
</html>
</xsl:template>

<xsl:template match="comet">
<td>

<table>
<tr><td rowspan="5">
<xsl:element name="img">
    <xsl:attribute name="src">images/comet<xsl:value-of
                                        select="@id"/>.gif</xsl:attribute>
    <xsl:attribute name="height">180</xsl:attribute>
    <xsl:attribute name="width">180</xsl:attribute>
    <xsl:attribute name="align">left</xsl:attribute>
</xsl:element>
```

LISTING 13.22   Continued

```
    </td>
    <td>
        <xsl:element name="h2">
            <xsl:attribute name="class"><xsl:value-of
                                        select="@class" /></xsl:attribute>
            <xsl:value-of select="./discovery/date" />
        </xsl:element>
    </td></tr>
    <tr><td>
        <xsl:element name="a">
            <xsl:attribute name="href"><xsl:value-of
                                        select="hunter/@homepage" /></xsl:attribute>
            <b><xsl:value-of select="discovery/hunter" /></b>
        </xsl:element>
        </td></tr>
    <tr><td><xsl:value-of select="discovery/description" /></td></tr>
    <tr><td><xsl:value-of select="discovery/magnitude" />
            <i><xsl:value-of select="discovery/vantage" /></i></td></tr>
    <tr><td>
    <xsl:apply-templates select="positions/datapoint" />
    </td></tr>
    </table>

    </td>

    </xsl:template>

    <xsl:template match="datapoint">
    <xsl:value-of select="date" /><xsl:text> </xsl:text>
    <xsl:value-of select="time" /><xsl:text> </xsl:text>
    <xsl:value-of select="position" />
    <br />
    </xsl:template>
    </xsl:stylesheet>
```

Because of the less-than sign (<), this will be a non-well-formed document if we don't enclose the script itself in a **CDATA** section. Unfortunately, if we do, and the transformation treats this like XML, we'll wind up with the following script in the final document:

```
<script type="text/javascript">

    function getStatus() {
        var today = new Date();
        var contest_end = new Date("7/1/2358");
        if (contest_end &lt; today) {
            alert("The contest is over.  No more entries will be accepted."); }
        };
    }

</script>
```

This takes care of the well-formedness problem, but now the script won't work. In addition, empty elements such as `<img>` and `<br>` are sometimes rendered as `<img></img>` and `<br></br>`.

The solution is to set the output method for the style sheet to HTML, as in Listing 13.23.

LISTING 13.23   Using the HTML Output Method

```
<?xml version="1.0"?>
<xsl:stylesheet xmlns:xsl="http://www.w3.org/1999/XSL/Transform" version="1.0">

<xsl:output method="html"/>

<xsl:template match="/">
<!DOCTYPE html PUBLIC "-//W3C//DTD XHTML 1.0 Transitional//EN"
                "http://www.w3.org/TR/xhtml1/DTD/xhtml1-transitional.dtd">
<html xmlns="http://www.w3.org/1999/xhtml">
<head><title>Comet Hunt Results</title>
...
```

The result is that `CDATA` sections are added to the document as is, and empty elements are rendered using the shorthand method (`<br/>` as opposed to `<br></br>`). In some cases, `meta` tags, which provide information about the document, may be added.

A `meta` tag is an element that can be used to specify information about the page. Search engines often check `meta` tags for information such as a title, keywords for searches in which this page should appear, and descriptions. A `meta` tag can also be used to redirect the browser to another location in the case of a site that is in the process of moving to a new address.

HTML DOM in the Browser

The Document Object Model originated as a way for Web authors to access information on an HTML page, such as the data in a form or the `src` attribute of an image. As such, browser scripting shouldn't be completely foreign to you if you understand the DOM for XML.

When it comes to the Document Object Model, however, all browsers are not created equal. Some support the actual Document Object Model from the W3C (to varying degrees) and some support a much earlier version known as DOM Level 0.

It's impossible to cover all the different permutations of browser support in one small section, so we're going to concentrate on the basics.

We'll look at two examples. First, we'll look at accessing form values, and then we'll look at changing content that's already on the page by setting a value for a block of HTML.

Accessing Form Values

First, we're going to take a look at the form for reporting a suspected comet. When the form is submitted, we want to pop up a window that shows each form element and its value, then asks whether to actually submit the data. Before we do that, however, let's talk about the actual structure of the page.

The document itself takes the form of the `document` object. That object has certain attributes, such as `url`, and certain methods, such as `write()`.

Some of the attributes are simple values, but some of them are `HTMLCollections`—array-like structures, such as `applets`, `images`, and `forms`. It's this last structure that we're interested in, in this case, but the general concepts are the same for all of them.

The `forms` array is an array of `form` objects, each of which consists of an array of `elements`. Each `element` has a `name` and a `value`.

In Listing 13.24, we're adding a script that loops through each element of the first `form` (number 0) and outputs its name and value.

LISTING 13.24   Looping Through `form` Elements

```
<!DOCTYPE html PUBLIC "-//W3C//DTD XHTML 1.0 Transitional//EN"
                "http://www.w3.org/TR/xhtml1/DTD/xhtml1-transitional.dtd">
<html xmlns="http://www.w3.org/1999/xhtml">
<head><title>Comet Report Form</title>

<script type="text/javascript">

<![CDATA[

function confirminfo() {

   var thisForm = document.forms[0];
   var numFields = thisForm.elements.length;
    var alertString = "";
   var y = 0;
   while (y < numFields) {
      alertString = alertString + thisForm.elements[y].name + "=";
      alertString = alertString + thisForm.elements[y].value + "\n";
    y = y + 1;
   }
   confirm(alertString);

}

]]>

</script>

</head>
<body>

<h2>Report a new suspected comet</h2>
<form action="report.php" method="get" onsubmit="return confirminfo()">
```

LISTING 13.24   Continued

```
<table>
...
```

Note that we're just adding the scripts to the existing form page, rather than creating a new page. Note also that some browsers (most notably IE 6.0) don't like the `<![CDATA[ ]]>` notation, even though it's correct XML.

In this script, we first get a reference to the first `form` in the `forms` array. From there, we find out how many elements are in the form by reading the `length` property of that `form`'s `elements` array.

Next, we initialize the `alertString` and `y` variables, which will hold the text to be output and determine when we've run out of fields, respectively. From here, we have a simple `while` loop that increments for each `element` and exits when they've all been evaluated.

Within the loop, we're retrieving two values and using them to build the alert string. The name of the field is the `name` attribute of the `y`th `element` in the `elements` array for the form. We determine the `value` in the same way.

The `\n` represents the newline character, so the result is a list of name-value pairs, as shown in Figure 13.18.

FIGURE 13.18

Looping through the elements on a form.

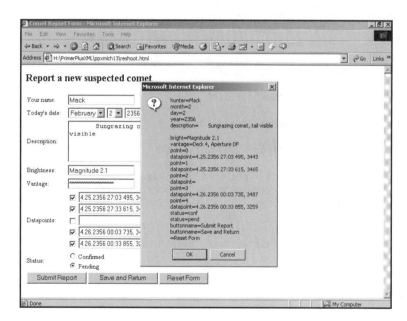

Each type of object has its own attributes. For instance, a `form` element has a `name` and `value`, and an `image` has `name`, `src`, `height`, `width`, and other attribute values that correspond to the attributes found on an `img` element.

Changing Page Content and Presentation

Once you've accessed the object representing a `form` element, changing its value is a straightforward process, but that's not all that you can do.

If the browser supports the DOM, which we'll check in this example, you can also change the content on the page without reloading.

In Listing 13.25, we're going to add a link to the pending comet report that allows an administrator (or contest judge) to remove this report from the page, substituting instead a notice that the claim has been rejected.

LISTING 13.25   Replacing Content

```html
<html>
<head><title>Comet Hunt Results</title>

<style type="text/css">

    .pending { color: red }
    * { font-family: Arial, Helvetica, sans-serif;
        font-size: x-small;}
    a {text-decoration: none}
    :hover {background-color: red}
    h1 { font-size: xx-large;
        margin: 50px }

</style>

<script type="text/javascript">

function clearPanel(panelid) {

   if (document.getElementById) {

      var theDiv = document.getElementById(panelid);
      theDiv.innerHTML = "<h1>Report Cleared</h1>";

   } else {

       alert("This browser doesn't support the DOM.");

   }

}

</script>

</head>
<body>

<table width="100%" border="0">
```

LISTING 13.25   *Continued*

```
<tr><td valign="top">
   <table border="0">
      <tr>
         <td rowspan="5">
            <img alt="Comet image DF1" src="images/cometDF1.gif" width="180"
                                        height="180" align="left" />
         </td>
         <td><h2 class="confirmed">4.28.2356</h2></td>
      </tr>
      <tr><td><a href="/pages/Mack.html"><b>Mack</b></a></td></tr>
      <tr><td>Sungrazing comet, tail visible</td></tr>
      <tr><td>Magnitude 2.1
      <i>Deck 4, Aperture DF</i></td></tr>

      <tr><td>
          4.25.2356 27:03 495, 3443<br />
          4.25.2356 27:33 615, 3465<br />
          4.26.2356 00:03 735, 3487<br />
          4.26.2356 00:33 855, 3259
      </td></tr>
   </table>
</td><td valign="top">
  <div id="pend">
     <table border="0">
        <tr>
           <td rowspan="5">
              <img alt="Comet image DF2" src="images/cometDF2.gif" width="180"
                                          height="180" align="left" />
           </td>
           <td><h2 class="pending">5.1.2356</h2></td>
        </tr>
        <tr><td><a href="/pages/Vega.html"><b>Vega</b></a></td></tr>
        <tr><td>Possible Kreutz comet</td></tr>
        <tr><td>Magnitude: faint
        <i>Deck 4, Aperture DF</i></td></tr>

        <tr><td>
            4.30.2356 09:03 2934, 1003<br />
            4.30.2356 09:33 2709, 1070<br />
            4.30.2356 10:03 2484, 1137<br />
            4.30.2356 10:33 2229, 1304
        </td></tr>
     </table>

     <h2 align="center">
        <a href="javascript:return false" onclick="clearPanel('pend')">
           Clear this report
        </a>
     </h2>
  </div>
 </td></tr>
</table>
```

LISTING 13.25 Continued

```
</body>
</html>
```

In this case, we've added a `div` element containing the pending table. This is an element that doesn't itself appear on the page, but acts as a block that holds other content. At the bottom of the `<div>`, we're adding a link that has an event handler, `onclick`. When the user clicks on the link, it executes the script specified by `onclick`. (The value `javascript: return false` keeps the link from activating its regular function.)

The script itself first checks to see whether the browser supports the DOM. If it doesn't, the `getElementById` function won't exist, so `document.getElementById` will return `null`, or `false`.

If the method does exist, we'll use it to retrieve the `<div>` object. Once we have it, we can set the `innerHTML` property. This is the property that defines the content of the `<div>`, so by setting it to a single heading, we change the content on the page, as shown in Figure 13.19.

FIGURE 13.19
Changing the content on the page.

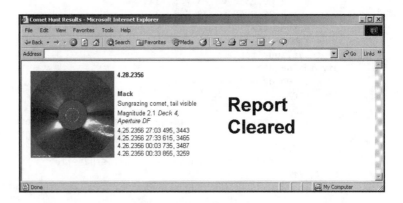

Notice that the CSS directives included on the page take effect for this "new" content.

Summary

Despite the control that CSS gives over XML, Web pages are usually built using HTML or its XML counterpart, XHTML. HTML is a defined set of tags that the browser understands, and XHTML is HTML forced to follow XML's rules.

A page contains an HTML element and `<head>` and `<body>` elements, with the content in the `<body>` element. Whitespace in the content is ignored, and must be added through the use of elements such as the paragraph and break tags.

Information can be styled using presentation-type tags such as bold and italics, or using structure-type tags such as headings.

Pages can be laid out using tables, which can also be used for tabular data. You can also create user forms, which accept information from users in a variety of ways.

Forms and other aspects of the page are accessible through scripting in a DOM-like structure.

Review Questions

1. What are the advantages of using HTML instead of XML and CSS?

2. Name three ways to add CSS information to an HTML page.

3. Name three differences between HTML and XHTML.

4. How can an HTML table aid in the layout of a Web page?

5. Can a table contain another table?

6. How can you limit the number of characters entered into a `<form>` text input? A `<textarea>`?

7. What is the difference between the `get` and `post` methods for submitting forms?

8. When transforming XML into HTML, how can you prevent problems with scripting that has been escaped using a `CDATA` section?

9. What is the main object representing an HTML page? How are its child objects represented?

Programming Exercises

1. Create an HTML page that includes an image that links to another page.

2. Create the page shown in Figure 13.20.

FIGURE 13.20

Hint: Use tables for layout.

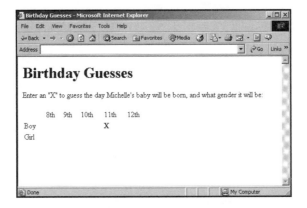

3. Add the form shown in Figure 13.21 to the page.

FIGURE 13.21
Hint: Use check boxes.

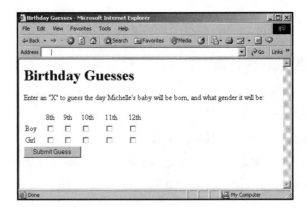

4. Create a page with three images. When the page loads, the body's `onload` event is triggered. When this event is triggered, the `src` attribute of the second image should appear in an alert box.

CHAPTER 14

XML LINKING LANGUAGE (XLINK)

You will learn about the following in this chapter:

- Simple links
- Extended links
- Using XLink to embed new information

- Linkbases
- Using extended links and linkbases to relate information
- XPointer points and ranges

*I*n the last two chapters, we talked about XML and the Web as it is now. You can create XHTML pages and display them in a browser, and you can (in some cases) take an XML file and display it directly in your environment of choice, as long as that environment supports Cascading Style Sheets. In this chapter, we're going to study the XML Linking Language (XLink), which takes things one step further into the future.

XML Linking Language (XLink) is like XHTML hyperlinks on steroids; not only can you create a link from one page to another, but you can also create a link back—even if you don't have write access to the remote page.

XLink has one simple purpose: to create relationships between different resources. Those resources might be something as simple as a text link and a page on another server (as in the case of a hyperlink), or they might be a collection of documents, each of which is related to the others in a specific way.

Some of these uses will require new applications very different from those we're using today. Others, such as artificial intelligence systems, won't involve us at all, and will instead use the information directly.

In this chapter, we're going to look at some simple weblog entries and examine the relationships between authors, entries, and the articles they reference. We'll start out with a traditional browser, then move to a sample XLink application that demonstrates more capabilities than browsers can currently handle.

We'll also talk about XML Pointer Language (XPointer), a related recommendation similar to XPath that allows you to address a portion of an XML document, rather than the whole document.

Versions

At the time of this writing, XLink 1.0 is a W3C Recommendation. XPointer is a Candidate Recommendation, so it's possible that minor details will have changed by the time you read this. Check Appendix A for the locations of the official recommendations.

XLink Overview

When you come right down to it, XLink is an attempt to bring the Web back to what it was in the beginning.

The concept of the World Wide Web originated in a 1948 article by Vannevar Bush entitled "As We May Think." The article described the memex, a way for users to leave "trails" through information that they found. Users following the trails could leave their own comments, or branch off into trails of their own. The result was a pool of information linked together in a logical way.

Fast-forward four decades or so to the genesis of the modern World Wide Web, when Tim Berners-Lee attempted to organize the information at CERN. Like HyperCard and some of the other prototypes that came before, the World Wide Web linked a single resource with another single resource. If you clicked a linked word, you got information related to that word. Collections of sorts could be made in the form of pages of links, but the Web still didn't organize resources into a reasonable facsimile of relationships.

An XLink is, at its heart, a relationship between two or more resources. Those resources can be any addressable information, such as Web pages or other types of Internet content, or even sections of a document. But while an XLink creates that relationship, it says absolutely nothing about how it is to be presented to the user. The user, in fact, is almost an afterthought.

XLink enables you to create complex relationships between documents, which are designed to be handled by an application. That application might hide the information from the user completely, as in the case of an artificial intelligence application that looks at linked resources for patterns and trends, or it might be geared toward the user, the way a browser is. In the latter case, the application takes the information and massages it into something a human can comprehend.

In both cases, it is the relationships that are important, and not the presentation. The presentation (or lack of it) is the application's problem.

In this section, we're going to take a quick look at some of the capabilities that XLink defines.

Link Types

In XLink, there are two basic types of links: *simple links* and *extended links*. Extended links can be gathered into collections called *linkbases*.

A simple link is much like a hyperlink that you might see on a Web page. It involves a local resource, such as a string of text that says "Click here for more information," and an external resource such as a brochure the user can download or a Web page with more information. Simple XLinks are beginning to show up in traditional browsers such as Netscape 6 and 7.

An extended link is a bit more generic, and thus more complex. Simply put, an extended link defines a relationship between two or more resources. These resources might be text within the link, or they might be content you have no control over. You might even link a single starting point to several endpoints. For example, a single link on an investment site might enable users to go to pages where they can research any of the stocks featured in a particular mutual fund.

Browsers and Extended Links

If a single string of text links to multiple potential destinations, the browser might pop up a window of choices, or it might provide a pull-down menu when you click the link; because nobody has yet implemented extended links in a browser, these decisions have yet to be made.

Linking to information beyond your control isn't so strange; you've probably been doing it for years with hyperlinks. But what if you could link *from* such a document, without ever having to edit it?

XLink also allows you to define links outside the documents themselves, in special structures called *link databases*, or *linkbases* for short. These linkbases can be loaded automatically, allowing you to make use of relationships between different resources without having to embed the actual links in them. You might create a structure that relates entire collections of information that is outside your control.

The actuate Attribute

XLinks give you the ability to decide when a particular link will be followed (traversed). For example, a typical hyperlink has an `actuate` value of `onRequest`. Nothing happens until you click it. On the other hand, there are certain situations in which you want a particular link to be loaded immediately. For example, you might want to immediately redirect a browser to another page as soon as the original page is loaded. This is a situation in which the actual value should be `onLoad`.

You should use `onLoad` in linkbases, where you may need the information immediately, and in situations where you're embedding information on the page.

The show Attribute

Hyperlinks are typically displayed in one of two ways. The most common is to replace the current window with the contents of the linked information. This allows you to work your way through a site. In some cases, however, an author might want the new information to pop up in a separate window so that the user still has access to the information in the original window.

Both of these situations are covered by the show attribute, which has among its possible values replace, which replaces the entire window in the same way as a traditional hyperlink, and new, which opens a new window but leaves the original window intact.

These are just some of the possibilities, however. An XLink can also be embedded in the page. For example, when you add an image to an HTML page, you're just adding a reference to that image into the actual HTML. The browser takes that reference, retrieves the image resource, and replaces the reference with the actual content so the user sees it in the browser window.

XLink allows you to do this with other content, as well. For example, you might have an article title on the page, and when the user clicks it, the content of the actual article is embedded within the page.

Seeing XLinks in Action

Despite its usefulness, XLink is still new enough that there aren't a lot of implementations out there for us to take a look at. Fortunately, Fujitsu has released an XLink processor that consists of an API. Even more fortunately, one of their sample applications is a rudimentary XLink "browser" that we can use to see how all of this actually works.

XLink Processor (XLiP) is a Java application, so if you don't have Java on your machine, you'll need to get it in order to see the examples. (If this is a problem, you have the option of just following along with the screenshots, of course.)

Once you've got Java installed, download XLiP from `http://www.labs.fujitsu.com/free/xlip/en/index.html` and install it. Next, download the XLink Tree Demo Application at `http://www.labs.fujitsu.com/free/xlip/en/sample1.html` and extract it. You should be able to start the application by double-clicking on the `XlinkDemo.jar` file, as shown in Figure 14.1.

FIGURE 14.1
The XLiP Tree Demo
application.

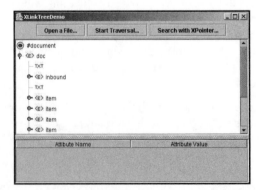

Once the application is open, you can click the Open a File button to load any of the examples—choose the `hub.xml` file in any given folder. The application allows you to look at the structure of a document, expanding and closing element nodes, and to traverse links within the documents. It also allows you to process XPointer expressions, which we'll discuss later in the chapter, but as of this writing support is still pretty rudimentary.

Link-Building Basics

Now let's get our hands dirty and start building some real live links. In this section we'll start with a traditional XHTML hyperlink, then see what it would look like as a simple XLink. From there, we'll look at embedding the linked information rather than replacing the original page.

Finally, we'll look at the difference in syntax between a simple and an extended link.

XHTML Hyperlinks

Chances are you're familiar with XHTML hyperlinks, even if it's just because you read about them in Chapter 13, "Browser-Based XML: XHTML."

A hyperlink is a specific element, `<a>`, with an `href` attribute that allows you to specify where the browser should look for the related content. You might also add a `target` attribute that allows you to open the content in a new window, as shown in Listing 14.1.

LISTING 14.1   Sample Hyperlinks

```
<html>
<head>
   <title>What were they thinking? (4.28.2356)</title>
</head>
<body>
   <h2>What were they thinking?</h2>
   <p><i>4.28.2356</i></p>

<p>So it seems that <a href="merlor.xml">Jasper Borkot is
Bumbledoop of Merlor</a>.  I don't know what the Merlorians
were thinking, but in my opinion, Shoopfuma the Irradiant
should have been the Bumbledoop.  Borkot couldn't win a mind
battle against a sneech.  My Great Aunt Kyleesey could do a
better job.  If you want proof, check out
<a href="merlor.xml" target="_blank">this
article</a>, where he promises to "build a monument to Flurowamp,
the greatest Merlorian of them all."  Nobody wants a monument to
Flurowamp! He wasn't that popular, and the guchucks to pay
for it will come from the Merlorians' hard earned wages.</p>

</body>
</html>
```

Here we have two different versions of the same link, distinguished by the `target` attribute. If we were to click each of them, we'd get a different result, as shown in Figure 14.2.

FIGURE 14.2
Hyperlinks can replace the information in the window, or they can cause the browser to open a whole new window.

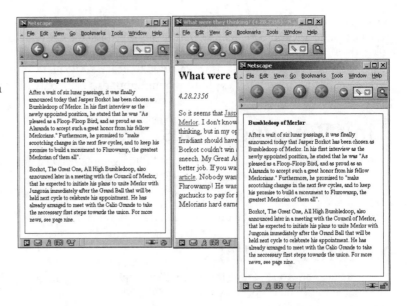

The first link behaves as you'd expect, replacing the content of the original window with the content found at the location specified by the `href` attribute, or the ending resource. The second link also tells the browser to retrieve the information at the location of the ending resource, but to display it in a new window. This is similar to some of the things we can do with simple XLinks.

The target Attribute

Strictly speaking, the `target` attribute isn't meant to be used specifically to open content in a new window. It's actually part of HTML frames, and as such is not part of XHTML Transitional (though it is part of XHTML Frameset). It's intended to send the content to a particular named target within a set of subwindows. The `_blank` value is a special keyword telling the browser to open a new window for the content, however, which is what I wanted to demonstrate here.

Simple XLinks

Simple XLinks are very similar to traditional hyperlinks, in that they consist of an element that may or may not contain text, and when the link is activated, the client application (that is, the browser) retrieves the information at the other end of the link and acts on it, typically by displaying it.

Before we go any further, it's useful to note that there are no "XLink elements." The capabilities of XLink are carried out entirely through attributes, all of which must be part of the XLink namespace, `http://www.w3.org/1999/xlink`. For example, Listing 14.2 shows the article from Listing 14.1, this time as an XML document using XLinks.

Namespace Issues

As always, it's the full namespace that counts, and not the prefix, but it's traditional to use `xlink:` as the prefix for XLinks to avoid confusion. Also, it's not necessary to declare the namespace on every single XLink. In some cases, you might want to declare the namespace on the root element to make the code a little more readable.

LISTING 14.2   Simple XLinks

```
<?xml-stylesheet href="blogs.css" type="text/css"?>
<entry>
<head>
   <title>What were they thinking?</title>
   <entrydate>4.28.2356</entrydate>
</head>
<body id="mainbody">

<paragraph>So it seems that <article xmlns:xlink="http://www.w3.org/1999/xlink"
xlink:type="simple" xlink:href="merlor.xml">Jasper Borkot is Bumbledoop of
Merlor</article>.  I don't know what the Merlorians were thinking, but in my
opinion, Shoopfuma the Irradiant should have been the Bumbledoop.  Borkot
couldn't win a mind battle against a sneech.  My Great Aunt Kyleesey could do
a better job.  If you want proof, check out <makemypoint
xmlns:xlink="http://www.w3.org/1999/xlink" xlink:type="simple"
xlink:href="merlor.xml" xlink:show="new">this article</makemypoint>,
where he promises to "build a monument to Flurowamp, the greatest Merlorian
of them all."  Nobody wants a monument to Flurowamp! He wasn't that popular,
and the guchucks to pay for it will come from the Merlorians' hard earned
wages.</paragraph>

</body>
</entry>
```

In this case, there's nothing special about the `article` or `makemypoint` elements as far as presentation is concerned. In fact, if we don't have the style sheet treat them differently, they'll look just like the rest of the text, as shown in Figure 14.3.

The client application, however, recognizes that this is now a link, as evidenced by the fact that it allows us to click on the relevant text.

In this case, we've also added an attribute to the second link, `show`, telling the browser to display the linked content in a new window.

Using Simple Links with Linkbases

Later, you'll see how you can use simple links to embed linkbases. Because of a special attribute called the `arcrole`, the client knows to treat them differently from regular links.

FIGURE 14.3
Without special treatment, XLinks look just like any other generic element.

The show Attribute: Replace, New, or Embed?

In the previous listing, we added the show attribute in order to tell the client to display the linked information in a new window. As you might have guessed, the default behavior is to replace the content that currently inhabits the window.

A third option, embed, is particularly exciting, in that it allows you to embed external content into your page without ever having to touch the file. For example, at the bottom of the log entry, we could add a link to the article itself that embeds the content into the document when it's clicked, as in Listing 14.3.

LISTING 14.3   Embedding Content: misha.xml

```
...
where he promises to "build a monument to Flurowamp, the greatest Merlorian of
them all." Nobody wants a monument to Flurowamp! He wasn't that popular, and the
guchucks to pay for it will come from the Merlorians' hard earned wages.
</paragraph>

<references xmlns:xlink="http://www.w3.org/1999/xlink" xlink:type="simple"
xlink:href="merlor.xml" xlink:show="embed" xlink:actuate="onRequest">View
the reference</references>

</body>
</entry>
```

Now, we could open this in Netscape 7 or a similar browser, but at the time of this writing, none of them supports embedded content, so it's time to go to XLiP. In the Tree Demo Application, click the Open a File button and choose the file you've created with this entry. (I've called it mishaluda1.xml, which will matter later, when we link back to the file.)

Click the icon next to each element to expand the file until you see the link element and its text reference, as shown in Figure 14.4.

FIGURE 14.4
Find the link in the XLiP window.

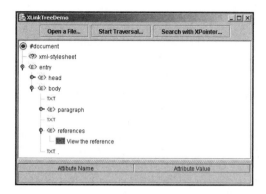

The client, in this case the XLiP demo, shows all links in red, so the text should be easy to pick out. To traverse the link, select it and click the Start Traversal button. The article should be embedded within the document, as shown in Figure 14.5. (You may have to expand some of the new nodes to get a result similar to the screenshot.)

FIGURE 14.5
Information can be embedded within a document.

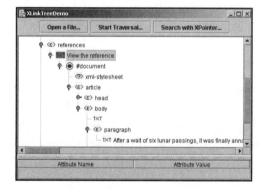

Other possible values for the **show** attribute are **none**, which indicates that the application should do nothing with the linked information, and **other**, which is undefined in the recommendation. It's assumed that a client that allows **other** as a value will also define other markup that gives the application instructions on what to do.

The actuate Attribute

You may have noticed that we also added the **actuate** attribute with a value of **onRequest**. The browser gives it this value as a default, but normally you'll want to specify it. The XLiP demo application, for example, requires it before traversing a link.

Support for **onLoad** is very limited at the time of this writing, so most of the time we'll be using **onRequest**. There are, however, notable exceptions, as you'll see when we get to linkbases.

Coexisting with XHTML

As noted before, the name of the element for an XLink is irrelevant because all the information is conveyed in attributes. Because of this, XLink can coexist nicely with older content, such as that written in XHTML. For example, we could have written the simple link in Listing 14.3 as

```
<a href="merlor_basic.html" xmlns:xlink="http://www.w3.org/1999/xlink"
    xlink:type="simple" xlink:href="merlor.xml">View the reference</a>
```

In this case, if the page were opened in a browser that understands XLink, clicking the link would send the browser to `merlor.xml`, but if the browser doesn't understand XLink, it would instead interpret the `<a>` element's `href` attribute and go to `merlor_basic.html`. Because they're in different namespaces, there's no conflict between `href` and `xlink:href`.

Extended XLinks

A simple type XLink is really just a special case of XLinks in general, which are normally expressed as extended links. Before we move on to extended links in their full glory, let's see what the previous example looks like as an extended link. In Listing 14.4, we'll create an extended link that performs the same function as the simple link.

LISTING 14.4   Using an Extended Link

```
...
Nobody wants a monument to Flurowamp! He wasn't that popular, and the guchucks to
pay for it will come from the Merlorians' hard earned wages.</paragraph>

<references xmlns:xlink="http://www.w3.org/1999/xlink" xlink:type="extended">
    <reflink xlink:type="resource" xlink:label="view"
                                            xlink:title="View Reference">
            View the reference
    </reflink>.
    <reflink xlink:type="locator" xlink:href="merlor.xml"
            xlink:label="merlorarticle" xlink:title="Borkot Made Bumbledoop" />
    <arcelement xlink:type="arc" xlink:from="view" xlink:to="merlorarticle"
                xlink:show="embed" xlink:actuate="onRequest"
                xlink:title="To article"  />
</references>

</body>
</entry>
```

We're going to discuss the pieces in detail in the next section, but for now understand that we created an extended link with two resources. One, the `View the reference` text, is local, and the other, the article, is remote. We then created an arc that ties them together. When the user clicks on the text, which is the starting point, the client should go to the article, or the ending point, and should embed the content within the original document.

Extended Links

A simple link, or even an extended version of a simple link, barely scratches the surface of XLink's capability to relate different resources. Extended links allow us to define relationships between multiple pieces of information, and to define directions for these links. This information can then be used in various ways, all of which are appropriate to the application currently using them.

Consider for a moment our example, in which users log interesting resources they've found so that others can also look at them. (This is known as *weblogging*, or *blogging*.)

Figure 14.6 illustrates the relationships between various pieces of information.

FIGURE 14.6
Relationships can be complex.

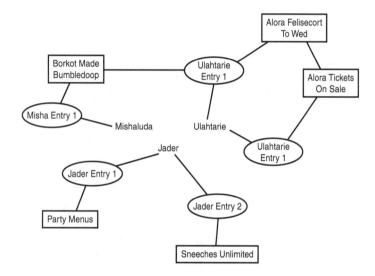

Suppose someone comes across Mishaluda's blog. They read the article about the All High Bumbledoop, and wonder what other people have to say about it. They might want to look at other entries that mention this article, such as the one by Ulahtarie. Finding that interesting, they might wonder what else she's written about, and look at her other blog entries. On the other hand, they might look at the second article cited by her entry, and from there move directly to the information on Alora Felisecort tickets.

With much of this information out of the developer's control, this kind of trail would be virtually impossible using only traditional XHTML.

Difficult, But Not Impossible

Nothing is impossible, of course. You could write a Web/database application that handles this work, but all by itself, XHTML wouldn't cut it.

In the next two sections, we're going to talk about extended links and look at the process of combining those extended links into linkbases.

Anatomy of an Extended XLink

Although an extended link can get complicated quickly as more and more information is added to it, the basic idea is straightforward. A link defines two or more resources, then links them together.

There are two different types of resources: local and remote. A local resource is one that is actually embedded within the link; it's part of the link element. Consider our previous example:

```
<references xmlns:xlink="http://www.w3.org/1999/xlink" xlink:type="extended">

    <reflink xlink:type="resource" xlink:label="view"
                                             xlink:title="View Reference">
             View the reference
    </reflink>.
    <reflink xlink:type="locator" xlink:href="merlor.xml"
             xlink:label="merlorarticle" xlink:title="Borkot Made Bumbledoop" />

    <arcelement xlink:type="arc" xlink:from="view" xlink:to="merlorarticle"
                xlink:show="embed" xlink:actuate="onRequest"
                xlink:title="To article"   />
</references>
```

Here the text, `View the reference`, is local, because it's part of the link itself. If we viewed the page in the browser, we'd see the link, as shown in Figure 14.7.

FIGURE 14.7

Local resources are part of the extended link element.

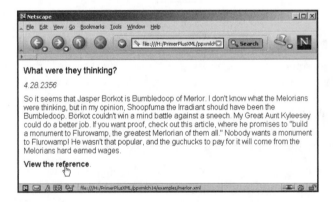

The style sheet (`blog.css`) makes any `reflink` elements bold, so we can clearly see them, but the other subelements don't have any text, so we don't see them.

Because this text is actually part of the link element (in this case, `references`) we don't have to tell the application where to find it. That's what makes it local, and that's why it has a `type` value of `resource`.

The article at the other end of our link is a remote resource, because the information is outside the link element (`references`). Note that a resource's classification as local or remote has nothing to do with whether it's actually in another file. As long as it's not in the actual link element, it's remote. For this reason, we have to tell the client where to find it using the `href` attribute, so it becomes a `locator`:

```
<references xmlns:xlink="http://www.w3.org/1999/xlink" xlink:type="extended">

    <reflink xlink:type="resource" xlink:label="view"
                                        xlink:title="View Reference">
            View the reference
    </reflink>.
    <reflink xlink:type="locator" xlink:href="merlor.xml"
            xlink:label="merlorarticle" xlink:title="Borkot Made Bumbledoop" />

    <arcelement xlink:type="arc" xlink:from="view" xlink:to="merlorarticle"
            xlink:show="embed" xlink:actuate="onRequest"
            xlink:title="To article"   />

</references>
```

Now that we've got the pieces, we need to put them together. To do so, we need to create an arc. Like the overall link and the previous definitions, it doesn't matter what we call the element, as long as the `type` attribute is `arc`.

```
<references xmlns:xlink="http://www.w3.org/1999/xlink" xlink:type="extended">

    <reflink xlink:type="resource" xlink:label="view"
                                        xlink:title="View Reference">
            View the reference
    </reflink>.
    <reflink xlink:type="locator" xlink:href="merlor.xml"
            xlink:label="merlorarticle" xlink:title="Barkot Made Bumbledoop" />

    <arcelement xlink:type="arc" xlink:from="view" xlink:to="merlorarticle"
            xlink:show="embed" xlink:actuate="onRequest"
            xlink:title="To article" />

</references>
```

It's the arc that actually creates the relationship between these two resources. In this case, we have a one-way link from the `View the reference` text (identified by its label, `view`) to the article (identified by its label, `merlorarticle`). The link is actuated `onRequest`, so nothing happens until you click on the `from` resource, `view`. When you do, the `show` attribute indicates that the new content should be embedded within the original document.

This is a very simple extended link. If we open this document in the client, the `references` element appears, but it's only the text of the first `reflink` element that's indicated as clickable, as shown in Figure 14.8.

FIGURE 14.8

The new extended link.

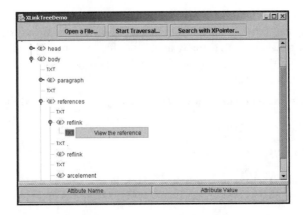

The text is known to be a link because there's an arc defined that specifies it as a `from` resource. When we click on it and start the traversal, we'll get a dialog box asking us which arc we want to follow, as shown in Figure 14.9. The text comes from the `title` attribute of the `arc` type element.

FIGURE 14.9

Choose an arc.

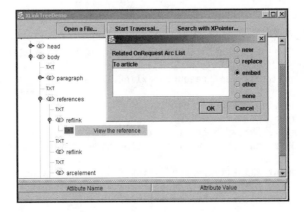

When you choose an arc, it automatically selects the value we added for `show` within the `arc` type element. In this case, the application allows you to change that, but there's nothing in the recommendation that mandates this opportunity for users.

Select the arc and click OK, and you'll see a list of choices for the endpoint of the link, as shown in Figure 14.10. Again, the text comes from the `title` element, and has nothing to do with the content of the actual linked file.

If you select the end point and then click `Traverse`, you'll see the article embedded in the document, as before (that is, unless you opted to change the value of `show`).

This may seem like an awful lot of work for what is essentially a simple link. But remember, extended links can do much more. A single resource can be the starting point for multiple arcs, and each arc can have an unlimited number of endpoints.

FIGURE 14.10

Choose an endpoint.

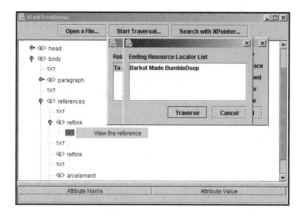

One Resource, Multiple Arcs

Let's start by looking at multiple arcs. Because we're defining the resources separately from the arcs themselves, there's no reason we can't have one resource that acts as the starting resource for more than one, as shown in Listing 14.5.

LISTING 14.5   Multiple Arcs

```
<?xml-stylesheet href="blogs.css" type="text/css"?>
<entry>
<head>
    <title>An unlikely alliance</title>
    <entrydate>4.28.2356</entrydate>
</head>
<body id="mainbody">

<paragraph>Jasper Borkot <link id="merlor"
xmlns:xlink="http://www.w3.org/1999/xlink" xlink:type="simple"
xlink:href="merlor.xml">says he's going to try and forge an alliance
with Jungonia</link>.  That means he's got to deal with Alora Felisecort,
now that she's <link id="marry" xmlns:xlink="http://www.w3.org/1999/xlink"
xlink:type="simple" xlink:href="alorawed.xml">marrying Sulligort the
Wise</link>.  "As the future Ruler of Jungonia, she will now make all
decisions for the planet."</paragraph>

<paragraph>Gorks, I hope she kicks the All High Bumbledoop's ickle when he
tries to make an alliance with her. It should be quite a contest. You can
also share your cosmic waves on this matter at <link id="share"
xmlns:xlink="http://www.w3.org/1999/xlink" xlink:type="simple"
xlink:href="http://www.QueeglesJungonianCosmicWaves.net">
QueeglesJungonianCosmicWaves.net</link>.</paragraph>

<references xmlns:xlink="http://www.w3.org/1999/xlink" xlink:type="extended">

    <reflink xlink:type="resource" xlink:label="view"
            xlink:title="View References">
```

LISTING 14.5   Continued

```
                    View the references
        </reflink>

        <reflink xlink:type="locator" xlink:href="merlor.xml#mainbody"
                xlink:label="merlorarticle" xlink:title="Borkot Made Bumbledoop"/>
        <reflink xlink:type="locator" xlink:href="alorawed.xml#mainbody"
                xlink:label="aloraarticle" xlink:title="Alora Felisecort To Wed" />
        <reflink xlink:type="locator" xlink:href=
                                "http://www.QueeglesJungonianCosmicWaves.net"
                xlink:label="queegles" xlink:title="QueeglesJungonianCosmicWaves.net" />

        <arcelement xlink:type="arc" xlink:from="view" xlink:to="merlorarticle"
                xlink:show="replace" xlink:actuate="onRequest"
                xlink:title="To Merlor Article" />
        <arcelement xlink:type="arc" xlink:from="view" xlink:to="aloraarticle"
                xlink:show="replace" xlink:actuate="onRequest"
                xlink:title="To Alora Article" />
        <arcelement xlink:type="arc" xlink:from="view" xlink:to="queegles"
                xlink:show="replace" xlink:actuate="onRequest"
                xlink:title="To Queegles" />
    </references>

    </body>
    </entry>
```

In this case, we have two different types of links. In the **body** of the **entry**, we have three simple links, one to each of the article destinations. The extended link at the bottom of the page, however, is a different matter.

Notice that all three **arc** type elements have as their starting point the resource labeled **view**, which is the local text **View the references**. If we load this document in the client application and traverse that link, the application lets us choose which arc to traverse, as shown in Figure 14.11.

FIGURE 14.11

Choose an arc.

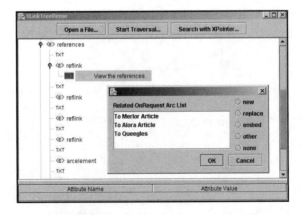

Here, each arc has only one possible destination, but that doesn't have to be the case.

One Arc, Multiple Destinations

The capability to create multiple arcs for a single resource can be convenient, but not nearly as convenient as the capability to group different resources so that a user can get to any of them from a single arc. For example, we can group the different destinations using labels, as in Listing 14.6.

LISTING 14.6   Grouping Resources by Label

```
...
share your cosmic waves on this matter at <link id="share"
xmlns:xlink="http://www.w3.org/1999/xlink" xlink:type="simple"
xlink:href="http://www.QueeglesJungonianCosmicWaves.net">
QueeglesJungonianCosmicWaves.net</link>.</paragraph>

<references xmlns:xlink="http://www.w3.org/1999/xlink" xlink:type="extended">

    <reflink xlink:type="resource" xlink:label="view"
                                    xlink:title="View References">
            View the references
    </reflink>

    <reflink xlink:type="locator" xlink:href="merlor.xml#mainbody"
        xlink:label="extlink" xlink:title="Borkot Made Bumbledoop"/>
    <reflink xlink:type="locator" xlink:href="alorawed.xml#mainbody"
        xlink:label="extlink" xlink:title="Alora Felisecort To Wed" />
    <reflink xlink:type="locator" xlink:href=
                        "http://www.QueeglesJungonianCosmicWaves.net"
        xlink:label="extlink" xlink:title="QueeglesJungonianCosmicWaves.net" />

    <arcelement xlink:type="arc" xlink:from="view" xlink:to="extlink"
                xlink:show="replace" xlink:actuate="onRequest"
                xlink:title="To Merlor Article" />

</references>

</body>
</entry>
```

Here we have just one arc with the text as a starting resource, but that one arc has as its destination any resource (remote or local) with `extlink` as its `label`. In this case, that's all three external links, as shown in Figure 14.12.

Not only can we group ending resources in this way, but we can also group starting resources. For example, rather than creating simple links within the text, we could have created each of them as resources with the label `view`, and each of them would have activated the same arc.

Local Versus Remote

Remember, the elements that are currently simple links within the body of the article are remote because they're not part of the link, even though they're part of the document.

FIGURE 14.12
Choose a destination.

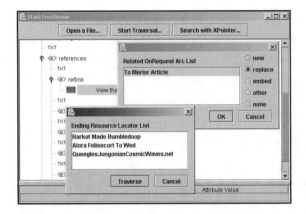

Multidirectional Links

So far, every link we've created has been unidirectional, or one-way. We can go from the blog entry to the article, but we can't come back (unless we use a Back button). One of XLink's strengths is that it enables us to do exactly that.

You may have noticed that the `simple` type link elements in the previous example had `id` attributes. These attributes allow us to directly reference these points with a `locator` type element, as in Listing 14.7.

LISTING 14.7   Creating One End of a Multidirectional Link

```
<?xml-stylesheet href="blogs.css" type="text/css"?>
<entry>
<head>
   <title>An unlikely alliance</title>
   <entrydate>4.28.2356</entrydate>
</head>
<body id="mainbody">

<paragraph>Jasper Borkot <link id="merlor">says he's going to try
and forge an alliance with Jungonia</link>.  That means he's got to
deal with Alora Felisecort, now that she's <link id="marry">marrying
Sulligort the Wise</link>.  "As the future Ruler of Jungonia, she
will now make all decisions for the planet."</paragraph>

<paragraph>Gorks, I hope she kicks the All High Bumbledoop's ickle
when he tries to make an alliance with her. It should be quite a
contest. You can also share your cosmic waves on this matter at
<link id="share">QueeglesJungonianCosmicWaves.net</link>.</paragraph>

<references xmlns:xlink="http://www.w3.org/1999/xlink"
xlink:type="extended">
    <link xlink:type="locator" xlink:href="ulahtarie2.xml#merlor"
          xlink:label="merlor" xlink:title="... alliance with Jungiona." />.
    <link xlink:type="locator" xlink:href="ulahtarie2.xml#marry"
```

LISTING 14.7 *Continued*

```
                 xlink:label="alora" xlink:title="... marrying Sulligort ..." />.
        <link xlink:type="locator" xlink:href="ulahtarie2.xml#share"
             xlink:label="toqueegles"
             xlink:title="QueeglesJungonianCosmicWaves.net." />.

        <link xlink:type="locator" xlink:href="merlor.xml#mainbody"
             xlink:label="merlorarticle" xlink:title="Borkot Made Bumbledoop"/>
        <link xlink:type="locator" xlink:href="alorawed.xml#mainbody"
             xlink:label="aloraarticle" xlink:title="Alora Felisecort To Wed" />
        <link xlink:type="locator" xlink:label="queegles"
             xlink:href="http://www.QueeglesJungonianCosmicWaves.net"
             xlink:title="QueeglesJungonianCosmicWaves.net" />

        <arcelement xlink:type="arc" xlink:from="merlor" xlink:to="merlorarticle"
                   xlink:show="replace" xlink:actuate="onRequest"
                   xlink:title="To Merlor Article" />
        <arcelement xlink:type="arc" xlink:from="alora" xlink:to="aloraarticle"
                   xlink:show="replace" xlink:actuate="onRequest"
                   xlink:title="To Alora Article" />
        <arcelement xlink:type="arc" xlink:from="toqueegles" xlink:to="queegles"
                   xlink:show="replace" xlink:actuate="onRequest"
                   xlink:title="To Queegles" />

        <arcelement xlink:type="arc" xlink:to="merlor" xlink:from="merlorarticle"
                   xlink:show="replace" xlink:actuate="onRequest"
                   xlink:title="From Merlor Article" />
        <arcelement xlink:type="arc" xlink:to="alora" xlink:from="aloraarticle"
                   xlink:show="replace" xlink:actuate="onRequest"
                   xlink:title="From Alora Article" />
        <arcelement xlink:type="arc" xlink:to="toqueegles" xlink:from="queegles"
                   xlink:show="replace" xlink:actuate="onRequest"
                   xlink:title="From Queegles" />
</references>


<references xmlns:xlink="http://www.w3.org/1999/xlink" xlink:type="extended">

  <reflink xlink:type="resource" xlink:label="view" xlink:title="View References">
          View the references
  </reflink>
...
</references>

</body>
</entry>
```

Notice that there's nothing wrong with having more than one extended link in a document, just as there's no limit to the number of hyperlinks on a Web page.

In this case, we remove the simple links and create `locator`s out of all three text references in the body of the entry, then out of each article. Don't worry if the syntax for the `href` attributes doesn't look familiar. We'll deal with it in detail in the section titled "XPointer," but understand for now that we're pointing to an element in `ulahtarie2.xml` (this file) with an `id` attribute that matches the value after the pound sign (#).

ID Values
Strictly speaking, an attribute is not considered to be of type ID unless it's declared within a DTD as an ID, but many processors (including XLiP) will look for attributes named `id` as a stopgap measure.

When we create the arcs, we make two sets: one from the entry to the article, and the other from the article to the corresponding point within the entry. It is this dichotomy that makes it a multidirectional link.

Let's think this through for a moment. We've got a file that will link to an article, and has a link from the article back to the entry defined in it, but once we go to the article, what happens to that reference? In all likelihood, that information is lost, unless the same link information is included in the article as well, as in Listing 14.8.

LISTING 14.8   The Other End of the Line

```
<article>
<head><title>Alora Felisecort to Wed</title></head>
<body id="mainbody">

<paragraph>The greatest violaphonatobia player in the
universe announced today that she is engaged to Suliggort the Wise,
leader of the entire Fullum Galaxy.  She will be Suliggort's Seventh
wife, which means that she will be the Royal Queen of the seventh
planet in the Fullum Galaxy, Jungonia. She and her fiance are planning
the Great Nuptial Ordeal Ceremony to take place on the 137th of
Brinkish.  As the future Ruler of Jungonia, she will now make all
decisions for the planet.  Her fans are thrilled to hear she will also
stage a violaphonatobia concert at the Nuptials as part of the Great
Ordeal.  Tickets will be seven Fnorks each and will go on sale in
three cycles.  She plans on playing her entire fifth symphony "Lolo,
Ifo, Doodah Mecido".  It looks like a sure bet that she will win the
Ordeal.  Suliggort plans on doing gymnastics and reciting from the
book of Ograpal the Prophet for his part of the Ordeal.</paragraph>

<references xmlns:xlink="http://www.w3.org/1999/xlink" xlink:type="extended">
    <link xlink:type="locator" xlink:href="ulahtarie2.xml#merlor"
          xlink:label="merlor" xlink:title="... alliance with Jungiona." />.
    <link xlink:type="locator" xlink:href="ulahtarie2.xml#marry"
          xlink:label="alora" xlink:title="... marrying Sulligort ..." />.
    <link xlink:type="locator" xlink:href="ulahtarie2.xml#share"
          xlink:label="toqueegles"
          xlink:title="QueeglesJungonianCosmicWaves.net." />.

    <link xlink:type="locator" xlink:href="merlor.xml#mainbody"
          xlink:label="merlorarticle" xlink:title="Borkot Made Bumbledoop"/>
    <link xlink:type="locator" xlink:href="alorawed.xml#mainbody"
```

LISTING 14.8 *Continued*

```
                    xlink:label="aloraarticle" xlink:title="Alora Felisecort To Wed" />
        <link xlink:type="locator" xlink:label="queegles"
              xlink:href="http://www.QueeglesJungonianCosmicWaves.net"
              xlink:title="QueeglesJungonianCosmicWaves.net" />

        <arcelement xlink:type="arc" xlink:from="merlor" xlink:to="merlorarticle"
                    xlink:show="replace" xlink:actuate="onRequest"
                    xlink:title="To Merlor Article" />
        <arcelement xlink:type="arc" xlink:from="alora" xlink:to="aloraarticle"
                    xlink:show="replace" xlink:actuate="onRequest"
                    xlink:title="To Alora Article" />
        <arcelement xlink:type="arc" xlink:from="toqueegles" xlink:to="queegles"
                    xlink:show="replace" xlink:actuate="onRequest"
                    xlink:title="To Queegles" />

        <arcelement xlink:type="arc" xlink:to="merlor" xlink:from="merlorarticle"
                    xlink:show="replace" xlink:actuate="onRequest"
                    xlink:title="From Merlor Article" />
        <arcelement xlink:type="arc" xlink:to="alora" xlink:from="aloraarticle"
                    xlink:show="replace" xlink:actuate="onRequest"
                    xlink:title="From Alora Article" />
        <arcelement xlink:type="arc" xlink:to="toqueegles" xlink:from="queegles"
                    xlink:show="replace" xlink:actuate="onRequest"
                    xlink:title="From Queegles" />
    </references>

    </body>
    </article>
```

Now let's look at what happens when we try to traverse these arcs. When we load the file, we see that the references are now highlighted as links even though we've removed the simple links. In fact, because of the way we've referenced it in the locator **type** element, the element itself is the link's starting point, and not the text, as shown in Figure 14.13.

FIGURE 14.13
The elements as links.

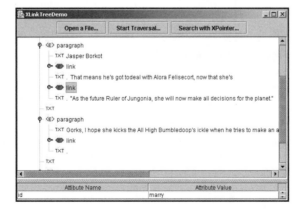

If we traverse the second link, we wind up at the article about Alora Felisecort's wedding. Notice that the **body** element (referenced in the **locator** type element) is highlighted as a link, as shown in Figure 14.14.

FIGURE 14.14
The destination can also be a link.

If we traverse this link, we wind up back at the original reference, as shown in Figure 14.15.

FIGURE 14.15
On the way back to the starting point.

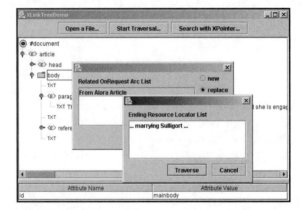

Note that this is not the same as simply pressing the Back button on your browser. The user might have gotten to the wedding article from a completely different starting point.

Using External Entities

Now let's take a moment to touch on a topic that's not really part of XLink, but might come in handy. You might have considered the fact that it is ludicrous to include lengthy extended link definitions in each and every document for which they apply. Instead, we have a couple of options. The first is to use an external entity that can be shared among files.

We touched briefly on external entities in Chapter 7, "Document Type Definitions (DTDs)," but the idea here is to create a single document that contains the link definitions, then define it as an external entity and reference that entity from each relevant document. For example, we might have a file, `extlinks.xml`, that includes the extended links, as in Listing 14.9.

LISTING 14.9   Creating the External File

```
<references xmlns:xlink="http://www.w3.org/1999/xlink" xlink:type="extended">
    <link xlink:type="locator" xlink:href="ulahtarie2.xml#merlor"
          xlink:label="merlor" xlink:title="... alliance with Jungiona." />
    <link xlink:type="locator" xlink:href="ulahtarie2.xml#marry"
          xlink:label="alora" xlink:title="... marrying Sulligort ..." />
    <link xlink:type="locator" xlink:href="ulahtarie2.xml#share"
          xlink:label="toqueegles"
          xlink:title="QueeglesJungonianCosmicWaves.net." />

    <link xlink:type="locator" xlink:href="merlor.xml#mainbody"
          xlink:label="merlorarticle" xlink:title="Borkot Made Bumbledoop"/>
    <link xlink:type="locator" xlink:href="alorawed.xml#mainbody"
          xlink:label="aloraarticle" xlink:title="Alora Felisecort To Wed" />
    <link xlink:type="locator" xlink:label="queegles"
          xlink:href="http://www.QueeglesJungonianCosmicWaves.net"
          xlink:title="QueeglesJungonianCosmicWaves.net" />

    <arcelement xlink:type="arc" xlink:from="merlor" xlink:to="merlorarticle"
                xlink:show="replace" xlink:actuate="onRequest"
                xlink:title="To Merlor Article" />
    <arcelement xlink:type="arc" xlink:from="alora" xlink:to="aloraarticle"
                xlink:show="replace" xlink:actuate="onRequest"
                xlink:title="To Alora Article" />
    <arcelement xlink:type="arc" xlink:from="toqueegles" xlink:to="queegles"
                xlink:show="replace" xlink:actuate="onRequest"
                xlink:title="To Queegles" />

    <arcelement xlink:type="arc" xlink:to="merlor" xlink:from="merlorarticle"
                xlink:show="replace" xlink:actuate="onRequest"
                xlink:title="From Merlor Article" />
    <arcelement xlink:type="arc" xlink:to="alora" xlink:from="aloraarticle"
                xlink:show="replace" xlink:actuate="onRequest"
                xlink:title="From Alora Article" />
    <arcelement xlink:type="arc" xlink:to="toqueegles" xlink:from="queegles"
                xlink:show="replace" xlink:actuate="onRequest"
                xlink:title="From Queegles" />
</references>

<references xmlns:xlink="http://www.w3.org/1999/xlink" xlink:type="extended">

    <reflink xlink:type="resource" xlink:label="view"
             xlink:title="View References">
             View the references
    </reflink>

    <reflink xlink:type="locator" xlink:href="merlor.xml#mainbody"
             xlink:label="extlink" xlink:title="Borkot Made Bumbledoop"/>
```

LISTING 14.9   Continued

```
        <reflink xlink:type="locator" xlink:href="alorawed.xml#mainbody"
              xlink:label="extlink" xlink:title="Alora Felisecort To Wed" />
        <reflink xlink:type="locator" xlink:label="extlink"
              xlink:href="http://www.QueeglesJungonianCosmicWaves.net"
              xlink:title="QueeglesJungonianCosmicWaves.net" />

        <arcelement xlink:type="arc" xlink:from="view" xlink:to="extlink"
                 xlink:show="replace" xlink:actuate="onRequest"
                 xlink:title="To Merlor Article" />
```

```
    </references>
```

We can then create a DTD file that defines it as an entity, as in Listing 14.10.

LISTING 14.10   linksentity.dtd

```
    <!ENTITY links SYSTEM "extlinks.xml">
```

Now all we need to do is reference this DTD from the files and reference the entity, as in Listing 14.11.

LISTING 14.11   ulahtarie2.xml

```
    <!DOCTYPE entry SYSTEM "linksentity.dtd">
    <?xml-stylesheet href="blogs.css" type="text/css"?>
    <entry>
    <head>
      <title>An unlikely alliance</title>
      <entrydate>4.28.2356</entrydate>
    </head>
    <body id="mainbody">
    ...
    <paragraph>Gorks, I hope she kicks the All High Bumbledoop's ickle when
    he tries to make an alliance with her. It should be quite a contest.
    You can also share your cosmic waves on this matter at <link id="share">
    QueeglesJungonianCosmicWaves.net</link>.</paragraph>

    &links;

    </body>
    </entry>
```

We can make a similar change to the second file, as in Listing 14.12.

LISTING 14.12   alorawed.xml

```
    <!DOCTYPE article SYSTEM "linksentity.dtd">
    <article>
    <head><title>Alora Felisecort to Wed</title></head>
    <body id="mainbody">
```

LISTING 14.12 Continued

```
<paragraph>The greatest violaphonatobia player in the
universe announced today that she is engaged to Suliggort the Wise,
leader of the entire Fullum Galaxy.  She will be Suliggort's Seventh
wife, which means that she will be the Royal Queen of the seventh
planet in the Fullum Galaxy, Jungonia. She and her fiance are planning
the Great Nuptial Ordeal Ceremony to take place on the 137th of
Brinkish.  As the future Ruler of Jungonia, she will now make all
decisions for the planet.  Her fans are thrilled to hear she will also
stage a violaphonatobia concert at the Nuptials as part of the Great
Ordeal.  Tickets will be seven Fnorks each and will go on sale in
three cycles.  She plans on playing her entire fifth symphony "Lolo,
Ifo, Doodah Mecido".  It looks like a sure bet that she will win the
Ordeal.  Suliggort plans on doing gymnastics and reciting from the
book of Ograpal the Prophet for his part of the Ordeal.</paragraph>

&links;

</body>
</article>
```

You may be wondering how we can use the same DTD for both files even though they have different structures, and how we can use it at all when it doesn't actually declare any of the elements or attributes. Remember, that only matters if the parser is a validating parser. If it isn't, the information in entities, attribute default values, and so on is simply added.

But (and this is a big *but*) a nonvalidating parser is not required to retrieve external entities like this one. The XLiP demo does, but there's no guarantee that other parsers will.

So what's a conscientious developer to do?

One solution is to use linkbases.

Linkbases

For various reasons, it's typically not convenient to include the actual links in every file for which they're relevant. Instead, you can use a link database, or linkbase.

Linkbases are collections of linking information that are typically not intended for navigation by humans. Linkbases are normally loaded with the document (using the `onLoad actuate` value) and by themselves have no means of presentation. Instead, they create links out of other information.

For instance, in the last two examples we had information on "third-party" links (links in which all the resources are remote, and not part of the link itself). There was, in fact, no reason to keep the link information in the file at all.

Instead, we could simply create a linkbase, then link the linkbase to the appropriate documents.

When the linkbase is loaded, it creates the relationships between various resources within application memory. Links on a page might be activated. In some cases, entire sections of content might be populated with embedded material.

In other cases, the linkbase might not have anything to do with the user. Perhaps it is used to define relationships between resources in a system that performs research or a search engine that keeps track of links between pages.

In this section, we're going to create a linkbase, link it into a document, and examine the results.

Creating a Linkbase

We've already created some of the relationships illustrated in Figure 14.6 in previous exercises. Listing 14.13 shows a section of the linkbase.

LISTING 14.13   The Linkbase, `blogbase.xml`

```
<?xml version='1.0'?>
<blogbase xmlns:xlink="http://www.w3.org/1999/xlink">
<people xlink:type="extended">
    <person xlink:type="locator" xlink:href="community.xml#jader"
            xlink:title="Jader's Log Entries" xlink:label="jader" />
    <person xlink:type="locator" xlink:href="community.xml#misha"
            xlink:title="Mishaluda's Log Entries" xlink:label="mishaluda" />
    <person xlink:type="locator" xlink:href="community.xml#ulahtarie"
            xlink:title="Ulahtarie's Log Entries" xlink:label="ulahtarie" />

    <entry xlink:type="locator" xlink:href="jader1.xml"
            xlink:title="What a Party!" xlink:label="jaderentry" />
    <entry xlink:type="locator" xlink:href="jader2.xml"
            xlink:title="Sneeches Unlimited" xlink:label="jaderentry" />

    <entry xlink:type="locator" xlink:href="mishaluka1.xml"
            xlink:title="What Where They Thinking?!" xlink:label="mishaentry" />

    <entry xlink:type="locator" xlink:href="ulahtarie1.xml#mainbody"
            xlink:title="Alora Felisecort Tickets On Sale"
            xlink:label="ulahtarieentry" />
    <entry xlink:type="locator" xlink:href="ulahtarie2.xml#mainbody"
            xlink:title="An Unlikely Alliance" xlink:label="ulahtarieentry" />

    <arcelement xlink:type="arc" xlink:from="jader" xlink:to="jaderentry"
        xlink:show="embed" xlink:actuate="onRequest"
        xlink:title="Jader's Log Entries" />
    <arcelement xlink:type="arc" xlink:from="mishaluda" xlink:to="mishaentry"
        xlink:show="embed" xlink:actuate="onRequest"
        xlink:title="Mishaluda's Log Entries" />
    <arcelement xlink:type="arc" xlink:from="ulahtarie"
        xlink:to="ulahtarieentry" xlink:show="embed" xlink:actuate="onRequest"
        xlink:title="Ulahtarie's Log Entries" />
```

LISTING 14.13   *Continued*

```
    <arc xlink:type="arc" xlink:to="jader" xlink:from="jaderentry"
        xlink:show="embed" xlink:actuate="onRequest"
        xlink:title="Jader's Log Entries" />
    <arc xlink:type="arc" xlink:to="misha" xlink:from="mishaentry"
        xlink:show="embed" xlink:actuate="onRequest"
        xlink:title="Mishaluda's Log Entries" />
    <arc xlink:type="arc" xlink:to="ulahtarie" xlink:from="ulahtarieentry"
        xlink:show="embed" xlink:actuate="onRequest"
        xlink:title="Ulahtarie's Log Entries" />

</people>

<references xlink:type="extended" id="ulahtarie2">
    <link xlink:type="locator" xlink:href="ulahtarie2.xml#merlor"
        xlink:label="merlor" xlink:title="... alliance with Jungiona." />
    <link xlink:type="locator" xlink:href="ulahtarie2.xml#marry"
        xlink:label="alora" xlink:title="... marrying Sulligort ..." />
    <link xlink:type="locator" xlink:href="ulahtarie2.xml#share"
        xlink:label="toqueegles"
        xlink:title="QueeglesJungonianCosmicWaves.net." />
    <link xlink:type="locator" xlink:href="ulahtarie2.xml"
        xlink:label="entry" xlink:title="An Unlikely Alliance" />

    <link xlink:type="locator" xlink:href="merlor.xml#mainbody"
        xlink:label="merlorarticle" xlink:title="Borkot Made Bumbledoop"/>
    <link xlink:type="locator" xlink:href="alorawed.xml#mainbody"
        xlink:label="aloraarticle" xlink:title="Alora Felisecort To Wed" />
    <link xlink:type="locator" xlink:label="queegles"
        xlink:href="http://www.QueeglesJungonianCosmicWaves.net"
        xlink:title="QueeglesJungonianCosmicWaves.net" />

    <link xlink:type="locator" xlink:href="merlor.xml#mainbody"
        xlink:label="extlink" xlink:title="Borkot Made Bumbledoop"/>
    <link xlink:type="locator" xlink:href="alorawed.xml#mainbody"
        xlink:label="extlink" xlink:title="Alora Felisecort To Wed" />
    <link xlink:type="locator" xlink:label="extlink"
        xlink:href="http://www.QueeglesJungonianCosmicWaves.net"
        xlink:title="QueeglesJungonianCosmicWaves.net" />

    <arcelement xlink:type="arc" xlink:from="merlor" xlink:to="extlink"
            xlink:show="replace" xlink:actuate="onRequest"
            xlink:title="To Other Resources" />
    <arcelement xlink:type="arc" xlink:from="alora" xlink:to="extlink"
            xlink:show="replace" xlink:actuate="onRequest"
            xlink:title="To Other Resources" />
    <arcelement xlink:type="arc" xlink:from="toqueegles" xlink:to="extlink"
            xlink:show="replace" xlink:actuate="onRequest"
            xlink:title="To Other Resources" />

    <arcelement xlink:type="arc" xlink:from="merlor" xlink:to="merlorarticle"
            xlink:show="replace" xlink:actuate="onRequest"
            xlink:title="To Merlor Article" />
```

LISTING 14.13   Continued

```
            <arcelement xlink:type="arc" xlink:from="alora" xlink:to="aloraarticle"
                        xlink:show="replace" xlink:actuate="onRequest"
                        xlink:title="To Alora Article" />
            <arcelement xlink:type="arc" xlink:from="toqueegles" xlink:to="queegles"
                        xlink:show="replace" xlink:actuate="onRequest"
                        xlink:title="To Queegles" />

            <arcelement xlink:type="arc" xlink:from="extlink" xlink:to="entry"
                        xlink:show="replace" xlink:actuate="onRequest"
                        xlink:title="To Log Entry" />
    </references>

    <references xlink:type="extended" id="mishaluda1">
        <link xlink:type="locator" xlink:href="mishaluda1.xml#Bumbledoop"
              xlink:label="bumble" xlink:title="... Bumbledoop of Merlor." />
        <link xlink:type="locator" xlink:href="mishaluda1.xml#thisarticle"
              xlink:label="bumble" xlink:title="... this article ..." />

        <link xlink:type="locator" xlink:href="ulahtarie2.xml"
              xlink:label="entry" xlink:title="What Were They Thinking?" />

        <link xlink:type="locator" xlink:href="merlor.xml#mainbody"
              xlink:label="merlor" xlink:title="Borkot Made Bumbledoop"/>

        <arcelement xlink:type="arc" xlink:from="bumble" xlink:to="merlor"
                    xlink:show="replace" xlink:actuate="onRequest"
                    xlink:title="To Other Resources" />

        <arcelement xlink:type="arc" xlink:to="bumble" xlink:from="merlor"
                    xlink:show="replace" xlink:actuate="onRequest"
                    xlink:title="To Log Entry" />
    </references>

    ...

</blogbase>
```

It would take much too much room to detail all the possibilities, but please note the `people` element. It contains references to elements in the `community.xml` document, and provides a way to link in all their entries.

I've included the links you've already seen, and after that come the similar links for other entries, which I'll leave up to you.

Using Linkbase Information on a Page

Okay, now you've got a linkbase, but it's not going to do you any good at all unless it's accessible from a document.

An application might already have a linkbase in memory, or it might load it from another source, but one common way to associate a linkbase with a document is through a simple link, as in Listing 14.14.

LISTING 14.14   Adding the Linkbase

```
<community>
<head><title>Community Blog Information</title></head>
<body>

<onRequestLinkbase xmlns:xlink="http://www.w3.org/1999/xlink"
        xlink:type="simple" xlink:href="blogbase.xml"
        xlink:actuate="onLoad"
        xlink:arcrole="http://www.w3.org/1999/xlink/properties/linkbase">
</onRequestLinkbase>

<author id="jader">
    Jader's Log
</author>

<author id="misha">
    Mishaluda's Log
</author>

<author id="ulahtarie">
    Ulahtarie's Log
</author>

</body>
</entry>
```

Here you see a `simple` type element link with the `actuate` element set to `onLoad`. This is, in fact, the only time (at present) we can load something with the `onLoad` handler.

But why would the application handle it differently? The secret is in the `arcrole` element. XLink defines two roles: the `arcrole` and the `role`.

Resources can have roles (created using the `role` attribute on the `locator` type or `resource` type element), such as reference and entry. Sometimes a single resource can carry multiple roles. For example, if Jader references Ulahtarie's blog entry from his own blog, Ulahtarie's entry will be an entry in some cases, and an article in others.

Using Roles to Indicate MIME Types

Roles can also be used to indicate MIME type for other media that might be loaded. For example, a JPEG image might have a role of `image/jpeg`.

At this point, we're more interested in the `arcrole` attribute on the `arc`-type element. By setting its value to the linkbase namespace (`http://www.w3.org/1999/xlink/properties/linkbase`), we're telling the application that it is, in fact, a linkbase, and that it should get the file and create any of the specified relationships.

Linkbase Behaviors

Linkbases are in many ways special cases, so let's take a moment and run down some of the special considerations when it comes to linkbases.

Linkbases have no presentation. Although they can be called using a simple link, any value other than `none` for the `show` attribute is ignored.

Second, linkbases can be chained together. For example, we could have started out with a linkbase that just defines the people involved, then loads a second linkbase with information about each entry. This second linkbase could be loaded via a simple link on the first linkbase.

It's possible that a linkbase (or series of chained linkbases) will have duplicate links—the same arcs pointing to the same resources and the same conditions. An application is expected to recognize this and skip any duplicates.

In our case, all the links we created were `onRequest`, rather than `onLoad`. So we'd have to specifically request Ulahtarie's entries, as shown in Figure 14.16.

FIGURE 14.16

Links created with a linkbase.

In an ideal world, the content would have been automatically embedded when the linkset was loaded, but unfortunately the demo application doesn't support this.

XPointer

In this example, all of our entries and articles were in different files. What would happen if they were in the same file? How could we, for example, reference just one blog entry in a file containing several hundred?

The answer is XPointer, a W3C recommendation related to and developed in conjunction with XLink. XPointer is a method of referring to specific locations within an XML document. These locations may be in the form of a point or a range. XPointer was separated from XLink so that it could be used with other specifications, just as XPath is separate from XSLT so it can be used with other applications. In fact, XPointer builds on XPath.

Support for XPointer is still sketchy, so we'll talk in general terms about it and try to give examples where possible.

Forms

There are three forms of XPointer expressions, and each has its own purpose. We've been using what is known as the bare names form of XPointer all along, when we pointed to specific nodes within the document using the `id` attribute.

In the linkbase, we pointed to the Jader author element as

```
... xlink:href="community.xml#jader" ...
```

The pound sign indicates that what comes next is an XPointer expression (in this case, `jader`).

When a name appears on its own like this, XPointer knows that we're referring to an ID value:

```
<author id="jader">
    Jader's Log
</author>
```

This is equivalent to the full XPointer expression

```
xpointer(id("jader"))
```

A second method of XPointer addressing is to use child sequences. In this case, we provide a series of integers that indicate the index of the node we want. For example, we could refer to this same element using the XPointer expression

```
/1/2/2
```

Like an XPath expression, an XPointer expression that begins with a slash starts with the document root as the context. The first child of the document root is the `community` element. The second child of the `community` element is the `body` element. The second child of the `body` element is Jader's `author` element.

This method doesn't look particularly useful until you realize that you may find yourself addressing parts of documents over which you have no control, and into which you cannot insert `id` values.

You can also combine the bare names and child sequences XPointer forms. For example, the expression

```
mainbody/2/1
```

refers to the first child of the second child of the element with an `id` of `mainbody`.

Finally, there's the full XPointer form. You can use this form when you have a full-blown XPath expression, or when you want to use some of the XPointer functions. For example:

```
xpointer(/community/body/author[@id='jader'])
```

Because we're using the full syntax, this expression produces the same result as an XPath expression with the same information. In other words, **community**, **body**, and so on are element names, rather than IDs.

XPath is based on the concept of node sets. Each XPath expression returns a node set, even if that set is empty or simply contains one node. (XPath functions are, of course, a notable exception.)

XPointer builds on XPath, adding the concepts of points and ranges.

Points

In XPointer, a point is defined by two pieces of information: the containing node and the index. Points are crucial in XPointer, because they provide not only a potential resource at either side of a link, but also the start and end of ranges. XPointer defines two types of points: node-points and character-points.

Consider, for example, the XML code in Listing 14.15.

LISTING 14.15   A Sample Document

```
<entry>
<head><title>Alora Tickets on Sale!</title></head>
<body id="mainbody">

  <paragraph>I just ordered tix online for Alora Felisecort's
   next concert. I can't wait to see it. She's so critsy and
   mulled. The whole Jinkers fanclub is going. Be there or be
   frobish. Don't forget to check out Alora Felisecort's new
   fan site: Alora Sees Us All at <article
   xmlns:xlink="http://www.w3.org/1999/xlink" xlink:type="simple"
   xlink:href="http://Nightobservers.com">Nightobservers.com</article>
  </paragraph>

</body>
</entry>
```

Node-Points

Let's start with node-points. Each node-point has a containing node and an index, which must be greater than or equal to zero and less than or equal to the number of child nodes the containing node has.

If the containing node were the entry element, an index of **0** would place the point immediately before the first child node, **head**. An index of **1** places it between the **head** and **body** elements, and an index of **2** places it after the second child, **body**. In short, an index of **N** places the node-point after the **N**th child of the containing node.

We could ask for the start point of the **body** element

```
xpointer(start-point(//body))
```

and get the point immediately before the **paragraph** element, as shown in Figure 14.17.

FIGURE 14.17
Selecting a point.

Notice that, like XPath and unlike DOM, XPointer doesn't consider ignorable whitespace a node.

Character-Points

In some cases, the containing node won't have node children. In the case of a text node, for instance, the points generated are character-points. Take the sample text node

```
I just ordered tix online for Alora Felisecort's next concert. I can't wait to
see it.
```

If this were the containing node, and the index were **6**, the character-point would be just after the **t** in **just**, but before the space. As with node-points, an index of **0** indicates the point before the first character, and an index of **N** indicates the point after the **N**th character.

Ranges

An XPointer range is a location that is defined by a start point and an end point. Notice that I haven't said anything about the types of start points and end points. A range might even encompass only part of a node. For example, we might have a range that starts at the top of the **body** element, but only runs to a character-point in the middle of a text node. At the very least, it's not well-formed XML—but that's not a problem.

Ranges are useful in XLink for both the start and end points of links. As an end point, they're useful if you want to extract just a portion of an XML file. As a start point, they're useful because they give the user something to click on.

For example, in the document

```
<entry>
<head><title>Sneech Supply</title></head>
<body id="mainbody">3
```

```
<paragraph>I found a great source for sneeches: <reference
xmlns:xlink="http://www.w3.org/1999/xlink" xlink:type="simple"
xlink:href="http://www.sneechesunltd.net">SneechesUnlimited.net</reference>.
They've got everything, including Slidads, dybons, accessories,
and more.  The prices seem reasonable, too.</paragraph>

</body>
</entry>
```

the linked text is actually a range. That range has a start point and an end point. Both points have the `reference` element as their containing node. The start point has an index of `0`, and the end point has an index of `21`, which puts it right after the `t` in `.net`.

Schemes, and Using XPointer in URIs

As I mentioned earlier, we've already been using XPointer expressions as part of URIs, but let's take a closer look. The expression

```
http://www.example.com/merlor.xml#mainbody
```

consists of the address of the file (`http://www.example.com/merlor.xml`), then a pound sign (`#`), then the XPointer expression (`mainbody`).

Because the bare names form of XPointer is intentionally similar to traditional XHTML notation, it's easy to miss the fact that this is, in fact, an XPointer expression, but we could just as easily have written

```
http://www.example.com/merlor.xml#xpointer(id("mainbody"))
```

We can even add more than one XPointer expression, and if the first one is unsuccessful (in that it doesn't find the requested material), the processor moves on to the next. One such common situation is IDs. As I've mentioned, without a DTD, we can't assume that IDs will be recognized. For that reason, we could write

```
http://www.example.com/merlor.xml#xpointer(
                        id("mainbody"))xpointer(//*[@id="mainbody"])
```

If the first expression doesn't recognize any ID values, the second will look for any element with an `id` attribute of `mainbody`.

This technique can be used to initialize values for namespace declarations, as well. For example:

```
http://www.example.com/viola.xml#xmlns(
                    v="http://example.com/viola")xpointer(//v:sheetmusic)
```

In this case, we're using the `xmlns` scheme, which will never find anything, because it's not looking for anything. The value is initialized, however, and will be used by the second expression, which uses the XPointer scheme.

The only two schemes defined by the XPointer Recommendation are `xpointer` and `xmlns`, but because of this "failover" behavior, an application can define its own scheme while providing a backup address in case it's not supported.

Functions

XPointer adds several functions to those already provided by XPath.

The `range(node-set)` function explicitly creates a range out of a particular node-set. For example, rather than specifying the body element by its ID value, we can create a locator that points to the covering range of the body element:

```
<entry xlink:type="locator" xlink:href="jader1.xml#xpointer(range(//body))"
       xlink:title="What a Party!" xlink:label="jaderentry" />
```

Perhaps even more useful than the `range()` function is the `string-range(node-set, string-to-match, start-index, length)` function, which enables you to choose a particular portion of text. For example, we could make a link out of every occurrence of the name `Alora` within the body of a document:

```
<entry xlink:type="locator" xlink:href="xpointer(string-range(//body, 'Alora'))"
       xlink:title="Reference to Alora" xlink:label="alora" />
```

In this case, the start-index takes its default value, 1 (defined here as the point before the first character—a difference from the normal zero-based index that may change in the final recommendation) and the length takes its default value as the length of the requested string. Note that the start-index is defined with respect to the found string, not the container node. If we used the function

```
string-range(//body, "Alora", 2)
```

we would only receive the string

```
lora
```

Other functions include `start-point()`, `end-point()`, and `range-to()`.

Summary

Today's hyperlinks barely scratch the surface of what is possible with information relationships. XLink improves on those capabilities by enabling you to create, among other things, links that lead to more than one potential destination and links that are multidirectional. Resources can be either local (part of the link itself) or remote (outside the link). Linked content may be displayed in place of the content that referenced it, embedded within it, or opened in a new context, such as a new window.

XLink also provides for link databases, or linkbases, which can create relationships between many different resources even if the author has no control over the resources themselves.

Finally, XLink integrates with XPointer, which provides the means for addressing both specific points and ranges within a document.

Review Questions

1. What are the XLink elements?

2. What is a simple link?

3. If a string of linked text is in the same document as an extended link, but not within the link element itself, is it local or remote?

4. How many resources can be involved in an extended link?

5. What does the `actuate` attribute do?

6. How does an application know to treat a linkbase differently from other linked resources?

7. How does XPointer relate to XPath?

8. What are the three forms of an XPointer?

Programming Exercises

1. Convert the hyperlinks (`<a></a>` elements) in the following code into simple XLinks.

```
<html>
<head><title>Wow, a party!</title></head>
<body>
<h1>Wow, a party!</h1>

<p>All High Bumbledoop is throwing a Grand Ball, and Manicpa's
got the <a href="http://www.example.com/menu.html">menu</a>.
Check it out, from Gillbrits to Quakles.</p>

</body>
</html>
```

2. Create a link with multiple starting resources but a single ending resource.

3. Create a link with multiple starting and ending points.

4. Create an XPointer expression that selects the main content in the solution to exercise 2.

5. Create an extended link that has as its origin the word Bumbledoop in exercise 2. Assume that the file is called `jader1.html`.

CHAPTER 15

XFORMS

- The purpose of XForms
- Separating content from presentation
- Creating an instance document
- Setting initial form values
- Validating forms
- Binding values
- Using multiple forms
- XML Events

A t this point, you've seen how XHTML forms enable you to accept information from a user, but if you've ever tried to build anything substantial with them, you've discovered limitations in their use. Aside from the fact that they can be difficult to move to platforms such as PDAs and cell phones, they can be cumbersome for large data sets, and they completely ignore the issue of validation, requiring you, the programmer, to write client-side scripting to make sure that nobody requests that their order be delivered on February 31.

The XForms Recommendation, maintained by the W3C, is an attempt to solve many, if not all, of these problems.

XForms Basics

At its heart, the promise of XForms is to integrate forms and XML by separating form from presentation. Along the way, it offers significant advances in validation and integration with XML Events.

Significantly, it also offers us the ability to manipulate an XML information set directly rather than taking in disparate pieces of data and trying to construct one.

In this chapter, we'll look at two forms. The first takes information about service calls made by the maintenance department, and the second performs calculations using data from multiple service calls.

One XForms, Two XForms

It's tempting to call a single XForms file an XForm, but it's also incorrect. A note from the editor on the W3C site declares that "XForms is a word with no singular form. Other such words in the English language are: ALMS, CATTLE, CLOTHES, PLIERS, SCISSORS, and SHORTS. It is considered a misspelling to use the term 'XForm' in a sentence."

A Simple Form

Creating a simple form isn't very difficult in XHTML. For example, using what we covered in Chapter 13, "Browser-Based XML: XHTML," we can create a simple login page, as shown in Listing 15.1.

LISTING 15.1 A Simple XHTML Page

```
<html xmlns="http://www.w3.org/1999/xhtml">
<head><title>Maintenance Login Page</title></head>
<body>

    <h1>Log In</h1>

    <form action="http://www.example.com/processlogin.jps" method="post">

    <p>Username:  <br /> <input type="text" name="username" /></p>
    <p>Password:  <br /><input type="password" name="password" /></p>

    <p><input type="submit" value="Log In" /></p>
    </form>

</body>
</html>
```

Overall, this is a pretty simple page that yields a form allowing a user to enter a username and password, as shown in Figure 15.1.

FIGURE 15.1
A simple XHTML form.

When a user submits this form, we'll get two name-value pairs. The actual values will depend on what the user enters.

That's all well and good for this particular purpose, but content and presentation are pretty tightly linked here. For example, what text goes with the `username` field? We can look at it on the screen and say it's the "Username:" text, but there's nothing in this document to indicate that fact. "Username:" is just a piece of text on the page, as far as the browser is concerned.

And what about the returned data? Name-value pairs are fine for programming in general, but we're talking about XML programming here. Wouldn't it be nice to be able to manipulate an XML document directly, or at least to get one back as a form result?

XForms allows us to do that, as shown in Listing 15.2.

XForms Versions

the code in this chapter is based on the January 18, 2002 Working Draft, and may change when the final document is released by W3C.

LISTING 15.2   A Simple XForms Form

```
<html xmlns="http://www.w3.org/1999/xhtml"
     xmlns:xforms="http://www.w3.org/2002/01/xforms">
<head>
    <title>Maintenance Login Page</title>

    <xforms:model>
        <xforms:submitInfo action="http://www.example.com/processlogin.jsp"
                                    method="post" mediaType="text/xml"/>
        <xforms:instance xmlns="">
            <information>
                <username/>
                <password/>
            </information>
        </xforms:instance>
    </xforms:model>

</head>
<body>

    <h1>Log In</h1>

    <p>
        <xforms:input ref="information/username">
            <xforms:caption>Username: </xforms:caption>
        </xforms:input>
    </p>
    <p>
        <xforms:secret ref="information/password">
            <xforms:caption>Password: </xforms:caption>
        </xforms:secret>
```

LISTING 15.2   Continued

```
    </p>

    <p>
        <xforms:submit>
            <xforms:caption>Log In</xforms:caption>
        </xforms:submit>
    </p>

</body>
</html>
```

Web Browser Error

Don't panic if you try to open this page in your usual Web browser and you get an error; at the time of this writing, a separate application is required. We'll discuss the process of installing it shortly.

The result is virtually identical to that of Listing 15.1, as shown in Figure 15.2, but the underlying theory is significantly different.

FIGURE 15.2
An XForms form.

The two major differences lie in what goes in and what comes out.

As far as what goes in, we're dealing with an ordinary XML document in which information such as the caption is actually associated with the element, so different applications can handle the inputs appropriately. For example, Figure 15.2 shows a Web browser–like application displaying the page, but any XML-aware application can use the actual form; the presentation is left out of the equation.

This separation helps even when we use the browser, as we can use CSS to control how the page looks through properties such as `caption-side`.

The major difference between the XForms example and the XHTML example lies in what comes out. Rather than name-value pairs, we can actually get an XML document, like this:

```
<?xml version="1.0" encoding="ISO-8859-1"?>
<information>
    <username>myusername</username>
```

```
        <password>mypassword</password>
    </information>
```

Does this structure look familiar? Notice that it matches the instance element. XForms allows you to specify an instance document, then "bind" form elements to it. When the user changes the value in the form, the value in the document changes.

Let's look at the overall structure of an XForms form.

Anatomy of an XForms Form

Before we get into specifics about how to build an XForms form, let's take a look at its overall structure. Listing 15.3 shows a skeleton XForms form embedded in an XHTML page.

XHTML Is Just the Beginning

Note that although we'll look at XForms embedded in XHTML in this chapter, part of the beauty of XForms is their ability to work with all sorts of structures, such as XSL Formatting Objects and Scalable Vector Graphics, without altering the structure of the actual form.

LISTING 15.3   A Skeleton Form

```
<html xmlns="http://www.w3.org/1999/xhtml"
      xmlns:xforms="http://www.w3.org/2002/01/xforms">
<head>
    <title>Page Title</title>

    <xforms:model>
        <xforms:submitInfo mediaType="..." action="..." />

        <xforms:schema>
            <!-- Form validation information -->
        </schema>

        <xforms:instance xmlns="">
            <!-- The initial and final XML instance document -->
        </xforms:instance>

        <!-- Binding information -->

        <!-- Event definitions -->
    </xforms:model>

</head>
<body>

    <!-- Actual forms controls reside in the body of the document. -->
    <!-- Controls for multiple forms can intermingle. -->

</body>
</html>
```

Notice first that the information about the form, such as the submission information and the instance document, is kept separate from the form controls themselves. An additional benefit of this structure is that it gives us the ability to mix controls from different forms in the same part of a page, a feat that's impossible with XHTML.

All the information about the form is part of the `model` element.

The `submitInfo` element contains the information that normally resides in the `form` element of an XHTML form, such as the `action` (defining what should happen when the user submits the form) and the structure in which the information is sent.

The `schema` element enables you to define constraints for the returned data. For example, you might define a particular piece of information as a `date`. Because these constraints are constructed with XML Schema, however, you can exert fairly fine control over the data, creating your own custom types to which it must conform. The `schema` element also allows you to link to an external document rather than defining the constraints inline.

The instance element contains the structure for the returned data. You can also use it to specify initial values, as you'll see in the section titled "Form Values."

Binding information allows you to easily specify types for information, relate different data elements together, and perform calculations without having to create client-side scripting.

XForms allow you to use XML Events by creating listeners and defining events and their targets, as you'll see in the "Form Events" section.

As you can see, we've got a lot of ground to cover, so let's get started!

Getting Ready

First you're going to need an application that understands XForms. At the time of this writing, mainstream browsers don't understand it, though there is a movement underway to add it to Mozilla, and thus to Netscape Navigator.

In the meantime, however, you can download any of the implementations listed at `http://www.w3.org/MarkUp/Forms/#implementations`. For the examples in this chapter, we'll be using X-Smiles, a Java implementation that not only allows us to easily see the submitted data, but also implements XSL Formatting Objects, which we'll be using in Chapter 16, "XML and Publishing: Formatting Objects with XSL."

Download the software and install it. It comes with a number of XForms demos so you can easily test whether or not it's working. (The demos are available online, so you don't have to download them to use them.)

Form Controls

In this section, we'll build a basic form that takes information about maintenance service calls. The form uses each of the different types of controls and creates an XML information set that represents all the data recorded about the call. In fact, we can start with a `model` that represents all the eventual data, as in Listing 15.4.

LISTING 15.4   The Basic Form

```
<html xmlns="http://www.w3.org/1999/xhtml"
      xmlns:xforms="http://www.w3.org/2002/01/xforms">
<head>
    <title>Maintenance Report Form</title>

    <xforms:model>

        <xforms:submitInfo method2="postxml" localfile="./temp.xml" />

        <xforms:instance xmlns="">
            <servicecall>
                <person pid="">
                    <empname></empname>
                    <password></password>
                </person>
                <visit>
                    <responsedate></responsedate>
                    <visitlength></visitlength>
                    <location>
                        <deck></deck>
                        <section></section>
                        <equipment></equipment>
                    </location>
                    <performed></performed>
                    <resolution>
                        <status></status>
                        <satisfaction></satisfaction>
                        <workaroundavail></workaroundavail>
                        <workarounddesc></workarounddesc>
                    </resolution>
                </visit>
                <comments></comments>
                <supportingdoc></supportingdoc>
            </servicecall>
        </xforms:instance>

    </xforms:model>

</head>
<body>

<h1>Maintenance Report Form</h1>

<p>
    <xforms:submit>
        <xforms:caption>Submit Report</xforms:caption>
    </xforms:submit>

    <xforms:button>
        <xforms:caption>Erase Changes</xforms:caption>
    </xforms:button>
</p>

</body>
</html>
```

Let's take this one step at a time. First, notice that we have two namespaces declared: the XHTML namespace, declared as the default namespace, and the XForms namespace. Note that this is the January 18, 2002 Working Draft namespace. By the time you read this, the "current" version may have changed.

Next, we have the `model` for the form. First in the `model` is the `submitInfo` element. Under normal circumstances, we'd have an `action`, `method`, and `mediaType` noted here, but in order to actually see the results, we're going to use the `method2` and `localfile` attributes, which are specific to X-Smiles. These attributes will cause the results to be written to the file `temp.xml`, which is then loaded in the main window for inspection. If you're using different software, check to see whether it's got similar capabilities.

Next comes the `instance` element. This is the placeholder for the actual data from the form. Notice that we have multiple levels of elements here, rather than simple name-value pairs. Notice also that we are undeclaring the default namespace. If we don't, all the elements in the instance will be part of the XHTML namespace, and that's definitely not what we want. We also have the option of declaring an explicit namespace for the data.

In the body of the document, we have the beginnings of the actual form. Notice that there is no `form` element, as there was with the XHTML form. Instead, we can use the XForms elements anywhere in the document, and because they're part of the `xforms` namespace they'll be handled properly. Here we're defining two buttons. The first is the `submit` button, with its text defined as part of the `caption` element. When clicked, this button submits the form. The second is a `button` button, which does nothing at the moment; later, we'll look at defining behaviors.

Now let's start adding form fields.

Text

The most common type of form field is a simple text element, and by default an `input` element is handled that way, as shown in Listing 15.5.

LISTING 15.5   Simple Text Fields

```
<html xmlns="http://www.w3.org/1999/xhtml"
     xmlns:xforms="http://www.w3.org/2002/01/xforms">
<head>
    <title>Maintenance Report Form</title>

    <xforms:model>

        <xforms:submitInfo method2="postxml" localfile="./temp2.xml" />

        <xforms:instance xmlns="">
            <servicecall>
                <person pid="">
                    <empname></empname>
                    <password></password>
```

LISTING 15.5 *Continued*

```
                    </person>
                    <visit>
                        <responsedate></responsedate>
                        <visitlength></visitlength>
                        <location>
                            <deck></deck>
                            <section></section>
                            <equipment></equipment>
                        </location>
                        <performed></performed>
                        <resolution>
                            <status></status>
                            <satisfaction></satisfaction>
                            <workaroundavail></workaroundavail>
                            <workarounddesc></workarounddesc>
                        </resolution>
                    </visit>
                    <comments></comments>
                    <supportingdoc></supportingdoc>
                </servicecall>
            </xforms:instance>

        </xforms:model>

</head>
<body>

<h1>Maintenance Report Form</h1>

<p>
    <xforms:input ref="servicecall/person/empname">
        <xforms:caption>Name: </xforms:caption>
    </xforms:input>
</p>

<p>

    <xforms:input ref="servicecall/visit/responsedate">
        <xforms:caption>Respond Time and Date: </xforms:caption>
    </xforms:input>

    <br />

    <xforms:input ref="servicecall/visit/visitlength" id="visit">
        <xforms:caption>Visit Length: </xforms:caption>
    </xforms:input>
</p>

<p>

    <xforms:input ref="servicecall/visit/location/equipment">
        <xforms:caption>Equipment:  </xforms:caption>
    </xforms:input>
</p>
```

LISTING 15.5   Continued

```
<p>
    <xforms:submit>
        <xforms:caption>Submit Report</xforms:caption>
    </xforms:submit>

    <xforms:button>
        <xforms:caption>Erase Changes</xforms:caption>
    </xforms:button>
</p>

</body>
</html>
```

Notice that, like the buttons, each of these text fields has a `caption` that provides a label for the field, as shown in Figure 15.3.

FIGURE 15.3
Text fields.

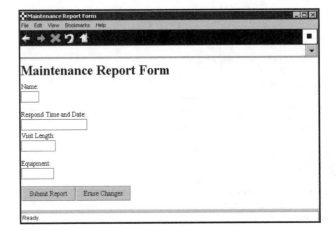

Notice also that instead of the `name` attribute you may have come to expect in an XHTML form, we have the `ref` attribute, which points back to a node in the `instance` element. Here we are using relative XPath expressions; the root for these expressions is the `instance` element, so

```
servicecall/visit/responsedate
```

is the equivalent of

```
/servicecall/visit/responsedate
```

When we add data to one of these fields, it's also added to the corresponding node in the instance document. For example, if we added data to the form and submitted it, we'd get a result like this:

```
<?xml version="1.0" encoding="ISO-8859-1"?>
            <servicecall>
                <person pid="">
```

```
            <empname>Nick</empname>
            <password/>
        </person>
        <visit>
            <responsedate>Wednesday, 2PM</responsedate>
            <visitlength>1 hour</visitlength>
            <location>
                <deck/>
                <section/>
                <equipment>Airlock</equipment>
            </location>
            <performed/>
            <resolution>
                <status/>
                <satisfaction/>
                <workaroundavail/>
                <workarounddesc/>
            </resolution>
        </visit>
        <comments/>
        <supportingdoc/>
    </servicecall>
```

Notice not only that the data was added to the document at the proper locations, but also that the entire instance document was submitted, even though the rest of it wasn't referenced by form controls. This enables you to use XForms to modify only part of a document.

The input control isn't the only way to accept direct data entry from the user. As with an XHTML form, you can use passwords and textareas.

Passwords: The `secret` Control

In an XHTML form, we use `type="password"` on an `input` element to enable users to type sensitive information without worrying that someone looking over their shoulder will see it. The same feat is accomplished in XForms using a `secret` control, as shown in Listing 15.6.

LISTING 15.6   The `secret` Control

```
...
<p>
    <xforms:input ref="servicecall/person/empname">
        <xforms:caption>Name: </xforms:caption>
    </xforms:input>

    <br />

    <xforms:secret ref="servicecall/person/password">
        <xforms:caption>Password: </xforms:caption>
    </xforms:secret>
</p>
...
```

Like the input control, the secret control references a node in the instance document. (Notice that the text entered in the Password field in Figure 15.4 is obscured.)

Textareas

Textareas follow the same format as input controls, as shown in Listing 15.7.

LISTING 15.7 Textareas

```
...
<p>
    <xforms:input ref="servicecall/visit/location/equipment">
        <xforms:caption>Equipment:  </xforms:caption>
    </xforms:input>
</p>

<p>
    <xforms:textarea ref="servicecall/visit/resolution/workarounddesc">
        <xforms:caption>Describe workaround: </xforms:caption>
    </xforms:textarea>
</p>
<p>
    <xforms:textarea ref="servicecall/comments">
        <xforms:caption>Comments: </xforms:caption>
    </xforms:textarea>
</p>

<p>
    <xforms:submit>
        <xforms:caption>Submit Report</xforms:caption>
    </xforms:submit>

    <xforms:button>
        <xforms:caption>Erase Changes</xforms:caption>
    </xforms:button>
</p>
...
```

In Figure 15.4, you can see that unless we apply CSS styling to adjust the size (which we haven't done yet), textareas are rendered as though they were text input controls. There is one major difference, however: A textarea is capable of holding more than one line of data.

FIGURE 15.4
Textareas and a `secret` field.

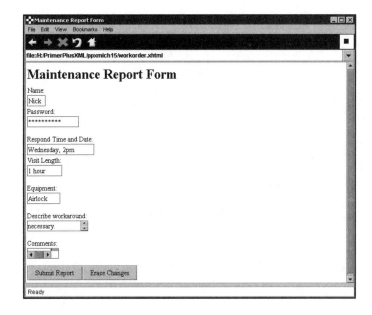

The data is submitted as is:

```
<?xml version="1.0" encoding="ISO-8859-1"?>
        <servicecall>
            <person pid=" ">
                <empname>Nick</empname>
                <password>myPassword</password>
            </person>
            <visit>
...

                <resolution>
                    <status/>
                    <satisfaction/>
                    <workaroundavail/>
                    <workarounddesc>Don't use the
airlock unless it's
absolutely
necessary.</workarounddesc>
                </resolution>
            </visit>
            <comments>User says that the workaround
doesn't work for them.</comments>
            <supportingdoc/>
        </servicecall>
```

Choices

Another common task for a form is to allow users to choose from a list of values. In XHTML, this takes the form of check boxes, radio groups, pull-down menus, and select lists, each of which has its own presentation requirements.

In XForms, there are two types of choices: `selectOne` and `selectMany`. Both can be constructed of a series of `item` elements, and how they're rendered depends on the `selectUI` attribute, as shown in Listing 15.8.

LISTING 15.8   `selectOne` and `selectMany`

```
...
<p>
    Location:  <br />

    <xforms:selectOne ref="servicecall/visit/location/deck" selectUI="listbox">
        <xforms:caption>Deck:    </xforms:caption>
        <xforms:item>
            <xforms:value>1</xforms:value>
            <xforms:caption>One</xforms:caption>
        </xforms:item>
        <xforms:item>
            <xforms:value>2</xforms:value>
            <xforms:caption>Two</xforms:caption>
        </xforms:item>
...
    </xforms:selectOne>

    <xforms:selectMany ref="servicecall/visit/location/section"
                                            selectUI="listbox">
        <xforms:caption>Section:    </xforms:caption>
        <xforms:item>
            <xforms:value>A</xforms:value>
            <xforms:caption>A</xforms:caption>
        </xforms:item>
        <xforms:item>
            <xforms:value>B</xforms:value>
            <xforms:caption>B</xforms:caption>
        </xforms:item>
...
    </xforms:selectMany>
</p>
<p>
    <xforms:input ref="servicecall/visit/location/equipment">
        <xforms:caption>Equipment:  </xforms:caption>
    </xforms:input>
<br/>
    <xforms:selectMany ref="servicecall/visit/performed" selectUI="checkbox">
        <xforms:caption>Action performed (Checkbox doesn't work properly in 0.6):
                                            </xforms:caption>
        <xforms:item>
            <xforms:value>repair</xforms:value>
            <xforms:caption>Repair </xforms:caption>
        </xforms:item>
        <xforms:item>
            <xforms:value>clean</xforms:value>
            <xforms:caption>Cleaning </xforms:caption>
```

LISTING 15.8   Continued

```
            </xforms:item>
            <xforms:item>
                <xforms:value>maint</xforms:value>
                <xforms:caption>Routine Maintenance</xforms:caption>
            </xforms:item>
        </xforms:selectMany>
</p>

<p>
    <xforms:selectOne ref="servicecall/visit/resolution/workaroundavail"
                                                selectUI="radio">
        <xforms:caption>Workaround available? </xforms:caption>
        <xforms:item>
            <xforms:value>Y</xforms:value>
            <xforms:caption>Yes</xforms:caption>
        </xforms:item>
        <xforms:item>
            <xforms:value>N</xforms:value>
            <xforms:caption>No</xforms:caption>
        </xforms:item>
    </xforms:selectOne>
<br />
    <xforms:textarea ref="servicecall/visit/resolution/workarounddesc">
        <xforms:caption>Describe workaround: </xforms:caption>
    </xforms:textarea>
</p>
...
```

Let's start with the first new field, the `selectOne` element. First, notice that in addition to `item` elements, it carries its own `caption` describing the overall field. Each item has a `caption`, as before, but because it is the `selectOne` element itself that returns a value, the `items` don't need a `ref` attribute. Instead, we're adding a value to the item element using a `value` element child. Just as in an XHTML form, the value and caption are independent of each other. If this were an XHTML form, we might write

```
<select name="deck>
    <option value="1">One</option>
    <option value="2">Two</option>
...
</select>
```

The `deck` and `section` values are both represented using the `listbox` user interface, as indicated by the `selectUI` attribute on the `selectOne` and `selectMany` elements, so they're both rendered the same, as shown in Figure 15.5. The difference is that the user can hold down a key such as Shift or Ctrl and select more than one option for the `selectMany` element.

In this case, we have two different elements with the same user interface, but we can also have two instances of the same element with different user interfaces. For example, the `workaroundavail` value is also a `selectOne`, but instead of the list box, we're choosing to use radio buttons. Similarly, we're choosing the `checkbox` user interface for the `performed selectMany`.

(Unfortunately, check boxes don't work properly in version 0.6 of X-Smiles, so you won't see the difference in the screenshots.)

FIGURE 15.5
Single and multiple choices.

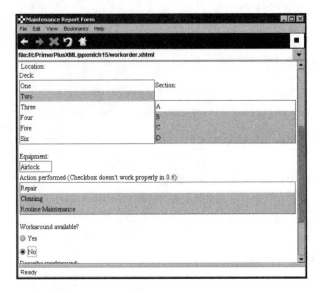

In this way, we can separate content and presentation, simplifying the process of changing either.

But what happens when multiple values are submitted? In this case, we have only a single placeholder element in the instance document, so the multiple values are submitted as space-delimited text within that element:

...

```
<location>
    <deck>2</deck>
    <section>B C D</section>
    <equipment>Airlock</equipment>
</location>
<performed>clean maint</performed>
<resolution>
    <status/>
    <satisfaction/>
    <workaroundavail>N</workaroundavail>
    <workarounddesc/>
</resolution>
```

...

Uploads

Another common task for a form is uploading files. While the `file` element is defined as part of XHTML, handling the data on the other end is a tedious chore that often involves third-party components.

XForms defines the `upload` element, as shown in Listing 15.9.

LISTING 15.9   The `upload` Element

```
...
<p>
    <xforms:textarea ref="servicecall/comments">
        <xforms:caption>Comments: </xforms:caption>
    </xforms:textarea>
</p>

<p>
    <xforms:upload ref="servicecall/supportingdoc">
        <xforms:caption>Supporting Documents</xforms:caption>
    </xforms:upload>
</p>

<p>
    <xforms:submit>
        <xforms:caption>Submit Report</xforms:caption>
    </xforms:submit>

    <xforms:button>
        <xforms:caption>Erase Changes</xforms:caption>
    </xforms:button>
</p>
...
```

Notice that there's nothing special about this element thus far. In a typical implementation, it's rendered as a button, which allows the user to choose a file, as shown in Figure 15.6.

FIGURE 15.6

Using the `upload` control.

The information is added to the instance document as binary data:

```
<comments/>
<supportingdoc>CQkJCQk8eGZvcm1zOnJlcGVhdCByZWY9InJlc3VsdHMvcHVyY2hhc2VvcmRlci9p
dGVtcy9pdGVtIiBpZD0icmVwZWF0MSIgeC1udW1iZXXI9IjQiHgtc3RhcnRRJbmRl
eD0iMSI+DQoJCQkJCQkJCQk8eGZvcm1zOnJhbmdlIHN0YXJ0PSIwIiBlbmQ9Ijlw
IiBzdGVwc2l6ZT0iMSIgcmVmPSJ1bml0cyI+DQoJCQkJCQkJPHhmb3Jtczpo
aW50PlRoZSB1bml0cyBvZiB0aGlzIGl0ZW08L3hmb3JtczpoaW50Pg0KCQkJCQkJ
CQkJPC94Zm9ybXM6cmFuZ2U+DQoJCQkJCQkJCQk8eGZvcm1zOmlucHV0IHJlZj0i
bmFtZSIgY2xhc3M3M9Im5hbWUiPg0KCQkJCQkJCQkJCQkJCQk8eGZvcm1z
OmhpbnQ+VGhlIG5hbWUgb2YgdGhpcyBpdGVtPC94Zm9ybXM6aGludD4NCgkJCQkJ
CQkJCTwveGZvcm1zOmlucHV0Pg0KCQkJCQkJPHhmb3JtczppbnB1dCBjb2xz
PSIzIiByZWY9InByaWNlIiBjbGFzcz0icHJpY2UiPg0KCQkJCQkJCTx4Zm9y
bXM6aGludD5UaGUGUgcHJpY2Ugb2YgdGhpcyBpdGVtPC94Zm9ybXM6aGludD4NCgkJ
CQkJCQkJCTwveGZvcm1zOmlucHV0Pg0KCQkJCQkJPHhmb3JtczpvdXRwdXQg
Y29scz0iNSIgcmVmPSJkaXNjb3VudCGY2xhc3M3M9InByaWNlIj4NCgkJCQkJCQkJ
CQk8eGZvcm1zOmhpbnQ+VGhlIGRpc2NvdW50IHZhbHVlIG9mIHRoZaoaXMgaXRlbTwv
eGZvcm1zOmhpbnQ+DQoJCQkJCQk8L3hmb3JtczpvdXRwdXQ+DQoJCQkJCQkJ
CQk8eGZvcm1zOm91dHB1dCBjb2xzPSI2IiByZWY9InRvdGFsGFsIiBjbGFzcz0icHJp
Y2UiPg0KCQkJCQkJCQkJCTx4Zm9ybXM6aGludD5UaGUgdG90YWwgdmFsdWUgb2Yg
dGhpcyBpdGVtPC94Zm9ybXM6aGludD4NCgkJCQkJCTwveGZvcm1zOm91dHB1
dD4NCgkJCQkJPC94Zm9ybXM6cmVwZWF0PC9zdXBwb3J0aW5nZG9jPg==
</supportingdoc>
      </servicecall>
```

Ranges

One type of form control that is new to XForms is the **range** control, shown in Listing 15.10. The way in which it is rendered depends on the application, but the idea is that it allows the user to enter only a very specific range of numbers, with specific increments.

LISTING 15.10   The **range** Control

```
...
        <xforms:item>
            <xforms:value>maint</xforms:value>
            <xforms:caption>Routine Maintenance</xforms:caption>
        </xforms:item>
    </xforms:selectMany>
</p>

<p>
    <xforms:range ref="servicecall/visit/resolution/satisfaction" start="0"
                                            end="10" stepsize="1">
        <xforms:caption>Customer satisfaction (0 = worst, 10 = best)
                                            </xforms:caption>
    </xforms:range>
<br />
    <xforms:selectOne ref="servicecall/visit/resolution/workaroundavail"
                                            selectUI="radio">
        <xforms:caption>Workaround available? </xforms:caption>
        <xforms:item>
```

LISTING 15.10   Continued

```
            <xforms:value>Y</xforms:value>
            <xforms:caption>Yes</xforms:caption>
        </xforms:item>
...
```

The user can move the slider along the **range** to select a value, as shown in Figure 15.7.

FIGURE 15.7
The **range** control.

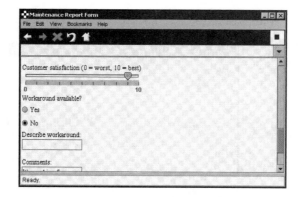

Boolean

Some questions (such as "Is the problem resolved?") simply require a yes-or-no answer. In XHTML, you can use a **checkbox**, but the **checkbox** is an all-or-nothing proposition; if it's checked, you get a value—if it isn't, you get nothing. XForms solves this problem by adding a **boolean** form control that works like a **checkbox** but returns a **true** or **false** value based on whether or not the control is checked.

Listing 15.11 shows the control in the form.

LISTING 15.11   Adding the **boolean** Control

```
...
        <xforms:item>
            <xforms:value>maint</xforms:value>
            <xforms:caption>Routine Maintenance</xforms:caption>
        </xforms:item>
    </xforms:selectMany>
</p>

<p>
    <xforms:selectBoolean ref="servicecall/visit/resolution/status">
        <xforms:caption>Resolved?</xforms:caption>
    </xforms:selectBoolean>
<br />
    <xforms:range ref="servicecall/visit/resolution/satisfaction" start="0"
                                            end="10" stepsize="1">
```

LISTING 15.11   Continued

```
            <xforms:caption>Customer satisfaction (0 = worst, 10 = best)
                                                        </xforms:caption>
        </xforms:range>
    <br />
    ...
```

This creates a check box, as shown in Figure 15.8.

FIGURE 15.8
The Boolean check box.

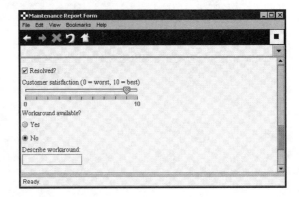

Submitting the Form

When XForms are completely implemented, you will have a great deal of control over what happens when the user submits the form. You will be able to control what parts of the instance data are submitted, whether the page or the data is replaced, and the form the data takes when it is submitted.

submitInfo

The `submitInfo` element is the "nerve center" that controls what happens when the user submits the form, which carries attributes that control various aspects of the application's behavior. These attributes include

- `action`—The destination for the data. Normally, this is some sort of script such as a JavaServer Page or CGI script.

- `method`—Our two XHTML methods, `get` and `post`, are back, and they retain the same meanings. It should be noted, however, that the `get` method, which puts all the data into the URL of the request, is deprecated and may be removed at some point.

- `replace`—This attribute controls whether the entire page is replaced, or just the data within the instance element. At first, this may seem pointless; because the instance document is updated as the form is updated, it should be in sync, right? Right, but submitting the form also causes the data to be validated and calculated, as you'll see, and reloading the instance document causes the form to reinitialize itself with the new data, potentially triggering other actions.

- **mediaType**—This attribute controls the serialization of the submitted information, as you'll see in the examples that follow. We've been dealing with `text/xml`, but it's also possible to send the information in more traditional ways.

- **omitXMLDeclaration**, **indent**, and **CDATASectionElements**—These attributes control the treatment of the actual XML data returned.

Let's take a look at some of the ways the form can return data.

mediaType=`"application/x-www-form-urlencoded"`

The `mediaType` controls the way in which the instance data is serialized. A value of `applica-tion/x-www-form-urlencoded` is similar to processing the data using the `get` method; it simply provides name-value pairs. For example, submitting our form using this method would provide results something like this:

```
empname=Nick
password=mypassword
responsedate=Wednesday, 2pm
section=B C D
visitlength=1 hour
equipment=Airlock
comments=No comments
deck=4
satisfaction=9
performed=clean maint
status=true
workaroundavail= N
workarounddesc=
supportingdoc = PHhzZDpzY2hlbWEgeG1sbnM6eHNkPSJodHRwOi8vd3d3LnczLm9yZy8yMDAxL1hN
TFNjaGVtYSI+DQoNCjx4c2Q6Y29tcGxleFR5cGUgbmFtZT0icmVzdWx0c1R5cGUi
Pg0KPHhzZDplbGVtZW50IG5hbWU9InBlcnNvbmlkIiB0eXBlPSJ4c2Q6c3RyaW5n
Ii8+DQo8eHNkOmVsZW1lbnQgbmFtZT0icGVyc29ubmFtZTSIgdHlwZT0ieHNkOnN0
cmluZyIvPg0KPKPC94c2Q6Y29tcGxleFR5cGU+DQoNCg0KPHhzZDplbGVtZW50IG5h
bWU9InJlc3VsdHMiIHR5cGU9InJlc3VsdHNUeXBlIi8+DQoNCg0KDQo8L3hzZDpl
bGVtZW50Pg0KDQogICAgICAgICAgPHJlc3VsdHM+DQogICAgICAgICAgICAgIDxw
ZXJzb25pZD5FNDQ0PC9wZXJzb25pZD4NCiAgICICAgICAgICAgICAgPHBlcnNvbm5h
bWU+ZW55bzwvcGVyc29ubmFtZT4NCiAgICICAgICA8L3Jlc3VsdHM+DQoNCg0K
PC94c2Q6c2NoZW1h
```

Not only is the hierarchical nature of the data lost, but we don't even see the `pid` attribute. (We don't have data in it now, but we will eventually.) Use of this serialization type results in lost attribute values, and this method is deprecated.

mediaType=`"multipart/form-data"`

This method is somewhat better; it at least provides attribute values and the overall structure. It doesn't arrive as an XML document, but at least all the information is there in case you want to reconstruct one.

The `multipart/form-data` type sends individual "parts," separated by a specified "boundary." For example, the data might be sent as

```
Content-Type: multipart/form-data; boundary=CwZ33b

--CwZ33b
  Content-Disposition: form-data; name="/servicecall/person/@pid"

E438
--CwZ33b
  Content-Disposition: form-data; name="/servicecall/person/empname"

Nick
--CwZ33b
  Content-Disposition: form-data; name="/servicecall/person/password"

mypassword
--CwZ33b
  Content-Disposition: form-data; name="/servicecall/visit/responsedate"

Wednesday, 2pm
--CwZ33b
  Content-Disposition: form-data; name="/servicecall/visit/visitlength"

1 hour
--CwZ33b
...
--CwZ33b-
```

Typically, server applications such as the ASP or JSP engine automatically translate these parts back into name-value pairs so you don't have to do it manually.

mediaType="text/xml"

This is the form of submission we've been dealing with so far, though we've been looking at it from a local perspective. In this case, the instance data is submitted as a single XML stream, which the application can handle appropriately.

Form Values

In this section, we're going to look at the form values themselves. First we're going to set the initial values for the form, then we're going to look at validating the form by creating a schema against which the entered values can be checked. Finally, we'll look at binding values, both to calculations and to each other.

Setting Initial Values

We'll start by setting initial values for the form. In XHTML forms, we did this mostly through the `value` attribute. In an XForms form, we're going to take advantage of the very nature of the form itself.

We've been saying all along that when we enter information into the form, the instance document is updated, so it should come as no surprise that if we start out with data in the instance document, it affects the form. In Listing 15.12, we add default data corresponding to the service call.

LISTING 15.12   Adding Initial Form Values

```
<html xmlns="http://www.w3.org/1999/xhtml"
      xmlns:xforms="http://www.w3.org/2002/01/xforms">
<head>
    <title>Maintenance Report Form</title>

    <xforms:model>

        <xforms:submitInfo action="http://localhost/test.asp" method="get"
                                                mediaType="text/xml" />

        <xforms:instance xmlns="">
            <servicecall>
                <person pid="">
                    <empname>Nick</empname>
                    <password>mypass</password>
                </person>
                <visit>
                    <responsedate>Wednesday, 2pm</responsedate>
                    <visitlength>1 hour</visitlength>
                    <location>
                        <deck>3</deck>
                        <section>B C D</section>
                        <equipment>Airlock</equipment>
                    </location>
                    <performed>clean maint</performed>
                    <resolution>
                        <status>true</status>
                        <satisfaction>9</satisfaction>
                        <workaroundavail>N</workaroundavail>
                        <workarounddesc></workarounddesc>
                    </resolution>
                </visit>
                <comments>It's working fine now.</comments>
                <supportingdoc></supportingdoc>
            </servicecall>
        </xforms:instance>

    </xforms:model>

</head>
<body>

<h1>Maintenance Report Form</h1>

<p>
    <xforms:input ref="servicecall/person/empname">
        <xforms:caption>Name: </xforms:caption>
```

LISTING 15.12   Continued

```
        </xforms:input>

        <br />

        <xforms:secret ref="servicecall/person/password">
            <xforms:caption>Password: </xforms:caption>
        </xforms:secret>
    </p>
    ...
```

When we load this page, the values are automatically filled in the form, as shown in Figure 15.9.

FIGURE 15.9
When we add values to the instance document, XForms adds them to the form automatically.

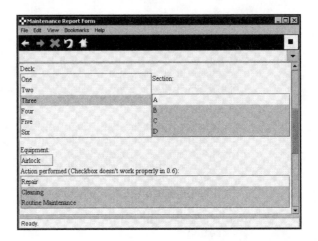

Before, we used the `ref` attribute to specify how to move the data from the input field to the instance document. In this case, the `ref` attribute works in the other direction. When loading the form, the application checks the `ref` attribute in order to determine the location from which it should draw the data. So the control

```
    <xforms:textarea ref="servicecall/comments">
        <xforms:caption>Comments: </xforms:caption>
    </xforms:textarea>
```

grabs the value of the `comments` child of the `servicecall` element and inserts it into the form control.

Schemas

In an XHTML form, guaranteeing that a particular field conforms to a certain requirement (such as the requirement that it is a valid date or is part of an enumerated list of variables) involves extensive client-side scripting that must be adapted for each potential client.

Because of its XML base, XForms allows you to perform validation much more easily by simply using XML Schema.

Listing 15.13 shows the schema to which we want the instance data to conform.

LISTING 15.13   The Schema

```
<xsd:schema xmlns:xsd="http://www.w3.org/2001/XMLSchema">

<xsd:simpleType name="employees">
<xsd:restriction base="xsd:string">
  <xsd:enumeration value="Nick"/>
  <xsd:enumeration value="maURO"/>
  <xsd:enumeration value="Kelemon"/>
  <xsd:enumeration value="Rhiannon"/>
</xsd:restriction>
</xsd:simpleType>

<xsd:element name="empname" type="employees"/>
<xsd:element name="password" type="xsd:string"/>
<xsd:element name="responsedate" type="xsd:date"/>
<xsd:element name="visitlength" type="xsd:integer"/>
<xsd:element name="deck" type="xsd:string"/>
<xsd:element name="section" type="xsd:string"/>
<xsd:element name="equipment" type="xsd:string"/>
<xsd:element name="performed" type="xsd:string"/>
<xsd:element name="status" type="xsd:string"/>
<xsd:element name="satisfaction" type="xsd:string"/>
<xsd:element name="workaroundavail" type="xsd:string"/>
<xsd:element name="workarounddesc" type="xsd:string"/>
<xsd:element name="comments" type="xsd:string"/>
<xsd:element name="supportingdoc" type="xsd:string"/>

<xsd:complexType name="persontype">
    <xsd:sequence>
        <xsd:element ref="empname" />
        <xsd:element ref="password" />
    </xsd:sequence>
    <xsd:attribute name="pid" type="xsd:string"/>
</xsd:complexType>

<xsd:complexType name="locationtype">
    <xsd:sequence>
        <xsd:element ref="deck" />
        <xsd:element ref="section" />
        <xsd:element ref="equipment" />
    </xsd:sequence>
</xsd:complexType>

<xsd:complexType name="resolutiontype">
    <xsd:sequence>
        <xsd:element ref="status" />
        <xsd:element ref="satisfaction" />
        <xsd:element ref="workaroundavail"/>
        <xsd:element ref="workarounddesc" />
```

LISTING 15.13 Continued

```
        </xsd:sequence>
    </xsd:complexType>

    <xsd:complexType name="visittype">
        <xsd:sequence>
            <xsd:element ref="responsedate" />
            <xsd:element ref="visitlength"/>
            <xsd:element ref="location" />
            <xsd:element ref="performed" />
            <xsd:element ref="resolution" />
        </xsd:sequence>
    </xsd:complexType>

    <xsd:complexType name="servicecalltype">
        <xsd:sequence>
            <xsd:element ref="person" />
            <xsd:element ref="visit"   />
             <xsd:element ref="comments" />
             <xsd:element ref="supportingdoc" />
        </xsd:sequence>
    </xsd:complexType>

    <xsd:element name="resolution" type="resolutiontype"/>
    <xsd:element name="location" type="locationtype" />
    <xsd:element name="servicecall" type="servicecalltype" />
    <xsd:element name="person" type="persontype" />
    <xsd:element name="visit" type="visittype" />

</xsd:schema>
```

Notice that the `responsedate` is now a date value, so `Wednesday, 2pm` is no longer acceptable. Similarly, the `visitlength` must be an `integer`, rather than a simple `string`.

In addition to built-in types, we can validate against custom types, so if we list the employees of the maintenance department as part of the `employees` type, we can restrict acceptable values to those on the list.

Now all we have to do is bind the schema to the form by way of the `schema` element, as in Listing 15.14.

LISTING 15.14 Linking to a Schema Document

```
<html xmlns="http://www.w3.org/1999/xhtml"
      xmlns:xforms="http://www.w3.org/2002/01/xforms">
<head>
    <title>Maintenance Report Form</title>

    <xforms:model>

        <xforms:submitInfo action="http://localhost/test.asp" method="get"
                                                 mediaType="text/xml" />
```

LISTING 15.14   Continued

```
<xforms:schema href="workorder.xsd"/>

<xforms:instance xmlns="">
    <servicecall>
        <person pid="">
            <empname>Nick</empname>
            <password>mypass</password>
        </person>
        <visit>
...
```

You can also define the schema inline as part of the **schema** element, but if the form specifies an external schema, the inline definitions will be ignored.

Linking
In a full implementation, you'll be linking to a schema document using simple XLink links.

With a schema bound to the form, the application attempts to keep the data in sync. In some cases, when the user changes a value, the application checks the values and may indicate invalid entries, as shown in Figure 15.10. When the user submits the form, the application validates the instance document against the schema, and if the document is invalid, the submission process stops, typically causing some sort of error message.

FIGURE 15.10
Schemas prevent invalid entries from being submitted, and can provide clues about data that might be a problem.

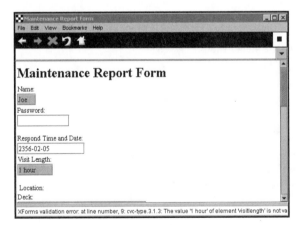

Binding

Binding can serve several functions within a document. First, it can literally bind two controls together, so that when one changes, the other changes as well. Second, it can bind a control to a particular predefined type. (This is similar to using schema validation.) Third, it can be used to define calculated values.

In Listing 15.15, we're creating a new form that calculates the cost of a service call based on the length of the visit and the hourly rate.

LISTING 15.15   Binding Calculations

```
<html xmlns="http://www.w3.org/1999/xhtml"
                 xmlns:xforms="http://www.w3.org/2002/01/xforms"
                    xmlns:xsd="http://www.w3.org/2001/XMLSchema">
<head><title>Maintenance Report Form</title>
<xforms:model>
    <xforms:submitInfo id="submit1" method2="postxml" localfile="./temp2.xml" />
      <xforms:instance xmlns="">
          <reports>
              <report>
                  <id>D33</id>
                  <service>Airlock service</service>
                  <length>1.5</length>
                  <rate>75</rate>
                  <total/>
              </report>
          </reports>
      </xforms:instance>

<xforms:bind ref="/reports/report/total" calculate="../rate * ../length"/>

</xforms:model>

</head>
<body>

<h1>Maintenance Report Summary</h1>

<p>

  <xforms:input ref="reports/report/id" cols="20">
    <xforms:caption>ID: </xforms:caption>
  </xforms:input>
  <xforms:input ref="reports/report/service" cols="20">
    <xforms:caption>Service: </xforms:caption>
  </xforms:input>
  <xforms:input ref="reports/report/length" cols="20">
    <xforms:caption>Length: </xforms:caption>
  </xforms:input>
  <xforms:input ref="reports/report/rate" cols="20">
    <xforms:caption>Rate: </xforms:caption>
  </xforms:input>
  <xforms:input ref="reports/report/total" cols="20">
    <xforms:caption>Total: </xforms:caption>
  </xforms:input>

</p>
<p>
```

LISTING 15.15   Continued

```
<xforms:submit>
  <xforms:caption>Submit Report</xforms:caption>
</xforms:submit>
</p>
</body>
</html>
```

When the application loads the form, it performs the calculation automatically. If either the rate or the duration changes, the total is automatically updated, as shown in Figure 15.11.

FIGURE 15.11
Bound calculations change automatically.

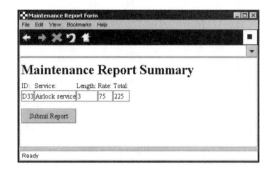

Relevance

Binding can also be used to determine relevance. For example, if there's no workaround available, there's no point in having a `workarounddesc` field. Using a binding expression, we can turn it on and off based on the value of the `workaroundavail` field, as shown in Listing 15.16.

LISTING 15.16   Using Relevance

```
...
            <comments>It's working fine now.</comments>
            <supportingdoc></supportingdoc>
        </servicecall>
    </xforms:instance>

    <xforms:bind ref="/servicecall/visit/resolution/workarounddesc"
                 relevant="../workaroundavail = 'Y'"/>

    </xforms:model>

</head>
<body>

<h1>Maintenance Report Form</h1>

...
```

When the value of the `workaroundavail` field is Y, the `workarounddesc` is relevant, so it appears. When it's not, the `workarounddesc` field disappears, as in Figure 15.12.

FIGURE 15.12
When there is no workaround, the workaround description isn't relevant, and disappears.

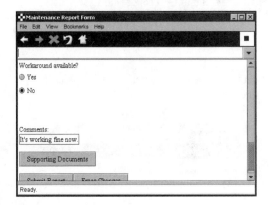

Binding works in this way because you're actually setting a value of **true** or **false** for the **relevant** attribute, but you're doing it using an expression based on another control.

Similarly, you can determine whether a particular entry is required using the **required** attribute.

Form Structures

Now that we've covered the basics, let's look at some XForms features that make your life easier. We'll discuss repeating structures and itemsets, which allow you to build a form based on the content of the instance document, and grouping, which allows you to set a context node for a group of elements.

Repeating Structures

First let's look at repeating structures. One of the most odious tasks in an XHTML form is creating fields for multiple rows of similar data. Not only is it a hassle to create elements for each item, but it can be a hassle to process the results, because each item must be correlated to its original.

XForms enables us to create a structure that takes a specific node and creates a set of controls for each child. In Listing 15.17, we'll create a form that shows three different service calls and summarizes their costs.

LISTING 15.17   Generating Repeated Form Controls

```
<html xmlns="http://www.w3.org/1999/xhtml"
        xmlns:xforms="http://www.w3.org/2002/01/xforms"
xmlns:xsd="http://www.w3.org/2001/XMLSchema">
<head><title>Maintenance Report Form</title>
```

LISTING 15.17   Continued

```
<xforms:model>

    <xforms:submitInfo id="submit1" method2="postxml" localfile="./temp2.xml" />

      <xforms:instance xmlns="">
          <reports>
              <report>
                  <id>D33</id>
                  <service>Airlock service</service>
                  <length>1.5</length>
                  <rate>75</rate>
                  <total/>
              </report>
              <report>
                  <id>F83</id>
                  <service>General maintenance</service>
                  <length>3</length>
                  <rate>35</rate>
                  <total/>
              </report>
              <report>
                  <id>K8283</id>
                  <service>Airlock service</service>
                  <length>1.5</length>
                  <rate>75</rate>
                  <total/>
              </report>
               <grandtotal/>
          </reports>
      </xforms:instance>

<xforms:bind ref="/reports/report/total" calculate="../rate * ../length"/>
<xforms:bind ref="/reports /grandtotal" calculate="sum(../report/total)"/>

</xforms:model>

</head>
<body>

<h1>Maintenance Report Summary</h1>

<xforms:repeat ref="reports/report">
<p>
  <xforms:input ref="id" cols="20">
    <xforms:caption>ID: </xforms:caption>
   </xforms:input>
  <xforms:input ref="service" cols="20">
    <xforms:caption>Service: </xforms:caption>
   </xforms:input>
  <xforms:input ref="length" cols="20">
    <xforms:caption>Length: </xforms:caption>
   </xforms:input>
```

LISTING 15.17   Continued

```
    <xforms:input ref="rate" cols="20">
      <xforms:caption>Rate: </xforms:caption>
    </xforms:input>
    <xforms:input ref="total" cols="20">
      <xforms:caption>Total: </xforms:caption>
    </xforms:input>
</p>
</xforms:repeat>
<p>
    <xforms:input ref="reports/grandtotal">
      <xforms:caption>Grand Total</xforms:caption>
    </xforms:input>
</p>
<p>
<xforms:submit>
  <xforms:caption>Submit Report</xforms:caption>
</xforms:submit>
</p>

</body>
</html>
```

For every `reports/report` element, the application creates each of the controls listed within the `repeat` element. Note that for each set, the context is the current `report` element, so the second instance of the `id` control points to **F83**, the second instance of `reports/report/id`, as shown in Figure 15.13.

FIGURE 15.13
The `repeat` element allows you to easily enter a set of controls.

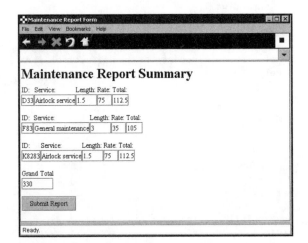

Itemsets and Attributes

Now we're going to take a look at itemsets, which are similar to repeating elements in that they allow you to iterate through multiple nodes in the instance document. We're also going to look at attributes as references.

Previously, we created a list of acceptable employee names. Ultimately, this will do the job of making sure that only actual employees are listed in the Employee field on the form, but it's not the best way to accomplish that goal. Instead, because we have the names anyway, it makes more sense to put them into some sort of menu the user can choose from.

In the following example, we'll add a list of employees to the instance document. We'll use that list to create the pull-down menu, but there's a twist: The employee ID is stored as an attribute, not as an element's text node, as shown in Listing 15.18.

LISTING 15.18 Using an Itemset and Attributes

```
<html xmlns="http://www.w3.org/1999/xhtml"
    xmlns:xforms="http://www.w3.org/2002/01/xforms">
<head>
    <title>Maintenance Report Form</title>

    <xforms:model>

        <xforms:submitInfo action="http://localhost/test.asp" method="get"
                                                mediaType="text/xml" />

        <xforms:schema href="workorder.xsd"/>

        <xforms:instance xmlns="">
            <servicecall>
                <people>
                    <person pid="E98">
                        <personname>Nick</personname>
                    </person>
                    <person pid="E234">
                        <personname>maURO</personname>
                    </person>
                    <person pid="E448">
                        <personname>Kelemon</personname>
                    </person>
                    <person pid="E4354">
                        <personname>Rhiannon</personname>
                    </person>
                </people>
                <person pid="">
                    <password></password>
                </person>
                <visit>

                </visit>
                <comments>It's working fine now.</comments>
                <supportingdoc></supportingdoc>
            </servicecall>
        </xforms:instance>

        <xforms:bind ref="/servicecall/visit/resolution/workarounddesc"
                    relevant="../workaroundavail = 'Y'"/>
```

LISTING 15.18   *Continued*

```
    </xforms:model>


</head>
<body>

<h1>Maintenance Report Form</h1>

<p>
    <xforms:selectOne ref="servicecall/person/@pid" selectUI="menu">
        <xforms:caption>Employee: </xforms:caption>
        <xforms:itemset  nodeset="servicecall/people/person">
            <xforms:caption ref="personname" />
            <xforms:value ref="@pid" />
        </xforms:itemset>
    </xforms:selectOne>

    <br />

    <xforms:secret ref="servicecall/person/password">
        <xforms:caption>Password: </xforms:caption>
    </xforms:secret>
</p>
...
```

Pay close attention to the context for each element reference. The form control itself has a reference of `servicecall/person/@pid`, so whatever value is selected for the control, that's where it'll go. In creating the control itself, however, we're using an itemset. The itemset represents a set of nodes, in this case defined as `servicecall/people/person`, the new data that we added to the instance document. (In the section titled "Multiple Forms and Form Submissions," we'll look at separating this data into a second structure.)

For each `servicecall/people/person`, an item is created with a caption that matches the `personname`, and a value that is the `pid` attribute. The control itself is a `selectOne` that we've specified as a `menu`, as shown in Figure 15.14, so the user has the opportunity to choose one of the appropriate options.

Keeping the Schema Updated

Note that because we've removed the `empname` element from `servicecall/person`, we have to update `workorder.xsd` to match the changes.

FIGURE 15.14

The itemset helps to create a pull-down menu listing the available employees and their employee codes.

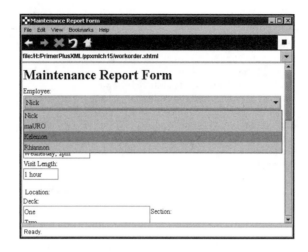

Grouping

In the previous example, we specified a context for the values and captions by adding a reference point for the itemset. But what if we want to set a context for a group of elements without having to use some kind of repeating mechanism?

The **group** element allows us to semantically and hierarchically group elements together. For example, in Listing 15.19, we are creating a group out of the **location**'s **deck** and **section** elements.

LISTING 15.19   Grouping Elements Together

```
...
    <xforms:input ref="servicecall/visit/visitlength" id="visit">
        <xforms:caption>Visit Length: </xforms:caption>
    </xforms:input>
</p>
<p>
<xforms:group ref="servicecall/visit/location">
<caption>Location:  </caption>

    <xforms:selectOne ref="deck" selectUI="listbox">
        <xforms:caption>Deck:    </xforms:caption>
        <xforms:item>
            <xforms:value>1</xforms:value>
            <xforms:caption>One</xforms:caption>
        </xforms:item>
        <xforms:item>
            <xforms:value>2</xforms:value>
            <xforms:caption>Two</xforms:caption>
        </xforms:item>
...
    </xforms:selectOne>
```

LISTING 15.19   Continued

```
            <xforms:selectMany ref="section" selectUI="listbox">
                <xforms:caption>Section:    </xforms:caption>
                <xforms:item>
                    <xforms:value>A</xforms:value>
                    <xforms:caption>A</xforms:caption>
                </xforms:item>
                <xforms:item>
                    <xforms:value>B</xforms:value>
                    <xforms:caption>B</xforms:caption>
                </xforms:item>
...
            </xforms:selectMany>
        </xforms:group>
    </p>
    <p>
        <xforms:input ref="servicecall/visit/location/equipment">
            <xforms:caption>Equipment:  </xforms:caption>
        </xforms:input>
    <br/>
    ...
```

	Reference Points

In version 0.6 of X-Smiles, the reference information doesn't carry through for a group element.

In Figure 15.15, you can see that the items have been grouped, because they now have a common `caption`, though of course in practice we'd probably want to set a style for that caption so that it appears on top of the elements, or in some more convenient location.

FIGURE 15.15
Grouping elements.

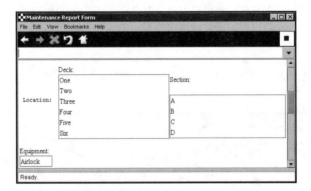

Multiple Forms and Form Submissions

One thing you can do with an XForms form that you can't do with an XHTML form is to intermingle information from two different forms. In this section, we're going to break the list of employees into a separate form `model`, which we'll then reference from the original form.

You can have any number of XForms forms on a single page, but you can only submit one at a time.

Creating a Second Form Model

Strictly speaking, you don't work with separate forms in XForms, but with separate form models. Each can have its own **submitInfo** (if appropriate), its own binding, and its own controls.

In Listing 15.20, we create a second **model** and give it an **id** attribute by which we can refer to it.

LISTING 15.20   Creating a Second Model

```
<html xmlns="http://www.w3.org/1999/xhtml"
    xmlns:xforms="http://www.w3.org/2002/01/xforms">
<head>
    <title>Maintenance Report Form</title>


    <xforms:model>

        <xforms:submitInfo method2="postxml" localfile="./temp.xml"/>

        <xforms:schema href="workorder.xsd"/>

        <xforms:instance xmlns="">
            <servicecall>
                <person pid="">
                    <password>mypassword</password>
                </person>
                <visit>
...
                </visit>
                <comments>It's working fine now.</comments>
                <supportingdoc></supportingdoc>
            </servicecall>
        </xforms:instance>

        <xforms:bind ref="/servicecall/visit/resolution/workarounddesc"
                relevant="../workaroundavail = 'Y'"/> —>

    </xforms:model>

    <xforms:model id="employees">
        <xforms:instance>
            <people xmlns="">
                <person pid="E98">
                    <personname>Nick</personname>
                </person>
                <person pid="E234">
                    <personname>maURO</personname>
                </person>
```

LISTING 15.20   Continued

```
                        <person pid="E448">
                            <personname>Kelemon</personname>
                        </person>
                        <person pid="E4354">
                            <personname>Rhiannon</personname>
                        </person>
                    </people>
                </xforms:instance>
            </xforms:model>

    </head>
    <body>
    ...
```

Here we've removed the `people` information from the first instance document and created a second instance document in a second form model, `employees`. Note that we've only named the second model; the first model needs no identifier.

Order Matters

The XForms Recommendation specifically references the "first form model" in the current Working Draft. Some applications interpret this phrase literally, and won't allow you to leave the second form unidentified, even if the first has an `id` attribute. This may change in the Final Recommendation.

Associating Controls with the Appropriate Form Model

In order to associate controls with a particular model, you'll need to set the `model` attribute, as shown in Listing 15.21.

LISTING 15.21   Associating Controls with a Model

```
...
<body>

<h1>Maintenance Report Form</h1>

<p>
    <xforms:selectOne ref="servicecall/person/@pid" selectUI="menu">
        <xforms:caption>Employee: </xforms:caption>
        <xforms:itemset model="employees" nodeset="people/person">
            <xforms:caption ref="personname" />
            <xforms:value ref="@pid" />
        </xforms:itemset>
    </xforms:selectOne>

    <br />

    <xforms:secret ref="servicecall/person/password">
```

LISTING 15.21   Continued

```
            <xforms:caption>Password: </xforms:caption>
        </xforms:secret>
</p>
...
```

In this case, we're explicitly pulling the `itemset` nodes from the `employees` model, rather than the default model. Because the `selectOne` element has no `model` attribute, however, it's still part of the original form, and its value will go into the main instance document.

Importing Additional Data

This separation into different forms enables us to "import" data from other files into our form. For example, In Listing 15.22, we reference an external file rather than defining the `people` element inline.

LISTING 15.22   Referencing an External Document

```
    ...
    </xforms:model>

    <xforms:model id="employees">
        <xforms:instance href="people.xml" />
    </xforms:model>

</head>
<body>
    ...
```

Form Events

The XML recommendations were meant to overlap, and one of the places where this happens is between XForms and XML Events. As forms become more complex, it often becomes necessary to trigger certain actions based on certain events. For example, X-Smiles automatically revalidates and recalculates values when any of the form data changes. This can also be triggered manually.

In this section, we're going to look at how events are structured, and how to trigger and listen for them with a simple example. On the summary form, we're going to warn people to check their numbers carefully if they try to change the hourly rate.

Events Overview

A traditional application starts at the beginning and responds to a user's actions in a way that is hopefully predictable. When the programmer is writing it, he or she has a pretty good idea of what can happen at any given time, and control stays with the main application. In events-base programming, control is passed to the objects themselves, which register events and act accordingly.

XML Events involve three entities: events, targets, and listeners. An event, such as a mouse click or validation of a form, has a target, such as a button or form model. That target may have one or more listeners waiting for that event to happen. When the listener is notified of that event, it takes some action.

Events have three phases: capture, arrival, and bubbling.

In the capture phase, the event is on its way to its target, and may be "captured" by any of the ancestors of the target. For example, if the target were a form button, the window would be an ancestor of the target. In the capture phase, the window would see an event such as a mouse click. If that ancestor had any listeners watching for a mouse click, those listeners would act on it and the event would be passed on until it reached its target.

When the event arrives at the target, any appropriate listeners take action.

When the target's listeners are finished, the bubbling phase begins. In the bubbling phase, children of the target get their chance to act on the event.

Not all events get through this entire life cycle, however. Most events can be canceled, in which case they go no further. Also, not all events can be captured, and not all events will bubble. Every application defines its own events and determines whether they can be captured, bubbled, or canceled.

In this example, we're looking at just one event: the pressing of the mouse button, known as mousedown. XForms provides a mechanism for designating an object as an observer and creating an event handler. That event handler has a specific action that it takes.

Creating the Action

In this case, the action we want to take is the creation of a message that is displayed for the user. We'll add it as part of the model, as in Listing 15.23.

LISTING 15.23   Adding the Event Handler

```
<html xmlns="http://www.w3.org/1999/xhtml"
                 xmlns:xforms="http://www.w3.org/2002/01/xforms">
<head><title>Maintenance Report Form</title>

<xforms:model>

    <xforms:submitInfo id="submit1" method2="postxml" localfile="./temp2.xml" />

    <xforms:instance xmlns="">
        <reports>
            <report>
                <id>D33</id>
                <service>Airlock service</service>
                <length>1.5</length>
                <rate>75</rate>
                <total/>
            </report>
```

LISTING 15.23   Continued

```
                <grandtotal/>
            </reports>
        </xforms:instance>

    <xforms:bind ref="/reports/report/total" calculate="../rate * ../length"/>
    <xforms:bind ref="/reports /grandtotal" calculate="sum(../report/total)"/>

    <xforms:message level="ephemeral" id="checkRate">
      Please make sure that the rate is correct.
      Your salary depends on these numbers!
    </xforms:message>

</xforms:model>

</head>
<body>
...
```

Other actions defined in the working draft include `dispatch`, `refresh`, `recalculate`, `revali-`
`date`, `setFocus`, `loadURI`, `setValue`, `submitInstance`, `resetInstance`, `setRepeatCursor`,
`insert`, `delete`, `toggle`, `script`, and `action`. Each has its own attributes. For example,
`resetInstance` needs to know what model to reset.

Create the Listener

From the description at the beginning of the "Form Events" section, you might think that the
process of creating the listener involves going to the target and creating it from there, but actually, the listener is created as an independent object, and the target, or **observer**, is specified as
part of it.

In fact, the listener is part of the XML Events namespace, as shown in Listing 15.24.

LISTING 15.24   Creating the Listener

```
<html xmlns="http://www.w3.org/1999/xhtml"
      xmlns:xforms="http://www.w3.org/2002/01/xforms"
      xmlns:ev="http://www.w3.org/2001/xml-events">
<head><title>Maintenance Report Form</title>

<xforms:model>
...
    <xforms:message level="ephemeral" id="checkRate">
      Please make sure that the rate is correct.
      Your salary depends on these numbers!
    </xforms:message>

    <ev:listener observer="hourlyRate" event="mousedown" handler="#checkRate"/>

</xforms:model>
```

LISTING 15.24   Continued

```
</head>
<body>

<h1>Maintenance Report Summary</h1>

<p>
...
  <xforms:input ref="/reports/report/length">
     <xforms:caption>Length: </xforms:caption>
   </xforms:input>
  <xforms:input ref="/reports/report/rate" id="hourlyRate">
     <xforms:caption>Rate: </xforms:caption>
   </xforms:input>
  <xforms:input ref="/reports/report/total">
     <xforms:caption>Total: </xforms:caption>
   </xforms:input>
</p>

<p>
<xforms:submit>
  <xforms:caption>Submit Report</xforms:caption>
</xforms:submit>
</p>

</body>
</html>
```

First, notice that we've added an `id` attribute to the form control itself, which we're referencing as the `observer`. For this reason, we can only have one `hourlyRate` control. Second, notice that the handler refers to the action by its XPointer address, `#checkRate`. Third, notice that we've specified the event that the observer is listening for as `mousedown`.

XForms defines two types of events: initialization events and interaction events.

Initialization events, which usually have the form model as their target, include `modelConstruct`, `modelInitialize`, `intializeDone`, `UIInitialize`, and `formControlInitialize`.

Interaction events cover most of the things that can happen when a user works with a form. These events include `next` and `previous`, `focus` and `blur`, `valueChanging` and `valueChanged`, `scrollFirst` and `scrollLast`, `insert` and `delete`, `select` and `deselect`, `help` and `hint`, `alert`, `valid` and `invalid`, `refresh`, `revalidation`, `recalculate`, and `reset`.

Triggering the Event

Finally, we're ready to trigger the event. Before we do, though, let's take a look at what's happening.

All we're going to do is click on a text field, but lots of things are actually happening. Every ancestor and descendant of that form control, from the window to the caption, is going to see that event, but the only object that has a listener attached at the moment is the button itself.

When we click the button, the listener calls the handler, message, as shown in Figure 15.16.

FIGURE 15.16
The event calls the message box.

Summary

XForms solve many of the problems left over from XHTML forms by separating content and presentation and allowing for much more robust data collection, validation, and event processing.

Data in an XForms form is held in an instance document, an XML information set that can contain multiple levels of children, attributes and other structures that are not possible using the name-value pairs of XHTML forms. On the other hand, the scripting and validation capabilities of an XForms form can also be used to provide traditional name-value pairs for legacy applications.

XForms also provides robust event handling that allows you to creating complex applications without having to engage in client-side scripting.

XForms has many more capabilities than we could possibly cover in a single chapter. For a complete look, and to see any changes that have been made to XForms, see the latest document at `http://www.w3.org/TR/xforms`.

Review Questions

1. How do XForms ease maintenance?

2. Where is the data in an XForms form stored while the user manipulates the data?

3. How can you ensure the type of data submitted in a particular field?

4. How do you add initial values to the form?

5. Where are the aspects of the form defined?

6. How many models can exist per page?

7. How are form controls associated with the instance document?

Programming Exercises

1. Create a form that allows users to enter their name and three favorite foods.

2. Alter the form in exercise 1 so that users choose one of a series of options using a radio button.

3. Alter the form in exercise 2 so that users choose one or more items from a list box.

4. Give the form initial values.

5. Create a form populated by a series of order items.

6. Create a binding that automatically totals each line item and creates a grand total.

7. Create form controls for payment information. The controls for credit card number and expiration date should only appear if the payment method is a credit card, in which case they should be mandatory.

CHAPTER 16

XML AND PUBLISHING: FORMATTING OBJECTS WITH XSL

You will learn about the following in this chapter:

- Paged media
- Creating page layouts
- Static content
- Styling content using properties
- Tables
- Lists

*I*n Chapter 9, "Extensible Stylesheet Language Transformations (XSLT)," we took a very brief look at the side of XSL known as XSL Formatting Objects (XSL-FO). Also known simply as XSL (as opposed to XSLT), formatting objects enable the definition not only of content, but also of its presentation.

In this chapter, we'll note similarities to some of the techniques already covered, such as XHTML and Cascading Style Sheets, as we create a file that can be translated into many different formats.

Overview

In Chapter 13, "Browser-Based XML: XHTML," we looked at XHTML as a means for defining the structure of content in a way that also incidentally has an effect on its presentation. In Chapter 12, "Browser-Based XML: Cascading Style Sheets (CSS)," we looked at properties that control presentation more precisely. In this chapter, we're going to look at a combination of these two topics.

Uses for XSL

Extensible Stylesheet Language (XSL) allows us to create content in such a way that its presentation is completely described. That's not to say, however, that its format is fixed.

Rather, once we've created an XSL file, or formatting object, that file can be translated into many different formats. For example, X-Smiles, with which we worked in Chapter 15, "XML

Forms Language (XForms)," can use formatting objects to lay out its pages. Formatting Objects Processor (FOP), the application we'll use in this chapter, can translate an XSL file into Adobe Portable Document Format (PDF) files, printer formats such as PCL and PostScript, Scalable Vector Graphics (SVG), Adobe FrameMaker's Maker Interchange Format (MIF), or ASCII text. You can also use the Abstract Window Toolkit (AWT) output to view the page inside a Java graphic or send the document right to a printer. Upcoming versions will also output to Rich Text Format (RTF).

XSL has other advantages as well. Like CSS and unlike XHTML, formatting objects give you complete control over where and how your content is presented.

Layouts, Flows, and Blocks

Using XSL, we can create a document such as the one shown in Figure 16.1 using interrelated definitions.

FIGURE 16.1

A simple XSL document, converted to PDF.

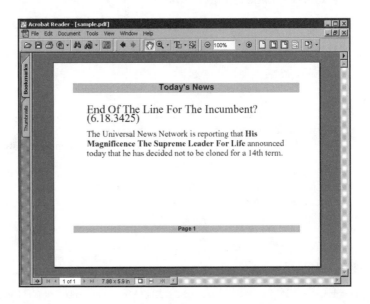

We're going to cover all of this in detail throughout the chapter, but let's take a quick look at the structure of this page. The size and margins of the page itself are determined by a *page master*, which also defines the size and other properties for each of the regions on the page. In this case, we have three regions: the body, and the sections before and after the body. The page master is plugged into a *page sequence master*, which is then referenced by the definition of the page itself, as shown in Listing 16.1, a partial version of the sample page.

LISTING 16.1　The Basic Framework

```
<?xml version="1.0" encoding="utf-8"?>
<fo:root xmlns:fo="http://www.w3.org/1999/XSL/Format">
```

LISTING 16.1   Continued

```
<fo:layout-master-set>
    <fo:simple-page-master master-name="mainpages">
            <fo:region-body/>
            <fo:region-before extent="2.75cm"/>
            <fo:region-after extent="1.5cm"/>
    </fo:simple-page-master>

    <fo:page-sequence-master master-name="pageMaster">
        <fo:single-page-master-reference master-reference="mainpages" />
    </fo:page-sequence-master>
</fo:layout-master-set>

<fo:page-sequence master-reference="pageMaster">
    <fo:static-content flow-name="xsl-region-before">
        <fo:block>Today's News</fo:block>
    </fo:static-content>

    <fo:static-content flow-name="xsl-region-after">
        <fo:block>Page <fo:page-number/></fo:block>
    </fo:static-content>

    <fo:flow flow-name="xsl-region-body">
        <fo:block>
                End Of The Line For The Incumbent? (6.18.3425)
        </fo:block>
...
    </fo:flow>
</fo:page-sequence>

</fo:root>
```

Notice that the size of the page doesn't conform to the length of the content, but rather to the size defined by the page master. In fact, this particular page is structured in such a way that if the content were longer than one page, it would automatically flow to a second page, with the headers and footers remaining intact.

We control the details of presentation using properties.

Properties

Because both the Cascading Style Sheets and Extensible Stylesheet Language Recommendations are maintained by the World Wide Web Consortium (W3C), it should come as no surprise that they interrelate. In fact, most of the properties accessible through XSL are the same properties that were available to us for use with CSS. They are also defined in much the same way, so the bounding box model we talked about in Chapter 12 applies here as well, though it's not fully implemented in the software we're using.

In an XSL file, however, properties are set as attributes rather than as CSS styles (see Listing 16.2).

LISTING 16.2 Properties

```
<?xml version="1.0" encoding="utf-8"?>
<fo:root xmlns:fo="http://www.w3.org/1999/XSL/Format">

    <fo:layout-master-set>
        <fo:simple-page-master master-name="mainpages"
                page-height="15cm" page-width="20cm" margin="1.5cm"
                margin-bottom="0.75cm" margin-top=".75cm">
                    <fo:region-body margin="1cm"/>
                    <fo:region-before extent="2.75cm" background-color="#CCCCCC"/>
                    <fo:region-after extent="1.5cm" background-color="#CCCCCC"/>
        </fo:simple-page-master>

        <fo:page-sequence-master master-name="pageMaster">
            <fo:single-page-master-reference master-reference="mainpages" />
        </fo:page-sequence-master>
    </fo:layout-master-set>

    <fo:page-sequence master-reference="pageMaster">
        <fo:static-content flow-name="xsl-region-before">
            <fo:block font-weight="bold" font-size="18pt" text-align="center">
                Today's News
            </fo:block>
        </fo:static-content>

        <fo:static-content flow-name="xsl-region-after">
            <fo:block font-weight="bold" text-align="center">
                Page <fo:page-number/>
            </fo:block>
        </fo:static-content>

        <fo:flow flow-name="xsl-region-body">
            <fo:block font-size="24pt" font-family="serif" line-height="20pt"
                    space-before.optimum="20pt" space-after.optimum="14pt">
                End Of The Line For The Incumbent? (6.18.3425)
            </fo:block>
            <fo:block font-size="18pt" space-after.optimum="3pt"
                                        font-family="serif">
                The Universal News Network is reporting that
                <fo:inline font-weight="bold">His Magnificence The
                Supreme Leader For Life</fo:inline> announced today
                that he has decided not to be cloned for a 14th term.
            </fo:block>
        </fo:flow>
    </fo:page-sequence>
</fo:root>
```

Setting Up

X-Smiles, the application we used in Chapter 15, supports XSL through an application called FOP, but unfortunately it supports a previous version of FOP that differs from the XSL 1.0 Recommendation, so in this chapter we're going to use the current version, which at the time of this writing is 0.20.4. FOP enables us to convert our formatting objects to PDF, which we can then view with the Adobe Acrobat Reader.

Download FOP from `http://xml.apache.org/fop/download.html` and install it. If you don't already have the free Acrobat Reader from Adobe installed, you can download it from `http://www.adobe.com/products/acrobat/readstep.html`. In addition to a browser plug-in, it installs a standalone application for viewing the files directly.

Prerequisites

FOP is a Java application, so at the very least you'll need the Java Runtime Environment, but if you used X-Smiles in Chapter 15, you've already got that covered. If for some reason you didn't, you can download a Java runtime environment from `http://java.sun.com`.

Creating a Basic Document

Let's get started with a fairly simple document that looks at the different aspects of building a page with XSL. In this section, we'll create a basic page to display station news, convert it to a PDF file, and then look at issues such as pagination and static content.

Creating the Page Master

The first step is to create the page master. This master defines the various sizes of objects such as the page and its regions. Together with the page sequence master we'll create in a moment, the page master in Listing 16.3 is part of the layout master set.

LISTING 16.3   Creating the Page Master

```
<?xml version="1.0" encoding="utf-8"?>
<fo:root xmlns:fo="http://www.w3.org/1999/XSL/Format">

    <fo:layout-master-set>

        <fo:simple-page-master master-name="mainLayout"
              page-height="10cm" page-width="15cm" margin="1.5cm"
              margin-bottom="0.75cm" margin-top=".75cm">

            <fo:region-body margin-top="2.0cm" region-name="body"/>
            <fo:region-before extent="2.75cm" region-name="header"/>
            <fo:region-after extent="1cm"  region-name="footer"/>
        </fo:simple-page-master>

    </fo:layout-master-set>

</fo:root>
```

Let's start by looking at the structure of the document itself. Note that an XSL document must start with a root element, and that all elements are in the Formatting Objects namespace, `http://www.w3.org/1999/XSL/Format`. As usual, the namespace alias is unimportant, but usually `fo` is used.

From here, we're beginning to define the layout of the document. A `simple-page-master` element defines the geometry of any page based on it, defining the `height` and `width`, the `margin`, and any regions that will be used. In this case, we're dealing only with the `region-body`, `region-before`, and `region-after`, but XSL also defines `region-start`, which generally appears to the left of the body, and `region-end`, which generally appears to the right of the body.

For the regions other than the body, we specify the size, or `extent` of the section. This is the maximum size of content in that area. For the body, we specify a margin that takes the potential side areas into account. Lengths can take the same units that they take in CSS, such as `pt` and `px`, but it's more common to use absolute lengths such as millimeters (`mm`) or centimeters (`cm`), as in this case, the intention is to be as definite as possible.

Direction

XSL takes into account the fact that not all languages run from left to right, as English does. For example, if the page were written in Hebrew, which runs right to left, `region-start` would appear on the right. Similarly, `region-start` and `region-end` depend on the orientation of the content.

We're also naming the regions so we can refer to them later. Even if we didn't, though, we'd still be able to use the default names (`xsl-region-start`, `xsl-region-body`, and so on).

Building the Page Sequence Master

A document consists of at least one page, but usually more than one. Later, we'll see how we can create a sequence of layouts that adapts to conditions such as title pages and odd/even processing, but for now we're going to create a page sequence master that consists of a reference to our page master (see Listing 16.4).

LISTING 16.4   Creating a Page Sequence Master

```
<?xml version="1.0" encoding="utf-8"?>
<fo:root xmlns:fo="http://www.w3.org/1999/XSL/Format">

    <fo:layout-master-set>
        <fo:simple-page-master master-name="mainLayout"
                page-height="10cm" page-width="15cm" margin="1.5cm"
                margin-bottom="0.75cm" margin-top=".75cm">
            <fo:region-body margin-top="2.0cm" region-name="body"/>
            <fo:region-before extent="2.75cm" region-name="header"/>
            <fo:region-after extent="1cm"  region-name="footer"/>
        </fo:simple-page-master>
```

LISTING 16.4   Continued

```
            <fo:page-sequence-master master-name="pageSeqMaster">
                <fo:single-page-master-reference master-reference="mainLayout" />
            </fo:page-sequence-master>
        </fo:layout-master-set>
...
```

Here we've created a page sequence master, `pageSeqMaster`, that references our `mainLayout` master. The `single-page-master-reference` element refers to a single instance of whatever layout is specified, so we've specified a one-page document.

Now we just have to add the actual page.

Generating the Page

We've defined a one-page sequence of pages that use a particular geometry, so it's time to use that definition.

Pages in XSL are added as **page-sequence**s, because they rarely consist of just a single object on a single page. Instead, a **page-sequence** can define content that flows from page to page, as well as static content that appears on each page, as you'll see in the sections titled "Controlling Page Flow and Page Breaks" and "Adding Static Content."

In Listing 16.5, we add a **page-sequence** with a single news item.

LISTING 16.5   A Simple Page

```
<?xml version="1.0" encoding="utf-8"?>
<fo:root xmlns:fo="http://www.w3.org/1999/XSL/Format">

    <fo:layout-master-set>
        <fo:simple-page-master master-name="mainLayout"
                page-height="10cm" page-width="15cm" margin="1.5cm"
                margin-bottom="0.75cm" margin-top=".75cm">
            <fo:region-body margin-top="2.0cm" region-name="body"/>
            <fo:region-before extent="2.75cm" region-name="header"/>
            <fo:region-after extent="1cm"  region-name="footer"/>
        </fo:simple-page-master>

        <fo:page-sequence-master master-name="pageSeqMaster">
            <fo:single-page-master-reference master-reference="mainLayout" />
        </fo:page-sequence-master>
    </fo:layout-master-set>

    <fo:page-sequence master-reference="pageSeqMaster">

        <fo:flow flow-name="body">

            <fo:block>
                End Of The Line For The Incumbent? (6.18.3425)
            </fo:block>
```

LISTING 16.5 *Continued*

```
        <fo:block>
            The Universal News Network is reporting that His
            Magnificence The Supreme Leader For Life announced today
            that he has decided not to be cloned for a 14th term.
        </fo:block>

    </fo:flow>

    </fo:page-sequence>

</fo:root>
```

Let's take a look at this from the outside in. First, we designate the content as a pair of blocks. Just as in Cascading Style Sheets, the rendering engine knows to start a new line before and after a `block` element, so adding content to a `block` element is like adding it to a `div` in XHTML. (We'll see the equivalent of `span`—`inline`—in the section titled "Text Properties.")

These blocks are part of the `flow` element. A `flow` element designates content that can flow from one page to the next. For example, in the next section, we'll add more content and see how it flows onto page two. We can have only one `flow` per `page-sequence`, and we must specify which region it belongs to. As with most flows, this one belongs with the body region.

The flow itself is part of the `page-sequence`. In order to determine how to display the `page-sequence`, the renderer checks to see which `page-sequence-master` the `page-sequence` belongs to. From there, it can determine the layout by checking the page master.

Finally, we have something to look at. FOP provides a command-line script that we can use to convert our documents.

First, save the file. I've named mine `news.fo`. Next, open a command prompt and go to the directory in which you installed FOP. For me, that's `d:\fop=0.20.4`. Finally, call the appropriate script. Both `fo.bat` and `fo.sh` are provided, so type either

```
fo {path}\news.fo {path}\news.pdf
```

for Windows or

```
fo {path}/news.fo {path}/news.pdf
```

for Unix.

Don't forget to change `{path}` to your actual path information!

If you haven't got any typos, you should see output similar to this:

```
[INFO] FOP 0.20.4
[INFO] building formatting object tree
[INFO] [1]
[INFO] Parsing of document complete, stopping renderer
```

Now open the `news.pdf` document, either in your browser or in Acrobat Reader. The results should look like Figure 16.2.

FIGURE 16.2

The basic page.

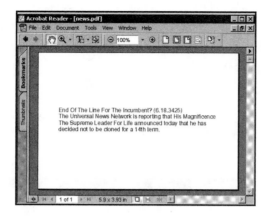

Controlling Page Flow and Page Breaks

Now that we've mastered a single page, let's move on to multiple pages. First, let's add a second page of content, as in Listing 16.6, and see what happens.

LISTING 16.6   Adding a Second Page

```xml
<?xml version="1.0" encoding="utf-8"?>
<fo:root xmlns:fo="http://www.w3.org/1999/XSL/Format">

    <fo:layout-master-set>
...
        <fo:page-sequence-master master-name="pageSeqMaster">
            <fo:single-page-master-reference master-reference="mainLayout" />
            <fo:single-page-master-reference master-reference="mainLayout" />
        </fo:page-sequence-master>
    </fo:layout-master-set>

    <fo:page-sequence master-reference="pageSeqMaster">

        <fo:flow flow-name="body">

            <fo:block>
                End Of The Line For The Incumbent? (6.18.3425)
            </fo:block>
            <fo:block>
...
            </fo:block>

            <fo:block>
                New Fall Lineup (6.19.3425)
            </fo:block>
            <fo:block>
                The Omega Channel has announced two new shows for its ...
            </fo:block>
```

LISTING 16.6   Continued

```
        </fo:flow>

      </fo:page-sequence>

  </fo:root>
```

Here we've added a second page master to the page sequence master, making room for the additional content, which we've added as part of the flow. The results are shown in Figure 16.3.

FIGURE 16.3
Adding another page.

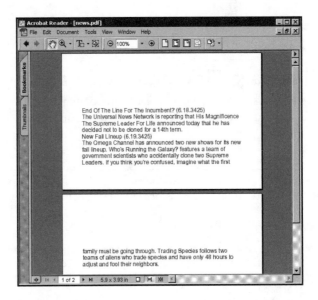

Notice that the flow has continued on to the next page. It's awfully messy, though. We can exert more control over page breaks as shown in Listing 16.7.

LISTING 16.7   Adding a Page Break

```
...

        <fo:block>
            The Universal News Network is reporting that His
            Magnificence The Supreme Leader For Life announced today
            that he has decided not to be cloned for a 14th term.
        </fo:block>

        <fo:block break-before="page">
            New Fall Lineup (6.19.3425)
        </fo:block>
        <fo:block>

...
```

Here we're telling the renderer that we want to insert a break before this block. The value of the `break-before` attribute determines the condition that the renderer is trying to achieve. For example, in this case, we've indicated that we want a new page, so the block is moved so that it appears on the first available new page, as shown in Figure 16.4.

FIGURE 16.4

Controlling the page break using the `break-before` attribute.

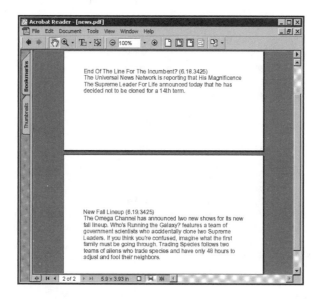

You can also set the value of `break-before` to `column`, `even-page`, or `odd-page`. For example, if we had set this value to `odd-page`, the renderer would have added a blank page so that the block could be on page 3, rather than page 2.

Similarly, you can use the `break-after` property to create a break after a particular block.

Adding Static Content

Now it's time to make use of that great big gap we left at the top of each page.

Most publishing projects involve information that remains constant for each page, such as chapter name, date, or the position of page numbers.

In this section, we're going to add a header to the pages. Listing 16.8 shows the addition of static content.

LISTING 16.8   Adding Static Content

```xml
<?xml version="1.0" encoding="utf-8"?>
<fo:root xmlns:fo="http://www.w3.org/1999/XSL/Format">

    <fo:layout-master-set>
        <fo:simple-page-master master-name="mainLayout"
                page-height="10cm" page-width="15cm" margin="1.5cm"
```

LISTING 16.8   Continued

```
                margin-bottom="0.75cm" margin-top=".75cm">
            <fo:region-body margin-top="2.0cm" region-name="body"/>
            <fo:region-before extent="2.75cm" region-name="header"/>
            <fo:region-after extent="1cm"  region-name="footer"/>
        </fo:simple-page-master>

        <fo:page-sequence-master master-name="pageSeqMaster">
            <fo:single-page-master-reference master-reference="mainLayout" />
            <fo:single-page-master-reference master-reference="mainLayout" />
        </fo:page-sequence-master>
    </fo:layout-master-set>

    <fo:page-sequence master-reference="pageSeqMaster">

        <fo:static-content flow-name="header">
            <fo:block font-weight="bold">
                Today's UNN Headlines
            </fo:block>
            <fo:block font-weight="bold">
                You give us 22 standard millirotations, we'll
                give you the universe
            </fo:block>
        </fo:static-content>

        <fo:flow flow-name="body">

            <fo:block>
                End Of The Line For The Incumbent? (6.18.3425)
            </fo:block>
...
        </fo:flow>

    </fo:page-sequence>

</fo:root>
```

Remember, we can only have one `flow` per `page-sequence`, but that's all right because we're adding static content using the `static-content` element. In order to let the renderer know where it goes, we're specifying the region we named `header`—`region-before`.

Because this region appears on every page that uses this page master, the static content will appear on every page, as shown in Figure 16.5.

We can add static content for each region defined in the `simple-page-master`.

FIGURE 16.5
Adding static content.

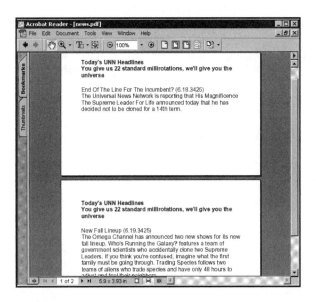

Inserting Page Numbers

Not all static information is necessarily constant. For example, we commonly want to add page numbers to the header or footer of every page. XSL defines the **page-number** element to make this possible, as shown in Listing 16.9.

LISTING 16.9   Adding a Page Number to the Footer

```
...
            give you the universe
        </fo:block>
    </fo:static-content>

    <fo:static-content flow-name="footer">
        <fo:block>
            Page <fo:page-number />
        </fo:block>
    </fo:static-content>

    <fo:flow flow-name="body">

        <fo:block>
            End Of The Line For The Incumbent? (6.18.3425)
        </fo:block>
...
```

Just as before, we add a **static-content** element, providing the region name for the **flow-name**. The **page-number** element simply returns a value, which is output to the page.

Notice that we've added the static content before the flow, even though it appears at the bottom of the page. We have to do this because even though the renderer is going to render some of the flow before the footer, it won't necessarily render all of it. In some cases, with some applications, this may not matter, but the XSL 1.0 Recommendation requires that all static content be defined before any flows so that an application can stream data if necessary.

Styling the Content

Now we've got the basic page layout. Because XSL is all about presentation, let's look at styling the content.

As I mentioned earlier, styling in XSL is similar to styling in Cascading Style Sheets, except that properties are set as attributes. Also, properties are set directly on the objects to which they apply, rather than using selectors to determine which elements should be affected by a particular set of properties, or style.

Types of Properties

Some of the properties we've already seen, such as `margin`, should already be familiar from our work with CSS. Others, such as `break-before`, are new, but they are in fact included in the CSS specification. The reason we haven't dealt with them before is that in all of our work prior to this chapter, we were dealing with continuous media, whereas we're now looking at paged media. This means that properties such as `widows` and `orphans`, which control how many lines of a paragraph may be left alone at the top or the bottom of a page, suddenly make sense in a way that they didn't before.

Does this mean that we're limited to paged media properties? Absolutely not. The whole idea of formatting objects is to provide a device-independent way of specifying presentation, so in addition to paged properties, the XSL 1.0 Recommendation specifically defines aural properties. Because we're dealing with a "paper" document here, we'll stick with properties appropriate to visual media, but be aware that the concepts are the same.

Text Properties

Adding text properties is as simple as adding attributes to the relevant elements, as shown in Listing 16.10.

LISTING 16.10 Adding Text Properties

```
<?xml version="1.0" encoding="utf-8"?>
<fo:root xmlns:fo="http://www.w3.org/1999/XSL/Format">
...
    <fo:page-sequence master-reference="pageSeqMaster">

        <fo:static-content flow-name="header">
            <fo:block font-size="18pt" font-family="sans-serif"
```

LISTING 16.10 *Continued*

```
                    font-weight="bold">
                    Today's UNN Headlines
                </fo:block>
                <fo:block font-size="14pt" font-family="sans-serif"
                    font-weight="bold">
                    You give us 22 standard millirotations, we'll
                    give you the universe
                </fo:block>
            </fo:static-content>

            <fo:static-content flow-name="footer">
                <fo:block font-family="serif">
                    Page <fo:page-number />
                </fo:block>
            </fo:static-content>

            <fo:flow flow-name="body">

                <fo:block font-size="18pt" font-family="serif">
                    End Of The Line For The Incumbent? (6.18.3425)
                </fo:block>
                <fo:block font-size="14pt" font-family="serif">
                    The Universal News Network is reporting that
                    <fo:inline font-weight="bold">His Magnificence The
                    Supreme Leader For Life</fo:inline> announced today
                    that he has decided not to be cloned for a 14th term.
                </fo:block>

                <fo:block font-size="18pt" font-family="serif" break-before="page">
                    New Fall Lineup (6.19.3425)
                </fo:block>
                <fo:block font-size="14pt" font-family="serif">
                    The Omega Channel has announced two new shows for its
                    new fall lineup. <fo:inline font-style="italic">Who's Running
                    the Galaxy?</fo:inline> features a team of government scientists
                    who accidentally clone two Supreme Leaders. If you think you're
                    confused, imagine what the first family must be going through.
                    <fo:inline font-style="italic">Trading Species</fo:inline> follows
                    two teams of aliens who trade species and have only 48 hours to
                    adjust and fool their neighbors.
                </fo:block>
            </fo:flow>
        </fo:page-sequence>
</fo:root>
```

All these properties should look familiar to you, as we used them in Chapter 12, where you can also find more information on available text- and font-related properties.

Also, because properties must be set on elements, or formatting objects, in addition to the `block` element, we're using the `inline` element to attach properties to our inline content.

Spacing

XSL gives us much more control over spacing than CSS does. XSL retains the spacing-related properties we used in Chapter 12, such as `margin` and `padding`, and adds more capabilities, such as those shown in Listing 16.11.

LISTING 16.11   Using Spacing

```xml
<?xml version="1.0" encoding="utf-8"?>
<fo:root xmlns:fo="http://www.w3.org/1999/XSL/Format">
...
    <fo:page-sequence master-reference="pageSeqMaster">

        <fo:static-content flow-name="header">
            <fo:block font-size="18pt" font-family="serif"
                font-weight="bold" line-height="24pt"
                text-align="center" padding-top="3pt">
                Today's UNN Headlines
            </fo:block>
            <fo:block font-size="14pt" font-family="serif"
                font-weight="bold" line-height="18pt"
                space-after.optimum=".5cm" text-align="center">
                You give us 22 standard millirotations, we'll
                give you the universe
            </fo:block>
        </fo:static-content>
...
        <fo:flow flow-name="body">

            <fo:block font-size="18pt" font-family="serif"
                line-height="20pt" space-before.optimum="10pt"
                space-after.optimum="14pt" >
                End Of The Line For The Incumbent? (6.18.3425)
            </fo:block>
            <fo:block font-size="14pt" font-family="serif"
                space-after.optimum="3pt">
                The Universal News Network is reporting that ...
            </fo:block>

            <fo:block font-size="18pt" font-family="serif"
                line-height="20pt" space-before.optimum="10pt"
                space-after.optimum="14pt" break-before="page">
                New Fall Lineup (6.19.3425)
            </fo:block>
            <fo:block font-size="14pt" font-family="serif"
                space-after.optimum="3pt">
                The Omega Channel has announced two new shows for its ...
            </fo:block>
        </fo:flow>

    </fo:page-sequence>
</fo:root>
```

The `space-before` and `space-after` properties have several components. Here we're using the `.optimum` component, which gives the renderer a goal. You can also use `.maximum` and `.minimum` to specify values that must be achieved. In some cases this can lead to a conflict. For instance, if one block has a `space-after.maximum` of `1cm` and the block after it has a `space-before.minimum` of `2cm`, the renderer has to choose which component to satisfy. In such cases, the `.precedence` value comes into play. The higher value "wins."

Borders

Borders work just the way they do for Cascading Style Sheets. Keep in mind that regions can't have a border, but the blocks within them can, as shown in Listing 16.12.

LISTING 16.12   Adding a Border

```
...
        <fo:static-content flow-name="header">
            <fo:block border="1px solid black" padding-left=".5cm"
                padding-right=".5cm">
                <fo:block font-size="18pt" font-family="serif"
                    font-weight="bold" line-height="24pt"
                    text-align="center" padding-top="3pt">
                    Today's UNN Headlines
                </fo:block>
                <fo:block font-size="14pt" font-family="serif"
                    font-weight="bold" line-height="18pt"
                    text-align="center">
                    You give us 22 standard millirotations, we'll
                    give you the universe
                </fo:block>
            </fo:block>
        </fo:static-content>
...
```

You can see the result in Figure 16.6.

FIGURE 16.6
Adding a border.

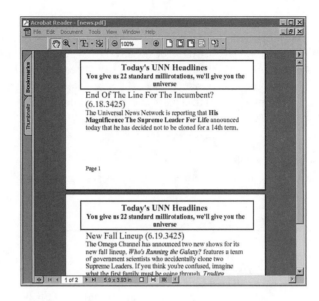

Colors

Colors are also handled the same way in XSL as they are in CSS, as you can see in Listing 16.13.

LISTING 16.13   Adding Color

```
...
        <fo:static-content flow-name="header">
            <fo:block border="1px solid black" padding-left=".5cm"
                padding-right=".5cm" background-color="blue"
                color="white">
                <fo:block font-size="18pt" font-family="serif"
                    font-weight="bold" line-height="24pt"
                    text-align="center" padding-top="3pt">
                    Today's UNN Headlines
                </fo:block>
                <fo:block font-size="14pt" font-family="serif"
                    font-weight="bold" line-height="18pt"
                    text-align="center">
                    You give us 22 standard millirotations, we'll
                    give you the universe
                </fo:block>
            </fo:block>
        </fo:static-content>
...
```

Figure 16.7 shows the results (though obviously, this book can only show black and white).

FIGURE 16.7
Adding color.

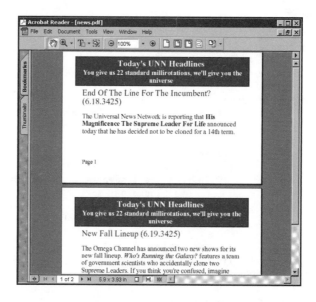

Tables and Lists

Two common XSL structures look more like XHTML than CSS: tables and lists. Like their XHTML counterparts, they provide structure to the content so it can be displayed in a predictable way.

Tables

Tables consist of columns and rows, and each row is made up of cells. Each cell takes up one or more columns within the row.

In Listing 16.14, we're creating a table of event information.

LISTING 16.14   Creating a Table

```
<?xml version="1.0"?>
<fo:root xmlns:fo="http://www.w3.org/1999/XSL/Format">

<fo:layout-master-set>
    <fo:simple-page-master master-name="mainLayout"
            page-height="12cm" page-width="15cm" margin-top="1cm"
            margin-bottom=".5cm" margin-left="1.5cm"
            margin-right="1.5cm">
        <fo:region-body margin-top="0.5cm"/>
    </fo:simple-page-master>

    <fo:page-sequence-master master-name="pageMaster">
        <fo:single-page-master-reference master-reference="mainLayout" />
    </fo:page-sequence-master>
</fo:layout-master-set>
```

LISTING 16.14   Continued

```
<fo:page-sequence master-reference="pageMaster">

    <fo:flow flow-name="xsl-region-body">
        <fo:block>
            <fo:table>
                <fo:table-column column-width="60mm"/>
                <fo:table-column column-width="60mm"/>

                <fo:table-header>
                    <fo:table-row>
                        <fo:table-cell number-columns-spanned="2">
                            <fo:block font-size="18pt" font-weight="bold"
                                                    text-align="center">
                                Station events for this week
                            </fo:block>
                        </fo:table-cell>
                    </fo:table-row>
                </fo:table-header>

                <fo:table-footer>
                    <fo:table-row>
                        <fo:table-cell number-columns-spanned="2">
                            <fo:block font-size="9pt" font-weight="bold"
                                                    text-align="center">
                                See Activities for signup
                            </fo:block>
                        </fo:table-cell>
                    </fo:table-row>
                </fo:table-footer>

                <fo:table-body>
                    <fo:table-row>
                        <fo:table-cell padding="3mm">
                            <fo:block font-weight="bold">
                                Making Friends With The Venusian Flu Virus
                            </fo:block>
                            <fo:block>
                                Dr. Biff Mercury discusses his theory on
                                coexisting with this useful organism.
                                (6.20.3425)
                            </fo:block>
                        </fo:table-cell>
                        <fo:table-cell padding="3mm">
                            <fo:block font-weight="bold">
                                Putting the Manners in Bedside Manner
                            </fo:block>
                            <fo:block>
```

LISTING 16.14   Continued

```
                              Dr. Zingzowpowie, the famous xenoneurosurgeon,
                              lectures on bedside manner and the benefits
                              of using cold tentacles during a physical.
                              (6.21.3425)
                          </fo:block>
                      </fo:table-cell>
                  </fo:table-row>
                  <fo:table-row>
                      <fo:table-cell padding="3mm" number-columns-spanned="2">
                          <fo:block font-weight="bold">
                              An Evening of Fun
                          </fo:block>
                          <fo:block>
                              This evening join us for the monthly "Identify
                              that Food" contest. (6.25.3425)
                          </fo:block>
                      </fo:table-cell>
                  </fo:table-row>
              </fo:table-body>
          </fo:table>
        </fo:block>
      </fo:flow>
  </fo:page-sequence>

</fo:root>
```

Here we have a table with two columns and two rows. The width of the columns is defined first. This allows the renderer to know how to set up the table without having to lay out all the content.

Next we have the table header and footer. If a table spans more than one page, the table header and footer appear at the top and bottom of the table on every page, in a manner similar to that of the static content we saw earlier. Both the header and footer contain table rows just as the body does, but there's no reason a cell can't span multiple columns using the `number-columns-spanned` property, as we're doing here. In most cases, however, headers and footers are used to label columns of data or provide totals.

Next comes the table body itself, which contains the table rows and their cells. Here again, the `number-columns-spanned` allows the cell in the last row to span the entire width of the table.

The XSL 1.0 Recommendation also defines a `table-caption` element, which, along with `table`, appears as the child of a `table-and-caption` element. (FOP version 0.20.4 doesn't support this.)

The resulting page is shown in Figure 16.8.

FIGURE 16.8
Creating a table for layout or data.

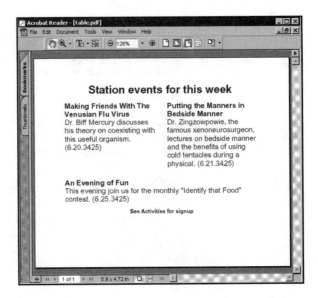

Lists

Lists bear some relation to their XHTML counterparts, but not quite as much as tables do. In an XHTML list, you can just set the type, such as ordered or unordered, and the renderer (that's the browser, in most cases) takes care of the rest. Using XSL's formatting objects, you don't have that option, but you do have much more control over what the renderer uses for each item, and how this label is placed in relation to the actual data.

Listing 16.15 shows the event data formatted as a bulleted list.

LISTING 16.15   Creating a List

```
<?xml version="1.0" encoding="utf-8"?>
<fo:root xmlns:fo="http://www.w3.org/1999/XSL/Format">

<fo:layout-master-set>
    <fo:simple-page-master master-name="mainpages"
                page-height="12cm" page-width="15cm" margin-top="1cm"
                margin-bottom=".5cm" margin-left="1.5cm"
                margin-right="1.5cm">
        <fo:region-body margin-top="0.5cm"/>
    </fo:simple-page-master>

    <fo:page-sequence-master master-name="pageMaster">
        <fo:single-page-master-reference master-reference="mainpages" />
    </fo:page-sequence-master>
</fo:layout-master-set>

<fo:page-sequence master-reference="pageMaster">
    <fo:flow flow-name="xsl-region-body">
        <fo:block>
            <fo:list-block>
                <fo:list-item>
```

LISTING 16.15   Continued

```
                    <fo:list-item-label end-indent="label-end()">
                        <fo:block>
                            <fo:inline font-family="Symbol">&#x2022;</fo:inline>
                        </fo:block>
                    </fo:list-item-label>
                    <fo:list-item-body start-indent="body-start()">
                        <fo:block font-weight="bold">
                            Making Friends With The Venusian Flu Virus
                        </fo:block>
                        <fo:block>
                            Dr. Biff Mercury discusses his theory on
                            coexisting with this useful organism.
                            (6.20.3425)
                        </fo:block>
                    </fo:list-item-body>
                </fo:list-item>
                <fo:list-item>
                    <fo:list-item-label end-indent="label-end()">
                        <fo:block>
                            <fo:inline font-family="Symbol">&#x2022;</fo:inline>
                        </fo:block>
                    </fo:list-item-label>
                    <fo:list-item-body start-indent="body-start()">
                        <fo:block font-weight="bold">
                            Putting the Manners in Bedside Manner
                        </fo:block>
                        <fo:block>
                            Dr. Zingzowpowie, the famous xenoneurosurgeon,
                            lectures on bedside manner and the benefits of using
                            cold tentacles during a physical.(6.21.3425)
                        </fo:block>
                    </fo:list-item-body>
                </fo:list-item>
                <fo:list-item>
                    <fo:list-item-label end-indent="label-end()">
                        <fo:block>
                            <fo:inline font-family="Symbol">&#x2022;</fo:inline>
                        </fo:block>
                    </fo:list-item-label>
                    <fo:list-item-body start-indent="body-start()">
                        <fo:block font-weight="bold">An Evening of Fun</fo:block>
                        <fo:block>
                            This evening join us for the monthly "Identify
                            that Food" contest. (6.25.3425)
                        </fo:block>
                    </fo:list-item-body>
                </fo:list-item>
            </fo:list-block>
        </fo:block>
    </fo:flow>
</fo:page-sequence>

</fo:root>
```

A list consists of a `list-block` and its `list-item` children. Each `list-item` has two children: the `list-item-label` and the `list-item-body`.

In XForms, labels are used to provide information about form elements, and typically contain explanatory text. XSL `list-item-labels` can be used that way—in a list of definitions, for example—but it's more common to use the label for bullets or for indicators of order or level, such as numbers, Roman numerals, or letters.

In this case, we're using bullets, as shown in Figure 16.9.

FIGURE 16.9
Creating a list.

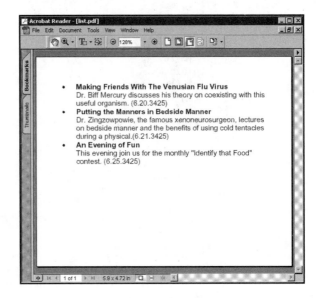

The `end-indent` attribute is used to tell the renderer to end the "column" at the edge of the label text, whereas the `start-indent` property tells the renderer to start rendering the `list-item-body` after the label and the incremental separation between the label box and the body box.

Here we're just using a single bullet for all list items, but there's no reason we can't generate sequential numbers or letters when generating the XSL file.

Images and Links

Now let's look at linking. As with XHTML pages, linking might refer to the inclusion of a hyperlink that the user clicks in order to get other material, a hyperlink that the user clicks to find material within the document, or other material altogether.

External Images

Adding external graphics to a document is straightforward, and simply involves the `external-graphic` element, as shown in Listing 16.16.

LISTING 16.16   Adding Images

```
...
            <fo:flow flow-name="body">

                <fo:block font-size="18pt" font-family="serif"
                    line-height="20pt" space-before.optimum="10pt"
                    space-after.optimum="14pt" >
                    End Of The Line For The Incumbent? (6.18.3425)
                </fo:block>
                <fo:block font-size="14pt" font-family="serif"
                    space-after.optimum="3pt">
                    The Universal News Network is reporting that ...
                </fo:block>
                <fo:block text-align="center" padding="10px">
                    <fo:external-graphic height="200px" width="200px"
                                                src="image1.jpg"/>

                </fo:block>

                <fo:block font-size="18pt" font-family="serif"
                    line-height="20pt" space-before.optimum="10pt"
                    space-after.optimum="14pt" break-before="page">
                    New Fall Lineup (6.19.3425)
                </fo:block>
                <fo:block font-size="14pt" font-family="serif"
                    space-after.optimum="3pt">
                    The Omega Channel has announced two new shows for its ...
                </fo:block>
                <fo:block text-align="center" padding="10px">
                    <fo:external-graphic height="200px" width="200px"
                                                src="image5.jpg"/>

                </fo:block>
            </fo:flow>

        </fo:page-sequence>

    </fo:root>
```

Image types

The `external-graphic` element is not limited to any particular type of graphic, but Scalable Vector Graphics (SVGs) are usually added using the `instream-foreign-object` element instead.

Just as on an XHTML page, we can set the height, width, and source of the graphic. Ultimately, we will also be able to float images as we did in Chapter 13.

The resulting image is shown in Figure 16.10.

FIGURE 16.10
Including an external graphic.

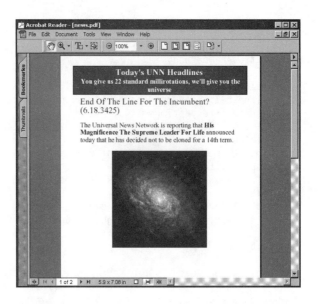

External Links

External links are also fairly simple to add using `basic-links`, as shown in Listing 16.17.

LISTING 16.17   Adding an External List

```
...
            <fo:block font-weight="bold">
                <fo:basic-link external-destination="signup.jsp?eventid=A335">
                    Making Friends With The Venusian Flu Virus
                </fo:basic-link>
            </fo:block>
...
            <fo:block font-weight="bold">
                <fo:basic-link external-destination="signup.jsp?eventid=B963">
                    Putting the Manners in Bedside Manner
                </fo:basic-link>
            </fo:block>
...
            <fo:block font-weight="bold">
                <fo:basic-link external-destination="signup.jsp?eventid=C934">
                    An Evening of Fun
                </fo:basic-link>
            </fo:block>
...
```

In this case, we've linked each title to a separate signup page, as you can see in Figure 16.11.

FIGURE 16.11

Linking to an external destination.

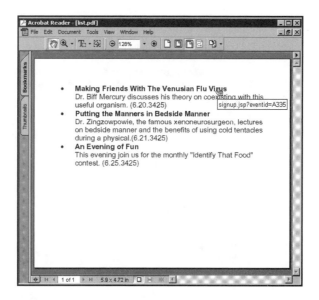

Internal Links

In many cases, you're linking not to an external destination, but rather to an object such as a block within the file itself.

In Listing 16.18, we create a table of contents for the news listings.

LISTING 16.18   Internal Links

```xml
<?xml version="1.0" encoding="utf-8"?>
<fo:root xmlns:fo="http://www.w3.org/1999/XSL/Format">

    <fo:layout-master-set>
        <fo:simple-page-master master-name="mainLayout"
                page-height="18cm" page-width="15cm" margin="1.5cm"
                margin-bottom="0.75cm" margin-top=".75cm">
            <fo:region-body margin-top="2cm" region-name="body"/>
            <fo:region-before extent="2.75cm" region-name="header"/>
            <fo:region-after extent="1cm"  region-name="footer"/>
        </fo:simple-page-master>

        <fo:page-sequence-master master-name="pageSeqMaster">
            <fo:single-page-master-reference master-reference="mainLayout"/>
            <fo:single-page-master-reference master-reference="mainLayout"/>
            <fo:single-page-master-reference master-reference="mainLayout"/>
        </fo:page-sequence-master>
    </fo:layout-master-set>

    <fo:page-sequence master-reference="pageSeqMaster">
...
        <fo:flow flow-name="body">
```

LISTING 16.18   Continued

```
                <fo:block space-before="1cm">
                    <fo:block>
                        <fo:basic-link internal-destination="newsitem1">
                            End Of The Line For The Incumbent? (6.18.3425)
                        </fo:basic-link>
                    </fo:block>
                    <fo:block>
                        <fo:basic-link internal-destination="newsitem2">
                            New Fall Lineup (6.19.3425)
                        </fo:basic-link></fo:block>
                </fo:block>

                <fo:block font-size="18pt" font-family="serif"
                    line-height="20pt" space-before.optimum="10pt"
                    space-after.optimum="14pt" break-before="page"
                    id="newsitem1">
                    End Of The Line For The Incumbent? (6.18.3425)
                </fo:block>
    ...
                <fo:block font-size="18pt" font-family="serif"
                    line-height="20pt" space-before.optimum="10pt"
                    space-after.optimum="14pt" break-before="page"
                    id="newsitem2">
                    New Fall Lineup (6.19.3425)
                </fo:block>
    ...
            </fo:flow>

        </fo:page-sequence>

    </fo:root>
```

Internal links point to blocks with a specific `id` value, so we've added an `id` attribute to the first block of each news story, then created a `basic-link` that points to each block by referencing it as an `internal-destination`.

We've also added another page, so we've added an additional master to the page sequence master. We can't go on doing that forever, however; we need a way to manage page sequences more effectively.

Advanced Page Management

In this section, we're going to solve several page-related problems. Specifically, we're going to create a document that can have any number of pages, and that can distinguish between the first, last, and other pages, as well as between odd and even pages, as is often necessary when creating documents that will ultimately be bound.

First, we'll look at using more than one `page-sequence-master` in order to accomplish the task manually, then we'll look at ways to let the renderer take care of it for us.

Multiple Page Sequence Masters

The simplest way to get different page sequences to use different layouts is to create different `page-sequence-masters` and reference them directly.

In Listing 16.19, we're going to create a new layout for the table of contents we just created, then reference it within the document.

LISTING 16.19   Using Multiple `page-sequence-masters`

```xml
<?xml version="1.0" encoding="utf-8"?>
<fo:root xmlns:fo="http://www.w3.org/1999/XSL/Format">

    <fo:layout-master-set>
        <fo:simple-page-master master-name="mainLayout"
                page-height="18cm" page-width="15cm" margin="1.5cm"
                margin-bottom="0.75cm" margin-top=".75cm">
            <fo:region-body margin-top="2cm" region-name="body"/>
            <fo:region-before extent="2.75cm" region-name="header"/>
            <fo:region-after extent="1cm"  region-name="footer"/>
        </fo:simple-page-master>

        <fo:simple-page-master master-name="firstPage"
                page-height="18cm" page-width="15cm" margin-top="1.5cm"
                margin-bottom="0cm" margin-left="0cm"
                margin-right="0cm">
            <fo:region-body margin-top="2.5cm" region-name="body"/>
            <fo:region-before extent="2.5cm" region-name="header"/>
            <fo:region-after extent="1cm" region-name="footer"/>
        </fo:simple-page-master>

        <fo:page-sequence-master master-name="firstPageMaster">
            <fo:single-page-master-reference master-reference="firstPage" />
        </fo:page-sequence-master>

        <fo:page-sequence-master master-name="pageSeqMaster">
            <fo:single-page-master-reference master-reference="mainLayout"/>
            <fo:single-page-master-reference master-reference="mainLayout"/>
        </fo:page-sequence-master>
    </fo:layout-master-set>

    <fo:page-sequence master-reference="firstPageMaster">

        <fo:static-content flow-name="header">
            <fo:block border="1px solid black" padding-left=".5cm"
                padding-right=".5cm" background-color="blue"
                color="white">
                <fo:block font-size="18pt" font-family="serif"
                    font-weight="bold" line-height="24pt"
                    text-align="center" padding-top="3pt">
                    Today's UNN Headlines
                </fo:block>
                <fo:block font-size="14pt" font-family="serif"
```

LISTING 16.19 *Continued*

```
                    font-weight="bold" line-height="18pt"
                    text-align="center">
                    You give us 22 standard millirotations, we'll
                    give you the universe
                </fo:block>
            </fo:block>
        </fo:static-content>

        <fo:flow flow-name="body">

            <fo:block margin="2.5cm">
                <fo:block>
                    <fo:basic-link internal-destination="newsitem1">
                        End Of The Line For The Incumbent? (6.18.3425)
                    </fo:basic-link>
                </fo:block>
                <fo:block>
                    <fo:basic-link internal-destination="newsitem2">
                        New Fall Lineup (6.19.3425)
                    </fo:basic-link></fo:block>
            </fo:block>

        </fo:flow>
    </fo:page-sequence>

    <fo:page-sequence master-reference="pageSeqMaster">
...
        <fo:flow flow-name="body">

            <fo:block font-size="18pt" font-family="serif"
                line-height="20pt" space-before.optimum="10pt"
                space-after.optimum="14pt" id="newsitem1">
                End Of The Line For The Incumbent? (6.18.3425)
            </fo:block>
...
        </fo:flow>

    </fo:page-sequence>

</fo:root>
```

Let's start from the bottom and work our way up. We've taken the table of contents out of the main **page-sequence** and put it into its own **page-sequence**, which uses **firstPageMaster** rather than **pageSeqMaster**. The **firstPageMaster** page sequence master then references the **firstPage** layout, which has no margins and no footer section. The result is that the renderer renders the first page using the **firstPage** layout, and the rest of the document using the original layout, as shown in Figure 16.12.

FIGURE 16.12

Using a different page sequence master.

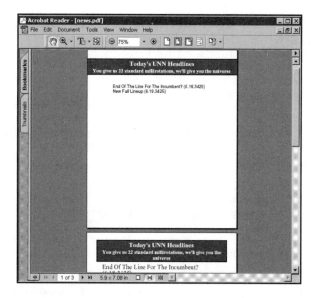

Multiple Pages

We could have accomplished the same thing with a single page sequence master by using a combination of `single-page-master-reference`s and `repeatable-page-master-references`.

For example, we could have defined `pageSeqMaster` as

```
<fo:page-sequence-master master-name="pageSeqMaster">
    <fo:single-page-master-reference master-reference="firstPage"/>
    <fo:repeatable-page-master-reference master-reference="mainLayout"/>
</fo:page-sequence-master>
```

In this case, the renderer fills the single page, then moves on to the next reference, which allows as many pages as necessary—or as many as specified by the optional `maximum-repeats` property.

Page Alternatives and Page Position

The process of manually getting different page sequences to use different layouts works, but it'd be much easier if we could just let the renderer take care of this for us. To do that, we need to use a different type of page sequence master, the `repeatable-page-master-alternatives`, combined with `conditional-page-master-reference`s.

In Listing 16.20, we're going back to a single `page-sequence-master` and allowing it to decide which masters to use.

LISTING 16.20   Conditional References

```
<?xml version="1.0" encoding="utf-8"?>
<fo:root xmlns:fo="http://www.w3.org/1999/XSL/Format">

    <fo:layout-master-set>
        <fo:simple-page-master master-name="mainLayout"
                page-height="18cm" page-width="15cm" margin="1.5cm"
                margin-bottom="0.75cm" margin-top=".75cm">
            <fo:region-body margin-top="2cm" region-name="body"/>
            <fo:region-after extent="1cm"  region-name="footer"/>
        </fo:simple-page-master>

        <fo:simple-page-master master-name="firstPage"
                page-height="18cm" page-width="15cm" margin-top="1.5cm"
                margin-bottom="0cm" margin-left="0cm"
                margin-right="0cm">
            <fo:region-body margin-top="2.5cm" region-name="body"/>
            <fo:region-before extent="2.5cm" region-name="header"/>
        </fo:simple-page-master>

        <fo:page-sequence-master master-name="pageSeqMaster">
            <fo:repeatable-page-master-alternatives>
                <fo:conditional-page-master-reference page-position="rest"
                                        master-reference="mainLayout"/>
                <fo:conditional-page-master-reference page-position="first"
                                        master-reference="firstPage"/>
                <fo:conditional-page-master-reference
                                        master-reference="otherPages"/>
            </fo:repeatable-page-master-alternatives>
        </fo:page-sequence-master>

    </fo:layout-master-set>

    <fo:page-sequence master-reference="pageSeqMaster">

        <fo:static-content flow-name="header">
            <fo:block border="1px solid black" padding-left=".5cm"
                padding-right=".5cm" background-color="blue"
                color="white">
                <fo:block font-size="18pt" font-family="serif"
                    font-weight="bold" line-height="24pt"
                    text-align="center" padding-top="3pt">
                    Today's UNN Headlines
                </fo:block>
                <fo:block font-size="14pt" font-family="serif"
                    font-weight="bold" line-height="18pt"
                    text-align="center">
                    You give us 22 standard millirotations, we'll
                    give you the universe
                </fo:block>
            </fo:block>
        </fo:static-content>
```

LISTING 16.20   Continued

```
            <fo:static-content flow-name="footer">
                <fo:block font-family="serif">
                    Page <fo:page-number />
                </fo:block>
            </fo:static-content>

            <fo:flow flow-name="body">

                <fo:block margin="2.5cm">
                    <fo:block>
                        <fo:basic-link internal-destination="newsitem1">
                            End Of The Line For The Incumbent? (6.18.3425)
                        </fo:basic-link>
                    </fo:block>
                    <fo:block>
                        <fo:basic-link internal-destination="newsitem2">
                            New Fall Lineup (6.19.3425)
                        </fo:basic-link></fo:block>
                </fo:block>

                <fo:block font-size="18pt" font-family="serif"
                    line-height="20pt" space-before.optimum="10pt"
                    space-after.optimum="14pt" id="newsitem1"
                    break-before="page">
                    End Of The Line For The Incumbent? (6.18.3425)
                </fo:block>
...
            </fo:flow>

        </fo:page-sequence>

</fo:root>
```

Figure 16.13 shows all three pages and the differences between them.

Notice that `pageSeqMaster` does *not* list the `firstPage` layout first. Instead, the `page-position` property makes sure that the renderer uses it only for the first page. In addition to the `rest` value for the `page-position`, as used here for any other pages, it's possible to specify the last page as a `page-position`. We've also specified a fallback position for any pages that don't have a named position by adding a `conditional-page-master-reference` without a `page-position` property.

Also notice what each page *doesn't* have. The first page layout doesn't have a footer region defined, so even though there's static content for one, it doesn't appear on the page. Similarly, we've removed the header region from the `mainpages` layout, so the header no longer appears on those pages.

We can use this ability to pick and choose which static sections to use in different situations.

FIGURE 16.13
Conditionally generated pages.

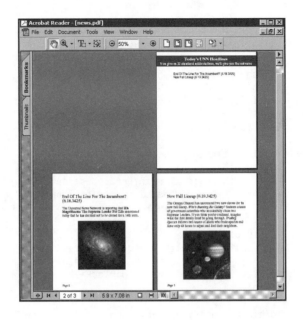

Odd/Even Pages

You might want to pick different sections to differentiate between even and odd pages. For example, if you were creating a bound document, you might want the page numbers to always appear on the "outside" edge.

In Listing 16.21, we'll use conditional references and named regions to accomplish this task.

LISTING 16.21   Distinguishing Between Even and Odd Pages

```xml
<?xml version="1.0" encoding="utf-8"?>
<fo:root xmlns:fo="http://www.w3.org/1999/XSL/Format">

    <fo:layout-master-set>
        <fo:simple-page-master master-name="evenLayout"
                page-height="18cm" page-width="15cm" margin="1.5cm"
                margin-bottom="0.75cm" margin-top=".75cm">
            <fo:region-body margin-top="2cm" region-name="body"/>
            <fo:region-after extent="1cm"  region-name="evenFooter"/>
        </fo:simple-page-master>

        <fo:simple-page-master master-name="oddLayout"
                page-height="18cm" page-width="15cm" margin="1.5cm"
                margin-bottom="0.75cm" margin-top=".75cm">
            <fo:region-body margin-top="2cm" region-name="body"/>
            <fo:region-after extent="1cm"  region-name="oddFooter"/>
        </fo:simple-page-master>

        <fo:simple-page-master master-name="firstPage"
                page-height="18cm" page-width="15cm" margin-top="1.5cm"
```

LISTING 16.21   Continued

```
                         margin-bottom="0cm" margin-left="0cm"
                         margin-right="0cm">
              <fo:region-body margin-top="2.5cm" region-name="body"/>
              <fo:region-before extent="2.5cm" region-name="header"/>

          </fo:simple-page-master>

          <fo:page-sequence-master master-name="pageSeqMaster">
              <fo:repeatable-page-master-alternatives>
                  <fo:conditional-page-master-reference page-position="rest"
                          odd-or-even="even" master-reference="evenLayout"/>
                  <fo:conditional-page-master-reference page-position="rest"
                          odd-or-even="odd" master-reference="oddLayout"/>
                  <fo:conditional-page-master-reference page-position="first"
                                              master-reference="firstPage"/>
                  <fo:conditional-page-master-reference
                                              master-reference="otherPages"/>
              </fo:repeatable-page-master-alternatives>
          </fo:page-sequence-master>

      </fo:layout-master-set>

      <fo:page-sequence master-reference="pageSeqMaster">

          <fo:static-content flow-name="header">
              <fo:block border="1px solid black" padding-left=".5cm"
                  padding-right=".5cm" background-color="blue"
                  color="white">
                  <fo:block font-size="18pt" font-family="serif"
                      font-weight="bold" line-height="24pt"
                      text-align="center" padding-top="3pt">
                      Today's UNN Headlines
                  </fo:block>
...
              </fo:block>
          </fo:static-content>

          <fo:static-content flow-name="evenFooter">
              <fo:block font-family="serif" text-align="left">
                  Page <fo:page-number />
              </fo:block>
          </fo:static-content>

          <fo:static-content flow-name="oddFooter">
              <fo:block font-family="serif" text-align="right">
                  Page <fo:page-number />
              </fo:block>
          </fo:static-content>

          <fo:flow flow-name="body">
...
          </fo:flow>
```

LISTING 16.21   Continued

```
    </fo:page-sequence>
</fo:root>
```

Here we have two layouts that are virtually identical. The only difference is in the names we've given to their `region-after`s. We've created conditional references within the page sequence master that not only specify that they're not the first page, but also whether they're an odd or even page in the layout.

Within the page sequence itself, we now have two static footer sections, each of which refers to the appropriate region name. When each page is rendered, only the appropriate sections, as defined in the `simple-page-master`, will show up, as shown in Figure 16.14.

FIGURE 16.14
Odd and even pages.

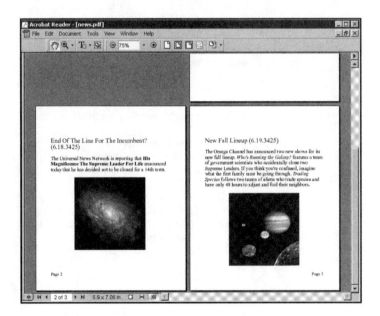

Summary

XSL formatting objects enable you to take control of the presentation of your content. They allow you to define the geometry of pages and the appearance of content within them with a fair amount of precision. XSL allows you to create pages that automatically flow from one page to another, with the renderer choosing the appropriate page layout based on criteria such as page position or the even or odd nature of the page number. It also allows you to specify static content that will appear on each page—but only if requested.

Review Questions

1. What is the difference between XSL Formatting Objects and XSL Transformations?

2. How does a formatting objects renderer know how to lay out the basic geometry of the page?

3. How are different page layouts combined in a single document?

4. What do you call content that appears at the same position on each page?

5. What structure allows content to span several pages?

6. How do you get a document that uses a different layout for the title page?

Programming Exercises

1. Create a document with a single page of content.

2. Create a document that can handle an undetermined number of pages that all use the same layout.

3. Add a footer to the document in exercise 2.

4. Create a document that uses a different layout for the first page than for other pages.

CHAPTER 17

XML AND WEB SERVICES

You will learn about the following in this chapter:

- The idea behind Web services
- The structure of SOAP messages
- How to send SOAP messages
- Web Services Description Language (WSDL) files
- Universal Description, Discovery, and Integration (UDDI)

Web services are applications that you can call by sending a specially formatted request to a particular URL and waiting (in most cases) for a response.

At the moment, a number of products are available that will build a Web service or a Web service client for you without requiring that you know what's going on behind the scenes. This isn't necessarily an advantage; when something goes wrong (notice that I said *when*, not *if*), it pays to understand what's actually happening. That's what we're going to cover in this chapter.

Overview

Taken at face value, Web Services seem like the Holy Grail of distributed computing. Any computer, anywhere, can make a request and get back a specified piece of information, or can send a command to a remote machine and have that command executed. It's all seamless and everybody's happy, right?

Well, no.

The concept of Web services has a lot of potential; all of those things are certainly possible...someday.

For now, however, we've got a cloud of disparate ideas and services that are rapidly coalescing into something that looks as if it will eventually be workable, but it pays to understand what's actually happening.

What Are Web Services?

It should be simple to come up with a general definition of a Web service, but unfortunately it isn't. For the purposes of this discussion, we're going to take the most technologically simple view: A Web service is an application that can be called from another location or application using a predictable means for sending input and receiving a reply, if there is one.

Web services typically fall into two categories: those that return information, and those that cause the server application to perform some sort of action. The latter are also known as *remote procedure calls (RPCs)*.

How Do You Use Web Services?

Although the actual implementation is frequently hidden from the programmer, Web services work by receiving information in a predictable format through a protocol such as HTTP.

Those of you who are already at least partially familiar with Web services may think I'm being overly general, but I'm not. The format in which messages are sent is usually some form of SOAP, but you can also use other methods such as MIME. The protocol used to call a Web service is usually HTTP, but messages can be sent in any number of ways, including through email.

The beauty of Web services is that they are so flexible, but in this chapter we're going to stick with the basics, and cover SOAP messages sent over HTTP.

When the service receives the message, it decodes it and takes some action, possibly returning information to the sender. For example, in this chapter we're going to make a call to a Web service that provides information on the oxygen level for a particular location within the station. To do that, we're sending the following SOAP message:

```
<soap-env:Envelope xmlns:soap-env="http://schemas.xmlsoap.org/soap/envelope/"
                   xmlns:xsd="http://www.w3.org/1999/XMLSchema">
   <soap-env:Header/>
   <soap-env:Body>
       <tns:getOxygenPercentage xmlns:tns="LifeSupportInformationSystem"
           soap-env:encodingStyle="http://schemas.xmlsoap.org/soap/encoding/">
          <deckId xmlns:xsi="http://www.w3.org/1999/XMLSchema-instance"
                  xsi:type="xsd:int">3</deckId>
          <section xmlns:xsi="http://www.w3.org/1999/XMLSchema-instance"
                  xsi:type="xsd:string">B</section>
       </tns:getOxygenPercentage>
   </soap-env:Body>
</soap-env:Envelope>
```

We'll talk more about the actual structure of SOAP messages in detail as we go on, but for now understand that the service interprets this message as a method call of getOxygenPercentage(3, "B"). This method returns a value, which is sent back within the following SOAP message:

```xml
<?xml version="1.0" encoding="UTF-8"?>
<SOAP-ENV:Envelope xmlns:SOAP-ENV="http://schemas.xmlsoap.org/soap/envelope/"
                   xmlns:xsi="http://www.w3.org/2001/XMLSchema-instance"
                   xmlns:xsd="http://www.w3.org/2001/XMLSchema">
    <SOAP-ENV:Body>
        <ns1:getOxygenPercentageResponse xmlns:ns1="LifeSupportInformationSystem"
            SOAP-ENV:encodingStyle="http://schemas.xmlsoap.org/soap/encoding/">
            <return xsi:type="xsd:double">0.62</return>
        </ns1:getOxygenPercentageResponse>
    </SOAP-ENV:Body>
</SOAP-ENV:Envelope>
```

We can then analyze the response to get the return value.

How Do You Find Web Services?

Once you've made the decision to use Web services, you'll have to find a service that provides the functionality you need. You can't just go around scanning every port you come into contact with hoping to find someone who sells extra large dog collars and takes electronic purchase orders, so how do you locate the appropriate company and find out how to interact with it?

Web services involve registries, where companies can enter information not only about the company and what it does, but also about the services (including Web services) it supports. These services might be as basic as picking up a telephone.

In this chapter, we're going to talk about Universal Description, Discovery, and Integration (UDDI) registries, which categorize business data and provide information that leads back to the specification of how to access any available Web services.

This information may be in the form of a Web Services Description Language (WSDL) document.

How Do You Secure Web Services?

Securing a Web service will probably continue to be a challenge for the next few years, at the very least. Technical specifications that involve encryption and other means of providing security are in the works, and companies such as IBM, Microsoft, and Sun have their own ideas about how to make everything secure.

The Web Server

Before we can even consider running a Web service, we need to set up the proper environment. In the previous section we looked at a very simple example; the client sends a SOAP message and receives one in return. While it's possible to write an application that does the translation from SOAP message to method call, it's much easier (and more common) to have a server environment that takes care of this for you.

For our example, we're going to use the Tomcat servlet engine, along with the SOAP Toolkit. Both applications are Apache projects.

You can run Tomcat within another Web server or as a standalone Web server, as we're going to do here.

Installing the Web Server

First, download the binaries from `http://jakarta.apache.org/tomcat/resources.html`. At the time of this writing, the latest release version is 4.0.4, so the following instructions assume that's the version you're using, but they should work for any 4.x version. If you're using a different version, check the documentation for differences.

Install the software, either by using the installer or by unzipping the binaries and placing them in the appropriate directory. To complete the installation, set the `JAVA_HOME` and `CATALINA_HOME` environment variables.

`JAVA_HOME` should be set to the main directory for your Java installation, such as `c:\j2sdk1.4.0`, and `CATALINA_HOME` should be set to the main directory for Tomcat, such as `c:\jakarta-tomcat-4.0.4`.

In Windows, you can set them from the System Control Panel by clicking the Advanced tab, then Environment. You can also set them from the command line using

```
set JAVA_HOME=c:\j2sdk1.4.0
set CATALINA_HOME=c:\jakarta-tomcat-4.0.4
```

Starting and Testing the Server

To start the server, open a command prompt window and type

```
cd %CATALINA_HOME%\bin
startup
```

The application should open a second command prompt window. After a few seconds, this second window should display the text

```
Starting service Tomcat-Standalone
Apache Tomcat/4.0.4
Starting service Tomcat-Apache
Apache Tomcat/4.0.4
```

Testing the Server

If the server starts up correctly, you will be able to test it by calling the main URL. By default, Tomcat runs on port 8080, so you can test it by pointing your browser to

```
http://localhost:8080
```

If all is well, you should see the main page, shown in Figure 17.1.

FIGURE 17.1

The Tomcat home page.

Click the Servlet Examples link and execute one of the samples to verify that the server is working correctly. If it isn't, check the Tomcat documentation for troubleshooting tips.

Once it's working, shut it down by returning to %CATALINA_HOME\bin and typing **shutdown**.

Installing the SOAP Toolkit

A J2EE server such as Tomcat consists of a number of self-contained Web applications, each of which can be started and stopped independently of the others, making it possible to develop one application without disturbing any others the server may be hosting.

In our case, we're going to install the Apache SOAP Toolkit application. This application consists of a special servlet, rpcrouter, that takes in a SOAP message and interprets it in order to determine where the request should go, and what parameters should go with it. In other words, rpcrouter acts as a proxy, forwarding requests to the appropriate resource and sending responses back to the original sender in the appropriate format.

The SOAP Toolkit is supplied as a Web archive (WAR) file, which will make your life easy when it comes to installing it. First download it from http://xml.apache.org/soap/index.html. Again, it's likely that one or more new versions will be released between the time I write this and the time you read it. (I'm using version 2.3.)

Unzip the archive file and place it in a convenient directory. The soap.war file is located in the SOAP Toolkit's webapps directory. Make a copy of soap.war and place it in

%CATALINA_HOME\webapps

Now restart Tomcat. The WAR file should be automatically expanded, creating a soap directory under webapps. This is the soap Web application, which includes not only rpcrouter, but also all the classes on which rpcrouter depends.

C++ and Visual Studio .NET

Web services are part of the core of Microsoft's .NET, so it will do us good to take a look at the .NET way of doing things. Although much of the underlying theory will be hidden, you can still get a good idea of what's happening underneath by reading the Java examples.

To develop Web services for C++ or Visual Basic, you will need to have a Web server that is configured with Internet Information Services (IIS) version 5.0 or 6.0 with FrontPage Server extensions and ASP.NET. You can configure your Web server to be either a local or a remote server. A local server allows you to create, run, and debug the Web service on your local machine. You can also use a remote server to host the Web service and connect to that machine via the network or Internet to access, run, and debug the Web service.

Web services developed using Visual Studio .NET have a few basic requirements. The Web server must be running Windows 2000, Windows XP, or Windows .NET Server. No other versions of Windows are supported. Microsoft also recommends that the Web server be installed on a computer formatted with the NTFS file system. You can use other file systems such as FAT or FAT32, but an NTFS installation is much more secure by default.

To configure a remote Web server for Visual Studio .NET, you will first need to run Visual Studio .NET Setup on the remote computer and select the first step to install the Windows Component Update. This installs to the system all the components that the .NET Framework needs to function. When it's done, the setup program will return to the main menu. Select step 2 on the setup menu. In the left pane of the setup window, clear all the options except Server Components. Expand the Server Components node and select the Web Development and Remote Debugger options. Then click the Install Now button to complete the installation.

After the Visual Studio .NET setup program is complete, you need to verify that the FrontPage Server Extensions are configured. On an NTFS-formatted computer, this is automatic. However, on a FAT or FAT32 system, you will need to configure the FrontPage Server Extensions. To do this, open the Control Panel and select the Administration Tools icon. Then select the Computer Management applet. Open the Services and Applications node and then open the Internet Information Service node as well. Open the Web Sites node and then right-click on the Default Web Site item. Select the Configure Server Extensions menu item. On systems where the Server Extensions have already been configured, the menu option will read Check Server Extensions. You may select that option to confirm that the Server Extensions are properly configured.

Finally, add user accounts for any users who will be creating Web projects on this server to the VS Developers group. This gives them the necessary security privileges to create projects. However, in order to debug applications on either a remote or local installation, it is necessary to be an administrator or a member of the Administrators group.

For a local Web server, it is necessary to make sure that the IIS and FrontPage Server Extensions are installed, configured, and running *prior* to running the setup program for Visual Studio .NET; otherwise, the system will not be configured properly to allow creation of local Web projects. Windows 2000 has IIS installed by default, but Windows XP and Windows .NET Server don't.

PHP

Because PHP is typically used as a Web server module, no separate server installation is needed. Simply put the PHP page that provides your SOAP service in your Web document tree like any other page, and you can access it as you would any other page.

Several SOAP toolkits are available for PHP. As of this writing, the SOAP toolkit that's included with PEAR (`http://pear.php.net`) is the most complete and easiest to install. If you have already installed the PEAR Web installer, just download the current SOAP distribution from the PEAR Web site and install with the `pear install` tool (this example is for version 0.6.2; the current version may be different):

```
pear install SOAP-0.6.2.tgz
```

PEAR's SOAP toolkit requires two other PEAR packages, `Mail_MIME` and `Net_DIME`, which you can install directly using the PEAR Web installer:

```
pear install Mail_MIME
```

```
pear install Net_DIME
```

It also requires that your PHP installation be built with the optional `bcmath` library.

Perl

Several SOAP toolkits are available for Perl as well. I've chosen to use SOAP::Lite for our examples because of its comprehensive server and client support, and excellent documentation. (Check out the guide and cookbook sections at `http://www.soaplite.com`.) You can install SOAP::Lite via CPAN.

SOAP::Lite can be used to provide a SOAP server in a CGI script, a `mod_perl` module or registry script, or a standalone HTTP daemon. We've used the daemon for our examples, because it requires no setup or configuration beyond the Perl script itself. However, the daemon can only answer one request at a time, and so is unsuitable for production use. As with just about any large-scale Perl application, if it will be used by a large number of people, you should run under `mod_perl`, or `fastCGI` if `mod_perl` is unavailable.

Testing the SOAP Installation

Now you're ready to test the SOAP installation. The easiest way is to simply call `rpcrouter` without any service information. Point your browser to

```
http://localhost:8080/soap/servlet/rpcrouter
```

This represents the `rpcrouter` servlet within the soap application running on `localhost` with a port of `8080`.

You may remember that in Chapter 13, "Browser-Based XML: XHTML," we talked about the difference between the `GET` method and the `POST` method for a form. In the `GET` method, all information is conveyed through the URL. In the `POST` method, most information comes in the form of HTTP headers. This is the kind of information the `rpcrouter` expects, and calling the servlet without it results in an error, as shown in Figure 17.2.

FIGURE 17.2
The `rpcrouter` servlet
expects `POST` information.

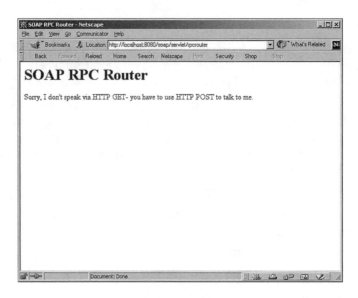

If you get this message, the soap application is working properly.

PHP

To test your PHP SOAP library installation, untar `SOAP-0.6.2.tar.gz` and copy the file
`server.php` from the `examples` directory to your Web server's document root and load the
page in your browser. If you see a message like

```
XML Parsing Error: junk after document element
```

SOAP is installed correctly.

Perl

Beyond the automated tests run by `make test` (you *did* run `make test`, didn't you?), the easiest way to test SOAP::Lite is to write a simple SOAP server and client, which, not coinciden-
tally, we'll do in the next section.

A Simple Web Service

In this section, we're going to build a simple Web service, then make a call to it via SOAP and
look at the response. In the next section, we'll document the interface to the service using
WSDL.

The Application

We're going to build a simple service that checks life support and environmental systems for
the space station. Each time we check a value, the application will also call a method to update
the "last checked" time, which we can also query.

It's a fairly simple application, but it symbolizes what you can do with any Web service: perform actions via remote procedure call, and/or retrieve information.

The Java class itself is shown in Listing 17.1a.

LISTING 17.1a   The Service Application in Java

```java
import java.util.GregorianCalendar;
import java.util.Date;

public class LifeSupportInfo {

    GregorianCalendar lastCheckedOxygen = new GregorianCalendar();
    GregorianCalendar lastCheckedTemperature = new GregorianCalendar();

    public double getOxygenPercentage (int deckId, String section) {

        if (deckId==3){
            if (section.equals("B")){
                lastCheckedOxygen.setTime(new Date());
                return .62;
            } else if (section.equals("C")) {
                lastCheckedOxygen.setTime(new Date());
                return .68;
            } else {
                return 0;
            }
        } else {
                return 0;
        }

    }

    public int getAvgHullTemperature (String side) {
        lastCheckedTemperature.setTime(new Date());
        return 45;
    }

    public GregorianCalendar getLastChecked(String systemType) {
        if (systemType.equals("oxygen")) {
            return lastCheckedOxygen;
        } else if (systemType.equals("temperature")) {
            return lastCheckedTemperature;
        } else {
            return null;
        }
    }

}
```

Here we have three methods, each of which takes at least one parameter and returns a simple value. Of course, these are extremely simplified versions, intended only to illustrate the service. In a real application, of course, the implementation would be more complex, getting information from databases and other systems.

Compile the application to create the `.class` file.

C++

Web services that are developed using Visual Studio .NET are high-level services that are tightly integrated with the .NET Framework, and that's one of the main thrusts of .NET. As a result, it's impossible to easily create an application that does the low-level SOAP transfer that you can do in Java or other languages. In this section, we'll re-create the Web service from Listing 17.1a and use the debugger to access it.

First, you need to create the Web service. Do this by creating a Managed C++ Web Service project found under the Visual C++ Projects project types. Select a Managed C++ Web Service project, change the name to `LifeSupportInformationSystem`, and click OK.

Open the `LifeSupportInformationSystem.asmx` file and change the text so that it looks like this:

```
<%@ WebService Class=LifeSupportInformationSystem.LifeSupportInfo %>
```

Next, open the `LifeSupportInformationSystem.h` file. This is where the Web service class is defined. Change the file so that it is like Listing 17.1b.

LISTING 17.1b   The Service Application in C++

```
#pragma once

#using <System.Web.Services.dll>

using namespace System;
using namespace System::Web;
using namespace System::Web::Services;

namespace LifeSupportInformationSystem
{
    public __gc
        class LifeSupportInfo : public WebService
    {
        public:
            [System::Web::Services::WebMethod]
            double getOxygenPercentage(int deckId, String *section);

            [System::Web::Services::WebMethod]
            int getAvgHullTemperature(String *side);

            [System::Web::Services::WebMethod]
            DateTime getLastChecked(String *systemType);

        private:
            DateTime lastCheckedOxygen;
```

LISTING 17.1b   Continued

```
                DateTime lastCheckedTemperature;
    };
}
```

Finally, we need to add the code that implements the class definition. To do this, open the LifeSupportInformationSystem.cpp file and change the existing code to match the following:

```
#include "stdafx.h"
#include "LifeSupportInformationSystem.h"
#include "Global.asax.h"

namespace LifeSupportInformationSystem
{
    double LifeSupportInfo::getOxygenPercentage(int deckId, String *section)
    {
        if (deckId == 3)
        {
            if (section->Equals("B"))
            {
                lastCheckedOxygen = lastCheckedOxygen.get_Now();
                return .62;
            }
            else if (section->Equals("C"))
            {
                lastCheckedOxygen = lastCheckedOxygen.get_Now();
                return .68;
            }
            else
                return 0;
        }
        else
            return 0;
    }

    int LifeSupportInfo::getAvgHullTemperature(String *side)
    {
        lastCheckedTemperature = lastCheckedTemperature.get_Now();
        return(45);
    }

    DateTime LifeSupportInfo::getLastChecked(String *systemType)
    {
        if (systemType->Equals("oxygen"))
            return lastCheckedOxygen;
        else if (systemType->Equals("temperature"))
            return lastCheckedTemperature;
        else
            return 0;
    }
};
```

You can now save the files and build the solution. Your Web service is now compiled, deployed, and ready for use.

Visual Basic .NET

Like our C++ examples, our Visual Basic .NET examples demonstrate the .NET way of doing things rather than relying on low-level SOAP calls.

First, create the Web service by creating an ASP.NET Web Service project (found under the Visual Basic Projects project types). Select an ASP.NET Web Service project and change the name to `http://localhost/LifeSupportInformationSystem`. Press OK.

Click on the link in the design view that switches you to the code view. We need to change the name of the class and of the default `.asmx` file. In the Solution Explorer, right-click on `Service1.asmx` and select Rename. Change the name to `LifeSupportInfo.asmx`. Then change the name of the class in the code view to `LifeSupportInfo`. It should look like this when you are done:

```
<WebService(Namespace:="http://tempuri.org/")> _
Public Class LifeSupportInfo
    Inherits System.Web.Services.WebService
```

Now add the code in Listing 17.1c to the file just under the region labeled "Web Services Designer Generated Code."

LISTING 17.1c   The Service Application in Visual Basic .NET

```
        Dim lastCheckedOxygen As Date
        Dim lastCheckedTemperature As Date

        <WebMethod()> Public Function getOxygenPercentage(ByVal deckId As Integer, _
                                                ByVal section As String) _
                                                As Double

            If (deckId = 3) Then
                If (section = "B") Then
                    lastCheckedOxygen = Now
                    Return 0.62
                ElseIf (section = "C") Then
                    lastCheckedOxygen = Now
                    Return 0.68
                Else
                    Return 0
                End If
            Else
                Return 0
            End If
        End Function

        <WebMethod()> Public Function getAvgHullTemperature(ByVal side As String) _
                                                    As Integer
            lastCheckedTemperature = Now
            Return 45
        End Function
```

LISTING 17.1c   Continued

```
<WebMethod()> Public Function getLastChecked(ByVal systemType As String) _
                                        As Date
    If (systemType = "oxygen") Then
        Return lastCheckedOxygen
    ElseIf (systemType = "temperature") Then
        Return lastCheckedTemperature
    Else
        Return Nothing
    End If
End Function
```

You can now save the files and build the solution. Your Web service is compiled, deployed, and ready for use.

PHP

To make a PHP page provide a SOAP service, simply define a class that implements the methods you want to make available, instantiate it, and pass it to a SOAP server object. You don't have to do anything special to deploy the application; just put it where your Web server can find it.

Because the PHP script is recompiled on each run, and the SOAP service object is reinstantiated each time, we can't use object properties or global variables to store the `last_checked` dates between requests. Instead, each time they're updated, we write the information to a temporary file, which is read on each instantiation of the object to set the object properties, as shown in Listing 17.1d. Of course, you could store this information in a SQL database or a DBM file.

LISTING 17.1d   The Service Application in PHP

```
<?php
require_once 'SOAP/Server.php';

$server = new SOAP_Server ();

class LifeSupportInfo
{
    var $last_checked_oxygen         = NULL;
    var $last_checked_temperature    = NULL;
    var $last_checked_oxygen_file    = '/tmp/lifesupport
                                            _last_checked_oxygen';
    var $last_checked_temperature_file = '/tmp/lifesupport
                                            _last_checked_temperature';

    var $method_namespace            = 'urn:LifeSupportInformationSystem';

    function LifeSupportInfo ()
    {
        $lco = @file($this->last_checked_oxygen_file);
        $lct = @file($this->last_checked_temperature_file);
```

LISTING 17.1d   Continued

```php
        $this->last_checked_oxygen      = is_array($lco)
                                            ? rtrim($lco[0]) : 'never';
        $this->last_checked_temperature = is_array($lct)
                                            ? rtrim($lct[0]) : 'never';
    }

    function getOxygenPercentage($deckid, $section)
    {

        if ($deckid == 3) {
            if ($section == 'B') {
                $this->set_last_checked('oxygen');
                return .62;
            } else if ($section == 'C') {
                $this->set_last_checked('oxygen');
                return .68;
            } else {
                return 0;
            }

        } else {
            return 0;
        }
    }

    function getAvgHullTemperature($side)
    {
        $this->set_last_checked('temperature');
        return 45;
    }

    function getLastChecked($systemtype)
    {
        if ($systemtype == 'oxygen') {
            return $this->last_checked_oxygen;
        } else if ($systemtype == 'temperature') {
            return $this->last_checked_temperature;
        } else {
            return null;
        }
    }

    function set_last_checked($systemtype)
    {
        $last_checked = date("Y-m-d H:i:s", time());
        $tempfile     = tempnam('/tmp',$systemtype);
        $storefile    = "last_checked_{$systemtype}_file";

        $fp = fopen($tempfile, "w");
        fwrite($fp,$last_checked);
        fclose($fp);
```

LISTING 17.1d   Continued

```
            copy ($tempfile,$this->$storefile);
            unlink($tempfile);
        }

    }

    $soap = new LifeSupportInfo();
    $server->addObjectMap($soap);
    $server->service($HTTP_RAW_POST_DATA);
    ?>
```

Perl

In addition to dispatching requests to a single class, SOAP::Lite allows you to dispatch requests to any Perl module in a given directory, with the module to use being determined by the URI requested by the client. When we are dispatching to a single class, as in Listing 17.1e, the class is loaded once, on server startup; that means we don't have to do anything tricky to make the `last_checked` dates work correctly, because, as package globals, they stick around for the lifetime of the server. (Of course, if this were a forking server, or a CGI, that wouldn't be the case.)

As with PHP, you don't have to do anything special to deploy the application; just run the script, which is shown in Listing 17.1e.

LISTING 17.1e   The Service Application in Perl

```
use SOAP::Transport::HTTP;

$SIG{PIPE} = $SIG{INT} = 'IGNORE';

my $server = new SOAP::Transport::HTTP::Daemon( LocalPort => 8000 );
$server->dispatch_to('LifeSupportInformationSystem');

print "Contact to SOAP server at ", $server->url, "\n";
$server->handle;

package LifeSupportInformationSystem;

$last_checked_oxygen      = undef;
$last_checked_temperature = undef;
$method_namespace         = 'urn:LifeSupportInformationSystem';

sub getOxygenPercentage {
    my ( $class, $deckid, $section ) = @_;

    if ( $deckid == 3 ) {
        if ( $section eq 'B' ) {
            $last_checked_oxygen = localtime(time);
            return .62;
```

LISTING 17.1e   Continued

```perl
        } elsif ( $section eq 'C' ) {
            $last_checked_oxygen = localtime(time);
            return .68;
        } else {
            return 0;
        }

    } else {
        return 0;
    }
}

sub getAvgHullTemperature {
    my ( $class, $side ) = @_;
    $last_checked_temperature = localtime(time);
    return 45;
}

sub getLastChecked {
    my ( $class, $systemtype ) = @_;
    if ( $systemtype eq 'oxygen' ) {
        return $last_checked_oxygen;
    } elsif ( $systemtype eq 'temperature' ) {
        return $last_checked_temperature;
    } else {
        return undef;
    }
}
```

Preparing for Deployment

If all we wanted to do was access the values of these methods, we could have created a simple servlet class and simply dropped it into the directory

`%CATALINA_HOME%\webapps\soap\WEB-INF\classes`

In this case, it's not that simple.

At no time will anybody be accessing this application directly; all access will be through the Web service. In order for this to work, we need to find a way to tell `rpcrouter` about the application so that it recognizes requests for it. This process is called *deploying the service*.

To see the list of services that have been deployed so far, point your browser to `http://local-host:8080/soap/admin/index.html` and click the `List` button. You should see an indication that there are not yet any services deployed, as in Figure 17.3.

Deployment consists of three steps. First, copy the `LifeSupportInfo.class` file to the directory

`%CATALINA_HOME%\webapps\soap\WEB-INF\classes`

FIGURE 17.3

No services are deployed yet.

Next, create the deployment descriptor file. This file is an XML document that contains the information `rpcrouter` will eventually need. In our case, the deployment descriptor file looks like Listing 17.2.

LISTING 17.2   The Deployment Descriptor File

```
<isd:service xmlns:isd="http://xml.apache.org/xml-soap/deployment"
                                 id="urn:LifeSupportInformationSystem">
    <isd:provider type="java" scope="Application"
            methods="getOxygenPercentage getAvgHullTemperature getLastChecked">
        <isd:java class="LifeSupportInfo" static="false"/>
    </isd:provider>
    <isd:faultListener>org.apache.soap.server.DOMFaultListener</isd:faultListener>
</isd:service>
```

What we're doing with this file is describing the actual service that we want to create. The `id` value is the name of the service, so it may seem as though *LifeSupportInformationSystem* would have been a better name, but later we're going to use this value as a namespace, so it makes sense to add the `urn:` prefix to turn this into a URI. Note, however, that the name doesn't actually have to correspond to anything else, such as the classname. I made them similar for the sake of clarity.

The actual service provider in this case is a Java class, as indicated by type, and the scope of all objects is the application, so they'll hold their state between requests, and between users. We're also specifying the methods we want to make available.

Finally, we're indicating the name of the class that will be supplying methods. We will not be using static values in our class, so we're setting `static` to `false`.

Deploying the Application

Apache SOAP provides two ways to deploy an application. The first is to use the Deploy form on the administration page, as shown in Figure 17.4.

FIGURE 17.4

Deploying an application using the Deploy form.

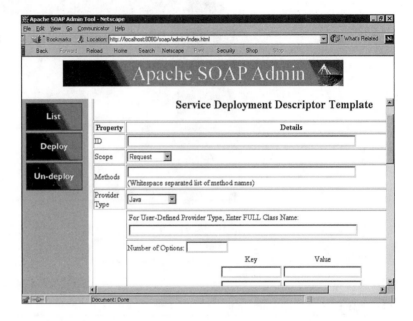

This can be extremely tedious, not to mention error-prone. Instead, we are going to use the `ServiceManagerClient` application.

Create the deployment descriptor file and save it to a convenient directory, then open a command prompt window and navigate to that directory.

Add the `soap.jar` file to your `classpath`. In most systems, you can do this with some variation on

```
set classpath=%CLASSPATH%;%SOAP_HOME%\lib\soap.jar;
```

where `SOAP_HOME` is the directory in which you installed the SOAP Toolkit, such as `c:\soap-2_3_1`.

Deploy the application by calling `ServiceManagerClient` and passing it the location of `rpcrouter` and the descriptor document:

```
java org.apache.soap.server.ServiceManagerClient
        http://localhost:8080/soap/servlet/rpcrouter
        deploy DeployLifeSupportInfo.xml
```

This should all be on one line, of course; it's simply wrapped here to fit on the page.

Check to make sure that the application was deployed by once again going to `http://localhost:8080/soap/admin/index.html` and clicking `List`. You should see the new service, as shown in Figure 17.5. Click the link to see information about the service.

FIGURE 17.5

The new service information.

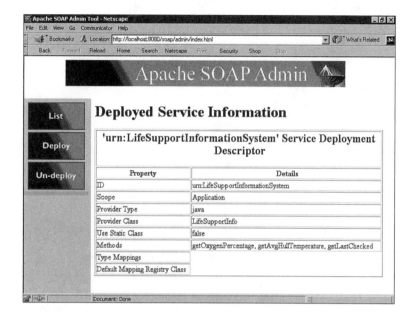

Using SOAP to Call a Web Service

Finally, we're ready to actually call the Web service. A number of products, including the SOAP Toolkit itself, have APIs that allow you to make a call to a Web service without ever having to touch the SOAP message, but because this book is about XML and not about programming, we are instead going to use a messaging API that creates the SOAP message, sends it, then examines the SOAP message that comes back.

What Is SOAP?

SOAP was originally intended as a means for passing information about objects back and forth, and carried the moniker Simple Object Access Protocol. The purpose of the technology has changed, however, and in the latest version as of this writing (version 1.2), SOAP is no longer considered an acronym.

The Origin of SOAP

A group that included Microsoft and IBM submitted SOAP 1.1 to the W3C as a note.

A SOAP message consists of an `Envelope` that holds a `Header` and `Body` elements, all of which belong to the SOAP namespace, `http://schemas.xmlsoap.org/soap/envelope/`. The header is optional in many cases, but if it's included, it generally carries one or more elements that provide more information about the message.

Accessing the SOAP Namespace (or Not)

Remember, namespaces are just unique names, and not necessarily valid Web addresses.

The `Body` element is where the fun is. The data contained in the `Body` element is known as the *payload*; it's the actual information being passed from sender to receiver.

When sending a SOAP message via HTTP, you send it as part of a `POST` action, so the service (or the application that's between the Web and the service, such as `rpcrouter`) receives information something like this:

```
POST /soap/servlet/rpcrouter HTTP/1.1
Host: localhost:8080
Content-Type: application/soap+xml; charset="utf-8"
Content-Length: ???
SOAPAction: http://localhost:8080/AirlockSystem


<?xml version='1.0' ?>
<soap-env:Envelope xmlns:soap-env="http://schemas.xmlsoap.org/soap/envelope/"
                   xmlns:xsd="http://www.w3.org/1999/XMLSchema">
    <soap-env:Header>
        <tns:maintenanceStation xmlns:tns="urn:AirlockSystem">
            <designation>5Y</designation>
        </tns:maintenanceStation>
    </soap-env:Header>
    <soap-env:Body>
        <tns:openAirlock xmlns:tns="LifeSupportInformationSystem"
                soap-env:encodingStyle="http://schemas.xmlsoap.org/soap/encoding/">
            <airlockId xmlns:xsi="http://www.w3.org/1999/XMLSchema-instance"
                       xsi:type="xsd:string">DR94</airlockId>
        </tns:openAirlock>
    </soap-env:Body>
</soap-env:Envelope>
```

Here we have a message with a special optional header, `SOAPAction`. This header not only tells the `rpcrouter` where to send this message, but it also gives an administrator a way to set a firewall to accept or reject these messages without having to read the entire message.

Notice that the `SOAPAction` header is optional. There are two styles of SOAP message, as we'll see, and one doesn't use `SOAPAction` at all. In fact, `SOAPAction` may be removed completely in SOAP 1.2, and replaced with a new action on the MIME type. Because there are so many services still using `SOAPAction`, however, we'll stick with it for the purposes of our examples.

The `Header` in a SOAP element can serve two purposes. It can provide information about the message itself, as it does here, or it can provide a way to implement multiparty processing. In this case, each party acts on the header element that it understands, then deletes it from the message and sends the new message down the line.

The Body carries the payload, the information that will actually be passed on to the Web service.

Let's see how all of this stacks up for our system.

The SOAP Message

In our case, we're going to use a SOAP message to interact with the LifeSupportInformation service, as in Listing 17.3.

LISTING 17.3   The Message to Send

```
<soap-env:Envelope xmlns:soap-env="http://schemas.xmlsoap.org/soap/envelope/"
                    xmlns:xsd="http://www.w3.org/1999/XMLSchema">
    <soap-env:Header/>
        <soap-env:Body>
            <tns:getOxygenPercentage xmlns:tns="urn:LifeSupportInformationSystem"
                    soap-env:encodingStyle=
                                    "http://schemas.xmlsoap.org/soap/encoding/">
            <deckId xmlns:xsi="http://www.w3.org/1999/XMLSchema-instance"
                        xsi:type="xsd:int">3</deckId>
            <section xmlns:xsi="http://www.w3.org/1999/XMLSchema-instance"
                        xsi:type="xsd:string">B</section>
        </tns:getOxygenPercentage>
    </soap-env:Body>
</soap-env:Envelope>
```

In this case, we're sending a message to the urn:LifeSupportInformationSystem service telling it to execute the getOxygenPercentage method with a deckId value of 3 and a section value of B.

SOAP Messaging

To send the message, we're going to use the Java API for XML Messaging, or JAXM. You can download it as part of the Java JAX Pack from http://java.sun.com/xml/downloads/javaxmlpack.html.

The process of sending the SOAP message consists of several steps:

1. Create the message.

2. Create the connection.

3. Send the message.

4. Read the reply.

Creating the SOAP Message

JAXM allows us to treat the message much like any DOM document, adding attributes and elements where we need them. We also have the option to read the SOAP message from a file to simply populate the overall message object.

In this case, we're going to build it by hand, so to speak, as in Listing 17.4a.

LISTING 17.4a   Creating the Message in Java

```java
import javax.xml.soap.MessageFactory;
import javax.xml.soap.SOAPMessage;
import javax.xml.soap.SOAPPart;
import javax.xml.soap.SOAPEnvelope;
import javax.xml.soap.SOAPBody;
import javax.xml.soap.SOAPElement;

public class SendSoapMessage {

    public static void main(String args[]) {

        try {

            //Create the actual message
            MessageFactory messageFactory = MessageFactory.newInstance();
            SOAPMessage message = messageFactory.createMessage();

            //Create objects for the message parts
            SOAPPart soapPart =        message.getSOAPPart();
            SOAPEnvelope envelope = soapPart.getEnvelope();
            SOAPBody body =            envelope.getBody();

        } catch(Exception e) {
            System.out.println(e.getMessage());
        }
    }
}
```

Here we're using a factory to create the actual **SOAPMessage** object, message. The **SOAPMessage** consists of up to three parts:

- MIME headers
- The XML representing the message
- Any attachments

The XML representing the message is the **SOAPPart** object, which we're retrieving with the **getSOAPPart()** method. From the **SOAPPart**, we're retrieving the **SOAPEnvelope**, which in turn provides access to the **SOAPBody**.

At this point, we have the following blank message:

```
<soap-env:Envelope xmlns:soap-env="http://schemas.xmlsoap.org/soap/envelope/">
    <soap-env:Header/>
    <soap-env:Body/>
</soap-env:Envelope>
```

Now it's time to populate it.

C++

In C++, we don't send SOAP messages from our client application to the Web service because of the highly integrated structure of .NET. Instead, the communication is done at a much higher level. In fact, accessing a Web service is similar to making a function call in an application. For this example, we will be using the Win32 Project type. Create a new Win32 project and name it `LSISClient`. Select the Application Settings tab, select Console Application and the ATL check box, and then press Finish.

After creating the application, create a Web reference to the Web service so that the client application is able to access it. This reference will build the necessary files to simplify access to the methods of the Web service. To do this, select the Project, Add Web Reference menu item. The Add Web Reference dialog box will appear. In the Address text box, enter the location of your Web service. For example: `http://localhost/LifeSupportInformationSystem/LifeSupportInformationSystem.asmx?wsdl`. When the Web service is listed in the Available References text box, press the Add Reference button at the bottom of the dialog. This will bring the information described in the WSDL file into the project.

Now open the `stdafx.h` file and make it look like the following:

```
#pragma once

#define WIN32_LEAN_AND_MEAN
#include <stdio.h>
#include <tchar.h>
#define _ATL_CSTRING_EXPLICIT_CONSTRUCTORS
#define ATL_SOCK_TIMEOUT INFINITE
#define _WIN32_WINDOWS 0x0410

#include <atlbase.h>
#include "LifeSupportInfo.h"
#include <conio.h>
#include <iostream>
```

Finally, open the `LSISClient.cpp` file and change it to look like the following:

```
#include "stdafx.h"

int _tmain(int argc, _TCHAR* argv[])
{
    using namespace std;
    double OxyPercent = 0.0;

    ::CoInitialize(NULL);
    LifeSupportInfo::CLifeSupportInfo ws;
    HRESULT hr = ws.getOxygenPercentage(3, L"B", &OxyPercent);
```

```
    if (SUCCEEDED(hr))
        cout << "The oxygen percentage is: " << OxyPercent << endl;
    else
        cout << "An error occurred: " << hr << endl;
    ::CoUninitialize();
    return 0;
}
```

Build the application and then press F5 to run it under the debugger. The application will print out the value of the oxygen percentage in the console.

Visual Basic .NET

Visual Basic is similar to C++ when accessing a Web service. We even have the choice of using a Web-based application or the more traditional Windows application for our client. For this example, we will be using the ASP.NET Web Application project type. Create a new ASP.NET Web Application project and name it `http://localhost/LSISClient`.

Next, create a Web reference to the Web service so that the client application is able to access it. This reference will build the necessary proxy files to simplify access to the methods of the Web service. To do this, select the Project, Add Web Reference menu item. The Add Web Reference dialog box will appear. In the Address text box, enter the location of your Web service. For example: `http://localhost/LifeSupportInformationSystem/LifeSupportInformationSystem.asmx?wsdl`. When the Web service is listed in the Available References text box, press the Add Reference button at the bottom of the dialog. This will bring the information described in the WSDL file into the project.

Now we need to design a quick form for our client application. From the Web Forms toolbox, select a button and text box controls. Name the button `btnO2Percent` and set the Text property to `Get Oxygen Percentage`. Next, name the text box `txtO2Value` and set the `ReadOnly` value to `True`. Now double-click the button to go to the code view for the button event method. Enter the code that appears in Listing 17.4b.

LISTING 17.4b   Accessing the Web Service via Visual Basic .NET

```
Private Sub btnO2Percent_Click(ByVal sender As System.Object,_
                               ByVal e As System.EventArgs)_
                               Handles btnO2Percent.Click
    Dim ws As New localhost.LifeSupportInfo()
    Dim OxyPercent As Double
    OxyPercent = ws.getOxygenPercentage(3, "B")
    txtO2Value.Text = OxyPercent
End Sub
```

In the Solution Explorer, right-click on the `LSISClient` node and select the Set As Startup Project menu item. Press the F5 key to execute the application in the debugger. Press the button and you will see the return value posted in the text box from the Web service.

PHP

PHP provides a higher-level interface to creating and sending SOAP messages, as shown in
Listing 17.4c.

LISTING 17.4c   Creating a SOAP Client in PHP

```php
<?php
 require_once 'SOAP/Client.php';

 $client = new SOAP_Client("http://localhost:8080/soap/lifesupport.php");
?>
```

Perl

Like PHP's interface, SOAP::Lite is at quite a high level, as shown in Listing 17.4d.

LISTING 17.4d   Creating a SOAP Client in Perl

```perl
use SOAP::Lite;

my $client = new SOAP::Lite
  proxy => 'http://localhost:8000/',
  uri   => 'urn:LifeSupportInformationSystem';
```

Populating the Message

Populating the message involves adding the appropriate elements, attributes, and namespaces,
as shown in Listing 17.5a.

LISTING 17.5a   Populating the Message

```
...
    //Create objects for the message parts
    SOAPPart soapPart =      message.getSOAPPart();
    SOAPEnvelope envelope = soapPart.getEnvelope();
    SOAPBody body =          envelope.getBody();

    envelope.addNamespaceDeclaration("xsd",
                        "http://www.w3.org/1999/XMLSchema");

    SOAPElement payloadElement =
            body.addChildElement(
                envelope.createName("getOxygenPercentage" ,
                        "tns",
                        "urn:LifeSupportInformationSystem"));

    payloadElement.setEncodingStyle(
                "http://schemas.xmlsoap.org/soap/encoding/");
```

LISTING 17.5a   *Continued*

```
    SOAPElement messageElement1 = payloadElement.addChildElement("deckId");
    messageElement1.addAttribute(
                        envelope.createName("type", "xsi",
                            "http://www.w3.org/1999/XMLSchema-instance"),
                                                    "xsd:int");
    messageElement1.addTextNode("3");

    SOAPElement messageElement2 = payloadElement.addChildElement("section");
    messageElement2.addAttribute(
                        envelope.createName("type", "xsi",
                            "http://www.w3.org/1999/XMLSchema-instance"),
                                                    "xsd:string");
    messageElement2.addTextNode("B");

    //Save the message
    message.saveChanges();

  System.out.println("\nREQUEST Message:\n");
  message.writeTo(System.out);
  System.out.println();

  } catch(Exception e) {
      System.out.println(e.getMessage());
      e.printStackTrace();
  }
 }
}
```

In our quest to duplicate the SOAP message in the previous example, we're first adding the XML Schema declaration to the envelope object. This will allow us to specify XML Schema data types within the payload.

Next, we're adding the main payload element. We're creating it by adding it directly to the body object using the `addChildElement()` method. Because the payload must specify the appropriate namespace, you can't just choose a simple `String` value for the name. Instead, you have to use a `javax.xml.soap.Name` object, returned by the `envelope.createName()` method.

The payload itself is destined for the namespace represented by the actual service, which in this case is `urn:LifeSupportInformationSystem`. (Remember, we mentioned that this would be used as a namespace at some point.) Here we're designating the service as the appropriate namespace, and giving it an alias of `tns` (This NameSpace). As always, the prefix is immaterial.

Next, we're setting the standard SOAP encoding as the encoding style for the payload. Later, we'll look at alternative ways of handling encoding.

The payload element name determines the method that we want to execute (in this case, `getOxygenPercentage`). The `getOxygenPercentage()` method takes two parameters, `deckId` and `section`. Each of these is added to the `payloadElement` as a new `SOAPElement` that has as its child the value of the parameter. For the value to be properly understood, however, we must specify the appropriate type, which we do by creating the `xsi:type` attribute, where `xsi:` represents the Schema-instance namespace.

Finally, we save all the changes that we made to the message object. To see the results, we can use the message's `writeTo()` method.

Compile and run the application. (Make sure the JAXM `.jar` files are in the `CLASSPATH`!) You should see the following output:

```
REQUEST Message:
```

```
<soap-env:Envelope xmlns:soap-env="http://schemas.xmlsoap.org/soap/envelope/" xm
lns:xsd="http://www.w3.org/1999/XMLSchema"><soap-env:Header/><soap-env:Body><tns
:getOxygenPercentage xmlns:tns="urn:LifeSupportInformationSystem" soap-env:encod
ingStyle="http://schemas.xmlsoap.org/soap/encoding/"><deckId xmlns:xsi="http://w
ww.w3.org/1999/XMLSchema-instance" xsi:type="xsd:int">3</deckId><section xmlns:x
si="http://www.w3.org/1999/XMLSchema-instance" xsi:type="xsd:string">B</section>
</tns:getOxygenPercentage></soap-env:Body></soap-env:Envelope>
```

It's not pretty, but you can see that the structure of the message is there. Now it's time to send it.

PHP

In PEAR's SOAP client interface, the "create" and "send" steps are inseparable, so we'll look at that next.

Perl

Using SOAP::Lite, the message will normally be created for you at send time. However, you can access the SOAP::Serializer directly to create the message out-of-band, if you want to. In Listing 17.5b, we're doing so, but purely for didactic purposes; you don't need to, and should not, do this in a production SOAP client.

LISTING 17.5b   Creating the Message in Perl

```
use SOAP::Lite;

my $client = new SOAP::Lite
  proxy => 'http://localhost:8000/',
  uri   => 'urn:LifeSupportInformationSystem';

print "REQUEST MESSAGE:\n";

my $deckid  = SOAP::Data->type( int    => 3 )->name('deckid');
my $section = SOAP::Data->type( string => 'B' )->name('section');

my $ser = $client->serializer;
print $ser->method( 'getOxygenPercentage', $deckid, $section ), "\n";
```

Sending the Message

When sending a message through JAXM, you have the option of sending it directly or using a messaging provider, which takes the message and forwards it to the recipient. The latter capability is useful in situations where the recipient is not reliably available at the time that the message is sent. In that case, the provider holds the message and sends it when appropriate.

In this case, we're going to use a direct connection, as shown in Listing 17.6a.

LISTING 17.6a   Sending the Message in Java

```
//Check the input
System.out.println("\nREQUEST Message:\n");
message.writeTo(System.out);
System.out.println();

//First create the connection
SOAPConnectionFactory soapConnFactory =
                    SOAPConnectionFactory.newInstance();
SOAPConnection connection =
                    soapConnFactory.createConnection();

//Set the destination
URLEndpoint destination =
    new URLEndpoint("http://localhost:8080/soap/servlet/rpcrouter");
//Send the message
SOAPMessage reply = connection.call(message, destination);

//Close the connection
connection.close();

} catch(Exception e) {
    System.out.println(e.getMessage());
    e.printStackTrace();
}
    }
}
```

Once again we're using a factory, in this case to create the connection itself. From there, we're creating the URLEndpoint, which represents the actual location of the service. In our case, the location is the rpcrouter, located at http://localhost:8080/soap/servlet/rpcrouter.

Now we're ready to send the message. To do so, we're going to use the SOAPConnection's call() method, feeding it the message object and the destination. Notice that the call() method returns a SOAPMessage in reply.

Finally, we close the connection.

PHP

Although you can't create the message outside of the "send" step, you can find out what message was sent (after the fact) by accessing the wire property of the SOAP client, as shown in Listing 17.6b.

LISTING 17.6b   Sending the message in PHP

```php
<?php
require_once 'SOAP/Client.php';

$client = new SOAP_Client("http://localhost:8080/soap/lifesupport.php");
$namespace = 'urn:LifeSupportInformationSystem';
$deckid    = 3;
$section   = 'B';

$ret = $client->call("getOxygenPercentage",
                     array ( "deckid"  => $deckid,
                             "section" => $section ),
                     $namespace);

echo "<xmp>\n";
echo $client->wire;
echo "</xmp>\n";
?>
```

Perl

You can use a neat trick involving Perl's AUTOLOAD facility to call the remote SOAP method as if it were a method belonging to the local SOAP client object. You can also pseudo-import all the remote functions into the main package so that you can call them with no object at all, as global functions. However, be aware that this will also trap all erroneous function calls in your script, which will then try to issue them as SOAP messages, which could be awfully confusing.

You won't actually see anything about AUTOLOAD in the main script, however, as shown in Listing 17.6c.

LISTING 17.6c   Sending the Message in Perl

```perl
use SOAP::Lite;

my $client = new SOAP::Lite
  proxy => 'http://localhost:8000/',
  uri   => 'urn:LifeSupportInformationSystem';

print "REQUEST MESSAGE:\n";

my $deckid  = SOAP::Data->type( int    => 3 )->name('deckid');
my $section = SOAP::Data->type( string => 'B' )->name('section');

my $ser = $client->serializer;
print $ser->method( 'getOxygenPercentage', $deckid, $section ), "\n";

my $call = $client->getOxygenPercentage( $deckid, $section );
```

Notice that there's no getOxygenPercentage() method in the client, so when we try to call $client->getOxygenPercentage(), the client calls AUTOLOAD and executes getOxygenPercentage() as a SOAP call, dispatching the desired function to the SOAP server.

Reading the Reply

We can read the `SOAPMessage` that represents the reply in one of several ways. We can use the `writeTo()` method, or we can break the message down into its component parts the same way we built them up in the original message, or we can treat the `reply` as XML from any other source, as in Listing 17.7a.

LISTING 17.7a   Reading the Reply in Java

```
...
import javax.xml.transform.TransformerFactory;
import javax.xml.transform.Transformer;
import javax.xml.transform.Source;
import javax.xml.transform.stream.StreamResult;

public class SendSoapMessage {

    public static void main(String args[]) {

        try {

...
            SOAPMessage reply = connection.call(message, destination);

            //Close the connection
            connection.close();

            System.out.println("\nRESPONSE:\n");
            //Create the transformer
            TransformerFactory transformerFactory =
                            TransformerFactory.newInstance();
            Transformer transformer =
                        transformerFactory.newTransformer();

            //Extract the content of the reply
            Source sourceContent = reply.getSOAPPart().getContent();

            //Set the output for the transformation
            StreamResult result=new StreamResult( System.out );
            transformer.transform(sourceContent, result);
            System.out.println();

        } catch(Exception e) {
            System.out.println(e.getMessage());
            e.printStackTrace();
        }
    }
}
```

Really, the only thing that's new here is the retrieval of the SOAP message content as a `Source` object using `getContent()`. Otherwise, this is just a typical XSLT identity transformation. If we wanted, we could create a style sheet that specifically retrieves the result, or we could transform the data into a DOM object, which we could then manipulate just like any other DOM object.

In this case, the entire contents are simply output, providing the results shown in Figure 17.6.

FIGURE 17.6

The results.

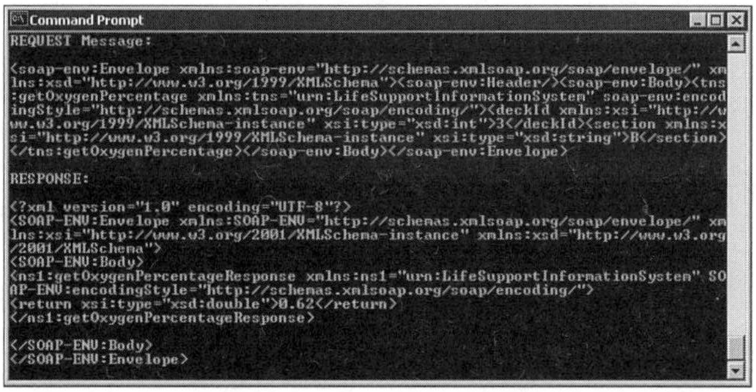

Notice that ultimately we do get our result: **0.62**. In an actual application, we would of course retrieve it and use it for further processing.

C++ and Visual Basic .NET

Visual Studio .NET provides a way to test and debug a new Web service without having to write a client application first. If you have a Web service project loaded in the IDE, it is simply a matter of setting the startup page to that Web service project (for example, **LifeSupportInfo.asmx**). To do this, right-click the **LifeSupportInfo.asmx** item in the Solution Explorer and select the Set As Start Page menu item. If you are using a managed C++ Web service, this step is unnecessary. Press F5 to begin debugging the project.

A new page is displayed in a browser window that has the name of the Web service and lists all the exposed functions of the Web service. (You can also see the generated WSDL description of the service, which we'll discuss later, by clicking the Service Description link at the top of the page.) For now, click the link to display a new page with quite a bit of information.

First is the Test section. This section has a simple user interface for all the variables exposed by the function as well as an Invoke button. By entering values into the text boxes, you can call the function and get a reply. Do this now by setting **deckID:** to **3** and **section:** to **B** and then clicking the Invoke button. You should receive a response that looks similar to this:

```
<?xml version="1.0" encoding="utf-8" ?>
<double xmlns="http://tempuri.org/">0.62</double>
```

The result from our Web service is **0.62**.

Let's look at the rest of the **getOxygenPercentage** test page. There is some really valuable information here as well. Under the SOAP section are the request and response SOAP messages that are generated by the test page and sent to the Web service. The only difference is that the bold text is replaced with the values that you put into the applicable text boxes, except for the length value, which is calculated before the message is sent. This allows you to examine the actual SOAP message that will be sent without having to use a spy utility.

Following the SOAP section are the HTTP **GET** and **POST** sections. These are similar to the **SOAP** section except that they show sample HTTP **GET** and **POST** messages that can be generated depending on the use of the Web service. Closing the browser window will end the debugging session with the Web service.

PHP

The value returned by `call()` is a fully parsed and translated value, as shown in Listing 17.7b.

LISTING 17.7b   Reading the Result in PHP

```php
<?php
require_once 'SOAP/Client.php';

$client = new SOAP_Client("http://localhost:8080/soap/lifesupport.php");
$namespace = 'urn:LifeSupportInformationSystem';
$deckid     = 3;
$section    = 'B';

$ret = $client->call("getOxygenPercentage",
                     array ( "deckid"  => $deckid,
                             "section" => $section ),
                     $namespace);

echo "<xmp>\n";
echo $client->wire;
echo "</xmp>\n";

echo "RESPONSE:<br />\n";
echo "$ret <br />\n";
?>
```

Perl

The result of the client method call is an internal SOAP::Lite object; to get the root result, use `$call->result`, as shown in Listing 17.7c.

LISTING 17.7c   Reading the Result in Perl

```perl
use SOAP::Lite;

my $client = new SOAP::Lite
  proxy => 'http://localhost:8000/',
  uri   => 'urn:LifeSupportInformationSystem';

print "REQUEST MESSAGE:\n";

my $deckid  = SOAP::Data->type( int    => 3 )->name('deckid');
my $section = SOAP::Data->type( string => 'B' )->name('section');

my $ser = $client->serializer;
```

LISTING 17.7c   Continued

```
print $ser->method( 'getOxygenPercentage', $deckid, $section ), "\n";

my $call = $client->getOxygenPercentage( $deckid, $section );

print "RESPONSE:\n";
print $call->result, "\n";
```

Web Services Description Language (WSDL)

Congratulations, you've built a Web service! Now it would be nice if other people actually used it.

If others are going to use your Web service, they need to know how. They need to know where the service is located, and they need to know what form their messages should take. What are the services available? What parameters do they take? What types are they? What kind of information is returned?

In this section, we're going to look at Web Services Description Language. WSDL is a structured way to describe all these issues. When a WSDL file is complete, it contains enough information that an application such as an integrated development environment (IDE) can automatically generate classes and applications that access the service.

In this section, we'll build a WSDL file for our **LifeSupportInfo** service.

The Overall Architecture

A WSDL document consists of a hierarchy of descriptions, each more granular than the one before. In this section, we'll look at the overall structure. In those that follow, we'll actually build each of these items for our service.

To start with, a service defines a series of ports. Each port consists of an end point, or URL at which the service can be found. The port also defines a binding.

Ports

While in some ways it serves a similar purpose as a receptacle for information, the "port" referred to by a WSDL document is just a conceptual location, as opposed to a traditional TCP port.

The binding consists of a transport, such as HTTP or SMTP, over which the messages will be sent, and a port type.

The port type defines the methods, or types of operations, that can be executed.

Operations define the type of action being taken and the input, output, and/or fault messages.

Messages define the types of content that must be sent, and the parts of the message they must occupy.

Finally, types define the information that is sent to and from the Web service, typically using XML Schema. These types can be primitive, or they can be entire `complexType`s or elements.

Now let's see this architecture in action.

Services

We'll start with a service, as defined in Listing 17.8.

LISTING 17.8   A Service

```
<?xml version="1.0" encoding="UTF-8"?>
<definitions name="LifeSupportInfoServiceDefn" targetNamespace=
        "http://localhost:8080/soap/wsdl/LifeSupportInfo-service.wsdl"
      xmlns="http://schemas.xmlsoap.org/wsdl/"
      xmlns:soap="http://schemas.xmlsoap.org/wsdl/soap/"
      xmlns:tns="http://localhost:8080/soap/wsdl/LifeSupportInfo-service.wsdl"
      xmlns:binding=
            "http://localhost:8080/definitions/LifeSupportInfoRemoteInterface">

   <service name="LifeSupportInfoService">
     <port name="LifeSupportInfoPort" binding="binding:LifeSupportInfoBinding">
       <soap:address location="http://localhost:8080/soap/servlet/rpcrouter"/>
     </port>
   </service>

</definitions>
```

Before we look at the actual service, let's take a quick look at the namespaces. Two of the namespaces—the default namespace and the `soap:` namespace—are standard. The rest are arbitrary values used simply for this document. It's important to notice, however, that the `targetNamespace` for the schema we'll eventually create and the `tns:` namespace are the same. This will allow us to create a reference to an element in the `targetNamespace` by using an alias. Remember, it's the actual URI, and not the alias, that's important!

As for the service itself, we're creating just one, with an arbitrary name and a single port. The port, `LifeSupportInfoPort`, references a SOAP address, which you may recognize as the end point for our service, and a binding.

We'll create the binding next.

Bindings

A binding binds a particular port type or series of operations to a particular transport. In our case, we're going to bind our operations to SOAP over HTTP, and we're going to use the RPC style. (We'll talk more about style in the next section.) In this section, we also determine any encodings, as shown in Listing 17.9.

LISTING 17.9   Bindings

```
...
  <binding name="LifeSupportInfoBinding" type="tns:LifeSupportInfoJavaPortType">
    <soap:binding style="rpc" transport="http://schemas.xmlsoap.org/soap/http"/>
    <operation name="getOxygenPercentage">
      <soap:operation soapAction="" style="rpc"/>
      <input name="getOxygenPercentageRequest">
        <soap:body use="encoded"
                        encodingStyle="http://schemas.xmlsoap.org/soap/encoding/"
                namespace="urn:LifeSupportInformationSystem"/>
      </input>
      <output name="getOxygenPercentageResponse">
        <soap:body use="encoded"
                        encodingStyle="http://schemas.xmlsoap.org/soap/encoding/"
                namespace="urn:LifeSupportInformationSystem"/>
      </output>
    </operation>
    <operation name="getAvgHullTemperature">
      <soap:operation soapAction="" style="rpc"/>
      <input name="getAvgHullTemperatureRequest">
        <soap:body use="encoded"
                        encodingStyle="http://schemas.xmlsoap.org/soap/encoding/"
                namespace="urn:LifeSupportInformationSystem"/>
      </input>
      <output name="getAvgHullTemperatureResponse">
        <soap:body use="encoded"
                        encodingStyle="http://schemas.xmlsoap.org/soap/encoding/"
                namespace="urn:LifeSupportInformationSystem"/>
      </output>
    </operation>
    <operation name="getLastChecked">
      <soap:operation soapAction="" style="rpc"/>
      <input name="getLastCheckedRequest">
        <soap:body use="encoded"
                        encodingStyle="http://schemas.xmlsoap.org/soap/encoding/"
                namespace="urn:LifeSupportInformationSystem"/>
      </input>
      <output name="getLastCheckedResponse">
        <soap:body use="encoded"
                        encodingStyle="http://schemas.xmlsoap.org/soap/encoding/"
                namespace="urn:LifeSupportInformationSystem"/>
      </output>
    </operation>
  </binding>
...
```

Here we have three operations: `getOxygenPercentage`, `getAvgHullTemperature`, and
`getLastChecked`. Notice that they correspond with the methods that we have available.

For each operation, we're specifying that the operation has no `SOAPAction` header and uses the
RPC style. We'll discuss both of these decisions in the next section. Each operation also has an
input and an output. Both are named, and both are specified to belong in the body of the message, to use the SOAP encoding style, and to be within the main service namespace.

The binding also refers to a `portType`, in this case `tns:LifeSupportInfoJavaPortType`. We'll define that next.

Port Types

In object-oriented terms, a binding is a concrete implementation of a port, but we must also define a `portType` that corresponds with it; you might think of it as the interface to which the binding conforms. Listing 17.10 shows the `portType` definition.

LISTING 17.10   The Port Type

```
<portType name="LifeSupportInfoJavaPortType">
  <operation name="getOxygenPercentage">
    <input name="getOxygenPercentageRequest"
                        message="tns:getOxygenPercentageRequest"/>
    <output name="getOxygenPercentageResponse"
                        message="tns:getOxygenPercentageResponse"/>
  </operation>
  <operation name="getAvgHullTemperature">
    <input name="getAvgHullTemperatureRequest"
                        message="tns:getAvgHullTemperatureRequest"/>
    <output name="getAvgHullTemperatureResponse"
                        message="tns:getAvgHullTemperatureResponse"/>
  </operation>
  <operation name="getLastChecked">
    <input name="getLastCheckedRequest" message="tns:getLastCheckedRequest"/>
    <output name="getLastCheckedResponse" message="tns:getLastCheckedResponse"/>
  </operation>
</portType>
```

Each operation lists the message, which defines the content that makes up the input or output, respectively. Before we move on to messages, though, we need to take a look at operations.

Operations

By definition, there are four types of operations:

- **Request/response**—By far the most common Web service, a request/response service involves the sender requesting information, which is then returned by the receiver. In a request/response situation, an operation lists an input element, then an output element.

- **One-way**—In this case, the sender simply sends an input to the service; there is no response, so the operation doesn't list an output element.

- **Solicit/response**—In this case, there's still an input and a response, but the Web service itself is calling a user, which then responds. In this case, the output method comes first, then an input message appears.

- **Notification**—In the case of notification, the sender sends out information, such as automated virus updates, but doesn't expect a response from the reader.

Keep in mind that this model requires you to think a little differently than you might when building a traditional client application. In some situations, you'll have to code your application to handle asynchronous responses. You might send a message and get a reply a week later.

Operations can include a **fault** element, which points to the built-in or custom elements. This message is displayed if the service doesn't successfully complete its mission.

Messages

Now we've specified the messages involved in each operation, so we need to define what's in each message, as shown in Listing 17.11.

LISTING 17.11 Messages

```
...
  <message name="getOxygenPercentageRequest">
    <part name="deckId" type="xsd:int"/>
    <part name="section" type="xsd:string"/>
  </message>
  <message name="getOxygenPercentageResponse">
    <part name="result" type="xsd:double"/>
  </message>
  <message name="getAvgHullTemperatureRequest">
    <part name="side" type="xsd:string"/>
  </message>
  <message name="getAvgHullTemperatureResponse">
    <part name="result" type="xsd:double"/>
  </message>
  <message name="getLastCheckedRequest">
    <part name="systemType" type="xsd:string"/>
  </message>
  <message name="getLastCheckedResponse">
    <part name="result" type="xsd:date"/>
  </message>
...
```

Here we've defined each of the messages we named within operations, determining what each part should be and what it should contain. For example, the getAvgHullTemperatureRequest message consists of one side element of type string. The getOxygenPercentageRequest message has two parts: one deckId (consisting of an int value) and one section (consisting of a string value).

Actually, we could have defined the getOxygenPercentageRequest message as a complex type, or as a particular element, as in Listing 17.12.

LISTING 17.12 An Alternative View

```
...
  <message name="getOxygenPercentageRequest">
    <part name="parameters" element="tns:getOxygenPercentageRequest"/>
```

LISTING 17.12 Continued

```
  </message>
  <message name="getOxygenPercentageResponse">
    <part name="result" type="xsd:double"/>
  </message>
...
```

In this case, we're saying that the parameters that are passed should be in the form of the `getOxygenPercentageRequest` element defined in the `tns:` namespace, which happens to be the target namespace for the schema document we're about to create.

Types

All the types mentioned so far, with one exception, are standard XML Schema types, so we don't need to define them. The exception is the `getOxygenPercentageRequest` element, which is defined in the types section of the document, as shown in Listing 7.13.

LISTING 17.13 Defining Types

```
<types>
    <xsd:schema elementFormDefault="qualified"
                              xmlns:xsd="http://www.w3.org/2001/XMLSchema">
      <xsd:element name="getOxygenPercentageRequest">
        <xsd:complexType>
          <xsd:sequence>
            <xsd:element minOccurs="0" maxOccurs="1" name="deckId"
                                                      type="xsd:int" />
            <xsd:element minOccurs="0" maxOccurs="1" name="section"
                                                      type="xsd:string" />
          </xsd:sequence>
        </xsd:complexType>
      </xsd:element>
    </xsd:schema>
</types>
```

Putting It Together

When all is said and done, you have a single document that provides all the information that a developer needs to access your Web service. The document looks something like Listing 7.14.

LISTING 17.14 The Complete Document

```
<?xml version="1.0" encoding="UTF-8"?>
<definitions name="LifeSupportInfoServiceDefn" targetNamespace=
        "http://localhost:8080/soap/wsdl/LifeSupportInfo-service.wsdl"
      xmlns="http://schemas.xmlsoap.org/wsdl/"
      xmlns:soap="http://schemas.xmlsoap.org/wsdl/soap/"
      xmlns:tns="http://localhost:8080/soap/wsdl/LifeSupportInfo-service.wsdl"
      xmlns:binding=
        "http://localhost:8080/definitions/LifeSupportInfoRemoteInterface">
```

LISTING 17.14   *Continued*

```
<types>
  <xsd:schema elementFormDefault="qualified"
                         xmlns:xsd="http://www.w3.org/2001/XMLSchema">
    <xsd:element name="getOxygenPercentageRequest">
      <xsd:complexType>
        <xsd:sequence>
          <xsd:element minOccurs="0" maxOccurs="1" name="deckId"
                                              type="xsd:int" />
          <xsd:element minOccurs="0" maxOccurs="1" name="section"
                                              type="xsd:string" />
        </xsd:sequence>
      </xsd:complexType>
    </xsd:element>
  </xsd:schema>
</types>
<message name="getOxygenPercentageRequest">
  <part name="parameters" element="tns:getOxygenPercentageRequest"/>
</message>
<message name="getOxygenPercentageResponse">
  <part name="result" type="xsd:double"/>
</message>
<message name="getAvgHullTemperatureRequest">
  <part name="side" type="xsd:string"/>
</message>
<message name="getAvgHullTemperatureResponse">
  <part name="result" type="xsd:double"/>
</message>
<message name="getLastCheckedRequest">
  <part name="systemType" type="xsd:string"/>
</message>
<message name="getLastCheckedResponse">
  <part name="result" type="xsd:date"/>
</message>
<portType name="LifeSupportInfoJavaPortType">
  <operation name="getOxygenPercentage">
    <input name="getOxygenPercentageRequest"
                          message="tns:getOxygenPercentageRequest"/>
    <output name="getOxygenPercentageResponse"
                          message="tns:getOxygenPercentageResponse"/>
  </operation>
  <operation name="getAvgHullTemperature">
    <input name="getAvgHullTemperatureRequest"
                          message="tns:getAvgHullTemperatureRequest"/>
    <output name="getAvgHullTemperatureResponse"
                          message="tns:getAvgHullTemperatureResponse"/>
  </operation>
  <operation name="getLastChecked">
    <input name="getLastCheckedRequest" message="tns:getLastCheckedRequest"/>
    <output name="getLastCheckedResponse" message="tns:getLastCheckedResponse"/>
  </operation>
</portType>
```

LISTING 17.14 Continued

```
    <binding name="LifeSupportInfoBinding" type="tns:LifeSupportInfoJavaPortType">
      <soap:binding style="rpc" transport="http://schemas.xmlsoap.org/soap/http"/>
      <operation name="getOxygenPercentage">
        <soap:operation soapAction="" style="rpc"/>
        <input name="getOxygenPercentageRequest">
          <soap:body use="encoded"
                     encodingStyle="http://schemas.xmlsoap.org/soap/encoding/"
                                namespace="urn:LifeSupportInformationSystem"/>
        </input>
        <output name="getOxygenPercentageResponse">
          <soap:body use="encoded"
                     encodingStyle="http://schemas.xmlsoap.org/soap/encoding/"
                                namespace="urn:LifeSupportInformationSystem"/>
        </output>
      </operation>
      <operation name="getAvgHullTemperature">
        <soap:operation soapAction="" style="rpc"/>
        <input name="getAvgHullTemperatureRequest">
          <soap:body use="encoded"
                     encodingStyle="http://schemas.xmlsoap.org/soap/encoding/"
                                namespace="urn:LifeSupportInformationSystem"/>
        </input>
        <output name="getAvgHullTemperatureResponse">
          <soap:body use="encoded"
                     encodingStyle="http://schemas.xmlsoap.org/soap/encoding/"
                                namespace="urn:LifeSupportInformationSystem"/>
        </output>
      </operation>
      <operation name="getLastChecked">
        <soap:operation soapAction="" style="rpc"/>
        <input name="getLastCheckedRequest">
          <soap:body use="encoded"
                     encodingStyle="http://schemas.xmlsoap.org/soap/encoding/"
                                namespace="urn:LifeSupportInformationSystem"/>
        </input>
        <output name="getLastCheckedResponse">
          <soap:body use="encoded"
                     encodingStyle="http://schemas.xmlsoap.org/soap/encoding/"
                                namespace="urn:LifeSupportInformationSystem"/>
        </output>
      </operation>
    </binding>
    <service name="LifeSupportInfoService">
      <port name="LifeSupportInfoPort" binding="binding:LifeSupportInfoBinding">
        <soap:address location="http://localhost:8080/soap/servlet/rpcrouter"/>
      </port>
    </service>

  </definitions>
```

Document Versus RPC

Our service is set up in a way that's oriented toward Remote Procedure Calls, rather than the actual exchange of information via SOAP. Because this book focuses on programming, that's a natural choice. But there are enough document-based services out there that it makes sense to look at the alternative—the document-style definition.

In RPC-style documents, such as the one we've been using, the method to be executed is easy to spot, because it's the name of the element that encloses the parameters. In the document style, however, the information is included in the **Body** element directly, so the SOAP message becomes

```
<soap-env:Envelope xmlns:soap-env="http://schemas.xmlsoap.org/soap/envelope/"
                   xmlns:xsd="http://www.w3.org/1999/XMLSchema">
    <soap-env:Header/>
        <soap-env:Body>
            <deckId xmlns:xsi="http://www.w3.org/1999/XMLSchema-instance"
                    xsi:type="xsd:int">3</deckId>
            <section xmlns:xsi="http://www.w3.org/1999/XMLSchema-instance"
                     xsi:type="xsd:string">B</section>
    </soap-env:Body>
</soap-env:Envelope>
```

But if the method and the namespace identifying the service aren't indicated by the element, how does the system know what to do with the data?

Well, remember that **SOAPAction** attribute we glossed over earlier, in the section titled "Bindings"? This is where it comes into play. As of SOAP 1.1, the **SOAPAction** header holds information that helps to route the request. For example, the request for the preceding message might contain the following MIME header:

```
SOAPAction: http://localhost:8080/soap/servlet/rpcrouter/getOxygenPercentage
```

JAXM and SOAPAction

To send the **SOAPAction** header with JAXM, add it to the **MIMEHeaders** property of the message itself, as in

```
MimeHeaders headers = message.getMimeHeaders();
headers.addHeader("SOAPAction",
    "http://localhost:8080/soap/servlet/rpcrouter/getOxygenPercentage");
message.saveChanges();
```

One thing to keep in mind is that the **SOAPAction** header might be removed from the SOAP 1.2 Recommendation and added instead to the MIME type information.

Universal Description, Discovery, and Integration (UDDI)

All right, you've created your Web service and you've documented its use. How are other people going to find it?

The idea behind registry proposals such as Universal Description, Discovery, and Integration (UDDI) is that businesses need some sort of registry in which they can store pointers to information about themselves. This information might be organized like the white pages, in which entries are arranged by company name. On the other hand, it might be organized like the yellow pages, in which different companies that are in the same industry or provide the same types of business services are grouped together.

Then again, it might be organized like the green pages. What are the green pages, you ask? Well, rather than classifying companies by their name or industry, the green pages organize companies by the service they provide.

More a concept than an entry in an actual physical directory, a green page listing doesn't necessarily correspond to business services. The green pages focus more on Web services. For example, you know how to find a company that sells tire irons, but how would you go about finding one that not only sells tire irons, but also allows you to pay online using a particular format? This is what the green pages do.

A UDDI registry provides information organized into green pages listings in addition to white pages and yellow pages.

Redundancy

Because a UDDI registry may contain mission-critical information for businesses, redundancy is crucial. It would be a political impossibility to get every company in the world to sign up for a service that belongs exclusively to one company or country. Instead, UDDI is arranged as a series of registry servers, with information from all of them being propagated to all the other vendor servers. Signing up with one partner makes your information available to all.

Business Information

The main object describing a business in a UDDI registry is a `businessEntity` object. The `businessEntity` includes a name, description, contacts, and several types of identifiers. Some, such as the DUNS number and tax identification number, begin as name-value pairs in the `identifierBag` value.

What's a DUNS Number?

A Data Universal Numbering System number, or DUNS number, is issued by the Dun & Bradstreet firm, which tracks business credit information. In this respect, it's much like a person's Social Security number.

All this information is tied to a single, universally unique identifier (UUID) known as the object's key.

Businesses are categorized by their taxonomy. For example, in the United States, a company might be classified by industry using the North American Industry Classification System (NAICS), or by product using the United Nations Standard Products and Services Code (UNSPSC).

Service Information

A business indirectly describes the services it hosts through the use of a `tModel`. A `tModel` can contain information on the actual service, but it's more likely that the `tModel` simply points to some other standard piece of information, such as the WSDL file.

That's not to say that the `tModel` isn't very useful—far from it. Once standard services begin to take hold, it will be necessary only to see whether a particular `tModel` refers to a particular standardized specification.

A `tModel` is tied to a `businessEntity` through binding information.

The UDDI API

In most cases, at least for the short term, users will access UDDI information through prebuilt interfaces, such as the Web-based approach at IBM. In other cases, however, you'll want to access the data directly.

Here you have several options. For example, Sun has created a program, JAXR, to read any sort of registry, and it's currently ready to read both UDDI and ebXML registries. JAXR has its own API, which roughly corresponds to the actual UDDI object model, although names and syntax are different.

You can also access the data directly using the actual UDDI API. The API is generally split into two sides of the same coin.

First, there are the `find_xxx` methods. These methods include `find_business`, `find_relatedBusiness`, `find_binding`, `find_service`, and `find_tModel`. The `find_xxx` models allow you to locate an object even if you don't know its key. Once you have its key, however, you can get more detailed information through the `get_xxx` methods.

The `get_xxx` methods take a UUID as a parameter, and allow you to retrieve all the information about an object. These methods include `get_bindingDetail`, `get_businessDetail`, `get_businessDetailExt`, `get_serviceDetail`, and `get_tModelDetail`.

Underneath, however, the application executes all these methods as SOAP messages.

Summary

Web services allow companies in different locations running different platforms and software packages to communicate with each other using a standard protocol such as SOAP. Messages can be sent via HTTP, SMTP, or any other method. As long as the server is properly configured to intercept the message and forward it to the responsible application, everything will work out just fine.

To document the Web service so that others can use it, we created a Web Services Description Language (WSDL) document that describes the available services, where they're located, and how to use them.

Finally, we discussed Universal Description, Discovery, and Integration (UDDI), an initiative that involves the creation of registry node operators that mirror information throughout the system. A business stores information within the registry (including technical information on how to use any Web services the company supports), and another company can find that information.

Review Questions

1. What is a Web service?

2. What is SOAP?

3. What is the SOAP header element typically used for?

4. What is WSDL?

5. Why is a WSDL file useful?

6. What is UDDI?

Programming Exercises

1. Create a SOAP message that requests a random number between 1 and 500.

2. Create a SOAP message that requests television listing information by sending a genre element and a timeslot element that includes date and time.

3. Create the response message for the television listing request.

4. Create a WSDL file that describes the service in the previous two exercises.

CHAPTER 18

XML DATA BINDING

You will learn about the following in this chapter:

- Marshalling and unmarshalling data
- Manipulating XML data as objects
- Controlling the structure of bound objects
- Altering bound data
- Using bound classes to create and delete information
- Using objects as properties of other objects

X ML data binding is a way of doing things that's not currently very prevalent, but I really think that's just because not many people know about it, or if they do, they haven't tried it.

Data binding isn't limited to XML; any time an application works with data across different systems (for instance, when C++ works with SQL data), the data must be "bound" in some way in order for the application to work with it. When you're using object-oriented languages such as Java or C++, XML data binding allows you to use your XML data as though it were an object (or a group of objects), setting and getting values through methods and function calls.

Every data binding product accomplishes this feat in its own way, but by the end of this chapter you should understand the overall concepts involved well enough to not only use the products featured here, but also to understand the differences between other products' documentation and adjust accordingly.

Overview

Before we look at the details, let's take a look at the overall XML data binding landscape in order to understand why you'd ever want to use it, and what you gain by doing so.

If you're reading this book, you probably have an interest in creating applications that utilize XML data. The fact that I say *probably* may seem silly to most of you, but some of you know exactly what I'm talking about.

In general, object-oriented programmers like to work with objects. All this DOM and SAX stuff probably doesn't appeal to them. They know how to design their applications using objects, and they don't necessarily want to change their way of thinking or doing things.

XML data binding provides these programmers the opportunity to work with XML without having to endure the pain of actually learning it. True, someone has to learn XML, even if it's just to set up the system, but data binding makes it possible for teams to work on a project without everyone having to learn XML.

Data binding does this by creating a hierarchy of objects that represent the data in the original XML document, including methods for retrieving, changing, adding, and deleting this information.

For example, consider the following XML document:

```
<?xml version="1.0"?>
<meal>
    <mealType>dinner</mealType>
    <food>chicken</food>
</meal>
```

It might become a class with the following methods:

```
public void setMealType(String arg){...};
public String getMealType(){...};
public void setFood(String arg) {...};
public String getfood(){...};
```

If a **meal** object already existed, you could output it to a file as XML. This process is known as *marshalling* the data. In the military, commanding officers marshal troops by organizing them for deployment. In data binding, you marshal the data by organizing it into XML for later use.

To load data into an object, you can reverse the process and *unmarshal* the data.

 Object Persistence

In object-oriented programming, the concepts of marshalling and unmarshalling data are commonly referred to as *serializing* and *deserializing* an object.

The important thing is this: Whatever changes you make to the object containing the data after you've unmarshalled it are represented in the XML data after you marshal it again.

How Bound Classes Can Be Used

Once the classes are created, they can literally be used just like any other class. Overall, the process works like this:

1. Binding schemas that equate the XML data with the classes are created. The way in which this is accomplished varies from product to product, but it's important to note that the structure of the object doesn't have to match the structure of the data, as you'll see in the section titled "The Binding Schema." The XML developer creates the binding schema.

2. The bound classes are created from the binding schema. Once these classes are compiled (or even before, if you're feeling adventurous) you can pass them on to another developer along with the XML source data.

3. The second developer creates an application that references and manipulates objects created from the classes provided. This application generally unmarshals the data to instantiate the objects with the appropriate information, manipulates them, and then marshals them back to the original source.

Because the second developer isn't touching the actual source data except to load it indirectly through the unmarshalling process, the type of data that the actual source represents isn't important. In this chapter we're covering XML, of course, but you can also perform data binding with databases or other sources, as long as the binding framework is up to the task.

Data Binding Products

A number of different frameworks for XML data binding are already available, in various states of maturity, including the Java products listed here:

- **Java Architecture for XML Binding (JAXB)**—JAXB is both an implementation provided by Sun Microsystems as part of the XML Developer Pack and a specification that other vendors can use to create their own applications. The examples in this chapter will use Sun's implementation. At the time of this writing it's not yet in general release, but it is stable and reliable (although it suffers from a lack of support for XML Schemas and XML Namespaces). You can download it from `http://java.sun.com/xml/jaxb/index.html`.

- **Castor**—This open source Java data binding framework supports binding not only to and from XML, but also to and from SQL databases and LDAP systems. You can find this project, which bases its XML binding capabilities on the JAXB Specification, at `http://www.castor.org/`.

Appendix A, "Resources," lists additional products.

Creating a Class

In this chapter, we're going to take the airlock system maintenance data we created in Chapter 7, "Document Type Definitions (DTDs)," and bind it to a series of objects, which we'll then manipulate.

In this section, we'll look at a simple example that just deals with employee data. We'll create the classes, instantiate the objects, unmarshal the data, look at the employee listings, transfer an employee to a different department, and hire and fire employees. In each case, we'll look at how the data is affected when we marshal it back to a file.

A Simplified Set of Data

We'll start out with a simple file that contains only information on station personnel (see Listing 18.1).

LISTING 18.1 The Simplified Data File

```xml
<?xml version="1.0" standalone="no"?>
<!DOCTYPE airlocksystem SYSTEM "airlocks.dtd">
<airlocksystem>
    <personnel badge="D59">
        <name>Angus Doyle</name>
        <department>Maintenance</department>
    </personnel>
    <personnel badge="R98">
        <name>Frank Welby</name>
        <department>Maintenance</department>
    </personnel>
</airlocksystem>
```

We'll need to alter the DTD from Chapter 7 to match the simplified structure.

The Simplified DTD

JAXB doesn't actually use the data file at all to determine the structure of classes to create. Instead, it goes by the DTD. To keep the generated classes simple in this first example, we'll strip out most of the contents of **airlocks.dtd**, keeping only what is necessary to accurately define our source file, as shown in Listing 18.2.

LISTING 18.2 The Simplified DTD

```dtd
<!ELEMENT airlocksystem (personnel+)>
<!ELEMENT personnel (name, department)>
<!ATTLIST personnel badge CDATA #REQUIRED>
<!ELEMENT name (#PCDATA)>
<!ELEMENT department (#PCDATA)>
```

Validation

It's always a good idea to validate the source file against the DTD to make sure that there are no differences. Otherwise, you'll be chasing down errors that seem to be coming from elsewhere, but are in fact simple data-related problems.

The Binding Schema

In order for the binding framework to create the new classes, it needs to understand how elements are mapped to objects. In JAXB, this mapping is accomplished through the use of a binding schema, or `*.xjs` file. The binding schema must at a minimum identify the root element of the document, as shown in Listing 18.3.

LISTING 18.3   The Minimal Binding Schema

```
<?xml version="1.0"?>
<xml-java-binding-schema version="1.0ea">

    <element name="airlocksystem" type="class" root="true" />

</xml-java-binding-schema>
```

In this case, we're telling JAXB that `airlocksystem` is the root element, and that we want it to be represented as a class. JAXB will read the structure of the document from there, making assumptions based on information within the DTD. We'll look at the actual structure of the classes in a moment, after we've generated them.

Generating the Classes

How the classes are actually generated depends on the product used.

Using JAXB, you can generate the class files by executing the JAXB JAR file, offering it the DTD, the binding schema, and the destination directory (specified by the `-d` switch), like this:

```
java -jar jaxb-xjc-1.0-ea.jar airlocks.dtd airlocks.xjs -d .
```

The result is a list of class files generated:

```
.\Airlocksystem.java
.\Personnel.java
```

The Generated Classes

Before we compile these classes, let's take a quick look at their structure.

According to the DTD, the `Airlocksystem` class can hold zero or more `Personnel` objects. It has these methods:

- `public List getPersonnel() {...}`—Returns a `List` of `Personnel` objects. As with any `List`, you can iterate through, add to, and remove objects from this `List`. This `List` is mutable, meaning that if you make changes to it, those changes affect the original `Airlocksystem` object.

- `public void deletePersonnel() {...}`—Removes all `Personnel` objects from the `Airlocksystem` object. For example, this method comes into play if the station is closing down and everyone gets fired.

- `public void emptyPersonnel() {...}`—Removes all existing `Personnel` objects and creates an empty `List` to take their place. For example, you'd use this method instead of `deletePersonnel()` if you were simply replacing the entire staff, rather than closing down permanently.

The `Personnel` class is a little simpler, because it holds only simple data:

- `public String getBadge() {...}`—Returns the value of the `badge` attribute of the `personnel` element represented by this `Personnel` object.

- `public void setBadge(String _Badge) {...}`—Sets the value of the `badge` attribute for the `personnel` element represented by this `Personnel` object.

- `public String getName() {...}`—Returns the value of the `name` child of the `personnel` element represented by this `Personnel` object.

- `public void setName(String _Name) {...}`—Sets the value of the `name` child for the `personnel` element represented by this `Personnel` object.

- `public String getDepartment() {...}`—Returns the value of the `department` child of the `personnel` element represented by this `Personnel` object.

- `public void setDepartment(String _Name) {...}`—Sets the value of the `department` child for the `personnel` element represented by this `Personnel` object.

In addition to these methods, the `Airlocksystem` and `Personnel` classes both have methods that allow you to validate the object to make sure that all data conforms to the DTD and to any additional constraints in the binding schema, and to marshal and unmarshal the data.

Controlling the Generated Structure

In the section titled "A Closer Look at Binding Structures," you'll see how to control the structure of the generated class, including method names. In most cases, however, the framework simply uses the names of the attributes and elements.

Using the Classes

Of course, the classes don't do a bit of good until you start using them within an application. In this section, we'll look at unmarshalling the data, making changes to it, and marshalling it again.

Note that before you can use the classes, you must make sure that they're compiled and that the XML data conforms to the DTD used to generate the classes.

Unmarshalling the Data

The first step in creating an application that makes use of the bound classes is to unmarshal the data, or load it into a newly created bound object, as in Listing 18.4.

LISTING 18.4   Unmarshalling the Data

```
import java.io.File;
import java.io.InputStream;
```

LISTING 18.4   Continued

```java
import java.io.FileInputStream;

public class PersonnelUpdate {

    public static Airlocksystem airlocksystem;

    public static void main(String[] args) {

        try {
            airlocksystem = new Airlocksystem();

            File airlocksFile = new File("airlocks.xml");
            InputStream inStream = new FileInputStream(airlocksFile);
            try {
                airlocksystem = airlocksystem.unmarshal(inStream);
            } catch (Exception e){
                System.out.println(e.getMessage());
            } finally {
                inStream.close();
            }

        } catch (Exception e) {
            e.printStackTrace();
        }

    }

}
```

The two important steps here revolve around the `Airlocksystem` object, `airlocksystem`. First we create it by simply calling the no-argument constructor, or the default constructor. We can then use it to unmarshal the data, loading it into the object.

In this case, `unmarshal()` loads all the data in the `airlocksystem` element, which is to say, everything.

Retrieving the Objects

Now that we've loaded the data into the main `airlocksystem` object, we want to retrieve the `personnel` information.

To retrieve the data stored in the `personnel` elements, we simply use the `getPersonnel()` method, as in Listing 18.5.

LISTING 18.5   Getting the `Personnel` Objects

```java
import java.io.File;
import java.io.InputStream;
import java.io.FileInputStream;
import java.util.List;
```

LISTING 18.5   Continued

```
import java.util.Iterator;

public class PersonnelUpdate {

    public static Airlocksystem airlocksystem;

    public static void main(String[] args) {

        try {
            airlocksystem = new Airlocksystem();

            File airlocksFile = new File("airlocks.xml");
            InputStream inStream = new FileInputStream(airlocksFile);
            try {
                airlocksystem = airlocksystem.unmarshal(inStream);
            } catch (Exception e){
                System.out.println(e.getMessage());
            } finally {
                inStream.close();
            }

            List personnelList = airlocksystem.getPersonnel();

            for (Iterator i = personnelList.iterator();
                i.hasNext();)
            {

                Personnel person;
                person = (Personnel)i.next();

                //Perform some action on the person
            }

        } catch (Exception e) {
            e.printStackTrace();
        }
    }
}
```

Remember, because there can be more than one `personnel` element, and thus more than one `Personnel` object, the `getPersonnel()` method returns a `List`, `personnelList`.

There's nothing special about `personnelList`. It's just a `List` of objects, and we can iterate through it just as we iterate through any Java `List`. It just so happens, however, that the objects that `personnelList` holds are instances of the `Personnel` class, so we can get information from them.

Reading the Data

Once we have the `Personnel` object, we can read its properties—otherwise known as data members—using the object's methods. `Personnel` is a simple class with three properties:

`badge`, `name`, and `department`. We can retrieve those values using the `get` methods, as in Listing 18.6.

LISTING 18.6 Getting the Data

```
...
            List personnelList = airlocksystem.getPersonnel();

            for (Iterator i = personnelList.iterator();
                i.hasNext();) {

                Personnel person;
                person = (Personnel)i.next();

                String personBadge = person.getBadge();
                String personName = person.getName();
                String personDepartment = person.getDepartment();

                System.out.println(personBadge + ")");
                System.out.print("Name: " + personName);
                System.out.println("    Department: " +
                                            personDepartment);

            }

        } catch (Exception e) {
            e.printStackTrace();        }
    }
}
```

In this case, we're taking each **person** object and simply retrieving the **String** values for the **badge** number, **name**, and **department**. Notice that there is no indication here whether this information was originally stored as attributes or element children; the programmer simply doesn't care. The `marshal()` and `unmarshal()` methods take care of all that. The programmer simply works with the properties he or she expects.

The result is a list containing personnel information:

```
D59)
Name: Angus Doyle      Department: Maintenance
R98)
Name: Frank Welby      Department: Maintenance
```

Changing Data

All this is nice, but of limited use in any practical sense. What happens if we want to actually change the data?

Data binding is useful in that it allows us to handle tasks such as transferring an employee to another department in a way that's more intuitive for OOP programmers.

In the real world, this action might involve many different steps, such as informing the employee's new boss, moving the employee's office, or even adjusting his salary. For that reason, it makes sense to segregate the action of transferring him to its own method, as shown in Listing 18.7.

In this case, we're going to separate the output from the previous exercise into its own method, then search for the appropriate `Personnel` object and act on it.

LISTING 18.7   Changing the Data

```
...
public class PersonnelUpdate {

    public static Airlocksystem airlocksystem;

    public static void main(String[] args) {

        try {
            airlocksystem = new Airlocksystem();

            File airlocksFile = new File("airlocks.xml");
            InputStream inStream = new FileInputStream(airlocksFile);
            try {
                airlocksystem = airlocksystem.unmarshal(inStream);
            } catch (Exception e){
                System.out.println(e.getMessage());
            } finally {
                inStream.close();
            }

            List personnelList = airlocksystem.getPersonnel();

            System.out.println("-------------");
            System.out.println("ORIGINAL DATA:");
            System.out.println("-------------");

            showPersonnel(airlocksystem);

            System.out.println("-------------");
            System.out.println("Transferring employee R98 to Activities "+
                                                    "department...");
            System.out.println("-------------");

            for (Iterator i = personnelList.iterator();
                    i.hasNext();) {

                Personnel person;
                person = (Personnel)i.next();

                String personBadge = person.getBadge();
                if (personBadge.equals("R98")){
                    transferPerson(person, "Activities");
```

LISTING 18.7   Continued

```
                }
            }

            System.out.println("-------------");
            System.out.println("REVISED DATA:");
            System.out.println("-------------");

            showPersonnel(airlocksystem);

        } catch (Exception e) {
            e.printStackTrace();
        }
    }

    public static void showPersonnel(Airlocksystem airlocksystem) {

        List personnelList = airlocksystem.getPersonnel();

        for (Iterator i = personnelList.iterator();
            i.hasNext();) {

            Personnel person;
            person = (Personnel)i.next();

            String personBadge = person.getBadge();
            String personName = person.getName();
            String personDepartment = person.getDepartment();

            System.out.println(personBadge + ")");
            System.out.print("Name: " + personName);
            System.out.println("    Department: " + personDepartment);
        }

    }

    public static void transferPerson(Personnel person, String department) {

        person.setDepartment(department);

    }
}
```

Notice how the objects are interrelated. We output the data to the screen, as before. This is the same code, but it's been moved to a method into which we pass the `airlocksystem` object.

We're still looping through each `Personnel` object, but this time, rather than outputting the data, we're looking for a specific `Personnel` object. When we find it, we're simply passing it to the `transferPerson()` method. As I said earlier, the actual process may involve a series of steps managed by this method, but we're just interested in the data.

Because `department` is a property of the `Personnel` object, we can change it by simply calling `setDepartment()` on the `Personnel` object.

Once that's done, we're outputting the data once more. The results show the change:

```
- - - - - - - - - - - - -
ORIGINAL DATA:
- - - - - - - - - - - - -
D59)
Name: Angus Doyle      Department: Maintenance
R98)
Name: Frank Welby      Department: Maintenance
- - - - - - - - - - - - -
Transferring employee R98 to Activities department...
- - - - - - - - - - - - -
- - - - - - - - - - - - -
REVISED DATA:
- - - - - - - - - - - - -
D59)
Name: Angus Doyle      Department: Maintenance
R98)
Name: Frank Welby      Department: Activities
```

This process works because when we pass the `Personnel` object in to `transferPerson()`, it's a reference to the actual `Personnel` object in the `personnelList` List. When we change its value, we're making a change to the object in the `List`. That `List` is part of the overall `Airlocksystem` object, so the change affects `airlocksystem` as well, as we can see when we print out the post-change contents.

Marshalling the Data

Now we're ready to marshal the data back to a file. In most cases, we'd go back to the original file, but for convenience we'll create a new file.

To marshal the data, we simply need to create a new `File` object and use the `marshal()` method to send the data to it, as in Listing 18.8.

LISTING 18.8   Marshalling the Data

```
import java.io.FileOutputStream;

import java.util.List;
import java.util.Iterator;

public class PersonnelUpdate {

    public static Airlocksystem airlocksystem;

    public static void main(String[] args) {
...
            showPersonnel(airlocksystem);

            airlocksystem.validate();
```

LISTING 18.8   Continued

```
            File saveAirlocksystem = new File("newairlocks.xml");
            FileOutputStream outStream = new FileOutputStream(saveAirlocksystem);
            try {
                airlocksystem.marshal(outStream);
            } catch (Exception e) {
                System.out.println(e.getMessage());
            } finally {
                outStream.close();
            }

        } catch (Exception e) {
            e.printStackTrace();
        }
    }
...
```

Note that when we make a change to the data, as we did by changing the `department` property, we need to validate the data held by the object before marshalling it back to the file. From there, we create the new file, then simply use the `marshal()` method to send the data to it.

The New Data

The result of all this manipulation is a file that contains the old and the new data, as shown in Listing 18.9.

LISTING 18.9   The Results of Changing the Data

```
<?xml version="1.0"?>
<airlocksystem>
  <personnel badge="D59">
    <name>Angus Doyle</name>
    <department>Maintenance</department>
  </personnel>
  <personnel badge="R98">
    <name>Frank Welby</name>
    <department>Activities</department>
  </personnel>
</airlocksystem>
```

Creating and Removing Elements

We're not limited to manipulating the data that we already have. We can also use bound classes to create and destroy elements. In this section, we're going to hire a new employee, adding her personnel record to the data, and then fire an existing employee, removing him from the document.

Creating and Adding a New Element

Just as we did when we transferred an employee, we'll break the functionality needed to hire a new employee into its own method, as shown in Listing 18.10.

LISTING 18.10   Hiring a New Employee

```
        ...
                        String personBadge = person.getBadge();
                        if (personBadge.equals("R98")){
                            transferPerson(person, "Activities");
                        }
                }

                System.out.println("-------------");
                System.out.println("Hiring employee S84 to replace R98...");
                System.out.println("-------------");

                hirePerson("Stevie Stickler", "Maintenance");

                System.out.println("-------------");
                System.out.println("REVISED DATA:");
                System.out.println("-------------");

                showPersonnel(airlocksystem);

                airlocksystem.validate();

        ...
            public static void transferPerson(Personnel person, String department) {

                    person.setDepartment(department);

            }

            public static void hirePerson(String personName, String personDepartment) {

                    Personnel person = new Personnel();
                    person.setName(personName);
                    person.setDepartment(personDepartment);

                    List personnelList = airlocksystem.getPersonnel();
                    personnelList.add(person);

            }
        }
```

Let's take a close look at what we're doing here. First, we're instantiating a new `Personnel` object using a simple constructor, then we're setting the `name` and `department` properties. From there, we're getting the `List` of `Personnel` objects from the main `Airlocksystem` object, and adding our new `person`.

Notice that we have not set the **badge** property. When the revised data is output by showPersonnel(), we can see the effects:

```
- - - - - - - - - - - -
ORIGINAL DATA:
- - - - - - - - - - - -
D59)
Name: Angus Doyle      Department: Maintenance
R98)
Name: Frank Welby      Department: Maintenance
- - - - - - - - - - - -
Transferring employee R98 to Activities department...
- - - - - - - - - - - -
- - - - - - - - - - - -
Hiring employee S84 to replace R98...
- - - - - - - - - - - -
- - - - - - - - - - - -
REVISED DATA:
- - - - - - - - - - - -
D59)
Name: Angus Doyle      Department: Maintenance
R98)
Name: Frank Welby      Department: Activities
null)
Name: Stevie Stickler     Department: Maintenance
```

When Good Data Goes Bad

We've created a new object/element and added it to the data, but all is not well. You may remember that the **badge** attribute was required by the DTD, so if we tried to save the new data without it, the document would be invalid (well-formed, yes, but not valid).

When that happens, it causes an error:

```
javax.xml.bind.MissingAttributeException: badge
        at Personnel.validateThis(Personnel.java:68)
        at javax.xml.bind.Validator.validate(Validator.java:344)
        at Airlocksystem.validate(Airlocksystem.java:60)
        at javax.xml.bind.Validator.validate(Validator.java:350)
        at javax.xml.bind.Validator.validateRoot(Validator.java:356)
        at javax.xml.bind.ValidatableObject.validate(ValidatableObject.java:124)
        at PersonnelUpdate.main(PersonnelUpdate.java:63)
```

Note that there was no problem until we tried to validate and marshal the data. This means that we can work with the object in any way or order we see fit, as long as we do what's necessary before saving the final document.

In this case, we can fix the problem by simply setting the **badge** property on the **person** object, as in Listing 18.11.

LISTING 18.11   Setting the `badge` Property

```
...
                System.out.println("-------------");
                System.out.println("Hiring employee S84 to replace R98...");
                System.out.println("-------------");

                hirePerson("S75", "Stevie Stickler", "Maintenance");

                System.out.println("-------------");
                System.out.println("REVISED DATA:");
                System.out.println("-------------");

...

        public static void transferPerson(Personnel person, String department) {

                person.setDepartment(department);

        }

        public static void hirePerson(String personBadge, String personName,
                                                String personDepartment) {

            Personnel person = new Personnel();
            person.setBadge(personBadge);
            person.setName(personName);
            person.setDepartment(personDepartment);

            List personnelList = airlocksystem.getPersonnel();
            personnelList.add(person);

        }
    }
```

Removing an Existing Element

Firing an employee, or removing the object that represents the employee from the system, may seem simple; all we have to do is remove the employee's object from the `List` of `personnel`. When we do that, however, we have to make sure that we're not causing other problems.

For example, trying to remove an object from a `List` while the application is iterating through the `List` causes an error. Fortunately, we don't need to know precisely where the object is in the list to remove it; we just need the object itself, as shown in Listing 18.12.

LISTING 18.12   Removing an Object

```
...
                hirePerson("S75", "Stevie Stickler", "Maintenance");

                System.out.println("-------------");
```

LISTING 18.12   *Continued*

```
              System.out.println("Firing employee D59...");
              System.out.println("- - - - - - - - - - - - -");

              firePerson("D59");

              System.out.println("- - - - - - - - - - - - -");
              System.out.println("REVISED DATA:");
              System.out.println("- - - - - - - - - - - - -");
...

     public static void firePerson(String personBadge) {

         Personnel personToFire = null;
         List personnelList = airlocksystem.getPersonnel();
         for (Iterator i = personnelList.iterator();
             i.hasNext();) {

             Personnel thisPerson;
             thisPerson = (Personnel)i.next();

             String thisBadge = thisPerson.getBadge();
             if (thisBadge.equals(personBadge)){
                 personToFire = thisPerson;
                 break;
             }
         }
         personnelList.remove(personToFire);

     }
}
```

A Closer Look at Binding Structures

Now that you've got the general idea, let's take a closer look at what we're doing here. Notice that nowhere in the `PersonnelUpdate` application do we deal with anything that has to do with the structure of the XML document. In fact, except for the filenames, there is no indication that we are even dealing with XML.

This separation provides an enormous amount of flexibility, in that once the application is built, it doesn't matter what the data actually looks like.

Because the binding schema information is a structure unto itself, an XML developer can change the entire structure and as long as the binding schema is updated, the generated classes will have the same structure and the application will still work.

The reason for this is the developer's ability, using a binding schema, to control the names and structures of the elements as they're translated into objects.

The Actual File

The first thing we need to look at is the actual structure of the binding schema. In the previous examples, we used the minimum required schema, and allowed JAXB to make assumptions about the rest of the structure based on the DTD. The actual structure of the schema JAXB used looks more like Listing 18.13.

LISTING 18.13   The Full Binding Schema

```
<?xml version="1.0"?>
<xml-java-binding-schema version="1.0ea">

    <element name="airlocksystem" type="class" root="true">
       <content>
            <element-ref name="personnel"/>
       </content>
    </element>

    <element name="personnel" type="class">
       <attribute name="badge"/>
       <content>
         <element-ref name="name"/>
         <element-ref name="department"/>
       </content>
    </element>

    <element name="name" type="value"/>
    <element name="department" type="value"/>

</xml-java-binding-schema>
```

Notice that each element in the original DTD is represented by an `element` element. Elements that have no attributes or element children, such as `name` and `department`, are represented as simple values, or as properties, as you saw in the `PersonnelUpdate` application. Elements that do have attributes or element children, such as `airlocksystem` and `personnel`, are represented as classes.

Notice also that attributes are listed directly within their elements, and that the content of the element is indicated in a `content` element. The `element-ref` elements point back to the definitions of the actual elements.

By making changes to this schema, we can control the names of generated classes and properties, and data that they contain.

The New Data Structure

For this example, we're going to assume that the station has changed over from its old Human Resources application to a new "Being Resources" application, and the structure of the data has changed to something more like Listing 18.14.

LISTING 18.14   The New Data

```xml
<?xml version="1.0" standalone="no"?>
<!DOCTYPE airlocksystem SYSTEM "airlocks.dtd">
<airlocksystem>
    <employee>
        <employeeid>D59</employeeid>
        <empname>Angus Doyle</empname>
        <dept>Maintenance</dept>
    </employee>
    <employee>
        <employeeid>R98</employeeid>
        <empname>Frank Welby</empname>
        <dept>Maintenance</dept>
    </employee>
</airlocksystem>
```

It's not a drastic change, but we have renamed virtually all the elements, and we've changed the employee identification number from the `badge` attribute to the `employeeid` element. The corresponding DTD looks like Listing 18.15.

LISTING 18.15   The New DTD

```
<!ELEMENT airlocksystem (employee+)>
<!ELEMENT employee (employeeid, empname, dept)>
<!ELEMENT employeeid (#PCDATA)>
<!ELEMENT empname (#PCDATA)>
<!ELEMENT dept (#PCDATA)>
```

Because the `airlocksystem` root element hasn't changed, we could create the binding with the minimal binding schema used in the previous example, but the classes and properties would all have different names. For example, rather than a `Personnel` class, the binding framework would create an `Employee` class. The problem with those changes is that they would break the `PersonnelUpdate` application.

Instead, we can create a custom binding schema.

The New Binding Schema

What we need the binding schema to do is to map our new element names to the classes and properties that were present in the original binding, as shown in Listing 18.16.

LISTING 18.16   The Custom Binding Schema

```xml
<?xml version="1.0"?>
<xml-java-binding-schema version="1.0ea">

    <element name="airlocksystem" type="class" root="true">
        <content>
            <element-ref name="employee" property="personnel"/>
        </content>
```

LISTING 18.16 Continued

```
    </element>

    <element name="employee" type="class" class="Personnel">
      <content>
        <element-ref name="employeeid" property="badge"/>
        <element-ref name="empname" property="name"/>
        <element-ref name="dept" property="department"/>
      </content>
    </element>

    <element name="employeeid" type="value"/>
    <element name="empname" type="value"/>
    <element name="dept" type="value"/>

</xml-java-binding-schema>
```

First we have the `airlocksystem` element. Rather than the `personnel` elements, it now holds `employee` elements, so we're referencing those instead. The objects that represent these child elements will be properties of the `Airlocksystem` class objects, so in order to ensure that they will be referred to as `Personnel`, we add the `property` attribute.

The `employee` element itself is still designated as a class, but we want the actual class created from it to be called `Personnel`, so we use the `class` attribute.

Similarly, we're referencing the new elements as properties of the `employee/Personnel` class, but making sure that they're named properly.

With this new schema, we can rebind the classes, recompile them, and use the `PersonnelUpdate` application with no changes, even though the structure of the source data is significantly different.

Multiple Levels and Datatypes

So far, we've used just a root element and simple string properties. To get a feel for how data binding works in the real world, we need to look at XML structures with multiple levels and data types.

In this section, we'll bring back the airlock data we stripped out at the beginning of the chapter and look at how it affects the binding schema and, more importantly, the final application. We'll create an application that "installs" a new airlock and creates the appropriate data for it.

The Full Structure

Let's start by looking at the full DTD. We've kept the `personnel` information and added the `airlocks` back in, as shown in Listing 18.17.

LISTING 18.17   The Full DTD

```
<!ELEMENT airlocksystem (airlock+,personnel+)>
<!ELEMENT airlock (size, type, location, status, maintenance, signage)>
<!ATTLIST airlock lockid CDATA #IMPLIED>
<!ELEMENT size (#PCDATA)>
<!ELEMENT type (#PCDATA)>
<!ATTLIST size height CDATA  #IMPLIED
               width CDATA  #IMPLIED>
<!ELEMENT location (#PCDATA)>
<!ELEMENT status (#PCDATA)>
<!ELEMENT maintenance (lastdone, frequency)>
<!ATTLIST maintenance responsible IDREF #REQUIRED>
<!ELEMENT frequency (#PCDATA)>
<!ELEMENT lastdone (#PCDATA)>
<!ELEMENT personnel (name, department)>
<!ATTLIST personnel badge ID #REQUIRED>
<!ELEMENT name (#PCDATA)>
<!ELEMENT department (#PCDATA)>
<!ELEMENT signage (signtext, checkscript)>
<!ELEMENT signtext (#PCDATA)>
<!ELEMENT checkscript (#PCDATA)>
```

Listing 18.18 shows the sample data.

LISTING 18.18   The Sample Data

```
<?xml version="1.0" standalone="no"?>
<!DOCTYPE airlocksystem SYSTEM "airlocks.dtd">
<airlocksystem>
    <airlock lockid="A23b">
        <size width="500" height="320" />
        <type>Bronson</type>
        <location>Level 2 aft</location>
        <status>open</status>
        <maintenance responsible="B59">
            <lastdone>2/23/2325</lastdone>
            <frequency>monthly</frequency>
        </maintenance>
        <signage>
            <signtext></signtext>
            <checkscript/>
        </signage>
    </airlock>
    <personnel badge="B59">
        <name>Angus Doyle</name>
        <department>Maintenance</department>
    </personnel>
    <personnel badge="R98">
        <name>Frank Welby</name>
        <department>Maintenance</department>
    </personnel>
</airlocksystem>
```

Binding to Different Types

With this data we have several "special cases." First, as mentioned earlier, any element that has attributes or element children will be treated as a class by default, rather than as a value. That means that the `airlock`, `size`, `maintenance`, `signage`, and `personnel` elements will all be represented as classes.

Second, we have type issues. The `size` element needs integers for its `height` and `width` attributes, and the `lastdone` element needs a date. We can't specify that in the DTD, but we can specify it in the binding schema, as shown in Listing 18.19.

LISTING 18.19   The Binding Schema

```
<?xml version="1.0"?>
<xml-java-binding-schema version="1.0ea">

    <element name="airlocksystem" type="class" root="true"/>

    <conversion name="date" type="java.util.Date"/>
    <element name="lastdone" type="value" convert="date"/>

    <element name="size" type="class">
        <attribute name="height" convert="int"/>
        <attribute name="width" convert="int"/>
    </element>

</xml-java-binding-schema>
```

Here we've added a new element, `conversion`, that defines a data type. In this case, we're using the `java.util.Date` type, but the conversion element can alias any type based on a class, even if it's one that you've created yourself.

Next, we make use of the type by adding the `convert` attribute to the element defining the `lastdone` property. Doing this tells JAXB to replace the methods

public **String** getLastdone()

and

public void setLastdone(**String** _lastdone)

with

public **java.util.Date** getLastdone()

and

public void setLastdone(**java.util.Date** _lastdone)

This enables us to more easily check to see whether an airlock is beyond its maintenance date. (I'll leave that as an exercise for you to do on your own.)

Because the size element's `height` and `width` attributes use a primitive data type, `int`, we don't need to define it using a conversion element, but we still set the types using the `convert` attribute.

The Generated Classes

Once the binding schema is complete, rebind the classes. JAXB generates the following classes:

```
.\Airlock.java
.\Airlocksystem.java
.\Maintenance.java
.\Personnel.java
.\Signage.java
.\Size.java
```

Compile the new classes.

Objects as Properties

In the first part of this chapter, we looked at creating a new **Personnel** object as part of the List of **Personnel** objects that was a property of the **Airlocksystem** object. In this section, we're going to do something similar with an **Airlock** object. The difference is that here, the **Airlock** object also has objects as properties.

In Listing 18.20, we'll create a new **Airlock** object and set its properties.

LISTING 18.20   Creating a New Airlock

```java
import java.io.File;
import java.io.InputStream;
import java.io.FileInputStream;
import java.io.FileOutputStream;

import java.util.List;

public class AirlockMaintenance {

    static Airlocksystem airlocksystem;
    public static void main(String[] args) {

        airlocksystem = new Airlocksystem();
        try {

            File airlocksFile = new File("airlocks.xml");
            InputStream inStream = new FileInputStream(airlocksFile);
            try {
                airlocksystem = airlocksystem.unmarshal(inStream);
            } catch (Exception e){
                System.out.println(e.getMessage());
            } finally {
                inStream.close();
            }

            installAirlock(3, "Level 4 aft");

            airlocksystem.validate();
```

LISTING 18.20 Continued

```
        File saveAirlocksystem = new File("newairlocks.xml");
        FileOutputStream outStream = new FileOutputStream(saveAirlocksystem);
        try {
            airlocksystem.marshal(outStream);
        } catch (Exception e) {
            System.out.println(e.getMessage());
        } finally {
            outStream.close();
        }

    } catch (Exception e) {
        System.out.println(e.getMessage());
        e.printStackTrace();
    }
}

public static void installAirlock(int airlockType, String loc) {

    Airlock newAirlock = new Airlock();
    switch (airlockType) {
        case 1: //;
        case 2: //;
        case 3: {

            newAirlock.setType("Genosin");
            newAirlock.setLocation(loc);
            newAirlock.setStatus("open");

                Size newAirlockSize = new Size();
                newAirlockSize.setHeight(500);
                newAirlockSize.setWidth(750);
                newAirlock.setSize(newAirlockSize);

            Maintenance maintenance = new Maintenance();
            maintenance.setLastdone(new java.util.Date());
            maintenance.setFrequency("monthly");
            newAirlock.setMaintenance(maintenance);

                Signage signage = new Signage();
                signage.setCheckscript("//New Script here");
                signage.setSigntext("<![CDATA[<DANGER> Open Airlock]]>");
                newAirlock.setSignage(signage);
        }
        case 4: //;
    }
}
}
```

Most of the `main()` method should look familiar, as it's taken directly from the
`PersonnelUpdate` application. All we've added is a call to `installAirlock()`, which assumes
that there are different types of airlocks, represented by an integer value, and takes the location
in which the airlock should be installed as a parameter.

As far as the `installAirlock()` method itself, we're assuming that there are four types of airlocks, but we're only worrying about type 3 at the moment. (In a real application, the actual installation would, of course, be broken out further into different methods.)

To "install" the airlock, we first create the actual `Airlock` object, just as we created the `Personnel` object earlier. From there, we set its properties.

The `type`, `location`, and `status` properties are straightforward; they're simply `String` values. Starting with `Size`, however, things get a little more complicated.

If we were to look at the interface for the `Airlock` class, we'd see that the `get` and `set` methods for the `size` property are

```
public Size getSize(){...};
```

and

```
public void setSize(Size _size){...};
```

This is because the `Size` property is itself a class, so the first thing we have to do is create a `Size` object, `newAirlockSize`. That object has its own properties, `height` and `width`. We set them on the `newAirlockSize` object to complete the necessary information. Remember, though, that we defined `height` and `width` to be `int` values (in angstroparsemeters, in case you're keeping track), so we need to set them appropriately.

From there, we're ready to set the `size` property for the `newAirlock` object. We use `setSize()` as though it were a `String`, but we use the `newAirlockSize` object instead.

We'll use the same strategy for the `maintenance` property (keeping in mind that the `Maintenance` object's `lastdone` property is a date value) and for the `signage` property.

Referential Integrity

We're not quite finished creating the `Airlock` object. You may have noticed that the `maintenance` object still has no value for its `responsible` property. This is because the way the DTD defines `responsible` prevents us from simply setting a `String` value.

If we look at the DTD, we see that `responsible` is defined as an `IDREF` linked back to the `personnel` element's `badge` attribute:

```
<!ELEMENT maintenance (lastdone, frequency)>
<!ATTLIST maintenance responsible IDREF #REQUIRED>
<!ELEMENT personnel (name, department)>
<!ATTLIST personnel badge ID #REQUIRED>
```

When the classes are bound, `responsible` is bound not to a `String`, but to the appropriate `personnel` element. In other words, the `Maintenance` class's `responsible` property is a `Personnel` object.

In order to set the `responsible` property, we have to locate the appropriate `Personnel` object, as shown in Listing 18.21.

LISTING 18.21   Finding the Responsible Person

```
...
import java.util.Iterator;

public class AirlockMaintenance {

...
    public static void installAirlock(int airlockType, String loc) {
...
            Maintenance maintenance = new Maintenance();

            Personnel person = findResponsiblePerson("R98");
            maintenance.setResponsible(person);

            maintenance.setLastdone(new java.util.Date());
            maintenance.setFrequency("monthly");
            newAirlock.setMaintenance(maintenance);
...
    }

    public static Personnel findResponsiblePerson(String badgeid) {

        List personnelList = airlocksystem.getPersonnel();
        for (Iterator i = personnelList.iterator();
            i.hasNext();) {

            Personnel person = (Personnel)i.next();
            if (person.getBadge().equals(badgeid)) {
                return person;
            }
        }

        }
        return new Personnel();
    }

}
```

In this case, we're assuming that all type 3 airlocks are maintained by the person with badge number R98, so we'll send that value as a parameter to findResponsiblePerson(). The findResponsiblePerson() method looks at each Personnel object, just as we did earlier in the chapter, and if it finds the appropriate person, it returns that object. If it doesn't, it returns an empty Personnel object.

Note that if this method returns an empty Personnel object the application won't break, but the data can't be marshalled because the document isn't valid; responsible must point to an existing personnel element.

Summary

In many ways, data binding can provide a more intuitive way for programmers to work with XML data than DOM or SAX, as it creates objects, methods, and properties that can be directly manipulated. These objects are populated with data from an external source such as an XML file via a process called unmarshalling. You can use the marshalling process to manipulate the objects and save the data back to the original data source (or to a different data destination).

The actual structure of the objects depends on the structure of the original data, and on any decisions that are made during the binding process (for instance, whether to use a binding schema or some other application-dependent method such as setting properties).

Data is represented as properties of objects. In some cases these properties are simple values, and in others they are objects which themselves have properties. There is no limit to the complexity that you can represent and manage in this way.

Review Questions

1. What is data binding?

2. Why is XML data binding helpful for programmers?

3. What does marshalling data entail?

4. What does unmarshalling data entail?

5. How is data stored within objects?

6. What if an element has element children of its own?

Programming Exercises

Exercises 1–3 apply to this example:

```
<?xml version="1.0"?>
<!DOCTYPE music SYSTEM "music.dtd">
<music>
    <song id="_1" accesses="49">
        <title>Old Rex</title>
        <durationSecs>180</durationSecs>
    </song>
    <song id="_2" accesses="5">
        <title>My Francine</title>
        <durationSecs>194</durationSecs>
    </song>
    <song id="_3" accesses="603">
        <title>Eager to Fight</title>
        <durationSecs>162</durationSecs>
    </song>
</music>
```

1. Create an application that unmarshals the data and outputs it to the screen.

2. Create an application that unmarshals the data, increments the number of times each song has been accessed by one, and marshals it back to the original source.

3. Create an application that unmarshals the data and adds a new song called "No One Knows What It's Like" that is 208 seconds long and has not yet been accessed.

Exercises 4 and 5 apply to this example:

```xml
<?xml version="1.0"?>
<!DOCTYPE music SYSTEM "music.dtd">
<music>
    <song id="_1" accesses="49">
        <title>Old Rex</title>
        <durationSecs>180</durationSecs>
        <writers>
            <writer>
                <name>Arry Tome</name>
                <percentage>100</percentage>
            </writer>
        </writers>
    </song>
    <song id="_2" accesses="5">
        <title>My Francine</title>
        <durationSecs>194</durationSecs>
        <writers>
            <writer>
                <name>Arry Tome</name>
                <percentage>90</percentage>
            </writer>
            <writer>
                <name>Robert Maxwell</name>
                <percentage>10</percentage>
            </writer>
        </writers>
    </song>
    <song id="_3" accesses="603">
        <title>Eager to Fight</title>
        <durationSecs>162</durationSecs>
        <writers>
            <writer>
                <name>Joon Station</name>
                <percentage>40</percentage>
            </writer>
            <writer>
                <name>Lars Hotts</name>
                <percentage>25</percentage>
            </writer>
            <writer>
                <name>Owen Steen</name>
                <percentage>35</percentage>
            </writer>
        </writers>
```

```
    </song>
</music>
```

4. Create an application that unmarshals the data and outputs it to the screen.

5. Create an application that unmarshals the data, determines which writer wrote the greatest percentage of each song, and gives that writer complete credit. The application should then marshal the data.

CHAPTER 19

XML AND DATABASES: RELATIONAL DATABASES

You will learn about the following in this chapter:

- Types of databases and their XML capabilities
- Relational databases
- Object-relational mapping
- Table mapping

- Storing XML as large objects (LOBs)
- XML capabilities of common relational databases

A t some point in your XML programming career—and probably early in your XML programming career—you'll be asked to work on a project that involves a database. You may be asked to store your information in a database to improve search capabilities, or to simply integrate legacy data with your application, or to carry out any number of other potential interactions that may or may not involve actually storing data in a database. What you do will depend on the particular situation. The options are numerous, and have as much to do with the nature of the data as with what you're going to do with it.

In this chapter, we're going to look at some of the various options and the factors that determine the direction in which you might go. We're also going to take a look at one of the two major categories of solutions: XML-enabled relational databases. We'll see the technologies involved in XML-enabling a relational database, and how they're integrated into three of the most commonly used relational database management systems: Oracle, IBM's DB2, and Microsoft SQL Server 2000. In Chapter 20, "XML and Databases: Native XML Databases," we'll look at some of the new languages that are emerging to solve current problems.

Types of Systems

Ronald Bourret, who is known for keeping the most comprehensive list of XML-related database programs on the Web (at `http://www.rpbourret.com/xml/XMLDatabaseProds.htm`), lists over one hundred products at the time of this writing. Each of these products interacts with XML in a different way, but we can generally group them into several broad categories. Be aware, however, that products that include multiple offerings typically fall into more than one of these categories.

Middleware

Middleware is a category that encompasses any software that can be used to transfer data from one general state to another. For example, middleware is frequently used between a database and a Web site, or between two applications that share data. You've more than likely written some sort of middleware yourself, though you might not have sold it to others for their use.

In this case, however, we're talking about products and APIs that are designed to make your life easier when you need to get data into or out of a database. We could be referring to any type of database, but in general we're talking about a relational database.

Middleware comes in many different flavors. For example, Microsoft's ActiveX Data Object, better known as ADO, can be considered middleware because it helps you get data out of a database and into your application. ADO also has some XML capabilities. Therefore, you can use it to transfer your data between the XML and relational forms.

A variety of middleware programs exist, both commercial and open source. Typically, middleware connects to the database using ODBC or JDBC, so the exact type of the underlying database isn't necessarily important.

Relational Databases

A relational database stores information in a number of different tables, and can "relate" information from one table to information in another table. For example, you might have a table of work order information. You don't want to list all the information for each responsible employee, because you'd wind up with a large amount of duplicate data. Instead, a relational database puts the redundant information in a separate table and simply points to it. Figure 19.1 shows how these relationships might work.

FIGURE 19.1
Relational databases allow tables to refer to each other for more information through primary and foreign keys.

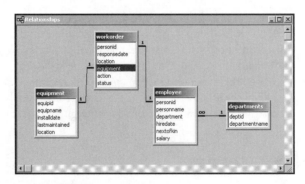

We'll discuss relationships involving primary and foreign keys in greater detail in the section titled "XML Relational Mapping Models."

All relational database management systems (RDBMSs) that have special capabilities for dealing with XML data are known as *XML-enabled databases*. But that's where the similarity stops. At least for now, database vendors are still finding their way when it comes to XML. They all know that they want to be involved, but the field is still fairly immature, so nobody knows quite how to best go about it.

In the section titled "XML Relational Mapping Models," we'll talk about the different ways in which you can use a relational database to store XML information.

Native XML Databases

A *native XML database (NXD)* looks at the problem from the other direction. Rather than trying to fit XML information into a relational database structure, it goes directly to the fact that this is XML data, and works with it appropriately. In a relational database, the smallest "complete unit of data" is the row, and rows are gathered together to form tables. In an NXD, the smallest complete unit of data is a document, and documents are gathered together to form a collection.

The advantage of an NXD lies in its capability to deal with the XML data in a way that's more natural for an XML programmer, enabling you to, for instance, select data using an XPath expression, or in the case of most NXDs, using a query language optimized for XML, such as XQuery.

In Chapter 20, we'll discuss XQuery in depth, along with XUpdate and XML:DB, a proposed API for NXDs.

Confusing Things Further...

Some of the relational database vendors are also adding features that mirror NXDs so that they can accommodate both types of data. For the purposes of discussion, we'll classify products by their primary purpose.

Other Options

These three categories (middleware, relational databases, and NXDs) in no way define the full range of products that are available for working with XML in the context of databases. Two other common categories are XML servers and application servers, and content management systems.

XML servers and application servers are arguably different categories, but the line between them is so blurry that we'll discuss them together. The purpose of an XML server or an application server is to retrieve information from a source, whatever that source may be, and deliver it to the destination, whatever that destination may be. For example, a business-to-business information exchange works in this way, taking information from one company's database and inserting it (hopefully with permission!) into another company's database.

A content management system is more user-oriented, typically providing a Web-based front end through which users can add, edit, or remove content that typically appears on a Web site, but (as it is XML) could appear anywhere.

Types of Data

What type of database you use will depend in large part on what type of data you have. If your XML is largely data-centric, you'll probably be better off using an XML-enabled relational database. If it's largely document-centric, you'll probably want to use a native XML database.

In this section, we're going to discuss the difference between data-centric XML and document-centric XML.

Data-Centric XML

As a programmer, you're probably more familiar with data-centric information than with document-centric information. This is information such as customer orders or employee information, which is not intended to be read in its raw form by a person. Rather, it was likely created by and destined for a software application. For example, Listing 19.1 shows a data-centric document.

LISTING 19.1   Data-Centric Event Information

```
<event>
    <eventName>The Great Nuptial Ordeal Ceremony</eventName>
    <eventType>wedding</eventType>
    <eventDate>Brinkish/137/2356</eventDate>
    <eventTime>16th Hour of Meire</eventTime>
    <wedders>
        <spouse>Alora Felisecort</spouse>
        <spouse>Suliggort the Wise</spouse>
    </wedders>
    <officiant>Hachalax The Three Headed Venusian</officiant>
    <entertainment>
        <warmup>Morpho and his Swinging Panorama Band</warmup>
        <headliner>Zaphrunda, the Effluviant Singing Head</headliner>
    </entertainment>
    <guests>
        <guest>
            <type>group</type>
            <quantity>37</quantity>
            <name></name>
            <title>High Sarino</title>
            <planet>Galundia</planet>
        </guest>
        <guest>
            <type>single</type>
            <quantity>1</quantity>
            <name>Narissa</name>
```

LISTING 19.1   Continued

```
                <title></title>
                <planet>Swobogda</planet>
            </guest>
            <guest>
                <type>single</type>
                <quantity>1</quantity>
                <name>Lars</name>
                <title>the Repulsive</title>
                <planet>Swobogda</planet>
            </guest>
            <guest>
                <type>single</type>
                <quantity>1</quantity>
                <name>Shoopfuma</name>
                <title>the Irradiant</title>
                <planet>Merlor</planet>
            </guest>
            <guest>
                <type>single</type>
                <quantity>1</quantity>
                <name>Borkot</name>
                <title>The Great One, All High Bumbledoop</title>
                <planet>Merlor</planet>
            </guest>
            <guest>
                <type>single</type>
                <quantity>1</quantity>
                <name></name>
                <title>Calio Grande</title>
                <planet>Jungonia</planet>
            </guest>
        </guests>
</event>
```

This document has several of the hallmarks of data-centric documents. Typically, each piece of actual data is self-contained. The `eventName` and `officiant` are segregated from the rest of the data within their own elements, as opposed to being part of mixed content.

Data-centric data typically has the following attributes:

- Documents are generated by an application, and either come from a database or are used to temporarily take the place of a database. The latter category includes documents in which XML is used solely to transport data between two applications.

- Atomic data is presented in the smallest possible units. In general, a data-centric document consists of individual data elements, rather than mixed content.

- Column order is unimportant. For example, it doesn't matter if the guest quantity comes before the guest type; the data is still meaningful. What's important is the overall hierarchy and structure, rather than the sibling order.

- Data conforms to a regular structure. Note that this distinction also encompasses documents that you might not consider to be data-centric, such as informational documents that are created using a template. For example, online greeting cards may not seem data-centric, because they generally contain a lot of non-data-like prose. Because they follow a strict template, however, they're considered data-centric.

Document-Centric XML

A document-centric document is one that was probably produced by hand or (more likely) by some page-oriented authoring tool or content management system, and is meant to be read by humans. For example, Listing 19.2 shows a document-centric document.

LISTING 19.2   Document-Centric Flyer Information

```
<flyer>
  <paragraph>
    Tickets now on sale for the Great Nuptial Ordeal
    of <person><name>Alora Felisecort</name></person> and
    <person><name>Suliggort</name> <title>the Wise</title></person>!
  </paragraph>
  <paragraph>
    This promises to be Alora's greatest concert ever.
    The Ordeal takes place on the 137th of Brinkish promptly
    at the 16th hour of Meire in the great hall of the Vanguard
    Station Resort. <calltoaction>Don't miss the greatest concert
    and ordeal of the millennium.  Tickets start at 80 Vazcreds for
    balcony seats.  Order now!</calltoaction></paragraph>
  <paragraph>
    Who will win the great Ordeal?  If you don't show,
    you won't know!
  </paragraph>
  <note>No bets taken after the Looloo Birds screech.</note>
  <tagline>Be there, or be frobish!</tagline>
</flyer>
```

Document-centric documents typically have traits that are the mirror image of the traits of data-centric documents:

- They have larger units of information, such as paragraphs, chapters, or sections. They are likely to consist of mixed content. In most cases, the document itself is the basic unit of information.

- They are generally produced by hand, rather than by a database or other data-oriented application.

- The order of information matters. If you switch around the paragraphs in a document-centric document, you've likely changed the meaning.

What the Type of Data Means to You

So why do we care whether a document is data-centric or document-centric? We care because it's going to make a big difference in how we treat it. In general, document-centric documents need a native XML database, or similar features within a relational database.

Data-centric documents, on the other hand, can be much more efficiently stored in a relational database, where they can be more quickly processed.

XML Relational Mapping Models

In this chapter, we're going to look at various ways to interact with relational databases. Notice that I didn't say that we're going to store XML in the database, though typically that's what happens. In some cases, rather than actually storing the information, what we really want to do is access relational data as if it's XML.

In either case, we're going to have to somehow "map" the XML structure to the relational structure. This section looks at some of the ways of thinking about that mapping.

CLOBs

The simplest possible mapping of XML to a relational database is the "brute force" method, in which you simply store the entire document in a single column of a content table. This column is known as a *large object (LOB)*. Typically LOBs fall into two categories: *character large objects (CLOBs)* and *binary large objects (BLOBs)*. (No, I'm not making that up.) For example, the table might look something like Figure 19.2.

FIGURE 19.2

We can store an XML document directly in a database column.

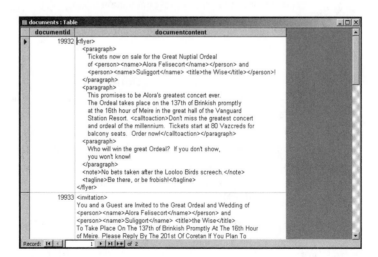

This is certainly the simplest way to store information in a relational database, and it does have its advantages, such as schema independence. It makes absolutely no difference what the structure of the data is in this case. But what happens if you actually want to find something?

The process of finding data stored as a CLOB (without having to search through a multitude of large documents) generally follows one of two schools of thought: storing all the data together as text or storing it in an object structure. The first, originally popularized by IBM's DB2 database, is to use *side tables* (separate indexes) in order to find the appropriate data. For example, if we knew that we would be looking for documents based on a person's name, we could store the names in side tables, as in Figure 19.3.

FIGURE 19.3

We can index data in a separate table that points back to the original table.

If we needed to find a particular document, we could search the side tables, and they would lead us to the original document. For example, to find any documents that mention Alora Felisecort, we could create the following simple SQL statement:

```
select documentid from document_personnames where personname = 'Alora Felisecort'
```

the `documentid`s returned from this SQL statement are for the document we want, which we can retrieve directly without ever having to search the documents table. Alternatively, we could create the following single SQL statement:

```
select documents.documentcontent
       from documents, document_personnames
       where document_personnames.personname = 'Alora Felisecort'
          and documents.documentid = document_personnames.documentid
```

Optimizing Queries

If you go this route, make sure that you understand how your database optimizes queries. You don't want to inadvertently cause it to look through all the content data that you're trying to avoid!

Of course, except for the actual indexed values, this doesn't make it very easy to find specific pieces of information. A second means of indexing the data is to create a side table that includes every possible XPath for the document and the data that it contains. This way, you can look for a particular XPath and the data is right at hand.

Neither of these methods is very relational, however. If you wanted to actually change any of the data in the document, you'd have to retrieve the entire document value, change it, and put it back. For this reason, this method is much better suited to document-centric documents.

Object-Relational Storage

A second way to store XML information in a relational database is to use concepts similar to those we used in Chapter 18, "XML Data Binding." In that chapter, we had an object with various properties. Some of those properties were actual data representing text nodes, and others were other objects representing child elements.

An object-relational database stores data in a similar way. For example, if we wanted to store the event information in Oracle in the object-relational manner, we could create a table called event using the script in Listing 19.3.

LISTING 19.3   Creating a Table with Object Types

```
CREATE TABLE event (
     eventId          NUMBER PRIMARY KEY,
     eventType        VARCHAR2(10),
     eventName        VARCHAR2(100),
     eventDate        VARCHAR2(50),
     eventTime        VARCHAR2(50),
     wedders          spouseList,
     officiant        VARCHAR2(100),
     entertainment    entertainmentType,
     guests           guestList
)
```

Notice that we have three types that are not standard SQL types. These are object types we have to create ourselves. For example, Listing 19.4 shows the script that creates the entertainmentType type, as well as the spouseType and guestType types, which you've not yet seen. We'll need them in a moment.

LISTING 19.4   Creating the entertainmentType Object Type

```
CREATE TYPE entertainmentType AS OBJECT
(
    warmup    VARCHAR2(100),
    headliner VARCHAR2(100)
);

CREATE TYPE spouseType AS OBJECT
(
    spouse VARCHAR2(100)
);

CREATE TYPE guestType AS OBJECT
(
    type      VARCHAR2(10),
    quantity  NUMBER,
    name      VARCHAR2(100),
    title     VARCHAR2(100),
    planet    VARCHAR2(100)
);
```

If you look back at Listing 19.1, you'll see that both the wedders and guests elements have multiple children, so we need to create the object equivalent of the array we used when data binding. In Oracle, we do this with a table type, as in Listing 19.5.

LISTING 19.5 Creating a Table Type

```
CREATE TYPE spouseList AS TABLE OF spouseType;
CREATE TABLE guestList AS TABLE OF guestType;
```

How the RDBMS actually manages this information is up to the database.

Collections of Tables

Finally, we come to the most, well, *relational* way to store information in a relational database: a collection of tables. In this case, each table has a primary key, which is a unique identifier for each particular record. The primary key can be referenced by another table, which refers to it as a foreign key (see Figure 19.4).

FIGURE 19.4
Data can be broken into a collection of tables.

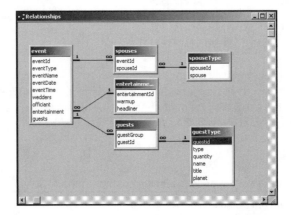

In this case, the one-to-many relationships between an **event** and its **spouses** and **guests** is managed through a separate table that links them together. Note that in a traditional relational application, these tables would most likely use the **eventId** rather than the **guestGroup** and **spouseGroup**, but the way the data is ultimately structured will, of course, depend on the database and any mapping that you do.

For those who have been working with relational data for a long time, this may seem like the most obvious way of storing XML data in a relational database, and in some ways it is. This method comes into play not so much when we're putting data into a relational database as when we're taking it back out again. In that case, we're starting off with information in different tables, and we're assembling it into an XML document. This method typically applies not only to XML-enabled relational databases, but also to middleware that accesses them.

XML-Enabled Databases

Now that you've got an idea of the various concepts and methods you can use to mix XML and relational data, let's take a look at how some of the major database vendors have chosen to integrate XML capabilities into their products.

Keep in mind that this is a snapshot of XML-enabled features for various products. As vendors try to find a niche, they will add and change these capabilities. Check for the latest features before making a decision!

Also keep in mind that some of these features are really more like native XML databases. This fact will become more obvious when we discuss NXDs in Chapter 20.

Oracle

At the time of this writing, support for XML in Oracle 9i goes in several different directions.

Object-Relational Tables

As you've already seen in the section titled "Object-Relational Storage," Oracle is an object-relational database that lends itself to this means for working with XML.

Oracle XML DB

Oracle 9i includes Oracle XML DB, which isn't actually a separate database, but rather a term to describe the XML capabilities native to the actual database server itself. Specifically, Oracle has created a new type, the `XMLType`, which you can use for all sorts of XML storage and retrieval. The `XMLType` interacts with applications, but also with the Oracle XML Registry, which consists of resources that are either containers (such as folders or directories) or files.

The registry stores XML Schemas, which can be associated with an instance of the `XMLType` to ensure that it's continuously validated; invalid data will never be entered into that column. Listing 19.6 shows a table with an `XMLType` column that must conform to an XML Schema in the file `events.xsd`. Note that we haven't created this file here; it's just an XML Schema like the ones we created in Chapter 8, "XML Schemas."

LISTING 19.6   Creating an `XMLType` Column

```
CREATE TABLE events(
eventId number,
event sys.XMLType
)
xmltype column event XMLSCHEMA "http://www.example.com/events.xsd"
element "event";
```

The `XMLType` works two ways. If a schema is associated with a value, as it is in Listing 19.6, the data will either be mapped to a particular structure or stored as a large object (LOB). This decision is up to the database administrator (DBA). If no schema is associated, the content can consist of any XML, which will be stored as a LOB. The Oracle database also allows you to use `XMLType` for other, non-XML data.

Inserting data into such a column involves a simple `INSERT` statement, such as

```
INSERT INTO events (eventId, event) values (23,
    xmltype('<event xmlns:xsi="http://www.w3.org/2001/XMLSchema-instance"
     xsi:noNamespaceSchemaLocation="http://www.example.com/events.xsd">
    <eventName>The Great Nuptial Ordeal Ceremony</eventName>
    <eventDate>Brinkish/137/2356</eventDate>
    <eventTime>16th Hour of Meire</eventTime>
    <wedders>
        <spouse>Alora Felisecort</spouse>
        <spouse>Suliggort the Wise</spouse>
    </wedders>
...'));
```

XML Developer's Kits

Along with Oracle 9i and Oracle Application Server 9i, Oracle ships the XML Developer's Kit for Java, C, C++, and Oracle's procedural language, PL/SQL. These kits have all the components necessary for working with XML, and more. The kits include

- **XML Parser**—This enables you to work with XML as both DOM objects and SAX streams.

- **XSL Processor**—This component enables you to perform XSL Transformations on XML data.

- **XML Schema Processor**—This processor enables you to create and work with schemas against which your XML data can be validated.

- **XML Class Generator**—This enables the use of XML data binding, just as JAXB did in Chapter 18. The XML Class Generator can create both Java and C++ objects based on a DTD or XML Schema.

- **XML Transviewer JavaBeans**—This is a set of beans that you can incorporate into your applications. These include the DOM Builder, Source Viewer, Tree Viewer, XSL Transformer, XML TransPanel, DBAccess, DBViewer, Compression, and Differ beans.

- **XML SQL Utility (XSU)**—Formerly a separate product, the XSU enables you to extract XML data from the database and insert XML into the database using SQL statements.

- **XSQL Servlet**—This servlet enables you to view XML data that resides in the database directly through a Web browser using a combination of SQL and XSLT executed on the server.

- **TransX Utility**—This utility enables you to encapsulate data within an XML document in order to facilitate loading it into the database.

- **Oracle SOAP Server**—Part of Oracle's Web Services strategy, the Oracle SOAP Server is a SOAP messaging server built right into the database server for applications that send and receive data using Web Services.

- **XML Compressor**—This component allows you to transfer data from one place to another in a compressed form. The database will only extract the information that is actually needed, resulting in a smaller memory footprint and faster transfer times.

As of this writing, Oracle has not yet implemented XQuery 1.0 (discussed in the next chapter) but has plans to do so.

DB2

The XML-enabled features of IBM's DB2 Universal Database are part of Net.DATA, a middleware product designed to transfer XML information to and from any ODBC-compatible relational database, and the XML Extender, an add-on that includes capabilities for working with data stored within DB2 itself.

The XML Extender is involved in three aspects of dealing with XML in relation to DB2: storing XML, extracting relational data as XML, and working with XML data stored in the database.

The XML Extender adds three new types to DB2: `XMLCLOB` and `XMLVARCHAR`, which provide CLOB and varchar columns for storing entire documents, and `XMLFile`, which stores the actual file on the local file system. A *data access definition (DAD)* defines what information is indexed. A DAD can also be used to create a mapping for those situations in which you don't actually want to store the document intact. Instead, DB2 allows you to divide the XML data into a set of separate relational tables, known as a *collection*. In this case, the user-defined functions `dxxGenXML()` and `dxxRetrieveXML()` can be used to insert or retrieve XML data. DADs can also define which columns of an XML document are indexed.

Terminology Alert!

In Chapter 20, we'll talk about collections in native XML databases. These are not the same as DB2 collections.

Listing 19.7 shows how a DAD might map the **events** structure into DB2 tables. For simplicity's sake, we'll leave out the guests and spouses.

LISTING 19.7 A Data Access Definition Mapping for `events.xml`

```
<?xml version="1.0"?>
<!DOCTYPE DAD SYSTEM "dad.dtd">
<DAD>
   <dtdid>events.dtd</dtdid>
   <validation>YES</validation>
   <Xcollection>
      <prolog>?xml version="1.0"?</prolog>
      <doctype>!DOCTYPE event SYSTEM events.dtd </doctype>
      <root_node>
         <element_node name="event">
            <RDB_node>
               <table name="events"/>
```

LISTING 19.7 Continued

```
              <table name="entertainment" key="entertainmentId"/>
              <condition>
                 events.entertainment=entertainment.entertainmentId
              </condition>
          </RDB_node>
          <element_node name="eventType">
              <text_node>
                 <RDB_node>
                    <table name="events"/>
                    <column name="eventType" type="VARCHAR(20)"/>
                 </RDB_node>
              </text_node>
          </element_node>
          <element_node name="eventName">
              <text_node>
                 <RDB_node>
                    <table name="events"/>
                    <column name="eventName" type="VARCHAR(100)"/>
                 </RDB_node>
              </text_node>
          </element_node>
          <element_node name="eventDate">
              <text_node>
                 <RDB_node>
                    <table name="events"/>
                    <column name="eventDate" type="VARCHAR(20)"/>
                 </RDB_node>
              </text_node>
          </element_node>
          <element_node name="eventTime">
              <text_node>
                 <RDB_node>
                    <table name="events"/>
                    <column name="eventTime" type="VARCHAR(20)"/>
                 </RDB_node>
              </text_node>
          </element_node>
          <element_node name="officiant">
              <text_node>
                 <RDB_node>
                    <table name="events"/>
                    <column name="officiant" type="VARCHAR(100)"/>
                 </RDB_node>
              </text_node>
          </element_node>
          <element_node name="entertainment">
              <element_node name="warmup">
                 <text_node>
                    <RDB_node>
                       <table name="entertainment"/>
                       <column name="warmup" type="VARCHAR(100)"/>
                    </RDB_node>
```

LISTING 19.7   Continued

```
                    </text_node>
                  </element_node>
                  <element_node name="headliner">
                    <text_node>
                        <RDB_node>
                          <table name="entertainment"/>
                          <column name="headliner" type="VARCHAR(100)"/>
                        </RDB_node>
                    </text_node>
                  </element_node>
                </element_node>
              </element_node>
          </root_node>
        </Xcollection>
      </DAD>
```

We start by creating the XML document's root element, events. That element defines the major tables, such as events and entertainment, so that you can relate them together. Simple elements consist of a text_node, but to set the content we reference a table and column in an RDB_node. The entertainment element isn't a simple element; it has child elements. Those children are defined directly within the element.

SQL Server

Since releasing SQL Server 2000, Microsoft has been making XML capabilities available via their Web Release program. Customers with SQL Server 2000 can go to the Microsoft Web site and download these new releases to augment their current capabilities. This section is based on Microsoft SQL Server 2000 Web Release 2 beta 3.

Queries

SQL Server 2000 has introduced a new extension to SQL queries: FOR XML. These queries are designed to select relational data from the database and return it as an XML document. Depending on the modifier given, the XML will be output as a series of row elements with columns as attributes (RAW), as a structure defined by specific nesting levels and attribute/element indicators (EXPLICIT), or as the compiler sees fit according to the data (AUTO).

For example, the query

```
select event.eventName, event.eventDate, spouseType.spouse
      from event, spouses, spouseType
      where event.wedders = spouses.spouseGroup
                          and spouses.spouseId = spouseType.spouseId
      for XML RAW
```

returns the XML shown in Listing 19.8.

LISTING 19.8   Raw XML Returned by SQL Server 2000

```
<row eventName="The Great Nuptial Ordeal" eventDate="137th of Brinkish"
                                     spouse="Suliggort the Wise"/>
<row eventName="The Great Nuptial Ordeal" eventDate="137th of Brinkish"
                                     spouse="Alora Felisecort"/>
```

Using **AUTO** instead of **RAW** causes the database to make a "best guess" at a structure, eliminating duplicate data such as the **eventName** and **eventDate** by nesting elements. You can also get more control over the structure of the output by using the **EXPLICIT** option. This option requires you to specify, for each piece of information, the nesting level, attribute or element presentation, and so on. The result is a query that's extremely complex and difficult to debug and maintain, so you'll only want to use it in situations where neither XSLT nor the other options discussed in this section are available.

One option that can make your life much simpler is to look at your data from the XML direction and use a mapping schema to define how the XML relates to the data in the database tables, and then use an XPath expression to actually select the data. When integrated with a normal XML Schema, a mapping schema, like a DB2 DAD, defines relationships between tables and between elements and attributes and table columns. For example, assuming that our database structure is similar to the structure shown in Figure 19.4 (with a few exceptions we'll discuss in a moment), we might have a mapping schema similar to Listing 19.9.

LISTING 19.9   Mapping to a SQL Server 2000 Database

```
<xsd:schema xmlns:xsd="http://www.w3.org/2001/XMLSchema"
        xmlns:sql="urn:schemas-microsoft-com:mapping-schema">

    <xsd:annotation>
        <xsd:appinfo>
            <sql:relationship name="event_entertainment"
                              parent="event"
                              parent-key="entertainment"
                              child="entertainmentType"
                              child-key="entertainmentId" />

            <sql:relationship name="event_spouses"
                              parent="event"
                              parent-key="wedders"
                              child="spouses"
                              child-key="spouseGroup" />

            <sql:relationship name="spouses_spouseType"
                              parent="spouses"
                              parent-key="spouseId"
                              child="spouseType"
                              child-key="spouseId" />

            <sql:relationship name="event_guests"
                              parent="event"
                              parent-key="guests"
```

LISTING 19.9   *Continued*

```
                                child="guests"
                                child-key="guestGroup" />

        <sql:relationship name="guests_guestType"
                          parent="guests"
                          parent-key="guestId"
                          child="guestType"
                          child-key="guestId" />

    </xsd:appinfo>
</xsd:annotation>
<xsd:element name="event" sql:relation="event" >
    <xsd:complexType>
        <xsd:sequence>
            <xsd:element name="eventType" sql:field="type"
                                                    type="xsd:string" />
            <xsd:element name="eventName" sql:field="name"
                                                    type="xsd:string" />
            <xsd:element name="eventDate" sql:field="dateOfEvent"
                                                    type="xsd:string" />
            <xsd:element name="eventTime" sql:field="eventTime"
                                                    type="xsd:string" />
            <xsd:element ref="wedders"  sql:relationship="event_spouses" />
            <xsd:element name="officiant" sql:field="officiant"
                                                    type="xsd:string" />
            <xsd:element ref="entertainment"
                                    sql:relationship="event_entertainment" />
            <xsd:element ref="guests" sql:relationship="event_guests" />
        </xsd:sequence>
    </xsd:complexType>
</xsd:element>

<xsd:element name="wedders" sql:relation="spouses" >
    <xsd:complexType>
        <xsd:sequence>
            <xsd:element name="spouse" sql:field="spouse"
                            maxOccurs="unbounded" type="xsd:string"/>
        </xsd:sequence>
    </xsd:complexType>
</xsd:element>

<xsd:element name="entertainment" sql:relation="entertainment" >
    <xsd:complexType>
        <xsd:sequence>
            <xsd:element ref="warmpup" type="xsd:string" />
            <xsd:element ref="headline" type="xsd:string" />
        </xsd:sequence>
    </xsd:complexType>
</xsd:element>

<xsd:element name="guests" sql:relation="guests" >
    <xsd:complexType>
```

LISTING 19.9   Continued

```
            <xsd:sequence>
                <xsd:element ref="guest" sql:relationship="guests_guestType"
                                        maxOccurs="unbounded" />
            </xsd:sequence>
        </xsd:complexType>
    </xsd:element>

    <xsd:element name="guest" sql:relationship="guestType">
        <xsd:complexType>
            <xsd:sequence>
                <xsd:element name="type" type="xsd:string" />
                <xsd:element name="quantity" type="xsd:string" />
                <xsd:element name="name" type="xsd:string" />
                <xsd:element name="title" type="xsd:string" />
                <xsd:element name="planet" type="xsd:string" />
            </xsd:sequence>
        </xsd:complexType>
    </xsd:element>

</xsd:schema>
```

In mapping, you typically have to deal with two situations: elements with element children that map to a table or combination of tables, and elements without element children that map to a table column. In this case, each element is mapped to a particular field or to a relationship that represents either a table or a join between two tables. The relationships that represent joins are defined in the `appinfo` section of the `annotation`.

Note that I've changed the names of a couple of columns for the main `event` table just to demonstrate that the names don't have to match. If they do match, however, you can leave out the `field` attribute, as I've done in most of the document, because the database is smart enough to figure it out.

This schema creates a conceptual look at the data known as an *XML view*.

To actually get an XML document from a query, we can use ADO just as we would with a traditional SQL query, but we can instead specify XPath as the "dialect" of the query, as shown in Listing 19.10.

LISTING 19.10   Using an XPath Query

```
...
Dim dbConn      As New ADODB.Connection
Dim dbCmd       As New ADODB.Command
Dim dataStream  As New ADODB.Stream

dbConn.Open "myDatabase"   'Can be a DSN, connection string or
                           'other connection information
Set dbCmd.ActiveConnection = dbConn
dbCmd.CommandType = adCmdText

dbCmd.Dialect = "{EC2A4293-E898-11D2-B1B7-00C04F680C56}"
```

LISTING 19.10   Continued

```
dbCmd.Properties("Mapping Schema") = "events.xsd"
dbCmd.CommandText = "/event"

dataStream.Open
dbCmd.Properties("Output Stream").Value = dataStream
dbCmd.Execute , , adExecuteStream

Debug.Print dataStream.ReadText
...
```

(This is just a fragment of a larger application to give you an idea of how it works.)

Updates

SQL Server 2000 has two different types of XML-related updating capabilities. The first, XML Bulkload, is a means for importing large amounts of data into the database.

To actually change data that's already in the database, however, you can use an *updategram*. Updategrams were designed for use in stateless environments such as Web services, where an application needs a way to determine whether the data has changed since it was originally queried. To solve that problem, an updategram contains two blocks of data: `before` and `after`. Before performing the update, the server checks to make certain that the data is still as it was when the original query was issued. (It's also how the database knows what to change!) If it's unchanged, the `after` block is applied. For example, Listing 19.11 changes the number of High Sarinos who will be attending the wedding.

LISTING 19.11   Using an Updategram

```
<ROOT xmlns:updg="urn:schemas-microsoft-com:xml-updategram">
<updg:sync mapping-schema="events.xsd" >
  <updg:before>
      <guest>
          <type>group</type>
          <quantity>37</quantity>
          <name></name>
          <title>High Sarino</title>
          <planet>Galundia</planet>
      </guest>
  </updg:before>

  <updg:after>
      <guest>
          <type>group</type>
          <quantity>40</quantity>
          <name></name>
          <title>High Sarino</title>
          <planet>Galundia</planet>
      </guest>
  </updg:after>
</updg:sync>
</ROOT>
```

Summary

Databases are a fact of programming life, and it's difficult to imagine a substantial application that won't ever have to interface in some way with a database management system of some type. Relational databases and native XML databases each have their strengths in dealing with certain types of data. Relational database management systems deal better with data-centric documents, such as are typically generated by a database or other application, and are not intended to be read by humans. Native XML databases work better for document-centric documents, where the content is ultimately intended for human eyes.

This chapter discussed various ways of integrating XML data with a relational database, from storing the document as a single column to creating an object-relational mapping to decomposing the document into a number of different tables. It also discussed the XML-enabled features of three of the most widely used relational database management systems: Oracle 9i, IBM DB2, and Microsoft SQL Server 2000.

Review Questions

1. Name one reason you might need to interact with a database management system in an XML-oriented application.

2. A document is loosely structured and contains a large number of mixed content elements. Is it likely data-centric or document-centric?

3. What does a side table do?

4. XML data binding is similar to what method of working with XML data in a relational database?

5. Name the type of software designed specifically to interface between an application and a database.

Programming Exercises

1. Determine the XML-enabled capabilities of your own database.

2. Insert an XML document into the database.

3. Perform a query on your data to retrieve part or all of the data.

XML AND DATABASES: NATIVE XML DATABASES

You will learn about the following in this chapter:

- The advantages of native XML databases
- Storing and retrieving XML strings
- Storing and retrieving DOM Documents
- Storing and retrieving SAX streams

- Using the XML:DB API to query resources
- XQuery FLWR statements
- XQuery 1.0 and XPath 2.0 functions
- XUpdate statements

*I*n Chapter 19, "XML and Databases: Relational Databases," we looked at some of the ways that vendors are trying to fit the square peg of XML data into the round hole of relational databases. In this chapter, we'll change the equation and look at the problem from the other side. The issue here is that the square hole isn't quite built yet. There are, to be sure, several native XML databases (NXDs) already on the market, and a few have been around for some time. As a whole, however, the industry hasn't quite reached a consensus on how things should be done. In this chapter, we'll look at some of the principles behind NXDs in general, and at some almost-standards in the field.

It's likely that some of this information is going to change within the lifetime of this book, but this chapter will give you a good feel for the issues and a good understanding of the underlying ideas so that the adjustment should be a simple matter of checking the documentation for specifics when you get stuck.

Overview of Native XML Databases

In this chapter, we're going to take a look at using native XML databases (NXDs) of various forms. NXD functionality runs the gamut from CLOBs in XML-enabled relational databases to persistent DOMs to separate applications from vendors that have developed their own proprietary text-based or model-based storage system, and as with XML-enabled relational databases, there still isn't a lot of agreement on how to do things.

In this section, we're going to look at some of the common denominators of NXDs and why you might want to use one instead of just a simple XML text file.

Why Use a Database at All?

The first question that generally comes to mind when talking about native XML databases is "Why do we need a database at all? Isn't an XML file a kind of database?"

Strictly speaking, it's true that an XML file is a database. In fact, when we use the term *database*, we're usually talking not about a collection of information, but about a database management system, or software that controls the storage of and access to that information. While an XML file is technically a database in the former sense, it certainly isn't a database in the latter sense.

A native XML database—in the latter sense—typically provides you with the following capabilities:

- **The ability to use the document as the standard unit of information**—NXDs are well suited for storing document-centric information. Whereas the basic unit of information in a relational database is a table row, the basic unit in an NXD is a document. Documents, which are analogous to table rows, can be aggregated into collections, which are analogous to tables, and individual document fragments, which are analogous to columns, can be retrieved if necessary.

- **Transactions**—Like a relational database management system, an NXD typically provides a mechanism for grouping various actions into transactions. In other words, you might have a group of actions that you want to take, but if one fails, you want to cancel the others. For example, you might want to delete an old version of a flyer—but only if the new version has been successfully stored.

- **Locking**—Similarly, an NXD usually provides some means of locking, or preventing users from overwriting each other. In other words, if I'm in the middle of making updates to a document, you shouldn't be able to make other changes until I'm finished and you've retrieved a copy with the new information. Some NXDs may choose to implement locking at a more granular level than the document.

- **Indexing**—NXDs provide a means for creating indexes of information contained within them, though how they accomplish this depends on their storage model. (See the next section, "Text-Based NXDs Versus Model-Based NXDs.") Indexing provides a fast way to find information for retrieval.

- **Programming API**—Whereas relational databases have ODBC and JDBC as standard APIs that programmers can use to access information, there currently isn't a standard way to programmatically access information within an NXD. (We'll look at a likely candidate, however, in the section titled "Using the XML:DB API.") In the meantime, most (if not all) NXDs provide some form of API that allows you to create applications to store and retrieve data.

- **Collections**—Finally, NXDs provide a way to combine data from several sources into a single location so that queries can easily be made across multiple documents.

Text-Based NXDs Versus Model-Based NXDs

One of the major differences between NXDs is the way in which they store information. In general, they fall into two categories: text-based and model-based.

In a text-based database, the file is stored intact, either as a file on the file system or as a single field in a database, such as a CLOB in an XML-enabled relational database. In fact, as we mentioned earlier, this is a situation where the line between the two types of databases blurs: Features surrounding a CLOB in an XML-enabled relational database are considered native XML features.

The second type of NXD is the model-based database. In this case, the database stores enough information about the document to re-create it. Models differ, but they all must contain information about elements present, the general hierarchy, the text nodes contained by each element, attributes present, and so on. A model-based NXD can use any number of different models, such as object-relational, XPath, variations on DOM, or even models based directly on the XML Information Set.

What's the difference, then, between an XML-enabled relational database that uses the object-relational model and a native XML database that uses the object-relational model? The difference lies in what the user sees. In an NXD, the user isn't aware that the database is using the object-relational model. The user simply interacts with the document as the unit of information, and the rest of the processing goes on behind the scenes.

There will typically be two situations in which you as a developer care whether an NXD is text-based or model-based. The first situation involves performance. If you typically deal with entire documents rather than fragments of documents, a text-based database can outperform a model-based database because the actual searching takes place in an index, and once the document involved is determined, it can be returned in one operation. By contrast, a model-based database has to recompose the document, which takes precious time.

The second situation where it may matter involves round-tripping.

Round-Tripping

Round-tripping is the capability of a database to return to you exactly the document you originally gave it, as opposed to a functionally equivalent but canonically different version. For example, the documents

```
<?xml version="1.0"?>
<options type="trip" occasion="vacation">
   <option1>Las Vegas</option1>
   <option2>Indianapolis</option2>
   <option3>Cleveland</option3>
</options>
```

and

```
<?xml version="1.0"?>
<options occasion="vacation" type="trip">
   <option2>Indianapolis</option2>
   <option3>Cleveland</option3>
   <option1>Las Vegas</option1>
</options>
```

are functionally equivalent because they contain the same information, but they don't have the same structure. For a data-centric document such as this one, that doesn't matter much; the information is the same. But consider these two document-centric documents:

```
<flyer>
   <paragraph>
      Tickets now on sale for the Great Nuptial Ordeal
      of <person><name>Alora Felisecort</name></person> and
      <person><name>Suliggort</name> <title>the Wise</title></person>!
   </paragraph>
   <paragraph>
      This promises to be Alora's greatest concert ever.
      The Ordeal takes place on the 137th of Brinkish promptly
      at the 16th hour of Meire in the great hall of the Vanguard
      Station Resort. <calltoaction>Don't miss the greatest concert
      and ordeal of the millennium.  Tickets start at 80 Vazcreds for
      balcony seats.  Order now!</calltoaction>
   </paragraph>
   <paragraph>
      Who will win the great Ordeal?  If you don't show,
      you won't know!
   </paragraph>
   <note>No bets taken after the Looloo Birds screech.</note>
   <tagline>Be there, or be frobish!</tagline>
</flyer>
```

and

```
<flyer>
   <note>No bets taken after the Looloo Birds screech.</note>
   <paragraph>
      This promises to be Alora's greatest concert ever.
      The Ordeal takes place on the 137th of Brinkish promptly
      at the 16th hour of Meire in the great hall of the Vanguard
      Station Resort. <calltoaction>Don't miss the greatest concert
      and ordeal of the millennium.  Tickets start at 80 Vazcreds for
      balcony seats.  Order now!</calltoaction>
   </paragraph>
   <paragraph>
      Who will win the great Ordeal?  If you don't show,
      you won't know!
   </paragraph>
   <tagline>Be there, or be frobish!</tagline>
   <paragraph>
      Tickets now on sale for the Great Nuptial Ordeal
      of <person><name>Alora Felisecort</name></person> and
      <person><name>Suliggort</name> <title>the Wise</title></person>!
   </paragraph>
</flyer>
```

The same information is in both files, and the overall hierarchy is unchanged. The only differences are in sibling order, but they are major differences.

Round-tripping is also an issue in nodes other than elements, attributes, and text. The way in which databases store information such as **CDATA** sections, processing instructions, and other nodes varies. In particular, entity references can be a problem. Are they expanded into the document before storage? If so, is the original reference lost? If not, what happens to the referenced information?

Different databases provide different levels of round-tripping, so be sure to understand what you need before choosing a product. In general, a text-based database will be more faithful to the original document than a model-based database.

Queries

Another advantage of an NXD is that it enables you to use queries that are much more natural for XML. Whereas a relational database uses SQL to retrieve data, as we saw in Chapter 18, "XML Data Binding," an NXD typically uses an XML-aware language such as XPath or XML Query (XQuery). These languages enable you to specify particular documents or document fragments with a precision that would be difficult to achieve with a SQL statement because of the difference in overall model.

We discussed XPath 1.0 extensively in Chapter 11, "Selecting Data: XML Path Language (XPath)," and in this chapter we'll discuss XML Query 1.0 (or XQuery) and XPath 2.0. XQuery, which shares a great deal of functionality with the upcoming XPath 2.0, is a query language that the World Wide Web Consortium is developing to act as a common query language for XML documents. We'll discuss it in detail in the section titled "XQuery 1.0 and XPath 2.0."

What's It Called Again?

W3C documents go back and forth between using the terms *XML Query Language* and *XQuery*, which can be confusing until you realize that XPath's full name is XML Path Language; XQuery is simply the standard abbreviation for XML Query Language. The two names are equivalent.

Updates

We've spent a great deal of time discussing the process of querying data and adding it to the database, but how do we change it once it's already in the database? Here again, it depends on the database. In many cases, the only way to alter a document that is already stored in a native XML database is to retrieve the document, alter it, and replace it within the database, but that's changing.

The XML:DB Initiative has created XUpdate, an XML-based language for specifying changes to an existing XML document without having to replace the entire contents. We'll discuss XUpdate in detail in the section titled "XUpdate."

Accessing the Database via an API

Typically, each database provides its own API for use in building applications to access it. Unfortunately, this severely limits interoperability between databases from different vendors. To solve this problem, the XML:DB Initiative has also created the XML:DB API, intended as a standard for accessing native XML databases. Several open source NXDs have already implemented XML:DB, and several commercial vendors are following suit, so it's likely that XML:DB (or a similar API) will become a de facto standard for storing and retrieving information from an NXD.

We'll discuss the XML:DB API in the section titled "Using the XML:DB API," but first, we need a database to access.

NXD Basics

In this section, we're going to install a native XML database, create a collection, and add and retrieve documents using command-line tools.

In addition to the open source NXD we'll use in this chapter, there are a number of other NXDs on the market, both commercial and open source. Some, such as Tamino from Software AG, and GoXML DB from XML Global, include the ability to integrate with local or remote relational information. Others, such as X-Hive/DB, concentrate fully on XML standards. For example, at the time of this writing, X-Hive/DB includes support not only for XQuery and XUpdate, but also for many of the features of XLink, such as linkbases, that are difficult to find elsewhere.

For a fairly comprehensive list of products and summaries of their capabilities, see Ronald Bourret's list at `http://www.rpbourret.com/xml/ProdsNative.htm`.

For the purposes of this chapter, you can install any database that supports the standards we're working on—most offer evaluation versions—but I'm going to assume that you're using Xindice 1.0, an open source version from the Apache project. It supports XML:DB and XUpdate as well as XPath 1.0. At the time of this writing, Xindice doesn't support XQuery, but by the time you read this, it might. (Xindice uses Xalan as its XPath implementation, so if Xalan supports XQuery, Xindice will too.)

Installing an XML Database

According to the Xindice Web site, "the name is pronounced zeen-dee-chay in your best faux Italian accent." Xindice started life as dbXML from the XML:DB Initiative, but was subsequently donated to the Apache project and renamed Xindice. It's Java-based, so you'll need a Java Virtual Machine to run it, but there are no operating system limitations.

Download the latest release of the Xindice database from `http://xml.apache.org/xindice/` and follow the instructions to install it. At the time of writing, this process involves several steps beyond simply uncompressing the files, so be sure to read the instructions—including the README file—for the current version carefully.

Creating a Collection

Once you've installed the database and performed any configuration necessary, make sure that you've actually started it, and that there are no errors.

Xindice, like many NXDs, stores XML documents in collections. These collections are analogous to relational database tables, but there's nothing that forces you to separate your documents into multiple collections. (Of course, it's good practice to do so.)

Xindice comes with two command-line programs: `xindiceadmin`, for performing administrative tasks, and `xindice`, for actually using the database. We'll start by using `xindiceadmin` to add a collection to the database.

Collections can form a hierarchy of their own, just like directories within a file system, but for now we're just going to create a single collection to hold documents related to the wedding of Alora Felisecort and Suliggort the Wise. From the command line, type the following:

```
xindiceadmin add_collection -c /db -n wedding
```

This command, which is the same as

```
xindiceadmin ac -c /db -n wedding
```

consists of several pieces common to Xindice command-line operations.

The application itself is `xindiceadmin`. After the application, we add the actual command, in this case `add_collection`. The `xindiceadmin` program also can delete collections, add objects to the database, import trees of documents from the file system, and perform other administrative functions.

Next, we specify the collection context using the `-c` switch. In this case, we're operating on the base context, `/db`. Finally, we're adding a collection called by the name (`-n`) `wedding`. You should see the following result:

```
Created : /db/wedding
```

Notice that the actual collection is `/db/wedding`, and not `wedding`. Verify that the collection was added by typing

```
xindiceadmin list_collections -c /db
```

Notice that we want to know about the collections in the `/db` context. You should see the following results:

```
        system
        wedding

Total collections: 2
```

Addressing the Matter

If you added the sample `addressbook` collection as part of installation, you should also see it in this list.

Now that we have a collection, we're ready to start adding documents to it.

Adding Documents

To actually add a document to the database, we'll use the `xindice` application. For example, the event information and guest list from Chapter 19 is stored in a file called `guests.xml`, so to add it to the database we could type

```
xindice add_document -c /db/wedding -f guests.xml -n guests
```

Let's take a look at what's happening here. As before, we've specified the program (`xindice`) and the action (`add_document`), as well as the collection context. In this case, the collection context is the `/db/wedding` collection that we added previously.

Next, using the `-f` switch, we've designated the file that we want to add. The final parameter, `-n guests`, specifies the name, or key, that is assigned to this resource. This key is crucial for retrieving the information later, so in most cases, you'll want to specify it directly. If you don't, the database will create a long random string to use as the key.

In some cases, however, specifying a key is not convenient. For example, we could add an entire directory of files using

```
xindice add_multiple_documents -c /db/wedding -f weddingdocs
```

In this case, the database adds all the files in the `weddingdocs` directory, assigning each a key that matches the filename.

We can also remove files from the database using the command line. For example, if the file `flyer.xml` had been in the `weddingdocs` directory when the preceding command was run, we could have removed it from the database using

```
xindice delete_document -c /db/wedding -n flyer.xml
```

In this case, `flyer.xml` refers to the key that was automatically assigned by the database, and not necessarily to the name of the original file, though of course in this case they're the same.

Retrieving Documents

All right, we've got at least one document in the database. Retrieving it is as simple as storing it:

```
xindice retrieve_document -c /db/wedding -n guests -f returnedguests.xml
```

Remember, when we originally stored this document, we gave it a key named `guests`, so that's what we use on the command line. In this case, we're outputting the results to a file, `returnedguests.xml`, but `xindice` will output the results to the screen if you don't provide a name.

Running Queries

You can also use the command-line interface to run a query against the database. For example, you can get the names of guests at the wedding:

```
xindice xpath -c /db/wedding -q /event/guests/guest/name
```

The result is a series of document fragments:

```
<?xml version="1.0"?>
<name xmlns:src="http://xml.apache.org/xindice/Query" src:col="/db/wedding"
                                       src:key="guests" />
<?xml version="1.0"?>
<name xmlns:src="http://xml.apache.org/xindice/Query" src:col="/db/wedding"
                                       src:key="guests">Narissa</name>
<?xml version="1.0"?>
<name xmlns:src="http://xml.apache.org/xindice/Query" src:col="/db/wedding"
                                       src:key="guests">Lars</name>
<?xml version="1.0"?>
<name xmlns:src="http://xml.apache.org/xindice/Query" src:col="/db/wedding"
                                       src:key="guests">Shoopfuma</name>
<?xml version="1.0"?>
<name xmlns:src="http://xml.apache.org/xindice/Query" src:col="/db/wedding"
                                       src:key="guests">Borkot</name>
<?xml version="1.0"?>
<name xmlns:src="http://xml.apache.org/xindice/Query" src:col="/db/wedding"
                                       src:key="guests" />
```

Each of these fragments is called a resource. (I've tweaked the formatting a little here to accommodate this book's line length restrictions.) Notice that a new namespace, aliased by `src:`, is present in each element and provides the collection information as well as the key for the document to which the element belongs. Later, when performing a query through the API, we can retrieve that information.

Using the XML:DB API

The database is useful for simply storing information and retrieving it again, but it would be much more useful if we could build these actions into an application. Specifically, it would be nice to be able to insert and retrieve information as DOM **Document**s or as SAX streams.

In this section, we're going to look at the XML:DB API. Developed by the XML:DB Initiative, it's intended as a common API for NXDs, and is implemented by most of the open source native XML databases. Commercial databases may or may not follow suit, but in any case, some sort of standard is needed, and that standard will likely look something like this in the end.

If you installed Xindice, you already have an XML:DB implementation available. If you installed another database that supports it instead, you may need to download the reference implementation from `http://www.xmldb.org/xapi/index.html`. (This page also includes a link to a version that sits on top of JDBC databases.)

At the time of this writing, the only implementation available is written in Java, but the concepts should be the same for any language.

Connecting to the Database and the Collection

Before we can do anything, of course, we need to connect to the database, and before we can do any actual work, we need to connect to a specific collection. Listing 20.1 shows the basic application.

LISTING 20.1   Connecting to the Database

```
import org.xmldb.api.base.Collection;
import org.xmldb.api.base.Database;
import org.xmldb.api.DatabaseManager;

public class ManageDocs {
    public static void main(String[] args) throws Exception {
        Collection collection = null;
        try {
            String driver = "org.apache.xindice.client.xmldb.DatabaseImpl";
            Class driverClass = Class.forName(driver);

            Database database = (Database)driverClass.newInstance();
            DatabaseManager.registerDatabase(database);
            collection =
                DatabaseManager.getCollection("xmldb:xindice:///db/wedding");

        } catch (Exception e) {
            System.out.println("Problem using database: "+e.getMessage());
        } finally {
            if (collection != null) {
                collection.close();
            }
        }
    }
}
```

Let's take this one step at a time. First, we need to determine the driver. As with SAX in Chapter 5, "XML Streams: The Simple API for XML (SAX)," the driver is the class that actually does the work. In the case of Xindice, that class is `org.apache.xindice.client.xmldb.DatabaseImpl`, but if you're working with another database you may need a different class name. From there, we can use the driver to get an instance of the `Database` object itself.

The `DatabaseManager` class includes a static method to register the database for use, so that when we use the `DatabaseManager` to request a collection, that's the database that it searches.

Next we have to get access to a specific collection. Like JDBC, XML:DB uses a URI to determine the location of the database and location. Let's take a closer look at the URI:

```
xmldb:xindice:///db/wedding
```

We can break this into several pieces:

- `xmldb:` is the main protocol, signaling that we're accessing a database using XML:DB.

- `xindice://` is the subprotocol, indicating that we're using the Xindice database. This is similar to the `jdbc:odbc:` chaining you see when you use a JDBC-ODBC bridge.

- `/db/wedding` is the actual collection context, just as we would have entered it on the command line.

In this way, we get access to the specific collection we're looking for.

Notice that we close the connection in the `finally` block. This way, even if there are errors, the connection should be released.

Adding a Resource

Now that we've got the basic application, we can start using it. The most basic task is to add resources to the database. We already added the wedding information and guest list using the command line, so in this section we're going to re-add the flyer (which we deleted) and add a menu and the XML for the invitation.

We've got three different options. The first is to simply add the document text, the second is to use a DOM object, and the third is to use a SAX stream. We'll see each in action.

First let's add the document directly, as shown in Listing 20.2.

LISTING 20.2   Adding the Document Directly

```
import org.xmldb.api.base.Collection;
import org.xmldb.api.base.Database;
import org.xmldb.api.DatabaseManager;
import org.xmldb.api.modules.XMLResource;

import java.io.File;
import java.io.FileInputStream;

public class ManageDocs {
    public static void main(String[] args) throws Exception {
        Collection collection = null;
        try {
            String driver = "org.apache.xindice.client.xmldb.DatabaseImpl";
            Class c = Class.forName(driver);

            Database database = (Database) c.newInstance();
            DatabaseManager.registerDatabase(database);
            collection =
                DatabaseManager.getCollection("xmldb:xindice:///db/wedding");

            String documentText = file2string("menu.xml");
            String documentKey = "menu";
```

LISTING 20.2   *Continued*

```
            XMLResource resource =
                (XMLResource) collection.createResource(documentKey,
                                                XMLResource.RESOURCE_TYPE);

            resource.setContent(documentText);
            collection.storeResource(resource);

        } catch (Exception e) {
            System.out.println("Problem using database: "+e.getMessage());
            e.printStackTrace();
        }
        finally {
            if (collection != null) {
                collection.close();
            }
        }
    }

    public static String file2string(String inFileName)
    {
        String outString = "";
        try {
            File inFile = new File(inFileName);
            FileInputStream inFileStream = new FileInputStream(inFile);

            byte[] streamBuffer = new byte[(int)inFile.length()];

            inFileStream.read(streamBuffer);
            inFileStream.close();

            outString = new String(streamBuffer);
        } catch (Exception e) {
            System.out.println("Problem reading the file: "+e.getMessage());
        }
        return outString;
    }

}
```

The idea here is to create a resource, which is then stored in the collection.

To create the resource itself, we need two pieces of information: the XML to be stored and the key to store it under. XML:DB takes the XML as a string, so I've included a simple `file2string()` method that takes the filename and returns a `String` object that represents the text within the file. Next, we designate the `menu` key.

We then create the resource itself through the collection's `createResource()` method. This method takes the key and a resource type. In this case, we're specifying that we want an `XMLResource`, but in practice, an NXD can store other information, such as binary files, as resources. The `createResource()` method creates the resource with the appropriate key, but we still have to populate it.

The **setContent()** method takes the **documentText** to populate the resource, which we then store using the collection's **storeResource()** method.

We can check to make sure that the document was stored from the command line by typing

```
xindice retrieve_document -c /db/wedding -n menu
```

Listing 20.3 shows the results.

LISTING 20.3   The Contents of `menu.xml`

```xml
<menu>
    <course coursename="hors d'oeuvres">
        <food>Greech Eggs</food>
        <food>Pyminca Squares</food>
        <food>Assorted Wagraphos</food>
        <food>Silraga Puffs</food>
        <food>Roasted Hagrop on Toasted Tenji</food>
    </course>
    <course coursename="soup">
        <food>Arvendo with Leaping Noodles</food>
    </course>
    <course coursename="main">
        <food>Floop Floop Bird Stuffed with Reckleberries</food>
        <food>Roasted Nera Beast</food>
        <food>Shivering Camdids</food>
        <food>Braised Tillentecks</food>
    </course>
    <course coursename="dessert">
        <food>Traditional Ordeal Pie</food>
        <food>Dewdotca Cake</food>
        <food>Candied Velpa Wings</food>
    </course>
</menu>
```

We also have the option to store a DOM **Document**. In Listing 20.4, we parse the `flyer.xml` file to create a **Document**, then use it to populate an **XMLResource**.

LISTING 20.4   Adding a DOM **Document**

```java
...
import javax.xml.parsers.DocumentBuilder;
import javax.xml.parsers.DocumentBuilderFactory;
import org.w3c.dom.Document;

public class ManageDocs {
    public static void main(String[] args) throws Exception {
...
        collection =
            DatabaseManager.getCollection("xmldb:xindice:///db/wedding");

        Document documentObject = null;
```

LISTING 20.4 Continued

```
        try {
            DocumentBuilderFactory dbf = DocumentBuilderFactory.newInstance();
            DocumentBuilder db = dbf.newDocumentBuilder();
            documentObject = db.parse("flyer.xml");
        } catch (Exception e) {
            System.out.print("Problem parsing the file.");
        }

        String documentKey = "flyer";

        XMLResource resource =
            (XMLResource) collection.createResource(documentKey,
                                                    XMLResource.RESOURCE_TYPE);

        resource.setContentAsDOM(documentObject);
        collection.storeResource(resource);

    } catch (Exception e) {
        System.out.println("Problem using database: "+e.getMessage());
    ...
    }
```

Overall, the process is the same as adding the document directly; we create a resource with the appropriate key, set the content, and store it in the database. The only difference here is that we need to create the actual DOM **Document**, but in practice this will be part of the overall application.

Adding a document using SAX is a little different, but still fairly straightforward, as shown in Listing 20.5.

LISTING 20.5 Adding a Document Using SAX

```
...
import org.xml.sax.XMLReader;
import org.xml.sax.helpers.XMLReaderFactory;
import org.xml.sax.ContentHandler;
import org.xml.sax.InputSource;

public class ManageDocs {
    public static void main(String[] args) throws Exception {
        Collection collection = null;
        try {
            String driver = "org.apache.xindice.client.xmldb.DatabaseImpl";
            Class c = Class.forName(driver);

            Database database = (Database) c.newInstance();
            DatabaseManager.registerDatabase(database);
            collection =
                DatabaseManager.getCollection("xmldb:xindice:///db/wedding");
```

LISTING 20.5   Continued

```
                 String documentKey = "invitation";
                 String documentName = "invitation.xml";

                 XMLResource resource =
                     (XMLResource) collection.createResource(documentKey,
                                                 XMLResource.RESOURCE_TYPE);

                 ContentHandler handler = resource.setContentAsSAX();

                 String parserClass = "org.apache.crimson.parser.XMLReaderImpl";
                 XMLReader reader = XMLReaderFactory.createXMLReader(parserClass);

                 reader.setContentHandler(handler);
                 reader.parse(new InputSource(documentName));

                 collection.storeResource(resource);

             } catch (Exception e) {
                 System.out.println("Problem using database: "+e.getMessage());
        ...
        }
```

As described in Chapter 5, using a SAX stream involves creating a parser, or XMLReader, that sends events to a ContentHandler. In this case, the ContentHandler is provided by the XMLResource object itself, and is returned by the setContentAsSAX() method. Once we have the handler, we create the XMLReader—don't forget to substitute the appropriate SAX driver class for your installation—and then set the handler object as the ContentHandler for the reader object. At this point, we can parse the file and the events will populate the resource.

Finally, we have a populated resource just like the first two, and we can store it in the collection as normal.

Returning a Resource

Now we've stored a full-text document, a DOM Document, and a SAX stream. How do we get them out again?

The process is actually very straightforward, as long as you know the key under which the information was stored in the first place. Basically, we retrieve the resource using the key, and then get the content using the appropriate method.

Listing 20.6 shows the retrieval as a string of text.

LISTING 20.6   Retrieving a Document as a String

```
import org.xmldb.api.base.Collection;
import org.xmldb.api.base.Database;
import org.xmldb.api.DatabaseManager;
import org.xmldb.api.modules.XMLResource;
```

LISTING 20.6 Continued

```
import java.io.File;
import java.io.FileInputStream;

import org.w3c.dom.Document;

import org.xml.sax.XMLReader;
import org.xml.sax.helpers.XMLReaderFactory;
import org.xml.sax.ContentHandler;
import org.xml.sax.InputSource;

public class ManageDocs {
    public static void main(String[] args) throws Exception {
        Collection collection = null;
        try {
            String driver = "org.apache.xindice.client.xmldb.DatabaseImpl";
            Class c = Class.forName(driver);

            Database database = (Database) c.newInstance();
            DatabaseManager.registerDatabase(database);
            collection =
                DatabaseManager.getCollection("xmldb:xindice:///db/wedding");

            String documentKey = "invitation";

            XMLResource resource = (XMLResource)collection.getResource(documentKey);
            String documentText = (String)resource.getContent();

            System.out.println(documentText);

        } catch (Exception e) {
            System.out.println("Problem using database: "+e.getMessage());
            e.printStackTrace();
        }
        finally {
            if (collection != null) {
                collection.close();
            }
        }
    }
}
```

Notice that the application is the same overall; the only change we're making is to the section that actually deals with the document. We simply retrieve the resource from the collection by its key, then retrieve the content from the resource. The results are shown in Listing 20.7.

LISTING 20.7 The Contents of the `invitation` Resource

```
<?xml version="1.0"?>
<invitation>
You and a Guest are Invited to the Great Ordeal and Wedding of
<person><name>Alora Felisecort</name></person> and
```

LISTING 20.7   Continued

```
<person><name>Suliggort</name> <title>the Wise</title></person>
To Take Place On The 137th of Brinkish Promptly At The 16th Hour
of Meire. Please Reply By The 201st Of Coretan If You Plan To
Attend.  The Reception Will Be Held Immediately Following The Ordeal
</invitation>
```

The process of retrieving the information as a DOM `Document` is virtually identical, as shown
in Listing 20.8.

LISTING 20.8   Retrieving a DOM `Document`

```
...
        collection =
            DatabaseManager.getCollection("xmldb:xindice:///db/wedding");

        String documentKey = "menu";

        XMLResource resource = (XMLResource)collection.getResource(documentKey);
        Document documentObject = (Document)resource.getContentAsDOM();

        System.out.println(documentObject.getDocumentElement().getNodeName());

    } catch (Exception e) {
        System.out.println("Problem using database: "+e.getMessage());
...
```

In this case, the only difference is that we're retrieving the content as a DOM `Document`, which
we can work with programmatically. In fact, we could easily retrieve a `Document` object,
manipulate it, and store it back in the database, as shown in Listing 20.9.

LISTING 20.9   Updating a DOM `Document`

```
...
        collection =
            DatabaseManager.getCollection("xmldb:xindice:///db/wedding");

        String documentKey = "menu";

        XMLResource resource = (XMLResource)collection.getResource(documentKey);
        Document documentObject = (Document)resource.getContentAsDOM();

        //Operations to work with the Document

        resource.setContentAsDOM(documentObject);
        collection.storeResource(resource);

    } catch (Exception e) {
        System.out.println("Problem using database: "+e.getMessage());
...
```

In this chapter, however, we'll stick to manipulating the data using XQuery and XUpdate.

Finally, we can retrieve the content of a resource as a SAX stream. In order to do that, however, we first need to create a `ContentHandler` class, as in Listing 20.10.

LISTING 20.10   The Retrieval `ContentHandler`

```
import org.xml.sax.helpers.DefaultHandler;

public class TextProcessor extends DefaultHandler
{
   public TextProcessor ()
   {
      super();
   }

   public void startDocument() {
      System.out.println("Start flyer text:");
      System.out.println("-----------------");
   }

   public void endDocument() {
      System.out.println("-----------------");
      System.out.println("End flyer text:");
   }

   public void characters (char[] ch, int start, int length)
   {
      System.out.println(new String(ch, start, length));
   }
}
```

In this case, we're dealing with a very simple `ContentHandler` that outputs start and end delimiters, as well as the text of any elements. To use it, we can send events to it, as in Listing 20.11.

LISTING 20.11   Retrieving the Data as a SAX Stream

```
   ...
           collection =
              DatabaseManager.getCollection("xmldb:xindice:///db/wedding");

           String documentKey = "flyer";

           ContentHandler textHandler = new TextProcessor();

           XMLResource resource = (XMLResource)collection.getResource(documentKey);
           resource.getContentAsSAX(textHandler);

        } catch (Exception e) {
           System.out.println("Problem using database: "+e.getMessage());

   ...
```

Listing 20.12 shows the results.

LISTING 20.12   The Results of the SAX Stream

```
Start flyer text:
- - - - - - - - - - - - - - - -



        Tickets now on sale for the Great Nuptial Ordeal
        of
Alora Felisecort
 and

Suliggort

the Wise
 !



        This promises to be Alora's greatest concert ever.
        The Ordeal takes place on the 137th of Brinkish promptly
        at the 16th hour of Meire in the great hall of the Vanguard
        Station Resort.
Don't miss the greatest concert
        and ordeal of the millennium.  Tickets start at 80 Vazcreds for
        balcony seats.  Order now!



        Who will win the great Ordeal?  If you don't show,
        you won't know!



No bets taken after the Looloo Birds screech.


Be there, or be frobish!



- - - - - - - - - - - - - - - -
End flyer text:
```

We can also retrieve portions of a document based on an XPath query.

Querying Resources

We've actually gotten quite a bit of use out of the API so far, and we haven't executed a single query. In fact, what we've seen so far is known as Level 0 compliance with the XML:DB API: the implementation of resources, and the ability to add and retrieve them.

Now we're going to look at Level 1, the implementation of services. At the time of this writing, there are two basic services—XPathQueryService and XUpdateService—but more could easily be added. The idea is that a service actually performs an operation on a collection.

In the section titled "XUpdate," we'll talk about using the application to perform updates, but for now we'll just look at the use of the XPathQueryService to retrieve resources (or parts of resources) based on an XPath query.

In Listing 20.13, we retrieve the names of all the wedding guests.

LISTING 20.13   Performing an XPath Query Using the API

```
import org.xmldb.api.base.Collection;
import org.xmldb.api.base.Database;
import org.xmldb.api.DatabaseManager;
import org.xmldb.api.modules.XMLResource;
import org.xmldb.api.modules.XPathQueryService;
import org.xmldb.api.base.ResourceSet;
import org.xmldb.api.base.ResourceIterator;

public class ManageDocs {
    public static void main(String[] args) throws Exception {
        Collection collection = null;
        try {
            String driver = "org.apache.xindice.client.xmldb.DatabaseImpl";
            Class c = Class.forName(driver);

            Database database = (Database) c.newInstance();
            DatabaseManager.registerDatabase(database);
            collection =
                DatabaseManager.getCollection("xmldb:xindice:///db/wedding");

            String xpathQueryString = "//name";

            XPathQueryService service =
                    (XPathQueryService)collection.getService("XPathQueryService",
                                                             "1.0");
            ResourceSet resultSet = service.query(xpathQueryString);

            ResourceIterator results = resultSet.getIterator();
            while (results.hasMoreResources()) {
                XMLResource resource = (XMLResource) results.nextResource();
                String resultText = (String)resource.getContent();
                System.out.println(resultText);
            }

        } catch (Exception e) {
            System.out.println("Problem using database: "+e.getMessage());
            e.printStackTrace();
        }
        finally {
            if (collection != null) {
```

LISTING 20.13 Continued

```
            collection.close();
        }
      }
    }
}
```

After creating the actual query string, we create the query service using the `getService()` method. We can use this method to create any supported service by using the correct service identifier.

Executing the query on the service returns a `ResourceSet`, which contains each of the returned nodes as document fragments. We can use this set to return an `Iterator` object. Using the `Iterator` object, we loop through each of the results, getting content from each and outputting it.

Listing 20.14 shows the results.

LISTING 20.14 The Query Results

```
<?xml version="1.0"?>
<name xmlns:src="http://xml.apache.org/xindice/Query" src:col="/db/wedding"
src:key="flyer">Alora Felisecort</name>
<?xml version="1.0"?>
<name xmlns:src="http://xml.apache.org/xindice/Query" src:col="/db/wedding"
src:key="flyer">Suliggort</name>
<?xml version="1.0"?>
<name xmlns:src="http://xml.apache.org/xindice/Query" src:col="/db/wedding"
src:key="guests" />
<?xml version="1.0"?>
<name xmlns:src="http://xml.apache.org/xindice/Query" src:col="/db/wedding"
src:key="guests">Narissa</name>
<?xml version="1.0"?>
<name xmlns:src="http://xml.apache.org/xindice/Query" src:col="/db/wedding"
src:key="guests">Lars</name>
<?xml version="1.0"?>
<name xmlns:src="http://xml.apache.org/xindice/Query" src:col="/db/wedding"
src:key="guests">Shoopfuma</name>
<?xml version="1.0"?>
<name xmlns:src="http://xml.apache.org/xindice/Query" src:col="/db/wedding"
src:key="guests">Borkot</name>
<?xml version="1.0"?>
<name xmlns:src="http://xml.apache.org/xindice/Query" src:col="/db/wedding"
src:key="guests" />
<?xml version="1.0"?>
<name xmlns:src="http://xml.apache.org/xindice/Query" src:col="/db/wedding"
src:key="invitation">Alora Felisecort</name>
<?xml version="1.0"?>
<name xmlns:src="http://xml.apache.org/xindice/Query" src:col="/db/wedding"
src:key="invitation">Suliggort</name>
```

Notice that these results come from several different documents. Because we weren't very specific about the XPath we were looking for, XML:DB returns every **name** element in the collection. Using the **getDocumentId()** method, we can programmatically determine the document that a resource is part of:

...

```
ResourceIterator results = resultSet.getIterator();
while (results.hasMoreResources()) {
   XMLResource resource = (XMLResource) results.nextResource();
   String thisResource = (String)resource.getDocumentId();
   System.out.println(thisResource);
}
```

...

XQuery 1.0 and XPath 2.0

Throughout this book, every time we've wanted to select a portion of a document, we've used XPath 1.0, and in general, it's served us well. In this section we're going to look at another type of query, XQuery 1.0. Why do we need it?

Well, after a couple of years of service, it's become clear that there are several areas that are lacking in XPath 1.0, including grouping, sorting, type management, and joins between information sets. XPath 1.0 also lacks a means for including markup within the results of an expression, and is in desperate need of a few more robust functions that will enable it to do such things as search for and replace strings. (The **translate()** function performed part of this task, but not very well, and only for single characters.)

The need for expanded capabilities led to the creation of XPath 2.0, and XQuery 1.0, which builds on it. In fact, the two are so tightly integrated that they come from the same Working Group—XPath 2.0 is a joint project of the XML Query Working Group and the XSL Working Group—and some of the recommendations share source documents.

In this section, we're going to look at XQuery 1.0, which at the time of this writing is at the Working Draft stage. (The current version is dated April 30, 2002.) At the moment, there are no good open source implementations, but several commercial databases such as X-Hive/DB have implemented it, and have online demos. These demos use a specific set of documents and queries known as the XML Query Use Cases, but while you can enter your own queries, you can't use your own source documents.

What all this means is that if you've downloaded a database that supports XQuery, you'll be able to run these queries directly. Otherwise, you'll need to just follow along for now and learn how the queries work so you'll be ready when your database does support them.

FLWR Statements

Perhaps the most noticeable difference between XPath 1.0 and XQuery 1.0 is the ability to create FLWR statements. FLWR (pronounced "flower") is an acronym for **for-let-where-return**, a set of clauses that can be mixed and matched to provide a powerful environment for selecting specific information.

In this section, we'll use the event information file listing guests of the wedding, reproduced in Listing 20.15.

LISTING 20.15   The Source File: `guests.xml`

```xml
<event>
    <eventName>The Great Nuptial Ordeal Ceremony</eventName>
    <eventType>wedding</eventType>
    <eventDate>Brinkish/137/2356</eventDate>
    <eventTime>16th Hour of Meire</eventTime>
    <wedders>
        <spouse>Alora Felisecort</spouse>
        <spouse>Suliggort the Wise</spouse>
    </wedders>
    <officiant>Hachalax The Three Headed Venusian</officiant>
    <entertainment>
        <warmup>Morpho and his Swinging Panorama Band</warmup>
        <headliner>Zaphrunda, the Effluviant Singing Head</headliner>
    </entertainment>
    <guests>
        <guest>
            <type>group</type>
            <quantity>37</quantity>
            <name></name>
            <title>High Sarino</title>
            <planet>Galundia</planet>
        </guest>
        <guest>
            <type>single</type>
            <quantity>1</quantity>
            <name>Narissa</name>
            <title></title>
            <planet>Swobogda</planet>
        </guest>
        <guest>
            <type>single</type>
            <quantity>1</quantity>
            <name>Lars</name>
            <title>the Repulsive</title>
            <planet>Swobogda</planet>
        </guest>
        <guest>
            <type>single</type>
            <quantity>1</quantity>
            <name>Shoopfuma</name>
            <title>the Irradiant</title>
            <planet>Merlor</planet>
        </guest>
        <guest>
            <type>single</type>
            <quantity>1</quantity>
            <name>Borkot</name>
            <title>The Great One, All High Bumbledoop</title>
```

LISTING 20.15   Continued

```
                <planet>Merlor</planet>
            </guest>
            <guest>
                <type>single</type>
                <quantity>1</quantity>
                <name></name>
                <title>Calio Grande</title>
                <planet>Jungonia</planet>
            </guest>
        </guests>
</event>
```

for and return

Let's start with a basic query using just **for** and **return** clauses, as in Listing 20.16.

LISTING 20.16   A Simple for/return Query

```
for $names in document("guests.xml")//guest/name
return {
    $names
}
```

We start out with a **for** clause, which binds a variable, **$names**, to each of the results of the XPath 2.0 query

```
document("guests.xml")//guest/name
```

This query starts with a data source that represents the document **guests.xml**. We'll talk more about sources in the section titled "Sources," but for now understand that the **document()** function returns the document root of that document. From there, we're simply getting all the **guest** descendants of the root, and their **name** child elements, just as in an XPath 1.0 query.

The **for** clause works like a **for-each** loop in other programming languages. For each node in the sequence returned by the expression, the **return** clause is executed.

Sequences Versus Node-sets

One of the major changes between XPath 1.0 and XPath 2.0 is the move from node-sets (unordered sets of nodes with no duplicates) to sequences (ordered sets of nodes in which duplicates are allowed).

Listing 20.17 shows the results.

LISTING 20.17   Results of a Simple for/return Statement

```
<name></name>
<name>Narissa</name>
<name>Lars</name>
```

LISTING 20.17   Continued

```
<name>Shoopfuma</name>
<name>Borkot</name>
<name></name>
```

In the XQuery expression, `$name` is a bound variable. It's bound to a node in the sequence. This means that we can include it within an XPath expression. For example, we could have achieved the same results with the statement

```
for $guests in document("guests.xml")//guest
return {
    $guests/name
}
```

In this case, the `$guests` variable is bound to each `guest` element, so each time the `return` clause is executed, the `name` child of the `$guests` variable is returned.

We can see the execution path a little more clearly if we add some structure to the results, as in Listing 20.18.

LISTING 20.18   Adding Structure to the Statement

```
<guests>
{
for $guests in document("guests.xml")//guest
return
    <person>{ $guests/name }</person>
}
</guests>
```

XQuery's capability to add elements to the output is similar to that of XSLT, though of course the two are meant to be complementary. Looking at the results in Listing 20.19, we can see that the `return` clause executes for each node in the sequence.

LISTING 20.19   Adding Structure to the Statement: Results

```
<guests>
    <person><name></name></person>
    <person><name>Narissa</name></person>
    <person><name>Lars</name></person>
    <person><name>Shoopfuma</name></person>
    <person><name>Borkot</name></person>
    <person><name></name></person>
</guests>
```

let

The `let` clause is similar to the `for` clause, but rather than binding to each individual node in the sequence, as the variable in a `for` clause does, the variable in a `let` clause binds to the entire set. We can see this effect if we run the query in Listing 20.20.

LISTING 20.20 Using a `let` Clause

```
let $guests := document("guests.xml")//guest
return
    <guestList>{ $guests/name } { $guests/title }</guestList>
```

The curly braces indicate content that should be evaluated, rather than simply output, as you can see in the results in Listing 20.21.

LISTING 20.21 Using a `let` Clause: Results

```
<guestList>
<name></name> <title>High Sarino</title>
<name>Narissa</name> <title></title>
<name>Lars</name> <title>the Repulsive</title>
<name>Shoopfuma</name> <title>the Irradiant</title>
<name>Borkot</name> <title>The Great One, All High Bumbledoop</title>
<name></name> <title>Calio Grande</title>
</guestList>
```

Notice a couple of things here. First of all, because the entire sequence of nodes is assigned to the `$guests` variable, there is only one `guestList` element, so the `return` clause executes only once. Second, we left a space between the two evaluated sections, and it appears within the document. You can use this to output any static content.

where

The `where` clause enables us to restrict the output to nodes that fulfill certain conditions. For example, we can restrict the output to only those guests who are coming as a group, as in Listing 20.22.

LISTING 20.22 Using a `where` Clause

```
<guests>
{
for $guests in document("guests.xml")//guest
where $guests/type = "group"
return
    <group>
        { $guests/title/text() }s of { $guests/planet/text() }: { $guests/text() }
    </group>
}
</guests>
```

In this case, each time `$guests` is bound to a `guest` element, the `where` clause determines whether the `return` statement should be executed. If the current value of `$guests` fulfills the `where` condition, `return` executes. If not, it doesn't. Listing 20.23 shows the results.

LISTING 20.23   Using a *where* Clause: Results

```
<guests>
    <group>
        High Sarinos of Galundia: 37
    </group>
</guests>
```

Sorting

XQuery also allows us to sort the sequence returned by a particular clause. For example, we can sort the returned data by `planet`, as in Listing 20.24.

LISTING 20.24   Sorting the Data

```
<guests>
{
for $guests in document("guests.xml")//guest
where not ($guests/name/text() = "")
return
    <person>
        { $guests/name }
        { $guests/title }
        { $guests/planet }
    </person>
sortby($guests/planet)
}
</guests>
```

Listing 20.25 shows the results, sorted by `planet`.

LISTING 20.25   Sorting the Data: Results

```
<guests>
    <person>
        <name></name>
        <title>High Sarino</title>
        <planet>Galundia</planet>
    </person>
    <person>
        <name></name>
        <title>Calio Grande</title>
        <planet>Jungonia</planet>
    </person>
    <person>
        <name>Shoopfuma</name>
        <title>the Irradiant</title>
        <planet>Merlor</planet>
    </person>
    <person>
        <name>Borkot</name>
        <title>The Great One, All High Bumbledoop</title>
```

LISTING 20.25   Continued

```
            <planet>Merlor</planet>
        </person>
        <person>
            <name>Narissa</name>
            <title></title>
            <planet>Swobogda</planet>
        </person>
        <person>
            <name>Lars</name>
            <title>the Repulsive</title>
            <planet>Swobogda</planet>
        </person>
    </guests>
```

FLWR Clause Mix and Match

There's no particular order required for the clauses in a FLWR statement. For example, Listing 20.26 shows a statement that gathers all the single guests and outputs their names in uppercase using the built-in upper-case() function.

LISTING 20.26   Mixing FLWR Clauses

```
<guestList>
{
    let $eventInfo := document("events.xml")/event
    for $guest in $eventInfo/guests/guest
    where $guest/type = "single"
    return
    {
        let $upperName := upper-case($guest/name/text())
        return
            <person>$upperName</person>
    }
}
</guestList>
```

In this case, the $eventInfo variable is bound to the sequence of one event node (because there is only one). The $guest variable is then bound to each guest element in the $eventInfo sequence, and for each one the where clause determines whether the return should be executed. If so, the nested let clause uses the upper-case() function (we'll discuss this and other functions in the upcoming "Functions" section) to bind a text value to $upperName, which is then returned by the nested return clause. The results are shown in Listing 20.27.

LISTING 20.27   Mixing FLWR Clauses: Results

```
<guestList>
    <person>NARISSA</person>
    <person>LARS</person>
```

LISTING 20.27   Continued

```
        <person>SHOOPFUMA</person>
        <person>BORKOT</person>
        <person></person>
</guestList>
```

Sources

One of the advantages XQuery and XPath 2.0 offer is the ability to accept input from a variety of sources. Specifically, functions that can determine the source of data for an expression include

- `document()`—The `document()` function returns the document root for the document specified by the URI used as an argument. For example, in this chapter we've used

  `document("guests.xml")`

  but we could just as easily have used

  `document("http://www.example.com/guests.xml")`

- `collection()`—The `collection()` function returns a collection of documents or document fragments. For example, if Xindice supported it, we might be able to evaluate the XPath expression

  `collection("/db/wedding")/menu/course/food`

- `input()`—The behavior of the `input()` function is determined largely by the application that implements it. Typically, it returns a sequence of nodes of some sort, which serves the same purpose as the sequence returned by `document()` or `collection()`. In other words, you might see an expression such as

  `input()//course`

Multiple Sources and Joins

One of the advantages of being able to explicitly set the source for an expression (rather than relying on the context document, as in XPath 1.0) is the ability to combine sources within a single query. For example, we could create a query that shows all the documents in the collection that mention any of the wedding guests' spouses, as in Listing 20.28.

LISTING 20.28   Combining Multiple Sources

```
for $spouse in document("guests.xml")//spouse
   for $mention in collection("/db/wedding")//person[name=$spouse]
   return
      <mention spouse="{$spouse}">
         { $mention/parent::node() }
      </mention>
```

In this case, we're starting out with all the `spouse` elements in the `guests.xml` document, and for each of them, we're checking all `person` elements in the `wedding` collection that have a `name` child that matches that `spouse`.

If we find one, we're outputting a `mention` element that includes the spouse's name as the value of the `spouse` attribute and the parent of the `person` element as the content. If we run this query, the results should look something like Listing 20.29.

LISTING 20.29 Combining Multiple Sources: Results

```
    <mention spouse="Alora Felisecort">
  <paragraph>
    Tickets now on sale for the Great Nuptial Ordeal
    of <person><name>Alora Felisecort</name></person> and
    <person><name>Suliggort</name> <title>the Wise</title></person>!
  </paragraph>
    </mention>
    <mention spouse="Alora Felisecort">
<invitation>
You and a Guest are Invited to the Great Ordeal and Wedding of
<person><name>Alora Felisecort</name></person> and
<person><name>Suliggort</name> <title>the Wise</title></person>
To Take Place On The 137th of Brinkish Promptly At The 16th Hour
of Meire. Please Reply By The 201st Of Coretan If You Plan To
Attend.  The Reception Will Be Held Immediately Following The Ordeal
</invitation>
    </mention>
```

The `$mention` variable refers to the `person` element, so the element containing the `person` element is output.

Notice here that we've run into a possible complication due to differing schemas for the two documents. Because Suliggort the Wise is listed as a spouse with his title, no matches come up for him because we're just looking for the value of the `name` element. This is one example of why it's important to have an organization-wide schema for your data.

Conditional Processing

Another advantage of XQuery over XPath 1.0 is the ability to do conditional processing. In addition to the `where` clause, we can add `if-then` statements to the `return` clause, as shown in Listing 20.30.

LISTING 20.30 Using an `if-then` Statement

```
<guests>
{
for $guests in document("guests.xml")//guest
return
  <person>
    {
```

LISTING 20.30   Continued

```
        if ($guests/name != "") {
            $guests/name
        }
    }{
        if ($guests/title != "") {
            $guests/title
        }
    }{ $guests/planet }
  </person>
sortby($guests/planet)
}
</guests>
```

This statement has three evaluated expressions. In the first, if the **name** is not empty, it's displayed. In the second, if the **title** isn't empty, it's displayed. In the third, the **planet** is displayed. Listing 20.31 shows the results.

LISTING 20.31   Using an `if`-`then` Statement: Results

```
<guests>
  <person>
    <title>High Sarino</title><planet>Galundia</planet>
  </person>
  <person>
    <title>Calio Grande</title><planet>Jungonia</planet>
  </person>
  <person>
    <name>Shoopfuma</name><title>the Irradiant</title><planet>Merlor</planet>
  </person>
  <person>
    <name>Borkot</name><title>The Great One, All High Bumbledoop</title><planet>
Merlor</planet>
  </person>
  <person>
    <name>Narissa</name><planet>Swobogda</planet>
  </person>
  <person>
    <name>Lars</name><title>the Repulsive</title><planet>Swobogda</planet>
  </person>
</guests>
```

Type Management

XPath 1.0 recognizes four types: node-sets, strings, Booleans, and numbers. If you want to do anything that involves other types, such as dates or durations, you have your hands full. XPath 2.0, on the other hand, incorporates all the built-in types that are part of XML Schema, such as **long**, **int**, **date**, **duration**, and so on, and includes functions for dealing with them, as discussed in the next section.

XQuery is also type-aware, in that it can recognize types that have been defined within an XML schema and react appropriately using the `typeswitch` expression. XQuery also offers the ability to cast a node from one type to another, as well as other type management abilities that are beyond the scope of this chapter.

Functions

Version 1.0 of XPath includes a grand total of 27 functions: 7 node-set functions, 10 string functions, 5 Boolean functions, and 5 number functions.

Version 2.0 of XPath includes 64 functions just for dealing with dates.

We could spend an entire chapter on the new functions, but we don't have that luxury, so let's just hit the highlights. XPath 2.0 functions fall into three categories:

- **Constructors** create a value of a particular type out of a value of another type. (For instance, a constructor can create an `integer` out of a `string` that represents an integer.)

- **Functions** return a value based on another single value (such as a function that returns the uppercase version of a `string`).

- **Operators and comparisons** typically return a value based on two or more values. (For example, an operator can return the product of two numbers.)

The XQuery 1.0 and XPath 2.0 Functions and Operators document further breaks functions into the following types:

- **Accessors** provide information about a node, such as its type (`node-kind()`) or text value (`string()`).

- **Constructors, functions, and operators on numbers** create values of types such as decimal and integer, perform numeric operations such as addition (`numeric-add()`) and division (`numeric-divide()` and `numeric-mod()`), and carry out comparisons (`numeric-equal()`, `numeric-less-than()`, `numeric-greater-then()`), while keeping the original numeric functions such as `floor()`, `ceiling()`, and `round()`.

- **Constructors and functions on strings** also include constructors such as `string()`, `normalizedString()`, and `ENTITY()`; comparisons such as `compare()`; and utility functions such as `concat()`, `starts-with()`, `substring-before()`, `normalize-space()`, `contains()`, `upper-case()`, `string-pad()`, and `replace()`.

- **Constructors, functions, and operators on Booleans** include the requisite `true()`, `false()`, and `not()`, as well as `boolean-from-string()`, `boolean-equal()`, `boolean-less-than()`, and `boolean-greater-than()`. These last two odd-looking functions take two values; the `boolean-less-than()` returns `true` if the first is `false` and the second is `true`, and vice versa.

- **Constructors, functions, and operators on durations, dates, and times** includes a rather lengthy list of constructors for all the built-in schema types relating to dates, durations, and times, such as `dateTime()`, `gMonthDay()`, and `dayTimeDuration-from-`

seconds(). It also includes comparisons such as duration-equal() and yearMonthDuration-less-than() and a bevy of functions for extracting particular components from a date or duration, such as get-days-from-dayTimeDuration(), get-month-from-date(), get-hours-from-time(), and get-timezone-from-time(). XPath 2.0 also provides for time-based arithmetic with functions such as add-yearMonthDurations(), add-days(), and subtract-yearMonthDuration-from-dateTime().

- **Functions and operators on nodes** have been greatly expanded to include sorely needed functions such as node-equal() (which checks whether the arguments are actually the same node), deep-equal() (which checks the content of the two argument nodes to see whether they're equivalent), and root() (which is especially handy now that we can deal with nodes from several different documents). It also includes if-absent() and if-empty(), which allow you to specify alternate content just in case a particular node is missing or empty, respectively.

- **Constructors, functions, and operators on sequences** include capabilities to insert nodes into and remove nodes from a sequence, to return only distinct-nodes() or distinct-values(), and to determine whether a sequence is empty(). It also includes functions that provide **set**-like operations such as union(), intersect(), and except() and aggregate functions such as count(), min(), and sum().

- **Context functions** include the already-familiar position() and last(), as well as new functions such as context-document() and current-dateTime().

- Five additional sections include constructors, operators, and functions for QNames (such as get-namespace-uri()); the anyURI type (such as resolve-URI()); base64Binary and hexBinary (such as hex-binary-equal()); and NOTATIONs (such as NOTATION-equal()); as well as functions that cast nodes from one type to another.

For a complete list of functions and their meanings, see the XQuery 1.0 and XPath 2.0 Functions and Operators document at http://www.w3.org/TR/xquery-operators. You can use these functions in an XPath expression just as you can use them in XPath 1.0. For example, Listing 20.32 shows two sequence functions.

LISTING 20.32   Using Built-in Functions

```
let $planets := distinct-values(document("guests.xml")//planet)
return
    <representatives>{ count($planets) }</representatives>
```

Custom Functions

In addition to providing an extensive list of built-in functions, XPath 2.0 enables us to build our own functions and use them within an expression. For example, Listing 20.33 shows the creation and use of a function that determines the number of guests invited to the wedding.

LISTING 20.33   Creating a Custom Function

```
define function countGuests(element guest* $guestsIn)
   returns element guestCount*
{
   let $countGuests := $guestsIn/quantity
   return
      <guestCount>{ sum($countGuests) }</guestCount>
}

let $guests := document("guests.xml")//guest
return
   <numberOfGuests>{ countGuests($guests) }</numberOfGuests>
```

The function `countGuests()` takes an argument consisting of one or more `guest` elements and returns one or more `guestCount` elements based on the FLWR statement in the function's body. The second FLWR statement calls the newly created function, feeding it the sequence of `guest` elements bound to `$guests`.

The result is a `numberOfGuests` element with a `guestCount` element child:

```
<numberOfGuests><guestCount>42</guestCount></numberOfGuests>
```

XUpdate

So far we've looked at interacting with a native XML database via a common API, and you've learned a new way to perform queries. This section covers the one area where XQuery and XPath are still lacking: updates.

The XML:DB Initiative has developed a proposed language for updating XML databases. Called XUpdate, it's an XML-based language for specifying information to be changed and the values to which it should be changed. Xindice and several other NXDs, including X-Hive/DB, support it.

In this section, we'll look at the different types of operations you can perform with XUpdate, including changing, adding, and removing information.

Using the XML:DB API with XUpdate

In order to execute the XUpdate statements, we'll need to use the `XUpdateQueryService` rather than the `XpathQueryService` in our `ManageDocs` application, as shown in Listing 20.34.

LISTING 20.34   Using an XUpdate

```
import org.xmldb.api.base.Collection;
import org.xmldb.api.base.Database;
import org.xmldb.api.DatabaseManager;
import org.xmldb.api.modules.XUpdateQueryService;

import java.io.File;
import java.io.FileInputStream;

public class ManageDocs {
```

LISTING 20.34 Continued

```java
public static void main(String[] args) throws Exception {
    Collection collection = null;
    try {
        String driver = "org.apache.xindice.client.xmldb.DatabaseImpl";
        Class c = Class.forName(driver);

        Database database = (Database) c.newInstance();
        DatabaseManager.registerDatabase(database);
        collection =
            DatabaseManager.getCollection("xmldb:xindice:///db/wedding");

        String xupdate = file2string("xupdate.xml");

        XUpdateQueryService updateService =
            (XUpdateQueryService) collection.getService("XUpdateQueryService",
                                                        "1.0");
        long result = updateService.update(xupdate);
        if (result == 0) {
            System.out.println("No resources to update.");
        } else {
            System.out.println("Resources updated.");
        }

    } catch (Exception e) {
        System.out.println("Problem using database: "+e.getMessage());
    }
    finally {
        if (collection != null) {
            collection.close();
        }
    }
}

public static String file2string(String inFileName)
{
    String outString = "";
    try {
        File inFile = new File(inFileName);
        FileInputStream inFileStream = new FileInputStream(inFile);

        byte[] streamBuffer = new byte[(int)inFile.length()];

        inFileStream.read(streamBuffer);
        inFileStream.close();

        outString = new String(streamBuffer);
    } catch (Exception e) {
        System.out.println("Problem reading the file: "+e.getMessage());
    }
    return outString;
}

}
```

The general process is similar to executing an XPath query. We instantiate the `XUpdateQueryService` object, then use it to perform the update. The XUpdate statement itself is stored in the `xupdate.xml` file so we don't have to constantly recompile the application. We've brought back the `file2string()` method to get the string value.

The `update()` method itself returns the number of nodes updated, so we can check the value to determine whether any changes were made.

The `XQueryUpdateService` also includes an `updateResource()` method that enables you to update just a particular document by including its key, like this:

```
long result = updateServiceUpdateResource("menu", xupdate);
```

Removing Information

Throughout the rest of the chapter, we're going to make changes to the menu for the wedding, the contents of which are shown in Listing 20.3.

Let's start simple, removing the Greech Eggs from the menu using the XUpdate statement in Listing 20.35.

LISTING 20.35   Removing a Node

```
<xupdate:modifications version="1.0" xmlns:xupdate="http://www.xmldb.org/xupdate">
    <xupdate:remove select="/menu/course/food[text() = 'Greech Eggs']"/>
</xupdate:modifications>
```

This query is simple, but it contains all the basic parts of an XUpdate document. First, notice that we're making use of namespaces; the `xupdate:` alias refers to the "official" XUpdate namespace, `http://www.xmldb.org/xupdate`. (Whether future changes will be signified by a change of namespace or a change in the `version` attribute is unclear at this time.)

The actual change, in this case, is signaled by the `remove` element, which indicates which node is affected via the `select` attribute. The `select` attribute uses a simple XPath expression to select a node.

The database determines the appropriate node based on the `select` attribute, and then performs the appropriate action on it (removal, in this case).

To execute the query, create the file `xupdate.xml` in the same directory as `ManageDocs.class` and run the application. You should get the following result:

```
Resources updated.
```

To verify that the change has been made, retrieve the document from the command line:

```
xindice rd -c /db/wedding -n menu
```

Listing 20.36 shows the results.

LISTING 20.36   Removing a Node: Results

```
<?xml version="1.0"?>
<menu>
    <course coursename="hors d'oeuvres">

        <food>Pyminca Squares</food>
        <food>Assorted Wagraphos</food>
        <food>Silraga Puffs</food>
        <food>Roasted Hagrop on Toasted Tenji</food>
    </course>
    <course coursename="soup">
        <food>Arvendo with Leaping Noodles</food>
    </course>
    <course coursename="main">
        <food>Floop Floop Bird Stuffed with Reckleberries</food>
        <food>Roasted Nera Beast</food>
        <food>Shivering Camdids</food>
        <food>Braised Tillentecks</food>
    </course>
    <course coursename="dessert">
        <food>Traditional Ordeal Pie</food>
        <food>Dewdotca Cake</food>
        <food>Candied Velpa Wings</food>
    </course>
</menu>
```

Notice the gap in the file where the element originally was. How your database handles this will depend on its model. In this case, the document is actually correct. Before the node removal, the Pyminca Squares element was preceded by a text node with a line feed, the Greech Eggs element, and another text node with a line feed. Now the Greech Eggs element is gone, but the two line feeds are still there.

Changing Information

Now that you understand the general structure of an XUpdate query, let's look at actually changing information. Listing 20.37 shows an XUpdate statement that changes the name of an attribute.

LISTING 20.37   Renaming an Attribute

```
<xupdate:modifications version="1.0" xmlns:xupdate="http://www.xmldb.org/xupdate">
    <xupdate:rename select="/menu/course/@coursename">courseType</xupdate:rename>
</xupdate:modifications>
```

The `rename` element indicates that we're going to change the name of a node or nodes. The node or nodes affected are indicated by the `select` attribute. In this case, we're actually talking about every `coursename` attribute in the document. The new name is contained within the `remove` element itself: `courseType`.

The complete effect is the renaming of the `coursename` attribute on every `course` element as `courseType`, as shown in Listing 20.38.

LISTING 20.38   Renaming an Attribute: Results

```xml
<?xml version="1.0"?>
<menu>
    <course courseType="hors d'oeuvres">

        <food>Pyminca Squares</food>
        <food>Assorted Wagraphos</food>
        <food>Silraga Puffs</food>
        <food>Roasted Hagrop on Toasted Tenji</food>
    </course>
    <course courseType="soup">
        <food>Arvendo with Leaping Noodles</food>
    </course>
    <course courseType="main">
        <food>Floop Floop Bird Stuffed with Reckleberries</food>
        <food>Roasted Nera Beast</food>
        <food>Shivering Camdids</food>
        <food>Braised Tillentecks</food>
    </course>
    <course courseType="dessert">
        <food>Traditional Ordeal Pie</food>
        <food>Dewdotca Cake</food>
        <food>Candied Velpa Wings</food>
    </course>
</menu>
```

A more common change, perhaps, is to update the actual content of a node, as shown in Listing 20.39.

LISTING 20.39   Updating an Element

```xml
<xupdate:modifications version="1.0" xmlns:xupdate="http://www.xmldb.org/xupdate">
    <xupdate:update select="//food[text()='Roasted Nera Beast']"
                                          >Broiled Nera Beast</xupdate:update>
</xupdate:modifications>
```

In this case, we're selecting an element, but XUpdate understands that when we say we want to update an element, we actually mean that we want to update the contents of the element. We could just as easily have updated the value of an attribute by designating an attribute node in the `select` attribute.

Listing 20.40 shows the results.

LISTING 20.40   Updating an Element: Results

```
...
   <course courseType="main">
     <food>Floop Floop Bird Stuffed with Reckleberries</food>
     <food>Broiled Nera Beast</food>
     <food>Shivering Camdids</food>
     <food>Braised Tillentecks</food>
   </course>
...
```

Creating New Information

Now let's up the ante a little bit and actually create some new information to insert into the document.

XUpdate enables you to add information using the `insert-before`, `insert-after`, or `append` elements. The new content can be elements, attributes, or other XML node types. For now, we'll add a new dessert (see Listing 20.41).

LISTING 20.41   Adding an Element

```
<xupdate:modifications version="1.0" xmlns:xupdate="http://www.xmldb.org/xupdate">
   <xupdate:append select="/menu/course[@courseType='dessert']">
      <xupdate:element name="food">Assorted Sweisal Tree Mints</xupdate:element>
   </xupdate:append>
</xupdate:modifications>
```

First, we're appending information. That means that the database will find the node indicated in the `select` attribute and add a new child to it. In this case, we've selected the dessert `course` element.

The information that we're appending is an element by the name of `food` that has text content. Listing 20.42 shows the results.

LISTING 20.42   Adding an Element: Results

```
...
   <course courseType="main">
     <food>Floop Floop Bird Stuffed with Reckleberries</food>
     <food>Broiled Nera Beast</food>
     <food>Shivering Camdids</food>
     <food>Braised Tillentecks</food>
   </course>
   <course courseType="dessert">
     <food>Traditional Ordeal Pie</food>
     <food>Dewdotca Cake</food>
     <food>Candied Velpa Wings</food>
     <food>Assorted Sweisal Tree Mints</food>
   </course>
</menu>
```

This is a simple element with just a text node child, but we can also nest elements or add attributes. For example, Listing 20.43 shows the addition of a salad course.

LISTING 20.42   Inserting a Nested Element

```
<xupdate:modifications version="1.0" xmlns:xupdate="http://www.xmldb.org/xupdate">
    <xupdate:insert-after select="/menu/course[@courseType='soup']">
        <xupdate:element name="course">
            <xupdate:attribute name="courseType">salad</xupdate:attribute>
            <food>Konkel Leaves with Smaste and Shredded Ossa Cheese</food>
        </xupdate:element>
    </xupdate:insert-after>
</xupdate:modifications>
```

In this case, we want to insert the new information in a very specific place: after the soup course. We select the soup course using the `insert-after` element's `select` attribute, and then specify the new information.

Inserts and Attributes

You can also use the `insert-before` and `insert-after` elements to insert a new attribute before or after another attribute.

The new information consists of an element named **course** that also includes an attribute named **courseType**, the value of which is set in the body of the **attribute** element.

The **food** element is added directly, but because it's not part of the **xupdate:** namespace, it's just output without being evaluated. Listing 20.44 shows the results.

LISTING 20.44   Inserting an Element: Results

```
...
    <food>Roasted Hagrop on Toasted Tenji</food>
  </course>
  <course courseType="soup">
    <food>Arvendo with Leaping Noodles</food>
  </course><course courseType="salad">
        <food>Konkel Leaves with Smaste and Shredded Ossa Cheese</food>
    </course>
  <course courseType="main">
    <food>Floop Floop Bird Stuffed with Reckleberries</food>
    <food>Broiled Nera Beast</food>
...
```

In addition to elements and attributes, XUpdate allows you to create text sections, processing instructions, and comments. For example, Listing 20.45 shows the creation of a comment.

LISTING 20.45   Creating a Comment

```
<xupdate:modifications version="1.0" xmlns:xupdate="http://www.xmldb.org/xupdate">
    <xupdate:insert-before select="/menu/course[@courseType='soup']">
        <xupdate:comment>
            The bride insists that the soup must come before the salad, and
            will not be swayed.
        </xupdate:comment>
    </xupdate:insert-before>
</xupdate:modifications>
```

Listing 20.46 shows the results.

LISTING 20.46   Creating a Comment: Results

```
<?xml version="1.0"?>
<menu>
    <course courseType="hors d'oeuvres">

        <food>Pyminca Squares</food>
        <food>Assorted Wagraphos</food>
        <food>Silraga Puffs</food>
        <food>Roasted Hagrop on Toasted Tenji</food>
    </course>
    <!—
        The bride insists that the soup must come before the salad, and
        will not be swayed.
    —>
    <course courseType="soup">
        <food>Arvendo with Leaping Noodles</food>
    </course><course courseType="salad">

            <food>Konkel Leaves with Smaste and Shredded Ossa Cheese</food>
    </course>
...
```

Variables

Finally, XUpdate, like XQuery and XSLT, allows the creation of variables that can be referenced elsewhere. For example, Listing 20.47 shows the creation of a variable that takes the value of the first dessert on the list, which is then added at the end of each of the other courses.

LISTING 20.47   Using a Variable

```
<xupdate:modifications version="1.0" xmlns:xupdate="http://www.xmldb.org/xupdate">
  <xupdate:variable name="predessertValue"
                    select="/menu/course[@courseType='dessert']/food[1]"/>

  <xupdate:insert-after select="/menu/course[@courseType!='dessert']/food[last()]">
    <xupdate:element name="predessert">
```

LISTING 20.47 Continued

```
      <xupdate:value-of select="$predessertValue"/>
    </xupdate:element>
  </xupdate:insert-after>

</xupdate:modifications>
```

The value for the variable is set based on an XPath expression. Note that while Xindice currently doesn't support it, in principle there's nothing to keep you from selecting a value from a completely different document in the collection and adding it to the current document.

Once the value is set, we insert a new element (named `predessert`) after the last food element in each course. The value of the new element is the `$predessertValue` variable, accessed via the `value-of` element.

Listing 20.48 shows the results.

LISTING 20.48 Using a Variable: Results

```
<?xml version="1.0"?>
<menu>
 <course courseType="hors d'oeuvres">

    <food>Pyminca Squares</food>
    <food>Assorted Wagraphos</food>
    <food>Silraga Puffs</food>
    <food>Roasted Hagrop on Toasted Tenji</food><predessert>
    <food>Traditional Ordeal Pie</food>
  </predessert>
  </course>
  <!--
       The bride insists that the soup must come before the salad, and
       will not be swayed.
     -->
  <course courseType="soup">
    <food>Arvendo with Leaping Noodles</food><predessert>
    <food>Traditional Ordeal Pie</food>
  </predessert>
  </course><course courseType="salad">
    <food>Konkel Leaves with Smaste and Shredded Ossa Cheese</food><predessert>
    <food>Traditional Ordeal Pie</food>
  </predessert>
  </course>
  <course courseType="main">
    <food>Floop Floop Bird Stuffed with Reckleberries</food>
    <food>Broiled Nera Beast</food>
    <food>Shivering Camdids</food>
    <food>Braised Tillentecks</food><predessert>
    <food>Traditional Ordeal Pie</food>
```

LISTING 20.48   *Continued*

```
    </predessert>
  </course>
  <course courseType="dessert">
    <food>Traditional Ordeal Pie</food>
    <food>Dewdotca Cake</food>
    <food>Candied Velpa Wings</food>
    <food>Assorted Sweisal Tree Mints</food>
  </course>
</menu>
```

Implementation Note

Version 1.0 seems to have a bug that causes the element to be added twice. It should, in fact, be added only once.

Summary

Native XML databases are better suited to handling document-centric data than their relational counterparts, though some relational databases have added native XML database capabilities by way of operations that act on a document that can be added to a single column within a table.

NXDs typically take one of two forms: text-based, in which the data is stored intact, and model-based, in which the database determines the structure of the document and stores it according to that information. A text-based NXD has a better chance of round-tripping, or faithfully representing the original data in its original structure, but in general, a user or developer should be unaffected by this choice, except perhaps in terms of performance.

Native XM databases have the document as their smallest unit of information. Those documents can be gathered together into a collection of documents.

Database designers are building a proposed common API from the XML:DB Initiative into various open source and commercial native XML databases to allow application developers to build programs that are database-independent.

If the database supports it, you can query XML data using XML Query Language (XQuery). XQuery supports a more robust XPath 2.0 as well as programming-like structures such as **if-then** statements and the capability to sort and group data. It can determine the structure of the output using **for-let-where-return** (FLWR) statements. You can update data in an XML native database using XUpdate, a language that uses XML elements and attributes to specify information to be changed, added, or removed from the document.

Review Questions

1. Name three advantages that a native XML database offers over a simple XML file.

2. What's the difference between a text-based and a model-based NXD?

3. What is round-tripping, and why is it important?

4. What is a collection?

CHAPTER 21

WHERE WE GO FROM HERE

You will learn about the following in this chapter:

- MathML
- Scalable Vector Graphics and Synchronized Multimedia Integration Language
- Resource Definition Framework Language
- Extensible User Interface Language
- Open eBook
- Wireless Markup Language
- XML-based User Interface Language
- Business Process Modeling Language

Wow, we've covered a lot of ground since you cracked open this book! By now you should have a good understanding of XML and the standards and recommendations that surround it. You should be ready to tackle your own projects, or to pick up where others have gone before.

In this chapter we're going to take one more long look over the landscape. We'll look at all the pieces of XML that we've already covered and how they fit together, and then we'll look at some of the situations and technologies in which you'll be able to put your newfound skills to work. Finally, we'll look at some of the work that's yet to be done in the business of XML specifications, and where it's likely to go in the next couple of years.

The 10,000-Foot View

First, let's take a look at where we are now, so we can see how the different recommendations and specifications complement or compete with each other.

Core Standards

First we have the core recommendations and specifications, on which everything else is based. These include

- The XML 1.0 Recommendation itself, which not only defines the types of nodes that can be part of a document, but also includes the definition of an XML Document Type Definition (DTD), making validation possible right out of the box. The XML Information Set Recommendation dovetails nicely with this recommendation, providing an alternative way to express the same information.

- The Document Object Model (DOM), in all of its various and sundry flavors, such as the Core module, which defines the basic concepts such as elements, nodes, and parents; the Traversal and Range module, which defines concepts such as `NodeFilter`s and `TreeWalker`s; and the HTML module, which allows you to represent an XHTML document as a DOM document structure while still accessing some of the properties that are normally set using DHTML.

- The Simple API for XML (SAX), which allows you to quickly and easily parse a document, then stop when you have all the information you need. SAX can be faster and much less memory-intensive than DOM, but is a read-only proposition.

- Namespaces, which allow you to mix data from different sources or with different purposes. Namespaces make applications such as Extensible Stylesheet Language Transformations (XSLT) possible.

All of this is useful, of course, but would be a lot less useful if it weren't for the recommendations and specifications that have sprung up around XML.

Associated Standards

Related recommendations and specifications are not necessarily crucial to using XML, but they certainly make your life a lot easier. These include

- **Extensible Stylesheet Language Transformations (XSLT)**—XSLT allows you to easily extract specific information from an XML document, or to transform it into another form, such as another XML structure, or even into something completely different.

- **XPath**—XSLT is only one recommendation that relies heavily on XPath, which provides a way to select specific information items from within an XML structure. XPath also provides a means for directly executing functions on XML data.

- **XML Schemas**—Schemas such as the W3C XML Schema Recommendation, RELAX NG, Schematron, and other related schema proposals, allow much greater control over the validation process. In addition to constraining datatypes and even data values, these recommendations and specifications provide the ability to validate data that might come from a number of different namespaces—a capability that's sorely lacking in DTDs.

Together with the core concepts, these related recommendations and specifications provide firm footing for XML-related applications.

Applications

When XML was first introduced, the common thought was, "That's great, but what can you *do* with it?" Today, nobody asks that question. XML as a technology is firmly established, and ends up in all sorts of places. Some uses for XML are informal, such as configuration files and data exchange. Others are more formalized.

Many XML applications are geared toward the Web, and toward HTML's traditional stomping ground. Some are complementary, such as XHTML's reformulation of HTML 4.01 into XML so that Web pages can benefit from some of the functionality available in an XML document. Others, such as XForms and XLink, are meant to enhance or replace various sections of HTML.

XML appears in publishing, providing an easy interchange format between different organizations and applications. In some ways, this is a return to its roots; SGML, on which XML is based, was heavily used in publishing. Recommendations such as Extensible Stylesheet Language Formatting Objects provide assistance here, as well.

And of course, XML has surfaced in the Web services arena. How better to implement a system that is platform-independent and application-independent than through XML?

Of course, in some cases, XML is the problem, not the solution. For example, data binding exists as (in some ways) an easier means of dealing with XML data, allowing you to treat it like any other object. Special databases have emerged to serve the developer with a large quantity of XML data to store in an organized fashion. Even traditional database vendors are getting into the act, XML-enabling relational databases such as Oracle, DB2, and SQL Server.

All these capabilities make XML a natural way of doing business in a wide range of situations.

Existing Vocabularies

With all these capabilities, it should come as no surprise that more and more individuals, companies, and industries are choosing XML to fill their needs. In some cases, this means custom development, but more common situations often involve the development of custom vocabularies. These vocabularies then go on to become "languages" of their own, with their own uses and developer communities. In this section, we'll take a quick look at some of them.

MathML

Considering that one of the early goals of HTML was to provide scientific researchers with the ability to pass information back and forth, it should come as no surprise that MathML is one of the "oldest" XML applications around, dating all the way back to 1999. (Don't you feel old now?)

MathML comes in two flavors: presentation MathML and full MathML. The former is intended to provide a way to convey mathematical information in such a way that a human can understand it; the latter enables a computer to understand its meaning.

For example, the expression E = mc² can be rendered for presentational purposes as

```
<mrow>
  <mi>E</mi>
  <mo>=</mo>
  <mrow>
    <mn>m</mn>
    <mo>&InvisibleTimes;</mo>
    <msup>
      <mi>c</mi>
      <mn>2</mn>
    </msup>
  </mrow>
</mrow>
```

or for content purposes as

```
<mrow>
<apply>
  <eq/>
  <apply>
    <apply>
      <times/>
      <cn>m</cn>
    <apply>
      <power/>
      <ci>c</ci>
      <cn>2</cn>
    </apply>
    </apply>
    <cn>4</cn>
  </apply>
  <cn>E</cn>
</apply>
</mrow>
```

Scalable Vector Graphics (SVG) and Synchronized Multimedia Integration Language (SMIL)

Scalable Vector Graphics (SVG) and Synchronized Multimedia Integration Language (SMIL—pronounced "smile") attempt to do for graphics and multimedia what HTML did for text-based content: provide a way to describe the content, using text, so that it can be used/read in a variety of environments. In fact, SVG allows you to describe quite detailed graphical elements, while SMIL allows you to create a fairly sophisticated presentation, including audio, text, and video, using a tag-based language that can be read by a variety of applications such as RealOne Player.

An additional advantage is a reduction of bandwidth; an SVG-based graphic can be represented by text that takes only a tiny fraction of the space that would be required by a binary format such as GIF or JPEG. Also, because they're text-based, these languages provide an easier means for providing accessibility to alternative clients such as audio systems, either through meta information attached to the content or through XSLT.

Resource Definition Framework (RDF)

The Resource Definition Framework provides a means for adding metadata to an XML document. Through the use of XML Namespaces, this information can be kept separate from the content, but still be available to other applications. RDF itself provides core objects, such as `RDF` and `Description`, which can be fleshed out with information as desired. Of course, RDF is only useful if the reader understands what it means, so for the sake of machine-readability, several different classification schemes have evolved. The Dublin Core, a set of metadata information items for describing content, used to be the most widely used RDF format, with information that might look something like this:

```
<rdf:RDF xmlns:rdf="http://www.w3.org/1999/02/22-rdf-syntax-ns#"
         xmlns:dc="http://purl.org/dc/elements/1.1/">
  <rdf:Description rdf:about="http://www.vanguardreport.com"
      dc:title="The Vanguard Station Status Page"
      dc:description="Current events, news, and updates for employees and guests."
      dc:creator="Nicholas Chase"
      dc:date="3425-18-06" />
</rdf:RDF>
```

These days, perhaps the most widely used "flavor" of RDF is RDF Site Summary (RSS). Sites use RSS to syndicate their headlines, or make them available to other sites. Because the format is standard (though there are significant differences between versions, which does cause problems on occasion), any site can take the RSS file and work with it to provide a list of headlines and links back to the original site. For example:

```
<?xml version="1.0" encoding="utf-8"?>
<rdf:RDF
  xmlns:rdf="http://www.w3.org/1999/02/22-rdf-syntax-ns#"
  xmlns="http://purl.org/rss/1.0/"
>

  <channel rdf:about="http:///www.vanguardreport.com/rss.rdf">
    <title>The Vanguard Report</title>
    <description>
        Find out what's going on on your home station.
    </description>
    <link>http://www.vanguardreport.com</link>
  </channel>

  <item rdf:about="http://www.vanguardreport.com/incumbent.html">
    <title>End Of The Line For The Incumbent?</title>
    <link>http://www.vanguardreport.com/incumbent.html</link>
  </item>

  <item rdf:about="http://www.vanguardreport.com/fall_lineup.html">
    <title>New Fall Lineup</title>
    <link>http://www.vanguardreport.com/fall_lineup.html</link>
  </item>

</rdf:RDF>
```

Wireless Markup Language (WML)

Browsers in mobile devices such as phones and PDAs are getting better, but you still can't serve your normal HTML pages to the vast majority of mobile users getting information on their pagers and phones. As a means of dealing with this limitation, the Wireless Application Protocol Forum, founded by Ericsson, Motorola, Nokia, and Unwired PlanetWML, maintains the Wireless Markup Language (WML).

WML organizes data into cards, and the cards into decks. The intent is to compensate for the low bandwidth, tiny display size, limited user-input capabilities, and limited memory these devices typically have. Cards can be linked together, and basic formatting options exist, but WML is definitely based on a different structure than HTML. For example, a document might look like this:

```
<?xml version="1.0"?>
<!DOCTYPE wml PUBLIC "-//WAPFORUM//DTD WML 1.1//EN"
                     "http://www.wapforum.org/DTD/wml_1.1.xml">
<wml>
  <card id="home" title="Station Home" newcontext="true">
    <p>
      <img src="resort.wbmp" alt="Station Logo" />
    </p>
    <p>
      <a href="#news">News</a><br/>
      <a href="#events">Events</a>
    </p>
  </card>
  <card id="news" title="News Page">
    <p>
      The news can be displayed here, or linked to a page <i>inside</i> or
      <b>outside</b> this deck.
    </p>
    <p align="center">
      <a href="#home">Home</a>
    </p>
  </card>
  <card id="events" title="News Page">
    <p>
      The events can be displayed here, or linked to a page inside or
      outside this deck.
    </p>
    <p align="center">
      <a href="#home">Home</a>
    </p>
  </card>
</wml>
```

The card method has never really caught on with developers, however, and as more capable devices are developed, WML is being replaced by a combination of XHTML and Cascading Style Sheets. For more information and a downloadable mobile browser, see `http://developer.openwave.com/`.

XML-based User Interface Language (XUL)

XUL (pronounced "zool") stands for XML-based User Interface Language. It's the means by which the user interface was built for Mozilla and all browsers based on it, such as Netscape 6.x and above. The idea was to provide an XML-based language that defines an actual user interface—the buttons, input boxes, windows, and so on as opposed to the content within them—in order to streamline development over different platforms.

An interface developed in XUL will work for any XUL-enabled system, and can be combined with CSS-style information to create different looks (called "skins") for the application.

Open eBook (OEB)

Open eBook (OEB) is a format designed for the creation of electronic books, or material that can be read on eBook-type devices, known as *reading systems*. On the surface, Open eBook is a language that closely resembles XHTML. Many of the structural and presentational elements are identical, and OEB uses CSS properties. But OEB adds its own wrinkles.

An OEB "document" may actually consist of a series of documents. These documents are all chronicled in the manifest. Documents also include a spine, which provides the "optimal" path through the content, and acts as a table of contents for the work.

What makes it interesting is that an author can also provide different views of the content through tours, in which different points of interest can be grouped together. For example, a reference book on gardening might have different tours for those interested in flowers and those interested in vegetables, and different tours can be organized for different regions of the world. The author can also create guides, which provide points of reference within the work.

Business Process Modeling Language (BPML)

In Chapter 17, "XML and Web Services," we briefly discussed ebXML, which is one of many systems that attempt to formalize the documentation of business processes. Business Process Modeling Language (BPML) is a slightly different take on the problem. While these systems attempt to describe business processes to external partners, BPML provides a means to describe them with regard to internal systems.

BPML is maintained by the Business Process Markup Initiative, which has also developed the Business Process Query Language.

Where We're Going

So what's left? We already have a fully functional set of recommendations and specifications, applications built on them, and languages sprouting everywhere. Where can we go from here?

In this section we'll look at current initiatives that are working their way through the World Wide Web Consortium (W3C).

Old Recommendations, New Versions

As you've probably noticed, many of the XML recommendations are interdependent. For example, XSLT, XPointer, XML Query, and XLink are all dependent in some way on XPath. Unfortunately, in the fast and furious world of the Web, inconsistencies have crept into these recommendations, despite the W3C's best efforts to keep everything synchronized.

To that end, the W3C's current strategy is to create new working groups and recommendations where they're really needed, but to also spend time cleaning up those that are already out there so that they mesh a bit more neatly. These efforts include new versions of existing recommendations that add new features and attempt to resolve remaining issues. For example:

- The Document Object Model Level 3 adds an XPath module that attempts to resolve the differences between the way in which each recommendation defines various nodes, such as the whitespace node issue we discussed in Chapter 11, "Selecting Data: XPath." It also adds the ability to load and save documents in a standardized way.

- XSLT 2.0 will provide for easier usage, and for better integration with XML Schema. It's also dependent on XPath 2.0.

- XPath 2.0 will provide additional functionality with respect to datatypes (moving it closer to XML Schema), as well as changes that integrate it more closely with XML Query.

Document Management

Two small specifications attempt to make it easier to modularize XML documents for later use. XML Fragments will provide a way for authors to reference a particular section of a document and pass it to the recipient without losing context information for the fragment. XML Include provides a way to combine data from several documents into a single information set.

Security

Even before global events mandated it, security-related protocols were underway at the W3C, particularly with the growing use of Web Services, which send data along traditionally unprotected routes. These initiatives include the following:

- A joint project between the W3C and the Internet Engineering Task Force (IETF), XML Signature is intended to provide a standard means for the sender to digitally "sign" a message (or part of a message) in such a way that the receiver can verify its authenticity and accuracy. Similarly, XML Encryption's goal is to provide an XML representation of content, both digital and text, that has been encrypted in such a way that the intended recipient (and only the intended recipient) can decrypt and read it.

- Both of these recommendations depend on the ability to retrieve the appropriate security key, and the XML Key Management Specification formalizes this process. This is also a joint project between the W3C and IETF. This project exists in two parts: the XML Key

Registration Service Specification, which defines how keys are stored, and the XML Key Information Service Specification, which defines how they are accessed.

Last Words

It's the nature of the computer industry—particularly when dealing with anything related to the World Wide Web—for things to change even before you can get used to them. The only way you could ever learn "everything" about a technology is if nothing new were being developed, and that would only happen if the technology were dead.

And so I leave you with the idea that you don't have to know everything. All you need is to understand how things work, and how they relate to each other. From there, you can delve deeper into whatever topic you need to master in order to solve whatever problem is vexing you on any particular day.

I hope that I've managed to impart a fairly deep understanding of the way things are right now, and more importantly, why they are that way. By the time you read this book, it's likely some things in it will have changed, perhaps significantly. That's all right. By now, you should understand the general concepts. You can find the specific details in the documentation.

Even if they haven't changed, you should now have a deep enough understanding to read through those incredibly long and (previously) confusing specifications and actually understand what they're talking about. Most people don't even try because they're intimidated, and they miss out. The really good stuff is in there, hidden, just waiting for you to find it.

And when you do, or if you have any questions, or if you just want to say hello and let me know that you made it to this last page in the last chapter of the book, you can contact me at `ppxml@nicholaschase.com`. I'm happy to help, but please remember that I didn't create any of the APIs or other applications that you downloaded, so please check with the appropriate groups and individuals if you're having trouble setting them up. You can also checkout my Web site at `http://www.nicholaschase.com` for updates and other information.

Now go out there and build something!

PART III

APPENDIXES

A Resources

B XML Information Set

C Answers to Review Questions and Sample Exercise Solutions

APPENDIX A

RESOURCES

*A*s its title indicates, this book is a primer on XML. Hopefully, it's given you a basic understanding of XML and related technologies, and that understanding will allow you to delve deeper into individual topics.

This appendix lists references that were mentioned within each chapter, as well as resources where you can find more information.

Introduction

- The XML 1.0 Recommendation: `http://www.w3.org/TR/REC-xml`

- James Clark's Comparison of SGML and XML: `http://www.w3.org/TR/NOTE-sgml-xml-971215`

- The XML home page: `http://www.w3.org/XML/`

- XML in 10 points: `http://www.w3.org/XML/1999/XML-in-10-points.html`

- The XML Cover Pages: `http://xml.coverpages.org/sgml-xml.html`

Chapter 1

- The XML-DEV mailing list: `http://www.xml.org/xml/xmldev.shtml`

- UTF-8 and Unicode FAQ for Unix/Linux: `http://www.cl.cam.ac.uk/~mgk25/unicode.html`

- The Online Edition of *The Unicode Standard, Version 3*: `http://www.unicode.org/unicode/uni2book/u2.html`

- "Acceptable" characters in an XML document: `http://www.w3.org/TR/REC-xml#charsets`

- The XML Cover Pages: Extensible Markup Language: `http://www.oasis-open.org/cover/xml.html`

- Namespaces in XML: `http://www.w3.org/TR/1999/REC-xml-names-19990114/`

Chapter 2

- XML Repositories: `http://www.xml.org`

- *Developing SGML DTDs: From Text to Model to Markup*, by Eve Maler and Jeanne El Andaloussi (Prentice Hall PTR, 1996, ISBN 0-13-309881-8)

- *Applied XML Solutions*, by Benôit Marchal (Sams, 2000, ISBN 0-672-32054-1)

- *Design Patterns: Elements of Reusable Object-Oriented Software*, by Erich Gamma, Richard Helm, Ralph Johnson, and John Vlissides (Addison-Wesley, 1995, ISBN 0-201-63361-2)

- *Pattern Hatching: Design Patterns Applied*, by John Vlissides (Addison-Wesley, 1998, ISBN 0-201-43293-5)

- *Case*Method: Entity Relationship Modelling*, by Richard Barker (Addison-Wesley Longman Limited, 1990, ISBN 0-201-41696-4)

- *Case*Method: Function and Process Modelling*, by Richard Barker and Cliff Longman (Addison-Wesley Longman Limited, 1992, ISBN 0-201-56525-0)

- *The XML & SGML Cookbook*, by Rick Jelliffe (Prentice Hall PTR, 1998, ISBN 0-13-614223-0)

Chapter 3

- The Document Object Model home page: `http://www.w3.org/DOM/`

- "Understanding DOM," by Nicholas Chase: `http://www-105.ibm.com/developerworks/education.nsf/xml-onlinecourse-bytitle/6B46D87B12C3FDE786256AB700730AF3?OpenDocument`

- XML Document Object Model (an index): `http://www.devx.com/upload/free/features/xml/objectmodel/xmldom1.asp`

- The DOM Cover Pages: `http://xml.coverpages.org/dom.html`

- "Effective XML processing with DOM and XPath in Java," by Parand Tony Darugar: `http://www-106.ibm.com/developerworks/xml/library/x-domjava/`

- Java XML Pack Summer 02 Release: `http://java.sun.com/xml/downloads/javaxmlpack.html`

- Xerces2 Java Parser: `http://xml.apache.org/xerces2-j/index.html`

- Xerces C++ Parser: `http://xml.apache.org/xerces-c/index.html`

- XML::Xerces (Perl API to the Xerces XML parser): `http://xml.apache.org/xerces-p/index.html`

- Microsoft XML Core Services 4.0 (also known as MSXML 4.0): `http://msdn.microsoft.com/downloads/default.asp?url=/downloads/sample.asp?url=/msdn-files/027/001/766/msdncompositedoc.xml`

- PHP documentation: `http://www.php.net/docs.php`

Chapter 4

- Canonical XML: `http://www.w3.org/TR/xml-c14n`

- "Let your DOM do the walking: A look at the DOM Traversal Module," by Brett McLaughlin: `http://www-106.ibm.com/developerworks/xml/library/x-dmtrv/index.html`

- "Just Over the Horizon ... a new DOM: A preview of DOM Level 3," by Brett McLaughlin: `http://www-106.ibm.com/developerworks/xml/library/x-dom3.html`

Chapter 5

- The SAX Project: `http://www.saxproject.org`

- "Understanding SAX," by Nicholas Chase: `http://www-105.ibm.com/developerworks/education.nsf/xml-onlinecourse-bytitle/02B719BE93D7655D86256AB9005FA8D6?OpenDocument`

- Serial Access with the Simple API for XML (SAX): `http://java.sun.com/xml/jaxp/dist/1.1/docs/tutorial/sax/`

- "SAX, the Simple API for XML," by Aaron Skonnard: `http://msdn.microsoft.com/msdnmag/issues/1100/xml/xml1100.asp`

- "Use the Simple API for XML," by Yasser Shohoud: `http://www.devx.com/upload/free/features/xml/2000/05win00/yy0005/yy0005.asp`

- The SAX Cover Page: `http://xml.coverpages.org/xml.html#saxAPI`

Chapter 7

- Complete list of ISO 639 language codes: `http://www.w3.org/WAI/ER/IG/ert/iso639.htm`

- DTD definition: `http://www.w3.org/TR/REC-xml#dt-doctype`

- *Inside XML DTDs* (ebook), by Simon St. Laurent and Robert J. Biggar (McGraw-Hill, 2002, ISBN B00005BBYE)

- "Validating XML," by Nicholas Chase: `http://www-105.ibm.com/developerworks/education.nsf/xml-onlinecourse-bytitle/7155C6A19EC801DB86256ACE006F5270?OpenDocument`

- "Customize a DTD with parameter entities," by Nicholas Chase: `http://www-106.ibm.com/developerworks/xml/library/x-tiparam.html?dwzone=xml`

- "Include external information with general entities," by Nicholas Chase: `http://www-106.ibm.com/developerworks/xml/library/x-tipgentity/index.html`

Chapter 8

- XML Schema home page: `http://www.w3.org/XML/Schema`

- The XML Cover Pages: `http://www.oasis-open.org/cover/schemas.html`

- The RELAX NG home page: `http://www.thaiopensource.com/relaxng/`

- RELAX NG Tutorial: `http://www.oasis-open.org/committees/relax-ng/tutorial-20011203.html`

- The Schematron home page: `http://www.ascc.net/xml/resource/schematron/schematron.html`

- XML Schema Validator: `http://www.w3.org/2000/06/webdata/xsv`

- "Analyzing XML schemas with the Schema Infoset Model," by Shane Curcuru: `http://www-106.ibm.com/developerworks/xml/library/x-schemimj/index.html?dwzone=xml`

- *Definitive XML Schema*, by Priscilla Walmsley (Prentice Hall PTR, 2001, ISBN 0-13-065567-8)

Chapters 9–10

- xalan-c: `http://xml.apache.org/xalan-c/index.html`

- XSL home page: `http://www.w3.org/Style/XSL/`

- XSLT Recommendation: `http://www.w3.org/TR/xslt`

- "Integrating data at run time with XSLT style sheets," by Andre Tost: `http://www-106.ibm.com/developerworks/xml/library/x-runxslt/index.html?dwzone=xml`

- "Manipulating data with XSL," by Nicholas Chase: `http://www-105.ibm.com/developerworks/education.nsf/xml-onlinecourse-bytitle/541CBB035C53F2CC86256AED006DE862?OpenDocument`

- XSL Cover Pages: `http://xml.coverpages.org/xsl.html`

- Adobe Acrobat Reader: `http://www.adobe.com/products/acrobat/readstep2.html`

- FOP: `http://xml.apache.org/fop`

- X-Smiles: `http://www.xsmiles.org/`

- The SAXON XSLT Processor: `http://saxon.sourceforge.net/`

- TransforMIIX: `http://www.mitre.org/mii/techproducts/transform.htm`

- XML::XSL: `http://xmlxslt.sourceforge.net/`

- Xalan-C++: `http://xml.apache.org/xalan-c/index.html`

- XSL processor for ColdFusion: `http://www.cfdev.com/xml/xslt`

- "An XSL Calculator: The Math Modules of FXSL," by Dimitre Novatchev: `http://fxsl.sourceforge.net/articles/xslCalculator/The FXSL Calculator.html`

- "XSL Transformation With PHP And Sablotron," by Harish Kamath: `http://www.devshed.com/Server_Side/XML/XSLTrans/print`

Chapter 11

- XPath Recommendation: `http://www.w3.org/TR/xpath`

- A transitive closure function for XPath: `http://www.cs.ucl.ac.uk/staff/c.nentwich/closure/`

Chapter 12

- The CSS home page: `http://www.w3.org/Style/CSS/`

- W3C CSS validation Service: `http://jigsaw.w3.org/css-validator/`

- CSS Colors: `http://www.w3schools.com/css/css_colors.asp`

- CSS2 Specification: `http://www.w3.org/TR/REC-CSS2/`

- CSS2 property index: `http://www.w3.org/TR/REC-CSS2/propidx.html`

- Converting binary and hexadecimal values: `http://www.computerhope.com/binhex.htm`

- CSS Tutorial: `http://www.w3schools.com/css/default.asp`

Chapter 13

- XHTML 1.0: `http://www.w3.org/TR/2000/REC-xhtml1-20000126/`

- XHTML Entity Sets: Latin-1 (`http://www.w3.org/TR/2000/REC-xhtml1-20000126/DTD/xhtml-lat1.ent`), special characters (`http://www.w3.org/TR/2000/REC-xhtml1-20000126/DTD/xhtml-special.ent`), and symbols (`http://www.w3.org/TR/2000/REC-xhtml1-20000126/DTD/xhtml-symbol.ent`)

- W3C HTML Validation Service: `http://validator.w3.org/`

- Web Content Accessibility Guidelines: `http://www.w3.org/TR/1999/WAI-WEBCONTENT-19990505/`

- Web Accessibility Initiative: `http://www.w3.org/WAI/`

- XHTML Strict DTD: `http://www.w3.org/TR/xhtml1/DTD/xhtml1-strict.dtd`

- XHTML Transitional DTD: `http://www.w3.org/TR/xhtml1/DTD/xhtml1-transitional.dtd`

- XHTML Frameset DTD: `http://www.w3.org/TR/xhtml1/DTD/xhtml1-frameset.dtd`

- HTML TIDY: `http://www.w3.org/People/Raggett/tidy/`

Chapter 14

- XLink: `http://www.w3.org/TR/xlink/`

- XPointer: `http://www.w3.org/TR/xptr/`

- Fujitsu XLink Processor (XLiP): `http://www.labs.fujitsu.com/free/xlip/en/index.html`

- XLink Tree Demo Application: `http://www.labs.fujitsu.com/free/xlip/en/sample1.html`

- XML Base: `http://www.w3.org/TR/xmlbase/`

- Annotea Project (a browser that uses XLink to keep a database of comments from you and other users): `http://www.w3.org/2001/Annotea/`

Chapter 15

- XForms Implementations: `http://www.w3.org/MarkUp/Forms/#implementations`

- X-Smiles: `http://www.x-smiles.org`

- XForms: `http://www.w3.org/TR/xforms-datamodel/`

Chapter 16

- XSL home page: `http://www.w3.org/Style/XSL/`

- XSL: `http://www.w3.org/TR/xsl/`

- "What is XSL-FO?" by G. Ken Holman: `http://www.xml.com/pub/a/2002/03/20/xsl-fo.html`

- "How to Develop Stylesheets for XML to XSL-FO Transformation":
  `http://www.antenna.co.jp/XML/downfree/howto1023/howtodevelop-en1025.pdf`

Chapter 17

- Tomcat: `http://jakarta.apache.org/tomcat/index.html`

- SOAP: `http://xml.apache.org/soap/index.html`

- HTTP Overview: `http://www.w3.org/Protocols/`

- The W3C Web Services Activity, including SOAP: `http://www.w3.org/2002/ws/`

- XMLP Requirements: `http://www.w3.org/TR/2002/WD-xmlp-reqs-20020626`

- "Discover and publish Web services with JAXR," by Kathy Walsh and Sang Shin:
  `http://www.javaworld.com/javaworld/jw-06-2002/jw-0614-jaxr.html`

- "Different Web Services Approaches": `http://www.it-director.com/article.php?id=2841`

- "Web Services Standards": `http://www.it-director.com/article.php?id=2840`

- The Liberty Alliance Project: `http://www.projectliberty.org/`

- "Web Services Security: A Political Battlefield," by Anne Chen: `http://www.eweek.com/article2/0,3959,169561,00.asp`

- "Web Services Architect Review," by Mark Waterhouse: `http://www.webservicesarchitect.com/content/articles/mark04.asp`

- "ebXML and Web Services—Friends or Foes?" by Dieter E. Jenz: `http://www.webservices.org/index.php/article/articleview/451/1/24/`

- "Rumble in the jungle: J2EE versus .NET, Part 1":
  `http://www.idg.net/ic_879962_1794_9-10000.html`

- Java Web Services Developer Pack: `http://java.sun.com/webservices/webservicespack.html`

- Java Web Services Tutorial: `http://java.sun.com/webservices/tutorial.html`

- Java XML Pack Summer 02 Release: `http://java.sun.com/xml/downloads/javaxmlpack.html`

Chapter 18

- The Castor Project: `http://www.castor.org/`

- Java XML Pack Summer 02 Release (including JAXB): `http://java.sun.com/xml/downloads/javaxmlpack.html`

- "Use XML data binding to do your laundry," by Sam Brodkin:
  `http://www.javaworld.com/javaworld/jw-12-2001/jw-1228-jaxb.html`

- XML Data Binding Resources: `http://www.rpbourret.com/xml/XMLDataBinding.htm`

- "XML in Java: Data Binding with Castor," by Dennis M. Sosnoski: `http://www-106.ibm.com/developerworks/xml/library/x-bindcastor/`

Chapter 19

- Ronald Bourret's XML/Database Links:
  `http://www.rpbourret.com/xml/XMLDBLinks.htm`

- "Mapping Objects To Relational Databases," by Scott W. Ambler:
  `http://www.ambysoft.com/mappingObjects.pdf`

- "XML and Databases," from the XML Cover Pages:
  `http://xml.coverpages.org/xmlAndDatabases.html`

- Oracle 9i Database Documentation: `http://otn.oracle.com/docs/products/oracle9i/content.html`

- "Using XML in Oracle Database Applications," from the Oracle Technology Network:
  `http://otn.oracle.com/tech/xml/htdocs/xml_in_oracle_apps.htm`

- "A Survey of Microsoft SQL Server 2000 XML Features," by Andrew Conrad:
  `http://msdn.microsoft.com/library/default.asp?url=/library/en-us/dnexxml/html/xml07162001.asp`

- XML information from the Microsoft Developer Network:
  `http://msdn.microsoft.com/library/default.asp?url=/nhp/default.asp?contentid=28000438`

- DB2 XML Extender information: `http://www-3.ibm.com/software/data/db2/extenders/xmlext/index.html`

Chapter 20

- Xindice: `http://xml.apache.org/xindice/`

- XML:DB API implementations: `http://www.xmldb.org/xapi/index.html`

- The X-Hive/DB online XQuery demo: `http://www.x-hive.com/xquery/index.html`

- The X-Hive/DB online XUpdate demo: `http://www.x-hive.com/xupdate/index.html`

- XML Query 1.0 and XML Path Language 2.0 drafts and recommendations:
  `http://www.w3.org/XML/Query`

- The GoXML DB Native XML Database from XML Global: `http://www.xmlglobal.com/prod/db/index.jsp`

- The Tamino Native XML Database from Software AG: `http://www.softwareag.com/tamino/default.htm`

- X-Hive/DB Native XML Database: `http://www.x-hive.com/products/db/`

Chapter 21

- MathML: `http://www.w3.org/Math/`

- SMIL: `http://www.w3.org/AudioVideo/`

- SVG: `http://www.w3.org/Graphics/SVG/`

- W3C RDF Validation Service: `http://www.w3.org/RDF/Validator/`

- XML Key Management Specification: `http://www.w3.org/TR/xkms2/`

- W3C XML Encryption Working Group: `http://www.w3.org/Encryption/2001/`

- "Enabling XML security: An introduction to XML encryption and XML signature," by Murdoch Mactaggart: `http://www-106.ibm.com/developerworks/xml/library/s-xmlsec.html/index.html`

- IETF/W3C XML Signature Working Group: `http://www.w3.org/Signature/`

- "An Introduction to XML Digital Signatures," by Ed Simon, Paul Madsen, and Carlisle Adams: `http://www.xml.com/pub/a/2001/08/08/xmldsig.html`

- RDF home page: `http://www.w3.org/RDF/`

- W3C RDF Validation Service: `http://www.w3.org/RDF/Validator/`

- "Dublin Core Metadata Element Set, Version 1.1: Reference Description": `http://purl.org/dc/about/element_set.htm`

- Frequently Asked Questions about RDF: `http://www.w3.org/RDF/FAQ`

- RDF Site Summary (RSS) 1.0: `http://groups.yahoo.com/group/rss-dev/files/specification.html#s5.2`

- "Writing RSS 1.0," by Rael Dornfest: `http://www.oreillynet.com/lpt/a/network/2000/08/25/magazine/rss_tut.html`

- The Platform for Privacy Preferences: `http://www.w3.org/P3P/`

- W3C Technical Reports and Publications (a complete list of W3C Recommendations and other documents): `http://www.w3.org/TR/`

- VoiceXML: `http://www.w3.org/TR/voicexml20/`

- CCXML: `http://www.w3.org/TR/ccxml/`

- P3P and Privacy FAQ: `http://www.w3.org/P3P/p3pfaq.html`

- WML Cover Page: `http://www.oasis-open.org/cover/wap-wml.html`

- Wireless Markup Language 2.0 information: `http://xml.coverpages.org/wap-wml.html`

- Wireless browser and information: `http://developer.openwave.com/`

- XML Messaging Cover Page: `http://xml.coverpages.org/xmsg.html`

- XUL Tutorial: `http://www.xulplanet.com/tutorials/xultu/intro.html`

- The Open eBook Forum: `http://www.openebook.org/`

- Open eBook 1.2 Proposed Specification: `http://www.openebook.org/oebps/oebps1.2/review/index.htm`

- BPML: `http://www.bpmi.org/bpml.esp`

XML INFORMATION SET

*T*he XML Information Set defines the basic structure of information that must be returned by an application or recommendation handling XML data. A collection of XML data is known as an *information set*. Each item within the set, such as an element or attribute, is known as an *information item*. Each information item has several properties with specific names, which may themselves refer to other information items or sets of items.

The document Information Item

The `document` information item has the following properties:

- `children`—A list that includes one `element` information item to represent the root element (also known as the *document element*), as well as one `comment` information item and `processing instruction` information item for each comment and processing instruction, respectively, that appears outside the root element.

- `document element`—An information item corresponding to the root element.

- `character encoding scheme`—The name of the encoding specified in the XML declaration.

- `standalone`—The `yes` or `no` value included in the XML declaration. If the standalone value is not included in the XML declaration, the `standalone` property has no value.

- `version`—The `version` value included in the XML declaration.

- `base URI`—The URI of the `document` itself.

- `notations`—The set of all `notation` information items included in the DTD.

- `unparsed entities`—The set of all `unparsed entity` information items included in the DTD.

- `all declarations processed`—This property specifies whether the entire DTD has been read. It's not really a part of the information set in that it doesn't contain data, but its value determines whether certain properties may still be unknown because they haven't yet been read.

The element Information Item

The `element` information item has the following properties:

- `local name`—The actual name of the `element`, not including any namespace prefix. The local name of the `<air:airlock></air:airlock>` element is `airlock`.

- `attributes`—A list of `attribute` information items, one for each attribute on the element, not including namespace declarations. Note that by definition, attributes are not returned in any particular order.

- `children`—A set of information items, one for each element, comment, processing instruction, entity reference (before expansion), and character that is directly contained by the element. These are added to the list in the order in which they appear in the document.

- `parent`—The `element` (or `document`) that contains this element.

- `base URI`—The URI of the element itself.

- `prefix`—The namespace alias attached to the element name. The `prefix` of the `<air:airlock></air:airlock>` element information item is `air`.

- `namespace name`—A string representing the full name for the namespace to which this element belongs (such as `http://www.example.com/air`), as opposed to the alias (such as `air`).

- `namespace attributes`—A set of `attribute` information items, one for each namespace declaration on the element.

- `in-scope namespaces`—A set of `namespace` information items, one for each namespace that is either declared in the element or inherited by it.

The attribute Information Item

The `attribute` information item has the following properties:

- `local name`—The actual name of the attribute, not including any namespace prefix. The local name of the `air:responsible` attribute is `responsible`.

- `normalized value`—The value of the attribute after whitespace has been converted and, if necessary, collapsed.

- `specified`—A flag indicating that the attribute was actually specified as part of an element and is not simply a default attribute from the DTD.

- `attribute type`—The declared type of the attribute (if any), such as `CDATA`, `ID`, or `IDREF`. If there is no declaration (for example, in the absence of a DTD), the application should behave as though this value were `CDATA`.

- references—In the case of certain attribute types, such as `IDREF` or `IDREFS`, this property contains an ordered list of `element`s or other information items to which the attribute refers.

- owner element—The element on which this attribute appears.

- prefix—The namespace alias attached to the attribute name. The prefix of the `air:responsible attribute` information item is `air`.

- namespace name—The full name for the namespace to which this attribute belongs, as opposed to the alias.

The processing instruction Information Item

The `processing instruction` information item has the following properties:

- target—A string representing the target for the processing instruction.

- content—A string representing the information to be passed to the target.

- parent—The document, DTD, or element that contains the processing instruction.

- base URI—The base URI of the processing instruction. If a processing instruction is included in an external entity and is subsequently saved as part of the final document, the base URI will change to the URI of the final document. If the original information is important to you, structure your documents accordingly.

- notation—The `notation` information item referred to by the processing instruction.

The unexpanded entity reference Information Item

The `unexpanded entity reference` information item (such as `&signagetext;`) contains the following properties:

- name—The name of the entity referenced. The name of the `&signagetext;` entity reference is `signagetext`.

- parent—The `element` information item that contains the reference.

- SYSTEM identifier—A string representing the system identifier as it appears in the entity definition within the DTD.

- declaration base URI—The base URI relative to which the system identifier should be resolved.

- PUBLIC identifier—A string representing the public identifier as it appears in the entity definition within the DTD.

The `character` Information Item

The `character` information item has the following properties:

- `parent`—The `element` information item that contains the character.
- `character code`—The ISO 10646 code for this character. These codes range from 0 to #x10FFFF.
- `element content whitespace`—This Boolean value specifies whether the character is a whitespace character. It's up to the application to handle the information accordingly.

The `comment` Information Item

The `comment` information item has the following properties:

- `content`—A string representing the content of the comment.
- `parent`—The `document` or `element` information item containing the comment.

The `Document Type Definition` Information Item

The `Document Type Definition` information item has the following properties:

- `children`—The list of any `processing instruction` information items, including definitions, that appear within the DTD. Internal processing instructions appear before those in an external subset.
- `parent`—The `document` information item.
- `SYSTEM identifier`—The system identifier for the external subset, if there is one.
- `PUBLIC identifier`—The public identifier for the external subset, if there is one.

The `unparsed entity` Information Item

The `unparsed entity` information item (such as a reference to a graphics file from within the DTD) has the following properties:

- `name`—A string representing the name of the entity.
- `notation name`—The notation name given by the entity definition.
- `notation`—The `notation` information item that corresponds to the notation name.
- `SYSTEM identifier`—The system identifier for the content that makes up the entity.

- **declaration base URI**—The base URI relative to which the system identifier should be resolved. This is the same as the base URI for the document that contains the entity declaration, whether it's internal to the document or part of an external subset.

- **PUBLIC identifier**—The public identifier for the content that makes up the entity, if one is given.

The notation Information Item

The notation information item has the following properties:

- **name**—A string representing the name of the notation.

- **SYSTEM identifier**—The system identifier for the notation.

- **declaration base URI**—The base URI relative to which the system identifier should be resolved. This is the same as the base URI for the document that contains the entity declaration, whether it's internal to the document or part of an external subset.

- **PUBLIC identifier**—The public identifier for the notation, if one is given.

The namespace Information Item

The namespace information item has the following properties:

- **prefix**—A string representing the alias used to identify the namespace, found after xmlns: in the declaration. For example, in the namespace declaration xmlns:air="http://www.example.com/airlock/", the prefix is air.

- **namespace name**—The actual namespace that the prefix represents. For example, in the namespace declaration xmlns:air="http://www.example.com/airlock/", the namespace name is http://www.example.com/airlock/.

APPENDIX C

QUESTIONS AND ANSWERS

Chapter 1

Review Questions

1. What is an XML element?

    ANSWER: An XML element is content that starts with a start tag and ends with an end tag. It may contain elements, text, or other content.

2. What is an attribute?

    ANSWER: An attribute is a name-value pair that appears in an element's start tag.

3. How do you nest elements?

    ANSWER: A nested element is contained completely between the start and end tag of the containing element.

4. How many root elements can there be in a document?

    ANSWER: One.

5. What is the difference between a well-formed document and a valid document?

    ANSWER: A well-formed document conforms to the rules of XML, while a valid document is well-formed and conforms to constraints defined in a DTD or XML Schema.

6. What is an entity?

    ANSWER: An entity is information that is predefined within a DTD and referenced within the document.

7. Give an example of a processing instruction.

    ANSWER: `<?xml-stylesheet href="airlocks.xsl" type="text/xsl"?>`

8. What is a DTD used for?

    ANSWER: A DTD defines entities and provides constraints against which validation can be performed.

9. What is a namespace?

    ANSWER: A namespace is a grouping of elements and attributes based on a unique identifier such as a URI or URN.

10. What is a child element?

ANSWER: A child element is an element that is nested within another element, known as the parent.

Programming Exercises

1. Create a simple XML document to describe yourself. Make sure that it is well-formed.

SOLUTION:

```
<?xml version="1.0"?>
<person>
    <fname>Nick</fname>
    <lname>Chase</lname>
    <height>5' 6"</height>
    <hair>black</hair>
</person>
```

2. Create an XML file to describe a hobby of yours. Make sure that the data is at least three levels deep.

SOLUTION:

```
<?xml version="1.0">
<hobby>
    <painting>
        <material>brushes</material>
        <material>paint</material>
        <material>canvas</material>
    </painting>
</hobby>
```

3. Create an XML file that uses ID and IDREF attributes to link elements together conceptually. (Do not include a DTD at this time.)

SOLUTION:

```
<?xml version="1.0"?>
<people>
    <person personid="B1">
        <name>Nick Chase</name>
        <spouse refid="A1"/>
    </person>
    <person personid="A1">
        <name>Sarah Chase</name>
        <spouse refid="B1"/>
    </person>
</people>
```

4. Add a second namespace to one of your documents and add information that is part of that namespace.

SOLUTION:

```xml
<?xml version="1.0"?>
<people xmlns:job="http://www.example.com/jobs">
    <person personid="B1" job:title="Chief Cook and Bottle Washer">
        <name>Nick Chase</name>
        <spouse refid="A1"/>
    </person>
    <person personid="A1" job:title="Boss">
        <name>Sarah Chase</name>
        <spouse refid="B1"/>
    </person>
</people>
```

Chapter 2

Review Questions

1. What's the difference between a goal and an objective?

   ANSWER: An objective is measurable.

2. What are the six roles involved in planning a design?

   ANSWER: Project manager, team leader, interviewer, recordist, subject matter experts, and stakeholders.

3. Can one person perform more than one of these functions?

   ANSWER: Yes.

4. What is the scope of a project?

   ANSWER: The scope of the project defines the general size and area covered.

5. What are three possible sources of data for an XML system?

   ANSWER: Any three of the following: legacy systems, paper documents, trading partners, new systems, direct input, databases.

6. What are three possible destinations for data in an XML system?

   ANSWER: Any three of the following: legacy systems, presentation to users, trading partners, databases, new systems.

7. What is an interchange structure?

   ANSWER: The structure in which data must exist for transfer to trading partners.

8. What is a reference structure?

   ANSWER: The overall structure to which data must ultimately conform, regardless of any intermediate steps.

9. What does function modeling document?

ANSWER: What a business does, and how it does it.

10. What is an event?

ANSWER: An event is an occurrence that causes an effect or makes it possible (or even necessary) to perform other actions.

11. When should you review the model with users?

ANSWER: Once the preliminary model is complete, and any time major changes are made to it. You should also review it with them prior to finalizing it.

12. What is a data entity?

ANSWER: A person or thing your system deals with.

13. What is a data attribute?

ANSWER: Information about a data entity.

14. What is a relationship?

ANSWER: A sentence describing how one data entity relates to another data entity.

15. What are you looking for when you cross-check the function hierarchy and entity-relationship diagrams?

ANSWER: Missing functions or entities.

16. What is the meaning of the ?, +, and * modifiers?

ANSWER: The ? modifier means that an element can appear zero or more times. The + modifier means that an element must appear at least once. The * modifier means that an element can appear any number of times.

17. What is data normalization?

ANSWER: Normalizing data is the process of structuring the data so that it's referenced in a single location, rather than repeated.

18. What is one reason for grouping similar elements using a container element?

ANSWER: To make the document conceptually simpler for authors, or to ease data access.

Programming Exercises

1. Create a function hierarchy diagram for making a major purchase, such as a car or a house.

SOLUTION:

FIGURE 2.E1
Buying a car.

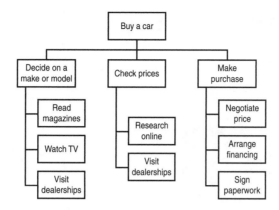

2. Create an entity-relationship diagram for a school.

    SOLUTION:

FIGURE 2.E2
ERD for a school.

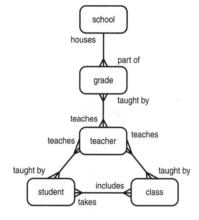

3. Translate the ERD in the previous exercise into an appropriate tree model.

    SOLUTION:

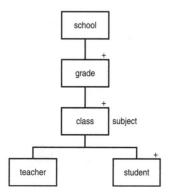

4. Create a sample document based on the model.

SOLUTION:

```xml
<school>
    <grade>
        <class subject="math">
            <teacher>Mrs. Lake</teacher>
            <student>John Smith</student>
            <student>Mary Jones</student>
            <student>Jack Ripper</student>
        </class>
        <class subject="english">
            <teacher>Mrs. Kastanis</teacher>
            <student>John Smith</student>
            <student>Mary Jones</student>
            <student>Jack Ripper</student>
        </class>
    </grade>
    <grade>
        <class subject="math">
            <teacher>Mrs. Chopper</teacher>
            <student>Frank Martin</student>
            <student>Sam Jackson</student>
        </class>
        <class subject="spanish">
            <teacher>Mrs. Dell</teacher>
            <student>Wayne Smith</student>
            <student>Margaret Eason</student>
            <student>Frank Martin</student>
        </class>
    </grade>
</school>
```

Chapter 3

Review Questions

1. What is the purpose of the Document Object Model?

    ANSWER: To create a standard API for developers.

2. What is the relationship between DOM and browsers?

    ANSWER: The DOM originated out of a need to standardize browser scripting, and many of the current modules are targeted toward that purpose.

3. What are the DOM Level 2.0 modules?

    ANSWER: Core, Style Sheets, Views, Traversal, HTML, and Events.

4. What is the main interface in the DOM Level 2.0 Core module?

   ANSWER: The `Node` interface.

5. Which interface is generally used to create nodes?

   ANSWER: `Document`.

6. Which interface is generally used to move nodes around?

   ANSWER: `Node`.

7. What two essential operations are not defined by DOM Level 2.0?

   ANSWER: Loading and saving documents.

8. How many nodes are involved with an element that has text content and two attributes?

   ANSWER: Six—one element node, two attribute nodes, and three text nodes.

Programming Exercises

These exercises assume that you have a file called `aliens.xml` with the following content:

```xml
<?xml version="1.0"?>
<aliens>
    <alien>
        <classification>GS3</classification>
        <species>Isaboreans</species>
        <planet>Isabore 3</planet>
        <range confirmed="yes">3000000</range>
    </alien>

    <alien>
        <classification>PPW</classification>
        <species>Rowaria</species>
        <planet>Roware 9</planet>
        <range confirmed="no">400000</range>
    </alien>

    <alien>
        <classification>IOPO</classification>
        <species>Discoria</species>
        <planet>Bearost 4</planet>
        <range confirmed="yes">9000</range>
    </alien>

</aliens>
```

1. Using your chosen language, create a `Document` object.

   SOLUTION (Java):

```java
import javax.xml.parsers.DocumentBuilder;
import javax.xml.parsers.DocumentBuilderFactory;
import java.io.File;
```

```
import org.w3c.dom.Document;

public class Exercises {
    public static void main (String args[]) {
        File docFile = new File("aliens.xml");
        Document doc = null;
        try {
            DocumentBuilderFactory dbf = DocumentBuilderFactory.newInstance();
            DocumentBuilder db = dbf.newDocumentBuilder();
            doc = db.parse(docFile);
        } catch (Exception e) {
            System.out.print("Problem parsing the file.");
        }
    }
}
```

2. Alter your application to retrieve the root element and output its name.

SOLUTION (Java):

```
import javax.xml.parsers.DocumentBuilder;
import javax.xml.parsers.DocumentBuilderFactory;
import java.io.File;
import org.w3c.dom.Document;
import org.w3c.dom.Element;

public class Exercises {
    public static void main (String args[]) {
        File docFile = new File("aliens.xml");
        Document doc = null;
        try {
            DocumentBuilderFactory dbf = DocumentBuilderFactory.newInstance();
            DocumentBuilder db = dbf.newDocumentBuilder();
            doc = db.parse(docFile);
        } catch (Exception e) {
            System.out.print("Problem parsing the file.");
        }

        Element root = doc.getDocumentElement();
        System.out.println(root.getNodeName());
    }
}
```

3. Display the species names.

SOLUTION (Java):

```
import javax.xml.parsers.DocumentBuilder;
import javax.xml.parsers.DocumentBuilderFactory;
import java.io.File;
import org.w3c.dom.Document;
import org.w3c.dom.Element;
import org.w3c.dom.Node;
import org.w3c.dom.NodeList;
```

```java
public class Exercises {
   public static void main (String args[]) {
      File docFile = new File("aliens.xml");
      Document doc = null;
      try {
         DocumentBuilderFactory dbf = DocumentBuilderFactory.newInstance();
         DocumentBuilder db = dbf.newDocumentBuilder();
         doc = db.parse(docFile);
      } catch (Exception e) {
         System.out.print("Problem parsing the file.");
      }

    Element root = doc.getDocumentElement();
      NodeList aliens = root.getElementsByTagName("alien");
      for (int i=0; i < aliens.getLength(); i++) {
         Element thisAlien = (Element)aliens.item(i);
         Node species = thisAlien.getElementsByTagName("species").item(0);
         String speciesText = species.getFirstChild().getNodeValue();
         System.out.println(speciesText);
      }
   }
}
```

4. For each `alien` element, display the name and text of each element node.

SOLUTION (Java):

```java
import javax.xml.parsers.DocumentBuilder;
import javax.xml.parsers.DocumentBuilderFactory;
import java.io.File;
import org.w3c.dom.Document;
import org.w3c.dom.Element;
import org.w3c.dom.Node;
import org.w3c.dom.NodeList;

public class Exercises {
   public static void main (String args[]) {
      File docFile = new File("aliens.xml");
      Document doc = null;
      try {
         DocumentBuilderFactory dbf = DocumentBuilderFactory.newInstance();
         DocumentBuilder db = dbf.newDocumentBuilder();
         doc = db.parse(docFile);
      } catch (Exception e) {
         System.out.print("Problem parsing the file.");
      }

    Element root = doc.getDocumentElement();
      NodeList aliens = root.getElementsByTagName("alien");
      for (int i=0; i < aliens.getLength(); i++) {
         Node thisAlien = aliens.item(i);
         NodeList children = thisAlien.getChildNodes();
         for (int j=0; j < children.getLength(); j++) {
            Node thisChild = children.item(j);
```

```
                    if (thisChild.getNodeType() == thisChild.ELEMENT_NODE) {
                        System.out.println("Name = "+thisChild.getNodeName());
                        System.out.println("Text = "+
                                    thisChild.getFirstChild().getNodeValue());
                    }
                }
            }
        }
    }
```

5. Make sure all confirmed attributes have a value of **yes**.

SOLUTION (Java):

```
import javax.xml.parsers.DocumentBuilder;
import javax.xml.parsers.DocumentBuilderFactory;
import java.io.File;
import org.w3c.dom.Document;
import org.w3c.dom.Element;
import org.w3c.dom.Node;
import org.w3c.dom.NodeList;

public class Exercises {
    public static void main (String args[]) {
        File docFile = new File("aliens.xml");
        Document doc = null;
        try {
            DocumentBuilderFactory dbf = DocumentBuilderFactory.newInstance();
            DocumentBuilder db = dbf.newDocumentBuilder();
            doc = db.parse(docFile);
        } catch (Exception e) {
            System.out.print("Problem parsing the file.");
        }

      Element root = doc.getDocumentElement();
        NodeList aliens = root.getElementsByTagName("alien");
        for (int i=0; i < aliens.getLength(); i++) {
            Element thisAlien = (Element)aliens.item(i);
            Element range =
                    (Element)thisAlien.getElementsByTagName("range").item(0);
            String rangeValue = range.getAttribute("confirmed");
            if (!rangeValue.equals("yes")){
                range.setAttribute("confirmed", "yes");
            }
        }
    }
}
```

Chapter 4

Review Questions

1. How does a `NodeIterator` traverse a document?

   ANSWER: Node by node, in document order.

2. How does a `TreeWalker` traverse a document?

   ANSWER: By traversing the children of a node before its siblings.

3. What does a `NodeFilter` do?

   ANSWER: It affects the nodes that are visible to a `NodeFilter` or `TreeWalker`.

4. What's the difference between the way a `NodeFilter` acts on a `NodeIterator` and the way it acts on a `TreeWalker`?

   ANSWER: A `NodeIterator` treats `FILTER_SKIP` and `FILTER_REJECT` in exactly the same way, whereas a `TreeWalker` skips all descendents of a node affected by `FILTER_REJECT`.

5. What does normalization do?

   ANSWER: Normalization removes empty text nodes and merges adjacent nodes.

6. What's the purpose of canonicalization?

   ANSWER: It provides a common way to represent data, allowing easier comparison of documents.

7. What's the purpose of the Load and Save portion of the DOM Level 3.0?

   ANSWER: To standardize these functions across implementations.

Programming Exercises

These exercises use the following source file:

```
<pets>
    <dog display="hidden"><name>Razzle</name><type>Yorkshire Terrier</type></dog>
    <dog display="hidden"><name>Sabre</name><type>German Shepherd Dog</type></dog>
    <cat display="hidden"><name>Tiger</name><type>Domestic Shorthair</type></cat>
    <bird display="hidden"><name>Frazzle</name><type>Quaker Parrot</type></bird>
    <fish><name display="hidden">Clark</name><type>goldfish</type></fish>
    <fish><name display="hidden">Lois</name><type>goldfish</type></fish>
</pets>
```

1. Write an application that uses a `NodeIterator` to display the text of a document.

   SOLUTION:

```
import javax.xml.parsers.DocumentBuilder;
import javax.xml.parsers.DocumentBuilderFactory;
import java.io.File;
```

```
import org.w3c.dom.Document;
import org.w3c.dom.Node;
import org.w3c.dom.traversal.DocumentTraversal;
import org.w3c.dom.traversal.NodeIterator;
import org.w3c.dom.traversal.NodeFilter;

public class ShowDocument {

    public static void main (String args[]) {
        File docFile = new File("pets.xml");

        Document doc = null;
        try {
            DocumentBuilderFactory dbf = DocumentBuilderFactory.newInstance();
            DocumentBuilder db = dbf.newDocumentBuilder();

            doc = db.parse(docFile);
        } catch (Exception e) {
            System.out.print("Problem parsing the file.");
        }
        Node root = doc.getDocumentElement();

        DocumentTraversal traversal = (DocumentTraversal)doc;
        int whattoshow = NodeFilter.SHOW_TEXT;
        NodeFilter nodefilter = null;
        boolean expandreferences = false;

        NodeIterator iterator = traversal.createNodeIterator(root,
                                                    whattoshow,
                                                    nodefilter,
                                                    expandreferences);

        Node thisNode = null;
        thisNode = iterator.nextNode();
        while (thisNode != null) {
            System.out.println(thisNode.getNodeValue());
            thisNode = iterator.nextNode();
        }
    }
}
```

2. Write a NodeFilter or TreeWalker that displays the text nodes of a document, but doesn't display "hidden" elements or their children.

SOLUTION:

```
import org.w3c.dom.traversal.NodeFilter;
import org.w3c.dom.Node;
import org.w3c.dom.Element;

public class ShowFilter implements NodeFilter {

    public short acceptNode(Node thisNode) {
        if (thisNode.getNodeType()==Node.ELEMENT_NODE) {
```

```
                Element thisElementNode = (Element)thisNode;
                if (thisElementNode.getAttribute("display")
                                   .equals("hidden")) {
                      return NodeFilter.FILTER_REJECT;
                }
            }
          return NodeFilter.FILTER_ACCEPT;
    }
}
--------------------------------------------------

import javax.xml.parsers.DocumentBuilder;
import javax.xml.parsers.DocumentBuilderFactory;
import java.io.File;
import org.w3c.dom.Document;
import org.w3c.dom.Element;
import org.w3c.dom.Node;
import org.w3c.dom.traversal.DocumentTraversal;
import org.w3c.dom.traversal.NodeIterator;
import org.w3c.dom.traversal.TreeWalker;
import org.w3c.dom.traversal.NodeFilter;

public class ShowDocument {

    public static void main (String args[]) {
        File docFile = new File("airlocks.xml");

        Document doc = null;
        try {
           DocumentBuilderFactory dbf = DocumentBuilderFactory.newInstance();
           DocumentBuilder db = dbf.newDocumentBuilder();

           doc = db.parse(docFile);
        } catch (Exception e) {
            System.out.print("Problem parsing the file.");
        }
        Node root = doc.getDocumentElement();

        DocumentTraversal traversal = (DocumentTraversal)doc;
        int whattoshow = NodeFilter.SHOW_ALL;
        NodeFilter nodefilter = new ShowFilter();
        boolean expandreferences = false;

        TreeWalker walker = traversal.createTreeWalker(root,
                                                 whattoshow,
                                                 nodefilter,
                                                 expandreferences);

        Node thisNode = null;
        thisNode = walker.nextNode();
        while (thisNode != null) {
           if (thisNode.getNodeType() == thisNode.TEXT_NODE) {
               System.out.println(thisNode.getNodeValue());
           }
```

```
                         thisNode = walker.nextNode();
                    }
               }
          }
```

3. Write an application that uses the DOM Level 3.0 to load a remotely located document.

SOLUTION:

```
import org.w3c.dom.Document;
import org.apache.xerces.dom.DOMImplementationImpl;
import org.apache.xerces.dom3.ls.DOMImplementationLS;
import org.apache.xerces.dom3.ls.DOMBuilder;
import org.apache.xerces.dom3.ls.DOMInputSource;
import org.w3c.dom.Node;

public class LoadSave {

    public static void main (String args[]) {

        Document doc = null;
        try {
            DOMImplementationLS DOMLS = new DOMImplementationImpl();
            short synch = 1;
            DOMBuilder db = DOMLS.createDOMBuilder(synch);
            DOMInputSource dinput = DOMLS.createDOMInputSource();
            dinput.setSystemId("http://www.nicholaschase.com/pets.xml");
            doc = db.parse(dinput);

            Node root = doc.getDocumentElement();
            System.out.println(root.getNodeName());

        } catch (Exception e) {
            System.out.print("Problem parsing the file.");
        }
    }

}
```

Chapter 5

Review Questions

1. What is an event-based API?

   ANSWER: An event-based API is one that reacts to events and the sequence in which they occur, rather than looking at the overall nature of a system.

2. Under what conditions would an event-based API be preferable to an object-based API?

   ANSWER: If only a small percentage of the data were required, particularly in situations where you needed to analyze a large amount of data. Other factors that make an event-based API preferable include read-only processing and situations where the overall structure of the data is not important.

3. Under what conditions would an object-based API be preferable to an event-based API?

ANSWER: If you needed to modify the original source, or if the same data were to be examined repeatedly.

4. What are the two main event handlers defined for SAX?

ANSWER: Content handlers and error handlers.

5. What does an `XMLReader` do?

ANSWER: It parses the document and sends events to event handlers.

6. What does an `XMLFilter` do?

ANSWER: It sits between the `XMLReader` and the event handlers and either passes events on unchanged or modifies them before passing them on.

Programming Exercises

1. Write an application that takes the simple XML document from this chapter, parses it using SAX, and outputs it to the screen. Whitespace is optional. If possible in your programming language, do this with a single class. Be sure to include the XML declaration and namespace definitions.

SOLUTION (Java):

```
import org.xml.sax.helpers.XMLReaderFactory;
import org.xml.sax.XMLReader;
import org.xml.sax.SAXException;
import org.xml.sax.InputSource;
import java.io.IOException;
import org.xml.sax.XMLFilter;
import org.xml.sax.helpers.DefaultHandler;
import org.xml.sax.Attributes;
import org.xml.sax.SAXParseException;

public class ExercisesClass extends DefaultHandler{

    public ExercisesClass ()
    {
        super();
    }

    public void startDocument() {
        System.out.println("<?xml version=\"1.0\"?>");
    }

    String thisNameSpaceDecl = "";
```

```
        public void startPrefixMapping (java.lang.String prefix,
                                        java.lang.String uri) {
          thisNameSpaceDecl = " xmlns:"+prefix+"=\""+uri+"\"";
          }

    StringBuffer thisText = new StringBuffer();
    public void startElement (String namespaceUri, String localName,
                     String qualifiedName, Attributes attributes) {
          System.out.print(thisText.toString());
          thisText.delete(0, thisText.length());
          System.out.print("<"+qualifiedName);
          for (int i = 0; i < attributes.getLength(); i++) {
             String qualAttName = attributes.getQName(i);
             String attValue = attributes.getValue(qualAttName);
             System.out.print(" " + qualAttName + "=\"" + attValue + "\"");
          }
          System.out.print(thisNameSpaceDecl);
          thisNameSpaceDecl = "";
          System.out.print(">");
    }

    public void endElement (String namespaceUri, String localName,
                     String qualifiedName) throws SAXException
    {
          System.out.print(thisText.toString());
          thisText.delete(0, thisText.length());
          System.out.println("</"+qualifiedName+">");
    }

    public void characters (char[] ch, int start, int length)
    {
          thisText.append(ch, start, length);
    }

     public void error (SAXParseException e) {
          System.out.println("Error: "+e.getMessage());
     }

     public void fatalError (SAXParseException e) {
          System.out.println("Fatal Error: "+e.getMessage());
     }

     public void warning (SAXParseException e) {
          System.out.println("Warning: "+e.getMessage());
     }

     public static void main (String[] args){

        try {

            String parserClass = "org.apache.crimson.parser.XMLReaderImpl";
            XMLReader reader = XMLReaderFactory.createXMLReader(parserClass);

            ExercisesClass thisContentHandler = new ExercisesClass();
```

```
          ExercisesClass thisErrorHandler = new ExercisesClass();

          reader.setContentHandler(thisContentHandler);
          reader.setErrorHandler(thisErrorHandler);

          InputSource file = new InputSource("votes.xml");
          reader.parse(file);

        } catch (IOException ioe) {
          System.out.println("IO Exception: "+ioe.getMessage());
        } catch (SAXException se) {
          System.out.println("SAX Exception: "+se.getMessage());
        }

    }

}
```

2. Create a filter that appends _test to the end of every element name. Use it with the solution to exercise 1.

SOLUTION (Java):

```
import org.xml.sax.helpers.XMLReaderFactory;
import org.xml.sax.XMLReader;
import org.xml.sax.SAXException;
import org.xml.sax.InputSource;
import java.io.IOException;
import org.xml.sax.XMLFilter;
import org.xml.sax.helpers.DefaultHandler;
import org.xml.sax.Attributes;
import org.xml.sax.SAXParseException;

public class ExercisesClass extends DefaultHandler{

    public ExercisesClass ()
    {
        super();
    }

    public void startDocument() {
        System.out.println("<?xml version=\"1.0\"?>");
    }

    String thisNameSpaceDecl = "";
    public void startPrefixMapping (java.lang.String prefix,
                                    java.lang.String uri) {
      thisNameSpaceDecl = " xmlns:"+prefix+"=\""+uri+"\"";
      }

    StringBuffer thisText = new StringBuffer();
    public void startElement (String namespaceUri, String localName,
                String qualifiedName, Attributes attributes) {
      System.out.print(thisText.toString());
```

```java
      thisText.delete(0, thisText.length());
      System.out.print("<"+qualifiedName);
      for (int i = 0; i < attributes.getLength(); i++) {
         String qualAttName = attributes.getQName(i);
         String attValue = attributes.getValue(qualAttName);
         System.out.print(" " + qualAttName + "=\"" + attValue + "\"");
      }
      System.out.print(thisNameSpaceDecl);
      thisNameSpaceDecl = "";
      System.out.print(">");
   }

   public void endElement (String namespaceUri, String localName,
                   String qualifiedName) throws SAXException
   {
      System.out.print(thisText.toString());
      thisText.delete(0, thisText.length());
      System.out.println("</"+qualifiedName+">");
   }

   public void characters (char[] ch, int start, int length)
   {
       thisText.append(ch, start, length);
   }

    public void error (SAXParseException e) {
        System.out.println("Error: "+e.getMessage());
    }

    public void fatalError (SAXParseException e) {
        System.out.println("Fatal Error: "+e.getMessage());
    }

    public void warning (SAXParseException e) {
        System.out.println("Warning: "+e.getMessage());
    }

    public static void main (String[] args){

       try {

          String parserClass = "org.apache.crimson.parser.XMLReaderImpl";
          XMLReader reader = XMLReaderFactory.createXMLReader(parserClass);

          XMLFilter filter = new ExerciseFilter();
          filter.setParent(reader);

          ExercisesClass thisContentHandler = new ExercisesClass();
          ExercisesClass thisErrorHandler = new ExercisesClass();

          filter.setContentHandler(thisContentHandler);
          filter.setErrorHandler(thisErrorHandler);

          InputSource file = new InputSource("votes.xml");
```

```
          filter.parse(file);

      } catch (IOException ioe) {
        System.out.println("IO Exception: "+ioe.getMessage());
      } catch (SAXException se) {
        System.out.println("SAX Exception: "+se.getMessage());
      }

   }

}
```

```
import org.xml.sax.XMLReader;
import org.xml.sax.helpers.XMLFilterImpl;
import org.xml.sax.Attributes;
import org.xml.sax.SAXException;

public class ExerciseFilter extends XMLFilterImpl
{

   public ExerciseFilter ()
   {
   }

   public ExerciseFilter (XMLReader parent)
   {
      super(parent);
   }

   public void startElement (String namespaceUri, String localName,
                 String qualifiedName, Attributes attributes)
                     throws SAXException
   {
      super.startElement(namespaceUri, localName+"_test",
                        qualifiedName+"_test", attributes);
   }

   public void endElement (String namespaceUri, String localName,
                 String qualifiedName) throws SAXException
   {
      super.endElement(namespaceUri, localName+"_test",
                             qualifiedName+"_test");
   }

}
```

3. Alter the sample program in this chapter to output voter comments and complete vote tallies. (Don't stop parsing when the winner is clear.)

SOLUTION (Java):

```
import org.xml.sax.XMLReader;
import org.xml.sax.helpers.XMLFilterImpl;
import org.xml.sax.Attributes;
```

```
import org.xml.sax.SAXException;

public class DataFilter extends XMLFilterImpl
{

   public DataFilter ()
   {
   }

   public DataFilter (XMLReader parent)
   {
      super(parent);
   }

   boolean isValidVote = false;
   boolean isVoteElement = false;
   public void startElement (String namespaceUri, String localName,
                     String qualifiedName, Attributes attributes)
                           throws SAXException
   {
      if (localName.equals("voter")) {
         if (attributes.getValue("status").equals("primary")){
            isValidVote = true;
         } else {
            isValidVote = false;
         }
      }
      if (localName.equals("vote")) {
         isVoteElement = true;
      } else {
         isVoteElement = false;
      }
      super.startElement(namespaceUri, localName, qualifiedName,
                                             attributes);
   }

   public void endElement (String namespaceUri, String localName,
                     String qualifiedName) throws SAXException
   {
      isVoteElement = false;
      super.endElement(namespaceUri, localName, qualifiedName);
   }

   public void characters (char[] ch, int start, int length)
                                             throws SAXException
   {

      if (isValidVote) {
         super.characters(ch, start, length);
      } else {
         if (isVoteElement) {
            super.characters(ch, start, 0);
         } else {
            super.characters(ch, start, length);
```

```
            }
        }
    }

}
------------------------------------------------------------
import org.xml.sax.helpers.DefaultHandler;
import org.xml.sax.Attributes;
import org.xml.sax.SAXException;

public class DataProcessor extends DefaultHandler
{
    public DataProcessor ()
    {
        super();
    }

    StringBuffer thisText = new StringBuffer();
    int sTally = 0;
    int dTally = 0;

    int totalVotes = 0;
    int votesLeft = 0;
    int votesDropped = 0;

    //---------------
    //UTILITY METHODS
    //---------------
    public static void println(String arg) {
        System.out.println(arg);
    }

    public void outputResults(){
        println("Sparkle: "+sTally+"   Dregraal: "+dTally);
    }

    //-------------
    //EVENT METHODS
    //-------------
    public void startDocument() { }
    public void endDocument() {
        outputResults();
    }

    public void ignorableWhitespace (char[] ch, int start, int length) { }

    public void startElement (String namespaceUri, String localName,
                    String qualifiedName, Attributes attributes) {
        thisText.delete(0, thisText.length());

        if (localName.equals("votes")) {
            totalVotes = Integer.parseInt(attributes.getValue("totalVotes"));
            votesLeft = totalVotes;
        }
```

```
        }

        public void endElement (String namespaceUri, String localName,
                     String qualifiedName) throws SAXException
        {
            if (localName.equals("comments")) {
                println(thisText.toString());
                println("----------------------");
            }
            if (localName.equals("vote")){
                if (thisText.toString().equals("Sparkle")){
                    sTally = sTally + 1;
                } else if (thisText.toString().equals("Dregraal")){
                    dTally = dTally + 1;
                } else if (thisText.toString().equals("")) {
                    votesDropped = votesDropped + 1;
                }
            }
            thisText.delete(0, thisText.length());
        }

        public void characters (char[] ch, int start, int length)
        {
            thisText.append(ch, start, length);
        }

    }
```

Chapter 6

Review Questions

1. What is validation?

   ANSWER: Validation is the process of ensuring that a document conforms to a particular structure.

2. Why is validation important?

   ANSWER: Validation is important because applications frequently depend on a particular structure when analyzing a document.

3. What are the two main validation languages?

   ANSWER: The two main validation languages are Document Type Definitions and XML schemas, which come in several varieties.

4. Can validation control the structure of a Document object after it's created?

   ANSWER: No. Once a Document is created, you can do anything to it, including making it invalid.

5. What do SAX features do?

ANSWER: SAX features are unique URIs that refer to tasks that a SAX parser should or should not perform.

Programming Exercises

1. Create an application that ignores warnings, but stops completely upon encountering any error.

SOLUTION (Java):

```java
import javax.xml.parsers.DocumentBuilder;
import javax.xml.parsers.DocumentBuilderFactory;
import org.w3c.dom.Document;
import java.io.File;
import org.xml.sax.SAXParseException;

public class DocumentListing {

    public static void main (String args[]) {

        File docFile = new File("votes.xml");
        Document doc = null;

        try {

            DocumentBuilderFactory dbf = DocumentBuilderFactory.newInstance();

            dbf.setValidating(true);

            DocumentBuilder db = dbf.newDocumentBuilder();
            db.setErrorHandler(new ErrorProcessor());

            doc = db.parse(docFile);

        } catch (Exception e) {
            exit(0);
        }

    }
}

- - - - - - - - - - - - - - - - - - - - - - - - - - - - - - - - - - - - -

import org.xml.sax.helpers.DefaultHandler;
import org.xml.sax.SAXParseException;

public class ErrorProcessor extends DefaultHandler
{

    public ErrorProcessor ()
```

```
    {
        super();
    }

    public void warning (SAXParseException e) {    }

    public void error (SAXParseException e) throws SAXParseException {
        throw e;
    }

    public void fatalError (SAXParseException e) throws SAXParseException {
        throw e;
    }

}
```

2. Create an application that displays the line and column number for warnings.

    SOLUTION (Java):

```
import org.xml.sax.helpers.DefaultHandler;
import org.xml.sax.SAXParseException;

public class ErrorProcessor extends DefaultHandler
{

    public ErrorProcessor ()
    {
        super();
    }

    public void warning (SAXParseException e) {
        System.out.println("Line number: "+e.getLineNumber());
        System.out.println("Column number: "+e.getColumnNumber());
        System.out.println();
    }
}
```

3. Using documentation, create a SAX parser that validates against an XML schema.

    SOLUTION: Implementation dependent. For an example, see Listing 6.19a–d.

Chapter 7

Review Questions

1. What is a DTD used for?

    ANSWER: A Document Type Definition defines the required structure of a document. It can also be used to provide additional content to a document in the form of entities.

2. Can a document have both an internal and an external DTD subset?

   ANSWER: Yes.

3. What are the possible data types for an attribute?

   ANSWER: `CDATA`, `ID`, `IDREF`, `IDREFS`, `NMTOKEN`, `NMTOKENS`, `ENTITY`, and `ENTITIES`.

4. Is it possible to create an element declaration that does not require elements to be present in a particular order?

   ANSWER: Yes, by allowing multiple choices.

5. What is a content model?

   ANSWER: A content model specifies what an element may contain.

6. What is a content model called if it includes both element and text content?

   ANSWER: Mixed content.

7. What is the difference between a general entity and a parameter entity?

   ANSWER: Both are defined within the DTD, but the general entity can only be used within the document and the parameter entity can only be used within the DTD.

8. What is a numeric entity?

   ANSWER: An entity that directly specifies a character using its decimal or hexadecimal number.

9. If a DTD specifies default values for an attribute and the document is processed by a nonvalidating parser, what happens to those values?

   ANSWER: If the values are specified in the internal DTD subset, they will be included in the document. If they're specified in the external DTD subset, they can be included, but will usually be ignored.

10. How does the value of the `standalone` attribute affect DTDs (specifically entity declarations)?

    ANSWER: If the document is specified as `standalone="yes"`, no external entities can be included.

11. What is the difference between a system identifier and a public identifier?

    ANSWER: A system identifier specifies a resource directly. A public identifier references a name that represents a resource location in a lookup table such as a catalog.

Programming Exercises

1. Create a DTD that includes a hierarchy of at least three elements, at least one of which has an enumerated attribute.

SOLUTION:

```
<!ELEMENT galaxies (solarsystem+)>
<!ELEMENT solarsystem (planet*)>
<!ELEMENT planet (#PCDATA)>
<!ATTLIST planet inhabitable (yes | no) #IMPLIED>
```

2. Create a DTD that includes a mixed-content element that cannot contain itself.

SOLUTION:

```
<!ELEMENT galaxies (solarsystem+)>
<!ELEMENT solarsystem (planet*)>
<!ELEMENT planet (#PCDATA | moon)*>
<!ATTLIST planet inhabitable (yes | no) #IMPLIED>
<!ELEMENT moon (#PCDATA)>
```

3. Create a DTD that includes an attribute that is optional, but if present must contain a value present within another defined attribute.

SOLUTION:

```
<!ELEMENT galaxies (solarsystem+)>
<!ELEMENT solarsystem (planet*)>
<!ELEMENT planet (#PCDATA | moon)*>
<!ATTLIST planet inhabitable (yes | no) #IMPLIED
                 moons IDREFS #IMPLIED>
<!ELEMENT moon (#PCDATA)>
<!ATTLIST moon moonid ID #REQUIRED>
```

4. Create a DTD that includes a section the author can turn on or off, and create a document that utilizes it.

SOLUTION:

```
<!ELEMENT solarsystem (planet*)>
<!ELEMENT planet (#PCDATA | moon)*>
<!ATTLIST planet inhabitable (yes | no) #IMPLIED
                 moons IDREFS #IMPLIED>
<!ENTITY % atmosphere "INCLUDE">
<![%atmosphere;[
    <!ATTLIST planet atmospressure CDATA #REQUIRED
                     gasses CDATA #REQUIRED>
]]>
<!ELEMENT moon (#PCDATA)>
<!ATTLIST moon moonid ID #REQUIRED>
<?xml version="1.0"?>
<!DOCTYPE solarsystem SYSTEM "solarsystem.dtd"
[
    <!ENTITY % atmosphere "IGNORE">
]>
<solarsystem>
    <planet inhabitable="yes">
        Earth
    </planet>
</solarsystem>
```

Chapter 8

Review Questions

1. List three advantages that XML Schema offers over Document Type Definitions.

   ANSWER: Any three of the following: namespace handling, multiple elements with the same names, type definition, data integrity.

2. What is a facet?

   ANSWER: A property of a simple type.

3. What does restriction do?

   ANSWER: Restriction limits the acceptable values for a base type based on supplied criteria.

4. What does extension do?

   ANSWER: Extension adds to the structure of a base type.

5. What is the difference between a simple type and a complex type?

   ANSWER: A simple type can't have element content or attributes.

6. What attribute or attributes specify how many times an element can appear in a document?

   ANSWER: `minOccurs` and `maxOccurs`.

7. What is a default value, and can it be applied to an element?

   ANSWER: A default value is a value added to an element or attribute if no value is provided.

8. What does *inlining* mean?

   ANSWER: Types can be created and named and then referenced, or they can be created within the definition of the element or attribute they describe. The latter is known as *inlining*.

Programming Exercises

1. Define a simple element that can take only integer values.

   SAMPLE SOLUTION:

   ```
   <?xml version="1.0" encoding="UTF-8"?>
   <xs:schema xmlns:xs="http://www.w3.org/2001/XMLSchema">
       <xs:element name="freethrows" type="xs:integer"/>
   </xs:schema>
   ```

2. Create an element that can contain at least two child elements, one of which is optional but can appear an unlimited number of times, and one of which must appear between 5 and 10 times.

SAMPLE SOLUTION:

```
<?xml version="1.0" encoding="UTF-8"?>
<xs:schema xmlns:xs="http://www.w3.org/2001/XMLSchema">

    <xs:element name="appointments">
        <xs:complexType>
            <xs:sequence>
                <xs:element name="dinner" type="xs:string" minOccurs="0"
                                                   maxOccurs="unbounded"/>
                <xs:element name="meeting" type="xs:string" minOccurs="5"
                                                   maxOccurs="10"/>
            </xs:sequence>
        </xs:complexType>
    </xs:element>
</xs:schema>
```

3. Create an element that can contain only date values and carries at least one attribute.

SAMPLE SOLUTION:

```
<?xml version="1.0" encoding="UTF-8"?>
<xs:schema xmlns:xs="http://www.w3.org/2001/XMLSchema">

    <xs:element name="dinnerDate">
        <xs:complexType>
            <xs:simpleContent>
                <xs:extension base="xs:date">
                    <xs:attribute name="alone" default="yes"/>
                </xs:extension>
            </xs:simpleContent>
        </xs:complexType>
    </xs:element>

</xs:schema>
```

4. Create an element that can contain its child elements in any order.

SAMPLE SOLUTION:

```
<?xml version="1.0" encoding="UTF-8"?>
<xs:schema xmlns:xs="http://www.w3.org/2001/XMLSchema">

    <xs:element name="appointments">
        <xs:complexType>
            <xs:all>
                <xs:element name="dinner" type="xs:string" minOccurs="0"
                                                   maxOccurs="unbounded"/>
                <xs:element name="meeting" type="xs:string" minOccurs="5"
                                                   maxOccurs="10"/>
            </xs:all>
```

```
            </xs:complexType>
        </xs:element>
</xs:schema>
```

5. Create an element that can contain mixed content.

SAMPLE SOLUTION:

```
<?xml version="1.0" encoding="UTF-8"?>
<xs:schema xmlns:xs="http://www.w3.org/2001/XMLSchema">

    <xs:element name="appointments">
        <xs:complexType mixed="true">
            <xs:all>
                <xs:element name="dinner" type="xs:string" minOccurs="0"
                                                maxOccurs="unbounded"/>
                <xs:element name="meeting" type="xs:string" minOccurs="5"
                                                maxOccurs="10"/>
            </xs:all>
        </xs:complexType>
    </xs:element>
</xs:schema>
```

6. Create an element that contains child elements and attributes that have been previously defined.

SAMPLE SOLUTION:

```
<?xml version="1.0" encoding="UTF-8"?>
<xs:schema xmlns:xs="http://www.w3.org/2001/XMLSchema">

    <xs:element name="dinner" type="xs:string"/>
    <xs:element name="meeting" type="xs:string"/>

    <xs:attribute name="marrative" type="xs:boolean"/>

    <xs:element name="appointments">
        <xs:complexType>
            <xs:all>
                <xs:element ref="dinner" type="xs:string" minOccurs="0"
                                                maxOccurs="unbounded"/>
                <xs:element ref="meeting" type="xs:string" minOccurs="5"
                                                maxOccurs="10"/>
            </xs:all>
            <xs:attribute ref="narrative"/>
        </xs:complexType>
    </xs:element>
</xs:schema>
```

7. Create a simple type that represents a specific set of numeric values.

SAMPLE SOLUTION:

```
<?xml version="1.0" encoding="UTF-8"?>
<xs:schema xmlns:xs="http://www.w3.org/2001/XMLSchema">
```

```
    <xs:simpleType name="reserved">
        <xs:restriction base="xs:integer">
            <xs:enumeration value="1"/>
            <xs:enumeration value="0"/>
            <xs:enumeration value="-1"/>
        </xs:restriction>
    </xs:simpleType>

</xs:schema>
```

8. Create a simple type that uses two or more facets. Create an element of that type.

    SAMPLE SOLUTION:

    ```
    <?xml version="1.0" encoding="UTF-8"?>
    <xs:schema xmlns:xs="http://www.w3.org/2001/XMLSchema">

        <xs:simpleType name="passwordType">
            <xs:restriction base="xs:string">
                <xs:minLength value="8"/>
                <xs:maxLength value="16"/>
            </xs:restriction>
        </xs:simpleType>

        <xs:element name="password" type="passwordType"/>

    </xs:schema>
    ```

9. Create a complex type and an element that references it.

    SAMPLE SOLUTION:

    ```
    <?xml version="1.0" encoding="UTF-8"?>
    <xs:schema xmlns:xs="http://www.w3.org/2001/XMLSchema">

        <xs:element name="dinner" type="xs:string"/>
        <xs:element name="meeting" type="xs:string"/>
        <xs:attribute name="narrative" type="xs:boolean"/>

        <xs:element name="appointments" type="appointmentType"/>

        <xs:complexType name="appointmentType">
            <xs:all>
                <xs:element ref="dinner" type="xs:string" minOccurs="0"
                                                          maxOccurs="unbounded"/>
                <xs:element ref="meeting" type="xs:string" minOccurs="5"
                                                          maxOccurs="10"/>
            </xs:all>
            <xs:attribute ref="narrative"/>
        </xs:complexType>
    </xs:schema>
    ```

10. Create a new type by extending it.

    SAMPLE SOLUTION:

```xml
<?xml version="1.0" encoding="UTF-8"?>
<xs:schema xmlns:xs="http://www.w3.org/2001/XMLSchema">

    <xs:element name="dinner" type="xs:string"/>
    <xs:element name="meeting" type="xs:string"/>
    <xs:attribute name="narrative" type="xs:boolean"/>

    <xs:element name="appointments" type="appointmentType"/>

    <xs:complexType name="appointmentType">
        <xs:all>
            <xs:element ref="dinner" type="xs:string" minOccurs="0"
                                                maxOccurs="unbounded"/>
            <xs:element ref="meeting" type="xs:string" minOccurs="5"
                                                maxOccurs="10"/>
        </xs:all>
        <xs:attribute ref="narrative"/>
    </xs:complexType>

    <xs:complexType name="personalAppointmentType">
        <xs:extension base="appointmentType">
            <xs:sequence>
                <xs:element name="movie" type="xs:string"/>
            </xs:sequence>
        </xs:extension>
    </xs:complexType>
</xs:schema>
```

11. Create a new type by restricting it.

SAMPLE SOLUTION:

```xml
<?xml version="1.0" encoding="UTF-8"?>
<xs:schema xmlns:xs="http://www.w3.org/2001/XMLSchema">

    <xs:element name="dinner" type="xs:string"/>
    <xs:element name="meeting" type="xs:string"/>
    <xs:attribute name="narrative" type="xs:boolean"/>

    <xs:element name="appointments" type="appointmentType"/>

    <xs:complexType name="appointmentType">
        <xs:all>
            <xs:element ref="dinner" type="xs:string" minOccurs="0"
                                                maxOccurs="unbounded"/>
            <xs:element ref="meeting" type="xs:string" minOccurs="5"
                                                maxOccurs="10"/>
        </xs:all>
        <xs:attribute ref="narrative"/>
    </xs:complexType>

    <xs:complexType name="businessReportType">
        <xs:restriction base="appointmentType">
            <xs:sequence>
```

```
                    <xs:element ref="meeting" type="xs:string" minOccurs="5"
                                                           maxOccurs="10"/>
                </xs:sequence>
                <xs:attribute ref="narrative"/>
            </xs:restriction>
        </xs:complexType>
    </xs:schema>
```

12. Create the same element with an inline, or anonymous, definition.

SAMPLE SOLUTION:

```
<?xml version="1.0" encoding="UTF-8"?>
<xs:schema xmlns:xs="http://www.w3.org/2001/XMLSchema">

    <xs:element name="dinner" type="xs:string"/>
    <xs:element name="meeting" type="xs:string"/>
    <xs:attribute name="narrative" type="xs:boolean"/>

    <xs:element name="appointments" type="appointmentType">

    <xs:complexType name="appointmentType">
        <xs:all>
            <xs:element ref="dinner" type="xs:string" minOccurs="0"
                                                maxOccurs="unbounded"/>
            <xs:element ref="meeting" type="xs:string" minOccurs="5"
                                                maxOccurs="10"/>
        </xs:all>
        <xs:attribute ref="narrative"/>
    </xs:complexType>

    <xs:element name="report">
        <xs:complexType>
            <xs:restriction base="appointmentType">
                <xs:sequence>
                    <xs:element ref="meeting" type="xs:string" minOccurs="5"
                                                           maxOccurs="10"/>
                </xs:sequence>
                <xs:attribute ref="narrative"/>
            </xs:restriction>
        </xs:complexType>
    </xs:element>
</xs:schema>
```

13. Create an instance document that references your schema. The data must not belong to a namespace.

SAMPLE SOLUTION:

```
<?xml version="1.0" encoding="UTF-8"?>
<report xmlns:xsi="http://www.w3.org/2001/XMLSchema-instance"
        xsi:noNamespaceSchemaLocation="reports.xsd"
        narrative="true">

    This week, I attended the <meeting>Board Meeting</meeting>, the
```

```
    <meeting>Marketing Meeting</meeting>, the <meeting>Insurance
    Meeting</meeting>, the <meeting>Advertising Meeting</meeting> and finally
    the <meeting>Morale Meeting</meeting>.

</report>
```

14. Create an instance document that references your schema. The data must belong to a namespace.

SAMPLE SOLUTION:

```
<?xml version="1.0" encoding="UTF-8"?>
<rep:report xmlns:xsi="http://www.w3.org/2001/XMLSchema-instance"
        xsi:schemaLocation="http://www.example.com/reports reports.xsd"
        xmlns:rep="http://www.example.com/reports"
        rep:narrative="true">

    This week, I attended the <rep:meeting>Board Meeting</rep:meeting>, the
    <rep:meeting>Marketing Meeting</rep:meeting>, the <rep:meeting>Insurance
    Meeting</rep:meeting>, the <rep:meeting>Advertising Meeting</rep:meeting>
    and finally the <rep:meeting>Morale Meeting</rep:meeting>.

</report>
```

Chapter 9

Review Questions

1. What is the difference between XSLT and XSL-FO?

   ANSWER: XSLT changes the structure of XML data. XSL-FO provides information on how XML data should be presented.

2. What is the main purpose of XSLT?

   ANSWER: To transform XML data from one structure into another.

3. What is the difference between the document root and the root element?

   ANSWER: The root element is just one child of the document root. The document root may have other children, such as comments and processing instructions.

4. What is the basic building block of an XSLT style sheet?

   ANSWER: The template.

5. What is the "current" node called?

   ANSWER: The context node.

6. How can you add information to the style sheet at runtime?

   ANSWER: By using parameters.

7. How do nodes propagate through different templates?

   ANSWER: Using the `apply-templates` element.

8. What happens if no template applies to a particular node?

   ANSWER: The default templates are applied. If there are no default templates, the data simply is not displayed.

9. What is the difference between a parameter and a variable?

   ANSWER: A parameter can be set from outside the style sheet, but its value cannot change. A variable can't have its value set from outside the style sheet, but its value can change within a template.

10. What is the difference between `value-of` and `copy-of`?

    ANSWER: The `value-of` element returns only the text value of an element. The `copy-of` element includes everything, including markup.

11. How can you prevent information from appearing in the resultset?

    ANSWER: Create an empty template that matches it.

Programming Exercises

1. Create a simple style sheet that outputs the text of an XML document.

   SAMPLE SOLUTION:

```
<?xml version="1.0"?>
<xsl:transform xmlns:xsl="http://www.w3.org/1999/XSL/Transform"
               version="1.0">

    <xsl:template match="/">
        <xsl:value-of select="."/>
    </xsl:template>

</xsl:transform>
```

The remaining exercises refer to the following document:

```
<?xml version="1.0"?>
<orders>
    <order>
        <customerid>2384</customerid>
        <status>pending</status>
        <item instock="Y" itemid="SD93">
            <name>Flying By Roller Skates</name>
            <price>25.00</price>
            <qty>25</qty>
        </item>
        <item instock="N" itemid="B12">
            <name>Bounce-o Ball</name>
            <price>.35</price>
```

```
            <qty>150</qty>
        </item>
    </order>
    <order>
        <customerid>5268</customerid>
        <status>complete</status>
        <item instock="Y" itemid="Q52">
            <name>Crash N Burn Skis</name>
            <price>20</price>
            <qty>10</qty>
        </item>
    </order>
</orders>
```

2. Create a style sheet that outputs a list of **customerid** values.

SAMPLE SOLUTION:

```
<?xml version="1.0"?>
<xsl:transform xmlns:xsl="http://www.w3.org/1999/XSL/Transform"
    version="1.0">

    <xsl:template match="/orders/order">
        <xsl:value-of select="customerid"/>
    </xsl:template>

</xsl:transform>
```

3. Create a style sheet that transforms the document to the following form:

```
<html>
<head>
<title>Order Status</title>
</head>
<body>
    <h2>Order Status</h2>

    <p>Customer number: 2384</p>
    <ul>
        <li>SD93: Flying By Roller Skates</li>
        <li>B12: Bounce-o Ball</li>
    </ul>

    <p>Customer number: 5268</p>
    <ul>
        <li>Q52: Crash N Burn Skis</li>
    </ul>

</body>
</html>
```

SAMPLE SOLUTION:

```
<?xml version="1.0"?>
<xsl:transform xmlns:xsl="http://www.w3.org/1999/XSL/Transform"
    version="1.0">
```

```
<xsl:template match="/">
    <html>
        <head><title>Order Status</title></head>
        <body>
            <h2>Order Status</h2>
            <xsl:apply-templates/>
        </body>
    </html>
</xsl:template>

<xsl:template match="order">
    <p><b>Customer number: <xsl:value-of select="customerid"/></b></p>
    <ul>
        <xsl:apply-templates select="item"/>
    </ul>
    <p>Status: <xsl:value-of select="status"/></p>
</xsl:template>

<xsl:template match="item">
    <li><xsl:value-of select="@itemid"/>:
                        <xsl:value-of select="name"/></li>
</xsl:template>

</xsl:transform>
```

4. Alter the style sheet in exercise 2 to show only pending orders.

SAMPLE SOLUTION:

```
<?xml version="1.0"?>
<xsl:transform xmlns:xsl="http://www.w3.org/1999/XSL/Transform"
    version="1.0">

<xsl:template match="/">
    <html>
        <head><title>Order Status</title></head>
        <body>
            <h2>Order Status</h2>
            <xsl:apply-templates
                    select="orders/order[status='pending']"/>
        </body>
    </html>
</xsl:template>

<xsl:template match="order">
    <p><b>Customer number: <xsl:value-of select="customerid"/></b></p>
    <ul>
        <xsl:apply-templates select="item"/>
    </ul>
    <p>Status: <xsl:value-of select="status"/></p>
</xsl:template>

<xsl:template match="item">
    <li><xsl:value-of select="@itemid"/>:
                        <xsl:value-of select="name"/></li>
```

```
      </xsl:template>

  </xsl:transform>
```

5. Alter the style sheet in exercise 2 to show only items that are in stock.

SAMPLE SOLUTION:

```
<?xml version="1.0"?>
<xsl:transform xmlns:xsl="http://www.w3.org/1999/XSL/Transform"
    version="1.0">

    <xsl:template match="/">
        <html>
            <head><title>Order Status</title></head>
            <body>
                <h2>Order Status</h2>
                <xsl:apply-templates
                         select="orders/order[status='pending']"/>
            </body>
        </html>
    </xsl:template>

    <xsl:template match="order">
        <p><b>Customer number: <xsl:value-of select="customerid"/></b></p>
        <ul>
            <xsl:apply-templates select="item"/>
        </ul>
        <p>Status: <xsl:value-of select="status"/></p>
    </xsl:template>

    <xsl:template match="item">
        <xsl:if test="@instock='Y'">
            <li><xsl:value-of select="@itemid"/>:
                             <xsl:value-of select="name"/></li>
        </xsl:if>
    </xsl:template>

</xsl:transform>
```

6. Alter the style sheet in exercise 2 to show backordered items in this form:

```
<li><i>B12: Bounce-o Ball</i></li>
```

SAMPLE SOLUTION:

```
<?xml version="1.0"?>
<xsl:transform xmlns:xsl="http://www.w3.org/1999/XSL/Transform"
    version="1.0">

    <xsl:template match="/">
        <html>
            <head><title>Order Status</title></head>
            <body>
                <h2>Order Status</h2>
                <xsl:apply-templates/>
```

```
                        </body>
                    </html>
                </xsl:template>

                <xsl:template match="order">
                    <p><b>Customer number: <xsl:value-of select="customerid"/></b></p>
                    <ul>
                        <xsl:apply-templates select="item"/>
                    </ul>
                    <p>Status: <xsl:value-of select="status"/></p>
                </xsl:template>

                <xsl:template match="item">
                    <xsl:choose>
                        <xsl:when test="@instock='Y'">
                            <li><xsl:value-of select="@itemid"/>:
                                              <xsl:value-of select="name"/></li>
                        </xsl:when>
                        <xsl:otherwise>
                            <li><i><xsl:value-of select="@itemid"/>:
                                          <xsl:value-of select="name"/></i></li>
                        </xsl:otherwise>
                    </xsl:choose>
                </xsl:template>

            </xsl:transform>
```

7. Convert the document to this form:

```
<?xml version="1.0" encoding="UTF-8"?>
<currentorders>
    <order custid="2384" status="pending">
        <inventory stocknumber="SD93" prodname="Flying By Roller Skates"
                                     quantity="25"/>
        <inventory stocknumber="B12" prodname="Bounce-o Ball"
                                     quantity="150"/>
    </order>
    <order custid="5268" status="complete">
        <inventory stocknumber="Q52" prodname="Crash N Burn Skis"
                                     quantity="10"/>
    </order>
</currentorders>
```

SAMPLE SOLUTION:

```
<?xml version="1.0"?>
<xsl:transform xmlns:xsl="http://www.w3.org/1999/XSL/Transform"
    version="1.0">

    <xsl:template match="/">
        <currentorders>
            <xsl:apply-templates/>
        </currentorders>
    </xsl:template>

    <xsl:template match="order">
```

```
    <xsl:element name="order">
        <xsl:attribute name="custid"><xsl:value-of
                        select="customerid"/></xsl:attribute>
        <xsl:attribute name="status"><xsl:value-of
                        select="status"/></xsl:attribute>
        <xsl:apply-templates select="item"/>
    </xsl:element>
</xsl:template>

<xsl:template match="item">
    <xsl:element name="inventory">
        <xsl:attribute name="stocknumber"><xsl:value-of
                        select="@itemid"/></xsl:attribute>
        <xsl:attribute name="prodname"><xsl:value-of
                        select="name"/></xsl:attribute>
        <xsl:attribute name="quantity"><xsl:value-of
                        select="qty"/></xsl:attribute>
    </xsl:element>
</xsl:template>

</xsl:transform>
```

Chapter 10

Review Questions

1. What are the three main components of an XSL transformation?

    ANSWER: The source, the style sheet, and the result.

2. What kind of object can act as the source of a transformation?

    ANSWER: Virtually any type. Specifically files (local or remote), character or byte streams, SAX streams, and DOM `Node`s.

3. What are the major steps involved in a transformation in your software?

    ANSWER: The correct answer varies for each implementation. For TrAX, the answer is

    1. Determine sources and results.
    2. Create the `TransformerFactory`.
    3. Determine the style sheet.
    4. Create the `Transformer`.
    5. Transform the document.

4. What should you do if you're going to perform several transformations with the same style sheet?

    ANSWER: Use a template or other compiled style sheet.

5. How can transformations be used with SAX?

ANSWER: A SAX stream can be the source or result, and a transformer can act as a `ContentHandler`. SAX can also be used to chain transformations together.

Programming Exercises

1. Create an application that transforms several source documents using a single style sheet.

SOLUTION:

```
import javax.xml.transform.stream.StreamSource;
import javax.xml.transform.stream.StreamResult;
import javax.xml.transform.TransformerFactory;
import javax.xml.transform.Source;
import javax.xml.transform.Transformer;
import javax.xml.transform.Templates;

public class TransformFile extends Object {
   public static void main (String args[]) throws Exception
   {
      String XMLFileName1 = "input1.xml";
      String XMLFileName2 = "input2.xml";
      String OutputFileName1 = "output1.xml";
      String OutputFileName2 = "output2.xml";

      StreamSource source1 = new StreamSource(XMLFileName1);
      StreamSource source2 = new StreamSource(XMLFileName2);
      StreamResult result1 = new StreamResult(OutputFileName1);
      StreamResult result2 = new StreamResult(OutputFileName2);

      TransformerFactory transFactory = TransformerFactory.newInstance();
      Source style = transFactory.getAssociatedStylesheet(source,
                                                null, null, null);

      Templates template = transFactory.newTemplates(style);
      Transformer trans = template.newTransformer();

      trans.transform(source1, result1);
      trans.transform(source2, result2);

   }
}
```

2. Create an application that transforms a DOM `Node`.

SOLUTION:

```
import javax.xml.parsers.DocumentBuilder;
import javax.xml.parsers.DocumentBuilderFactory;
import java.io.File;
import org.w3c.dom.Document;
import javax.xml.transform.TransformerFactory;
```

```
import javax.xml.transform.Transformer;
import javax.xml.transform.dom.DOMSource;
import javax.xml.transform.stream.StreamSource;
import javax.xml.transform.stream.StreamResult;
import javax.xml.transform.Source;
import java.io.FileOutputStream;
import javax.xml.transform.Templates;

public class TransformFile extends Object {

public static void main (String args[]) throws Exception
{
   String XMLFileName = "votes.xml";
   String XSLFileName = "votes.xsl";

   Document doc = null;
   try {
      DocumentBuilderFactory dbf = DocumentBuilderFactory.newInstance();
      DocumentBuilder db = dbf.newDocumentBuilder();
      doc = db.parse(XMLFileName);
   } catch (Exception e) {
      System.out.println(e.getMessage());
   }

   DOMSource source = new DOMSource(doc);
   StreamSource style = new StreamSource(XSLFileName);
   StreamResult result = new StreamResult(System.out);

   TransformerFactory transFactory = TransformerFactory.newInstance();

   Transformer transformer = transFactory.newTransformer(style);

   transformer.transform(source, result);

}
}
```

3. Create a transformer as a serializer for a SAX stream.

   SOLUTION:

```
import org.xml.sax.helpers.XMLReaderFactory;
import org.xml.sax.XMLReader;
import org.xml.sax.XMLFilter;
import org.xml.sax.SAXException;
import org.xml.sax.InputSource;

import javax.xml.transform.Source;
import javax.xml.transform.sax.SAXSource;
import javax.xml.transform.stream.StreamResult;
import javax.xml.transform.TransformerFactory;
import javax.xml.transform.Transformer;
```

```
public class MainSaxApp {

    public static void main (String[] args){

        try {

            XMLReader reader =
                        XMLReaderFactory.createXMLReader(
                                "org.apache.xerces.parsers.SAXParser");
            SAXSource source = new SAXSource(reader,
                                        new InputSource("infile.xml"));

            StreamResult result = new StreamResult("outfile.xml");

            TransformerFactory transFactory = TransformerFactory.newInstance();
            Transformer trans = transFactory.newTransformer();

            trans.transform(source, result);

        } catch (Exception e) {
            System.out.println(e.getMessage());
        }

    }

}
```

4. Create an application that chains three transformations together.

SOLUTION:

```
import javax.xml.transform.stream.StreamSource;
import javax.xml.transform.stream.StreamResult;
import javax.xml.transform.sax.SAXResult;
import javax.xml.transform.TransformerFactory;

import org.xml.sax.helpers.XMLReaderFactory;
import org.xml.sax.XMLReader;
import org.xml.sax.InputSource;
import org.xml.sax.SAXException;
import javax.xml.transform.sax.SAXTransformerFactory;
import javax.xml.transform.sax.TransformerHandler;

public class TransformFile extends Object {
    public static void main (String args[]) throws Exception
    {

        try {
            String XMLFileName = "votes.xml";
            String OutputFileName = "finalvotes.xml";

            StreamSource source = new StreamSource(XMLFileName);
            StreamSource style1 = new StreamSource("style1.xsl");
            StreamSource style2 = new StreamSource("style2.xsl");
```

```
        StreamSource style3 = new StreamSource("style3.xsl");

        StreamResult result = new StreamResult(OutputFileName);

        TransformerFactory transFactory = TransformerFactory.newInstance();

        SAXTransformerFactory saxTransFactory =
                                (SAXTransformerFactory)transFactory;
        TransformerHandler trans1 =
                        saxTransFactory.newTransformerHandler(style1);
        TransformerHandler trans2 =
                        saxTransFactory.newTransformerHandler(style2);
        TransformerHandler trans3 =
                        saxTransFactory.newTransformerHandler(style3);

        trans1.setResult(new SAXResult(trans2));
        trans2.setResult(new SAXResult(trans3));
        trans3.setResult(result);

        String parserClass = "org.apache.crimson.parser.XMLReaderImpl";
        XMLReader reader = XMLReaderFactory.createXMLReader(parserClass);

        reader.setContentHandler(trans1);

        reader.parse(XMLFileName);

    } catch (SAXException e) {
        System.out.println(e.getMessage());
    }

  }
}
```

Chapter 11

Review Questions

1. What are the three parts of a location step?

   ANSWER: The axis, the node test, and an optional predicate

2. Name three axes.

   ANSWER: Any three from `child`, `self`, `parent`, `ancestor`, `ancestor-or-self`, `descendant`, `descendant-or-self`, `following-sibling`, `preceding-sibling`, `attribute`, or `namespace`.

3. What does a node test do?

   ANSWER: It narrows the resultset based on the name or type of node.

4. What does a predicate do?

ANSWER: It narrows the resultset based on an expression, such as a particular attribute or child, or a particular value.

5. What's the difference between an absolute and a relative expression?

ANSWER: An absolute expression uses the document root as its first context node, and will always give the same result no matter what the application has as the current context node. A relative expression is evaluated with regard to the current context node, and can change when the context node changes.

6. How does an element get converted to a text value?

ANSWER: All descendant text nodes are concatenated together in document order.

7. Which axis is used in two location steps in the expression

```
/horse/race
```

ANSWER: The child axis.

8. What axis selects all of a node's children and their children?

ANSWER: The descendant axis.

Programming Exercises

The following exercises use the source document from Chapter 9:

```xml
<?xml version="1.0"?>
<content>
<events>
    <eventitem eventid="A335">
        <eventdate>6.20.3425</eventdate>
        <title>Making Friends With The Venusian Flu Virus</title>
        <description>Dr. Biff Mercury discusses his theory on
        coexisting with this useful organism.</description>
    </eventitem>

    <eventitem eventid="B963" optional="no">
        <eventdate>6.21.3425</eventdate>
        <title>Putting the Manners in Bedside Manner</title>
        <description>Dr. Zingzowpowie, the famous xenoneurosurgeon
        lectures on Bedside Manner and the benefits of using cold
        tentacles during a physical.</description>
    </eventitem>

    <eventitem eventid="C934" optional="yes">
        <eventdate>6.25.3425</eventdate>
        <title>An Evening of Fun</title>
        <description>This evening join us for the monthly "Identify
```

```
            that Food" contest.</description>
        </eventitem>

</events>
<news>
    <newsitem itemnum="1">
        <newsdate>6.18.3425</newsdate>
        <title>End Of The Line For The Incumbent?</title>
        <body>
            The Universal News Network is reporting that <person>His
            Magnificence The Supreme Leader For Life</person>
            announced today that he has decided not to be cloned for
            a 14th term.
        </body>
    </newsitem>

    <newsitem itemnum="2">
        <newsdate>6.19.3425</newsdate>
        <title>New Fall Lineup</title>
        <body>
            The Omega Channel has announced two new shows for its new
            fall lineup. <program>Who's Running the Galaxy?</program>
            features a team of government scientists who accidentally
            clone two Supreme Leaders. If you think you're confused,
            imagine what the first family must be going through.
            <program>Trading Species</program> follows two teams of
            aliens who trade species and have only 48 hours to adjust
            and fool their neighbors.
        </body>
    </newsitem>
</news>
</content>
```

1. Write an absolute expression that selects only the event title nodes.

   SOLUTION:

   `//eventitem/title`

   or

   `/content/events/eventitem/title`

2. Write a relative expression that selects the body of news item number 1, assuming that the news element is the context node.

   SOLUTION:

   `newsitem[@itemnum='1']/body`

3. Write an expression that returns the **eventitem** element for any event that mentions Dr. Zingzowpowie in the description.

   SOLUTION:

   `//description[contains(self::node(), 'Zingzowpowie')]/parent::*`

4. Write an expression that assumes that the news element is the context node, and returns the title of any news item that has a program element in the description.

SOLUTION:

```
newsitem/body[program]/preceding-sibling::title
```

Chapter 12

Review Questions

1. What do Cascading Style Sheets do?

   ANSWER: Cascading Style Sheets give a Web page author control over the presentation of content.

2. How can a style sheet be associated with an XML document?

   ANSWER: A style sheet can be associated with an XML document using the `xml-stylesheet` processing instruction, but the value of the `type` attribute must be `text/css`.

3. How many declarations can a rule contain?

   ANSWER: A rule can contain an unlimited number of declarations, as long as they are separated by semicolons.

4. What happens if a particular property isn't specified for an element?

   ANSWER: The browser will use the default value for that property, or if it's available, the property value for its parent.

5. What happens if more than one rule applies to an element?

   ANSWER: If different properties are specified, they will both be applied. If the same property is specified in both rules, the rule with the most specific selector takes precedence.

6. What is the difference between relative and absolute positioning?

   ANSWER: With relative positioning, the object is placed relative to the position it would normally have been in. With absolute positioning, the object is removed from the normal flow and placed relative to its containing block.

7. Why is it a good idea to specify more than one font family choice?

   ANSWER: Different operating systems use different fonts. If one isn't available, the browser will use the next.

Programming Exercises

1. Create an XML file and a style sheet that sets all of its text to a cursive font.

   SOLUTION:

   XML file (`ex.xml`):

   ```
   <?xml version="1.0"?>
   <?xml-stylesheet href="ex_styles.css" type="text/css"?>
   <comets>
     <comet class="confirmed" id="DF1">
       <discovery>
           <date>4.28.2356</date>
           <hunter>Mack</hunter>
           <description>Sungrazing comet, tail visible</description>
           <brightness>Magnitude 2.1</brightness>
           <vantage>Deck 4, Aperture DF</vantage>
       </discovery>
     </comet>
   </comets>
   ```

   Style sheet (`ex_styles.css`):

   ```
   * { font-family: monospace; }
   ```

2. Modify the style sheet so that only the text of a particular element is light blue, bold, and italic.

   SOLUTION:

   ```
   description { color: #BBBBFF; font-weight: bold; font-style: italic; }
   ```

3. Add a dotted pink border 3 pixels wide to the text that is now light blue.

   SOLUTION:

   ```
   description { color: #BBBBFF; font-weight: bold; font-style: italic;
                 border: 3px dotted #FFBBBB; }
   ```

4. Set the style sheet so that the content occupies a box that is 200 pixels wide, with the upper-right corner 50 pixels to the left of the right-hand edge of the window, no matter what the window size is.

   SOLUTION:

   ```
   description { color: #BBBBFF; font-weight: bold; font-style: italic;
                 border: 3px dotted #FFBBBB; }
   comet { display: block;
           width: 200px;
           position: absolute;
           right: 50px; }
   ```

Chapter 13

Review Questions

1. What are the advantages of using HTML instead of XML and CSS?

   ANSWER: The browser already understands what to do with HTML. Besides, not all browsers support XML and CSS.

2. Name three ways to add CSS information to an HTML page.

   ANSWER: You can add CSS information to an HTML page using the `<style>` element, the `<link>` element, or the `style` attribute of an individual element.

3. Name three differences between HTML and XHTML.

   ANSWER: XHTML requires all opening tags to have closing tags; HTML doesn't. XHTML requires all attributes to have quotes; HTML doesn't. XHTML requires all attributes to have values; HTML allows "minimized" attributes, where the values are assumed. XHTML is case sensitive; HTML isn't. XHTML requires documents to be well-formed; HTML doesn't.

4. How can an HTML table aid in the layout of a Web page?

   ANSWER: HTML tables make it possible to create columns and rows in which blocks of information of different sizes are lined up.

5. Can a table contain another table?

   ANSWER: Yes. This is called *nesting* the tables.

6. How can you limit the number of characters entered into a `<form>` text input? A `<textarea>`?

   ANSWER: You can limit the size of text input fields using the `maxlength` attribute. There is no way to limit the number of characters submitted using a `<textarea>` element.

7. What is the difference between the `get` and `post` methods for submitting forms?

   ANSWER: With `get`, all form values are appended to the URI. With `post`, form values are sent as HTTP headers, which is more secure.

8. When transforming XML into HTML, how can you prevent problems with scripting that has been escaped using a `CDATA` section?

   ANSWER: Use the `xsl:output` element with the `html` method.

9. What is the main object representing an HTML page? How are its child objects represented?

   ANSWER: The `document` object represents the page. Objects within it are represented as arrays.

Programming Exercises

1. Create an HTML page that includes an image that links to another page.

   SOLUTION:

   ```
   <html>
   <head><title>Exercise</title></head>
   <body>
       <a href="mypage.html"><img src="myimage.gif" alt="My Image"/></a>
   </body>
   </html>
   ```

2. Create the page shown in Figure 13.20.

FIGURE 13.20

Hint: Use tables for layout.

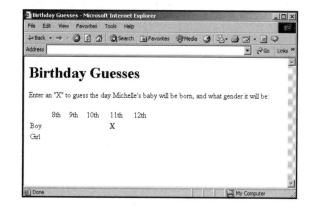

   SOLUTION:

   ```
   <html>
   <head><title>Birthday Guesses</title></head>
   <body>

   <h1>Birthday Guesses</h1>

   <p>Enter an "X" to guess the day Michelle's baby will be born,
   and what gender it will be:</p>

   <table width="50%">
   <tr><td></td><td>8th</td><td>9th</td><td>10th</td>
                                       <td>11th</td><td>12th</td></tr>
   <tr><td>Boy</td><td colspan="3"></td><td><b>X</b></td></tr>
   <tr><td>Girl</td><td colspan="5"></td></tr>
   </table>

   </body>
   </html>
   ```

3. Add the form shown in Figure 13.21 to the page.

FIGURE 13.21

Hint: Use check boxes.

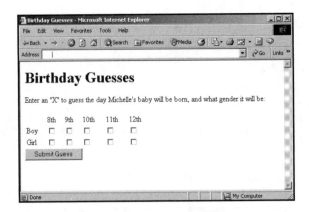

SOLUTION:

```html
<html>
<head><title>Birthday Guesses</title></head>
<body>

<h1>Birthday Guesses</h1>

<p>Enter an "X" to guess the day Michelle's baby will be born,
and what gender it will be:</p>

<form action="birthday.jsp" method="post">
<table width="50%">
<tr><td></td><td>8th</td><td>9th</td><td>10th</td>
                         <td>11th</td><td>12th</td></tr>
<tr><td>Boy</td>
<td><input type="checkbox" name="guess" value="8b"/></td>
<td><input type="checkbox" name="guess" value="9b"/></td>
<td><input type="checkbox" name="guess" value="10b"/></td>
<td><input type="checkbox" name="guess" value="11b"/></td>
<td><input type="checkbox" name="guess" value="12b"/></td></tr>
<tr><td>Girl</td>
<td><input type="checkbox" name="guess" value="8g"/></td>
<td><input type="checkbox" name="guess" value="9g"/></td>
<td><input type="checkbox" name="guess" value="10g"/></td>
<td><input type="checkbox" name="guess" value="11g"/></td>
<td><input type="checkbox" name="guess" value="12g"/></td></tr>

</table>
<input type="submit" value="Submit Guess" />
</form>

</form>


</body>
</html>
```

4. Create a page with three images. When the page loads, the body's `onload` event is triggered. When this event is triggered, the `src` attribute of the second image should appear in an alert box.

SOLUTION:

```
<html>
<head><title>Comet Hunt Results</title>
<script type="text/javascript">

function getImage(imagenum){

    alert(document.images[1].src);

}

</script>

</head>
<body onload="getImage();">
  <img alt="Comet image DF1" src="images/cometDF1.gif" width="180"
                                     height="180" align="left" />
  <img alt="Comet image DF2" src="images/cometDF2.gif" width="180"
                                     height="180" align="left" />
  <img alt="Comet image DF3" src="images/cometDF3.gif" width="180"
                                     height="180" align="left" />
</body>
</html>
```

Chapter 14

Review Questions

1. What are the XLink elements?

   ANSWER: There are no specific XLink elements. Because all XLink functionality is provided by attributes, any element can be an XLink element.

2. What is a simple link?

   ANSWER: A simple link is an XLink that uses the simple type. It has as its start point a local resource, and as its end point a remote resource.

3. If a string of linked text is in the same document as an extended link, but not within the link element itself, is it local or remote?

   ANSWER: Because it must be referenced with the `href` attribute, it's remote.

4. How many resources can be involved in an extended link?

   ANSWER: An unlimited number of resources can be involved in an extended link.

5. What does the `actuate` attribute do?

   ANSWER: The `actuate` attribute determines whether the link is traversed when the document is loaded or when the user performs some action, such as clicking on the start point.

6. How does an application know to treat a linkbase differently from other linked resources?

   ANSWER: The `arcrole` attribute contains a special value indicating that it's a linkbase.

7. How does XPointer relate to XPath?

   ANSWER: It encompasses XPath and adds the concepts of points and ranges.

8. What are the three forms of an XPointer?

   ANSWER: Bare names, child sequences, and full XPointer.

Programming Exercises

1. Convert the hyperlinks (`<a></a>` elements) in the following code into simple XLinks.

```
<html>
<head><title>Wow, a party!</title></head>
<body>
<h1>Wow, a party!</h1>

<p>All High Bumbledoop is throwing a Grand Ball, and Manicpa's
got the <a href="http://www.example.com/menu.html">menu</a>.
Check it out, from Gillbrits to Quakles.</p>

</body>
</html>
```

SOLUTION:

```
<html>
<head><title>Wow, a party!</title></head>
<body>
<h1>Wow, a party!</h1>

<p>All High Bumbledoop is throwing a Grand Ball, and Manicpa's
got the <a href="http://www.example.com/menu.html"
xmlns:xlink="http://www.w3.org/1999/xlink" xlink:type="simple"
xlink:href="http://www.example.com/menu.html">menu</a>.
Check it out, from Gillbrits to Quakles.</p>

</body>
</html>
```

2. Create a link with multiple starting resources but a single ending resource.

   SOLUTION:

```
<references xmlns:xlink="http://www.w3.org/1999/xlink" xlink:type="extended">
    <link xlink:type="locator" xlink:href="#firstPoint"
        xlink:label="startingend" xlink:title="First Point" />
    <link xlink:type="locator" xlink:href="#secondPoint"
        xlink:label="startingend" xlink:title="Second Point" />
    <link xlink:type="locator" xlink:href="#thirdPoint"
        xlink:label="startingend" xlink:title="Third Point" />

    <link xlink:type="locator" xlink:href="destination.xml"
        xlink:label="endingpoint" xlink:title="Summary" />

    <arcelement xlink:type="arc" xlink:from="startingpoint"
                xlink:to="endingpoint" xlink:show="replace"
                xlink:actuate="onRequest" xlink:title="To Summary" />
</references>
```

3. Create a link with multiple starting and ending points.

SOLUTION:

```
<references xmlns:xlink="http://www.w3.org/1999/xlink" xlink:type="extended">
    <link xlink:type="locator" xlink:href="#firstPoint"
        xlink:label="startingend" xlink:title="First Point" />
    <link xlink:type="locator" xlink:href="#secondPoint"
        xlink:label="startingend" xlink:title="Second Point" />
    <link xlink:type="locator" xlink:href="#thirdPoint"
        xlink:label="startingend" xlink:title="Third Point" />

    <link xlink:type="locator" xlink:href="destination.xml"
        xlink:label="endingpoint" xlink:title="Summary" />
    <link xlink:type="locator" xlink:href="details.xml"
        xlink:label="endingpoint" xlink:title="Details" />

    <arcelement xlink:type="arc" xlink:from="startingpoint"
                xlink:to="endingpoint" xlink:show="replace"
                xlink:actuate="onRequest" xlink:title="To Summary" />
</references>
```

4. Create an XPointer expression that selects the main content in the solution to exercise 2.

SOLUTION:

```
/1/2/2
```

or

```
xpointer(/html/body/p)
```

5. Create an extended link that has as its origin the word Bumbledoop in exercise 2.
   Assume that the file is called jader1.html.

SOLUTION:

```
<references xmlns:xlink="http://www.w3.org/1999/xlink" xlink:type="extended">
    <link xlink:type="locator"
        xlink:href="jader1.html#xpointer(string-ranger(/html/body/p,
                                                        'Bumbledoop'))"
```

```
                    xlink:label="startingend" xlink:title="Start" />

        <link xlink:type="locator" xlink:href="destination.xml"
              xlink:label="endingpoint" xlink:title="Summary" />

        <arcelement xlink:type="arc" xlink:from="startingpoint"
                    xlink:to="endingpoint" xlink:show="replace"
                    xlink:actuate="onRequest" xlink:title="To Destination" />
    </references>
```

Chapter 15

Review Questions

1. How do XForms ease maintenance?

    ANSWER: By separating content from presentation.

2. Where is the data in an XForms form stored while the user manipulates the data?

    ANSWER: In the instance document.

3. How can you ensure the type of data submitted in a particular field?

    ANSWER: By building the field to a type or by creating a schema against which to validate the form.

4. How do you add initial values to the form?

    ANSWER: Add values to the instance document.

5. Where are the aspects of the form defined?

    ANSWER: In the model.

6. How many models can exist per page?

    ANSWER: An unlimited number.

7. How are form controls associated with the instance document?

    ANSWER: The `ref` attribute uses XPath expressions.

Programming Exercises

1. Create a form that allows users to enter their name and three favorite foods.

    SOLUTION:

```
<html xmlns="http://www.w3.org/1999/xhtml"
      xmlns:xforms="http://www.w3.org/2002/01/xforms">
<head>
    <title>Favorites Form</title>
```

```
    <xforms:model>

        <xforms:submitInfo method2="postxml" localfile="./temp.xml"/>

        <xforms:instance xmlns="">
            <favorites>
                <username></username>
                <favorite1></favorite1>
                <favorite2></favorite2>
                <favorite3></favorite3>
            </favorites>
        </xforms:instance>

    </xforms:model>

</head>
<body>

<h1>Enter your three favorite foods</h1>

<p>
    <xforms:input ref="favorites/username">
        <xforms:caption>Your name: </xforms:caption>
    </xforms:input>
</p>

<p>
    <xforms:input ref="favorites/favorite1">
        <xforms:caption>Favorite 1: </xforms:caption>
    </xforms:input>

    <br />

    <xforms:input ref="favorites/favorite2">
        <xforms:caption>Favorite 2: </xforms:caption>
    </xforms:input>

    <br />

    <xforms:input ref="favorites/favorite3">
        <xforms:caption>Favorite 3: </xforms:caption>
    </xforms:input>
</p>

<p>
    <xforms:submit>
        <xforms:caption>Submit Report</xforms:caption>
    </xforms:submit>
</p>

</body>
</html>
```

2. Alter the form in exercise 1 so that users choose one of a series of options using a radio button.

SOLUTION:

```
<html xmlns="http://www.w3.org/1999/xhtml"
      xmlns:xforms="http://www.w3.org/2002/01/xforms">
<head>
    <title>Favorites Form</title>

    <xforms:model>

        <xforms:submitInfo method2="postxml" localfile="./temp.xml"/>

        <xforms:instance xmlns="">
            <favorites>
                <username></username>
                <favorite></favorite>
            </favorites>
        </xforms:instance>

    </xforms:model>

</head>
<body>

<h1>Enter your three favorite foods</h1>

<p>
    <xforms:input ref="favorites/username">
        <xforms:caption>Your name: </xforms:caption>
    </xforms:input>
</p>

<p>
    <xforms:selectOne ref="favorites/favorite" selectUI="radio">
        <xforms:caption>Favorite 1: </xforms:caption>
        <xforms:item>
            <xforms:caption>Ice cream</xforms:caption>
            <xforms:value>ic</xforms:value>
        </xforms:item>
        <xforms:item>
            <xforms:caption>Lasagna</xforms:caption>
            <xforms:value>l</xforms:value>
        </xforms:item>
        <xforms:item>
            <xforms:caption>Peanuts</xforms:caption>
            <xforms:value>p</xforms:value>
        </xforms:item>
    </xforms:selectOne>
</p>

<p>
    <xforms:submit>
```

```
            <xforms:caption>Submit Report</xforms:caption>
        </xforms:submit>
    </p>

    </body>
    </html>
```

3. Alter the form in exercise 2 so that users choose one or more items from a list box.

SOLUTION:

```
<html xmlns="http://www.w3.org/1999/xhtml"
      xmlns:xforms="http://www.w3.org/2002/01/xforms">
<head>
    <title>Favorites Form</title>

    <xforms:model>

        <xforms:submitInfo method2="postxml" localfile="./temp.xml"/>

        <xforms:instance xmlns="">
            <favorites>
                <username></username>
                <favorite></favorite>
            </favorites>
        </xforms:instance>

    </xforms:model>

</head>
<body>

<h1>Enter your three favorite foods</h1>

<p>
    <xforms:input ref="favorites/username">
        <xforms:caption>Your name: </xforms:caption>
    </xforms:input>
</p>

<p>
    <xforms:selectMany ref="favorites/favorite" selectUI="listbox">
        <xforms:caption>Favorite 1: </xforms:caption>
        <xforms:item>
            <xforms:caption>Ice cream</xforms:caption>
            <xforms:value>ic</xforms:value>
        </xforms:item>
        <xforms:item>
            <xforms:caption>Lasagna</xforms:caption>
            <xforms:value>l</xforms:value>
        </xforms:item>
        <xforms:item>
            <xforms:caption>Peanuts</xforms:caption>
            <xforms:value>p</xforms:value>
```

```
        </xforms:item>
      </xforms:selectMany>
  </p>

  <p>
      <xforms:submit>
          <xforms:caption>Submit Report</xforms:caption>
      </xforms:submit>
  </p>

  </body>
  </html>
```

4. Give the form initial values.

SOLUTION:

```
<html xmlns="http://www.w3.org/1999/xhtml"
      xmlns:xforms="http://www.w3.org/2002/01/xforms">
<head>
    <title>Favorites Form</title>

    <xforms:model>

        <xforms:submitInfo method2="postxml" localfile="./temp.xml"/>

        <xforms:instance xmlns="">
            <favorites>
                <username>Enter your name here</username>
                <favorite>1 ic</favorite>
            </favorites>
        </xforms:instance>

    </xforms:model>

</head>
<body>

<h1>Enter your three favorite foods</h1>

<p>
    <xforms:input ref="favorites/username">
        <xforms:caption>Your name: </xforms:caption>
    </xforms:input>
</p>

<p>
    <xforms:selectMany ref="favorites/favorite" selectUI="listbox">
        <xforms:caption>Favorite 1: </xforms:caption>
        <xforms:item>
            <xforms:caption>Ice cream</xforms:caption>
            <xforms:value>ic</xforms:value>
        </xforms:item>
        <xforms:item>
```

```
            <xforms:caption>Lasagna</xforms:caption>
            <xforms:value>l</xforms:value>
        </xforms:item>
        <xforms:item>
            <xforms:caption>Peanuts</xforms:caption>
            <xforms:value>p</xforms:value>
        </xforms:item>
    </xforms:selectMany>
</p>

<p>
    <xforms:submit>
        <xforms:caption>Submit Report</xforms:caption>
    </xforms:submit>
</p>

</body>
</html>
```

5. Create a form populated by a series of order items.

SOLUTION:

```
<html xmlns="http://www.w3.org/1999/xhtml"
      xmlns:xforms="http://www.w3.org/2002/01/xforms">
<head>
    <title>Favorites Form</title>

    <xforms:model>

        <xforms:submitInfo method2="postxml" localfile="./temp.xml"/>

        <xforms:instance xmlns="">
            <order>
                <item>
                    <itemnum>1</itemnum>
                    <itemname>FirstItem</itemname>
                    <unitprice>10</unitprice>
                    <quantity>5</quantity>
                    <total/>
                </item>
                <item>
                    <itemnum>3</itemnum>
                    <itemname>SecondItem</itemname>
                    <unitprice>30</unitprice>
                    <quantity>5</quantity>
                    <total/>
                </item>
                <item>
                    <itemnum>5</itemnum>
                    <itemname>ThirdItem</itemname>
                    <unitprice>5</unitprice>
                    <quantity>8</quantity>
                    <total/>
```

```
                            </item>
                        </order>
                    </xforms:instance>

            </xforms:model>

    </head>
    <body>

    <h1>Please check your order</h1>

    <p>
        <xforms:repeat ref="order/item">
            <xforms:input ref="itemnum">
                <xforms:caption>Item number: </xforms:caption>
            </xforms:input>
            <xforms:input ref="itemname">
                <xforms:caption>Item name: </xforms:caption>
            </xforms:input>
            <xforms:input ref="unitprice">
                <xforms:caption>Unit price: </xforms:caption>
            </xforms:input>
            <xforms:input ref="quantity">
                <xforms:caption>Quantity: </xforms:caption>
            </xforms:input>
            <xforms:input ref="total">
                <xforms:caption>Total: </xforms:caption>
            </xforms:input>
            <br />
        </xforms:repeat>
    </p>

    <p>
        <xforms:submit>
            <xforms:caption>Submit Report</xforms:caption>
        </xforms:submit>
    </p>

    </body>
    </html>
```

6. Create a binding that automatically totals each line item and creates a grand total.

    SOLUTION:

```
<html xmlns="http://www.w3.org/1999/xhtml"
      xmlns:xforms="http://www.w3.org/2002/01/xforms">
<head>
    <title>Favorites Form</title>

    <xforms:model>

        <xforms:submitInfo method2="postxml" localfile="./temp.xml"/>
```

```
            <xforms:instance xmlns="">
                <order>
                    <item>
                        <itemnum>1</itemnum>
                        <itemname>FirstItem</itemname>
                        <unitprice>10</unitprice>
                        <quantity>5</quantity>
                        <total/>
                    </item>
                    <item>
                        <itemnum>3</itemnum>
                        <itemname>SecondItem</itemname>
                        <unitprice>30</unitprice>
                        <quantity>5</quantity>
                        <total/>
                    </item>
                    <item>
                        <itemnum>5</itemnum>
                        <itemname>ThirdItem</itemname>
                        <unitprice>5</unitprice>
                        <quantity>8</quantity>
                        <total/>
                    </item>
                    <grandtotal/>
                </order>
            </xforms:instance>
            <xforms:bind ref="order/item/total"
                            calculate="../unitprice * ../quantity"/>
            <xforms:bind ref="order/grandtotal" calculate="sum(../item/total)"/>
        </xforms:model>

</head>
<body>

<h1>Please check your order</h1>

<p>
    <xforms:repeat ref="order/item">
        <xforms:input ref="itemnum">
            <xforms:caption>Item number: </xforms:caption>
        </xforms:input>
        <xforms:input ref="itemname">
            <xforms:caption>Item name: </xforms:caption>
        </xforms:input>
        <xforms:input ref="unitprice">
            <xforms:caption>Unit price: </xforms:caption>
        </xforms:input>
        <xforms:input ref="quantity">
            <xforms:caption>Quantity: </xforms:caption>
        </xforms:input>
        <xforms:input ref="total">
            <xforms:caption>Total: </xforms:caption>
        </xforms:input>
```

```
                <br />
            </xforms:repeat>
    </p>


    <p>
        <xforms:input ref="order/grandtotal">
            <xforms:caption>Grand Total</xforms:caption>
        </xforms:input>
    </p>


    <p>
        <xforms:submit>
            <xforms:caption>Submit Report</xforms:caption>
        </xforms:submit>
    </p>


    </body>
    </html>
```

7. Create form controls for payment information. The controls for credit card number and expiration date should only appear if the payment method is a credit card, in which case they should be mandatory.

SOLUTION:

```
<html xmlns="http://www.w3.org/1999/xhtml"
      xmlns:xforms="http://www.w3.org/2002/01/xforms">
<head>
    <title>Favorites Form</title>


    <xforms:model>


        <xforms:submitInfo method2="postxml" localfile="./temp.xml"/>


        <xforms:instance xmlns="">
            <order>
                <item>
                    <itemnum>1</itemnum>
                    <itemname>FirstItem</itemname>
                    <unitprice>10</unitprice>
                    <quantity>5</quantity>
                    <total/>
                </item>
                <item>
                    <itemnum>3</itemnum>
                    <itemname>SecondItem</itemname>
                    <unitprice>30</unitprice>
                    <quantity>5</quantity>
                    <total/>
                </item>
                <item>
                    <itemnum>5</itemnum>
                    <itemname>ThirdItem</itemname>
                    <unitprice>5</unitprice>
```

```
                    <quantity>8</quantity>
                    <total/>
                </item>
                <grandtotal/>
                <paymentinfo>
                    <paymethod/>
                    <ccnumber/>
                    <expmonth/>
                    <expyear/>
                </paymentinfo>
            </order>
        </xforms:instance>
        <xforms:bind ref="order/item/total"
                                    calculate="../unitprice * ../quantity"/>
        <xforms:bind ref="order/grandtotal" calculate="sum(../item/total)"/>

        <xforms:bind ref="order/paymentinfo/ccnumber"
                                        relevant="../paymethod='cc'"/>
        <xforms:bind ref="order/paymentinfo/expmonth"
                                        relevant="../paymethod='cc'"/>
        <xforms:bind ref="order/paymentinfo/expyear"
                                        relevant="../paymethod='cc'"/>

        <xforms:bind ref="order/paymentinfo/ccnumber"
                                        required="../paymethod='cc'"/>
        <xforms:bind ref="order/paymentinfo/expmonth"
                                        required="../paymethod='cc'"/>
        <xforms:bind ref="order/paymentinfo/expyear"
                                        required="../paymethod='cc'"/>

    </xforms:model>

</head>
<body>

<h1>Please check your order</h1>

<p>
    <xforms:repeat ref="order/item">
        <xforms:input ref="itemnum">
            <xforms:caption>Item number: </xforms:caption>
        </xforms:input>
        <xforms:input ref="itemname">
            <xforms:caption>Item name: </xforms:caption>
        </xforms:input>
        <xforms:input ref="unitprice">
            <xforms:caption>Unit price: </xforms:caption>
        </xforms:input>
        <xforms:input ref="quantity">
            <xforms:caption>Quantity: </xforms:caption>
        </xforms:input>
        <xforms:input ref="total">
            <xforms:caption>Total: </xforms:caption>
```

```
                </xforms:input>
                <br />
            </xforms:repeat>
    </p>

    <p>
        <xforms:input ref="order/grandtotal">
            <xforms:caption>Grand Total</xforms:caption>
        </xforms:input>
    </p>

    <p>
        <xforms:selectOne ref="order/paymentinfo/paymethod" selectUI="radio">
            <xforms:item>
                <xforms:caption>Credit Card</xforms:caption>
                <xforms:value>cc</xforms:value>
            </xforms:item>
            <xforms:item>
                <xforms:caption>Bill Me</xforms:caption>
                <xforms:value>bill</xforms:value>
            </xforms:item>
        </xforms:selectOne>
    </p>

    <p>
        <xforms:input ref="order/paymentinfo/ccnumber">
            <xforms:caption>Credit Card Number</xforms:caption>
        </xforms:input>

        <xforms:input ref="order/paymentinfo/expmonth">
            <xforms:caption>Month</xforms:caption>
        </xforms:input>

        <xforms:input ref="order/paymentinfo/expyear">
            <xforms:caption>Year</xforms:caption>
        </xforms:input>
    </p>

    <p>
        <xforms:submit>
            <xforms:caption>Submit Report</xforms:caption>
        </xforms:submit>
    </p>

    </body>
    </html>
```

Chapter 16

Review Questions

1. What is the difference between XSL Formatting Objects and XSL Transformations?

   ANSWER: XSL Transformations change the actual data contained in an XML file. XSL Formatting Objects control the way in which data is presented.

2. How does a formatting objects renderer know how to lay out the basic geometry of the page?

   ANSWER: Through the use of a `simple-page-master`.

3. How are different page layouts combined in a single document?

   ANSWER: They are combined through the use of a `page-sequence-master`.

4. What do you call content that appears at the same position on each page?

   ANSWER: Static content.

5. What structure allows content to span several pages?

   ANSWER: A flow.

6. How do you get a document that uses a different layout for the title page?

   ANSWER: Use `repeatable-page-master-alternatives` and set the `page-position` property.

Programming Exercises

1. Create a document with a single page of content.

   SOLUTION:

```
<?xml version="1.0" encoding="utf-8"?>
<fo:root xmlns:fo="http://www.w3.org/1999/XSL/Format">

    <fo:layout-master-set>
        <fo:simple-page-master master-name="simplePage"
                page-height="18cm" page-width="15cm" margin-top="1cm"
                margin-bottom="1cm" margin-left="1cm"
                margin-right="0cm">
                    <fo:region-body/>
        </fo:simple-page-master>

        <fo:page-sequence-master master-name="simplePageMaster">
            <fo:single-page-master-reference master-reference="simplePage" />
        </fo:page-sequence-master>

    </fo:layout-master-set>

    <fo:page-sequence master-reference="simplePageMaster">
```

```
            <fo:flow flow-name="xsl-region-body">

                <fo:block>
                    A page can be as simple as a single page with a single flow.
                </fo:block>

            </fo:flow>
        </fo:page-sequence>

    </fo:root>
```

2. Create a document that can handle an undetermined number of pages that all use the same layout.

SOLUTION:

```
<?xml version="1.0" encoding="utf-8"?>
<fo:root xmlns:fo="http://www.w3.org/1999/XSL/Format">

    <fo:layout-master-set>
        <fo:simple-page-master master-name="simplePage"
                page-height="5cm" page-width="15cm" margin-top="1cm"
                margin-bottom="1cm" margin-left="1cm"
                margin-right="0cm">
                    <fo:region-body/>
        </fo:simple-page-master>

        <fo:page-sequence-master master-name="simplePageMaster">
            <fo:repeatable-page-master-reference
                    master-reference="simplePage" />
        </fo:page-sequence-master>

    </fo:layout-master-set>

    <fo:page-sequence master-reference="simplePageMaster">

        <fo:flow flow-name="xsl-region-body">

            <fo:block>
                A page can be as simple as a single page with a single flow,
                or it can use multiple pages.
            </fo:block>

        </fo:flow>
    </fo:page-sequence>

</fo:root>
```

3. Add a footer to the document in exercise 2.

SOLUTION:

```
<?xml version="1.0" encoding="utf-8"?>
<fo:root xmlns:fo="http://www.w3.org/1999/XSL/Format">
```

```
<fo:layout-master-set>
    <fo:simple-page-master master-name="simplePage"
            page-height="5cm" page-width="15cm" margin-top="1cm"
            margin-bottom="1cm" margin-left="1cm"
            margin-right="0cm">
            <fo:region-body/>
            <fo:region-after extent="1cm"/>
    </fo:simple-page-master>

    <fo:page-sequence-master master-name="simplePageMaster">
        <fo:repeatable-page-master-reference
                master-reference="simplePage" />
    </fo:page-sequence-master>

</fo:layout-master-set>

<fo:page-sequence master-reference="simplePageMaster">

    <fo:static-content flow-name="xsl-region-after">
        <fo:block text-align="center">
            <fo:page-number/>
        </fo:block>
    </fo:static-content>

    <fo:flow flow-name="xsl-region-body">

        <fo:block>
            A page can be as simple as a single page with a single flow,
            or it can use multiple pages.
        </fo:block>

    </fo:flow>
</fo:page-sequence>

</fo:root>
```

4. Create a document that uses a different layout for the first page than for other pages.

SOLUTION:

```
<?xml version="1.0" encoding="utf-8"?>
<fo:root xmlns:fo="http://www.w3.org/1999/XSL/Format">

    <fo:layout-master-set>
        <fo:simple-page-master master-name="firstPageMaster"
                page-height="18cm" page-width="15cm" margin-top="1cm"
                margin-bottom="1cm" margin-left="1cm"
                margin-right="0cm">
                <fo:region-body/>
        </fo:simple-page-master>

        <fo:simple-page-master master-name="otherPageMaster"
                page-height="5cm" page-width="15cm" margin-top="1cm"
                margin-bottom="1cm" margin-left="1cm"
```

```
                    margin-right="0cm">
                        <fo:region-before extent="1cm"/>
                        <fo:region-body margin-top="1.5cm"/>
                        <fo:region-after extent="1cm"/>
            </fo:simple-page-master>

            <fo:page-sequence-master master-name="multiplePageMasterSequence">
                <fo:repeatable-page-master-alternatives>
                    <fo:conditional-page-master-reference
                            page-position="first"
                            master-reference="firstPageMaster"/>
                    <fo:conditional-page-master-reference
                            master-reference="otherPageMaster"/>
                </fo:repeatable-page-master-alternatives>

            </fo:page-sequence-master>

    </fo:layout-master-set>

    <fo:page-sequence master-reference="multiplePageMasterSequence">

        <fo:static-content flow-name="xsl-region-before">
                <fo:block text-align="center">
                    Heading off into the document...
                </fo:block>
        </fo:static-content>

        <fo:static-content flow-name="xsl-region-after">
                <fo:block text-align="center">
                    <fo:page-number/>
                </fo:block>
        </fo:static-content>

        <fo:flow flow-name="xsl-region-body">

            <fo:block>
                A page can be as simple as a single page with a single flow,
                or it can use multiple pages.
            </fo:block>

        </fo:flow>
    </fo:page-sequence>

</fo:root>
```

Chapter 17

Review Questions

1. What is a Web service?

    ANSWER: A Web service is any transaction that can take place over the Web, but in general the term is used to refer to transactions that take place using a messaging system such as SOAP.

2. What is SOAP?

    ANSWER: Simple Object Access Protocol (SOAP) is a standard format for Web services messages.

3. What is the SOAP header element typically used for?

    ANSWER: The SOAP header element is typically used to provide more information about the message.

4. What is WSDL?

    ANSWER: Web Services Description Language (WSDL) provides a standard way of describing a Web service.

5. Why is a WSDL file useful?

    ANSWER: A WSDL file is useful because it lets other developers know how to access your Web service.

6. What is UDDI?

    ANSWER: Universal Description, Discovery, and Integration (UDDI) is a system of registry information that provides pointers to individual Web services.

Programming Exercises

1. Create a SOAP message that requests a random number between 1 and 500.

    SOLUTION:

    ```
    <soap-env:Envelope xmlns:soap-env="http://schemas.xmlsoap.org/soap/envelope/"
                   xmlns:xsd="http://www.w3.org/1999/XMLSchema">
       <soap-env:Header/>
       <soap-env:Body>
          <tns:getRandomNumber xmlns:tns="RandomeNumberGenerator"
    soap-env:encodingStyle="http://schemas.xmlsoap.org/soap/encoding/">
             <min xmlns:xsi="http://www.w3.org/1999/XMLSchema-instance"
                   xsi:type="xsd:int">1</min>
             <max xmlns:xsi="http://www.w3.org/1999/XMLSchema-instance"
                   xsi:type="xsd:int">500</max>
          </tns:getRandomNumber>
    ```

```
        </soap-env:Body>
    </soap-env:Envelope>
```

2. Create a SOAP message that requests television listing information by sending a genre element and a timeslot element that includes date and time.

SOLUTION:

```
<?xml version="1.0" encoding="UTF-8" ?>
<SOAP-ENV:Envelope xmlns:SOAP-ENV="http://schemas.xmlsoap.org/soap/envelope/"
                   xmlns:SOAP-ENC="http://schemas.xmlsoap.org/soap/encoding/"
                   xmlns:xsi="http://www.w3.org/2001/XMLSchema-instance"
                       xmlns:xsd="http://www.w3.org/2001/XMLSchema"
SOAP-ENV:encodingStyle="http://schemas.xmlsoap.org/soap/encoding/">
<SOAP-ENV:Body>
    <search:getListingSearchRequest xmlns:search="urn:SearchSystem">
        <genre xsi:type="xsd:string">news</genre>
        <timeslot xsi:type="m:timeSlot">
            <date>10/28/2004</date>
            <time>22:30</time>
        </timeslot>
    </search:getListingSearchRequest>
</SOAP-ENV:Body>
</SOAP-ENV:Envelope>
```

3. Create the response message for the television listing request.

SOLUTION:

```
<?xml version="1.0" encoding="UTF-8"?>
<SOAP-ENV:Envelope xmlns:SOAP-ENV="http://schemas.xmlsoap.org/soap/envelope/"
                   xmlns:xsi="http://www.w3.org/2001/XMLSchema-instance"
                   xmlns:xsd="http://www.w3.org/2001/XMLSchema">
    <SOAP-ENV:Body>
        <ns1:getListingSearchResponse xmlns:ns1="urn:SearchSystem"
            SOAP-
ENV:encodingStyle="http://schemas.xmlsoap.org/soap/encoding/">
            <program xsi:type="m:programInfo">
                <title>The 10:30 News</title>
                <length>30 minutes</length>
            </program>
            <program xsi:type="m:programInfo">
                <title>The Nightly News</title>
                <length>60 minutes</length>
            </program>
        </ns1:getListingSearchResponse>
    </SOAP-ENV:Body>
</SOAP-ENV:Envelope>
```

4. Create a WSDL file that describes the service in the previous two exercises.

SOLUTION:

```
<?xml version="1.0" encoding="UTF-8"?>
<definitions name="LifeSupportInfoServiceDefn" targetNamespace=
        "http://localhost:8080/soap/wsdl/LifeSupportInfo-service.wsdl"
    xmlns="http://schemas.xmlsoap.org/wsdl/"
    xmlns:soap="http://schemas.xmlsoap.org/wsdl/soap/"
    xmlns:tns=
        "http://localhost:8080/soap/wsdl/LifeSupportInfo-service.wsdl"
    xmlns:binding=
"http://localhost:8080/definitions/LifeSupportInfoRemoteInterface"
    xmlns:typens=
        "http://localhost:8080/definitions/LifeSupportInfoRemoteInterface">
<types>
    <xsd:schema targetNamespace=
    "http://localhost:8080/definitions/LifeSupportInfoRemoteInterface"
xmlns:xsd="http://www.w3.org/2001/XMLSchema" >
        <xsd:complexType name="ListingSearchRequestType">
          <xsd:sequence>
            <xsd:element name="genre" type="xsd:string"/>
            <xsd:element name="timeSlot">
              <xsd:complexType>
                <xsd:sequence>
                    <xsd:element name="date" type="xsd:string" />
                    <xsd:element name="time" type="xsd:string" />
                </xsd:sequence>
              </xsd:complexType>
            </xsd:element>
          </xsd:sequence>
        </xsd:complexType>
        <xsd:complexType name="ListingSearchResponseType">
          <xsd:sequence>
            <xsd:element name="program" maxOccurs="unbounded">
              <xsd:complexType>
                <xsd:sequence>
                    <xsd:element name="title" type="xsd:string" />
                    <xsd:element name="length" type="xsd:string" />
                </xsd:sequence>
              </xsd:complexType>
            </xsd:element>
          </xsd:sequence>
        </xsd:complexType>
    </xsd:schema>
  </types>
  <message name="getListingSearchRequest">
    <part name="getListingSearchRequest"
type="typens:ListingSearchRequestType"/>
  </message>
  <message name="getListingSearchResponse">
    <part name="getListingSearchResponse"
        type="typens:ListingSearchResponseType"/>
  </message>
  <portType name="LifeSupportInfoJavaPortType">
```

```
        <operation name="getListingSearch">
          <input name="getListingSearchRequest"
                message="tns:getListingSearchRequest"/>
          <output name="getListingSearchesponse"
                message="tns:getListingSearchResponse"/>
        </operation>
      </portType>
      <binding name="ListingSearchBinding"
  type="tns:LifeSupportInfoJavaPortType">
        <soap:binding style="rpc"
  transport="http://schemas.xmlsoap.org/soap/http"/>
        <operation name="getListingSearch">
          <soap:operation soapAction="" style="rpc"/>
          <input name="getListingSearchRequest">
            <soap:body use="encoded"

  encodingStyle="http://schemas.xmlsoap.org/soap/encoding/"
                              namespace="urn:ListingSearchSystem"/>
          </input>
          <output name="getListingSearchResponse">
            <soap:body use="encoded"

  encodingStyle="http://schemas.xmlsoap.org/soap/encoding/"
                              namespace="urn:ListingSearchSystem"/>
          </output>
        </operation>
      </binding>
      <service name="ListingSearchService">
        <port name="ListingSearchPort" binding="binding:ListingSearchBinding">
          <soap:address location="http://localhost:8080/soap/servlet/rpcrouter"/>
        </port>
      </service>
  </definitions>
```

Chapter 18

Review Questions

1. What is data binding?

   ANSWER: The creation of classes that mimic the structure of data so that it can be accessed or altered directly.

2. Why is XML data binding helpful for programmers?

   ANSWER: It provides a more "natural" environment than traditional XML programming for object-oriented programmers, and allows bound objects to interact with other application objects.

3. What does marshalling data entail?

   ANSWER: Persisting objects back to a source such as an XML document.

4. What does unmarshalling data entail?

ANSWER: Loading the data in order to populate objects.

5. How is data stored within objects?

ANSWER: Data is stored as properties of the object.

6. What if an element has element children of its own?

ANSWER: An element with element children is treated as a class.

Programming Exercises

Exercises 1–3 apply to this example:

```
<?xml version="1.0"?>
<!DOCTYPE music SYSTEM "music.dtd">
<music>
   <song id="_1" accesses="49">
        <title>Old Rex</title>
        <durationSecs>180</durationSecs>
   </song>
   <song id="_2" accesses="5">
        <title>My Francine</title>
        <durationSecs>194</durationSecs>
   </song>
   <song id="_3" accesses="603">
        <title>Eager to Fight</title>
        <durationSecs>162</durationSecs>
   </song>
</music>
```

1. Create an application that unmarshals the data and outputs it to the screen.

SOLUTION:

music.dtd:

```
<!ELEMENT music (song+)>
<!ELEMENT song (title, durationSecs)>
<!ATTLIST song id ID #REQUIRED
               accesses CDATA #REQUIRED>
<!ELEMENT title (#PCDATA)>
<!ELEMENT durationSecs (#PCDATA)>
```

music.xjs:

```
<?xml version="1.0"?>
<xml-java-binding-schema version="1.0ea">

    <element name="music" type="class" root="true"/>

    <element name="song" type="class">
        <attribute name="id"/>
        <attribute name="accesses" convert="int"/>
```

```
            <content>
                <element-ref name="title"/>
                <element-ref name="durationSecs"/>
            </content>
        </element>

        <element name="durationSecs" type="value" convert="int"/>

</xml-java-binding-schema>
```

MusicApp.java:

```java
import java.io.File;
import java.io.InputStream;
import java.io.FileInputStream;

import java.util.List;
import java.util.Iterator;

public class MusicApp {

    public static void main(String[] args) {

        Music music;
        music = new Music();
        try {

            File musicFile = new File("music.xml");
            InputStream inStream = new FileInputStream(musicFile);
            try {
                music = music.unmarshal(inStream);
            } catch (Exception e){
                System.out.println(e.getMessage());
            } finally {
                inStream.close();
            }

            List songList = music.getSong();

            for (Iterator i = songList.iterator();
                    i.hasNext();) {

                Song song = (Song)i.next();

                String songId = song.getId();
                int songAccesses = song.getAccesses();
                String songTitle = song.getTitle();
                int songDuration = song.getDurationSecs();

                System.out.println(songId + ")");
                System.out.println(songTitle+": "+songAccesses+" accesses, "+

                                    songDuration+" seconds each");
            }
```

```
        } catch (Exception e) {
                System.out.println(e.getMessage());
            e.printStackTrace();
        }
    }

}
```

2. Create an application that unmarshals the data, increments the number of times each song has been accessed by one, and marshals it back to the original source.

SOLUTION:

```
import java.io.File;
import java.io.InputStream;
import java.io.FileInputStream;
import java.io.FileOutputStream;

import java.util.List;
import java.util.Iterator;

public class MusicApp {

    public static void main(String[] args) {

        Music music;
        music = new Music();
        try {

            File musicFile = new File("music.xml");
            InputStream inStream = new FileInputStream(musicFile);
            try {
                music = music.unmarshal(inStream);
            } catch (Exception e){
                System.out.println(e.getMessage());
            } finally {
                inStream.close();
            }

            List songList = music.getSong();

            for (Iterator i = songList.iterator();
                 i.hasNext();) {

                Song song = (Song)i.next();

                int songAccesses = song.getAccesses();
                song.setAccesses(songAccesses + 1);

            }

            music.validate();

            File savemusic = new File("newmusic.xml");
```

```
                FileOutputStream outStream = new FileOutputStream(savemusic);
                try {
                    music.marshal(outStream);
                } catch (Exception e) {
                    System.out.println(e.getMessage());
                } finally {
                    outStream.close();
                }

            } catch (Exception e) {
                    System.out.println(e.getMessage());
                e.printStackTrace();
            }
        }

    }
```

3. Create an application that unmarshals the data and adds a new song called "No One Knows What It's Like" that is 208 seconds long and has not yet been accessed.

SOLUTION:

```
import java.io.File;
import java.io.InputStream;
import java.io.FileInputStream;
import java.io.FileOutputStream;

import java.util.List;
import java.util.Iterator;

public class MusicApp {

    public static void main(String[] args) {

        Music music;
        music = new Music();
        try {

            File musicFile = new File("music.xml");
            InputStream inStream = new FileInputStream(musicFile);
            try {
                music = music.unmarshal(inStream);
            } catch (Exception e){
                System.out.println(e.getMessage());
            } finally {
                inStream.close();
            }

            List songList = music.getSong();

            Song newSong = new Song();
            newSong.setId("_4");
            newSong.setAccesses(0);
            newSong.setTitle("No-one Knows What It's Like");
```

```
                newSong.setDurationSecs(208);
                songList.add(newSong);

                music.validate();

                File savemusic = new File("newmusic.xml");
                FileOutputStream outStream = new FileOutputStream(savemusic);
                try {
                    music.marshal(outStream);
                } catch (Exception e) {
                    System.out.println(e.getMessage());
                } finally {
                    outStream.close();
                }

            } catch (Exception e) {
                    System.out.println(e.getMessage());
                e.printStackTrace();
            }
        }

    }
```

Exercises 4 and 5 apply to this example:

```
<?xml version="1.0"?>
<!DOCTYPE music SYSTEM "music.dtd">
<music>
    <song id="_1" accesses="49">
        <title>Old Rex</title>
        <durationSecs>180</durationSecs>
        <writers>
            <writer>
                <name>Arry Tome</name>
                <percentage>100</percentage>
            </writer>
        </writers>
    </song>
    <song id="_2" accesses="5">
        <title>My Francine</title>
        <durationSecs>194</durationSecs>
        <writers>
            <writer>
                <name>Arry Tome</name>
                <percentage>90</percentage>
            </writer>
            <writer>
                <name>Robert Maxwell</name>
                <percentage>10</percentage>
            </writer>
        </writers>
    </song>
    <song id="_3" accesses="603">
        <title>Eager to Fight</title>
```

```
                <durationSecs>162</durationSecs>
                <writers>
                    <writer>
                        <name>Joon Station</name>
                        <percentage>40</percentage>
                    </writer>
                    <writer>
                        <name>Lars Hotts</name>
                        <percentage>25</percentage>
                    </writer>
                    <writer>
                        <name>Owen Steen</name>
                        <percentage>35</percentage>
                    </writer>
                </writers>
            </song>
    </music>
```

4. Create an application that unmarshals the data and outputs it to the screen.

SOLUTION:

music.dtd:

```
<!ELEMENT music (song+)>
<!ELEMENT song (title, durationSecs, writers)>
<!ATTLIST song id ID #REQUIRED
                accesses CDATA #REQUIRED>
<!ELEMENT title (#PCDATA)>
<!ELEMENT durationSecs (#PCDATA)>
<!ELEMENT writers (writer+)>
<!ELEMENT writer (name, percentage)>
<!ELEMENT name (#PCDATA)>
<!ELEMENT percentage (#PCDATA)>
```

music.xjs:

```
<?xml version="1.0"?>
<xml-java-binding-schema version="1.0ea">

    <element name="music" type="class" root="true"/>

    <element name="percentage" type="value" convert="int"/>

</xml-java-binding-schema>
```

MusicApp.java:

```
import java.io.File;
import java.io.InputStream;
import java.io.FileInputStream;

import java.util.List;
import java.util.Iterator;

public class MusicApp {
```

```java
public static void main(String[] args) {

    Music music;
    music = new Music();
    try {

        File musicFile = new File("music.xml");
        InputStream inStream = new FileInputStream(musicFile);
        try {
            music = music.unmarshal(inStream);
        } catch (Exception e){
            System.out.println(e.getMessage());
        } finally {
            inStream.close();
        }

        List songList = music.getSong();

        for (Iterator i = songList.iterator();
            i.hasNext();) {

            Song song = (Song)i.next();

            String songId = song.getId();
            String songAccesses = song.getAccesses();
            String songTitle = song.getTitle();
            String songDuration = song.getDurationSecs();
            Writers songWriters = song.getWriters();

            System.out.println(songId + ")");
            System.out.println(songTitle+": "+songAccesses+" accesses, "+
                               songDuration+" seconds each");
            System.out.println("Writers:");
            List writerList = songWriters.getWriter();
            for (Iterator j = writerList.iterator();
                j.hasNext();) {
                Writer thisWriter = (Writer)j.next();
                String writerName = thisWriter.getName();
                int percentage = thisWriter.getPercentage();

                System.out.println("   "+writerName+", "+percentage+"%");
            }
            System.out.println("---------");
        }

    } catch (Exception e) {
            System.out.println(e.getMessage());
        e.printStackTrace();
    }
}

}
```

5. Create an application that unmarshals the data, determines which writer wrote the greatest percentage of each song, and gives that writer complete credit. The application should then marshal the data.

SOLUTION:

```java
import java.io.File;
import java.io.InputStream;
import java.io.FileInputStream;
import java.io.FileOutputStream;

import java.util.List;
import java.util.Iterator;

public class MusicApp {

    public static void main(String[] args) {

        Music music;
        music = new Music();
        try {

            File musicFile = new File("music.xml");
            InputStream inStream = new FileInputStream(musicFile);
            try {
                music = music.unmarshal(inStream);
            } catch (Exception e){
                System.out.println(e.getMessage());
            } finally {
                inStream.close();
            }

            List songList = music.getSong();

            for (Iterator i = songList.iterator();
                    i.hasNext();) {

                Song song = (Song)i.next();

                Writers songWriters = song.getWriters();

                Writer primaryWriter = null;
                int primaryPercentage = 0;
                List writerList = songWriters.getWriter();
                for (Iterator j = writerList.iterator();
                        j.hasNext();) {

                    Writer thisWriter = (Writer)j.next();
                    int percentage = thisWriter.getPercentage();
                    if (percentage > primaryPercentage) {
                        primaryPercentage = percentage;
                        primaryWriter = thisWriter;
                    }
                }
```

```
                primaryWriter.setPercentage(100);
                songWriters.emptyWriter();
                writerList = songWriters.getWriter();
                writerList.add(primaryWriter);

            }

            music.validate();

            File savemusic = new File("newmusic.xml");
            FileOutputStream outStream = new FileOutputStream(savemusic);
            try {
                music.marshal(outStream);
            } catch (Exception e) {
                System.out.println(e.getMessage());
            } finally {
                outStream.close();
            }

        } catch (Exception e) {
                System.out.println(e.getMessage());
            e.printStackTrace();
        }
    }

}
```

Chapter 19

Review Questions

1. Name one reason you might need to interact with a database management system in an XML-oriented application.

   ANSWER: You might need to interact with a relational database management system in order to improve search capabilities, use legacy data, or combine data from multiple systems.

2. A document is loosely structured and contains a large number of mixed content elements. Is it likely data-centric or document-centric?

   ANSWER: Document-centric.

3. What does a side table do?

   ANSWER: A side table provides a means to index data within a document stored as a single column.

4. XML data binding is similar to what method of working with XML data in a relational database?

   ANSWER: XML data binding is similar to object-relational XML mappings.

5. Name the type of software designed specifically to interface between an application and a database.

    ANSWER: Middleware.

Programming Exercises

(No solutions are provided because no product is specified.)

1. Determine the XML-enabled capabilities of your own database.

2. Insert an XML document into the database.

3. Perform a query on your data to retrieve part or all of the data.

Chapter 20

Review Questions

1. Name three advantages that a native XML database offers over a simple XML file.

    ANSWER: NXDs provide transactional capabilities and locking, the ability to group documents together into collections, indexing, and the ability to easily access the data programmatically through an API.

2. What's the difference between a text-based and a model-based NXD?

    ANSWER: A text-based database stores the document in its entirety, whereas a model-based database breaks it up according to an internal model and stores the information.

3. What is round-tripping, and why is it important?

    ANSWER: Round-tripping is a database capability that enables you to get back the exact document you put in, attribute and sibling order, ignorable whitespace, and all.

4. What is a collection?

    ANSWER: A collection is a logical grouping of documents or document fragments.

INDEX

Symbols

\# (pound sign), 631
& (ampersand), 28-29
<!— (comment tag), 32
<?. See processing instructions, 31
?xml (XML declaration indicator), 19

A

absolute positioning, 544
absolute property, 542
Abstact Schemas
   advantages of, 369
   creating, 369-370
   overview, 369
Acrobat Reader, downloading, 685
all declarations processed property, 879
ampersand, 310, 314
analysis phase of planning, 51
ANY elements, DTDs, 301
Apache, XIndice product, 818
Apache project
   SOAP Toolkit, 721-723
   Tomcat servlet engine, 721-723
   Web services using, 721-723
   XSLT, 421

apostrophe, 314
application servers, 795
applications of XML, 859
arcs, XLink, 613-617
attribute information items, 880-881
attribute type property, 880
attributes
   CDATA type, 26
   default namespaces with, 42
   default values, 303-305
   defined, 25, 885
   DOM, 112
   DOM interface for, 90
   DTDs for, 257
   DTSs, declaring in, 303-306
   duplicated names for, 44
   elements, replacing with, 72-73
   ENTITY, 310-317
   enumerated, 305-306
   fixed value, 305
   groups, specifying, 344-345
   ID and IDREF, 307-309
   ID type, 26-27
   IDREF type, 26-27
   implied, 303-304
   namespaces for, 44-45
   naming, 25
   NMTOKEN, 309-310
   normalizing data, 73, 75

order in DTDs, 303
purpose of, 25
quotation marks for, 36
required, 304
retrieving in DOM, 145-146
SAX parsing of, 193-199
Schemas, adding to, 340, 342-345
types of, 26-27
value restrictions, 26
whitespace in, 26
XPath navigation to, 389
XSL, 683
attributes property, 880
attributes, data modeling. See data attributes, 61
authoring structures, 54

B

background-color property, 533
base URI property, 879-881
binary data types, 327
binding. See data binding
BLOBs (binary large objects), 799
blogging, XLink for, 611-612
books, electronic, OEB for, 863
boolean controls, 655-656
boolean data type, 327
border properties, CSS, 537-539
border-color property, 533
bound data. See data binding
bounding box model, XSL, 683
bounding box size properties, 540-541
Bourret, Ronald, 793, 818
BPML (Business Process Modeling Language), 863
browser-based XML. See XHTML
browsers
    extended links in, 603
    graceful degradation, 581
    mobile, 862
    Mozilla, 863
    XForms support, 640
    XSLT, support for, 589
Bush, Vannevar, 602
business functions, determining, 55-56
Business Process Modeling Language (BPML), 863

C

C++
    content handlers, 271-274
    DOM elements, accessing, 104-105
    DOM feature support test, 99-100
    DOM navigation using siblings, 137-138
    error handlers, 282-285, 288
    MySAXContentHandler example, 212
    parsing DOM documents, 96
    saving documents, 125-126
    SAX attribute events, 195-196
    SAX content handlers, 170-173
    SAX data, changing, 240-243
    SAX error handling, 183-185
    SAX events, capturing, 189
    SAX exceptions, 217
    SAX filters, 225-233
    SAX parser creation, 165-166
    SAX parsing method , 180
    SAX text events, 202
    SAX validation support, 260
    schemas for validation, 270-271, 275-277
    SOAP messaging, 741-742
    stopping SAX parses, 212-218
    Web services application example, 728-730
    Web services, configuring, 724
    Web services with, 749-750
    XMLReader creation, 165-166
    XSLT extension functions, 462-463
    XSLT, invoking, 420
    XSLT templates, 434
    XSLT with, 422-424, 427, 432, 436
    XSLT with SAX, 442, 447-449
canonical XML, 147-148
Cascading Style Sheets. See CSS
Castor, 765
Castor Project, 875
CDATA
    attribute type, 26
    DOM interface for, 90
    DOM, outputting content, 145
    normalization of, 147
    sections of, 30-31
CDATA sections, XHTML with, 592-593
cell phones, XML for, 862

cells, 571
chaining transformations, 455-459, 471, 926-927
character code property, 882
character data, example of, 18
character encoding scheme property, 879
character information items, 882
character large objects (CLOBs), 799-800
character sets
    illegal characters, 37
    Unicode, 37
    XML declarations, attribute of, 19
character-points, 633
characters, numeric entities for, 313
check boxes
    XForms, 649-651, 655-656
    XHTML forms, 580, 585
child elements
    attributes, replacing with, 72-73
    defined, 886
    DOM, 104
    Schema creation of, 329-331
    selectors for, CSS, 529
child nodes, DOM, 114-115
children property, 879-882
class selectors, 530-531
classes, XSLT, external, 468-470
clear property, 547
CLOBs (character large objects), 799-800
collections
    NXDs use of, 819
    of tables for data storage, 802
color
    CSS for setting, 533-534
    XSL, 698-699
columns, data attributes as, 61
comet.xml source file, 524-525
comment information items, 882
comments, 32-33
    XPath node tests for, 497-498
committee members, 50
container elements, 75-76
content management systems, 796
content models, 256, 296, 321
content modifiers, 297-299
content property, 881-882
context nodes, 386, 388
conversion structures, 54

core recommendations, 857-858
Cover Pages, 869
CSS (Cascading Style Sheets)
    absolute positioning, 544
    alternative media properties, 532, 550
    associating documents with, 526
    background-color property, 533
    border properties, 537-539
    border-color property, 533
    bounding box size properties, 540-541
    browser support for, 524
    children selectors, 529
    class selectors, 530-531
    clear property, 547
    color properties, 532
    color, setting, 533-534
    combining properties, 532
    descendant selectors, 528-529
    display property, 538, 548-549
    element selectors, 528
    float property, 546
    font properties, 535-537
    formatting properties, 532
    generated content properties, 532
    id selectors, 530-531
    margin property, 532, 539-540
    outline-color property, 533
    padding property, 539-540
    page flow, 545-547
    position property, 542-545
    properties, 532
    pseudoclasses, using in with, 575
    purpose of, 523-524
    reference sites, 873
    referencing style sheets, 526
    rule priority, 528
    selectors, 527-531
    shorthand property, 532
    sibling selectors, 530
    text properties, 532
    text size properties, 535-536
    text shadow properties, 533
    text/css type, 527
    visibility property, 547-548
    width property, 540-541
    XHTML using, 573-575
cursive fonts, 537, 551, 931

custom entities, 311-313
custom types, 352-354

D

data attributes, 61-65
data binding
    adding elements, 776-777
    advantages of, 779, 789, 956
    binding schemas, 764-767, 780-782
    binding schemas type issues, 784
    Castor framework, 765
    class creation, 766-767
    classes
        uses for, 764-765
        using, 768-775
    convert attribute, 784
    Custom Binding Schema example, 781-782
    defined, 789, 956
    development steps, 764-765
    DTD for Full example, 782-783
    DTD for New Data example, 781
    DTD for simplified data sample, 766
    editing data, 771-774
    elements, treating as classes, 784
    full binding schema example, 780-782
    Full DTD example, 782-783
    generating classes, 767, 785
    hierarchical nature of, 764
    IDREFs, 787-788
    invalid data, 777
    JAXB framework, 765
    loading data into objects, 768-769
    marshalling data, 764, 774-775, 790-791, 959-960, 964-965
    missing data, 777
    New Data example, 780-781
    object-oriented nature of, 764
    objects as properties, 785-787
    outputting to screen, 773, 791, 962-963
    overview, 763-765
    products for, 765
    properties as objects, 785-787
    properties, 777, 787-788
    purpose of, 763

reading data members, 770-771
reference sites, 875-876
referential integrity, 787-788
removing objects, 778-779
retrieving data from objects, 769-770
schemas, 764-767, 780-782
separation of XML structure, 779
simplified data sample, 766
structure of classes, 767-768
summary, 789
type issues, 784
unmarshalling data, 764, 768-769, 790-791, 957-965
using classes, 768-775
data entities, 61-63, 69
data entities, 69. *See also* ERDs (Entity Relationship Diagrams)
data entity information forms, 65
data integrity
    Schemas vs. DTDs, 358
    unique keys, 358-359
data modeling
    attributes, 61-65
    completeness checks, 69
    cross checking models, 68
    data entity information forms, 65
    entities, 61-63
    ERDs, 66-69
    normalizing data, 73-75
    redundant entities, 69
    relationships, 61, 65-69
    user review, 69-70
data sources, planning, 52-53
data-centric XML, 796-798
databases
    application servers, 795
    choosing a type, 796
    content management systems, 796
    data-centric XML, 796-798
    document-centric XML, 798
    middleware, 794
    NXDs (native XML databases), 795
    object-relational databases, 801-802
    products, Web site listing, 793
    reference sites, 876-877
    relational. *See* relational databases
    summary, 812

types of data in, 796, 799
XML
    files as, 814
    servers, 795
XML-enabled. *See* XML-enabled databases
DB2, XML Extender, 805-807
declaration base property, 883
declaration base URI property, 881-883
decomposing business functions, 56-57
deploying Web services, 734-737
descendant selectors, 528-529
deserializing data, 764
designing at the keyboard, 48
designing. *See also* planning
destinations, data, planning, 52-53
display property, 538, 548-549
DOCTYPE, 292-293
DOCTYPE declarations
    defined, 20
    XHTML, 555-556
DOCTYPE definitions. *See* DTDs
DOCTYPE keyword, 256
document element property, 879
document information items, 879
document management, new specifications, 864
Document Object Model. *See* DOM (Document Object Model)
document roots, 388-389
Document Type Definition information items, 882
Document Type Definitions. *See* DTDs
document-centric XML, 798
documentation
    planning required, 48
    of XML Schemas, 324-325
DOM (Document Object Model)
    accessing form values, 593-595
    APIs for, 87
    Attr interface, 90
    attribute values, changing, 119, 131, 894
    attributes, 112, 145-146
    browser support for, 593, 598
    C++
        accessing elements with, 104-105
        parsing with, 96
        saving documents with, 125-126
        sibling navigation, 137-138
        support test, 99-100

canonical XML, 147-148
CDATA sections, 145
CDDATASection interface, 90
child elements, 104
    adding , 121
child nodes, 109
    testing for, 114-115
Comment interface, 90
construction methods, 121
content modification, 120-121
content of elements, 103
content, changing, 117-119
defined, 87
DOCTYPE nodes, 145
document creation, 122-124, 131, 891
Document interface, 90
document roots, 104
document structure, 101-107
DocumentFragment interface, 91
DocumentType interface, 90
DOMBuilder, 156-157
DOMImplementation interface, 91-92, 98-101
element creation, 120-121
Element interface, 88, 90
element, adding to structure, 121-122
elements, 101-107
    retrieving by ID, 115-117
    retrieving by name, 109-111
Entity interface, 90
Events module, 91
exceptions interfaces, 91
feature support, testing for, 98
hasChildNodes() method, 114-115
home page, 870
HTML module, 91
ID, retrieving by, 115-117
implementations available, 93
interfaces defined by, 88-89
Java, accessing elements with, 102-104
    parsing with, 95
    saving documents with, 124-125
    sibling navigation, 136-137
    support test, 98-99
Level 3 recommendation, 864
Level 3.0 Load and Save, 156-158
levels of, 87-88
Load and Save module, 92, 156-159, 898

modifying content, 120-121
modules, testing for, 98-101
MSXML SDK support, 93
NamedNodeMap interface, 91, 111
node types, 108
    examining, 143
NodeFilters, 153-155, 159, 895-896
NodeIterator, 148-151, 155, 159, 895
NodeList interface, 91, 108-111
nodes, 89-90, 101-107, 130
normalization, 147
Notation interface, 90
origins of, 88
outputting tree contents, 141-146
parent-child relationship of nodes, 101-107
parsing documents, 94-98
Perl NodeIterators, 150-151
Perl
    accessing elements with, 107
    parsing with, 97-98
    saving documents with, 128-129
    sibling navigation, 140
    support test, 101
PHP
    accessing elements with, 106-107
    parsing with, 97
    saving documents with, 126-128
    sibling navigation, 139
    support test, 101
Processing Instructions, 145
Processing Instructions interface, 90
programming language for, 93
purpose of, 593
reference materials, 870-871
root elements, 104, 124, 131, 892
saving documents, 124-129, 157-158
SAX, compared to, 161-163
setAttribute() method, 119
setNodeValue(), 118
siblings, 134-141
source document for examples, 93-94, 133
stepping through trees with siblings, 134-141
Style Sheets module, 91
summary, 130
synchronous vs. asynchronous, 157
Text interface, 90
text nodes, 113

text, changing, 117-119
transformations, Java, 124
Traversal and Range module, 91
Traversal module, 148-153
TreeWalker, 148, 151-153, 159, 895-896
validation, 266-267
Validation module, 92
validation with, 265
version supported, determining, 92
Views module, 91
Visual Basic
    accessing elements with, 105-106
    parsing with, 96
    saving documents with, 126
    sibling navigation, 138-139
    support test, 100
whitespace in, 300-301
XPath module, 92
DTDs (Document Type Definitions)
ANY elements, 301
attribute declarations, 303-306
attribute default values, 303-305
attribute specification, 257
author customization, 319, 321-322, 910
conditional decisions with, 318-319
content models, 256, 296, 321
content modifiers, 297-299
content, mixed, 299-301
custom entities, 311-313
DOCTYPE, 292-293
DOCTYPE keyword, 256
Document Type Definition information items, 882
element choice indicator, 298
element content models, 256-257
element declarations, 296-297
element modifiers, 297-299
empty elements, 301-303
ENTITY attributes, 310-317
entities, external, 624
enumerated attributes, 305-306
external, 258, 291-295
external entities, 314-317
fixed value attributes, 305
formal public identifiers for, 293-294
frequency of elements, 299
history of, 291
ID attributes, 307-309

IDREF attributes, 307-309
implied attributes, 303-304
information items, 882
internal, 292, 295
language indicators, 294
mixed content, 299-301
names of, 294
NMTOKEN attributes, 309-310
notations, 316
numeric entities, 313-314
optional elements, indicating, 297
or operator (pipe), 298
parameter entities, 317-321
parsed entities, 314-316
PCDATA in, 300
percent sign, 317
PUBLIC identifiers, 258
purpose of, 33-36, 256, 321
reference sites, 871-872
referencing, 292-294
root elements, setting, 293
standards indicators, 294
SYSTEM identifiers, 258, 293
unparsed entities, 316-317
URIs, referencing with, 293
whitespace, 300-301
Dublin Core, 861

E

element content whitespace property, 882
element declarations, DTD, 296-297
element information items, 880
element selectors, 528
elements
    attributes, replacing with, 72-73
    child elements, 886
    components of, 20
    content models for, 256-257
    defined, 20-21, 885
    DOM interface for, 90
    DTD modifiers, 297-299
    empty, DTDs for, 301-303
    extension, XSLT, 464-468
    naming, 21
    nesting, 21

ellipses, 37
em dashes, 37
empty elements
    DTDs for, 301-303
    XHTML use of, 554
encryption, reference sites, 877-878
entities
    custom, 311-313
    defined, 310, 885
    DOM interface for, 90
    external, 36, 314-317
    general. See general entities
    need for, 28
    normalizing data, 73-75
    numeric, 313-314
    parameter. See parameter entities
    parsed, 314-316
    table of, 29-30
    unparsed, 316-317
entities, data. See data entities
ENTITY attributes, 310-317
entity-relationship diagrams. See ERDs
enumerated attributes, 305-306
enumeration, Schemas for, 349
ERDs (Entity-Relationship Diagrams), 66-70
error handling
    SAX, 182-186
    validation using, 262-266, 281-290
errors, validation, 255, 264-267, 290, 907-908. See also
    error handling, validation using
escape characters, 28-29
event-based approach. See SAX (Simple API for XML)
events
    business, 58-59
    XForms, 675-679
extended links
    arcs, 613-617
    blogging, 611-612
    defined, 603
    external entities with, 622-625
    id attributes, 620
    local resources, 612
    multidirectional, 618-622
    multiple arcs, 615-616
    multiple destinations, 617
    remote resources, 613
    resources, 612-613
    simple links converted to, 610
    syntax, 612-613

Extensible Stylesheet Language (XSL), 375
extension elements, XSLT, 464-468
extension functions, XSLT, 459-464
external DTDs (Document Type Definitions)
    defined, 258
    PUBLIC identifiers, 258
    SYSTEM identifiers, 258
external entities, 314-317, 622-625

forms, 637
    problems with XHTML, 639
    See also XForms
    XHTML. *See* XHTML forms
function hierarchy models, 55-56
function/process modeling, 54-59, 68
functions
    functions, XSLT, 459-464
    XPath. *See* XPath, functions

F

facets, 348-351
fantasy fonts, 537
fatal errors,validation, 264-267
filters, SAX
    appending names with, 253, 901-903
    C++, 225-232, 240-243
    inserting into streams, 238-239
    Java, 225, 239-240
    overview, 224
    Perl, 237, 248-251
    PHP, 237, 246-247
    Visual Basic .NET, 233-236, 243-245
fixed property, 542
fixed value attributes, 305
float property, 546
FLWR statements, 834-840
fonts
    generic families, 537
    properties, CSS, 535-537
footers
    XSL, 693, 701, 717, 950
FOP
    command-line script, 688
    defined, 682
    downloading, 684
foreign keys, 802
    Schema designation of, 360-361
formal public identifiers, 293-294
formatting
    objects. *See* XSL-FO (XSL Formatting Objects)
    XHTML, 561-563
Formatting Objects namespace, 686
Formatting Objects Processor. *See* FOP

G-H

gathering information planning step, 51-54
general entities, 310-317, 321
get method, XForms, 656-657
goals, defining, 48-49
graceful degradation, 581
graphics links, XSL, 704-705
graphics, vector. *See* Scalable Vector Graphics (SVG)

handlers, SAX, 163, 169-179
HTML
    relation to XML, 553-554
    tagged nature of, 554
    XHTML, differences from, 599, 932
    XML extension of. See XHTML, 553
    XSLT transformations to, 590-593
HTML (Hypertext Markup Language), 523
hyperlinks, 601. *See also* XLink (XML Linking Language)
    XHTML, 605

I-J

ID attributes, 307-309
id selectors, 530-531
ID type, 26-27
IDREF attributes, 307-309
IDREF type, 26-27
IIS (Internet Information Server), Web services, configuring for, 724

image links, XSL, 704-705
image tags, as empty elements, 301
images, XHTML, inserting in, 566-569
implied attributes, 303-304
include files, 314
indexes, NXDs with, 814
industry standards for XML, 53-54
information items, 879
information sets, 879
infoset augmentation, 305
instance documents, 325
interchange structures, 54
internal DTDs, 295
Internet Explorer, XML, display of, 526
interviewers, 50

Java
    chaining transformations, 455-457
    DOM feature support test, 98-99
    DOM navigation using siblings, 136-137
    error handlers, 262, 281-282, 287-288
    NodeFilter with, 154-155
    NodeIterator, 148-150
    parsing DOM documents, 95
    saving documents, 124-125
    SAX
        attribute events, 193-195
        content handlers, 169-170
        data, changing, 239-240
        error handling, 182-183
        events, capturing, 188-189
        exceptions, 212
        filters, 225
        parse method, 179-180
        parser creation, 164-165
        text events, 199, 201
    schemas for validation, 269-270
    SOAP messaging, 740-741
    stopping SAX parses, 210-212
    Web services application example, 726-728
    Web services in, 746-749
    XMLFilters in, 457-459
    XSLT
        extension functions, 459-462
        templates, 433-434
        with Java, 422-427, 431-432, 436-438
        with SAX, 440-442
Java Architecture for XML Binding (JAXB), 765

keys
    foreign keys, 360-361
    unique keys, 358-359
    XML Key Management Specification, 864

L-M

languages
    localization, 69
    Schemas, type for, 328
legal requirements, planning for, 53
Liberty Alliance Project, 875
line break element, 559-561
link databases. See linkbases
linkbases, 603, 625-630
links, 601. See also XLink (XML Linking Language)
    XHTML, 563-566, 605
    XSL, 704-706, 708
list boxes, XForms, 651, 680, 941-942
list type, 350-351
lists, XSL, 702-704
LOBs (large objects), 799-800
local name property, 880
local resources, 612
localization, planning, 69
locations in documents, pointing to. See XPointer

mapping models, XML to database, 799
margin property, 539-540
    CSS, 532
markup, defined, 18
marshalling data
    defined, 764
    examples, 774-775, 790-791, 959-960, 964-965
MathML, 859-860
meta tags, 593
metadata, RDF for, 861
methodology, planning, 51
Microsoft SQL Server, XML capabilities, 807-811
middleware, database, 794
mixed content
    Schemas for, 373, 913
    Schemas indicating, 333
mixed content, DTDs for, 299-301
mobile devices, XML for, 862

mode-based databases, 815
modeling
  completeness checks, 69
  cross checking models, 68
  data. *See* data modeling
  function/process, 54-59
  normalizing data, 73-75
  reviewing models, 58-59
  tree diagrams, 70, 72
  user review, 69-70
monospace fonts, 537
Mozilla, XUL, 863
MSXML
  parsing in Visual Basic, 96
  transformations,invoking, 420
  XSLT extension functions, 462-463
  XSLT with, 436
MSXML SDK, 93
MyContentHandler.vb sample, 218
MySAXContentHandler example, 212

N

name property, 881-883
name tokens, 309
name-value pairs. *See* attributes
named templates, XSLT, 408-409
named types, 346-347
namespace attributes property, 880
namespace information items, 883
namespace name property, 880-883
namespaces
  adding to documents, 491
  attributes with, 44-45
  declaring, 39
  default, 41-44
  emptying, 44
  multiple, 40
  multiple, in Schemas, 367-368
  no location, in Schemas, 362
  purpose of, 38
  referencing target namespaces, 366
  SAX parsing of, 193-195, 207, 222
  Schema features for, 361-368
  Schemas, declaring in, 323-324

scope of, 42-44
searching for with XPath, 493
specifying, 39-40
target namespaces, Schemas, 362-367
URI vs. URL, 40-41
URNs, 40
XForms, 644
XLink, 607
xsl, 38-39
naming
  attributes, 25
  elements, 21
native XML databases (NXDs), 795
nested elements, 21, 885
nesting
  elements, 75-76
  requirement for well-formedness, 36
Net.DATA, 805
Netscape Navigator, XML, display of, 525
NMTOKEN attributes, 309-310
node-points, 632-633
nodes
  DOM, 89-90, 130
  types, DOM, 108
normalization, 147
normalized value property, 880
normalizing data, 73-75
notation information items, 883
notation name property, 882
notation property, 881-882
notations, 316
notations property, 879
numeric entities, 313-314
NXDs (native XML databases), 795
  adding documents, 820
  adding DOM documents, 825-826
  adding resources, 823-827
  adding SAX documents, 826-827
  advantages of, 856, 966
  APIs for, 814, 818
  basic operations, 818
  capabilities of, 814-815
  categories of, 815
  collection creation, 819
  collections in, 815
  collections, specifying, 822
  connecting to databases, 822-823

documents as standard units, 814
entity reference problem, 817
indexes, 814
installing, 818
key specification, 820
locking system, 814
model-based, 815, 855, 966
object-relational model, 815
performance issues, 815
products for, 818
queries, 817
queries, running, 820-821
querying using XPath, 832-834
removing files from database, 820
resource fragments, 821
retrieving documents, 820, 827-828
retrieving DOM documents, 829-830
retrieving SAX documents, 830-831
round-tripping, 815-817, 856, 966
services, implementing, 832
summary, 855
text-based, 815, 855, 966
transactional ability, 814
updating data, 817
updating DOM documents, 829
vendors, 818
XIndice, 818-821
XML\, DB, 818, 821-834
XPath queries, 817
XPathQueryService, 832-834
XQuery, 817
XQuery with. See XQuery, 834
XUpdate. See XUpdate, 846

O-P

object-relational databases, 801-803
objectives, defining, 48-49
Open eBook (OEB), 863, 878
Oracle, XML-enabled databases, 803-805
outline-color property, 533
owner element property, 881

padding property, 539-540
page masters, 682, 685-686
page sequence masters, 682, 686-687, 709-713
paragraph tags, 557-559

parameter entities, 317-321
parameterized DTDs, 319-320
parent property, 880-882
parsed entities, 314-316
parsers
    SAX. See SAX (Simple API for XML)
    validating vs. non-validating, 37
    validation, turning on, 265
parsing, defined, 18
passwords
    XForms for, 647-648
    XHTML forms for, 577
PCDATA, order in declarations, 300
PDAs, XML for, 862
PDF (Portable Document Format), 376
    Acrobat Reader, 685
    FOP with XSL for, 684-685
percent sign, 317
Perl
    chaining transformations, 457
    creating documents, 128
    DOM elements, accessing, 107
    DOM feature support test, 101
    DOM navigation using siblings, 140
    error handlers, 263-264, 286-288
    NodeFilter with, 155
    NodeIterators, 150-151
    parsing DOM documents, 97-98
    saving documents, 128-129
    SAX
        attribute events, 198-199
        content handlers, 178
        data, changing, 248-251
        events, capturing, 190
        exceptions, 222
        filters, 237
        parse method, 181
        parsers, 168-169
        text events, 205-206
        validation with, 261
    schema validation, 281
    SOAP messaging, 743
    stopping SAX parses, 222-224
    Web services example, 733-734
    Web services
        accessing, 743
        using, 725-726, 745-747, 750-751
    XSLT
        extension functions, 463-464

external classes, 470
packages, 421
templates, 435
with Perl, 423, 429-431, 437-439
with SAX, 442-443, 453-455
persistence, 119
PHP
DOM elements, accessing, 106-107
DOM feature support test, 101
DOM navigation using siblings, 139
dump method dangers, 127
parsing DOM documents, 97
saving documents, 126-128
SAX
attribute events, 197-198
content handlers, 175-178
data, changing, 246-248
events, capturing, 190
filters, 237
parsers, 167-168
parsing method, 181
text events, 204-205
SOAP
messaging, 743
services, 731-733
stopping SAX parses, 220, 222
validation support, 260
Web services
accessing, 743
application example, 731-733
using, 725-726, 746-747, 750
XSLT
extension functions, 463-464
invoking, 421
with PHP, 423, 428-429, 435-436
with SAX, 442, 452-453
planning
analysis phase, 51
at the keyboard, 48
authoring structures, 54
basic business functions, determining, 55-56
committee members, 50
conversion structures, 54
data entity information forms, 65
data modeling. *See* data modeling
data sources, 52-53
decomposing functions, 56-57

destinations, data, 52-53
documentation as deliverable, 48
elements vs. attributes, 72-73
events, business, 58-59
feedback, importance of, 48
function hierarchy models, 55-56
function/process modeling, 54-59
gathering information step, 51-54
gathering the team, 50-51
goals, defining, 48-49
grouping elements, 75-76
importance of, 47
industry standards, 53-54
interchange structures, 54
interviewers, 50
legal requirements, 53
localization, 69
measurable steps, 49
methodology, determining, 51
models, reviewing, 58-59
nesting elements, 75-76
normalizing data, 73, 75
objectives, 48-49
potential data structures, 54
project managers, 50
recordists, 50
reference structures, 54
relationship diagrams. *See* ERDs (Entity-Relationship Diagrams)
scope of projects, 52
second-level parsing, 76-77
stakeholders, 50
steps in, basic, 48
subject matter experts, 50
team leaders, 50
team roles, 50-51
testing final structures, 79
tightness of structure, 77
tree diagrams, 70, 72
ultimate deliverable, 51
user review, 69-70
users, skill of, 52
pointing to locations in documents. *See* XPointer
points, 632-633
pop-up windows
XHTML for, 605
XLink, 604, 607-608

Portable Document Format (PDF), 376
ports, Web services using, 751-754
position property, 542-545
post method, XForms, 656
pre tags, 23
predicates. *See* XPath, predicates
prefix property, 880-883
preformatted text, 23
pretty printing, 21
primary keys, 802
processing instruction information items, 881
processing instructions
    <?, 31
    defined, 31-32
    referencing style sheets, 526
    SAX parsing of, 207
    stylesheet, 589
    targets, 31
    XPath processing-instruction() node tests, 497-498
    XSLT creation of, 404
project management. *See* planning
project managers, 50
properties, XSL, 683
properties, CSS
    absolute property, 542
    alternative media, 532, 550
    borders, 537-539
    bottom, 542-544
    bounding box size, 540-541
    clear, 547
    color, 533-534
    combining properties, 532
    display, 538, 548-549
    fixed property, 542
    float, 546
    fonts, 535-537
    left, 542-544
    margin, 539-540
    padding, 539-540
    position, 542-545
    relative property, 542
    right, 542-544
    shorthand properties, 532
    static property, 542
    text size, 535-536
    top, 542-544
    types of, 532
    visibility, 547-548
    width, 540-541
pseudoclasses, XHTML, using in, 575
PUBLIC identifier property, 881-883
PUBLIC identifiers, 258

Q-R

qualified names, 327
queries
    NXD, 817, 820-821
    running in XIndice, 820-821
    XPath for, 832-834
queries, 836. *See also* XQuery

radio buttons, XForms, 651, 680, 940-941
radio groups, XHTML forms, 580, 585
range controls, 654-655
RDBMSs (relational database management systems).
    See relational databases
RDF (Resource Definition Framework), 861
RDF Site Summary (RSS), 861
reading systems, 863
recommendations, 294
    associated standards, 858
    core, 857-858
recordists, 50
redirection, XLink for, 603
reference structures, 54
references property, 881
referential integrity, data binding, 787-788
relational databases
    CLOB mapping model, 799-800
    collections of tables, 802
    defined, 794
    foreign keys, 802
    object-relational storage model, 801-803
    one-to-many relationships, 802
    primary keys, 802
    RDBMSs, 795
    side tables, 800
    XML mapping models, 799
    XML-enabled. *See* XML-enabled databases
relationships
    arcs, 613
    diagrams of. *See* ERDs (Entity-Relationship
      Diagrams)
    extended links, 603

XLink, 602
relationships, data modeling, 61, 65-69
relative property, 542
RELAX NG, 370-371
remote procedure calls. *See* RPCs (remote procedure calls)
remote resources, 613
Resource Definition Framework (RDF), 861
root elements, defined, 20
round-tripping, 815-817
RPCs (remote procedure calls)
    defined, 720
    document-style alternative, 759
    document-style definitions, compared to, 759
RSS (RDF Site Summary), 861

S

Sablotron, 421, 429-431, 435, 442-443, 453-455, 463-464, 470
sans-serif fonts, 537
SAX (Simple API for XML)
    advantages of, 163
    affecting data, 239-243-251
    attribute events, 193-199
    C++
        attribute events, 195-196
        exceptions, 217
        filters, 225-233
        for parsing documents, 180
        handlers, 170-173
        stopping parsing, 212-218
        XMLReader creation, 165-166
    changing data, 239-243, 245-251
    DeclHandler, 186
    DefaultHandler class, 169, 182, 189
    defined, 161
    detecting specific events, 208-209
    DOM, compared to, 161-163
    DTDHandler, 186
    element events, 191-193
    endDocument events, 188-191
        detecting, 209-210
    error handling, 182-186

event-based API nature of, 253, 898-899
events
    capturing, 188-191, 207
    detecting, 208-209
exceptions, 212, 222
externally defined entities, 207
features, standard, 258-259
filters, 224-253, 901-903
handlers, 163, 169-179, 186
ignorableWhitespace event, 206-207
Java
    attribute events, 193-195
    drivers, 164-165
    filters, 225
    for parsing documents, 179-180
    handlers, 170
    stopping parsing, 210-212
    XMLReader creation, 164-165
LexicalHandler, 186
namespace events, 193-195, 207, 222
parser components, 163
parsing documents, 179-181
Perl
    attribute events, 198-199
    content handlers, 178
    filters, 237
    parse method, 181
    parser creation, 168-169
    stopping parsing, 222-224
PHP
    attribute events, 197-198
    content handlers, 175-178
    filters, 237
    parser creation, 167-168
    parsing method, 181
    stopping parsing, 220-222
processing instruction events, 207
read-only nature of, 163
reference sites, 871
simple streams, 162-163
source document example, 187-188
startDocument events, 188-191
stopping parsing, 210-224
stream-of-events model, 161-162
summary, 252
text events, 199-206

turning on validation feature, 259-262
validation error handling, 281
validation with, 258-259
Visual Basic .NET
    attribute events, 196-197
    filters, 233-237
    handlers, 174-175
    parsing method, 180-181
    stopping parsing, 218-220
    XMLReader creation, 166-167
whitespace, 206-207
XMLFilters, 224-239
XMLReader, 163-169
XSLT with, 421, 439-455
Scalable Vector Graphics (SVG), 860
schema documents, 323-324
Schemas
Abstract. *See* Abstract Schema
advantages of, 911
all elements, requiring, 330
annotations, 325
anyType, 334-335
appinfo element, 325
attribute extention of types, 351-352
attribute groups, 344-345
attributes
    adding, 340-345
    custom, 352-354
backward compatibility to DTDs, 338
binary data types, 327
boolean data type, 327
child elements, 329-331
choice keyword, 330-332, 340
complex elements, 329
custom types, 352-354
data integrity, 358
data type specification, 326
data types, built in, 326-328
date data, 327
default attribute values, 342-343
default values, 328-329
documentation, 324-325
documents, 323-324
DTD compatibility types, 327
elements, 329
elements of, 325-326

enumeration, 349
extending types, 351-352, 373, 914
facets, 348-351
fixed attribute, 342-343
fixed values, 328-329
foreign keys, 360-361
global attributes, 343-344
global element creation, 335-337
groups of attributes, 344-345
groups of elements, 339-340
inlining, 329, 373, 911, 916
instance documents, 325
keyrefs, 361
language type, 328
linking to, 325
list type, 350-351
maxOccurs, 331-332
minOccurs, 331-332
mixed content, 333, 373, 913
multiple namespaces, 367-368
Name type, 328
named attributes, 343-344
named types, 346-347
namespace declarations, 323-324
namespace-related types, 327
namespaces with, 361-368
noNamespaceSchemaLocation, 362
number of occurrences of elements, 331-332
numeric data, 326-327
optional attribute values, 342-343
predefined data types, 325
predefined elements, referencing, 335-337
prohibited attributes, 343
qualified names, 327
referencing target namespaces, 366
RELAX NG, 370-371
restricting complex types, 354-357
restriction types, 347-348, 373, 915
scope in, 337-338
sequencing elements, 329
simple content, 352
simple elements, 325-326
structure of, 323-324
summary, 372
target namespaces, 362-367
text data, 326

token data, 326

type creation, 345-349

types, adding attributes to, 351-352

types, built in, 326-328

unique keys, 358-359

use attribute, 342-343

XPath with, 359

xs prefix, 324

xsd prefix, 324

xsi prefix, 362

schematron, 260, 371-372

scope

of namespaces, 42-44

planning step, 52

second-level parsing, 76-77

security

current initiatives in, 864

reference sites, 877-878

Web services, 721

XML Encryption, 864-865

XML Key Management Specification, 864

XML Signature, 864-865

selectors

* asterisk, 527

all elements, selecting, 527

children, restricting to, 529

class, 530-531

defined, 527

descendant, 528-529

element, 528

id, 530-531

rule priority, 528

semicolons, 528

sibling, 530

syntax, 527

serializing data, 764

serif fonts, 537

sibling selectors, 530

side tables, 800

Simple API for XML. *See* SAX (Simple API for XML)

simple content, 352

simple links, 603, 606-607, 636, 935

SMIL (Synchronized Multimedia Integration Language), 860

SOAP

binding to ports, 752-754

C++ for messaging, 741-742

components of messages, 738

defined, 737, 762, 953

deploying Web services, 736-737

headers, 738-739, 759

installation, testing, 725-726

Java for messaging, 740-741

message creation, 739-743, 762, 953-954

payloads, 738

Perl for messaging, 743

Perl toolkits for, 725-726

PHP for messaging, 743

PHP server applications, 731-733

PHP toolkits for, 725

populating messages, 743-745

replies, reading, 748-751

sending messages, 746-747

sending via HTTP, 738

SOAPAction attribute, 759

Toolkit, Apache, 721-723

Visual Basic .NET for messaging, 742

Web services with, 720-721

SOAP, 731-733. *See also* Web services

sorting, XQuery with, 839-840

space attribute, 23-24

specified property, 880

stakeholders, 50

standalone declarations, 19, 37

standalone documents, DTDs, 295

standalone property, 879

standards

indicators, 294

recommendations as, 294

static property, 542

stream-of-events XML model, 161-162

structure of XML

attributes, 25

character data, 18

comments, 32-33

DOCTYPE declarations, 20

elements, 20-21

markup, 18

nesting, 21

overall, 18

parent-child hierarchy, 17

processing instructions, 31-32

root elements, 20

summary, 45

well-formed data, 18
whitespace, 21-24
XML declarations, 19-20
style sheets
    See XSLT (XSL Transformations)
    XHTML, converting to. See XHTML, XSLT
        conversions to
stylesheet processing instruction, 589
subject matter experts, 50
SVG (Scalable Vector Graphics), 860
Synchronized Multimedia Integration Language (SMIL), 860
SYSTEM identifier property, 881-883
SYSTEM identifiers, 258, 293

T

tables
    data entities as, 61
    XHTML, in, 570-573
    XSL, 699-701
target property, 881
team leaders, 50
team roles, 50-51
templates, XSLT, 391-398, 433
testing final structures, 79
text
    nodes, DOM, 113
    properties, CSS, 535-536
text-based databases, 815
text-shadow property, 533
Tomcat servlet engine, 721-723
transformation engines, 385
transformations. See XSLT
TrAX (Transformation API for XML)
    SAX as input, 440-443
    source data example for SAX, 439
    source XML, 422-423
    steps for using, 420
    style sheet example for SAX, 440
    templates, 433
tree diagrams, 70, 72
Tree Regular Expressions for XML (TREX), 370
TREX (Tree Regular Expressions for XML), 370
types
    adding attributes to, 351-352
    custom, 352-354
    facets, 348-349, 351
    restricting complex, 354-357
    Schemas, creating for, 345, 347-349

U-V

UDDI (Universal Description, Discovery and Integration), 760
    API for, 761
    business information, 760-761
    redundancy of registries, 760
    service information, 761
unexpanded entity reference information items, 881
Unicode, legal characters, 37
Universal Description, Discovery and Integration.
    See UDDI (Universal Description, Discovery and Integration)
unmarshalling data, 764, 790-791, 957-965
unparsed entities, 316-317
unparsed entities property, 879
unparsed entity information items, 882-883
updategrams, 811
uploading files with XForms, 652-653
URIs (uniform resource identifiers)
    defined, 40
    protocols, designating, 565
    Schemas, type for, 328
    XHTML links with, 565
URNs (uniform resource names), namespaces using, 40
UTF-8 and Unicode FAQ, 869

valid documents
    defined, 33
    well-formed files, compared to, 33-36
validation
    adding invalid information, 289-290
    C++
        error handlers, 282-285, 288
        schemas, 270-271, 275-277
        support for, 260
    content handlers in C++, 271-274
    defined, 255-256
    DOCTYPE definitions. See DTDs
    DOM, 265-267
    error handler creation, 262-264

error handling, 266, 281-290
errors, 264-267, 290, 907-908
exception IDs, 288
fatal errors, 264-267
importance of, 290, 906
Java error handlers, 281-282, 287-288
Java schemas, 269-270
Perl error handlers, 286-288
Perl support for, 261
Perl with schemas, 281
PHP support for, 260
SAX events, handling, 275-277
SAX for, 258-259
schematron, 260
summary, 290
turning on SAX feature, 259-262
Visual Basic .NET
    error handlers, 285-288
    schemas, 277-281
warnings, 264-267, 290, 907-908
well-formed documents, compared to, 256
XForms for, 660-663
XHTML, 555-556
XML 1.0 Recommendation, 258
variables, XSLT, 411-412
vector graphics, XSL with, 705
vector graphics. *See* Scalable Vector Graphics (SVG)
version property, 879
visibility property, 547-548
Visual Basic
    DOM elements, accessing, 105-106
    DOM feature support test, 100
    DOM navigation using siblings, 138-139
    parsing DOM documents, 96
    saving documents, 126
Visual Basic .NET
    error handlers, 285-288
    MyContentHandler.vb sample, 218
    SAX
        attribute events, 196-197
        data, changing, 243-246
        error handling, 185-186
        events, capturing, 189-190
        filters, 233-237
        handlers, 174-175
        parser creation, 166-167
        parsing method, 180-181
        text events, 203-204

validation, 277-281
schemas for validation, 277-281
SOAP messaging, 742
stopping parsing, 218-220
Web services
    accessing, 742
    application example, 730-731
    configuring, 724
    with Visual Basic .NET, 749-750
XMLReader creation, 166-167
XSLT
    extension functions, 462-463
    invoking, 420
    templates, 435
    with Visual Basic .NET, 423-424, 428, 433, 436
    with SAX, 442, 450-451
Visual C++, parsing DOM documents, 96
Visual Studio .NET, Web services, 724

W

W3C (World Wide Web Consortium), 17-18
warnings, validation, 264-267, 290, 907-908
Web services
    advertising to users. *See* UDDI()
    building applications, 726-734
    C++ application example, 728-730
    C++ for, 741-742, 749-750
    calling with SOAP, 737
    defined, 719-720, 762, 953
    deployment, 734-737
    deployment descriptor files, 735
    describing for users. *See* WSDL()
    document-style definitions, 759
    finding, 721
    Java application example, 726-728
    Java for, 740-741, 746, 748-749
    .NET, configuring, 724
    overview, 719
    Perl application example, 733-734
    Perl for, 725-726, 743-747, 750-751
    PHP application example, 731-733
    PHP for, 725-726, 743, 746-747, 750
    populating messages, 743-745
    ports for, 751-754

protocols for calling, 720
reference sites, 875
registries of. *See* UDDI()
replies, reading, 748-751
RPCs. *See* RPCs (remote procedure calls)
security, 721
sending messages, 746-747
simple example, 726-734
SOAP messages, 739-743
SOAP Toolkit, 721-723
SOAP, calling with, 720-721, 737
summary, 762
UDDI, 760-761
using, 720-721
Visual Basic .NET, 742
Visual Basic .NET application example, 730-731
Visual Basic .NET for, 749-750
Web servers for, 721-723
WSDL. See WSDL(), 751
Web Services Description Language.
    See WSDL(Web Services Description Language)
Weblogging, 611
well-formed documents
    defined, 18, 33
    element requirement, 20
    requirements for, 36-37
    valid documents, compared to, 33-36
    validation, compared to, 256
whitespace
    attributes with, 26
    collapsing, 22
    defined, 21-22
    DTD treatment of, 300-301
    element content whitespace property, 882
    facet for, 349
    preformatted text, 23
    SAX parsing of, 206-207
    space attribute, 23-24
    XHTML, in, 556-561
width property, 540-541
Wireless Markup Language (WML), 862
World Wide Web Consortium (W3C), 17-18
    current initiatives at, 863-865
World Wide Web, origin of, 602
WSDL (Web Services Description Language)
    architecture of, 751-752
    bindings, 752-754
    defined, 751, 953

document-style definitions, 759
file creation, 762, 954-956
messages, 751, 755-756
notification operations, 754
one-way operations, 754
operations, 751, 754-755
ports, 751-754
request/response operations, 754
sample document, 756-758
services, 752
solicit/response operations, 754
types, 752, 756

X-Z

X-Smiles
    FOP, 684
    XForms under, 642
    XSL support, 684
X-Smiles browser, 382
Xalan processor, 385
Xalan XSLT, 421
Xerces, references, 870
XForms
    action attribute, 656
    adding data to fields, 646-647
    advantages of, 637
    arrival phase, 676
    attributes as references, 668-670
    binding, 642, 663-666, 680, 944-946
    boolean controls, 655-656
    browser support for, 640
    bubbling phase, 676
    buttons, defining, 644
    call maintenance example, 642-644
    captions, 646, 651
    capture phase, 676
    check boxes, 649-651, 655-656
    choosing values with, 649-652
    controls, associating with models, 674-675
    default data in, 658-660
    demos, 642
    destination of data, 656
    downloading implementations, 642
    embedding in XHTML, 641
    event handlers, 676-677, 679

events, 675-679
file elements, 652-653
get method, 656-657
grouping elements, 671-672
importing external data, 675
initial values, setting, 658-660, 680, 942-943
initialization events, 678
input controls, 644-647
input elements, 644-646
installing, 642
instance documents, 679, 938
instance elements, 642-644
interaction events, 678
itemsets, 668-670
links to schemas, 663
list boxes, 651, 680, 941-942
listeners, 676-679
localfile attribute, 644
mediaType attribute, 657-658
method attribute, 656
method2 attribute, 644
mixing controls, 642
model attribute, 674-675
model elements, 642-644
models, multiple, 673-675
multipart/form-data type, 657-658
multiple forms on a page, 672-675
multiple nodes, iterating through, 668-670
multiple rows with, 666
namespaces, 644
order of models, 674
output as XML, 640
passwords, 647-648
phases of events, 676
post method, 656
purpose of, 637
radio buttons, 651, 680, 940-941
range controls, 654-655
ref attribute, 646, 660
reference sites, 874
relative XPath expressions, 646
relevance, 665-666
repeating structures, 666-668
replace attribute, 656
required entries, 666, 680, 946-948
schema elements, 642
schemas, 660-663

secret controls, 647-648
selecting values with, 649-652
showing results, 644
simple form example, 639-641
structure of forms, 641-642
submitInfo elements, 642-644, 656-658
submitting forms, 656-658
summary, 679
targets, 676-678
text areas, 648-649
text elements, 644-646
triggering events, 678
uploading files, 652-653
validation, 660-663
Working Draft site, 679
X-Smiles for, 642
XHTML forms, compared to, 640
XML Events with, 642, 675-676

XHTML
a tags, 563-566
alternate text attribute, 567
block formatting, 557, 559
body element, 554
bolding text, 561-563
browser support for XSLT, 589
browser XSLT conversions, 589
CDATA sections, 592-593
content, 563
CSS, adding to, 573-575
defined, 554
DOCTYPE declarations, 555-556
empty elements, 554
formatting, 561-563
forms. *See* XHTML forms
Frameset version, 555
graceful degradation, 581
head element, 554
heading tags, 561-562
headline tags, 563
html element, 554
HTML, differences from, 599, 932
HTTP protocol with, 565-566
HTTPS protocol with, 565
images, tags for, 566-569
italic text, 561-563
line break element, 559-561
links, creating, 563-566

meta tags, 593
nested formatting elements, 563
page structure, 554
paragraph tags, 557-559
positioning with tables, 570
presentation, 563
pseudoclasses, using in with, 575
reference sites, 873-874
root element of, 554
scripts, adding, 590-592
Strict version, 555
structure, basic, 554
style sheets for converting to. See XHTML,
   XSLT conversions to, 587
style sheets, adding to, 573-575
tables in, 570-573
tags in, 554
target attribute, 605-606
Transitional version, 555
URI's in, 564-566
validating documents, 555-556
versions of, 555
whitespace, 556-561
XLink with, 610
XSLT conversions to, 587-593
XHTML forms
  accessing form values, 593-595
  action attribute, 585
  buttons, submission, 581-582
  check boxes, 580, 585
  choice elements, 578-579
  default field values, 583-585
  DOM for, 593-595
  fields, 577
  form elements, 577, 585-587
  forms arrays, 594-595
  get method, 585-586, 599, 932
  graceful degradation, 581
  hidden elements, 587
  input elements, 577
  labels, 580
  looping through form elements, 594-595
  method attribute, 585-587
  name attributes, 578
  option elements, 579
  passwords, 577
  post method, 587, 599, 932

purpose of, 576
radio groups, 580, 585
replacing contents, 596-598
reset buttons, 581-582
scripts with, 594-595
select elements, 579, 585
sizing fields, 578
submitting forms, 581-582, 585-587
text-based elements, 576-578
textarea elements, 578, 585
type attribute, 577
URIs, 586
XIndice
  adding
    documents, 820
    DOM documents, 825-826
    resources, 823-827
    SAX documents, 826-827
  administrative tasks with, 819
  collection creation, 819
  command lines, 819
  connecting to databases, 822-823
  context for collections, 819
  driver class, 822
  features of, 818
  installing, 818
  key specification, 820
  queries, running, 820-821
  querying using XPath, 832-834
  removing files from database, 820
  retrieving documents, 820, 827-828
  retrieving DOM documents, 829-830
  retrieving SAX documents, 830-831
  updating DOM documents, 829
  XML\, DB, 821-834
  XPathQueryService, 832-834
  XUpdate. See XUpdate
XLink (XML Linking Language)
  actuate attribute, 603, 609
  arcroles, 629
  arcs, 613-617
  attributes, 606
  blogging, 611-612
  browser display of, 603
  browsers for, 604
  embedding, 604, 608-609
  extended links, 603, 610-622

external entities with, 622-625
id attributes, 620
linkbases, 603, 625-630
local resources, 612
locator elements, 618-622
multidirectional links, 618-622
multiple arcs, 615-616
multiple destination, 617
namespace for, 607
new windows, opening, 604, 607-608
overview, 602
pop-up windows, 604, 607-608
purpose of, 601
Recommendation, 602
redirection, 603
reference sites, 874
relationships, 602-603, 613
remote resources, 613
resources, 612-613
roles, 629
show attribute, 604, 607-609
simple links, 603, 606-607
syntax of extended links, 612-613
types of links, 603
XHTML with, 610
XLiP, 604
XLink Processor. See XLiP (XLink Processor), 604
XLiP (XLink Processor)
    embedded links, 608-609
    installing, 604
    purpose of, 605
XML 1.0 Recommendation, 869
XML\
    DB
        adding DOM documents, 825-826
        adding resources, 823-827
        adding SAX documents, 826-827
        collections, specifying, 822
        connecting to databases, 822-823
        Level 0 API compliance, 831
        querying using XPath, 832-834
        retrieving documents, 827-828
        retrieving DOM documents, 829-830
        retrieving SAX documents, 830-831
        services, implementing, 832
        updating DOM documents, 829
        URI syntax, 822

uses for, 821
        XPathQueryService, 832-834
        XUpdate. See XUpdate, 846
        XUpdateQueryService, 846-848
    DB Initiative, 818
XML-based User Interface Language (XUL), 863
XML declarations
    character set attribute, 19
    components of, 19-20
    standalone attribute, 19
    version attribute, 19
XML-DEV mailing list, 869
XML-enabled databases
    ADO for, 810
    DB2, 805-807
    defined, 795
    IBM, 805-807
    mapping, typical, 810
    Microsoft SQL Server, 807-811
    object-relational model, 803
    Oracle, 803-805
    Oracle XML DB, 803
    SOAP Server, 804
    TransX Utility, 804
    updategrams, 811
    vendors, 803-805
    XML Bulkload, 811
    XML Class Generator, 804
    XML Compressor, 805
    XML Developer's Kits, 804-805
    XML Parser, 804
    XML Processor, 804
    XML Schema Processor, 804
    XML Schemas, 803, 808
    XML Transviewer JavaBeans, 804
    XSQL Servlet, 804
    XSU (SQL Utility), 804
XML Encryption, 864-865
XML Events, XForms with, 642, 675-676
XML Fragments, 864
XML home page, 869
XML Include, 864
XML Information Set, 879
    attribute information items, 880-881
    character information items, 882
    comment information items, 882
    document information items, 879

Document Type Definition information items, 882
element information items, 880
namespace information items, 883
notation information items, 883
processing instruction information items, 881
unexpanded entity reference information items, 881
unparsed entity information items, 882-883
XML Information Set Recommendation, 17
XML Key Management Specification, 864
XML Pointer Language. See XPointer (XML Pointer Language), 630
XML Schema
    overview, 267-268
    reference sites, 872
    specifying schemas, 268
    validation, turning on, 268-281
    XForms, used in, 642
XML Schemas. *See* Schemas
XML servers, 795
XML Signature, 864-865
XML-to-XML mappings with XSLT, 401-402
XMLFilters, chaining transformations, 457-459
XMLReader
    C++ for, 165-166
    defined, 163
    Java, 164-165
    namespace awareness, 193
    Perl equivalent, 168-169
    PHP equivalent, 167-168
    VISUAL BASIC .NET for, 166-167
XPath
    (brackets), 506
    (double slashes), 504
    * node test, 493
    * node tests, 498
    . (period), 505
    .. (parent abbreviation), 505
    2.0. See XQuery, 834
    @ (attribute axis), 504
    abbreviated expressions, 504-505
    absolute expressions, 505, 518, 928
    absolute paths, 388-389
    addressing mechanism utility feature, 473
    all nodes, selecting, 498-499
    ancestor axes, 486-488
    ancestor-or-self axes, 488

attribute axes, 490-491, 504
attribute nodes, 499
attribute parents, 482
attributes, 389
axes, 476-493
boolean data type, 478
boolean functions, 512-513
Boolean values, converting, 514
brackets, 389
case conversion, 516-517
ceiling function, 517
child axes, 476, 478-480, 504
children, navigating, 388
combining location steps, 499-500
comment() node tests, 497-498
concat function, 514-515
contains function, 515
context, 477
context nodes, 386-388, 477, 499
context position, 511
context size, 511
count function, 513
criteria, adding, 389-391
data manipulation feature, 473
default axes, 504
descendant axes, 477, 485-486
descendant-or-self axes, 488, 504
descendents, 386-388
disadvantages of, 834
document root specification, 388-389
DOM module for, 92
element values, 509
equality predicates, 509-510
example document for, 475
existence predicates, 506-509
expressions, parts of, 476
false function, 512
filtering for attributes, 389
filtering instructions, 474
floor function, 517
following axes, 488-489
following-sibling axes, 483-484
for-each loops, 491
functions, 477-478, 511-517, 844-845
functions. See also XPath, predicates, 506
how it works, 474
id function, 514
lang function, 513

last function, 513
leading slashes, 505
local-name function, 514
location paths, 499-504
location steps, 476-477, 499-500
mechanism of, 474
name function, 514
name node tests, 493-494
namespace axes, 491-493
namespace-uri function, 514
namespaces in context scope, 477
navigating, 388
node functions, 513-514
node tests, 476-477, 493-499
node() node test, 498-499
node-set data type, 478
nonabbreviated expressions, 476
normalize-space function, 516
not function, 512
number data type, 478
number functions, 517
number values, 514
NXD queries with, 817
overview, 359
parent axes, 481-482
parent location steps, 505
parent-child relationship expression, 416
position function, 513
preceding axes, 488-489
preceding-sibling axes, 483-484
predicate context, 511
predicates, 477, 506, 509-511, 518, 928
principal node types for axes, 493
processing-instruction() node tests, 497-498
purpose of, 473
queries in XML\, DB, 832-834
Recommendation, 873
relative expressions, 505, 518, 928
result sets, 474-476, 506
returned data types, 478
root element, 389
round function, 517
self axes, 480-481
self node, 505
sibling axes, 483-484
starts-with function, 515
string data type, 478

string functions, 514-517
string-length function, 516
style sheet example for, 474
substring function, 516
substring-after function, 516
substring-before function, 515
sum function, 517
summary, 518
testing expressions, 474-476
testing for attributes, 390
text() node tests, 495-496
translate function, 516-517
true function, 512
URIs, compared to, 388
value-of elements, 514
values, testing for, 509-510
XPath 2.0, 864
XPointer (XML Pointer Language)
(pound sign), 631
actuate attribute, 636, 936
bare names form, 631, 634
character-points, 633
child sequences, 631
forms of expression, 631
full expressions, 631
full form, 631
functions, 635
IDs with, 634
integer sequences, 631
node-points, 632-633
points, 632-633
purpose of, 630
range function, 635
ranges, 633-634
schemes, 634
simple links, 636, 935
string-range function, 635
URIs, in, 634
XQuery
accessor functions, 844
adding elements to output, 837
Boolean functions, 844
collections, returning, 841
combining sources, 841-842
conditional processing, 842-843
context functions, 845
custom functions, 845-846

document() function, 841
FLWR statements, 834-840
for clauses, 836-837
functions, 844-845
if-then statements, 842-843
input() function, 841
let clauses, 837-838
miscellaneous functions, 845
node functions, 845
node sequences, returning, 841
node-sets vs. sequences, 836
number functions, 844
NXD queries with, 817
purpose of, 834
return clauses, 836-837
root, returning, 836, 841
sequence functions, 845
sorting, 839-840
source-detecting functions, 841
string functions, 844
time functions, 844
type management, 843-844
upper-case() function, 840
where clauses, 838
X-Hive/DB product, 834
xs prefix, 324
xsd prefix, 324
XSL (Extensible Stylesheet Language), 375
   Formatting Objects. See XSL-FO, 681
   home page, 874
   reference sites, 874
XSL Formatting Objects. See XSL-FO
XSL Transformations. See XSLT (XSL Transformations)
XSL-FO
XSL-FO (XSL Formatting Objects), 375, 681
   advanced page management concepts, 708
   attributes, 683
   basic-links, 706-707
   blocks, 688
   border properties, 697
   bounding box model, 683
   browser support for, 382
   colors, 698-699
   content, adding, 691-692
   CSS, relation to, 683
   defined, 375
   direction, reading, 686

extent, defining, 686
external graphics links, 704-705
external links, 706-707
file format conversions, 681-682
flow elements, 688-690
footers, 693, 701, 717, 950
FOP for, 684-685, 688
Formatting Objects namespace, 686
generating pages, 687-688
geometry of pages, 686
headers, 691-692, 713
image links, 704-705
internal links, 707-708
layout, 686
line height properties, 696-697
links, 704-708
lists, 702-704
multiple page sequence masters, 709-710
multiple pages, 689-690, 711, 717, 950
object size, defining, 685-686
odd/even pages, 714-716
page breaks, 690-691
page masters, 682, 685-686, 689-690
page numbers, adding, 693-694
page sequence masters, 682, 686-687, 709-713
page-sequences, 687-688
paged vs. continuous media, 694
PDF documents, 684-685
positions of pages, 713
properties, 683
purpose of, 681-682
reference sites, 874
repeatable page master alternatives, 711-713
root elements, 686
simple-page-master elements, 686
spacing properties, 696-697
static content, 691-692
structure of documents, 682-683
styling content, 694-698
tables, 699-701
text properties, 694-695
vector graphics with, 705
XSLT for generating, 378, 381-382
XSLT (XSL Transformations)
   advantages of, 419
   all nodes, processing, 398
   Apache Project, C++, 421

apply-templates element, 396
attribute element, 400
attribute parameters, 409-410
basic style sheet example, 383-384
browser support for, 589
built-in templates, 397-398
C++ for extension functions, 462-463
C++ with, 422-424, 427, 432-436, 442, 447-449
C++, invoking from, 420
call-template elements, 408
chaining transformations, 455-459, 471, 926-927
choose elements, 413-414
command lines, 385
commenting out, 403
comments, adding, 402-403
components of, 470, 923
content creation, 398-400
content handlers for transformers, 443-444
content, outputting all, 398
context nodes, 393
copy-of element, 407
customized content, 414
defined, 375-376
DOM nodes, 422-424, 467, 471, 924-925
dynamic attributes, 400
dynamic elements, 399
element creation, 398-400
element element, 399
elements, extension, 464-468
empty templates, 417, 918
engine substitution, 425
extension elements, 464-468
extension functions, 459-464
external classes, 468-470
flow control, 412-414
for-each elements, 405
HTML link creation, 398
HTML output method, 593
HTML, transformations to, 590-593
if elements, 412-413
input parameters, 410
Java extension functions, 459-462
Java with, 422-427, 431-438, 443-446
Java with SAX, 440-442
looping, 405
match attribute, 391-392, 396
methodologies, 420-421

mode attribute, 415-416
modularization with templates, 395
MSXML with, 420, 436
multiple template application, 393-397
multiple transformation, 437-439
multiple transformations, 471, 924
name attribute, 399-400
named template parameters, 410-411
named templates, 408-409
namespace declarations, 384
namespaces for extension functions, 460-461
namespaces, searching for, 493
node-set, copying, 407
order of output, 404-405
otherwise elements, 413-414
output from templates, 393
output, specifying, 384-385
param element, 409
parameters, 409-410, 417, 918
    named template, 410-411
    setting, 435-437
Perl for extension functions, 463-464
Perl packages for, 421
Perl with, 423, 429-431, 435, 437-439, 453-455, 470
Perl with SAX, 442-443
Perl, chaining with, 457
PHP for extension functions, 463-464
PHP with, 423, 428-429, 435-436, 442, 452-453
PHP, invoking from, 421
processing instruction creation, 404
programming constructs, 408
programming with style sheets, 459-464
purpose of, 417, 917
referencing param element, 409
reference sites, 872-873
results, creating, 424-425
root elements, 384
Sablotron, 421, 429-431, 435, 442-443, 453-455, 463-464, 470
SAX
    as input, 440-443
    as result, 445-455
    for style sheets, 443-444
    streams with, 421, 471, 925-926
select attribute, 385
select element, 396

selecting nodes, 391-392
sort element, 404-405
source data example for SAX, 439
Source interface, 422-423
sources, 470, 923
steps in, 470, 923
style sheet determination, 426-431
style sheet example for SAX, 440
stylesheet element, 384
subtemplates, 396
summary, 416, 470
templates, 391-393, 395-398, 433-435
test attributes, 412-413
testing style sheets, 385-386
transform element, 383-384
transformation engines, 385
Transformer creation, 431-433
TransformerFactory objects, 425
TrAX. *See* TrAX (Transformation API for XML)
value-of element, 384-385, 405-407
variables, 411-412, 417, 918
Visual Basic .NET for extension functions, 462-463
Visual Basic .NET with, 420, 423-424, 428,
    433-436, 442, 450-451
when elements, 413-414
Working Draft, 386
working draft, 589
Xalan, 421
Xalan processor, 385
XHTML, conversions to, 377-378, 587-593
XML-to-XML mappings, 401-402
XMLFilters for chaining, 457, 459
XSL-FO, conversions to, 378, 381-382
XSLT 2.0, 864
XUL (XML-based User Interface Language), 863
XUpdate
    adding elements, 851-852
    changing information, 849-851
    comment creation, 852-853
    elements, updating, 850-851
    executing queries, 848
    inserting nodes, 851-852
    purpose of, 846
    removing nodes, 848-849
    renaming attributes, 849-850
    variables, 853-855
    XUpdateQueryService, 846-848

Other Related Titles

**Sams Teach Yourself
CSS in 24 Hours**
Kynn Bartlett
ISBN: 0-672-32409-1
$24.99 US/$38.99 CAN

**Sams Teach Yourself
Perl in 21 Days**
*Laura Lemay and
Richard Colburn*
ISBN: 0-672-32035-5
$34.99 US/$54.99 CAN

**Sams Teach Yourself
Web Publishing with
HTML and XHTML in 21
Days, Professional
Reference Edition**
*Laura Lemay and
Rafe Colburn*
ISBN: 0-672-32204-8
$49.99 US/$77.99 CAN

Java 2 Unleashed
*Stephen Potts and
Alex Pestrikov*
ISBN: 0-672-32394-X
$49.99 US/$77.99 CAN

SAMS
www.samspublishing.com

**Sams Teach Yourself
Java 2 in 21 Days**
*Laura Lemay and
Rogers Cadenhead*
ISBN: 0-672-32370-2
$39.99 US/$62.99 CAN

**PHP and MySQL Web
Development**
*Laura Thomson and
Luke Welling*
ISBN: 0-672-31784-2
$49.99 US/$77.99 CA

All prices are subject to change.